FREE MOVEMENT OF PERSONS IN THE ENLARGED EUROPEAN UNION

AUSTRALIA
Law Book Co.
Sydney

CANADA and USA
Carswell
Toronto

HONG KONG
Sweet & Maxwell Asia

NEW ZEALAND
Brookers
Wellington

SINGAPORE and MALAYSIA
Sweet & Maxwell Asia
Singapore and Kuala Lumpur

FREE MOVEMENT OF PERSONS IN THE ENLARGED EUROPEAN UNION

By

Nicola Rogers

and

Rick Scannell

LONDON
Sweet and Maxwell
2005

Published in 2005 by Sweet & Maxwell Limited of
100 Avenue Road
London NW3 3PF
www.sweetandmaxwell.co.uk

Typeset by J&L Composition, Filey, North Yorkshire
Printed and bound in Great Britain by Athenaeum Press Ltd., Gateshead

No natural forests were destroyed to make this product; only farmed timber
was used and replanted

British Library Cataloguing in Publication Data

A CIP catalogue record for this book is available from the British Library.

ISBN: 0421 875704

Sweet and Maxwell Limited, London
2005

FOREWORD

The past 10 years have seen a dramatic rise in the importance of EU law in the field of immigration. When Denis Martin and I published a book on the subject of free movement of persons in 1996, the legal framework was substantially different from what it is now in 2004. It is, therefore, a great pleasure to introduce this book on free movement of persons in the EU which fills a critical gap in the field at the moment. The authors are particularly well placed to explain to legal practitioners in the UK and elsewhere the meaning and implications of EU law in this area by reference to the problems of individuals seeking to move and reside in Europe. They have both practiced in the field of domestic immigration and asylum law at the English bar for many years and have increasingly taken into account the EU developments. Indeed, they have both appeared before the courts in some of the cases referred to in this book which cases have changed our understanding of the law. My pleasure in introducing this book is enhanced by the fact that the authors are both not only highly respected colleagues but also personal friends of long standing. Indeed, Nicola Rogers and I have jointly chaired the European Sub Committee of the Immigration Law Practitioners Association for many years with every assistance from Rick Scannell, chair of the Association.

First and foremost this is an indispensable book for practitioners. It is still the case that some English lawyers go slightly pale when faced with an EC directive or regulation. This book reminds those who have forgotten of the sources of Community law and how it fits into the English legal framework. The first two chapters set out clearly and simply all the English adviser needs to know to answer the question: why does that apply here. Secondly, as a matter of fundamental importance all too often overlooked in practitioners' texts on EU law, the authors place the EU legal regime in the framework of supra national human rights law. It is not possible to apply EU law in this field without looking over one's shoulder all the time to the European Convention on Human Rights and the Court of Human Rights in order to ensure that the application of the EU rules is consistent with the Strasbourg law and jurisprudence. Just as UK domestic law no longer provides the final word on migration rights, so too EU law must be read in the light of international human rights instruments to which the Member States are parties.

Thirdly, this book provides a clear and immediately applicable explanation of the law of citizenship of the Union and the right of free movement of such citizens. The vast majority of the European Court of Justice's jurisprudence in the field of migration is exactly about the right of movement and the conditions attached to them which these citizens of the Union are entitled to exercise. On reading these chapters, one is startled at how often the UK authorities are parties in the cases which come before the European Court of Justice. One begins to wonder whether this is the result of a particularly awkward administration which has trouble applying EU law correctly (where other Member States are more obedient) or evidence of the excellence of

English practitioners who struggle so strenuously for the rights of their clients. Here the explanation of the right to family reunification with third country national family members provides the reader with an extremely valuable tool for the day-to-day practice of immigration law in the UK.

The third part of this book admirably covers one of the most contentious areas of EU migration law: the rights accruing to nationals of third countries by virtue of agreements with those states and the EU. Even occasional practitioners of immigration law are surprised by the extent of the residence rights of, for instance, Turkish workers under the subsidiary legislation adopted under the EC–Turkey Association Agreement. Specialists are also sometimes surprised to discover, for instance, that there are elements of free movement in the EC Agreement with Chile. This part of the book is invaluable not just for the general practitioner but for the expert as well, providing an overview of which agreements include provisions of interest in the field of immigration and the extent of those provisions. Where clarification from the European Court of Justice is still outstanding, the authors have included references so that the reader can check on the progress of the litigation.

Without doubt this book will rapidly become a well-thumbed resource on the shelf of all practitioners working in the field of immigration, a position it well deserves. I welcome wholeheartedly this contribution to the field and recommend this book to the reader as an indispensable part of the practice of immigration law in Europe.

Elspeth Guild
Professor of European Migration Law
Radboud University, Nijmegen

Partner
Kingsley Napley, London

October 18, 2004.

PREFACE

The right of freedom of movement for persons is the cornerstone of the principle of European integration lying at the heart of the European Union. The right is reflected by Articles 2 and 3(1)(c) EC Treaty which provide that, for the purpose of establishing a common market and the promotion of the harmonious development of economic activities between Member States, obstacles to the free movement of persons between Member States shall be abolished[1]. Since the Maastricht Treaty the right has been has been given articulation by the establishment of citizenship of the Union contained in Article 17 EC Treaty and the right of every citizen of the Union to move and reside freely contained in Article 18 EC Treaty.

There are at present 25 Member States of the European Union. When the 10 new States[2] joined on May 1st, 2004 the scale of the enlargement of the European Union went far beyond what had gone before. In more than a 30-year period the four previous Accession Treaties had accounted for a total of nine new Member States[3]. Further, of the other three candidate countries, Bulgaria and Romania are expected to become full members in 2007 and if Turkey succeeds in meeting the requisite political and economic criteria for membership the end of the decade could see a European Union of some 28 Member States[4].

Enlargement in itself provides ample justification for the timing of the publication of a book on freedom of movement of persons, but it is the expectation of some that such enlargement would increase dramatically the exercise of free movement rights by Union Citizens which gives the timing particular poignancy.

For the eight Eastern European countries which became members on May 1st, 2004 the path to accession began with the fall of the Berlin Wall in 1989 after which the European Community quickly established diplomatic relations with the countries of Central and Eastern Europe. But until accession a number of these countries continued to produce significant numbers of

---

[1] The roots of the "common market" can be seen in the 1951 Treaty Establishing the European Coal and Steel Community [ECSC], although free movement rights were limited to skilled employment (Article 69 ECSC refers).

[2] Cyprus, the Czech Republic, Estonia, Hungary, Latvia, Lithuania, Malta, Poland, the Slovak Republic and Slovenia.

[3] Under the terms of the first accession treaty signed on January 22,1972 Denmark, Ireland, Norway and the United Kingdom joined the six Member States from January 1, 1973 to make a Community of nine Member States; the second accession treaty saw the Member States grow to ten with the admission of Greece with effect from January 1, 1981; the third accession treaty accounted for Portugal and Spain who became full members from January 1, 1986 and with effect from January 1, 1995 the 12 Member States became 15 with the fourth accession treaty by which Austria, Finland and Sweden.

[4] The figure could be higher still with applications for membership from both Croatia and Macedonia still pending.

asylum seekers within the European Union. Certainly this fact contributed to the xenophobic fears about enlargement in the period immediately prior to accession with predictions of large scale migration[5]. These predictions would appear to have been unfounded. Nevertheless it is clear that enlargement *will* lead to an increase in the exercise of free movement rights amongst Union Citizens.

This book provides comprehensive analysis of the EU legislation and ECJ case law on freedom of movement of person for both EU nationals and their family members. It deals also with the Association Agreements. Although we have devoted a chapter to social security this is intended to be only an outline and general guide to social security provisions in Community law. In the absence of harmonisation amongst Member States of social security provisions more detailed analysis is beyond the scope of this work.

Our intention has been to focus on EU law, rather than the UK's implementation and application of it. We have in fact devoted Part IV of the book to the UK's approach, although that Part is not intended to be used in isolation. Our hope is to engender a discipline which regrettably appears all too often to be lacking of having primary regard to substantive EU law provisions, rather than the UK's interpretation of those provisions. In examining the scope of the right of the freedom of movement of persons the supremacy of Community law must always be kept in mind, as must the fact that most concepts, procedures and rights are spelt out in detail by Community law itself.

The book is divided into four parts.

Part I identifies in four chapters the fundamental principles of EU law. Perhaps the most significant question in the context of the freedom of movement of persons is the true reach of Articles 17 and 18 EC Treaty. In Chapter 4 (Union Citizenship) we consider two questions. Firstly, whether anything of value has been added to the rights of individuals by the creation of Union citizenship. Secondly, we consider the impact on the free movement rights of Union citizens made by the inclusion of the "right to move and reside freely."

Part II examines the substantive provisions in EU law for free movement of Union citizens and their family members. We deal discretely in Chapter 6 (Enlargement of the European Union) with the accession of the ten new Member States. We deal with the economically active free movers in Chapters 7 and 8 (workers and those exercising the freedom of establishment and the freedom to provide and receive services) and those who are economically inactive in Chapter 9 (retired persons, persons of independent means and students for whom specific provisions is made not in the EC Treaty itself but in directives). In addition we consider the rights of family members of all free movers in Chapter 10. Separate chapters are devoted to the right of residence,

---

[5] Such xenophobia is well demonstrated by the reporting of the Daily Express which on January 20, 2004 began its campaign against Roma migration from Eastern Europe claiming on its front page that "1.6 million Gypsies" were "ready to flood in". The newspaper predicted a "great invasion" in which gypsies would head to to Britain "to leech on us".

to discrimination and other obstacles to freedom of movement, to access to social security (as observed in outline and in general) and to exclusion.

Part III deals with agreements with third countries insofar as they impact on the freedom of movement of persons. Since the early 1990s the EU has broadened its relations to include a degree of co-operation with nearly all regions of the world and signed agreements and conventions with a wide range of partners. Detailed consideration however is limited to the Europe Agreements (concluded with Eastern European countries as the precursor to accession) and the EC-Turkey Association Agreement. It is these agreements which have most significance (for nationals of Romania, Bulgaria and Turkey) in the context of the freedom of movement of persons.

Part IV deals with UK law and practice implementing Community law provisions on the free movement of persons. However as already made clear it is not intended to be able to be used in isolation of the analysis of Community law contained in Parts I–III. The focus of Part IV is on contentious areas where UK law and practice appears to diverge from Community law standards.

We have also provided comprehensive appendices which—with one exception—contain either the full text or relevant extracts of both primary and secondary European Community law. Both for reasons of length and treatment of the subject matter Regulation 1408/71 on social security is not included. We have produced also the relevant materials dealing with Agreements with Third Countries and materials which will be of interest only to the UK reader.

Particular mention should be made of the Citizens' Directive[6] which comes into force on April 30, 2006. This Directive repeals a whole raft of secondary legislation which is the subject of much of this book. The differences between the Directive and such secondary legislation are identified briefly in a table at Appendix 30. To a large extent the Directive mirrors existing provisions, albeit consolidated. In other respects the Citizens' Directive reflects case law developments and does represent a progression towards greater free movement. However such Directive even when in force does not necessarily represent the full extent of free movement rights which will fall to be determined by the ECJ on a case by case basis and in accordance with the substantive principles of Community law discussed in this book.

We must thank Professor Elspeth Guild who provided invaluable comments on parts of the text and kindly agreed to write the Foreward. Thanks are extended also to Chris Randall, Fiona Lindsley, Tim Mitchell, Jawaid Zuqmani and Martin Soorjoo. We are particularly indebted to John Walsh for helping us to refine the text at short notice.

Thanks are due also to our clerks (particularly Lesley Perrott, Matthew Archer and Lisa O'Leary) and our colleagues in Chambers, for their patience and understanding of our absence for substantial periods of time during

---

[6] Directive 2004/38, OJ L 158/77.

2004. In July 2004 as our deadline for submission of the substantive text loomed the pressure of the task caused Nicola to miss a family holiday with her parents and Pippa and Charles and made Rick unbearable company for his wife Sona and children Liam and Vida. Our apologies for such behaviour and our thanks for our families' understanding. Finally we are indebted to Sweet & Maxwell for publishing this book and particularly Sue Lewis for agreeing to take this on and Steven Jackson for his forbearance.

The law is as stated as at October 2004. Responsibility for any errors or omission are ours and ours alone.

Nicola Rogers & Rick Scannell
2 Garden Court
Middle Temple
London
EC4Y 9BL

October 2004

CONTENTS

PART ONE—FUNDAMENTAL PRINCIPLES OF EU LAW

Chapter 1: Treaty Foundations and Institutions

Chapter 9: The Economically Inactive

Chapter 16: Association Agreements in Community Law

Chapter 29: Agreements with Third Countries

PART FIVE—APPENDICES

CONTENTS

GLOSSARY

Ankara Agreement	EC-Turkey Association Agreement signed in Ankara in 1963
Amsterdam Treaty	Treaty amending the EC and EU Treaties signed in Amsterdam in 1997
CEEC	Central and Eastern European Countries
CFI	Court of First Instance
EEA	European Economic Area, created by the EEA Agreement, now comprising all EU Member States and Norway, Iceland and Liechtenstein
EEC	European Economic Community now replaced by the European Community (EC)
EC	European Communities (representing the First Pillar of the European Union)
ECHR	European Convention on Human Rights signed in Rome in 1950
ECJ	European Court of Justice
ECSC	European Coal and Steel Community (ECSC)
ECtHR	European Court of Human Rights
EURATOM	European Atomic Energy Community
EC Treaty	Treaty establishing the Community (replacing the Treaty of Rome) as amended by the Amsterdam and Nice Treaties
EU	European Union; a political union of States comprising Austria, Belgium, Cyprus, Czech Republic, Denmark, Estonia, Finland, France, Germany, Greece, Hungary, Ireland, Italy, Latvia, Lithuania, Luxembourg, Malta, Netherlands, Poland, Portugal, Slovak Republic, Slovenia, Spain, Sweden and United Kingdom.
EU national	National of an EU Member State; Union Citizen
EU Treaty	Treaty establishing the European Union, signed in Maastricht in 1992 as amended by the Amsterdam and Nice Treaties (also referred to as TEU)
Maastricht Treaty	Treaty establishing the European Union signed in Maastricht in 1992
Treaty of Nice	Treaty amending the EC and EU Treaties, signed in Nice in 2001

Treaty of Rome	Treaty establishing the European Economic Community (EEC) signed in Rome in 1957
UDHR	Universal Declaration of Human Rights
Union Citizen	National of an EU Member State

TABLE OF EUROPEAN CASES

TABLE OF UK CASES

TABLE OF EUROPEAN COMMUNITY TREATIES

[xli]

TABLE OF REGULATIONS

TABLE OF DIRECTIVES

TABLE OF DECISIONS

TABLE OF INTERNATIONAL TREATIES AND CONVENTIONS

TABLE OF NATIONAL LEGISLATION

[li]

TABLE OF STATUTORY INSTRUMENTS

Part One
FUNDAMENTAL PRINCIPLES
OF EU LAW

CHAPTER 1

TREATY FOUNDATIONS AND INSTITUTIONS

This chapter examines the foundation stones of Community law and charts the development of the Treaties establishing the European Community and the European Union. The principal Community institutions are described, as are their powers.

1. TREATY FOUNDATIONS

(a) *Introduction*

The creation of the European Union as a political and economic collective of   **1–01**
states has been a gradual process that began in 1950 in the wake of the
Second World War. The six original Member States[1] of the European Coal
and Steel Community (ECSC) aimed to use European integration to ensure
that the events of the Second World War would not be repeated.[2]

The European Union is now a body comprising of 25 Member States.[3] It rep-   **1–02**
resents one of the most powerful trading blocs in the world, with a total population of just under half a billion people. Whilst originally the ECSC and
then the European Economic Community were concerned principally with
economic co-operation, leaving civil and political co-operation to the
Council of Europe, the European Union is now involved in a range of political areas including freedom, security and justice, defence and environmental
protection.

Co-operation between the Member States of the European Union is based on   **1–03**
four founding Treaties:

(a)   the Treaty establishing the European Coal and Steel Community
      (ECSC), which was signed on April 18, 1951 in Paris, entered into force
      on July 23, 1952 and expired on July 23, 2002 (see para. 1–07 below);

(b)   the Treaty establishing the European Atomic Energy Community
      (EAEC), which was signed (along with the EEC Treaty) in Rome on
      March 25, 1957, and entered into force on January 1, 1958 (see paras
      1–08 to 1–09 below);

---

[1] Germany, France, Belgium, Netherlands, Luxembourg and Italy.
[2] It was first proposed by the French Foreign Minister Robert Schumann in a speech on May 9, 1950. This date, the "birthday" of what is now the EU, is celebrated annually as Europe Day.
[3] Denmark, Ireland and the United Kingdom joined in 1973, Greece in 1981, Spain and Portugal in 1986, Austria, Finland and Sweden in 1995. On May 1, 2004 the largest enlargement took place with 10 new countries joining: Estonia, Latvia, Lithuania, Slovenia, Slovakia, Czech Republic, Malta, Cyprus, Poland and Hungary. Bulgaria, Romania and Turkey are likely to join the EU in 2007.

(c)   the Treaty establishing the European Economic Community (EEC) ("the Treaty of Rome") (see paras 1–10 to 1–15 below);

(d)   the Treaty on European Union, which was signed in Maastricht on February 7, 1992, entered into force on November 1, 1993 ("the Maastricht Treaty") (see paras 1–18 to 1–21 below).

Each of these Treaties is analysed in further detail below.

1–04   The Maastricht Treaty changed the name of the European Economic Community to simply "the European Community" ("the EC"). It also introduced new forms of co-operation between the Member State governments— for example on defence and in the area of "justice and home affairs". By adding this intergovernmental co-operation to the existing "Community" structure, the Maastricht Treaty created a new structure with three "pillars", and expanded the scope of that co-operation to include political as well economic areas. This is the European Union ("the EU").

1–05   The founding Treaties have been amended on several occasions, in particular when new Member States acceded in 1973 (Denmark, Ireland, United Kingdom), 1981 (Greece), 1986 (Spain, Portugal), 1995 (Austria, Finland, Sweden) and finally 2004 (Estonia, Latvia, Lithuania, Slovenia, Slovakia, Czech Republic, Malta, Cyprus, Poland and Hungary).

1–06   There have also been more far-reaching reforms bringing major institutional changes and introducing new areas of responsibility for the European institutions through further Treaties:

(a)   the Merger Treaty, signed in Brussels on April 8, 1965, in force since July 1, 1967, provided for a single Commission and a single Council of the then three European Communities;

(b)   the Single European Act (SEA), signed in Luxembourg and the Hague, entered into force on July 1, 1987, provided for the adaptations required for the achievement of the internal market (see paras 1–16 to 1–17 below);

(c)   the Treaty of Amsterdam, signed on October 2, 1997, entered into force on May 1, 1999, it amended and renumbered the EU and EC Treaty. The Treaty of Amsterdam changed the articles of the EU Treaties, identified by letters A to S, into numerical form (see paras 1–22 to 1–24 below);

(d)   the Treaty of Nice, signed on February 26, 2001, entered into force on February 1, 2003, amended certain provisions in the EU and EC Treaties (see paras 1–25 to 1–26 below).

Further changes will inevitably result from the draft Treaty establishing a Constitution for Europe (see paras 1–27 to 1–28 below).

(b) *The Treaty Establishing the European Coal and Steel Community*

The Treaty establishing the European Coal and Steel Community (ECSC)   **1–07**
was signed on April 18, 1951 in Paris and entered into force on July 23, 1952.
It contained a chapter on workers and movement of workers (Chapter VIII).
The provisions were restricted to those employed in the coal and steel industries. Although provisions relating to discrimination in remuneration and
working conditions are replicated throughout subsequent Treaty of Rome
provisions, the free movement provisions themselves were much weaker than
those contained in the Treaty of Rome. In the ECSC Treaty Member States
retained their competence as regards the free movement of workers whereas
in the Treaty of Rome competence in this area was ceded to the Community.[4]
The ECSC Treaty expired on July 23, 2002 and its significance is now only
historical.[5]

(c) *The Treaty Establishing the European Atomic Energy Community*

The Treaty establishing the European Atomic Energy Community (EAEC)   **1–08**
was signed along with the Treaty of Rome on March 25, 1957, and entered
into force on January 1, 1958. As with the ECSC Treaty, Art.232(2) of the
Treaty of Rome provides that its provisions do not derogate from those of the
Euratom Treaty.

In the field of free movement of persons, Art.96 EAEC contains a provision   **1–09**
on the free movement of those working in the field of nuclear energy.
Member States were required to abolish all restrictions on the free movement
of workers in the nuclear industry. In 1962 a directive was adopted by the
Euratom Council to give effect to Art.96.[6] Its scope is limited to those in
skilled employment in the field of nuclear energy. Skilled employment is confined to those with specialist knowledge or undertaking particular tasks in
the industry. The 1962 Directive is a very short directive and provides only
that Member States will adopt measures for the "automatic granting of
authorisations" of any skilled employment in the field. The Directive makes
clear that all other aspects of free movement are to be regulated by measures
taken generally in relation to the free movement of workers pursuant to the
Treaty of Rome.[7]

(d) *The Treaty Establishing the European Economic Community*

The Treaty establishing the European Economic Community is more com-   **1–10**
monly referred to as the Treaty of Rome. It was the central plank of the

---

[4] Art.69(1) and (3) ECSC Treaty.
[5] Art.232 (1) of the Treaty of Rome stated that its provisions did not affect those of the ECSC
Treaty. Thus whilst the ECSC Treaty remained in force those falling within the personal scope of
Art.69 of that Treaty would not be governed by the Treaty of Rome or more recently the EC
Treaty.
[6] EAEC Council Directive on freedom to take skilled employment in the field of nuclear energy
[1962] O.J. P 057 1650.
[7] In principle this means that the free movement of those employed in the nuclear energy industry is governed by Reg. 1612/68 and Dir. 68/360 other than where the 1962 Directive applies.

European Economic Community ("the EEC"). Art.2, which was amended by the Maastricht Treaty, laid down the objectives of the EEC: to establish a common market and economic and monetary union in order to promote throughout the Community development of economic activities, social cohesion, high levels of employment and social protection and to raise the standard of living in the Member States.

1–11 The creation of a "common market" would involve the elimination of obstacles to trade between Member States to create conditions as close as possible to an internal market. National frontiers therefore were intended to be abolished as regards the transaction of commerce.

1–12 Article 3(c) sets out the four freedoms which are the cornerstone of creation of that internal market:

(a) free movement of goods;

(b) free movement of persons;

(c) free movement of services;

(d) free movement of capital.

1–13 Article 5 directed Member States to take all appropriate measures to ensure the fulfilment of the obligations arising out of the Treaty or resulting from actions taken by the institutions of the Community.[8] Article 7 contained a general prohibition on non-discrimination on grounds of nationality in areas of application of the Treaty.[9]

1–14 It is the provisions in the Treaty on the free movement of persons which are of principal interest in this book. Free movement rights were clearly confined to areas of economic activity. Articles 48 to 50[10] provided for the free movement of workers which are discussed in detail in Chapter 7. Articles 52 to 58[11] contained provisions relating to the right of establishment. Articles 59 to 66[12] provided for the freedom to provide services. Both the freedom of establishment and freedom to provide services are discussed in detail in Chapter 8 (paras 8–01 to 8–61).

The Treaty contains provisions establishing the institutions of the European Community including the European Commission and the European Court of Justice. The principal Community institutions are discussed in paras 1–29 *et seq.* below.

1–15 Whilst many of the subsequent Treaties amended wording and numbering of the provisions contained within the Treaty of Rome, its principal provisions

---

[8] See further discussion in paras 2–27 to 2–35 on the Community legal order. The provision has been reworded post Amsterdam Treaty significantly defining the competence of the Community.
[9] Now Art.12 EC Treaty post Amsterdam Treaty. See further discussion in paras 2–63 to 2–66 on non-discrimination.
[10] Now Arts 39 to 42 EC Treaty post Amsterdam Treaty.
[11] Now Arts 43 to 48 EC Treaty post Amsterdam Treaty.
[12] Now Arts 49 to 55 EC Treaty post Amsterdam Treaty.

relating to the four freedoms remain at the heart of the Treaty today. Whilst the core activities of the Community have expanded[13] and the creation of the European Union has added a political dimension to the co-operation between the Member States, the internal market remains of key interest.

(e) *The Single European Act*

The Single European Act was signed in February 1986. The principal objective of the Act was the completion of the internal market by the end of 1992. To that end Art.13 of the Act inserted Art.8a[14] into the Treaty of Rome which stated that the Community would adopt measures with the aim of progressively establishing the internal market over a period expiring on December 31, 1992. It further stated that:

1–16

> "The internal market shall comprise an area without internal frontiers in which the free movement of goods, persons, services and capital is ensured in accordance with the provisions of this Treaty".

Article 13 of the Act has been the cause of considerable controversy since there is a divergence in understanding of that provision between Member States. The UK Government maintains the position that the provision means that since not all persons are covered by the internal market principle, border checks must remain in place. Other Member States considered it meant the abolition of all checks.

To some extent this controversy has been alleviated by the creation of the Schengen Agreement (1985) and the Schengen Convention (1990) which create a border free area for the participating Member States.

1–17

(f) *The Maastricht Treaty*

The Treaty on European Union was signed in Maastricht on February 7, 1992 and entered into force on November 1, 1993 (the "Maastricht Treaty"). The Maastricht Treaty created the European Union which was founded on the European Communities and was to represent "a new stage in the processing of creating an ever closed union".[15]

1–18

Title II of the Maastricht Treaty contained provisions amending the Treaty of Rome with a view to establishing the European Community ("the EC"). Thereafter the Treaty of Rome was to be referred to as the Treaty establishing the European Community. The most significant amendment to that Treaty was the inclusion of Art.8[16] which signified the creation of the European Union citizen and Art.8a[17] which granted the right of every citizen

1–19

---

[13] Art.3 EC Treaty now lists the core 21 aims of the Community including interests as wide ranging as protection of the environment and consumer protection to increasing industrial competitiveness.
[14] Now Art.14 EC Treaty post Amsterdam Treaty.
[15] Art.A of Title I of the Maastricht Treaty, now Art.1 TEU post Amsterdam.
[16] Now Art.17 EC Treaty post Amsterdam Treaty.
[17] Now Art.18 EC Treaty post Amsterdam Treaty.

of the European Union to move freely within the territory of the Union. These provisions are discussed in detail in Chapter 4 below. Together with Titles III and IV of the Maastricht Treaty which contained amended provisions of the ECSC Treaty and the EAEC this constituted the "first pillar" of the European Union.

1–20   The second pillar was set out in Title V which contained provisions on common foreign and security policies. Member States agreed to co-operate in areas of foreign policy and security and to support the Union's external foreign and securities policies.

1–21   The third pillar was set out in Title VI which contained provisions on co-operation in the fields of justice and home affairs. Of principal interest was the creation of a list of areas of common interest for the Member States including asylum policies, immigration policies relating to external borders and admission of third country nationals and matters relating to policing and judicial co-operation in both civil and criminal matters. The inclusion of this third pillar was significant since it demonstrated a broadening of the areas of interest beyond the internal market. As a result of the inclusion of Title VI the Member States made a number of resolutions in the areas of justice and home affairs such as the London Resolutions on asylum.[18] However third pillar measures made under Title VI were considered as soft law and did not fall within Community competence until the Amsterdam Treaty.

(g) *The Amsterdam Treaty*

1–22   The Treaty of Amsterdam was signed on October 2, 1997 and entered into force on May 1, 1999. It amended both the Maastricht Treaty and the Treaty establishing the European Community.[19] To avoid confusion we refer to these Treaties as the EU Treaty and the EC Treaty, respectively, following the Amsterdam Treaty since a significant number of the changes were in the numbering of both the EU and EC Treaty provisions.

1–23   Under the Amsterdam Treaty the third pillar of the Maastricht Treaty was moved to be included in the Treaty establishing the European Community thus bringing the areas of justice and home affairs within the competence of the Community. The Community would thus be able to make directives and regulations in areas such as asylum and the immigration of third country nationals. This significantly broadened the scope of the EC Treaty.

1–24   These provisions are not the subject of this book since they are not generally concerned with the rights of free movement within the Community or the rights of EU citizens. Rather they are concerned with the movement and rights of third country nationals from outside the European Union to within

---

[18] The London Resolutions include the conclusion on countries in which there is generally no serious risk of persecution; Resolution on manifestly unfounded applications for asylum; and Resolution on a harmonised approach to questions concerning host third countries: London, November 30, and December 1, 1992 (SN 2836/93 (WG1 1505)).
[19] Originally the Treaty of Rome, renamed by Maastricht Treaty.

it. To date the Council has adopted a number of asylum measures.[20] As regards immigration measures these have included measures relating to the common visa list,[21] the rights of long-term resident third country nationals in the European Union[22] and the right to family reunification for certain third country nationals resident in the European Union.[23] However none of the measures adopted creates rights of entry or stay for third country nationals, nor do any encroach upon the competence of Member States to determine the entry and stay of third country nationals. Even proposed measures currently under negotiation on labour migration[24] and third country national students and volunteers[25] are unlikely to create any rights of entry or stay. Rather they will guide Member States on the minimum standards and procedures to be adopted in these areas, whilst maintaining significant control over their own migration policies.

(h) *Treaty of Nice*

The Treaty of Nice was signed on February 26, 2001 and entered into force   **1–25**
on February 1, 2003. It amended a number of provisions of the EC and EU Treaties. The Treaty of Nice was prepared anticipating the accession of 10 new Member States due in May 2004 and thus it made particular institutional amendments which would incorporate those Member States into the Council and Parliament.

Revision of the Treaties took place in four key areas: **1–26**

(a)   size and composition of the Commission;

(b)   weighting of votes in the Council;

(c)   extension of qualified-majority voting; and

(d)   enhanced co-operation.

---

[20] Asylum measures adopted under Title IV include:

    1. Dec.2000/596/EC on European refugee fund [2000] O.J. L252/12.
    2. Reg.2725/2000 on Eurodac [2000] O.J. L316/1: applied from January 15, 2003.
    3. Dir.2001/55 on temporary protection [2001] O.J. L 212/12): implement by December 31, 2002.
    4. Reg.407/2002 implementing Eurodac Regulation [2002] O.J. L62/1.
    5. Dir.2003/9 on reception conditions [2003] O.J. L31/18.
    6. Dublin II Reg.343/2003 [2003] O.J. L50/1: in force September 1, 2003.
    7. Reg.1560/2003 implementing Dublin II [2003] O.J. L222/3: in force September 6, 2003.
    8. Dir.2004 (not adopted yet) on the definition of a refugee and person in need of subsidiary protection (not yet published); adopted by April 29, 2004 JHA Council.

A directive on asylum procedures (COM (2000) 578; amended COM (2002) 362) has also been agreed to at April 29, 2004 JHA Council. The European Parliament is to be reconsulted.
[21] Reg.539/2001 establishing visa list [2001] O.J. L81/1; see also Reg.2414/2001 moving Romania to "white list" not requiring visas [2001] O.J. L327/1 and Reg.453/2003 on visa list [2003] L69/10. The UK and Ireland have opted out of all these measures.
[22] Long term migrants directive [2004] O.J. L16/44. The UK has opted out of this measure.
[23] Dir. 2003/86 on family reunification [2003] O.J. L251/12). The UK has opted out of this measure.
[24] Economic migration directive (COM (2001) 386) which the UK is unlikely to opt into.
[25] Directive on migration of third-country students and volunteers, COM (2002) 548 final which was generally agreed at the April 29, 2004 JHA Council. The UK will opt out of this measure.

There were no major institutional or legal changes brought about by the Treaty of Nice but rather adjustments to address deficiencies in the functioning of the Community and possible imbalance which could result from enlargement by 10 new Member States.

(i) *The Constitution for Europe*

1–27   The EU constitutional "Convention" was convened in February 2002 and met until July 2003 under the chairmanship of former French President Valéry Giscard d'Estaing. It consisted of delegates from national parliaments, the European Parliament, the Commission and EU Member States' governments, including the parliaments and governments of states which have applied to join the European Union. Following on from a declaration to the Treaty of Nice and a later declaration agreed by the European Council summit meeting in Laeken in December 2001, the Convention had the task of examining the current EU and EC Treaties and suggesting possible changes. It decided to draft an EU Constitution merging the current EU and EC Treaties, based on the existing texts but making a number of important changes.

1–28   A draft of the Treaty establishing a Constitution for Europe, which consolidates and amends the existing Treaties, was agreed by Member States at an Intergovernmental Conference (IGC) in June 2004. The final version of the EU Constitution is to be signed at the end of 2004.[26] Thereafter the EU Constitution will need to be approved by national parliaments and national referenda and the text is therefore unlikely to come into force before 2006. The draft EU Constitution does not appear to make any significant changes in the field of free movement of persons in the European Union although changes are made to decision-making processes. There are however notable additions to the Treaties in the areas of asylum and immigration (presently under Title IV of the EC Treaty[27]).

2. THE EU INSTITUTIONS

(a) *Introduction*

1–29   The EU's decision-making process involves three main institutions:

(a)   the European Parliament which represents the European Union's citizens and is directly elected by them;

(b)   the Council of the European Union which represents the individual Member States;

---

[26] See Appendix 30 for a table of the key EC and EU Treaty provisions and their corresponding provisions in the draft EU Constitution.

[27] For a full analysis of the evolution of the draft Treaty establishing a Constitution for Europe readers are referred to the Statewatch (website:*www.statewatch.orgleuconstitution.htm*) from which the information in this section is obtained.

(c) the European Commission, which seeks to uphold the interests of the Union as a whole.

These three bodies together produce the policies and laws (directives, regulations and decisions) that apply throughout the European Union. In principle, it is the Commission that proposes new EU laws and it is the Parliament and Council that adopt them.

There are two other institutions of principal importance: **1–30**

(a) the European Court of Justice which upholds the rule of law in the European Union; and

(b) the Court of Auditors which checks the financing of the Union's activities.

All five institutions were set up under the Treaties outlined above. The Treaties themselves are agreed by the key political figures in the Member States and ratified by their national Parliaments. They lay down the rules and procedures that the EU institutions must follow.

(b) *The European Parliament*

The Parliament consists of "representatives of the peoples of the States   **1–31**
brought together in the Communities". The representatives are known as Members of the European Parliament (MEPs). They are elected for terms of five years.[28] The number of MEPs is currently 786, organised into seven political rather than national groups.

The European Parliament operates from France, Belgium and Luxembourg.   **1–32**
The monthly plenary sessions, which all MEPs attend, are held in Strasbourg, France. Parliamentary committee meetings and any additional plenary sessions are held in Brussels (Belgium), whilst Luxembourg is home to the administrative offices (the "General Secretariat").

Parliament has three main roles. First it shares with the Council the *power to legislate*. Secondly it exercises *democratic supervision* over all EU institutions, and in particular the Commission. It has the power to approve or reject the nomination of Commissioners, and it has the right to censure the Commission as a whole. Finally it shares with the Council *authority over the EU budget* and can therefore influence EU spending.

(i) *The Power to Legislate*

The influence and power that the European Parliament exerts over the   **1–33**
legislative process depends on the legal basis of the act in question. The different procedures are set out in Arts 251 to 255 EC Treaty.

Whenever the Council is required to consult the Parliament before adopting   **1–34**
a binding measure, the balance of power clearly lies with the Council.

---

[28] Art.190 EC Treaty.

However the Parliament's influence in such cases is not nugatory. If the Parliament is not properly consulted on the legislation in question, it will be void.[29]

1–35   Article 252 EC Treaty sets out a *"co-operation procedure"*. In contrast to the consultation procedure which does not give the Parliament the power to force any amendments or prevent the adoption of a measure, the co-operation procedure gives the Parliament greater power. At the conclusion of the first reading of a measure, the Council will adopt a "common position" which is communicated to the Parliament. The Parliament may then approve the common position in which case the Council must adopt the measure in accordance with the common position. Alternatively the Parliament may reject the common position in which case the Council may still adopt the measure but it can only do so on the basis of unanimity. Thirdly the Parliament may propose amendments to the common position. In such a case the Commission is required to re-examine the measure and either adopt or reject the Parliament's amendments. The re-examined measure is then returned to the Council, which may adopt it by qualified majority or amend it only by unanimity.

1–36   The most common procedure for adopting EU legislation is *"co-decision"* as laid down in Art.251 EC Treaty. This places the European Parliament and the Council on more of an equal footing and the laws passed using this procedure are joint acts of the Council and Parliament. The procedure applies to legislation in a wide range of fields. As with the co-operation procedure the Council adopts a "common position" which is communicated to the Parliament. At the second reading the Parliament must take a position on the common position. If the Parliament by absolute majority rejects the common position, the Council is informed. The Council may then convene a meeting of the "Conciliation Committee" which is composed of equal numbers of representatives from the Council and Parliament. The Committee is required to reach agreement on the joint text within six weeks.[30] Agreement will only be reached by qualified majority of the Council representatives and absolute majority of the Parliament representatives. If either of the two institutions fail to agree within the time period, the measure is deemed not to be adopted.

(ii) *Democratic Supervision*

1–37   Parliament exercises democratic supervision over the other European institutions. It does so in several ways. First, when a new Commission is to be appointed, Parliament interviews all the prospective new members and President of the Commission (nominated by the Member States). They cannot be appointed without Parliament's approval.[31] Secondly, the Commission is politically answerable to Parliament, which can pass a "motion of censure" calling for its mass resignation.[32] For a motion to be carried there must be a two-thirds majority of the votes cast.

---

[29] Case 138/79 *Roquette v Council* [1980] E.C.R. 3333.
[30] Art.251(5) EC Treaty.
[31] Art.241 EC Treaty.
[32] Art.201 EC Treaty.

More generally, Parliament exercises control by regularly examining reports **1–38**
sent to it by the Commission (general reports, reports on the implementation
of the budget, the application of Community law, etc.). Moreover, MEPs regularly ask the Commission written and oral questions. The members of the
Commission attend plenary sessions of Parliament and meetings of the parliamentary committees, maintaining a continual dialogue between the two
institutions. Parliament can also exercise democratic control by examining
petitions from citizens and setting up temporary committees of inquiry.

Finally, Parliament provides input to every EU summit (the European **1–39**
Council meetings). At the opening of each summit, the President of
Parliament is invited to express Parliament's views and concerns about
topical issues and the items on the European Council's agenda.

(iii) *The Budgetary Powers*

The European Union's annual budget is decided jointly by Parliament and **1–40**
the Council of the European Union. Parliament debates it in two successive
readings, and it does not come into force until it has been signed by the
President of Parliament. Parliament's Committee on Budgetary Control
(COCOBU) monitors how the budget is spent, and each year Parliament
decides whether to approve the Commission's handling of the budget for the
previous financial year. This approval process is technically known as
"granting a discharge".

The division of powers between the Council and Parliament depends on **1–41**
whether the expenditure is "compulsory expenditure", which includes all
expenditure to enable the Community to meet its obligations under the
Treaties, or non-compulsory expenditure, which consists mainly of expenditure on the common agricultural policy and aid to non-European countries.
The Parliament has the final control over the non-compulsory expenditure.

(c) *The Council of the European Union*

(i) *Organisation of the Council*

The Council is the EU's main decision-making body responsible for policy **1–42**
and legislative decisions. It represents the Member States, and its meetings
are attended by one minister from each of the EU's national governments.
Attendance by particular ministers at meetings depends on what subjects are
on the agenda.

Altogether there are nine different Council configurations: **1–43**

(a)   General Affairs and External Relations;

(b)   Economic and Financial Affairs ("ECOFIN");

(c)   Justice and Home Affairs;

(d)   Employment, Social Policy, Health and Consumer Affairs;

(e)   Competitiveness (Internal Market, Industry and Research);

(f)   Transport, Telecommunications and Energy;

(g)   Agriculture and Fisheries;

(h)   Environment;

(i)   Education, Youth and Culture.

Nevertheless, the Council remains one single institution. Each minister in the Council is empowered to commit his or her government. In other words, the minister's signature is the signature of the whole government. Moreover, each minister in the Council is answerable to his or her national parliament and to the citizens whom that parliament represents. This ensures the democratic legitimacy of the Council's decisions.

(ii) Powers of the Council

1–44   The Council has a wide range of powers and responsibilities which are laid down in Art.202 EC Treaty and which include legislative powers shared with the European Parliament. The legislative process is examined in paras 1–33 to 1–36 above. In principle, the Council acts on a proposal from the Commission, and the Commission normally has responsibility for ensuring that EU legislation, once adopted, is correctly applied.

1–45   Each year the Council "concludes" (*i.e.* officially signs) a number of agreements between the European Union and non-EU countries, as well as with international organisations. These agreements may cover broad areas such as trade, co-operation and development or they may deal with specific subjects such as textiles, fisheries, science and technology, transport, etc.

1–46   It is the Council's duty to co-ordinate the broad economic policies of the Member States and to approve the European Union's budget with the Parliament. The Council is also charged with developing the European Union's Common Foreign and Security Policy and co-ordinating co-operation between the national courts and police forces in criminal matters. These two responsibilities in foreign and security policy and police matters relate largely to areas in which the Member States have not delegated their powers to the Community but are co-operating at an inter-governmental level.[33]

(iii) The Council Presidency

1–47   The Presidency of the Council rotates every six months amongst all Member States. During its Presidency each EU Member State in turn takes charge of the Council agenda and chairs all the meetings for a six-month period, promoting legislative and political decisions and brokering compromises between the Member States.

---

[33] Post Amsterdam co-operation on foreign and security policy and co-operation in policing remain under "second" and "third pillars" of the Treaty on European Union and therefore outside of the competence of the Community.

(iv) *Decision-making in the Council*

Decisions in the Council are taken by vote. The bigger the country's popula-   **1–48**
tion, the more votes it has. But the number is not strictly proportional: it is
adjusted in favour of the less populous countries. The number of votes that
each Member State is allocated in the Council is set out in Art.205 EC Treaty.
From May 1, 2004 (when 10 new Member States joined the European Union)
until October 31, 2004, there are transitional arrangements for changing the
weighting of votes.

From November 1, 2004, the number of votes each country can cast (including   **1–49**
the new Member States) is as follows:

Germany, France, Italy and the United Kingdom	29
Spain and Poland	27
Netherlands	13
Belgium, Czech Republic, Greece, Hungary and Portugal	12
Austria and Sweden	10
Denmark, Ireland, Lithuania, Slovakia and Finland	7
Cyprus, Estonia, Latvia, Luxembourg and Slovenia	4
Malta	3

The most common voting procedure in the Council is "qualified majority   **1–50**
voting" (QMV). This means that, for a proposal to be adopted, it needs the
support of a specified minimum number of votes. From November 1, 2004, a
qualified majority will be reached if a majority of Member States (in some
cases a two-thirds majority) approve and if a minimum of votes is cast in
favour—which is 72.3 per cent of the total. In addition, a Member State may
ask for confirmation that the votes in favour represent at least 62 per cent of
the total population of the Union. If this is found not to be the case, the
decision will not be adopted.

(d) *The European Commission*

The Commission is the politically independent institution that represents and   **1–51**
upholds the interests of the European Union as a whole. It is the driving force
within the European Union's institutional system: it proposes legislation,
policies and programmes of action and it is responsible for implementing the
decisions of Parliament and the Council.

Like the Parliament and the Council, the European Commission was set up   **1–52**
in the 1950s under the EU's founding Treaties. It is now provided for in Arts
211 to 219 EC Treaty.

(i) *Constitution and Organisation of the Commission*

1–53 The term "Commission" is used in two senses. First, it refers to the members of the Commission—namely the team ("College of Commissioners") appointed by the Member States and Parliament to run the institution and take its decisions. Secondly, the term "Commission" refers to the institution itself and to its staff.

Informally, the members of the Commission are known as "commissioners". Generally they will have all held political positions in their countries of origin, and many have been government ministers, but as members of the Commission they are committed to acting in the interests of the Union as a whole and not taking instructions from national governments.

1–54 A new Commission is appointed every five years, within six months of the elections to the European Parliament.[34] From November 2004 there will be 25 members of the Commission, as each Member State will have one commissioner.[35]

The Commission remains politically answerable to Parliament, which has the power to dismiss it by adopting a motion of censure.[36] The Commission attends all the sessions of the European Parliament, where it must clarify and justify its policies. It also replies regularly to written and oral questions posed by MEPs. The day-to-day work of the Commission is done by its administrative officials, experts, translators, interpreters and secretarial staff. The Commission is based in Brussels although it has representations in all EU Member States and delegations in other countries around the world.

1–55 The Commission's staff are organised into departments, known as "Directorates-General" (DGs) and "services" (such as the Legal Service). Each DG is responsible for a particular policy area and is headed by a Director-General who is answerable to one of the commissioners.

(ii) *The Functions of the Commission*

1–56 The European Commission has four main roles:

(a) to propose legislation to Parliament and the Council;

(b) to manage and implement EU policies and the budget;

(c) to enforce European law (jointly with the Court of Justice);

(d) to represent the European Union on the international stage, for example by negotiating agreements between the Eurpoean Union and other countries.

---

[34] Art.214 EC Treaty.
[35] Art.213 EC Treaty.
[36] See para. 1–37 above.

Proposing new legislation

Under the Treaty, the Commission has the "right of initiative". It is responsi- **1–57**
ble for drawing up proposals for new European legislation, which it presents to
Parliament and the Council. Before making any proposals, the Commission is
obliged to consult two advisory bodies: the Economic and Social Committee
(made up of employers' and trade unions' representatives) and the Committee
of the Regions (made up of representatives of local and regional authorities).
It also seeks the opinions of national Parliaments and governments.

Implementing EU policies and the budget

As the European Union's executive body, the Commission is responsible for **1–58**
managing and implementing the EU budget and the policies and programmes adopted by Parliament and the Council. Most of the actual work
and spending is done by national and local authorities, but the Commission
is responsible for supervising it.

The Commission handles the budget under the supervision of the Court of **1–59**
Auditors. Both institutions aim to ensure good financial management. Only
if it satisfied with the Court of Auditors' annual report does the European
Parliament grant the Commission discharge for implementing the budget.

Enforcing European law

The Commission acts as "guardian of the Treaties". This means that the **1–60**
Commission, together with the Court of Justice, is responsible for making
sure EU law is properly applied in all the Member States.

Article 226 EC Treaty provides that if the Commission considers that a par- **1–61**
ticular Member State has failed to fulfil a particular obligation under the
Treaty, it may take action against that Member State. In the first instance the
Commission launches a legal process called the "infringement procedure",
which involves notifying the Member State of the alleged breach of
Community law and giving the Member State an opportunity to respond.
The Commission will then deliver a reasoned opinion.

If the Member State fails to comply with Commission's opinion the latter
must then refer the matter to the European Court of Justice, which has the
power to impose penalties.

Representing the EU on the international stage

A central aspect of the Commission's functions revolves around its conduct **1–62**
of EU's external trade relations. The Commission also has the responsibility
of negotiating international agreements on behalf of the European Union.[37]

---

[37] The Contonou Agreement discussed in paras 15–67 to 15–70 was negotiated by the
Commission for instance.

CHAPTER 2

THE COMMUNITY LEGAL ORDER

This chapter examines the sources of Community law and the system and context in which Community law operates. The inter-relationship between Community law and national legal systems is considered as are fundamental principles which are applied in the Community legal order.

1. SOURCES OF COMMUNITY LAW

Before considering the way in which Community law interacts with the legal systems of the individual Member States of the European Union it is necessary to briefly examine the five sources of Community law. These include: **2–01**

(a)   Treaties;

(b)   Secondary legislation including regulations, directives and decisions;

(c)   Agreement with third countries;

(d)   Rulings of the European Court of Justice and Court of First Instance; and

(e)   General Principles of Community law.

(a) *Treaties*

The primary source of Community is the EC and EU Treaties as amended by various other Treaties such as the Single European Act and the Treaty of Nice. These Treaties and their evolution are discussed in detail in Chapter 1. **2–02**

(b) *Secondary Legislation*

The Community institutions are given the power under Art.249 EC Treaty to adopt three types of secondary legislation in order to give effect to the provisions of the Treaty Regulations, Directives and Decisions: **2–03**

Article 249 EC Treaty

In order to carry out their task and in accordance with the provisions of this Treaty, the European Parliament acting jointly with the Council, the Council and the Commission shall make regulations and issue directives, take decisions, make recommendations or deliver opinions.

A regulation shall have general application. It shall be binding in its entirety and directly applicable in all Member States.

A directive shall be binding, as to the result to be achieved, upon each Member State to which it is addressed, but shall leave to the national authorities the choice of form and methods.

A decision shall be binding in its entirety upon those to whom it is addressed. Recommendations and opinions shall have no binding force.

2–04 There is a considerable volume of secondary legislation in general in Community law and the field of free movement of persons is no exception to that. Part II of this book will focus on the primary and secondary legislation which specifically relates to the free movement of persons within the European Union.

As is evident the three different types of secondary legislation are different in their effect.

2–05 *Regulations* are the most powerful form of secondary legislation that the institutions can make. As is discussed further in paras 2–44 to 2–47 below, regulations are directly applicable in all the Member States. Regulations are not addressed to Member States or private individuals specifically. They do not require any implementation into the national legal systems of the Member States in order to make them effective. In fact as will be seen Member States are not permitted to adopt national implementing measures unless the regulation itself requires it or it is necessary in order to give effect to the regulation in the national legal system.

2–06 *Directives* in contrast are weaker forms of secondary legislation. They are addressed to the Member States and impose an obligation on the Member States to which they are addressed to adopt all the measures necessary to ensure that the objectives of the directive are given full effect. Member States are entitled to choose how to implement a directive and therefore implementing measures do vary from Member State to Member State. The direct effect of directives is discussed in paras 2–48 to 2–53 below.

2–07 *Decisions* of the Community institutions are addressed to specific Member States or particular individuals. They take effect upon communication to the person or Member State to whom they are addressed. Decisions addressed to a Member State are binding on all the organs of that State, including the courts. Decisions differ from regulations in that they are addressed to specific states or individuals. Only the addressees are bound by the decision. Decisions differ from directives in that they are directly effective rather than merely setting out the objectives to be achieved. Examples of where decisions may be passed are in relation to competition policy, state aid and imposition of fines.

(c) *Agreements with Third Countries*

2–08 The European Union is not simply a supranational body confined to internal activities, it interacts considerably within the international arena representing both a powerful trade bloc as well as an influential political body. The European Union concludes agreements with third countries as well as international bodies to give effect to its trade, customs, social, political and economic aims within the international arena. There are three types of agreements which are of particular importance: Association Agreements, Co-operation Agreements and Trade Agreements.

Association agreements have been concluded with a wide variety of non-EU **2–09** countries. Such agreements go beyond mere trade or aid agreements and are expressions of political and economic co-operation between Member States. Association agreements are often used as a pre-accession tool to prepare third countries to possible accession to the European Union. The European Union has association agreements with Bulgaria, Romania and Turkey; the EU has a stabilisation and association agreement with Macedonia; and is in the process of negotiating such agreement with other states in the western Balkans.

Co-operation agreements are not as far reaching as association agreements in **2–10** that they are only aimed at economic co-operation at an intensive level. The European Union has co-operation agreements with Algeria, Morocco and Tunisia.

Trade agreements have been concluded with a very large number of countries **2–11** and international bodies. The most important trade agreements are with the World Trade Organisation (WTO) and the multilateral agreements deriving from it including the General Agreement on Trade and Tariff (GATT).

Part Three of this book will focus on agreements with third countries. It will **2–12** examine agreements which have provisions which potentially impact on the free movement of persons and provide detailed analysis of certain association agreements, namely those with Bulgaria, Romania and Turkey exploring the free movement provisions in those individual agreements.

(d) *Rulings by the ECJ and CFI*

At the heart of the Community legal system is the European Court of Justice **2–13** (ECJ) and the Court of First Instance (CFI). Judgments of these courts are binding on nationals courts. They are the only courts with judicial authority over Community law. The ECJ is the highest judicial authority. Since the Treaty of Nice the CFI has power to determine a wider range of actions in order to alleviate the pressure on the ECJ.

There are a several types of action that can be brought before the ECJ and **2–14** CFI. It is important to note that there is no mechanism for individuals to take direct action against Member States for failure to act in conformity with Community law.[1] An individual with a complaint that a Member State has failed to implement Community law correctly or has breached Community law would have two mechanisms for bringing the matter before the ECJ. The individual could either bring the matter to the attention of the Commission (or another Member State) in order that the Commission (or the other Member State) might bring infringement proceedings against the offending state under Art.226 EC Treaty or the individual would have to bring legal proceedings in the national legal system and request a reference by the national court under Art.234 EC Treaty.

---

[1] This is entirely different from the procedures before the European Court of Human Rights where for instance an aggrieved individual who has exhausted all possible domestic remedies has a right of individual petition to that court.

2–15 There are however two exceptions to the principle that individuals may not bring direct actions in the ECJ or CFI. First where a decision is individually directed at a person an action for annulment under Art.230 EC Treaty might be brought. Secondly, where the person has suffered damage as a result of the action of EC staff an action for damages under Art.235 would be appropriate.

All procedures before the ECJ and CFI, including those mentioned above, are described briefly below.

(i) *Treaty Infringement Proceedings (Article 226 EC Treaty)*

2–16 These are proceedings for establishing whether a Member State failed to fulfil an obligation imposed upon it by Community law. These must be preceeded by a preliminary procedure in which the Member State concerned is given an opportunity to defend its action or lack of action. If the matter is not settled at this stage either the Commission or another Member State can institute proceedings against the Member State concerned in the ECJ. The ECJ will then determine whether the Member State has breached an obligation of Community law. Most actions are brought by the Commission.

2–17 The Commission has brought a number of infringement proceedings against the Member States in the free movement field.[2] This mechanism is unsatisfactory for an individual aggrieved by the infringement of Community law by a Member State since it will result in no compensation or individual determination regarding his particular situation.

(ii) *Actions for Annulment (Article 230 EC Treaty)*

2–18 These actions can be brought against a Community institution in order to annul a legally binding measure. If an action is brought by an individual it must be brought in the CFI. Individuals or companies can only bring such direct action against decisions personally addressed to them.[3] Actions must be based on allegations of *ultra vires*, breach of procedural requirements or breach of Community law. Actions for annulment must be brought within two months of the impugned decision.

(iii) *Complaints for Failure to Act (Article 232 EC Treaty)*

2–19 Complaints for failure to act may be taken against the Commission, the Council, the Parliament or the European Central Bank. When actions are brought by individuals or companies it will be for a breach of Treaty obligations in failing to address a decision to them as required by the Treaty.

---

[2] For instance Case C–424/98 *Commission v Italy* [2000] E.C.R. I–4001. See Commission's First Report to the Council and Parliament on the implementation of Directives 90/364, 90/365 and 93/96 (right of residence) where the Commission describes the number of proceedings that were commenced for incorrect implementation of the self-sufficient directives.

[3] A person named on the Taliban sanctions list might for instance bring such action if they considered that the inclusion of their name on that list was *ultra vires* or procedurally incorrect.

(iv) *Actions for Damages (Articles 235 and 288(2) EC Treaty)*

Individuals and companies who suffer damage as a result of the action of EC **2–20**
staff can bring actions before the CFI. Member States which suffer such
damage may bring actions before the ECJ. The complainant would need to
demonstrate that there had been an unlawful act by a Community institution
or a member of its staff in the exercise of his functions. Actual harm must
have been suffered.

(v) *Actions by Community Staff (Article 236 EC Treaty)*

This is a mechanism for Community staff to bring actions before the CFI in **2–21**
relation to disputes regarding their employment relationship.

(vi) *Appeals Procedure (Article 225(1) EC Treaty)*

There is a right of appeal against decisions of the CFI to the ECJ on points **2–22**
of law. The appeal must be on grounds of lack of competence by the CFI, a
breach of procedure or a breach of Community law.

(vii) *Provisional Legal Protection (Articles 242 and 243 EC Treaty)*

Actions before the CFI or the ECJ do not automatically have suspensive effect. **2–23**
It is possible to apply the CFI or the ECJ to have the contested act suspended.
Applications for provisional legal protection will be considered on the basis of
prospects of success of the main action, urgency of the order and weighing
of the interests of the complainant against the interests of the Community
in implementation of the measure and any third parties' interests.

(viii) *Preliminary Rulings (Article 234 EC Treaty)*

This is the mechanism whereby national courts can seek the guidance of the **2–24**
ECJ on matters of Community law. The national court will stay proceedings
pending reference to the ECJ on questions of interpretation of Community
law or regarding the validity of a Community law measure. The ECJ
responds with a judgment which is a mandatory ruling binding on all
Member States whether or not they were party to proceedings. The objective
of the preliminary ruling procedure is to ensure uniform application of
Community law across the Member States. It is a mechanism whereby individuals and companies can ensure the proper application of Community law
before national courts. Once the ECJ has given its judgment the matter
returns to the national court for final ruling on the case and determination of
issues such as costs and damages.

The subject-matter of a preliminary reference must be confined to **2–25**
Community law measures only. The ECJ will not entertain references
concerning the interpretation or application of national law.

The reference procedure is available to all courts of the Member States. In **2–26**
this sense "court" means any independent institution which is empowered to
resolve disputes under due process of law. Thus a "court" may range from the
Constitutional court to a tribunal or adjudicator. Whether a court makes a
reference to the ECJ will depend on a number of factors, primarily whether

the matter is *"acte clair"*[4] and therefore whether the Community law measure requires any further interpretation by the ECJ.[5] Where a question of Community is considered by the final court of appeal in any Member State that court is obliged to refer to the ECJ unless the referral would make no material difference to the outcome of proceedings, or if the question has already been answered by the ECJ or if the interpretation of the Community law provision is not open to reasonable doubt.[6]

2. PRINCIPLES OF COMMUNITY LAW

(a) *Introduction*

2–27   The legal system created by the European Union is unique and the inter-relationship between the Community legal order and national legal systems is not reflective of any other supranational arrangements. A national legal system is self-contained. By contrast the Community legal order relies on the support of the national legal systems. It is the national legal systems which bring EU law into the lives of people living within the Member States.

2–28   European Union law is founded on a number of basic principles which assist in understanding the inter-relationship between the Member States and the Community. It clearly imposes obligations on Member States as well as the Community and it is important that those obligations as well as the system for enforcement are defined and adhered to. The ECJ has played a very significant role in defining the principles which guide the interpretation and application of EU law. Equally the EU and EC Treaties themselves codify many of the principles which underpin EU law.

(b) *Supremacy*

2–29   Numerous provisions of the EU and EC Treaties and secondary legislation impose obligations on Member States requiring them to ensure that their national legislation is in conformity with these obligations. Either the Commission or another Member State could bring an action before the ECJ for breach of such obligations by a Member State. Failure by the Member State to abide by the order of the ECJ will result in a financial penalty.

---

[4] The term *"acte clair"* means that national courts, bearing in mind the risk of divergences in judicial decisions within the Community, must be convinced that the interpretation or resolution of an issue taken by the national court is equally obvious to the court of the other Member States or the ECJ: see Case 283/81 *CILFIT* [1982] E.C.R. 3415.
[5] For the test to be applied by UK courts, see *R. v International Stock Exchange Ex p. Else* [1993] 1 All E.R. 420
[6] The procedure for preliminary references to the ECJ is not the subject-matter of this book. Readers are referred to the comprehensive book entitled, *References to the European Court* by D. Anderson Q.C. and M. Demetriou (2nd ed, Sweet and Maxwell, 2002).

Article 10 EC Treaty states: 2–30

> "Member States shall take all appropriate measures, whether general or particular, to ensure fulfilment of the obligations arising out of this Treaty or resulting from action taken by the institutions of the Community. They shall facilitate the achievement of the Community's tasks. They shall abstain from any measure which could jeopardise the attainment of the objectives of this Treaty."

Whilst it is not made express in either the Treaty of Rome or the subsequent amendments to that Treaty, the ECJ has repeatedly referred to the supremacy of Community law. According to the ECJ national courts of Member States are under an obligation to make their judgments in line with the ECJ. In a number of decisions the ECJ has established the primacy of Community law.

In *Van Gend en Loos*[7] the ECJ stated: 2–31

> ". . . the Community constitutes a new legal order of international law for the benefit of which the states have limited their sovereign rights, albeit within limited fields . . . ".

The doctrine of supremacy was further explained in *Costa v ENEL*[8] where 2–32
the ECJ held:

> "By creating a Community of unlimited duration, having its own institutions, its own personality, its own legal capacity and capacity of representation on the international plane and, more particularly, real powers stemming from a limitation of sovereignty or a transfer of powers from the States to the Community, the Member States have limited their sovereign rights, albeit within limited fields, and have thus created a body of law which binds both their nationals and themselves.
>
> The integration into the laws of each Member State of provisions, which derive from the Community, and more generally the terms and the spirit of the Treaty, make it impossible for the States, as a corollary, to accord precedence to a unilateral and subsequent measure over a legal system accepted by them on the basis of reciprocity."

As the ECJ stated in *Costa v ENEL*, the Treaty: ". . . has created its own legal 2–33
system which . . . became an integral part of the legal systems of the Member States and which their courts are bound to apply."

The ECJ went even further in *Internationale Handelsgesellschaft*[9] in making 2–34
clear that national courts will be obliged to disapply any national law provision or practice which contradicts a Treaty provision. As put by the ECJ "the law born from the Treaty . . . [cannot] . . . have the courts opposing to it rules of national law of any nature whatever".

The consequence of the doctrine of supremacy is that Community law has a 2–35
very significant impact both on the legislation and the administrative and

---

[7] Case 26/62 *Van Gend en Loos v Nederlandse Administratie der Berlastingen* [1963] E.C.R.1.
[8] Case 6/64 *Costa v ENEL* [1964] E.C.R. 585.
[9] Case 11/70 *Internationale Handelsgesellschaft v Einfuhr-und Vorratssteelle für Getreide und Futtermittel* [1970] E.C.R. 1125.

judicial practices of the Member States. Where an EU law provision has direct effect any provision of domestic law that conflicts with that EU law is rendered automatically inapplicable. This principle applies regardless of whether the national law takes the form of primary or secondary legislation and whether the national law came into force before or after the EU law provision. National courts are prevented from applying any national law which conflicts with the EU law provision. Any provision of domestic law, and any administrative or judicial practice, which might prevent Community laws from taking their full effect must be set aside.[10]

(c) *Direct Effect*

(i) *Meaning of "direct effect"*

2–36   It is well established in Community law that in certain instances Community law has primacy over Member States' domestic laws. This is where the provisions of Community law are said to have direct effect. The consequence of a provision having direct effect is that it grants rights to natural and legal persons. The provision can be relied upon by that individual before the national courts and authorities of the Member States regardless of any other provisions in domestic law and without the need for incorporation of the provision into domestic law.

2–37   The doctrine of direct effect was established by the ECJ in *Van Gend en Loos*.[11] In order for a provision of Community law to be considered to be directly effective the following three conditions must be satisfied:

(1)   the provision must be clear and precise;

(2)   the provision must be capable of conferring rights on individuals;

(3)   its operation must not be dependent on further action being taken by the Community or the national authorities or any other body and is thus "unconditional".

2–38   In essence the criteria seek to identify whether a provision is capable as it stands of judicial enforcement. Not all provisions of EU law will be directly effective. Provisions which lay down general objectives for instance will not be directly effective. The Commission produced a list of all direct effect measures in 1983 which has not been updated.[12]

2–39   Where the individual seeks to rely on the direct effect against other individuals, the provision is described as being *horizontally* effective. Where on the other hand the reliance is against a Member State, the provision is described as being *vertically* effective. In the area of free movement of persons it is primarily the vertical effect of a provision that is of concern as it is in the main

---

[10] In *R. v the Secretary of State for Transport Ex p. Factortame Ltd* (No.2) [1991] A.C. 603, the UK courts granted an interim injunction suspending the application of primary English law pending the outcome of a legal suit based on an argument that that English law was contrary to Community law.

[11] Case 26/62 *Van Gend en Loos v Nederlandse Administratie der Berlastingen* [1963] E.C.R.1.

[12] [1983] O.J. C177/13.

state authorities and courts which may facilitate or frustrate free movement rights. However the actions of private individuals such as employers might interfere with directly effective free movement rights.[13]

It is important to distinguish between a provision which may be "directly applicable" and one which may be "directly effective". A provision may be directly applicable in that it can be applied by a national court or authority. However that same provision might not be directly effective if for instance further legislative measures are required to make it effective. Directly applicable but not directly effective provisions can be regarded as binding on Member States although they may be too vague to form the direct source of rights and obligations for individuals, and still other provisions are too incomplete and require extended measures of implementation before they can be fully effective in law.[14] **2–40**

The direct effect of various EU law provisions are discussed below.

(ii) *Treaty Provisions*

In *Van Gend en Loos* the ECJ said that certain provisions of Community law create ". . . individual rights which national courts must protect". In that case the ECJ concluded that a "new legal order" had been created by the Treaty which ". . . independently of the legislation of Member States . . . not only imposes legislation upon individuals but is also intended to confer upon them rights which become part of their legal heritage". **2–41**

The ECJ has determined that a large number of EC Treaty provisions are directly effective. Of particular importance in the free movement field, the ECJ has held Art.39 EC Treaty on the free movement of workers, Art.43 EC Treaty on the freedom of establishment and Art.49 EC Treaty on the freedom to provide services to have direct effect. **2–42**

This means that not only do the relevant Treaty provisions provide the framework for the free movement of persons, they also provide specific rights that can be relied upon by individuals before their national courts and authorities to assert specific rights. This can be significant particularly where there is no secondary legislation to cover the area of concern or the secondary legislation itself is not directly effective.[15] Thus for instance the free movement of work-seekers is said to derive directly from Art.39 EC Treaty in the absence of any secondary legislation specifically referring to the situation of work-seekers.[16] **2–43**

---

[13] It is to be noted that directives do not have horizontal effect. See further para. 2–53 below.

[14] There is considerable academic debate about the true distinction between "direct applicability" and "direct effect". Some have argued that the drafters of the Treaty must have intended that regulations alone had direct effect. However the ECJ has gone out of its way to find that other measures and provisions are capable of direct effect so the distinction between the Treaty reference to "applicability" which applies only to regulations and "direct effect" is drawn. See for instance Craig, Paul and de Búrca, Gráinne, *EU Law: Text, Cases and Materials* 2nd ed, (Oxford University Press, 1998); and Pescatore, Pierre, "*The Doctrine of Direct Effect: An Infant Disease of Community Law*" (1983) 8 E.L. Rev. 155–177.

[15] This might be the case with certain directives. Further discussion of the direct effect of directives, see below.

[16] See further paras 7–44 to 7–48 on workers.

(iii) *Regulations*

2–44 Article 249 EC Treaty provides that a regulation "shall be binding in its entirety and directly applicable in all Member States". There is therefore no need for national implementation of regulations. Regulations are automatically part of national law. Any national implementing legislation must be consistent with the meaning given to the regulation by the ECJ. In *Bussone*[17] the ECJ stated:

> "The direct applicability of a regulation requires that its entry into force and its application in favour of or against those subject to it must be independent of any measure of reception into national law".

2–46 In *Commission v Italy*[18] the ECJ held for the first time that national implementing measures can be considered contrary to Community law because the Community nature of the provision is obscured by national implementation. That is not to say that the ECJ considers that national implementation of any regulation is generally impermissible but in general best practice would dictate that the national measure reflects accurately the precise wording of the regulation it purports to implement.[19]

2–47 Not all regulations will have direct effect. All will depend on the terms of the regulation itself. Where for example a regulation itself provides for implementing measures to be taken by a Community institution or Member State then its terms may mean that it, although binding and directly applicable, may not have direct effect. This would be the position where a provision of a regulation is not sufficiently precise or is too conditional.

(iv) *Directives*

2–48 Article 249 EC Treaty provides that: ". . . a directive shall be binding, as to the result to be achieved, upon each Member State to whom it is addressed, but shall leave to the national authorities the choice of form and methods".

At first sight the wording of Art.249 EC Treaty might suggest that directives could not have direct effect because although binding, implementation is at the choice of each Member State. But this does not mean that Member States can chose not to implement a directive, nor to do so in diluted form.

2–49 In *Van Duyn v Home Office*,[20] the ECJ found that it would be incompatible with the binding effect of a directive to exclude the possibility that an obli-

---

[17] Case 31/78 *Bussone v Ministère Italien de l'agriculture* [1978] E.C.R. 2429.
[18] Case 168/85 *Commission v Italy* (1986) E.C.R. 2945.
[19] Some commentators such as Hartley consider that national implementation can be useful for instance where national rules purport to codify the law in a particular area and thus give a complete statement of all the relevant legal rules. However in the interests of clarity and consistency it is important that the national measures import the precise wording of the regulation in question. Hartley, *The Foundations of European Community Law. An Introduction to the Constitutional and Administrative Law of the European Community* (Oxford University Press, 4th ed, 1998), p.199.
[20] Case 41/74 *Van Duyn v Home Office* [1974] E.C.R. 1337.

gation which a directive imposes may be invoked by the individuals concerned. Ms Van Duyn sought to rely on Art.3 of Directive 64/221 which provides that measures taken on grounds of public policy shall be based exclusively on the personal conduct of the individual concerned. She had been refused leave to enter the United Kingdom to take up employment as a secretary to the Church of Scientology on the basis of a general government policy that the activities of the Church of Scientology were socially harmful. Article 3 of Directive 64/221 had not been implemented anywhere in UK law and the decision in her case was not sought to be justified by reference to her own conduct.

The ECJ held that Ms Van Duyn could rely on Art.3 of Directive 64/221 **2–50** because it was sufficiently precise and unconditional. Remarking generally on the status of directives the ECJ stated:

> "where the Community authorities have, by directive, imposed on Member States the obligation to pursue a particular course of conduct, the useful effect of such an act would be weakened if individuals were prevented from relying on it before their national courts and if the latter were prevented from taking it into consideration as an element of Community law".

The direct effect of directives is not the norm. This is because the Member State to whom the directive is addressed must incorporate that directive into its own national law. The position thus contrasts with regulations which are directly applicable without the need for national implementing measures. Only the failure to implement a directive correctly or within the time-frame required by the directive will result in the individual being able to (or indeed needing to) rely on the provisions of the directive.[21]

In *Francovich*,[22] the ECJ held that provisions of a directive would be directly **2–51** effective if they contained rights which were both identifiable and were attributable to individuals. Where the delay in implementation causes loss, the individual affected can bring an action based on the provisions of the directive. In certain circumstances a Member State would have to recompense an individual for the loss suffered by that individual due to the failure to implement a directive correctly. In that case the directive in question dealing with the rights of employees upon insolvency had not been implemented by Italy. It was not directly effective as it was not sufficiently precise as to who was to pay the sums it had guaranteed in the case of insolvency.

However, the ECJ relied on Art.10 EC Treaty which provides that: "Member **2–52** States shall take all appropriate measures, whether general or particular, to ensure fulfilment of the obligations arising out of this Treaty . . .".

The ECJ laid down three conditions that must be met before the individual can successfully claim damages against the Member State which fails to implement a directive correctly or in time.

---

[21] Case 152/84 *Marshall v Southampton and South-West Hampshire Area Health Authority* [1986] E.C.R. 723. If there is ambiguity in the meaning of a particular provision the national implementing measure then the Community law interpretation should be applied.
[22] Joined Cases C 6 & 9/90 *Francovich v Italy* [1991] E.C.R. I-5357.

(1)   The result laid down by the directive involves the attribution of rights attached to individuals.

(2)   The contents of those rights must be capable of identification from the provisions of that directive.

(3)   A causal link must exist between the failure to implement and the damage suffered.

2–53   Directives do not have horizontal direct effect. This was confirmed by the ECJ in the case of *Marshall*[23] in which it stated:

"With regard to the argument that a directive may not be relied upon against an individual, it must be emphasized that according to Article . . . [249] of the E.C. Treaty the binding nature of a directive, which constitutes the basis for the possibility of relying on the directive before a national court, exists only in relation to 'each Member State to which it is addressed'. It follows that a directive may not of itself impose obligations on an individual and that a provision of a directive may not be relied upon as such against such a person . . .".[24]

The definition of "Member State" in this context however is broadly defined and thus all directives are binding upon all public bodies including nationalised industries,[25] police authorities[26] and health authorities.[27]

(v) *Decisions*

2–54   According to Art.249 EC Treaty a decision is "binding in its entirety upon those to whom it is addressed". Whilst the provision makes no reference to the direct effect of decisions. However the ECJ has held that decisions can be directly effective.[28]

(d) *Indirect Effect*

2–55   Where provisions of Community law are found not have direct effect they must still be taken into account by national courts when interpreting relevant national legislation. This reflects the obligation of good faith imposed on the Member States by Art.10 EC Treaty. This concept of "indirect effect" was relied upon by the ECJ in *Marleasing*[29] where the action was between private operators. The ECJ reiterated that directives cannot impose obligations on individuals. However the ECJ qualified this by holding that the authorities of

---

[23] Case 152/84 *Marshall v Southampton and South-West Hampshire Area Health Authority* [1986] E.C.R. 723.
[24] Case C–152/84 *Marshall v Southampton and South West Hampshire Area Health Authority* [1986] E.C.R. 723, para.48.
[25] Case C-188/89 *Foster v British Gas plc* [1990] E.C.R. I-3313, para. 20.
[26] Case 222/84 *Johnston v Chief Constable of the Royal Ulster Constabulary* [1986] E.C.R. 1651.
[27] Case 152/84 *Marshall v Southampton and South-West Hampshire Area Health Authority* [1986] E.C.R. 723.
[28] See discussion in Craig and de Búrca, *EU Law: Text, Cases and Materials* (2nd ed., Oxford University Press, 1998), p.178.
[29] Case C–106/89 *Marleasing SA v La Comercial Internacional de Alimentación SA* [1990] E.C.R. I–4135.

the Member States have an obligation to give effect to the aims and objectives laid down in a directive, and this obligation is binding on all authorities in the state, including the courts. Therefore when applying national law, whether passed before or after the directive, a national court is required to interpret national law as far as possible so as to be in conformity with the directive.

The obligation on the national courts is thus to construe a national law in accordance with Community law as far as it is possible to do so. Where there are two possible interpretations of a provision in national law, only the one which is consistent with the Community law provision should be adopted.[30] **2–56**

The duty to interpret national law in accordance with Community law extends beyond the strict scope of the Community law provision in question. The national court will be required to interpret national law in accordance with all the general principles of Community law which are discussed below.[31] **2–57**

(e) *General Principles*

When the ECJ examines the application or interpretation of the Treaties or secondary legislation it does so by reference to a number of general principles. These general principles are derived from the Treaties[32] themselves and other acts of the Community including resolutions of the Parliament and decisions of the ECJ and CFI. General principles may not be expressly recognised in the legal systems of all Member States. However they reflect the principles generally accepted in the legal systems of the majority of Member States. **2–58**

(i) *Proportionality*

The principle of proportionality is one which underpins many of the ECJ's decisions. The principle requires that individuals are not subjected to excessive burdens or interferences. The means employed to achieve a particular aim must therefore correspond to the importance of that aim and must be necessary to achieve that aim. Consideration must also be given to whether there was a less intrusive or harsh manner of achieving the aim. **2–59**

Although the principle of proportionality was first developed by the ECJ in cases such as *Granaria*[33] and *Sagulo*[34] the principle is now embodied in Art.5(b) EC Treaty itself which provides that "any action by the Community shall not go beyond what is necessary to achieve the objectives of this Treaty". **2–60**

The principle of proportionality may be used to challenge measures adopted by Community institutions and the legislation enacted by Member States to give effect to Community law.

---

[30] *Webb v Emo Air Cargo (UK) Ltd* [1993] W.L.R. 49.
[31] Case C–168/95 *Lucian Arcaro* [1996] E.C.R. I–4705.
[32] For instance Art.12 EC Treaty on non-discrimination.
[33] Case 116/76 *Granaria BV v Council of Ministers and Commission of the EC* [1977] E.C.R. 1247.
[34] Case 8/77 *Re (Criminal Proceedings) Sagulo* [1977] E.C.R. 1495.

(ii) *Legal Certainty and Legitimate Expectation*

2-61   The principles of legal certainty and legitimate expectation are closely related. The principle of legal certainty means that those subject to Community law should not be placed in a situation of uncertainty as to their legal rights and obligations. Therefore measures directed at individuals or companies must be clear and precise. They must be able to ascertain the time at which the measure comes into effect so that they may bring annulment proceedings under Art.230 EC Treaty within the strict two-month time-limit. Linked to this principle is the principle of non-retroactivity. This provides that Community measures should not take effect before they are published. There are exceptions to this rule where there is justification for retroactivity. It should be noted however that nearly all judgments of the ECJ are retrospective unless the ECJ expressly limits the retroactive effect under the doctrine of temporal effects.[35]

2-62   The principle of legitimate expectation dictates that an individual should be able to act in reliance that Community law will be properly applied to him.[36] The principle is generally used whether decisions are directed at individuals or companies for instance in cases concerning the recovery of State aid, pension levels for Community staff and compensation. Additionally it may have more general application where for instance the individual had an expectation that a directive would be given proper effect through national measures. Where the Member State has a degree of discretion however in Community law there can be no legitimate expectation of how that discretion will be exercised.

(iii) *Non-Discrimination*

2-63   The fundamental character and importance of the principle of equal treatment (or "equality" or "non-discrimination"[37]) is beyond doubt. The principle is reflected in the preamble to the Universal Declaration of Human Rights (UDHR) which characterises the "equal and inalienable rights of all members of the human family" as the foundation of freedom, justice and peace in the word. The principle is confirmed by Art.1 UDHR which provides that "all human beings are born free and equal in dignity and right" and by Art.2 UDHR which provides the entitlement of "everyone . . . to all rights and freedoms without distinction of any kind" (such as race, colour, sex, language, religion, political or other opinion, national or social origin, property, birth or other status). Further, Art.7 UDHR provides that "all are equal before the law and are entitled without any discrimination to equal protection of the law." Moreover the right is a rule of customary international law and is the cornerstone of international human rights law.[38]

---

[35] See for instance Case C–184/99 *Grzelczyk and Centre public d'aide sociale d'Ottignies-Louvain-la-Neuve* [2001] E.C.R. I–6193.

[36] See for instance Case 350/88 *Société française des Biscuits Delacre v Commission* [1990] E.C.R. I–418 and Case C–368/89 *Crispoltoni v Fattoria Autonoma Tabacchi* [1991] E.C.R. I–3715.

[37] The principle is variously described as "the principle of equality", "equal treatment" or "non-discrimination", used herein without distinction.

[38] For an example of a case decided in the refugee context by the House of Lords in the UK on the basis of the fundamental principle on non discrimination, see *Islam v Secretary of State for the Home Department; R. v Immigration Appeal Tribunal and Secretary of State for the Home Department Ex p. Shah* [1999] 2 A.C. 629.

The importance of the fundamental principle of non-discrimination to the   2–64
people of the European Union was revealed by the result of a 1997
Eurobarometer poll.[39] Such results might be thought to be surprising since—
despite the fundamental importance of the principles in the context of
human rights protection—there is a counter-tradition at work. As explained
by Gerard Quinn, this counter-tradition can be described as an archaic
European tendency to "exclude those who are significantly different, and
consign them to the margins of the social and economic mainstream".[40]
Quinn continues:

> "Our societies seem to be constructed on concentric circles of graduated exclusion
> . . . In large measure this process is unconscious . . . and therefore has the appear-
> ance of naturalness and inevitability, [and this] makes it all the hard to reveal the
> implicit exclusion, much less reform it".[41]

There is at least one other reason why the importance ascribed to the princi-   2–65
ple by Europeans is surprising. This is that although the principle is rightly
regarded as a cornerstone of all human rights protection it is correct to
observe that the principle generally finds articulation through other rights.
Thus in the context of the European Convention on Human Rights for example, non-discrimination is not a free-standing right itself, but rather one
linked to the enjoyment of the other discrete Convention rights.[42]

However the poll result does indeed reflect the importance of the principles   2–66
in the context of the Community legal order. The non-discrimination principle lies at the very heart of the European Union. The principle underpins the
exercise of free movement rights conferred on persons by the EC Treaty. The
application of the principle in the context of free movement rights will be
dealt with in detail in Chapter 12.

(iv) *Fundamental Human Rights*

Fundamental human rights have been recognised expressly in the Treaties   2–67
and by the ECJ on a number of occasions. In the field of the free movement
of persons, fundamental human rights have a significant impact and will be
examined in detail in Chapter 3.

---

[39] The poll revealed that 90 per cent of Europeans ranked equality in the eyes of the law as a right
to be respected at all times, and more than 80 per cent believed in a right to legal protection
against discrimination. By contrast, a mere 66 per cent thought the right to vote should be
respected under all circumstances (source: Eurobarometer OP No.47 (1997), 1).
[40] See G. Quinn "The Human Rights of People with Disabilities Under EU Law" in *The EU and
Human Rights* (ed. by P. Alston, Oxford University Press, 1999), Chapter 9.
[41] See G. Quinn "The Human Rights of People with Disabilities Under EU Law" in *The EU and
Human Rights* (ed. by P. Alston, Oxford University Press, 1999), Chapter 9.
[42] Art.14 ECHR provides that "the enjoyment of the rights and freedoms set forth in this
Convention shall be secured without discrimination on any grounds such as sex, race, colour,
language, religion, political or other opinion, national or social origin, association with a
national minority, property, birth or other status".

CHAPTER 3

RELATIONSHIP BETWEEN EU AND HUMAN RIGHTS LAW

This chapter examines the impact on EU law of international human rights law and specific EU provisions on human rights. Over recent years human rights law has come to play an ever more significant role in decisions concerning free movement of persons.

1. THE SOURCES OF HUMAN RIGHTS IN EU LAW

(a) *The Treaty on European Union*

The protection of fundamental human rights is clearly provided for in Art.6 of the Treaty on European Union (EU Treaty) which states: **3–01**

Article 6 EU Treaty

1. The Union is founded on the principles of liberty, democracy, respect for human rights and fundamental freedoms, and the rule of law, principles which are common to the Member States.

2. The Union shall respect fundamental rights, as guaranteed by the European Convention for the Protection of Human Rights and Fundamental Freedoms signed in Rome on 4 November 1950 and as they result from the constitutional traditions common to the Member States, as general principles of Community law.

3. The Union shall respect the national identities of its Member States.

4. The Union shall provide itself with the means necessary to attain its objectives and carry through its policies.

Further provision for protection of human rights is made elsewhere in the EU Treaty. Article 7 EU Treaty provides for a mechanism for the suspension of the application of certain Treaty rights in a Member State, including voting rights, should the Council conclude that the Member State has been in serious and persistent breach of the principles outlined in Art.6(1) EU Treaty. Article 11 EU Treaty provides that the development of human rights forms an objective of the EU's common foreign and security policy. Article 49 EU Treaty provides that applicants for membership of the European Union should respect the principles laid down in Art.6(1) EU Treaty. **3–02**

As is plain from Art.6(1) EU Treaty, the European Convention on Human Rights (ECHR) is central to the European Union's human rights commitment. As all Member States of the European Union are parties to the ECHR and the ECHR has legally binding standards, the reference to the ECHR in the Treaty is logical. However there is inevitable tension caused by reference to the standards of an international instrument which is already supervised **3–03** and enforced by other international bodies, namely the Council of Europe and the European Court of Human Rights (ECtHR). The interrelationship between the ECHR and EU law is discussed in greater detail below.

(b) *The Charter on Fundamental Rights*

3–04   The prospect of the European Union having its own human rights instrument has been under discussion for a number of years. The furthest that the Union has got in attaining that object is the EU Charter on Fundamental Rights (the EU Charter).

3–05   The EU Charter is a statement of the principles and values which underpin the European Union. On December 7, 2000, the Presidents of the European Parliament, the Council and the Commission signed the EU Charter in Nice on behalf of the three institutions. However no reference to the EU Charter was included in the Treaty of Nice. The EU Charter thus remains without any binding legal force. The current negotiations surrounding the Constitution for Europe include the possibility of making the EU Charter part of that Constitution and therefore legally binding.

3–06   The EU Charter is broad in content bringing together in one document all of the rights previously found in a variety of legislative instruments, including national laws and international conventions from the Council of Europe, the United Nations and the International Labour Organisation.

3–07   The EU Charter contains a preamble and 54 articles, grouped into seven chapters:

- Chapter I: *Dignity* (human dignity, the right to life, the right to the integrity of the person, prohibition of torture and inhuman or degrading treatment or punishment, prohibition of slavery and forced labour);

- Chapter II: *Freedoms* (the right to liberty and security, respect for private and family life, protection of personal data, the right to marry and found a family, freedom of thought, conscience and religion, freedom of expression and information, freedom of assembly and association, freedom of the arts and sciences, the right to education, freedom to choose an occupation and the right to engage in work, freedom to conduct a business, the right to property, the right to asylum, protection in the event of removal, expulsion or extradition);

- Chapter III: *Equality* (equality before the law, non-discrimination, cultural, religious and linguistic diversity, equality between men and women, the rights of the child, the rights of the elderly, integration of persons with disabilities);

- Chapter IV: *Solidarity* (workers' right to information and consultation within the undertaking, the right of collective bargaining and action, the right of access to placement services, protection in the event of unjustified dismissal, fair and just working conditions, prohibition of child labour and protection of young people at work, family and professional life, social security and social assistance, health care, access to services of general economic interest, environmental protection, consumer protection);

- Chapter V: *Citizens' rights* (the right to vote and stand as a candidate at elections to the European Parliament, the right to vote and stand as a candidate at municipal elections, the right to good administration, the right of access to documents, the ombudsman, the right to petition, freedom of movement and residence, diplomatic and consular protection);

- Chapter VI: *Justice* (the right to an effective remedy and a fair trial, the presumption of innocence and the right of defence, principles of legality and proportionality of criminal offences and penalties, the right not to be tried or punished twice in criminal proceedings for the same criminal offence);

- Chapter VII: *General provisions* (including rights specifically relating to citizenship of the European Union such as free movement rights).

(c) *Relationship Between the ECHR and the EU Charter*

Whilst the text of the EU Charter largely mirrors that of the ECHR, it is more generous than the ECHR with respect to certain rights, particularly social and economic rights, such as the right to engage in work (Art.15), the right to education (Art.14) and collective labour rights (Art.12). For historical and political reasons the ECHR did not originally have at its core any social or economic rights. However with the passing of time such rights have come to be seen as increasingly fundamental. **3–08**

There are inherent limits to the EU Charter. In particular Art.51 EU Charter states: **3–09**

1. The provisions of this Charter are addressed to the institutions and bodies of the Union with due regard for the principle of subsidiarity and to the Member States only when they are implementing Union law. They shall therefore respect the rights, observe the principles and promote the application thereof in accordance with their respective powers.

2. This Charter does not establish any new power or task for the Community or the Union, or modify powers and tasks defined by the Treaties.

and Art.52 EU Charter states:

1. Any limitation on the exercise of the rights and freedoms recognised by this Charter must be provided for by law and respect the essence of those rights and freedoms. Subject to the principle of proportionality, limitations may be made only if they are necessary and genuinely meet objectives of general interest recognised by the Union or the need to protect the rights and freedoms of others.

2. Rights recognised by this Charter which are based on the Community Treaties or the Treaty on European Union shall be exercised under the conditions and within the limits defined by those Treaties.

3. In so far as this Charter contains rights which correspond to rights guaranteed by the Convention for the Protection of Human Rights and Fundamental Freedoms, the meaning and scope of those rights shall be the same as those laid down by the said Convention. This provision shall not prevent Union law providing more extensive protection.

3–10   Articles 51 and 52 make clear that the EU Charter does not alter the system of rights conferred by the EU and EC Treaties and is not applicable in situations not covered by the Treaties. The more general protection offered by the ECHR in all areas is therefore not mirrored by the EU Charter.

3–11   Article 52(3) defines the relationship between the EU Charter and the ECHR. Its purpose is to ensure the necessary consistency between the EU Charter and the ECHR by establishing the principle that, in so far as the rights in the present Charter also correspond to rights guaranteed by the ECHR, the meaning and scope of those rights, including authorised limitations, are the same as those laid down by the ECHR. However, as seen, the scope of the EU Charter is clearly broader than the ECHR, with greater emphasis on social and economic rights than the ECHR. Article 52 does not in any way prohibit this more extensive protection of rights.

2. The Protection of Human Rights by the European Court of Justice

(a) *The Path to Human Rights Protection*

3–12   In its early case law the ECJ did not see itself as a guardian of human rights and rejected any submission that a Community measure should be struck down for non-compliance with human rights provisions enshrined in national constitutions or in international agreements to which the relevant Member State was a signatory.[1] Member States were thus left to ensure compliance with own their human rights obligations even in areas falling within the scope of the Treaties.

3–13   This position taken in these early cases was clearly not sustainable in light of the ECJ's view of the primacy of Community law and its precedence over national law. Such supremacy could only be maintained if Community law was itself able to guarantee the protection of basic human rights in compliance with Member States' international obligations. It was only to be a matter of time before the European Court of Human Rights asserted its scrutiny of compliance with ECHR standards and found that the transfer of power to a supranational body would not absolve a contracting party to the ECHR from its obligations under the ECHR.[2]

---

[1] Joined Cases 16 & 18/59 *"Geitling" Ruhrkohlen-Verkaufsgesellschaft mbH, "Mausegatt" Ruhrkohlen-Verkaufsgesellschaft mbH "Präsident" Ruhrkohlen-Verkaufsgesellschaft mbH and Associated Companies v High Authority of the European Coal and Steel Community*; Case 40–64 *Sgarlata v Commission* [1965] E.C.R. 215.

[2] Indeed in 1999 in the case of *Matthews v United Kingdom* (Application no.24833/94, February 18, 1999) the European Court of Human Rights stated unequivocally that Member States will be responsible for Community acts under the ECHR.

The potential then for conflict between the ECJ and the ECtHR would be **3–14** great if the ECJ continued to assert the supremacy of Community law without regard to human rights. The first attempt by the ECJ to resolve this potential conflict was in the case of *Stauder*[3] where it referred to "fundamental human rights enshrined in the general principles of Community law and protected by the Court". Although on its facts the ECJ did not consider that the question of a violation of fundamental rights was necessary to determine, this judgment represented a significant shift in the ECJ's approach to the protection of human rights in Community law.

In the years that followed the ECJ began to develop its protection of human **3–15** rights. Initially this was by reference to the constitutions of the Member States. In *Internationale Handelsgesellschaft*,[4] the ECJ referred to the fact that its protection of fundamental rights was "inspired by the constitutional traditions common to the member states". On the facts the ECJ stated that the impugned regulation should have its validity judged by reference to the fundamental rights which it said formed "an integral part of the general principles of Community law protected by the Court of Justice".

In *Nold*,[5] the ECJ went slightly further in referring to "*i*nternational treaties **3–16** for the protection of human rights" as representing an additional source of the Court's new general principles. In the years that followed the ECJ was presented with arguments which hinged on the application of specific provisions of both constitutional human rights and international human rights instruments.[6]

These incremental developments culminated within about a decade in the **3–17** position reached in *Cinetheque*[7] by which time the ECJ saw itself as duty bound to ensure the observance of fundamental rights in the field of Community law. This was in an era prior to the EU Treaty and therefore prior to a time when human rights were even alluded to in the Treaties governing the Community. As commentators have observed "respect for and protection of human rights were, thus, conceived as an integral, inherent, transverse principle forming part of all objectives, functions, and powers of the Community"[8] albeit without any discernable Treaty basis for such principle.

Of further significance in *Wachauf*,[9] the ECJ held that as a consequence of **3–18** the place that fundamental human rights held in the Community legal order the Community could not accept measures which are incompatible

---

[3] Case 29/69 *Stauder v City of Ulm* [1969] E.C.R. 419.
[4] Case 11/70 *Internationale Handelsgesellshaft mbH v Einfuhr-und Vorratstelle für Getreide und Futtermittel* [1970] E.C.R. 1125.
[5] Case 4/73 *Nold KG v Commission* [1974] E.C.R. 491.
[6] In both Case 36/75 *Rutili v Minister for the Interior* [1975] E.C.R. 1219 and Case 130/75 *Prais v Council* [1976] E.C.R. 1589, the ECJ made reference to specific provisions of the ECHR.
[7] Joined Cases 60 & 61/84 *Cinetheque SA v Federation Nationale des Cinemas Francais* [1985] E.C.R. 2605, para.26.
[8] See Weiler and Fries "EC and EU Competences in Human Rights" in *The EU and Human Rights* (ed. by Philip Alston, Oxford University Press, 1999), p.157.
[9] Case 5/88 *Wachauf v Federal Republic of Germany* [1989] E.C.R. I–2609, para.19.

with observance of human rights protected by national constitutions and international human rights standards.

(b) *The Special Protection of the ECHR*

3–19   The particular significance of the ECHR in the protection of fundamental human rights in Community law has been repeated by the ECJ on a number of occasions. In 1986 in the case of *Johnston*,[10] the ECJ underlined the special significance that the ECHR had in protection of fundamental human rights in Community law. As the ECJ explained in *ERT*:

> "the Court has consistently held, fundamental rights form an integral part of the general principles of law, the observance of which it ensures. For that purpose the Court draws inspiration from the constitutional traditions common to the Member States and from the guidelines supplied by international treaties for the protection of human rights on which the Member States have collaborated or of which they are signatories (see, in particular, the judgment in Case C-4/73 *Nold v Commission* [1974] ECR 491, paragraph 13). The European Convention on Human Rights has special significance in that respect".[11]

3–20   In *Kremzow*,[12] the ECJ pointed to the importance of the ECHR as the foundation of the fundamental rights which are the integral part of the general principles of Community law.[13] Reiterating earlier jurisprudence in *Wachauf* the ECJ held:

> "The Convention (*i.e.* the ECHR) has special significance . . . [I]t follows that measures are not acceptable in the Community which are incompatible with observance of the human rights thus recognised and guaranteed".[14]

(c) *Consequences Today for Free Movement of Persons*

3–21   Undoubtedly the specific reference to the ECHR in Art.6(3) EU Treaty has fortified the ECJ in its approach to the ECHR. In recent years in the field of free movement of persons the ECJ has made increasing use of the rights protected by the ECHR, in particular Art.8, to justify its conclusions.

3–22   In *Carpenter*,[15] the ECJ considered the position of the family member (a spouse) of a provider of services who had infringed the immigration laws of

---

[10] Case 222/84 *Johnston v Chief Constable of the Royal Ulster Constabulary* [1986] E.C.R. 1651, para. 18.
[11] Case C–260/89 *Elliniki Radiophonia Tiléorassi AE ("ERT") and Panellinia Omospondia Syllogon Prossopikou v Dimotiki Etairia Pliroforissis and Sotirios Kouvelas and Nicolaos Avdellas* [1991] E.C.R. I–2925, para.41.
[12] Case C–299/95 *Kremzow v Austria* [1997] E.C.R. I-2629.
[13] See most recently Case C–71/02 *Herbert Karner Industrie-Auktionen GmbH and Troostwijk GmbH*, March 25, 2004 in a case concerning advertising restrictions placed on a company and the compatibility of such restrictions with Art.10 ECHR: freedom of expression.
[14] Case C–299/95 *Kremzow v Austria* [1997] E.C.R. I-2629, at 2645.
[15] Case C-60/00 *Carpenter v Secretary of State for the Home Department* [2002] E.C.R. I–6279.

the United Kingdom. Notwithstanding the breach of nationals laws the ECJ held that she was entitled to reside in the territory with the provider. In doing so, the ECJ read Art.49 EC Treaty in light of the fundamental right to respect for family life so as to infer a right of residence for the family member.

In *MRAX*,[16] the ECJ ruled, *inter alia*, that a Member State may not refuse to **3–23** issue a residence permit to a third country national married to a national of a Member State who entered the territory of that Member State lawfully on the sole ground that the visa expired before they applied for a residence permit.[17]

These two cases illustrate the determination of the ECJ to ensure the protec- **3–24** tion of the family life of Member State nationals in order to eliminate obstacles to the exercise of the fundamental freedoms guaranteed by the Treaty, even in the face of contrary domestic legislation. *Carpenter*[18] in particular is indicative also of the ECJ's willingness to interpret the Treaty obligations in light of the rights protected by the ECHR. In its judgment the ECJ explicitly relied on the right to respect for family life as guaranteed by Art.8(1) ECHR and concluded that:

> "[t]he decision to deport Mrs Carpenter constitutes an interference with the exercise by Mr Carpenter of his right to respect for his family life within the meaning of Article 8 of the Convention for the Protection of Human Rights and Fundamental Freedoms, signed at Rome on 4 November 1950, which is among the fundamental rights which, according to the Court's settled case-law, restated by the Preamble to the Single European Act and by Article 6(2) E.U., are protected in Community law".[19]

The ECJ took a similar stance in *Baumbast*[20] in holding that the requirements **3–25** of Reg.1612/68 on the free movement of workers had to be interpreted "in light of the requirement of respect for family life protected by Article 8 [ECHR]". As a consequence the ECJ found it to be an infringement of the rights of the child to enter into education if he is to be deprived of the right to live with his primary carer.

(d) *The Impact of the EU Charter on Fundamental Rights*

As stated above at the present time the EU Charter is not legally binding in **3–26** Community law and is not referred to in the Treaties. The ECJ and CFI have not tended to use the EU Charter as a primary source of fundamental rights but more an ancillary source.

---

[16] Case C–459/99 *Mouvement contre le racisme, l'antisémitisme et la xénophobie ASBL (MRAX)* [2002] E.C.R. I–6591.
[17] See paras 11–08 to 11–10.
[18] C–60/00 *Carpenter v Secretary of State for the Home Department* [2002] E.C.R. I–6279.
[19] C–60/00 *Carpenter v Secretary of State for the Home Department* [2002] E.C.R. I–6279, para. 41.
[20] Case C–413/99 *Baumbast and R. v Secretary of State for the Home Department* [2002] E.C.R. I–7091.

3–27 In the few cases in which the CFI has even referred to the EU Charter it has referred to the fact that fundamental rights in Community law are based on the common constitutional traditions of the Member States and the ECHR which are "affirmed" by the Charter.[21]

3–28 Despite the number of times that the Advocates-General refer to the EU Charter in their opinions,[22] the ECJ itself has yet to draw on the EU Charter as a source of specific inspiration for the protection of fundamental human rights in the Community legal order. This is somewhat surprising and leaves the ECJ out of step with the European Court of Human Rights which has itself referred to the EU Charter and specifically drawn inferences from the wording of specific provisions. In *Goodwin v United Kingdom*[23] the European Court of Human Rights considered the rights of transsexuals to marry and referred to the fact that Art.9 EU provides the right to marry without the inclusion of the words "men and women" which appears in the equivalent provision in Art.12 ECHR.

3–29 It is not just to that the ECJ is out of step with the ECtHR in this respect. In *KB*,[24] a case which followed on from the European Court of Human Rights' decision in *Goodwin*, the ECJ failed to even refer to the EU Charter thereby demonstrating its ingrained resistance to reliance on the EU Charter.

(e) *The Future for Human Rights Protection in the Community Legal Order*

3–30 Despite the ECJ's apparent willingness to adhere to fundamental human rights, particularly more recently the standards of the ECHR, there are certainly criticisms that can be made of the ECJ's approach. There have been occasions when the interpretation given by the ECJ to human rights provisions is more restrictive than that afforded by the ECtHR. By way of example there is a clear conflict between *Hoechst* (ECJ)[25] and *Niemitz* (ECtHR)[26] over whether the right to privacy as guaranteed by Art.8 ECHR extended to business premises.

3–31 There are a number of occasions when the ECJ has failed to address a fundamental human rights questions raised by a litigant in proceedings.[27] It may not be necessary for the ECJ to address a human rights issue every time it is

---

[21] Case T–177/01 *Jégo-Quéré et Cie SA v Commission* [2002] E.C.R. II–2365, paras 41, 42 and 47; see also Case T–54/99 *Max Mobil v Commission* [2002] E.C.R. II–313.

[22] According to the European Institutions website the A.G. have referred to the EU Charter in more than 100 of their opinions since it was agreed in 2000: Source *http://europa.eu.int/scadplus/leg/en/lvb/l33501.htm.*

[23] *Goodwin v UK* (2002) 35 E.H.R.R. 18, para. 100.

[24] Case C–117/01 *KB v (1) National Health Service Pensions Agency (2) Secretary of State for Health (2004)* judgment of January 7, 2004, not yet reported.

[25] Case T–10/89 *Hoechst AG v Commission* [1992] E.C.R.II–629.

[26] *Niemitz v Germany*, December 16, 1992, Series A 251–B.

[27] Case 136/79 *National Panasonic (UK) Limited v Commission* [1980] E.C.R. 2057, Case C–168/91 *Christos Konstantindis v (1) Stadt Altensteig (2) Landratsamt Calw—Ordnungsamt,* [1993] E.C.R. I–1191 and C–159/90 *Society for the Protection of the Unborn Child v Grogan,* [1991] E.C.R. I–4685. For further analysis see Spielmann in P. Alston (ed.), *The EU and Human Rights* (Oxford University Press, 1999), p.764.

raised, particularly if the answer to the questions referred by the national court can be provided by reference to other Community law principles. However it leaves a sense that the ECJ relies on human rights principles when it has no other arguments to employ in achieving its aims.[28] If such analysis is correct then the consequence is likely to be one in which human rights protection will not be consistent. This is potentially a serious criticism since human rights protection must be consistently available, interpreted and applied if it is to be real and meaningful and not illusory.[29]

There is also an apparent reluctance on the part of the ECJ to find **3–32** Community institutions, as opposed to individual Member States, in breach of fundamental rights.[30] This is a particular cause for concern since absolving Community institutions from fundamental human rights obligations undoubtedly creates a framework in which there is no incentive for Community institutions to act compatibly with fundamental human rights. The application by the European Parliament to strike down a council directive on the basis that it does not conform with human rights demonstrates the frustration of at least one Community institution that fundamental human rights are not at the heart of all acts of the Community.[31]

These problems might be resolved however in the near future by the incor- **3–33** poration of the EU Charter into the Constitution for Europe and the possible accession of the European Union as a legal entity to the ECHR. Inclusion of the EU Charter into the Constitution for Europe will undoubtedly strengthen the Charter's position in the Community legal order and make its provisions legally binding on the Member States and institutions of the Community.

However inconsistency between the ECJ and ECtHR will not be resolved by **3–34** incorporation alone; neither will the reluctance of the ECJ to answer human rights questions necessarily disappear. There are some who therefore have argued for the accession of the European Union to the ECtHR.[32]

---

[28] Coppell and O'Neill, who in "The European Court of Justice, Taking Rights Seriously?" (1992) 29 C.M.L.Rev.669; state "[e]vidently it is economic integration, to be achieved through the acts of Community institutions, which the Court sees as its fundamental priority. In adopting and adapting the slogan of protection of human rights the court has seized the moral high ground. However, the high rhetoric of human rights protection can be seen as no more than a vehicle for the Court to extend the scope and impact of European law".

[29] *Artico v Italy* [1980] 3 E.H.R.R. 1.

[30] See criticisms made by Persaud in C.A. Gearty (ed.), *European Civil Liberties and the European Convention on Human Rights* (Kluwer, 1997) p.364 at p.376, of the *Wachauf* case where the ECJ held a Regulation valid despite the fact that it had the effect of depriving a lessee of the fruits of his labour without compensation (in breach of Art.1, Protocol 1 ECHR) and chose instead to criticise the German implementing measure since it is Member States which "must, as far as possible, apply those rules in accordance with those requirements" of fundamental human rights.

[31] See Action by the Parliament against the Council of the European Union in respect of Council Directive 2003/86/EC (Case C-540/03) in which the Parliament alleges that the Directive on Family Reunification for Third Country Nationals is in certain respects "unacceptable" in view of human rights obligations and argued that the Court should annul, pursuant to Art.230 EC Treaty, the last sub-para. of Arts 4(1), (6) and 8 of the Directive. This case is pending.

[32] See for instance the House of Lords' European Select Committee's Eight Report in the Session 1999/2000 on the EU Charter of Fundamental Rights, May 24, 2000, HL 67, ISBN 0 10 406700 4.

3–35   In its Opinion 2/94 the ECJ held that as the law stood at the time, the Community had no competence to accede to the ECHR and that accession to the ECHR would entail a substantial change in the Community legal system for the protection of human rights in that it would involve the Community entering into a distinct international institutional system.

3–36   However the significance of such issues of competence will disappear with the inclusion of Art.I-7(2) in the EU Constitution which states:

> "The Union shall accede to the European Convention for the Protection of Human Rights and Fundamental Freedoms. Such accession shall not affect the Union's competences as defined in the Constitution".

The EU Constitution was agreed in June 2004 although it is still to be signed and ratified by all Member States.[33]

---

[33] The official signature of the EU Constitution is planned to take place before the end of 2004 according to the conclusions of the June 2004 EU summit meeting (European Council). Thereafter national Parliaments must ratify the Constitution, a process that could take some years to conclude. See discussion above at paras 1–27 to 1–28 on Treaty Foundations.

CHAPTER 4

UNION CITIZENSHIP

This chapter examines the creation of Union citizenship and the rights given to Union citizens flowing from such citizenship. The interpretation given by the ECJ to these rights will determine the true reach of free movement rights for persons throughout the EU.

Article 17 EC Treaty

1. Citizenship of the Union is hereby established. Every person holding the nationality of a Member State shall be a citizen of the Union. Citizenship of the Union shall complement and not replace national citizenship.

2. Citizens of the Union shall enjoy the rights conferred by this Treaty and shall be subject to the duties imposed thereby.

Article 18 EC Treaty

1. Every citizen of the Union shall have the right to move and reside freely within the territory of the Member States, subject to the limitations and conditions laid down in this Treaty and by the measures adopted to give it effect.

2. If action by the Community should prove necessary to attain this objective and this Treaty has not provided the necessary powers, the Council may adopt provisions with a view to facilitating the exercise of the rights referred to in paragraph 1. The Council shall act in accordance with the procedure referred to in Article 251.

3. Paragraph 2 shall not apply to provisions on passports, identity cards, residence permits or any other such document or to provisions on social security or social protection.

1. INTRODUCTION

The principal concern of this chapter is the analysis of the impact on the rights of nationals of the Member States of the establishment of Union citizenship conferred by Art.17 EC Treaty and of the right of Union citizens to move and reside freely contained in Art.18 EC Treaty. The uniqueness and potential enormity of these provisions—based on the creation of the novel concept of citizenship of a supranational body—should be acknowledged.   **4–01**

As well as examining the historical background to inclusion in the EC Treaty of a discrete part entitled "Citizenship of the Union", two questions are considered. Firstly, whether the creation of Union citizenship has added anything of value to the rights of nationals of Member States. Secondly, whether the right to move and reside contained in Art.18 EC Treaty creates discrete rights for Union citizens beyond those already contained elsewhere in the EC Treaty or secondary legislation.   **4–02**

2. HISTORICAL BACKGROUND

4–03   As already acknowledged, Union citizenship and the rights accompanying it mark a huge advance on the ethos and dynamics of the process of European integration launched by the Treaty establishing the European Economic Community signed in Rome in 1957 (see generally Chapter 1). Originally the right to move freely within the European Community was linked closely to the performance by nationals of Member States in the territories of other Member States of economic activity—whether as employee, self-employed or service provider.

4–04   However, as observed by the Commission[1] such state of affairs could not be allowed to continue indefinitely since it did not fully comply with the objective contained in Art.3c of the Treaty of Rome of "the abolition, as between Member States, of obstacles to the free movement of . . . persons". Such objective is not one linked to the performance of economic activity. Moreover, such state of affairs did not meet the political aspiration expressed at the Paris Summit in 1974 to move towards a "citizens' Europe".[2]

4–05   The first step away from the necessity to carry out economic activity as the precondition of the exercise of free movement rights was the Commission proposal of 1979[3] to extend the freedom of movement of persons to those *not* economically active. The proposal—later withdrawn—was seen by the Commission as an important step towards the completion of the internal market. But it was the adoption of the Single European Act signed in February 1986[4] which provided the impetus towards the adoption of directives providing for the right of residence for the economically non active. In 1989 the Commission put forward three proposals covering students, retired persons and others not engaged in economic activity[5] which culminated in the adoption on June 28, 1990 of Directives 90/364, 90/365 and 90/366.[6]

4–06   The final stage in attaining the general right to movement and residence now contained in Art.18(1) EC Treaty was the incorporation of the provisions on Union Citizenship contained in Part II of Maastricht Treaty signed on February 7, 1992. The provisions (Arts 8 and 8a–e of the Maastricht Treaty)

---

[1] See Report from the Commission to the Council and the European Parliament of March 17, 1999 on the implementation of Dirs 90/364, 90/365 and 93/96 (Right of Residence) (COM(99) 127 final).

[2] Report from the Commission to the Council and the European Parliament of March 17, 1999 on the implementation of Dirs 90/364, 90/365 and 93/96 (Right of Residence) (COM(99) 127 final), above and Report from the Commission on the Citizenship of the Union of December 21, 1993 (COM(93) 702 final).

[3] (COM(79) 215 final), [1979] O.J. C207.

[4] The single European Act stated that the Community would adopt measures with the aim of progressively establishing an internal market by December 31, 1992 and wrote provisions into the Treaty of Rome to establish an area without frontiers and to abolish checks on persons at internal frontiers.

[5] [1989] O.J. C207.

[6] Directive 90/364 on the right of residence; Dir. 90/365 on the right of residence of employees and self-employed persons who have ceased their occupational activity and 90/366 on the right of residence for students (the latter replaced by Dir. 93/96 after annulment of Dir. 90/366 by the ECJ in Case C–295/90 *Parliament v Council*[1992] E.C.R. I–4193).

came into force on November 1, 1993. After the signing of the Treaty, the Declaration by the Birmingham European Council in October 1992 stated that ". . . citizenship of the Union brings our citizens additional rights and protection without in any way taking the place of their national citizenship". A Declaration attached to the Treaty setting up the European Community notes that "the question whether an individual possesses the nationality of a Member State shall be settled solely by reference to the national law of the Member State concerned".

However, the rights of free movement and residence throughout the Union   **4–07** do not represent the totality of rights enjoyed by Union citizens. Specific provision is made also in Part II EC Treaty for:

- the right of every Union citizen residing in another Member State to vote and stand as a candidate in municipal elections and in elections to the European Parliament in the state where the Union citizen resides (Art.19 EC Treaty);

- the right of every Union citizen in the territory of a third country to protection by the diplomatic or consular authorities of any Member State where the state of which the person is a national is not represented in the non-member third country (Art.20 EC Treaty); and

- the rights of every citizen of the Union to petition the European Parliament, to apply to the Ombudsman and to write to EU institutions or bodies in their own language and have an answer in the same language (Art.21 EC Treaty).

Moreover, citizens of the Union, and indeed third country nationals residing   **4–08** in the European Union, also enjoy fundamental rights. Such rights, and their inter-relationship with the community legal order, are considered in Chapter 3. The Amsterdam Treaty completed the list of civic rights of Union citizens and clarified the link between national citizenship and European citizenship.[7]

3. ARTICLE 17 EC TREATY: A NEW FORM OF CITIZENSHIP

(a) *Introduction*

The creation of the Union citizen was heralded as the dawn of a new era in   **4–09** Community law, with Union citizenship 'destined to be the fundamental status of nationals of the Member States'. Two particular questions arise in relation to Union citizenship.

---

[7] Art.17 EC Treaty was amended to clarify the link between European and national citizenship with the addition of the unequivocal text that "citizenship of the Union shall complement and not replace national citizenship". Further the Amsterdam Treaty established the new right (contained in Art.21) for European citizens to write to the European Parliament, the Council, the Commission , the Court of Justice, the Court of Auditors, the Economic and Social Committee, the Committee of the Regions or the Ombudsman in one of the languages of the Treaties and receive an answer in the same language.

4–10   Firstly, what rights and benefits are there for holders of Union citizenship over and above those that accrue as a result of other rights contained in the EC Treaty? In summary the answer to this question is that under certain circumstances Union citizens will enjoy the protection of the non-discrimination provision contained in Art.12 EC Treaty whether or not they are exercising free movement rights.

4–11   Secondly, what is the relationship between Union citizenship and national citizenship? Whilst Union citizenship is not intended to replace national citizenship, if rights accrue to its holders then Union citizenship plainly enhances national citizenship. At the same time, however, Union citizenship undoubtedly also creates a potential tension with national authorities, particularly where such citizenship has consequences for Member States which are wider than anticipated.

(b) *Rights and benefits flowing from Union citizenship*

(i) *Non-discrimination and Article 12 EC Treaty*

4–12   Union citizens may find themselves residing in Member States other than that of their nationality for different reasons. Where unambiguosly exericising Treaty rights the obligations consequently imposed on Member States in which they reside is the subject matter of Part II of this book and, for the most part laid down in primary and secondary legislation. At the very least Union citizens who exercise free movement rights provided for in the EC Treaty enjoy the right to equal treatment entailing the right (as stated by the ECJ in *Bickel and Franz*[8]) to "be placed on an equal footing with nationals of the [host] Member State".

4–13   However, where Union citizens do not fall within such primary or secondary legislation as free movers, their rights and the obligations owed to them by the Member States in which they reside are far more contentious. Prior to the inclusion of Art.17 in the EC Treaty such persons obtained no rights as a matter of Community law since their status in such other Member State had no Community nexus. Moreover, still less were Member States under any obligation to treat such persons any differently than they would other third country nationals.

---

[8] Case C–274/96 *Bickel and Franz* [1998] E.C.R. I–7637. The case concerned the trials in Italy of (respectively) an Austrian lorry driver charged with driving while under the influence of alcohol and a German tourist charged with possession of a prohibited knife. The issue was whether Mr Bickel and Mr Franz could rely on the principle of non-discrimination on grounds of nationality in order to be granted the right to have the criminal proceedings conducted in a language other than Italian where that right is granted to certain Italian nationals. Although the Advocate General had pointed to the lack of any obvious link with Community law[8] the ECJ—basing itself on its earlier decision in *Cowan* (Case 186/87 *Cowan v Trésor public* [1989] E.C.R. 195) held that the situations of both Mr Bickel and Mr Franz fell within the scope of the Treaty. This was because the situations governed by Community law included those covered by the freedom for the recipients of services to go to another Member State in order to receive services there under Art.59 EC Treaty. As such they were "entitled, pursuant to Art.6 [now 12] of the Treaty, to treatment no less favourable than that accorded to nationals of the host State so far as concerns the use of languages which are spoken there" (para. 16).

There is no doubt that the creation of Union citizenship has fundamentally **4–14**
changed this position. Union citizenship now provides the Community law
nexus through which Union citizens gain the protection of Art.12 EC Treaty
and are thereby able to access a range of benefits and rights on a non-
discriminatory basis in other Member States. This protection arises without
the Union citizen needing to establishing a Community law right of residence
in those States.

Since the creation of Union citizenship the ECJ has consistently affirmed the **4–15**
importance of this interrelationship between Arts 17 and 12 EC Treaty.[9] As
the ECJ stated in *D'Hoop*:[10]

> "Union citizenship is destined to be the fundamental status of nationals of the
> Member States, enabling those who find themselves in the same situation to enjoy
> with the scope *ratione materiae* of the Treaty the same treatment in law irrespective
> of their nationality, subject to such exceptions as are expressly provided for."

In spite of such affirmation, however, the protection against discrimination **4–16**
for Union citizens is not without its limits. To date the ECJ has found that
Union citizens only benefit from Art.12 EC Treaty when they are "lawfully
resident", albeit that such lawful residence may result from the application of
national laws and practices and need not result from the exercise of a free
movement right in Community law. As discussed below "lawful residence" is
a difficult concept to define bearing in mind that the ECJ is here deferring to
national state practice and there is huge variation in practice between
Member States.[11]

Furthermore, Union citizens will only receive protection from discrimination **4–17**
in areas which fall within the scope of the EC Treaty. Whether a matter falls
within the scope of the Treaty is a difficult question which will plainly be
answered in a more limited way where the Union citizen is not exercising a
free movement right. For those that *are* exercising free movement rights
Community law places an overriding obligation on Member States to facilitate the exercise of such rights. In this context the scope of Art.12 EC Treaty
will extend to any matter which affects the exercise of the free movement
right concerned. By contrast, for those *not* exercising free movement rights
but who are nevertheless resident in another Member State, the scope of
Art.12 EC Treaty is potentially more limited because of the absence of the
exercise of any underlying EC Treaty right.

The case of *Sala*[12] was the first to identify the benefit that Art.17 EC Treaty, **4–18**
taken together with Art.12 EC Treaty, would bring to Union citizens. *Sala*[13]
concerned a Spanish national who had lived in Germany since 1968.
Although in employment doing various jobs until 1989, she had since then

---

[9] Case C-184/99 *Grzelczyk v Centre Public d'aide sociale d'Ottignies-Louvain-la-Neuve* [2001]
E.C.R.I–6193; Case C–413/99 *Baumbast and R. v Secretary of State for the Home Department*
[2002] E.C.R. I–7091; Case C-224/98 *D'Hoop v Office national de l'emploi* [2002] E.C.R. I–6191.
[10] Case C-224/98 *D'Hoop v Office national de l'emploi* [2002] E.C.R. I–6191, para.28
[11] See paras 4–25 to 4–29 below.
[12] Case-85/96 *Martinez Sala v Freistat Bayern* [1998] E.C.R. I–2691.
[13] Case-85/96 *Martinez Sala v Freistat Bayern* [1998] E.C.R. I–2691.

been in receipt of social assistance. In January 1993 an application made for child-raising allowance was refused on the ground that she did not have German nationality, a residence entitlement or a residence permit.[14]

4–19 The ECJ had no doubt that child-raising allowance fell within the material scope of Community law. This was the case both as a family benefit within the meaning of Art.4(1)(h) of Reg. 1408/71 and as a social advantage within the meaning of Art.7(2) of Reg. 1612/68.[15] As regards personal scope, if the referring court were to conclude either that Mrs Sala retained the status of worker[16] or of employed person[17] her unequal treatment would be unlawful. But what if Mrs Sala retained neither status? The Commission had argued that Mrs Sala would be able to rely on her Art.18 EC Treaty right without more to bring herself within the personal scope of the Treaty.[18] However, according to the ECJ it was not necessary to decide whether Mrs Sala could rely on Art.18 EC Treaty to obtain recognition of "a new right to reside" in Germany since she had "already been authorised to reside there".[19] According to the ECJ she was within the personal scope of the EC Treaty provisions on Union citizenship as a national of a Member State lawfully residing in the territory of another Member State. As such she was entitled under Art.12 EC Treaty not to suffer discrimination on grounds of nationality in matters falling within the material scope of the Treaty (which as stated included child raising allowance). In the words of the ECJ:

> "63. . . . [A] citizen of the European Union, such as the appellant in the main proceedings, lawfully resident in the territory of the host Member State, can rely on Article 6 of the Treaty in all situations which fall within the scope ratione materiae of Community law, including the situation where that Member State delays or refuses to grant to that claimant a benefit that is provided to all persons lawfully resident in the territory of that State on the ground that the claimant is not in possession of a document which nationals of that same State are not required to have and the issue of which may be delayed or refused by the authorities of that State."

---

[14] Until May 19, 1984 Mrs Sala obtained residence permits running more or less without interruption; thereafter she obtained only documents certifying that the extension of her residence permit had been applied for. However the European Convention on Social and Medical Assistance of December 11, 1953 did not allow her to be deported. A residence permit expiring on April 18, 1995 was issued on April 19, 1994 (which was extended for a further year on April 20, 1995).

[15] Case-85/96 *Martinez Sala v Freistat Bayern* [1998] E.C.R. I–2691, para.57.

[16] Within the meaning of Art.39 EC Treaty and of Reg. 1612/68.

[17] Within the meaning of Reg. 1408/71.

[18] A.G. La Pergola also focussed on Art.18 EC Treaty. In his opinion since the entry into force of Art.8a: "The right of residence can no longer be considered to have been created by [Directive 90/364]. . . . The right to move and reside freely throughout the whole of the Union is enshrined in an act of primary law and does not exist or cease to exist depending on whether or not it has been made subject to limitations under other provisions of Community law, including secondary legislation. The limitations in Art.8a itself concern the actual exercise but not the existence of the right . . . Art.8a extracted the kernel from the other freedoms of movement—the freedom which we now find characterised as the right, not only to move, but also to reside in every Member State: a primary right, in the sense that it appears as the first of the rights ascribed to citizenship of the Union". (para.18).

[19] Case-86/96 *Martinez Sala v Freistat Bayern* [1998] E.C.R. I–2691, para.60: see discussion at paras 4–25 to 4–29 for the relevance and meaning of being "authorised" to reside in the host Member State.

Sala was novel insofar as it provided the link between Arts 17 and 12 EC   **4–20**
Treaty with the consequence that Union citizens lawfully residing in other
Member States fall to be treated on an equal footing with own nationals. It is
to be emphasised that *Sala* concerned a benefit that was expressly provided
for in secondary legislation and therefore that the benefit fell within the scope
of the EC Treaty was less open to question. However more difficult questions
would arise if the Union citizen sought protection against discrimination in
an area which did not so obviously fall within the scope of the EC Treaty.

Where a Union citizen is exercising free movement rights in another   **4–21**
Member State that Member State is expected to comply with Community
law, and in particular to prevent discrimination, even when exercising
competence in areas that fall outside Community law and within the exclusive competence of the Member States themselves.[20] But how should this
principle apply in situations where the Union citizen is not exercising free
movement rights?

The ECJ had to grapple with this question in *Avello*. [21] The case concerned a   **4–22**
dispute between Mr Avello and the Belgian State concerning an application
to change the surname of his children who were dual Belgian and Spanish
nationals.[22] The ECJ expressly acknowledged that the subject-matter of the
dispute (namely the rules governing a person's surname) was one falling
within the exclusive competence of the Member States rather than the
Community.[23] However, according to the ECJ the fact that the Union citizen
children were residing in another Member State provided them with a sufficient link to Community law enabling them to be afforded protection under
Art.12 EC Treaty. Such a conclusion was not undermined by the fact that
they also held the nationality of the host Member State to which the host
Member State wished to give preference to.[24]

Whilst the Belgian authorities were entitled to apply their own rules as   **4–23**
regards surnames to their own nationals, where those nationals also held the
nationality of a second Member State, the Belgian authorities were not entitled to treat them as if they were Belgian nationals alone without permitting
them to benefit from the holding of their second state nationality. If a

---

[20] Case- C–224/02 *Pusa v Osuuspankkien Keskinainen Vakuutusyhtio*, judgment of April 29, 2004
concerned the taxation of a Union citizen who was exercising the right to move and reside in
another Member State. Whilst taxation is not harmonised at Community law level and therefore
is normally said to fall with the exclusive competence of the individual Member States, the ECJ
held that such competence must be exercised in compliance with Community law and thus in
Art.12 EC Treaty. Similarly in *Elsen* (Case C–135/99 *Elsen v Bundesversicherungsanstalt fur
Angestellte*) the ECJ considered the rules relating to the calculation of old age pension allowance
fell within the competence of Member States. However such legislation must be compatible with
Community law. If national legislation is disadvantageous to those who have exercised their free
movement rights such legislation would be incompatible with Community law.
[21] Case C–148/02 *Avello v Belgium*, judgment of October 2, 2003.
[22] Mr Garcia Avello, a Spanish national, and Ms I. Weber, a Belgian national reside in Belgium
where they married in 1986. Applying provisions of Belgian law the registrar entered the
patronymic surname of their father ("Garcia Avello") on their certificates as their own surname.
An application to change the surname to "Garcia Weber" (in accordance with well-established
usage in Spanish law) was refused.
[23] Case C–148/02 *Avello v Belgium* [2004] C.M.L.R.1, para.25.
[24] For a discussion on dual nationality, see Chapter 5 below.

Spanish national were residing in Belgium he would be entitled to have his surname conferred in accordance with Spanish law. A dual Belgian/Spanish national should not be in a *worse* position by virtue only of holding such dual nationality.

4–24 Further development of the relationship between Arts 12 and 17 EC Treaty is to be found in the decision of the ECJ in *Trojani*.[25] The case concerned a French national residing at a Salvation Army hostel in Belgium where he undertook various jobs in return for board, lodging and some "pocket money". He approached the Belgian authorities for payment of the minimum subsistence allowance (the minimex) which was refused on the grounds that he was not Belgian and was not a worker. The ECJ left the determination of the question whether Mr Trojani was a worker to the national court.[26] In the event that the national court were to conclude Mr Trojani was not a worker, and since due to his lack of resources he could not derive any other benefit from Art.18 EC Treaty, the ECJ considered his position as a Union citizen alone. Mr Trojani was in possession of a residence permit issued to him by the Belgian authorities. The ECJ held that a Union citizen in such a situation could rely on Art.12 EC Treaty in order to be granted a social assistance benefit such as the minimex. The ECJ canvassed the possibility of the Member State taking measures to remove a person who has recourse to public funds.[27] However, any such measures could be undertaken by the Member State only subject to two important caveats. First, the ECJ recalled that removal must not be the automatic consequence of having recourse to public funds.[28] Secondly, and most importantly in the present context, the ECJ emphasised that whilst the person continues to reside in the host Member State he is entitled to benefit from the fundamental principle of equal treatment.

(ii) *Lawful residence*

4–25 The ECJ appears to make as a precondition to the benefit of the principle of equal treatment guaranteed by Art.12 EC Treaty that the Union citizen is "lawfully resident" in the host Member State.[29] Lawful residence for these purposes is defined by reference to national laws and practices. Inevitably therefore there is scope for significant divergence of approach as regards what constitutes lawful residence as between the various Member States. If "lawful residence" is an absolute precondition to access Art.12 EC Treaty protection there is a potential for Member States with restrictive immigration laws and practices to limit the benefits of Union citizenship for Union citizens residing in their territories. Whether the ECJ would countenance such divergence is doubtful. Moreover, the case law suggests that lawful residence is not to be strictly construed.

---

[25] Case C–456/02 *Trojani v Centre public d'aide sociale de Bruxelles (CPAS)*, judgment of September 7, 2004.
[26] See further Chapter 7.
[27] Case C–456/02 *Trojani v Centre public d'aide sociale de Bruxelles (CPAS)*, judgment of September 7, 2004, at para.45.
[28] See Case C-184/99 *Grzelczyk v Centre Public d'aide sociale d'Ottignies-Louvain-la-Neuve* [2001] E.C.R. I–6193.
[29] See further Case C–456/02 *Trojani v Centre public d'aide sociale de Bruxelles (CPAS)*, judgment of September 7, 2004, para.39.

In *Sala*,[30] Mrs Sala at the relevant time could not be removed by virtue of   **4–26**
provisions contained in the European Convention on Social and Medical
Assistance. She had only documents confirming that an application had been
made for a residence permit. Although the ECJ describes her as having been
"authorised to reside", her situation was in fact not one of authorisation, but
rather one of toleration on the part of the host Member State.

There may be a wide variety of situations in which Union citizens reside in   **4–27**
the territories of other Member States without having fulfilled administrative
formalities and in which their presence there is apparently tolerated. Firstly,
bearing in mind the administrative difficulties of actually seeking to enforce
the removal of Union citizens who do not possess residence permits, such toleration is likely to be common in Member States. Secondly, in light of the
breadth of the concepts of (for example) worker and work seeker, there will
frequently be a very fine line between who is and who is not in fact exercising
free movement rights. Thirdly, it may also occasionally be the case that Union
citizens will have moved to Member States *intending* to exercise a particular
free movement right, without ever actually doing so.

The *Sala*[31] decision therefore apparently includes in the beneficiaries of pro-   **4–28**
tection of Art.12 EC Treaty a broad spectrum of Union citizens residing in
Member States who are not in possession of residence permits. Plainly this is
to be welcomed if Union citizens are not to be socially excluded and
disadvantaged in other Member States.

Even however if the foregoing analysis of residence and toleration is too   **4–29**
broad, and lawful residence *is* required, such lawful residence need not have
been continuous or for a predetermined period of time in order that the Union
citizen is able to benefit from the protection of Art.12 EC Treaty. In *Trojani*
the ECJ expressly stated that the benefit of Art.12 EC Treaty was to be enjoyed
by those who have been lawfully resident in a Member State "for a certain
period of time".[32] Thus for example, a person whose residence was initially
lawful as a work seeker, but who fails within a reasonable period to find work
and who thereafter ceases to fall within the scope of the free movement
provisions, should on the ECJ's analysis nonetheless benefit from Art.12 EC
Treaty.

(iii) *Scope of Article 12 EC Treaty*

The scope of situations in which Union citizens have benefited from the equal   **4–30**
treatment provision contained in Art.12 EC Treaty has been both broad and
varied. It has included non-discriminatory access to: the minimex (*Trojani*);
child-raising allowance (*Sala*) and the ability to change surnames (*Avello*).
Moreover as *Avello*[33] makes clear, the ECJ has even been prepared to extend
the scope of Art.12 EC Treaty for Union citizens into areas that fall within
the exclusive competence of Member States. However, in particular in such

---

[30] Case-85/96 *Martinez Sala v Freistat Bayern* [1998] E.C.R. I–2691.
[31] Case-85/96 *Martinez Sala v Freistat Bayern* [1998] E.C.R. I–2691.
[32] Case C–456/02 *Trojani v Centre public d'aide sociale de Bruxelles (CPAS)*, judgment of September 7, 2004, para.43.
[33] Case C-148/02 *Avello v Belgium* [2004] C.M.L.R.1, para.25.

areas falling within the exclusive competence of Member States it is to be emphasised that the protection provided by Art.12 EC Treaty is not absolute and will be subject to objective justification invoked by Member States. In contentious areas of social policy, for example, a Member State would seek to guard jealously its right to maintain and uphold such policy. A degree of deference would likely be given by the ECJ to such pleas.

Moreover, there will plainly be limits to the ECJ willingness to extend further the material scope of Art.12 for Union citizens. Where the Union citizen seeks non-discriminatory access to a right or benefit whose provisions do not have financial ramifications for the Member State concerned the ECJ will require substantial objective justification for the discriminatory treatment. Where on the other hand there are financial consequences for the host Member State from the provision of any such right or benefit, the ECJ is likely to take a more restrictive approach. Such analysis is not contradicted by the ECJ's decision in *Trojani*[34] which concerned non-discriminatory access to the minimex (a non-contributory means tested benefit), since the minimex is a benefit guaranteeing only a minimum level of subsistence which if not given arguably engages the Member State's human rights obligations.

4-31 Whilst the development of the relationship between Arts 12 and 17 EC Treaty is to be welcomed, it remains the case that it will normally better avail the Union citizen if able to bring himself within the scope of a free movement right. The material scope of Art.12 EC Treaty is plainly broader if the Union citizen is exercising free movement rights since, as already emphasised, in those cases it is the obligation of Member States to facilitate the exercise of such rights and to eliminate any obstacles to free movement.[35] All rights or benefits which in any way impact on the ability of Union citizens to exercise the right to move and reside in other Member States must fall within the scope of Art.12 EC Treaty since such Union citizens must not be disadvantaged by their having moved.[36]

(c) *Tension between Union and national citizenship*

4-32 As identified above, the creation of citizenship of a supranational body undoubtedly creates a potential tension with national authorities, particularly where such citizenship has consequences for Member States which might be considered to be wider than anticipated. Such tension will be at its most acute where Member States are obliged to shoulder additional financial responsibility.

4-33 In its original form as it appeared in the Maastricht Treaty, Art.8(1) [now Art.17(1) EC Treaty] contained no reference to Union citizenship complementing rather than replacing national citizenship. It was the Amsterdam

---

[34] Case C–456/02 *Trojani v Centre public d'aide sociale de Bruxelles (CPAS)*, judgment of September 7, 2004
[35] See for example Case C-138/02 *Collins v Secretary of State for Work and Pensions*, judgment of March 23, 2004 where the ECJ held that a work seeker was entitled to job-seeker's allowance on a non-discriminatory basis.
[36] See Case C–135/99 *Elsen v Bundesversicherungsanstalt für Angestellte* [2000] E.C.R. I–10409, para.34.

Treaty signed more than five years later[37] which clarified the link between European and national citizenship adding to Art.17(1) EC Treaty the unequivocal statement that "citizenship of the Union shall complement and not replace national citizenship".

If such clarification was not reassurance enough for Member States, the ECJ has reaffirmed the sovereignty of Member States as regards the right of Member States to determine the acquisition of nationality and also the conferring of the status of Union citizenship.[38] As made clear in Chapter 5, the nationality of the Member States is determined by reference to the domestic law of the individual Member States alone. A Member State may change its laws relating to the acquisition of nationality without reference to any EU or other body, and it is permissible also for Member States to define which of their nationals are to be considered EU citizens for the purposes of EU law. Nationality is thus a matter exclusively within the competence of the Member States, although where a Member State wishes to preclude some of its nationals from obtaining EU law benefits it must do so by means of a declaration.[39]

4–34

Despite such reassurance however the tension remains. It is well shown by the June 11, 2004 citizenship referendum in Ireland which was proposed by Irish Justice Minister Michael McDowell to end what he claimed was an incentive for foreign mothers to give birth in Irish hospitals, so called 'baby tourists'.[40] When the Advocate General gave his opinion in *Chen* [41] Mr McDowell took the opportunity to appeal to voters to support the Government's referendum stating that the Advocate General's decision sent out a clear message that if people do not want to be sent home, "all they have to do is get to either part of Ireland and have a child there".[42]

4–35

It is not inconceivable that the holding of the Irish referendum was motivated in part by pressure put on the Irish by other Member States.

---

[37] The Amsterdam Treaty was signed on October 2, 1997 and came into force on May 1, 1999: see Chapter 1 above.
[38] See Case C-256/99 *Cheung Chiu Hung*, judgment of July 12, 2001 and Case C-192/99 *The Queen v Secretary of State for the Home Department Ex p. Manjit Kaur* [2001] All E.R. (EC) 250.
[39] The UK's declaration means that the following are to be considered as "nationals" for the purposes of EU law: a) British citizens; b) British subjects with the right of abode in the UK and c) British Dependant Territories citizens who acquire that citizenship as a result of a connection to Gibraltar. January 28, 1983 [1983] O.J. C23, p 1, (Cmnd 9062, 1983).
[40] See Art. "'Baby tourist' vote in June" by Deborah Condon (posted on April 7, 2004 on the website *www.irishhealth.com*). On April 11, 2004 in an Art. by Mark Brennock in *The Irish Times* ("McDowell spells out plans to restrict rights to citizenship") Mr Brennock refers to Mr McDowell having "shifted his argument for the holding of the referendum, saying it was necessary 'to protect the integrity of the Irish citizenship law'." The article continues: "Last month he and his Department based their case for change on suggestions the growing number of non-national births in Ireland to 'citizenship tourists' was causing a crisis in maternity hospitals. Yesterday, however, he said: 'This is not an issue about maternity hospitals. Ireland could not be the only EU state offering national—and therefore EU-wide—citizenship rights to babies whose parents came here solely for this purpose'."
[41] Case C-200/02 *Man Lavette Chen v Kunqian Catherine Zhu v Secretary of State for the Home Department*, opinion of May 18, 2004.
[42] See "Ruling 'justifies' citizenship referendum" by Deborah Condon (posted on May 19, 2004 on the website *www.irishhealth.com*).

4–36   In theory a Member State could seek to prevent its citizens from obtaining the benefits of Union citizenship the greater such benefits become. However, whilst such concerns might well dictate the wishes of certain national authorities to curtail rights, the reality is that it is too late. It is not possible[43] to dissociate Union citizenship from the citizenship of Member States so as to create categories of persons who could enjoy the free movement rights of the economically active and inactive, but not the rights associated with Union citizenship. This does not mean, however, that a Member State might not seek to enter a declaration which would have the effect of depriving its nationals of all benefits of EU law (as for example in the case of the UK's declarations), nor that a Member State would not seek to amend its citizenship laws as Ireland has done.

4. ARTICLE 18 EC TREATY: THE RIGHT OF UNION CITIZENS TO MOVE

(a) *Introduction*

4–37   The insertion of Art.8a (Art.18(1) EC Treaty) into the Maastricht Treaty was symbolically important. It placed at the heart of the EC Treaty a right for all Union citizens to move and reside freely in the Member States. Whilst free movement rights had always been core to the EC Treaty, the original intended beneficiaries were the economically active. Until the Maastricht Treaty, the substance of free movement rights for the economically inactive was described only by secondary legislation.

4–38   The extent to which Art.18(1) EC Treaty was more than merely symbolic is a question that the ECJ is still answering. There is potentially a range of interpretations which could be given to Art.18(1) EC Treaty:

- Art.18 EC Treaty adds nothing of substance to free movement rights which are conferred exclusively by (other) existing EC Treaty provisions and secondary legislation. The conditions and limitations laid down in those other provisions are to be strictly construed and applied (a "restrictive interpretation").

- Art.18(1) EC Treaty provides an interpretative obligation requiring Member States to apply such limitations and conditions in compliance with the limits imposed by Community law and in accordance with the general principles of that law, in particular the principle of proportionality. Thus the "limitations and conditions" that are found in EC Treaty provisions and secondary legislation are to be construed against a backdrop of the fundamental right to move and reside contained in Art.18(1) EC Treaty (an "interpretative obligation").

- Art.18(1) EC Treaty itself founds the right to move and reside without reference to any need to establish that the right is already provided for

---

[43] Subject of course to Treaty amendment.

elsewhere in the pre-existing specific provisions contained in the Treaty or secondary legislation relating to free movement (a "free standing right").

Each is considered in turn below.

(b) *A restrictive interpretation*

The narrowest interpretation of Art.18(1) EC Treaty would deprive the pro- **4–39** vision of any legal impact at all, in effect characterising it as having little more than political significance. Such approach is reflected by (for example) the submissions made to the ECJ in *Grzelczyk*[44] by the Belgian and Danish Governments that Union citizens did not obtain through Art.18 EC Treaty rights that were "new" or "more extensive" than those already derived from the EC Treaty and secondary legislation. As the ECJ itself characterised their submissions: "The principle of citizenship of the Union has no autonomous content, but is merely linked to other provisions in the Treaty".[45]

The ECJ's response to such exhortations by some Member States has been **4–40** one of resounding rejection. As stated by the ECJ in *Baumbast*[46] (and as consistently restated thereafter), Art.18 EC Treaty grants a right to reside which is conferred directly on every Union citizen. Although the ECJ acknowledges that the right conferred is subject to limitations and conditions, the application of those limitations and conditions is subject to judicial review. The narrow approach advocated by some Member States is thus plainly not one which the ECJ approves.

(c) *An interpretative obligation*

The majority of the cases to date in which the ECJ has considered Art.18 EC **4–41** Treaty reflect "the interpretative approach". This approach sees the "limitations and conditions" referred to in Art.18 EC Treaty as those provided for in existing primary and secondary legislation, but insists that they must be construed against the backdrop of the fundamental right to move and reside.

The cases of *Grzelczyk*[47] and *Baumbast*[48] provide good examples of this approach.

Grzelczyk[49] concerned a French student studying in Belgium who during the **4–42** final year of his studies was refused payment of the minimum subsistence

---

[44] Case C-184/99 *Grzelczyk v Centre Public d'aide sociale d'Ottignies-Louvain-la-Neuve* [2001] E.C.R. I–6193.
[45] Case C-184/99 *Grzelczyk v Centre Public d'aide sociale d'Ottignies-Louvain-la-Neuve* [2001] E.C.R. I–6193, para.21.
[46] Case C-413/99 *Baumbast and R. v Secretary of State for the Home Department* [2002] E.C.R. I–7091.
[47] Case C-184/99 *Grzelczyk v Centre Public d'aide sociale d'Ottignies-Louvain-la-Neuve* [2001] E.C.R. I–6193.
[48] Case C-413/99 *Baumbast and R. v Secretary of State for the Home Department* [2002] E.C.R. I–7091
[49] Case C-184/99 *Grzelczyk v Centre Public d'aide sociale d'Ottignies-Louvain-la-Neuve* [2001] E.C.R. I–6193.

allowance known as the minimex because he was not a Belgian national. The ECJ emphasised that Union citizenship was "destined to be the fundamental status of nationals of the Member States, enabling those who find themselves in the same situation to enjoy the same treatment in law irrespective of their nationality, subject to such exceptions as are expressly provided for".[50] Such situations included those involving the exercise of the fundamental freedoms guaranteed by the Treaty and those involving the exercise of the right to move and reside freely in another Member State as conferred by Art.18 EC Treaty.

4–43 In the context of Art.18(1) EC Treaty the limitations and conditions relevant to Mr Grzelczyk were those contained in the Student Directive.[51] However, reading those limitations in conjunction with Art.18(1) EC Treaty the ECJ emphasised the following features of the Directive:

- whilst Art.3 makes clear that the directive does not establish any right to payment of maintenance grants, there are no provisions in the directive that preclude those to whom it applies from receiving social security benefits;

- as to resources, Art.1 does not require resources of any specific amount, nor that they be evidenced by specific documents: rather the Art. refers merely to a declaration (or equivalent alternative means) enabling the student to satisfy the national authority as to the availability of sufficient resources (the truthfulness of which fell to be assessed only as at the time when made); and

- the directive thereby differed from Directives 90/364 and 90/365 which do indicate the necessary minimum level of available income.

4–44 Such factors did not prevent a Member State from taking the view that a student who has recourse to social assistance no longer fulfils the conditions of his right of residence or from taking measures, within the limits imposed by Community law, either to withdraw his residence permit or not to renew it. However, according to the ECJ "in no case may such measures become the automatic consequence of a student who is a national of another Member State having recourse to the host Member State's social assistance system." In these circumstances the ECJ held that:

"Articles 6 [now 12] and 8 [now 18] of the Treaty preclude entitlement to a non-contributory social benefit, such as the minimex, from being made conditional, in the case of nationals of Member States other than the host State where they are legally resident, on their falling within the scope of Regulation No 1612/68 when no such condition applies to nationals of the host Member State".[52]

---

[50] Case C-184/99 *Grzelczyk v Centre Public d'aide sociale d'Ottignies-Louvain-la-Neuve* [2001] E.C.R. I-6193 para.31. Such aspirational statement has been repeated frequently by the ECJ since first used in this case. However, there are no transitional provisions contained in Pt II of the EC Treaty and whilst perhaps understandable that the ECJ's attitude to Art.18(1) EC Treaty should reflect incremental change, it is difficult to see what possible justification there could be for any notion that Union Citizenship should be confined to something aspirational as opposed to something which is real and effective.

[51] Dir. 93/96 [1993] O.J. L317/59.

[52] Case C-184/99 *Grzelczyk v Centre Public d'aide sociale d'Ottignies-Louvain-la-Neuve* [2001] E.C.R. I-019, para.46.

Whilst Member States might have previously construed the Student Directive **4-45**
as placing an absolute bar on access to social assistance, the ECJ has made
clear by reference to Art.18 EC Treaty that such a narrow interpretation is
no longer open.

In *Baumbast*[53] the ECJ considered the limitations found in the general right **4-46**
of Residence Directive.[54] The limitations and conditions contained in that
Directive require that those wishing to enjoy the right to reside (and members
of their families) must be covered by sickness insurance in respect of *all* risks
in the host Member State and have sufficient resources to avoid becoming a
burden on the social assistance system of the host Member State during their
period of residence.[55]

Mr Baumbast satisfied the condition relating to sufficient resources. At issue **4-47**
was whether his sickness insurance covered all risks.[56] However, whatever the
actual position as regards sickness insurance (a matter for determination by
the national tribunal), the ECJ acknowledged that the limitations and conditions laid down by Directive 90/364 were based on the notion that the exercise of the right of residence could be sub-ordinated to the legitimate
interests of the Member States which (according to the fourth recital in the
preamble to Directive 90/364) included the requirement that beneficiaries of
the right must not become an "unreasonable" burden on the public finances
of the host Member State.

However, reflective of the interpretative approach the ECJ held that such lim- **4-48**
itations and conditions were to be applied "in compliance with the limits
imposed by Community law and in accordance with the general principles of
that law, in particular the principle of proportionality".[57] This meant that
national measures adopted were required to be both necessary and appropriate to attain the objective pursued. Applying the principle of proportionality
the ECJ stated:[58]

> "92. In respect of the application of the principle of proportionality to the facts of
> the *Baumbast* case, it must be recalled, first, that it has not been denied that Mr
> Baumbast has sufficient resources within the meaning of Directive 90/364; second,
> that he worked and therefore lawfully resided in the host Member State for several
> years, initially as an employed person and subsequently as a self-employed person;
> third, that during that period his family also resided in the host Member State and
> remained there even after his activities as an employed and self-employed person in
> that State came to an end; fourth, that neither Mr Baumbast nor the members of
> his family have become burdens on the public finances of the host Member State
> and, fifth, that both Mr Baumbast and his family have comprehensive sickness
> insurance in another Member State of the Union.

---

[53] Case C-413/99 *Baumbast and R. v Secretary of State for the Home Department* [2002] E.C.R.
I–7091.
[54] Dir. 90/364 [1990] O.J. L180/26.
[55] Dir. 90/364, Art.1(1).
[56] It had been found by the UK first instance court that Mr Baumbast's sickness insurance could
not emergency treatment given in the UK: Case C-413/99 *Baumbast and R. v Secretary of State
for the Home Department*, [2002] E.C.R. I-7091, para.89.
[57] Case C-413/99 *Baumbast and R. v Secretary of State for the Home Department*, [2002] E.C.R.
I-7091 para.91.
[58] Case C-413/99 *Baumbast and R. v Secretary of State for the Home Department* [2002] E.C.R.
I-7091.

93. Under those circumstances, to refuse to allow Mr Baumbast to exercise the right of residence which is conferred on him by Article 18(1) EC by virtue of the application of the provisions of Directive 90/364 on the ground that his sickness insurance does not cover the emergency treatment given in the host Member State would amount to a disproportionate interference with the exercise of that right."

(d) *A free standing right*

4-49   The most liberal interpretation of Art.18(1) EC Treaty sees it as a discrete provision founding the right to move and reside for those not catered for by the free movement provisions otherwise contained in the EC Treaty or secondary legislation.

Opponents of such interpretation would doubtless maintain that the interpretation would render entirely otiose the phrase in Art.18 EC Treaty that the right is "subject to the limitations and conditions laid down in this Treaty and by the measures adopted to give it effect". In fact the interpretation is more nuanced.

4-50   Such approach was first articulated by Advocate General Geelhoed in *Baumbast*.[59] Identifying the economically active and the economically non-active by reference to two discrete sets of rules[60] Advocate General Geelhoed stated that Art.18 EC Treaty added to such sets of rules "a general right of residence in favour of citizens of the European Union" which he described as "a fundamental right in favour of citizens of the European Union to move and reside freely within it".

4-51   In Advocate General Geelhoed's view Art.18 EC Treaty has substantive significance in two respects. Firstly, the unconditional nature of the first part of Art.18(1) EC Treaty entails that the right of residence must be a recognisable right of substance for citizens. Whilst the provision lays down requirements to be met such requirements must be neither arbitrary, nor deprive the right of residence of its substantive content. Any limitations must respect the essence of the rights and freedoms, be proportionate and be made only if necessary and genuinely meeting objectives of general interest recognised by the Union. Secondly, the provision imposes an obligation on the Community legislature to ensure that a citizen of the European Union can actually enjoy the rights conferred on him under Art.18 EC Treaty.

The approach is summarised Advocate General Geelhoed[61] in these terms:

"Finally, the unambiguous nature of Article 18(1) EC entails that a person not entitled to a right of residence under other provisions of Community law can none the less acquire such a right by reliance on Article 18. Since there is no single general

---

[59] Case C-413/99 *Baumbast and R v Secretary of State for the Home Department*, [2002] E.C.R. I-7091.
[60] Arts 39 *et seq* EC Treaty dealing with the economically active and Dirs 90/364, 90/365 and 93/96 dealing with the economically non-active—para. 104.
[61] Case C-413/99 *Baumbast and R. v Secretary of State for the Home Department*, opinion July 5, 2001.

and all-embracing set of rules concerning the exercise of the right of residence in Community law recourse must be had in cases for which the Community legislature has made no provision to Article 18 EC. However, that does not mean that an unrestricted right of residence is recognised in those—special—cases. The conditions and limitations imposed on that right by EC law must be applied by analogy as far as possible to persons who derive their right to reside directly from Article 18 EC. The wording of the second part of Article 18(1) EC forms the basis for that."

The first (and to date only) example of a case in which the ECJ has embraced this approach is *D'Hoop*[62] in which the ECJ considered the position of a Belgian national who had completed her secondary education in France before commencing university studies in Belgium. After she had completed her university studies she applied for a "tide-over allowance"—a social benefit intended for young unemployed people in search of their first job. The allowance was refused by the Belgian national employment office because Ms D'Hoop had completed her secondary education in France.   **4–53**

In assessing the provisions on Union citizenship the ECJ—as it had done in *Grzelczyk*—emphasised both that Union citizenship was destined to be the "fundamental status" of nationals of the Member States[63] and that the situations falling within the scope of Community law included those involving the exercise of the fundamental freedoms guaranteed by the Treaty "in particular those involving the freedom to move and reside within the territory of the Member States, as conferred by Article 18 EC Treaty".[64]   **4–54**

Of particular relevance for present purposes is the that the ECJ characterised Ms D'Hoop as someone who had exercised "the opportunities offered by the Treaty in relation to freedom of movement".[65] She had exercised her fundamental right to move having undertaken her secondary education in France. This was an entirely novel approach. Shortly stated this is because there is no specific right recognised in the EC Treaty (or secondary legislation) to move for the purposes of secondary education.[66] Whilst the decision of the ECJ in *Raulin*[67] requires equal treatment as regards *vocational* training, the principle does not apply to general secondary education. Although Art.12 of Regulation 1612/68 provides a discrete right for the children of workers to be admitted to a Member State's 'general education, apprenticeship and vocational training courses' there is no indication that Ms D'Hoop was exercising her own discrete right of access to secondary education as the child of a worker. Thus—at least by implication—*D'Hoop*[68] can be characterised as the first case in which the ECJ treated Art.18 EC Treaty itself as founding the right to move and reside.   **4–55**

---

[62] Case C-224/98 *D'Hoop v Office national de l'emploi*, judgment of July 11, 2002.
[63] Case C-224/98 *D'Hoop v Office national de l'emploi*, para.28: as stated at para.31 of *Grzelczyk*, the ECJ stated that the status enabled those who find themselves in the same situation to enjoy within the scope *ratione materiae* of the Treaty the same treatment in law irrespective of their nationality, subject to such exceptions as are expressly provided for.
[64] Case C-224/98 *D'Hoop v Office national de l'emploi*, para.29, as the ECJ had stated in Case C-274/96 *Bickel and Franz* [1998] E.C.R. I-7637, paras 15 and 16, and *Grzelczyk*, para.33.
[65] Case C-224/98 *D'Hoop v Office national de l'emploi* judgment of July 11, 2002, paras 30 and 33.
[66] Save for the Art.12 right contained in Reg. 1612/68 considered below.
[67] Case C-357/89 *Raulin v Minister van Onderwijs en Wetenschappen* [1992] E.C.R. I–1027.
[68] Case C-224/98 *D'Hoop v Office national de l'emploi* judgement of July 11, 2002.

4–56   Furthermore, it is important to appreciate the significance of the ECJ's finding that although not in force at such time the provisions on Union citizenship could be taken into account enabling assessment to be made of the present effects of a situation which had arisen previously.[69] It is clear that without such finding and an ability to rely on Art.18(1), Ms D'Hoop could not have been characterised as having exercised Treaty opportunities when she undertook her secondary education in France.

(e) *The future of Article 18 EC Treaty*

4–57   As Advocate General Geelhoed has stated, Art.18 EC Treaty provides the free movement right for those not already covered by primary and secondary education. In essence those not covered are twofold: children and the poor.

(i) *Children*

4–58   As regards children, without Art.18 EC Treaty they enjoy no specific free movement rights, other than as the consequence of being the children of parents exercising free movement rights[70] or students in vocational training.[71] In *D'Hoop*[72] the ECJ plainly remedied the lacuna, at least for children in secondary education. It did so by reference to the specific inclusion of Art.149 in the EC Treaty aimed at encouraging the mobility of students. Since Art.149 applies to education generally and not only to secondary education, there is no reason why the ECJ's reasoning should not apply equally to children in primary education.

4–59   This leaves a potential lacuna only for those children who are not in education and do not have EU national parents.

4–60   This category of children was considered by the ECJ in *Chen*.[73] The case concerned a Chinese couple who decided that their second child should be born abroad. To this end Mrs Chen traveled to the United Kingdom and gave birth on September 16, 2000 to her daughter Catherine in Belfast, Northern Ireland, having been advised by lawyers that the child would thereby be Irish by birth. After the birth Mrs Chen moved to Cardiff with her child and applied to the UK authorities for residence permits which were refused.

4–61   The principal issue was whether the infant child could rely on the provisions of Directive 90/364 (providing the right of residence for the self-sufficient). It was argued by the Irish Government that because of her tender age the child was incapable of independently exercising the right to choose a place of residence in the United Kingdom and to establish herself there in the context of the Directive. The ECJ held that it was sufficient for nationals of Member States simply to "have" the necessary resources in order to benefit from the

---

[69] Case C-224/98 *D'Hoop v Office national de l'emploi*, judgment of July 11, 2002, paras 21–26.
[70] See for example Arts 10 and 12 of Reg. 1612/68.
[71] Dir. 93/96 on the right of residence for students..
[72] Case C-224/98 *D'Hoop v Office national de l'emploi*, judgment of July 11, 2002.
[73] Case C-200/02 *Man Lavette Chen and Kunqian Catherine Zhu v Secretary of State for the Home Department*, October 19, 2004.

right of residence given by Directive 90/364. That Directive lays down no requirement whatsoever as to the origin of such resources.[74] Furthermore, as regards the child's mother and carer, the ECJ applied *Baumbast*[75] and held that unless Mrs Chen was able to reside with her daughter this would deprive the child's right of residence of any useful effect.[75A]

The result in *Chen* is unsurprising. As regards sufficiency of resources, the   **4–62** Commission has long held the view that Directives 90/364 and 90/365 do not mean that the requirement must be satisfied by the beneficiaries *own* resources, or indeed resources originating from any dependents.[75B] There is no reason why the position should be different for an EU national child with resources, whatever the *origin* of such resources. As regards the position of the child's carer, the judgment in *Chen* reinforces the firmly established principles that family members facilitate the exercise of EC Treaty rights and that a child will usually be unable to exercise free movement rights without being accompanied by a primary carer. The ECJ was clearly fortified in its views by the existence of the child's Article 18 EC Treaty right to move and reside in another Member State.

This decision will undoubtedly be of considerable benefit to EU national   **4–63** children whose parents are not themselves EU nationals. The ECJ in *Chen* was clear that the primary carer of such children should have a right of residence. Such right of residence must include the right to work, which has long been recognised in secondary legislation as a corollary to the right of residence of family members. In assessing the ability of the child to meet the resources requirement of Directive 90/364 the income derived form any work by the carer should be included in considering the level of available resources.

(ii) *The poor*

The present position (children aside) is that those who are not economically   **4–64** self-sufficient or economically active do not benefit from free movement rights. Clearly this is a deliberate choice made by the Community institutions in determining the beneficiaries of free movement rights.

As discussed above, the "lawfully resident" and even just tolerated Union cit-   **4–65** izens are able, by virtue of Arts 12 and 17 EC Treaty, to obtain a non-contributory benefit payable to own nationals on a non-discriminatory basis, thereby facilitating their further residence in other Member States.

It would undoubtedly be a considerable step forward for the ECJ to establish   **4–66** a free movement right for the poor from Art.18(1) EC Treaty, although it is to be acknowledged that such step would for some Member States be both

---

[74] Case C–200/02 *Man Lavette Chen and Kunqian Catherine Zhu v Secretary of State for the Home Department* October 19, 2004, para.30
[75] Case C–413/99 *Baumbast and R. v Secretary of State for the Home Department* [2002] E.C.R. I-7091.
[75A] Case C–200/02 *Man Lavette Chen and Kunqian Catherine Zhu v Secretary of State for the Home Department* October 19, 2004, para.45.
[75B] See Chapter 9 at paras 9–12 to 9–18.

particularly objectionable and a step too far. However, it remains to be seen how much longer the ECJ is prepared to countenance the regrettable situation in which the already socially excluded find themselves discriminated against further by Community law.

(iii) *Limitations and conditions*

4-67   If Art.18 is to provide a free standing free movement right for those not already covered by Community law, there must plainly be limitations and conditions on the exercise of such right. Art.18(1) EC Treaty itself refers expressly to conditions and limitations and, as Advocate General Geelhoed observed, in respect of the "special cases" for which Community law has made no provision there is not an "unrestricted right of residence". There are (at least) two possible categories of limitations and conditions.

4-68   Firstly, the limitations are likely to include some financial constraints. As a general principle it would doubtless be said that the exercise of EC Treaty rights ought not place an unreasonable financial burden on Member States. Certainly such principle is one expressed (for example) in the preambles to the three directives concerning the economically inactive.[76] However, it is well settled that such principle could not be interpreted so as to exclude all access to any financial benefits. Indeed, such proposition is vouchsafed by the fact that *Sala*,[77] *Grzelczyk*[78] and *D'Hoop*[79] each concerned access to financial resources. Thus financial limitations will not *always* operate so as to defeat the exercise of the right to move and reside freely where such free mover is (or becomes) impecunious. The conditions and limitations already laid down in existing secondary legislation relating to the economically inactive provide a useful yardstick in this respect, subject also to the interpretative gloss placed upon them by the ECJ (in for example *Baumbast*[80]).

4-69   Secondly, it is plain that the limitations justified on grounds of public policy, public security and public health—as provided expressly for example in relation to workers by Art.39(3) EC Treaty—must apply to any free mover.

---

[76] The preambles to Dirs 90/364, 90/365 and 93/96 each contain the following recital: Whereas the beneficiaries of the right of residence must not become an unreasonable burden on the public finances of the host member state.

[77] Case C-85/96 *Martinez Sala v Freistat Bayern* [1998] E.C.R. I-2691.

[78] Case C-184/99 *Grzelczyk v Centre Public d'aide sociale d'Ottignies-Louvain-la-Neuve* [2001] E.C.R. I-6193.

[79] Case C-224/98 *D'Hoop v Office national de l'emploi*, judgment of July 11, 2002.

[80] Case C-413/99 *Baumbast and R. v Secretary of State for the Home Department* [2002] E.C.R. I-7091.

Part Two

FREE MOVEMENT OF EU CITIZENS AND THEIR FAMILY MEMBERS

CHAPTER 5

BENEFICIARIES OF FREE MOVEMENT PROVISIONS

In this chapter we consider who benefits from the EC Treaty provisions on free movement of persons. The primary focus is the identification of EU nationals although we also examine which third country nationals have rights in the context of free movement law.

1. CITIZENSHIP OF THE UNION

(a) *The Union Citizen*

The historical and conceptual basis of citizenship of the Union has been discussed in Chapter 4, Art.17. EC Treaty makes clear that Union citizenship is dependent on holding the nationality of one of the Member States. In other words, anyone who is a national of a Member State is considered to be a Union citizen but the European Union itself cannot confer status on a non-national of a Member State: **5–01**

Article 17 EC Treaty

1. Citizenship of the Union is hereby established. Every person holding the nationality of a Member State shall be a citizen of the Union. Citizenship of the Union shall complement and not replace national citizenship.

2. Citizens of the Union shall enjoy the rights conferred by this Treaty and shall be subject to the duties imposed thereby.

Such an approach concords with the well defined principle of international law that the granting of nationality is the ultimate act of state sovereignty,[1] relating to notions of diplomatic and consular protection which only a state is considered able to provide. Since the European Union is not equitable to a nation state, and has not replaced the state in terms of international responsibility,[2] it is therefore logical that Union citizenship should be wholly deferential to that of the Member States.   **5–02**

The specific and detailed rights and duties conferred on Union citizens are laid down in the EC Treaty. In addition since the Maastricht Treaty Union citizenship has conferred four special rights: **5–03**

- freedom to move and take up residence anywhere in the Union;
- the right to vote and stand in local government and European Parliament elections in the country of residence;

---

[1] *Nottebohm*, Case (*Liechtenstein v Guatamala*) ICJ Reports (1955), p.4
[2] *Matthews v UK* [1999] 28 E.H.R.R. 361: *T.I. v UK* [2000] I.N.L.R. 211. At the same time it is not impossible that the EU would replace the nation State in international law terms, *e.g.* if the EU were to accede to international covenants as a State party.

- diplomatic and consular protection from the authorities of any Member State where the country of which a person is a national is not represented in a non-Union country; and

- the right of petition and appeal to the European Ombudsman.

It is the Art.18(1) EC Treaty freedom to move and reside in other Member States that is of principal concern in this book.

5–04   The extension of free movement rights to EEA nationals through the EEA Treaty is discussed in Chapter 15. It is important to note however that EEA nationals are not Union citizens for the purposes of Art.18(1) EC Treaty. Whilst EEA nationals therefore do enjoy the free movement rights discussed in this Part, they do not enjoy the additional rights that flow from Art.18(1) EC Treaty itself.

(b) *Nationals of Member States*

(i) *Who is a National?*

5–05   Nationality of the Member States is determined by reference to domestic law of the individual Member States alone. As the ECJ held in *Micheletti*[3] "[u]nder international law, it is for each Member State, having due regard to Community law, to lay down the conditions for the acquisition and loss of nationality". It is possible for a Member State to change its laws relating to the acquisition of nationality without reference to any EU or other body. The fact that it is much easier to acquire the nationality of some Member States[4] as compared others[5] does not alter the position in Community law.

5–06   Moreover, it is also permissible for Member States to define which of their nationals are to be considered Union citizens for the purposes of Community law. For most Member States this has no relevance at all and all their nationals are to be treated as Union citizens and accordingly acquire full free movement rights within the European Union. However for the Member States such as the United Kingdom, which wish to preclude some of their nationals from obtaining the benefits from Community law, the European Union must be put on notice by means of a declaration.[6]

5–07   This and other such declarations by Member States were generally made at the time of the Member State joining the European Union and were understood to define who nationals of Member State were for the purposes of Treaty provisions such as the provision on freedom of establishment contained in Art.43 EC Treaty which refers to "nationals of a Member State". When the Maastricht Treaty then developed the concept of the Union citizen

---

[3] Case C-369/90 *Micheletti v Delegación del Gobierno en Cantabria* [1992] E.C.R. I-4239.
[4] *e.g.* Greece/Ireland.
[5] *e.g.* France/Germany.
[6] The UK's declaration means that the following are to be considered as "nationals" for the purposes of EU law: (a) British citizens; (b) British subjects with the right of abode in the UK and (c) British Dependant Territories citizens who acquire that citizenship as a result of a connection to Gibraltar, January 28, 1983 [1983] O.J. C23 Cmnd. 9062 (1983).

in Art.17 EC Treaty there was debate as to whether the declarations were valid for interpretation of that provision.

In *Hung*,[7] the UK courts referred a question to the ECJ on the interpretation **5–08** of "every person holding the nationality of a Member State" in Art.17 EC Treaty. Without reference to the full court, the President of the ECJ (First Chamber) ruled that in order to determine whether a person was a national of a Member State for the purposes of Community law, it was necessary to refer to any declarations made by the government of that Member State on the definition of the term "nationals", thereby confirming that EU citizenship could be limited by declaration in the same way as "national of a Member State" was.

In *Kaur*,[8] the ECJ was also referred questions on the validity of the UK dec- **5–09** laration[9] and whether Art.17 EC Treaty conferred any rights on persons who were not defined as "nationals" under the terms of such a declaration. The ECJ was categorical in its response that Union citizenship was conferred only on "nationals of Member States" and the declarations entered by the United Kingdom defining who its "nationals" are for the purposes of Community law were valid and unchallengeable.[10]

It is difficult to see what positive outcome there could have been for Mrs **5–10** Kaur. Whatever answer the ECJ had given about the validity of the UK declaration, it was unlikely to conclude that Mrs Kaur could obtain any benefit from Arts 17 and 18 EC Treaty. Mrs Kaur, a British Overseas Citizen, was seeking to derive a right to remain in the United Kingdom from Community law having never exercised or sought to exercise free movement rights in another Member State. Given the ECJ's constant jurisprudence on internal situations, namely that Union citizens cannot benefit from Community law in their own Member State, even if she had been recognised as a Union citizen within the meaning of Arts 17 and 18 EC Treaty she would have derived no right to reside in the United Kingdom given such absence of Community law nexus. The position might have been different if she had been seeking to move to and reside in another Member State in which case being treated as a Union citizen could have availed her.

(ii) *Internal Situations/Own Nationals*

It is well established in the case law of the ECJ that in order to fall within the **5–11** scope of the Treaty, there must be a "Community law nexus" between the activity and the Treaty. Community law will have no bearing on matters that

---

[7] Case C-256/99 *The Queen v Secretary of State for the Home Department Ex p. Cheung Chui Hung*, [2001] E.C.R. I-1237.

[8] Case C-192/99 *The Queen v Secretary of State for the Home Department Ex p. Kaur* [2001] E.C.R. I-1237.

[9] The validity of the 1982 Declaration was questioned as it was made without any statutory authority or parliamentary approval.

[10] The ECJ does not grapple with the discriminatory treatment of British nationals originating from East Africa reinforced by the United Kingdom's declaration. For a critique of the *Kaur* decision in this context see Prof. Guild, *The Legal Elements of European Identity* (Kluwer Law International, 2004), pages 75–76.

fall outside its scope. The ECJ has stated that a situation will be "wholly internal" to a Member State where "there is no factor connecting them to any of the situations envisaged by Community law".[11]

5–12 Prior to the creation of Union citizenship, the ECJ had repeatedly held that in order for nationals of Member States to benefit from the rules relating to free movement and rights of residence contained in the Treaty and secondary legislation, they must generally be outside their own Member State.[12] As the following chapters discuss, Union citizens who exercise their Treaty rights to move and reside in another Member State, acquire a number of rights as a result. These include the right to install family members and the right, in certain circumstances, to tax and social benefits. Subject to the exceptions set out below, as a general rule Union citizens residing in their own Member State cannot benefit from these rights as a matter of Community law.

5–13 It might have been thought that the creation of the concept of Union citizenship would bring benefits to all Union citizens, even in their own Member States. However the inclusion of Arts 17 and 18 EC Treaty has not altered the ECJ's approach to the question of internal situations. In *Uecker and Jacquet*,[13] the ECJ confirmed that Art.17 EC Treaty had not been intended to extend the material scope to include internal situations. Moreover, absent an express amendment to the EC Treaty, Art.47 EU Treaty makes clear that nothing in that Treaty will affect the EC Treaty.

(iii) *Exceptions to the "Internal Situations" Rule*

5–14 There are two exceptions to "internal situations" rule where own nationals might benefit from free movement provisions in their own Member State:

(a)   where the person is a dual national; or

(b)   where the person has exercised Treaty rights outside their own Member State: "the *Surinder Singh*" principle.

In other areas of Community law, provisions are transposed into domestic law and will apply to own nationals. For instance provisions relating to sex discrimination in employment apply to all EU nationals irrespective as to whether they have exercised free movement.[14]

---

[11] Case 175/78 *The Queen v Saunders* [1979] E.C.R. 1129.

[12] Joined Cases 35 & 36/82 *Morson and Jhanjan v State of the Netherlands* [1982] E.C.R. 3723, para.16; Case 147/87 *Zaoui v Cramif* [1987] E.C.R. 5511, para.15; Case C-332/90 *Steen v Deutsche Bundespost* [1992] E.C.R. I-341, para.9; Case C-153/91 *Petit v Office National des Pensions* [1992] E.C.R. I-4973, para.8; and Case C-206/91 *Koua Poirrez v Caisse d'Allocations Familiales* [1992] E.C.R. I-6685, para.11.

[13] Joined Cases C 64 & 65/96 *Land Nordrhein-Westfalen v Uecker and Jacquet v Land Nordrhein Westfalen* [1997] E.C.R. I-3171.

[14] See for example Pannick, Lewis & Hewson "Community Law, Employment and Discrimination" (Chapter 14) in *Practitioners' Handbook of EC Law* (ed. Barling and Brearley, Trenton Publishing, 1998).

Dual nationality

It is now well established that a dual national of two Member States may still   **5–15**
rely on their second nationality to obtain rights under Community law in a
Member State of which they may also be a national, irrespective of whether
the person has ever resided in the second Member State.[15] Those rights might
include the right to non-discrimination as well as general free movement rights.
The ECJ has confirmed that these principles will apply even in situations where
a dual national has never exercised free movement rights outside the Member
State of which they are also a national.

In *Avello*,[16] the ECJ examined the situation of dual Spanish and Belgian   **5–16**
national children who were born and lived all their lives in Belgium. Their
father brought an action in the Belgium courts in respect of the failure of the
Belgian authorities to allow the alteration of the children's surnames in
accordance with Spanish practices. The three Governments which intervened
in the case argued that as the children had been born in Belgium and never
moved outside of it, their dispute with the Belgian authorities was "wholly
internal" and thus outside the scope of Community law. The Advocate
General argued that their situation was inextricably linked with the exercise
of free movement rights by their father, a Spanish national with whom they
resided, and thus Community law must apply to their situation. The case and
its wider impact is discussed in detail in Chapter 4.

For present purposes it is to be emphasised that the ECJ held that the children   **5–17**
were entitled to benefit from Community law. However the ECJ's reasoning
differed from that of the Advocate General. The ECJ concentrated on the fact
that the children were nationals of one Member State residing in another
Member State, regardless of where they were born.[17] The ECJ did not make
any reference to the link between the exercise of free movement rights by their
father and the rights of residence of the children. The ECJ made it clear that
by refusing to treat the children as Spanish nationals the Belgium authorities
would be in effect adding additional conditions for the recognition of that
nationality. *Avello* thus clearly confirms that dual nationals may benefit from
Community law even where they have not exercised free movement rights and
were born and reside in one of the Member States of their nationality.

In addition, although somewhat trite it must be emphasised that to dual   **5–18**
nationals of a Member State and a non-Member State are able to rely on
their Member State nationality in obtaining free movement rights in the rest
of the Community.[18] Such dual nationals cannot be treated as third country
nationals in other Member States.

---

[15] Case C-122/96 *Saldanha v Hiross Holding AG* [1997] E.C.R. I-5325.
[16] Case C-148/02 *Garcia Avello v Belgium*, judgment of October 2, 2003, not yet reported.
[17] The ECJ did not link the children's right to the exercise of free movement rights by their father
which would make its decision equally applicable in cases where there had been no actual movement by the individual or his or her parents. Take for example the situation where a child is a
dual British/Irish national born in the UK. Even if her father (through whom Irish nationality
had been acquired) had never moved to the UK, the ECJ's decision would suggest that the
situation of the child would not be "wholly internal" to the UK.
[18] Case C-369/90 *Micheletti v Delegación del Gobierno en Cantabria* [1992] E.C.R. I-4239.

"Returning" nationals: The first cases

5–19   EU free movement law is principally concerned with the removal of obstacles
that would deter a Union citizen from exercising the right to move and reside
in another Member State.[19] The landmark case of Surinder Singh[20] established that a national of a Member State must not be deterred from exercising free movement rights by facing conditions on return to the national's own
Member State which are more restrictive than Community law. The conditions in that case related to the right of entry and residence of the third country national spouse of a British citizen on the couple's return to the United
Kingdom following a two year period of residing in Germany where the
British citizen had worked. The ECJ held that the third country national
spouse should attain at least the same rights as if accompanying the EU
national to another Member State.

5–20   Since the ECJ's judgment in *Surinder Singh* focused on the specific regulation
and directives relating to the free movement of workers, some national
authorities attempted to limit the application of the *Surinder Singh* principle
to nationals who exercise their rights of free movement as workers for a substantial period of time in another Member State. However the ECJ has now
extended this principle to students[21] and to the self-employed and service
providers.[22] The principle must apply equally to all free movers.

5–21   Furthermore since the ECJ's decision in *Carpenter*[23] there is no requirement
for the EU national to exercise the right to live in another Member State
before invoking Community law in his own Member State, provided that the
EU national can show that failure to grant an equivalent to the Community
law right in question would constitute an obstacle to the fundamental right
of free movement. Mr Carpenter, a British citizen residing in the United
Kingdom with his third country national spouse, argued that his situation
and that of his spouse was covered by Community law as he provided services, albeit on a short-term periodic basis, in other Member States whilst
retaining his residence in the United Kingdom. The ECJ concluded that as
Mr Carpenter was availing himself of the right to provide services guaranteed by Art.49 EC Treaty his situation was covered by Community law. The
fact that Mr Carpenter remained established in the United Kingdom, his
own Member State, did not affect the outcome. The ECJ recalled its own
decisions where it had found that the rights flowing from Art.49 EC Treaty
could be relied on by a provider in the State in which he is established, if the
services are provided for persons established in other Member States.[24]

---

[19] Case 118/75 *Watson and Belmann* [1976] E.C.R. 1185, para.16.
[20] Case C-370/90 *The Queen v Immigration Appeal Tribunal Ex p. Surinder Singh* [1992] E.C.R.
I-4265.
[21] Case C-224/98 *D'Hoop v Office national de'emploi* [2002] E.C.R. I-6191. This decision may be
more far reaching than first thought given the ECJ suggests that a secondary school student has
exercise a fundamental free movement right, arguably going beyond the scope of the students'
Directive 93/96.
[22] Case C-60/00 *Carpenter v Secretary of State for the Home Department* [2000] E.C.R. I-6279.
[23] Case C-60/00 *Carpenter v Secretary of State for the Home Department* [2000] E.C.R. I-6279.
[24] Case C-384/93 *Alpine Investments* [1995] E.C.R. I-1141, paras 15–22.

Akrich—A step backwards?

Progression by the ECJ in its approach to the question of internal situations 5–22
and the application of the *Surinder Singh* principle has not been a consistent
move forwards. Indeed the judgment in the case of *Akrich*[25] might represent
a significant regression. The case concerned a Moroccan national who, after
two prior deportations from the United Kingdom, entered the United
Kingdom again clandestinely and married a British citizen. Facing a further
deportation order, he then moved to Ireland with the British citizen. After a
period of residence in Ireland the couple then sought to move back to the
United Kingdom. During the entry clearance process, it was admitted that
they had gone to Ireland in order to put themselves in a position to enter the
United Kingdom lawfully. The UK Government argued that this admission
meant Mrs Akrich was not a genuine worker in Ireland, and the Immigration
Appeal Tribunal asked whether these circumstances constituted an abuse of
Community law. The ECJ confirmed its consistent position that motives
prompting the exercise of the Community rights were irrelevant to determining whether Community law applied to the situation.

However, entirely unprovoked by the national court's questions, the ECJ con- 5–23
sidered whether the spouse of an EU national who had been unlawfully present in the EU national's own Member State could rely on Community law to
enter and reside in another Member State. The ECJ stated that the illegality
precluded such reliance on Community law:

"In order to be able to benefit in a situation such as that at issue in the main proceedings from the rights provided for in Article 10 of Regulation No 1612/68, a
national of a non-Member State married to a citizen of the Union must be lawfully
resident in a Member State when he moves to another Member State".

At first blush it is extremely difficult to see how the statement that a third 5–24
country national spouse must be *lawfully* resident in one Member State
before reliance can be placed on Regulation 1612/68 can stand with the recent
judgment in *MRAX*.[26] The ECJ was clear in *MRAX* in holding that the failure to comply with immigration controls (and specifically unlawful entry into
the territory) would not be a ground for refusal of a residence permit for the
spouse of an EU national exercising free movement rights.

Indeed the statement regarding legality of residence is entirely at odds with 5–25
long-established principles of Community law: first, the principle that
Community law accords directly effective rights to EU nationals who are
exercising Treaty rights in other Member States[27] and secondly, the principles
that Member States act proportionality and with respect for human rights
when applying Community law.[28] The ECJ cannot have intended to erode

---

[25] Case C-109/01 *Secretary of State for the Home Department v Akrich*, September 23, 2003.
[26] Case C-459/99 *Mouvement contre le racisme, l'antisemitisme et la xénophobie ASBL (MRAX)
v Belgium State* [2002] E.C.R. I-6591.
[27] Case C-292/89 *The Queen v Immigration Appeal Tribunal, Ex P. Antonissen* [1991] E.C.R.
I-745.
[28] Case C-459/99 *Mouvement contre le racisme, l'antisemitisme et la xénophobie ASBL (MRAX)
v Belgium State* [2002] E.C.R. I-6591.

these fundamental principles of Community law. Indeed by applying the principles of proportionality and respect for human rights to the *Akrich* judgment the consequences of the decision are minimal.

5–26   Moreover, at worst the judgment could be considered as a refinement of the *Surinder Singh* principle such that a returning national should be no worse off than he would have been if he had not left his Member State to exercise free movement rights. It might be said that since Mr. Akrich had been a serious immigration offender and Mrs Akrich did not enjoy the benefit of having her husband lawfully residing with her in the United Kingdom before she left for Ireland, she is not "worse off" if her husband is not to be treated as lawful upon return to the United Kingdom.[29] However even if she is not worse off than before she left the United Kingdom, the refusal to admit her husband might still constitute a breach of Community law for other reasons; namely human rights and proportionality.

5–27   **The human rights caveat**   The ECJ itself provides a significant caveat to its judgment which arguably renders questions of illegal residence largely redundant except in cases where there are very significant public policy reasons for exclusion.[30] The ECJ stated that where the marriage is genuine and where the couple resided together in another Member State, on return to the Member State of which the EU national is a citizen, regard must be had for the right to respect for family life under Art.8 ECHR. Recalling the ECtHR's decisions in *Boultif*[31] and *Amrollhi*,[32] the ECJ reiterated that there are limits to the right of the State to interfere in the right to family life, even where criminal offences have been committed.

5–28   **Proportionality**   The decision in *Akrich* can be easily particularised on its facts, in that the ECJ distinguishes between cases where a person has been deported twice and has criminal convictions (*Akrich*) from cases where the person has merely failed to abide by formalities laid down in national law (such as obtaining entry clearance in *Carpenter*) or Community law (*MRAX*). Applying principles of proportionality, illegality in the country of origin may only have any consequence if it is grave making, the interference with free movement rights proportionate to safeguards that states are entitled to have in place against abuse.

5–29   **Can the ECJ have intended further consequences?**   It might be suggested that the ECJ has created a precedent that permits Member States to question the legal status of the third country national spouse of an EU national in the Member State of origin. The ECJ cannot have intended that *Akrich* would

---

[29] It might have been difficult for the ECJ to suggest that failure to admit a serious immigration offender might constitute an obstacle to free movement although it is not entirely clear why the ECJ felt it even necessary to address this question when it had not been posed by the national court nor formed any part of the oral or written procedure.

[30] Chapter 14 outlines the public policy exception. It is to be noted that the public policy exceptions is to be very narrowly construed

[31] *Boultif v Switzerland* (2001) 33 E.H.R.R. 50.

[32] *Amrollahi v Denmark* (Application no. 56811/00, July 11, 2002). See also *Sen v the Netherlands* (Application no. 31465/96, December 20, 2001) and *Yildiz v Austria* (Application no. 37295/97, October 31, 2002).

have any further reach than suggested above for two reasons. Firstly, if it were correct that Member States were permitted to refuse entry to a third country national spouse on the basis that he was not lawfully resident in the home Member State of the EU national, these facts would have to be verified. The ECJ cannot have intended to create further bureaucratic hurdles to the free mover when it has previously been so clear that the only facts that need to be proved are those referred to in Directive 68/360.[33] Lawfulness of residence in the previous Member State is not one of them.

Secondly, it would create the following absurd situation. The consequences of **5–30** *Akrich* could be avoided by the third country national spouse travelling to his country of origin (or another non EU Member State) and from there travelling to the Member State where his spouse is residing. Following *MRAX*, he would have to be granted entry on arrival in that Member State, even if he failed to obtain any necessary visas or complete formalities in order to enter. It surely cannot be the case that the third country national spouse is in a better position by entering from a non-EU State, rather than seeking to enter with his spouse from within the Community.[34]

The procedural deficiencies Whatever the intended consequences of the **5–31** decision, it is extremely surprising that the ECJ should have chosen to embark on this unprecedented path without first inviting the parties and interveners, including the Commission, to address it fully on these issues.[35] The judgment was made without the minimum level of procedural standards in terms of right of access to a court protected by the ECHR and the Charter on Fundamental Rights. It is questionable whether the ECJ would regard a decision of a national court made in such a way as reliable authority.

A final note on Mr Akrich's position What consequences the decision will **5–32** have for Mr and Mrs Akrich themselves remains to be seen. The judgment is focused on Mr Akrich's legal position in Ireland which was not an issue that the ECJ had been called upon to determine since the Irish authorities had given Mr Akrich a residence document. The legal position in Ireland was thus irrelevant to the UK referring court. Even if that had not been the case, it would be a matter for the Irish, as opposed to the UK authorities or courts to determine his legality. The UK referring court would certainly not be able to go behind the decision of the Irish authorities. If Mr Akrich is considered legal in Ireland, then the judgment can have no consequence for his return to the United Kingdom.

---

[33] See Chapter 11 at paras 11–11 *et seq.*
[34] *Cf.* C-459/99 *Mouvement contre le racisme, l'antisemitisme et la xénophobie ASBL (MRAX) v Belgium State* [2002] E.C.R. I-6591, where the ECJ was extremely clear in its conclusion that the failure to comply with formalities by obtaining visas or residence permits would not be grounds for exclusion or refusal of a residence permit.
[35] The line of argument followed by the Court was introduced in the Opinion given by the Advocate General.

(c) *Third Country Nationals*

5–33 As a general rule third country nationals are not the direct beneficiaries of EU free movement law save in certain limited circumstances, namely where they are:

(a)   the family members of EU nationals;

(b)   stateless persons and refugees;

(c)   employees of national companies.

(i) *The Family Members of EU Nationals*

5–34 One of the immediate benefits for EU nationals exercising their rights of free movement is that they have the right to install their family members with them. As the secondary legislation itself makes clear, the right to install family members exists irrespective of the nationality of the family members. The rights of family members are considered in Chapter 11.

(ii) *Stateless Persons and Recognised Refugees*

5–35 Stateless persons and those who have been recognised as refugees in one Member State do not enjoy free movement rights under the EC Treaty or secondary legislation. However if they are admitted to another Member State they are entitled to bring with them any accrued social security benefits in the same way as EU nationals are within the terms of Regulation 1408/71. There is no right of admission although some commentators have suggested that the Council has given a clear indication of the favourable treatment that stateless persons and refugees should be accorded if they wish to move around the Community.[36] The rights to social security benefits are considered in Chapter 13.

(iii) *Employees of National Companies*

5–36 Companies registered in a Member State are entitled to exercise rights of establishment and provide services in other Member States. In so doing they are entitled to transport employees under the umbrella of their organisation in order to fulfil the provision of services in the other Member State. Those employees might be third country nationals previously employed in the Member State where the company is registered[37] or in a third country outside of the Community.[38] These principles are considered in Chapter 8.

---

[36] The European Agreement on the abolition of visas for refugees (1959), does abolish the requirement to obtain visas for the purpose of visiting another contracting state for three years. However this is not a Community law instrument and therefore does not affect the position of refugees under EU law.

[37] Case C-113/89 *Rush Portugesa Lda v ONI* [1990] E.C.R. I-1417.

[38] Case C-43/93 *Vander Elst v OMI* [1994] E.C.R. I-3803.

2. THE FREE MOVEMENT RIGHTS

(a) *The Right to Move and Reside: The Basics*

Article 18 EC Treaty was included in the Treaty following the Maastricht **5–37**
summit. It contains the clearest expression of the free movement rights of
EU citizens and would appear to signal the completion of the internal market as regards the free movement of persons:

Article 18 EC Treaty

1. Every citizen of the Union shall have the right to move and reside freely within
the territory of the Member States, subject to the limitations and conditions laid
down in this Treaty and by the measures adopted to give it effect.

2. If action by the Community should prove necessary to attain this objective and
this Treaty has not provided the necessary powers, the Council may adopt provisions with a view to facilitating the exercise of the rights referred to in paragraph 1.
The Council shall act in accordance with the procedure referred to in Article 251.

The reference to the "limitations and conditions" in the Treaty and second- **5–38**
ary legislation adopted to give it effect suggest that those provisions should
be the first reference point for the establishment of any specific free movement rights. Primary and secondary legislation however does not reflect the
full scope of free movement rights. As discussed in Chapter 4, Art.18 EC
Treaty has the potential to go beyond that legislation.

(b) *The Specified Free Movement Rights*

The Treaty of Rome included the right of free movement for workers[39] and **5–39**
those wishing to establish themselves[40] or to provide and receive services
within the Community[41]: in other words the "economically active". This is
unsurprising given the origins of the Community as an economic union
designed to foster cross-fertilisation of economies and skills.

Following case law developments of the ECJ, free movement rights were **5–40**
extended in the 1990s through secondary legislation to the economically inactive but self-sufficient: students,[42] the self-sufficient[43] and the retired persons.[44]

The rights of all these categories of person are discussed in detail in this Part. **5–41**
For discussion of the historical context of the development of these free
movement rights see Chapter 4.

---

[39] Contained in Art.39 EC Treaty and EC Regulation 1612/68
[40] Arts 43–45 EC Treaty and Council Dir. 73/148.
[41] Arts 49–50 EC Treaty and Council Dir. 73/148.
[42] Council Dir. 93/96.
[43] Council Dir. 90/364.
[44] Council Dir. 90/365.

(c) *Qualifying the Limitations and Conditions*

5–42 As will be seen in the chapters which follow, the Treaty provisions themselves and the more detailed secondary legislation attach conditions and limitations to the exercise of the free movement rights which are not intended to be over-ridden by Art.18 EC Treaty. Such conditions include in certain cases the requirement to obtain sickness insurance for all risks in order to obtain the benefits of certain free movement provisions[45] or the requirement to engage in "genuine and effective" economic activity in order to obtain the benefits of a worker.[46]

5–43 Whereas Member States have tended to treat these conditions and limitations as absolutes, the ECJ's recent case law would suggest that Art.18 EC Treaty has meant a softening of the approach to be taken. Whilst Member States may expect an EU national to abide by the conditions and limitations laid down in the Treaty and secondary legislation, the application of such conditions must be in conformity with general principles of Community law, principally that of proportionality. Thus the failure of an EU national to obtain sickness insurance in compliance with Directive 90/364 might not be fatal to the establishment of his right of residence, if he has generally complied with other conditions laid down in that Directive.[47]

(d) *Beyond the Basic Free Movement Rights*

5–44 Article 18 is now recognised by the ECJ as having direct effect. In *Baumbast*, the ECJ considered Art.18(1) EC Treaty to contain "a clear and precise provision of the EC Treaty".[48]

5–45 It is arguable that Art.18(1) EC Treaty provides that any EU citizen should have the right to move and reside in the territory of another Member State simply by virtue of being a Union citizen. The true reach of Art.18(1) EC Treaty has yet to be settled by the ECJ – although as we discuss in Chapter 4 recent decisions give cause for optimism that Art.18(1) EC Treaty does indeed establish a discrete right of free movement for a person not previously catered for by Community law. However despite this optimism it is quite clear that the first port of call will always be the substantive provisions of the Treaty and secondary legislation which both unambiguously give specific free movement rights, as well as other attendant rights.

(e) *The Citizen's Directive*

5–46 The remainder of this Part of the book will examine the Treaty provisions and secondary legislation applicable to both the economically active and econom-

---

[45] See for instance the Council Directive on the economically inactive but self-sufficient categories.

[46] See for instance *Levin*, etc.

[47] Case C-413/99 *Baumbast and R. v the Secretary of State for the Home Department* [2002] E.C.R. I-7091.

[48] Case C-413/99 *Baumbast and R. v the Secretary of State for the Home Department* [2002] E.C.R. I-7091, para.84.

ically non-active free movers. Much discussion therefore necessarily involves detailed analysis of regulations and directives which have been passed to implement and facilitate the exercise of free movement rights. This secondary legislation will be substantially replaced by the Citizens' Directive[49] which Member States must have implemented by April 30, 2006. In Appendix 30, the corresponding provisions in the Citizens' Directive to those contained in the regulations and directives considered below are identified.

Readers will need to be aware that after April 30, 2006 it will no longer be appropriate to refer to many of the existing regulations and directives as the source of rights since the Citizens' Directive repeals a number of the original measures.[50] However the interpretation given to the provisions in existing secondary legislation will in many cases be determinative of the meaning to be given to the new provisions.   **5-47**

---

[49] Dir. 2004/38/EC of the European Parliament and of the Council of April 29, 2004 on the rights of citizens of the Union and their family members to move and reside freely within the territory of the Member States amending Reg. 1612/68 and repealing Dir. 64/221, 68/360, 73/148, 75/34, 75/35, 90/364, 90/365 and 93/96, [2004] O.J. L158/77.
[50] Art.38 of the Citizens' Directive provides that Dires 64/221, 68/360, 73/148, 75/34, 75/35, 90/364, 90/365 and 93/96 as well as Arts 10 and 11 of Reg. 1612/68 will be repealed on April 30, 2006.

ENLARGEMENT OF THE EUROPEAN UNION 2004

This chapter considers the background to the accession of the 10 new Member States which joined the European Union on May 1, 2004. Detailed considera-tion is given also to the provisions of the Treaty of Accession which as will be seen have most impact as regards the free movement rights of workers.

1. Background

(a) *Introduction*

On May 1, 2004 Cyprus, the Czech Republic, Estonia, Hungary, Latvia, Lithuania, Malta, Poland, the Slovak Republic and Slovenia became Members of the European Union. **6–01**

The scale of enlargement created by the fifth Treaty of Accession goes far beyond the previous four accession treaties which taken together in more than a 30-year period accounted for a total of nine new Member States[1] (although the figure would have been 11 had applications to join made by Norway and Switzerland in 1992 not proved abortive—the former after a ref-erendum in which 52.2 per cent voted against membership). Of the other three candidate countries, Bulgaria and Romania are expected to become full members in 2007 and if Turkey succeeds in meeting the requisite political and economic criteria for membership, the end of the decade could see a European Union of some 28 Member States.[2] **6–02**

Undoubtedly such enlargement is to be welcomed and the achievement rep-resented by the successful accession of a further 10 Member States from May 1, 2004 cannot be underestimated. However it is regrettable that the EU insti-tutions have been apparently less interested in the accession countries' record on human rights than their ability to offer economic benefits to the Union and that the European Union did not take full opportunity to address some **6–03**

---

[1] Under the terms of the first Accession Treaty signed on January 22, 1972 Denmark, Ireland, Norway and the UK joined the six Member States from January 1, 1973 to make a Community of nine Member States; the second Accession Treaty saw the Member States grow to 10 with the admission of Greece with effect from January 1, 1981; the third Accession Treaty accounted for Portugal and Spain who became full members from January 1, 1986 and with effect from January 1, 1995 the 12 Member States became 15 with the fourth Accession Treaty by which Austria, Finland and Sweden.

[2] The figure could be higher still. In January 2004 Croatia (which has been regarded as a "poten-tial" candidate country since June 2000) voiced the hope that it would become an official candi-date country in June 2004. However there are a number of problems standing in Croatia's way, including the need fully to co-operate with the UN war crimes tribunal at The Hague, problems with minority rights, reform of the judiciary and the resolution of a border row with Slovenia. See further Chapter 15.

of the deep-rooted problems in some of the accession countries, particularly relating to the Roma Community.

6–04 Nationals of the 10 accession states who became members of the European Union on May 1, 2004 at the same time became Union citizens. As such, they are entitled by Art.17 EC Treaty to enjoy the rights conferred by the EC Treaty.[3] However, not all are treated in the same way. The accession provisions draw a distinction between Cyprus and Malta on the one hand, and the Central Eastern European Countries (CEECs) on the other. To all intents and purposes it is only Cyprus and Malta whose nationals enjoy 'full' free movement rights from May 1, 2004.

6–05 In relation to the CEECs the Annexes to the Treaty of Accession enable the 15 Member States[4] to derogate—potentially for up to seven years—from the obligation to guarantee freedom of movement for workers (and, in certain circumstances, freedom of movement for service providers). The detail is considered below. Shortly stated all will depend on the extent to which national measures give access to the labour markets of the 15 Member States. Ireland and the United Kingdom are the only Member States which have provided access to their labour markets for CEEC nationals.

6–06 However, the situation of workers and certain service providers apart, it is to be emphasised that derogations cannot be made in relation to the freedom of establishment of the self-employed, nor to the freedom of movement of the economically non-active (students, the retired or self-sufficient).

6–07 Accession arrangements have always accompanied enlargement (indeed for Portugal and Spain there was a phasing-in period of 7 to 10 years, albeit subsequently shortened). The different accession arrangements as between Cyprus and Malta on the one hand and the CEEC's on the other reflect the vastly different positions in terms of their own and the Community's history.

6–08 Moreover, as will be seen, in order to address serious disturbances in specific sensitive sectors of the labour markets in Austria and Germany, special provision is made in the legislation enabling those countries to derogate from Art.49 EC Treaty for up to seven years. These arrangements reflect the fact that throughout the negotiation process account was taken of the particular sensitivities of Austria and Germany. Such sensitivities are shown by the results of research published in 2000 and 2001 showing that the two countries—which between them share borders with Poland, the Czech Republic, the Slovak Republic, Hungary and Slovenia—are expected to

---

[3] Art.17(2) EC Treaty provides that "Citizens of the Union shall enjoy the rights conferred by this Treaty and shall be subject to the duties imposed thereby." See generally Chapter 4.
[4] In the Annexes reference is made to "present" Member States to distinguish between the 15 Member States at time of signature of the Treaty and the 10 joining on accession. In this chapter the Member States *before* accession are referred to as the "15" Member States (namely Belgium, Denmark, Germany, Greece, Spain, France, Ireland, Italy, Luxembourg, the Netherlands, Austria, Portugal, Finland, Sweden and the United Kingdom).

absorb 77 per cent of the total migration flow from the new Member States.[5] When speaking in Weiden in December 2000 Germany's Chancellor Gerhard Schroeder had publicly demanded a seven-year transition period for workers. As Ziegler noted in 2002[6] this viewpoint was "difficult to ignore in Brussels"—as proved to be the case in light of the actual terms of the Treaty of Accession which do make potential provision for a seven-year phasing-in period.

(b) *From Co-operation to Association*

The establishment of diplomatic relations between the European Community 6–09 and the CEECs had quickly followed the fall of the Berlin Wall in 1989. The Community removed long-standing import quotas on various products, extended the Generalised System of Preferences (GSP) and during the course of the following years concluded Trade and Co-operation Agreements with Bulgaria, the former Czechoslovakia, Estonia, Hungary, Latvia, Lithuania, Poland, Romania and Slovenia. At the same time the Community's PHARE Programme began to provide financial support to enable the CEECs to reform and rebuild their economies. Initially launched in 1989 to assist Hungary and Poland the PHARE Programme provided technical expertise and investment support for the CEECs and before long was the world's largest assistance programme in the region.

During the 1990s the European Community and its Member States progres- 6–10 sively concluded Association Agreements with the CEECs. These association agreements are referred to also as "Europe Agreements". The first of these, concluded with Hungary and Poland, were signed on December 16, 1991 and came into force on February 1, 1994. The Polish Agreement, which contains provisions relating to employed workers, establishment and services, provides the model on which the agreements with the other CEECs are based (although the Art.41(3) provision relating to the granting of work permits to Polish nationals already holding residence permits in Member States is unique). Similar agreements signed on various dates were concluded with the Czech Republic, Slovakia, Romania and Bulgaria which came into force on February 1, 1995. On June 12, 1995 agreements were signed with Lithuania, Estonia and Latvia which came into force on February 1, 1998. And finally on June 10, 1996 an agreement was signed with Slovenia which came into force on February 1, 1999. The Europe Agreements provided the legal basis for bilateral relations between the CEECs and the Community. The Community had already established Association Agreements with Turkey (1963), Malta (1970) and Cyprus (1972). In the case of Turkey, a

---

[5] See para.4.3.4.1 of G. Ziegler, "Enlargement" is *Handbook on European Enlargement: A Commentary on the Enlargement Process* (A. Ott and K. Inglis, eds, T.M. Asser Press, 2002). Research by Brucker and Boeri was commissioned by DG Employment and Social Affairs of the European Commission, Berlin and Milano European Integration Consortium 2000 and research by Sin *et al.* was commissioned by the Federal Ministry of Labour and Social Affairs, Munchen/Bonn, 2001. The research estimated migratory flows from the Eastern European States at 200,000–240,000 per year with an expected decline to 85,000–125,000 during the first 10 years following accession.

[6] See para.4.3.4.1 of G. Ziegler, "Enlargement" is *Handbook on European Enlargement: A Commentary on the Enlargement Process* (A. Ott and K. Inglis, eds, T.M. Asser Press, 2002).

Customs Union entered into force in December 1995. Association Agreements are considered in detail in Part Three.

(c) *From Association to Accession: the Copenhagen Criteria*

6–11 In the meantime at the landmark June 1993 meeting of the European Council[7] in Copenhagen an ambitious process was launched with the underlying objective of overcoming the legacy of conflict and division in Europe. Of fundamental importance was the agreement by the Council that "the associated countries in Central and Eastern Europe that so desire shall become members of the European Union". Subject to the wishes of each particular country, it was no longer a question of *if* the CEECs would become part of the European Union, but *when*.

6–12 The Council agreed that accession would take place as soon as an associated country was able "to assume the obligations of membership by satisfying the economic and political conditions required". Those membership conditions—known as the "Copenhagen criteria"—require that the candidate country has achieved:

(a) stability of institutions guaranteeing democracy, the rule of law, human rights and respect for and protection of minorities;

(b) the existence of a functioning market economy as well as the capacity to cope with competitive pressure and market forces within the Union; and

(c) the ability to take on the obligations of membership including adherence to the aims of political, economic and monetary union.

6–13 The Council would closely follow the progress made in each associated country towards fulfilling these criteria. Moreover, future co-operation with the CEECs would be "geared to the objective of membership which has now been established". In this context the Council approved a proposal that the CEECs would enter into "a structured relationship with the Institutions of the Union within the framework of a reinforced and extended multilateral dialogue and concentration on matters of common interest".

6–14 The Council agreed to regular meetings between its President and the President of the Commission with their counterparts from the associated countries, as well as joint meetings of all the Heads of State and Government to discuss specific issues. Further, the Council recognised "the crucial importance of trade in the transition to a market economy" and agreed to accelerate the Community's efforts to open up its markets. It was expected that this would "go hand in hand with further development of trade between those countries themselves and between them and their traditional trading partners". Specific trade concessions were approved. The Community would "continue to devote a considerable part of the budgetary resources foreseen for external action to the [CEECs], in particular through the PHARE

---

[7] The meeting took place on June 21–22, 2003.

programme". The Community would also "make full use of the possibility foreseen under the temporary lending facility of the European Investment Bank (EIB) to finance trans-European network projects" and "where appropriate, part of the resources under the PHARE programme may be used for major infrastructural improvements".

The Council welcomed the participation of the CEECs in Community pro-   **6–15**
grammes and invited the Commission to make proposals before the end of the year for opening up further programmes. The Council underlined the importance of approximation of laws in the CEECs to those applicable in the Community. To this end it agreed that officials from the CEECs should be offered training in Community law and practice and decided that a task force composed of representatives of the Member States and the Commission shall be established to co-ordinate and direct this work. In the context of accession such approximation was of fundamental importance in relation to the protection of workers, the environment and consumers.

The decision that the eight CEECs were to join the European Union in 2004   **6–16**
was endorsed at the Copenhagen European Council meeting on December 12 and 13, 2002. The Presidency Conclusions characterise the meeting[8] as marking an "unprecedented and historic milestone" in completing the process begun in Copenhagen in 1993 with the conclusion of the accession negotiations with Cyprus, the Czech Republic, Estonia, Hungary, Latvia, Lithuania, Malta, Poland, the Slovak Republic and Slovenia. The conclusions looked forward to "welcoming these States as members from 1 May 2004". The conclusions include the following statements:

> This achievement testifies to the common determination of the peoples of Europe to come together in a Union that has become the driving force for peace, democracy, stability and prosperity on our continent. As fully fledged members of a Union based on solidarity, these States will play a full role in shaping the further development of the European project.[9]

> The current enlargement provides the basis for a Union with strong prospects for sustainable growth and an important role to play in consolidating stability, peace and democracy in Europe and beyond. In accordance with their national ratification procedures, the current and the acceding States are invited to ratify the Treaty in due time for it to enter into force on 1 May 2004.[10]

(d) The Other Candidate Countries and Accession

The Copenhagen meeting also considered the positions of the other candi-   **6–17**
date countries. In relation to Bulgaria and Romania, the Presidency Conclusions refer to the successful conclusion of the accession negotiations

---

[8] The conclusions are available at *www.europa-web.de/europa/03euinfl10councl/copconcl.htm*;
para.3.
[9] Para.3.
[10] Para.9.

with 10 other candidates as lending "new dynamism to the accession of Bulgaria and Romania as part of the same inclusive and irreversible enlargement process".[11] The stated objective was "to welcome Bulgaria and Romania as members of the European Union in 2007".[12]

2. TREATY OF ACCESSION

(a) *Introduction*

6–18   The Treaty of Accession was signed on April 16, 2003 in Athens. The views of the signatories are reflected by the following "One Europe" declaration annexed to the Final Act to the Treaty:

> "Today is a great moment for Europe. We have today concluded accession negotiations between the European Union and Cyprus, the Czech Republic, Estonia, Hungary, Latvia, Lithuania, Malta, Poland, Slovakia and Slovenia. 75 million people will be welcomed as new citizens of the European Union.

> We, the current and acceding Member States, declare our full support for the continuous, inclusive and irreversible enlargement process. The accession negotiations with Bulgaria and Romania will continue on the basis of the same principles that have guided the negotiations so far. The results already achieved in these negotiations will not be brought into question. Depending on further progress in complying with the membership criteria, the objective is to welcome Bulgaria and Romania as new members of the European Union in 2007. We also welcome the important decisions taken today concerning the next stage of Turkey's candidature for membership of the European Union.

> Our common wish is to make Europe a continent of democracy, freedom, peace and progress. The Union will remain determined to avoid new dividing lines in Europe and to promote stability and prosperity within and beyond the new borders of the Union. We are looking forward to working together in our joint endeavour to accomplish these goals.

> Our aim is One Europe."

(b) *The General Scheme of the Treaty*

6–19   The Treaty of Accession itself contains three articles. Article 1 lists the 10 States which "become members of the European Union and Parties to the Treaties on which the Union is founded". Article 2 deals with ratification (to take place by April 30, 2004) and entry into force (on May 1, 2004). Article 3 deals only with the formality of deposit of the original signed texts of the Treaty ("in the archives of the Government of the Italian Republic").

---

[11] *www.europa-web.de/europa/03euinfl10councl copconcl.htm*; para.13.
[12] *www.europa-web.de/europa/03euinfl10councl copconcl.htm*; para.14.

(c) *The Act of Accession*

The Treaty's implementation is dealt with by the Act of Accession which is   **6–20**
annexed to the Treaty. The provisions of that Act, as stated in Art.1(2) of the
Treaty, is an integral part of the Treaty. Part IV of the Act entitled
"Temporary Provisions" consists of two titles ("transitional measures" and
"other provisions").

(i) *The Transitional Provisions*

Of particular relevance under the first title is Art.24 which provides that   **6–21**
"the measures listed in Annexes [V–XIV] to this Act shall apply in respect of
the new Member States under the conditions laid down in those Annexes".
The Annexes deal separately with each new Member State and set out the
detail of the transitional provisions, in particular in relation to freedom of
movement for persons. The detail is considered below in paras 6–31 to 6–72.

(ii) *Other Provisions: Protective Measures*

The second title makes provision for transitional measures to be taken in   **6–22**
specified circumstances for up to three years in areas related to criminal law
or civil matters (Art.39), the application of the common agricultural policy
(Art.41) or the application of Community veterinary and phytosanitary rules
(Art.42).

Of more potential interest in the context of the free movement of persons are   **6–23**
Arts 37 and 38.

Article 37 enables protective measures to be taken for up to three years in the   **6–24**
event of serious economic difficulties in any sector of the economy of the
accession Member States. Such protective measures may be applied for by
any accession State or any of the 15 Member States "with regard to one or
more of the new Member States". Such protective measures are taken "in
order to rectify the situation and adjust the sector concerned to the economy
of the common market". Decisions on such measures are to be taken by the
Commission and may involve derogations "from the rules of the EC Treaty
and from this Act to such an extent and for such periods as are strictly necessary." Moreover, priority must be given to such measures "as will least
disturb the functioning of the common market".

Article 38 makes similar provision for measures to be taken where a new   **6–25**
Member State has failed to implement commitments undertaken in the context of the accession negotiations causing "a serious breach of the functioning of the internal market". The Czech Republic, Estonia, Lithuania, Poland,
the Slovak Republic and Slovenia made a joint declaration annexed to the
Final Act which states their understanding that "the notion 'has failed to
implement commitments undertaken in the context of the accession negotiations' only covers the obligations that are arising from the original Treaties
applicable to [those countries] under the conditions laid down in the Act of
Accession, and the obligations defined in this Act". The declaration goes on
to state the understanding of those countries "that the Commission will

consider application of Art.38 only in cases of alleged violations of the obligations referred to".

6–26   In view of the transitional provisions relating to workers, it is difficult to anticipate Art.38 measures, being invoked in the area of free movement of persons. However, the potential breadth of such measures should be recognised. Subject always to proportionality and the safeguards mentioned, they could apply in principle to any EU nationals and could include derogations from any rights and guarantees otherwise given by the EC Treaty.

(d) *The Protocols*

6–27   There are 10 Protocols to the Treaty. These deal with specific sectoral issues. A number of these deal with matters of relevance to the free movement of persons. These are Protocol No.3 (on the Sovereign Base Areas of the United Kingdom of Great Britain and Northern Ireland in Cyprus), Protocol No.5 (on the transit of persons by land between the region of Kaliningrad and other parts of the Russian Federation), Protocol No.6 (on the acquisition of secondary residences in Malta) and Protocol No.10 (on Cyprus[13]).

(e) *The Declarations in the Final Act*

6–28   The Final Act to the Treaty of Accession contains 44 declarations. Nine relate to freedom of movement for workers. There are specific identically worded declarations for each acceding CEEC which state (using that made in relation to the Czech Republic[14]) as follows:

> "The EU stresses the strong elements of differentiation and flexibility in the arrangement for the free movement of workers. Member States shall endeavour to grant increased labour market access to Czech nationals under national law, with a view to speeding up the approximation to the acquis. As a consequence, the employment opportunities in the EU for Czech nationals should improve substantially upon the Czech Republic's accession. Moreover, the EU Member States will make best use of the proposed arrangement to move as quickly as possible to the full application of the acquis in the area of free movement of workers."

6–29   In relation to Malta there is a declaration which states that, should Malta's accession give rise to "difficulties" relating to the free movement of workers, the matter may be brought before the institutions of the Union in order to obtain a solution to this problem.[15] There is no such declaration in relation to Cyprus.

---

[13] This principal relevance of this protocol is apparent from Art.1(1) which provides that "the application of the acquis shall be suspended in those areas of the Republic of Cyprus in which the Government of the Republic of Cyprus does not exercise effective control".
[14] Declaration 6.
[15] See further para. 6–66 below.

3. Free Movement of Persons Under the Accession Treaty

(a) Rights of Free Movement

6–30 Of principal interest in the context of the free movement of persons is the examination of the transitional provisions for workers and (in certain specific circumstances) companies providing services who send workers to Member States from the CEECs. It must be borne in mind that the transitional provisions are exhaustive in their identification of the restrictions on the exercise of free movement rights. Workers and posted workers apart, derogations from the EC Treaty provisions cannot be made in relation to the freedom of establishment nor to the freedom of movement of the economically non-active (students, the retired or self-sufficient).[16] Moreover, even in relation to workers and posted workers, derogation is permitted only to the extent specified in the transitional provisions. This means, for example, that from the date of accession the non-discrimination provision contained in Art.12 EC Treaty may be invoked by nationals of all accession states in relation to the future effects of all situations, including those arising prior to the new Member States' accession.[17]

(b) Derogation from Free Movement for Workers and Services: the Transitional Provisions

(i) Introduction

6–31 In relation to the eight CEECs, the Annexes to the Act of Accession, each contains an identical section dealing with "freedom of movement for persons". Commentary herein is based on Annex V which deals with the Czech Republic, although the same comments apply in relation to each CEEC. There is no such section in Annex VII for Cyprus. Annex XI which deals with Malta does contain provisions dealing with freedom of movement for persons,[18] although these relate not to an ability for pre-existing Member States to limit access to their labour markets of Maltese nationals, but rather to the ability of Malta to derogate from Art.39 EC Treaty by taking measures to protect its own labour market if Malta "undergoes or foresees disturbances on its labour market which could seriously threaten the standard of living or level of employment in a given region of occupation".[19] Malta may resort to such procedures for seven years following the date of accession.

---

[16] Subject to the possibility of the taking of the measures referred to in Arts 37 and 38 of the Act of Accession referred to above at paras 6–22 to 6–26.

[17] See Case C-122/96 *Saldhana and MTS v Hiross Holding AG*, October 2, 1997, para.12–14.

[18] Section 2, Annex XI.

[19] Broadly stated Malta is obliged to inform the Commission and other Member States of such eventuality and may request that the Commission suspend wholly or partly Arts 1 to 6 of Reg. 1612/68 "in order to restore to normal the situation in that region or occupation." Malta may also "in urgent and exceptional cases" itself suspend the application of Arts 1 to 6 "followed by a reasoned ex-post notification to the Commission." In order to have advance warning of any such situation Malta may retain its work permit system for nationals of other Member States, although work permits must be issued automatically.

(ii) *Transitional Arrangements for Workers and Posted Workers from the CEECs*

6–32   Paragraph 1 of Annex V (the Czech Republic) provides that freedom of movement for Czech workers is subject to the transitional provisions laid down in paras 2 to 14 of the Annex. The same is true for Czech "posted workers" (that is to say workers sent to Member States by Czech companies providing services[20]). Paragraphs 2 to 12 and 14 of the Annex apply to workers; para.13 applies to posted workers. However, the provisions relating to posted workers enabling derogation from the first paragraph of Art.49 EC Treaty "in order to address serious disturbances or the threat thereof in specific sensitive sectors" apply *only* to Germany and Austria.

(iii) *The Transitional Scheme in Outline*

6–33   In broad terms, the scheme in outline is as follows:

- for the first two years following accession national laws will govern the right of access to the labour market for CEECs seeking to exercise rights of free movement as workers;

- during this initial two-year period national authorities will have exclusive jurisdiction over the scope of application of such right of access since this is a matter of the national law of each of the 15 Member States concerned rather than a matter of Community law;

- national laws may be kept in place by the 15 Member States for up to five years upon notification to the Commission *before* the end of the first two years following accession;

- for those Member States which retain national laws for five years, such laws may continue to be applied for a further two years (making a total of seven years) in case of serious disturbance to the labour market of such Member States;

- after two years any of the 15 Member States may choose to apply provisions of Community law to the right of access to the labour market;

- from the date of accession Community law applies to all CEEC workers as regards matters other than access (for example conditions of work, social and tax advantages, rights of residence of family members); and

- in cases where family members accompany CEEC workers during the period when national measures are in place, access to the labour market for those family members is restricted.

(iv) *National Measures for the First Two Years for Workers*

6–34   Paragraph 2 of Annex V establishes the principle that for two years the position of Czech national workers entering the labour markets of the 15 Member States will be governed by national measures (or those resulting from bilateral agreements). The two-year period may be extended by the 15 Member States to five years.

---

[20] As defined in Art.1 of Dir. 96/71 of the European Parliament and of the Council of December 16, 1996 concerning the posting of workers in the framework of the provision of services.

(v) *The Scope of the Derogation*

The application of national immigration law to workers for two years, with   **6–35**
the possibility extension to five years, is to "derogation from Arts 1 to 6 of
Reg. 1612/68" (which lay down rights of access to the labour market of
Member States for workers exercising free movement rights). The scope of
the derogation is further extended by para.9 which provides for derogation
also from provisions of Directive 68/360 which cannot be dissociated from
those of Reg. 1612/68. Thus, for example, that Directive's obligation to grant
workers a right of residence evidenced by a residence permit[21] could not be
relied by a Czech worker otherwise unable to access the labour market of one
of the 15 Member States because of the derogation from Arts 1 to 6.

It must be emphasised however—consistent also with the principle that   **6–36**
restrictions on the exercise of a fundamental freedom must be narrowly
construed—that the other provisions contained in Reg. 1612/86 (namely Arts
7 to 9 dealing with workers' rights of equal treatment and Arts 10 and 12[22]
dealing with the rights of the workers' family members) will apply where a
Czech worker is in employment in a Member State.

The proposition is put beyond question by *Lopes de Veiga*[23] in which the ECJ   **6–37**
considered the scope of Art.216(1) of the Portuguese Act of Accession. This
provision delayed application of Arts 1 to 6 of Regulation 1612/68 in
Portugal with regard to nationals of the other Member States and in the
other Member States with regard to Portuguese nationals until January 1,
1993. As the ECJ stated at para.9 of its judgment:

> "It follows from an a contrario interpretation of that provision that Article 7 *et seq.*
> of the regulation, which are not covered by that derogating provision, apply as from
> 1 January 1986, the date on which the Act of Accession came into force".

Such interpretation was consistent with the ratio of the transitional arrange-   **6–38**
ments suspending the application of the provisions of Arts 1 to 6 of Reg.
1612/68 until January 1, 1993 (in the words of the ECJ) "in order to prevent
disruption of the labour markets of the old Member States through a mas-
sive influx of Portuguese nationals seeking employment". But there was no
reason to refuse to allow the provisions of Arts 7 to 12 of the Regulation
(dealing with employment and equality of treatment), nor those of Directive
68/360 (on the right of residence) to be applied to Portuguese workers who
were already employed in the territory of one of the old Member States.[24]

---

[21] Art.4.
[22] Art.11—which deals with the right of access to the labour market of family members—is
qualified by para.8 of the Annex where the application of Arts 1 to 6 is suspended. The effect of
para.8 is to limit the right of family members of workers to work. The detail of this is discussed
below at paras 6–56 *et seq.* This is unsurprising where the right of access to the labour market of
the principal worker is governed by national measures.
[23] Case 9/88 *Lopes da Veiga v Staatssecretaris van Justitie* [1989] E.C.R. 2989.
[24] Note also, as stated by the ECJ in *Lopes* at para.11 of its judgment, in relation to the similar
provisions of the Act concerning the Conditions of Accession of the Hellenic Republic, the ECJ
ruled, in its May 30, 1989 judgment in Case 305/87 *Commission v Greece* [1989] E.C.R. 1461, that
"although the transitional arrangements suspended the application of a number of provisions of

6–39 The correctness of the proposition is yet further confirmed by the content of para.8 to Annex V which spells out the scope of the derogation permissible from Art.11 of Reg. 1612/68. The detail is considered below but the necessity to derogate expressly from Art.11 demonstrates how specific the derogations are. Contrary to the view of at least one Member State derogation is not in respect of the entirety of Reg. 1612/68 (or indeed Art.39 EC Treaty) but goes no further than expressly provided for.

6–40 Moreover, attempts of the kind apparently contemplated by the UK Government in February 2004[25] to single out CEEC nationals for discriminatory measures (such as the denial of benefits otherwise available to EU national workers and work seekers) would similarly be unlawful as outwith the limited scope of derogation. Indeed, the publicity about such proposals prompted a European Commission spokesman to issue the following warning on February 13, 2004:[26]

> "Any member state putting into place [welfare] rules that discriminate according to nationality, that discriminate between members of the existing member states and the new member states, we would have to look at those rules very carefully, as it is quite possible there could be a contravention of existing Community law".

6–41 Member States can elect to apply national law measures which have the effect in practice of guaranteeing full rights of free movement to Czech workers. Indeed, para.12 states expressly that any one of the 15 Member States applying national measures "may introduce, under national law, greater freedom of movement than that existing at the date of accession, including full labour market access".

(vi) *Justiciability of Access Provisions*

6–42 For the first two years at least during which time "by way of derogation" from Arts 1 to 6 of Reg. 1612/68 "the [15] Member States *will* apply national measures", any question arising about the right of access to the labour market would not be a matter within the jurisdiction of the ECJ. Rather this would be a matter of national law in the Member State concerned. Indeed, there is no discretion to *apply* Community law rules relating to access during the first two years. This is clear not only from the terms of para. 2, but also the second sentence of para. 12 which states that "from the third year following the date of accession, any [one of the fifteen] Member State[s] applying national measures may at any time decide to apply Articles 1 to 6 of Regulation (EEC) No 1612/68 instead".

Regulation No 1612/68 defining the rights guaranteed under Arts 48 and 49 of the Treaty, they did not suspend the application of those articles, in particular in regard to workers from other Member States who were lawfully employed in the Hellenic Republic before 1 January 1981 and continued to be employed there after that date or those who were lawfully employed there for the first time after that date".

[25] In response to widespread unfavourable media attention being given to the UK's plans to allow CEEC national workers access to the labour market.

[26] See D. Lumsden, "Post-enlargement welfare curbs may break EU law" on the EU's website *www.eupolitix.com/EN/News/200402/74095623–a83b-4878–ad07–71776eb1e9ca.htm*, February 13, 2004.

Such limitation of the ECJ's jurisdiction however would not apply as regards   **6-43**
other matters. As emphasised above the derogation applies only as regards
Arts 1 to 6 of Reg. 1612/68 dealing with access to the labour market. Matters
arising for example in relation to other provisions (namely Arts 7 to 9 dealing with workers' rights of equal treatment and Arts 10 and 12 dealing with
the rights of the workers' family members) would be justiciable before the
ECJ since these are remain quintessentially matters of Community law and
thus within the ECJ's competence. Moreover, the ECJ will retain jurisdiction
over the interpretation of the Treaty of Accession itself (and any Annexes).
Thus for example were a dispute to arise as to whether a matter fell within the
scope of Arts 1 to 6 of Reg. 1612/68 it would fall to the ECJ to resolve such
dispute. This is because the resolution of such dispute would involve the
interpretation of a Community law instrument.

(vii) *CEECs Working Legally in One of the 15 Member States on Accession
or Permitted to Do so*

Paragraph 2 of Annex V provides also that Czech nationals legally working in   **6-44**
one of the 15 Member States at the date of accession and admitted to the
labour market of that Member State for an uninterrupted period of 12 months
or longer will enjoy access to the labour market of *that* Member State.
However it is emphasised that the right of access does not extend to the labour
markets of *other* Member States. Thus for example a Czech national who had
been given a one-year permit to live and work in a specific job in a Member
State for 12 months prior to accession must be allowed to continue to reside
and work there in any capacity or for any employer. Since this may be at odds
with the national law provisions otherwise in force in one of the 15 Member
States such a person's position would be governed by Community law.

The rights of access to the labour market are given also to Czech nationals   **6-45**
admitted to the labour market of a Member State for an uninterrupted
period of 12 months or longer following accession. The right of access will
be to the labour market of *that* Member State. The worker will also have the
right of access to the labour markets of any other Member State which is no
longer applying national measures.[27]

Czech nationals cease to enjoy such rights of access to the labour market of   **6-46**
the Member State in which they work if they "voluntarily leave" the labour
market of the Member State in question. Although not defined, "leaving"
should not be construed literally enabling a Member State to deny such rights
where (for example) the Czech worker returns to the Czech Republic for a
holiday. Any such interpretation would at the very least offend the principle
of broad construction already identified.

For those Czech nationals legally working in a Member State on accession   **6-47**
(or during a period when national measures are being applied), but who have
been admitted to the labour market of that Member State for a period of *less
than 12 months*, para.2 states expressly that such rights are not enjoyed.

---

[27] It is to be recalled that two years after accession Member States choose whether to continue
to apply national measures. Before May 2006 however only national measures will apply.

(viii) *Periods of Employment Before Accession Relevant to Social and Tax Advantages*

6–48   In *Österreichischer Gewerkschaftsbund*,[28] the ECJ considered provisions of Austrian law providing that previous periods of employment spent in Austria are treated differently from those spent in other Member States for the purpose of determining the pay of contractual teachers and teaching assistants. The third question considered by the ECJ sought to determine whether periods of employment spent by such staff before Austria's accession had to be taken into account. The ECJ noted that the case did not concern the recognition of rights under Community law allegedly acquired before the accession, but rather current discriminatory treatment of migrant workers. In the absence of specific transitional provisions concerning free movement of workers, the ECJ held that "previous periods of employment must necessarily be taken into account." This case is thus important in establishing the proposition that time spent as a worker prior to accession must be taken into account in calculating access to social and tax advantages in Community law.[29]

(ix) *Period of Application of National Measures: from Two to Five Years*

6–49   Whether national measures are extended beyond two years will be entirely at the discretion of each individual Member State. However, the Council is required to carry out a review. Such review is non-binding. The provisions are as follows.

6–50   Paragraph 3 of Annex V requires that the Council, acting on the basis of a report from the Commission and before the end of the two-year period following the date of accession, shall review the functioning of the para.2 transitional provisions. On completion of this review, and no later than at the end of the two-year period following the date of accession, the 15 Member States shall notify the Commission whether they will continue applying national measures or measures resulting from bilateral agreements, or whether they will instead apply Arts 1 to 6 of Reg. 1612/68. In the absence of any such notification, Arts 1 to 6 of Reg. 1612/68 shall apply. Paragraph 2 of Annex V makes clear that the continuation of national measures is permitted for a further three years until May 2009.

6–51   Despite the non-binding nature of the Council's review, its findings ought not to be thereby regarded as completely irrelevant. Early indications are that accession has not substantially affected the labour markets of the two Member States which have given the right of access to their labour markets (Ireland and the United Kingdom). Nor do there appear to have been problems experienced by Austria and Germany with large numbers of Accession State nationals exercising other Treaty rights. Indeed the Saxon State Minister in charge of European Affairs, Stanilaw Tillich said in July 2004 that his region of Germany desperately needed Polish and Czech workers despite its unemployment rate of 20 per cent to service particular industries.

---

[28] Case C–195/98 *Österreichischer Gewerkschaftsbund, Gewerkschaft öffentlicher Dienst v Austria* [2000] E.C.R. I–10497.
[29] This is a further example of the application of the principle identified at para. 6–30 above by reference to Case C–122/96 *Saldanha v Hiross Holding AG* [1997] E.C.R. I-5325.

Mr Tillich stated "Our automobile, IT and health sections suffer from a shortage of highly qualified employees, whereas Saxony's own unemployed consist mainly of poorly or non-qualified workers".[30] If such apparent trend continues it would be difficult to regard the continued withholding of the right of access to the labour market as justified.

(x) *Extension of National Measures to Seven Years in Cases of Serious Disturbance*

Paragraph 5 of Annex V makes provision for a further two-year extension of **6–52** national measures, potentially until May 2011, thereby enabling the maintenance of national measures for a total of seven years from accession. However, the provision applies only to Member States maintaining national measures (or measures resulting from bilateral agreements) beyond the first two years to the end of the five-year period. Such a Member State[31] may, in case of serious disturbances to its labour market or threat thereof and after notifying the Commission, continue to apply these measures until the end of the seven-year period following the date of accession. In the absence of such notification, Arts 1 to 6 of Reg. 1612/68 shall apply.

Similar comments can be made here as made above about the apparent trends **6–53** which have followed accession. In view of the need for the Member State to demonstrate actual or threatened serious disturbance to the labour market, the question may not simply be whether continued use of national measures is politically justified but rather whether it is lawful. However it is difficult to anticipate how the necessary threshold could be established by a Member State which has not given access to its labour market.

(xi) *Labour Market Disturbances Which Seriously Threaten Standard of Living or Level of Employment in Given Region or Occupation*

The limitation on the possibility of extension of national measures to seven **6–54** years to those Member States who have extended the initial two-year period to five years does not however mean that the 15 Member States are powerless in the event of serious disturbances to their labour markets. Paragraph 7 of Annex V makes provision for the situation where a Member State undergoes or foresees disturbances on its labour market which could seriously threaten the standard of living or level of employment in a given region or occupation. The procedures can be invoked for seven years following accession by Member States in which Arts 1 to 6 of Reg. 1612/68 *apply* as regards Czech nationals. However, not only is the threshold of disturbance arguably higher than under para.5, but the decision is generally taken by the Commission. Such difference is more than justified by reason of the fact that Member States relying on this provision will already have ceased derogating from Arts 1 to 6.

---

[30] M Beunderman, "German Border Region Presses for Labour Mobility" available at *http://euobserver.com*, July 14, 2004.
[31] Namely "A Member State maintaining national measures or measures resulting from bilateral agreements at the end of the five year period indicated in paragraph 2."

6–55 Such a Member State is required to inform the Commission and the other Member States of the situation and to supply all relevant particulars. The Member State may request the Commission to state that the application of Arts 1 to 6 of Reg. 1612/68 be wholly or partially suspended "in order to restore to normal the situation in that region or occupation." The Commission must decide on the suspension and on the duration and scope thereof not later than two weeks after receiving such a request. The Council must be informed of such a decision. Within two weeks from the date of the Commission's Decision, any Member State may request the Council to annul or amend the Decision. The Council must act on such a request within two weeks, by qualified majority. In "urgent and exceptional cases" a Member State may itself suspend the application of Arts 1 to 6 of Reg. 1612/68 "followed by a reasoned ex-post notification to the Commission."[32]

(c) *Family Members of CEEC Nationals*

(i) *The Right to Install Themselves with the Worker*

6–56 Article 10 of Reg. 1612/68 gives the right to family members to install themselves with a worker who is a national of a Member State. The right exists irrespective of the nationality of family members and extends to spouses and their descendants under 21 or dependants, and dependant relatives in the ascending line.[33] As already observed the scope of derogation is limited to Arts 1 to 6 of the Reg. 1612/68 relating to access. Thus if CEEC workers—even if in accordance with national law provisions—are residing in a Member State they will be able to be joined by their family members.

(ii) *The Right to Work*

6–57 Paragraph 8 of Annex V deals with the rights of family members, whether EU citizens or third country nationals, to work in the host state.[34]

6–58 The provisions apply without prejudice to more favourable measures applicable under national law (or resulting from bilateral agreements) for as long as the application of Arts 1 to 6 of Reg. 1612/68 is suspended. The only family members covered are the spouse and descendants under 21 years of age or dependants[35] (not dependant relatives in the ascending line).

6–59 What these family members get depends on whether they are legally residing with the worker in the territory of a Member State at accession or from a date later than accession during the period of application of the transitional provisions. In the former case, upon accession the family members shall have immediate access to the labour market of the host Member State. However this right does not apply to family members of a worker legally admitted to the labour market for a period of less than 12 months. In the latter case, the

---

[32] This power mirrors that given to Malta.

[33] Arts 10(1)(a) and (b).

[34] This is by reference to Art.11 of Reg. 1612/68 (giving the right to work to family members of those "pursuing an activity as employed or self employed person") which applies under the conditions spelt out in para.8.

[35] As defined by Art.10(1)(a) of Reg. 1612/68.

family members shall have access to the labour market of the Member State concerned once they have been resident there for at least 18 months or from the third year following accession, whichever is the earlier.

It is to be noted that para.8 thus limits the scope of application of Art.11 **6–60** of Reg. 1612/68 (which otherwise gives *all* family members the right to work *whenever* a national of a Member State pursues an activity as an employed or self-employed person). This is however not surprising since the ability of the principal worker to access the labour market at all is a matter of national law (namely whilst the application of Arts 1 to 6 of Reg. 1612/68 is suspended).

What then is the position of the family members of a CEEC worker who **6–61** benefits from para.2 of the Annex (having been legally working in a Member State at the time of accession for 12 months and thus enjoys access to the labour market of that Member State)? Despite the fact that the CEEC national has obtained free access to the labour market of the Member State concerned, the family members are still governed by para.8 and are thus limited in their access to the labour market because para.8 is dependant on national measures being in place in general (namely "as long as the application of Arts 1 to 6 . . . is suspended"). However, any dispute about such question would be a matter of Community law relating to the true scope of para.8 and thus justiciable before the ECJ.

(d) *Measures to be Taken by Accession Countries*

(i) *Equivalent measures Taken by the Czech Republic*

Paragraph 10 of Annex V makes provision for equivalent measures to be **6–62** taken by the Czech Republic "whenever national measures, or those resulting from bilateral agreements, are applied by the [15] Member States by virtue of the transitional provisions". In these circumstances the Czech Republic "may maintain in force equivalent measures with regard to the nationals of the Member State or States in question."

For Czech workers for the first two years after accession derogation from the **6–63** rights of access to the labour markets of 15 Member States is automatic. By contrast, if the Czech Republic does not take equivalent measures full Community law provisions will apply in relation to workers from the 15 Member States. Thus any EU national of the 15 Member States would be able to exercise full free movement rights in the Czech Republic.

(ii) *Disturbances Which Seriously Threaten Standard of Living or Level of Employment in Given Region or Occupation in the Czech Republic*

Paragraph 11 of Annex V provides that the Czech Republic may resort to the **6–64** procedures laid down in para.7 of Annex V[36] with respect to Estonia, Latvia, Lithuania, Hungary, Poland, Slovenia or Slovakia. Such resort may be had

---

[36] See paras 6–54 to 6–55 above.

by the Czech Republic "if the application of Articles 1 to 6 of Reg. 1612/68 is suspended by any of the [15] Member States".

6–65　　Thus for example if the Czech Republic is—by reason of particularly stringent national laws laid down by one of the 15 Member States—prevented from having its workers go to such Member State, it can likewise at that time protect its own labour market from influxes from other CEECs (the nationals of each of which will be similarly prevented from accessing the same Member State).

(iii) *Freedom of Movement Amongst Accession States*

6–66　　It is clear that, subject to the triggering of para.11 measures by a particular CEEC as against other CEECs, there is free movement as between CEECs. Paragraph 11 of Annex V is exhaustive of the limitations which are able to be placed on the exercise of free movements rights of workers between CEECs. As regards the CEECs on the one hand and Cyprus and Malta on the other, there is nothing in the transitional provisions which limits access of workers to their respective labour markets. It should be recalled however that such observations are subject to the possibility for three years of the taking of the protective measures contained in Arts 37 and 38 of the Act of Accession.[37] Moreover,[38] Malta may also take measures to protect its own labour market.

(e) *Posted Workers*

6–67　　Paragraph 13 of Annex V deals with posted workers, that is workers sent to Member States by Czech companies providing services. In relation to such workers sent by Czech Republic companies to Germany and Austria *only* this paragraph makes provision for derogation from the first paragraph of Art.49 EC Treaty[39] "in order to address serious disturbances or the threat thereof in specific sensitive service sectors on their labour markets, which could arise in certain regions[40] from the transnational provision of services" (as defined in Art.1 of Directive 96/71).

6–68　　Austria and Germany may so derogate for as long as national measures (or those resulting from bilateral agreements) are being applied to Czech workers. They may do so "after notifying the Commission". Paragraph 13 lists the service sectors in which there may be derogation. In relation to Germany the

---

[37] Referred to at paras 6–22 to 6–26 above.

[38] As referred to at paras 6–28 to 6–29 above.

[39] Art.49 EC Treaty provides: "Within the framework of the provisions set out below, restrictions on freedom to provide services within the Community shall be prohibited in respect of nationals of Member States who are established in a State of the Community other than that of the person for whom the services are intended".

[40] See Joint Declaration 19 to the Final Act by Germany and Austria which states as follows: "The wording of point number 13 of the transitional measures on the free movement of workers under Dir. 96/71/EC in Annexes V, VI, VIII, IX, X, XII, XIII and XIV is understood by the Federal Republic of Germany and the Republic of Austria in agreement with the Commission as meaning that 'certain regions' may, where appropriate, also comprise the entire national territory".

sectors are construction (including related branches); industrial cleaning and activities of interior decorators. In relation to Austria the same sectors are specified, plus horticultural service activities; cutting, shaping and finishing of stone; manufacture of metal structures and parts of structures; security activities; social work and activities without accommodations and home nursing. To the extent that Germany or Austria derogate under this provision, the Czech Republic may also, "after notifying the Commission, take equivalent measures".

There is also a "standstill" provision in para.13 of Annex V. Application of the paragraph must not result in conditions for the temporary movement of workers in the context of the transnational provision of services between Germany or Austria and the Czech Republic which are more restrictive than those existing on the date of signature of the Treaty of Accession.[41]   **6–69**

It is to be emphasised that this derogation applies to workers employed by Czech companies (or indeed companies established in other CEEC Accession States). It does not however apply to companies established in the 15 Member States who may indeed seek to post Czech or other CEEC national employees. This is however subject to satisfaction of the criteria that such employees have been habitually employed by the company established in one of the 15 Member States. Thus for example a company established in the UK could post a Czech employee in Germany in order to fulfil a contract for construction. The only pre-condition would be that the Czech employee had prior to such posting, been habitually employed by the UK company. For discussion of the posted workers requirements see Chapter 8.   **6–70**

(f) The 'Standstill' Provision and Other Measures

A similar standstill provision to that contained in para.13 is contained in para.14 of Annex V in relation to workers. This provides that the application of paras 2 to 5 and 7 to 12 must not result in conditions for access of Czech nationals to the labour markets of the 15 Member States which are more restrictive than those prevailing on the date of signature of the Treaty of Accession.[42]   **6–71**

Moreover, para.14 provides also that during any period when national measures are being applied preference must be given to workers who are nationals of the Member States over workers who are nationals of third countries as   **6–72**

---

[41] April 16, 2003 (as opposed to the date of accession).
[42] For the approach of the ECJ to the standstill clause in relation to Portugal and Spanish accession see Case C-279/89 *Commission v United Kingdom* [1992] E.C.R. I-5785, (a case in which the Commission sought a declaration that by imposing certain fishing licence conditions the UK had failed to fulfil its Treaty obligations). The ECJ held that "by excluding in the same way those same nationals where they are employed fishermen, the Member State also infringes Art.48 of the Treaty [now Art.39], since, in the case of restrictions which did not exist prior to the accession of Spain and Portugal, it fails to comply with the standstill clause in Arts 56(1) and 216(1) of the Act of Accession of 1985, or, in the case of the application of those restrictions to the Spanish or Portuguese members of the families of nationals of other Member States, it fails to respect the rights derived by them from Regulation No 1612/68 or Regulation No 1251/70 irrespective of the transitional provisions of the Act of Accession of 1985".

regards access to the labour market. The paragraph further provides Czech workers and their families legally resident and working in another Member State (or workers from other Member States and their families legally resident and working in the Czech Republic) shall not be treated in a more restrictive way than those from third countries resident and working in that Member State (or the Czech Republic). Furthermore, in accordance with the principle of Community preference, workers from third countries resident and working in the Czech Republic shall not be treated more favourably than nationals of the Czech Republic.

CHAPTER 7

WORKERS

This chapter identifies the concept of "workers" in the context of the free movement of persons.

1. INTRODUCTION

(a) *Fundamental Importance of Free Movement for Workers*

The freedom of movement for workers is one of the foundations of the EC **7–01**
Treaty.[1] This is reflected by Arts 2 and 3(1)(c) EC Treaty which provide that, for the purpose of establishing a common market and the promotion of the harmonious development of economic activities between Member States, obstacles to the free movement of persons between Member States shall be abolished.[2] Assuming that economic activities are being undertaken the freedom applies to all workers of all Member States regardless of occupation. Such free movement provision contrasts the narrower rights of free movement contained in the 1951 Treaty Establishing the European Coal and Steel Community (ECSC) and the Treaty establishing the European Atomic Energy Community (EAEC) which concerned economic integration in the fields of coal, steel and nuclear energy and gave limited free movement rights only in those sectors.[3]

(b) *Treaty Provisions on Workers*

The EC Treaty provisions on workers are contained in Chapter 1 (Workers) **7–02**
of Title III (Free movement of persons, services and capital). Broadly the scheme is as follows. Article 39 EC Treaty provides the principal means by which the abolition of obstacles to free movement of workers is achieved. As Art.39 EC Treaty makes clear, the abolition of any discrimination based on nationality between workers is of fundamental importance.[4] Such importance is reflected by the principle that the concepts which define "the field of application" of the freedom of movement for workers "may not be

---

[1] In the original text of the Treaty (as done in Rome on March 25, 1957) "Part Two" of the Treaty (which included the Title III provisions on free movement of persons, services and capital) was entitled "Foundations of the Community". The title was dropped in 1992 when amendments made by the Treaty on European Union substituted the title (for "Part Three") "Community Policies".

[2] The roots of the "common market" can be seen in the 1951 Treaty Establishing the European Coal and Steel Community (ECSC), although free movement rights were limited to skilled employment (Art.69 ECSC).

[3] See Art.69 ECSC and Art.96 EAEC, see further Chapter 1.

[4] See Chapter 9.

interpreted restrictively".[5] Article 39 EC Treaty itself gives meaning to the concept of "freedom of movement for workers" by the specific identification of the rights to accept employment offers made, to move freely within Member States for such purpose and to stay in Member States, both for employment and after having been employed:

Article 39 EC Treaty

1. Freedom of movement for workers shall be secured within the Community.

2. Such freedom of movement shall entail the abolition of any discrimination based on nationality between workers of the Member States as regards employment, remuneration and other conditions of work and employment.

3. It shall entail the right, subject to limitations justified on grounds of public policy, public security or public health:

(a)   to accept offers of employment actually made;
(b)   to move freely within the territory of Member States for this purpose;
(c)   to stay in a Member State for the purpose of employment in accordance with the provisions governing the employment of nationals of that State laid down by law, regulation or administrative action;
(d)   to remain in the territory of a Member State after having been employed in that State, subject to conditions which shall be embodied in implementing regulations to be drawn up by the Commission.

4. The provisions of this article shall not apply to employment in the public service.

7–03   Article 40 EC Treaty requires the Council to issue directives or make regulations to bring about the freedom of movement for workers as defined in Art.39 EC Treaty.

7–04   Article 41 EC Treaty requires that Member States shall, within the framework of a joint programme, encourage the exchange of young workers. Finally Art.42 EC Treaty requires the Council to adopt such measures in the field of social security as are necessary to provide freedom of movement for workers.[6]

(c) *Secondary Legislation*

7–05   The Art.40 EC Treaty obligation referred to above has resulted in two principal measures implementing the rights of free movement for workers. These are Reg. 1612/68 (freedom of movement for workers within the Community) and Directive 68/360 (abolition of restrictions on movement and residence within the Community for workers of Member States and their families).

---

[5] Case 53/81 *Levin v Staatssecretaris van Justitie* [1982] E.C.R. 1035, para.13. See also for example Case 66/85 *Lawrie-Blum v Land Baden-Württemberg* [1986] E.C.R. 2121, para.16: "since it defines the scope of that fundamental freedom, the community concept of a 'worker' must be interpreted broadly."
[6] Reg. 1408/71 (on the application of social security schemes to employed persons and their families moving within the Community). For discussion of social security measures see Chapter. 13.

(d) *The Community Concept of Worker*

The interpretation of who is a worker for the purposes of the free movement **7–06** provisions is a matter Community law which, in light of the fundamental importance of the field in which such interpretation arises, must not be interpreted restrictively.[7] Moreover the Community concept of worker for these purposes must not take flavour from national concepts. This principle was established over 40 years ago in *Hoekstra*[8] where the ECJ considered the interpretation of the concept of "wage-earner or assimilated worker" in a provision concerning social security for migrant workers.[9] As the ECJ stated,[10] if the definition were a matter within the competence of national law, "it would be possible for each Member State to modify the meaning of the concept of 'migrant worker' and to eliminate at will the protection afforded by the treaty to certain categories of person". The ECJ has constantly emphasised that the definition of worker has a Community meaning ever since.[11]

(e) *Community Concept of Worker Depends on Context*

There is no single definition of worker in Community law. Rather the defini- **7–07** tion varies according to the area in which it is to be applied. For example, as recognised by the ECJ in *Sala*,[12] the definition of worker used in the Art.39 EC Treaty context does not *necessarily* coincide with the definition applied in relation to measures adopted by the Council under Art.42 EC Treaty in the field of social security, notwithstanding that the focus of both is the freedom of movement for workers.

2. THE DEFINITION OF WORKER

(a) *Generally*

In *Lawrie-Blum*,[13] the ECJ identified the three essential criteria which deter- **7–08** mine whether there is an employment relationship and, in turn, whether the person concerned is a worker for the purposes of Art.39 EC Treaty:

---

[7] See Case 53/81 *Levin v Staatssecretaris van Justitie* [1982] E.C.R. 1035, para.13.
[8] Case 75/63 *Hoekstra v The Netherlands* [1964] E.C.R. 177.
[9] Council Reg. No. 3 concerning social security for migrant workers J.O. 561/58.
[10] Case 75/63 *Hoekstra v The Netherlands* [1964] E.C.R. 177, para 3.
[11] See for example Case 53/81 *Levin v Staatssecretaris van Justitie* [1982] E.C.R. 1035, "the term 'worker' in Article 48 [now Art.39] has a community meaning". See also Case C-188/00 *Kurz v Land Baden-Württemberg* [2002] E.C.R. I–10691 in the context of the Turkish Association Agreement (where reference is made to the interpretation of the concept of worker under Community law for the purposes of determining the scope of the same concept under the Agreement).
[12] Case C-85/96 *Martinez Sala v Freistaat Bayern* [1998] E.C.R. I–2691, para.31. See also for example Case C-443/93 *Ioannis Vougioukas v Idryma Koinonikon Asfalisseon (IKA)* [1995] E.C.R. I–4033 in which the meaning of civil servants was distinguished from persons in public service.
[13] Case 66/85 *Lawrie-Blum v Land Baden-Württemberg* [1986] E.C.R. 2121.

- Firstly, the person must perform services of some economic value. As will be seen this requirement has come to be qualified by the ECJ[14] which has emphasised that such services must be effective and genuine (and not marginal and ancillary).

- Secondly, the performance of such services must be for and under the direction of another person.

- Thirdly, in return, the person concerned must receive remuneration.

These requirements are exhaustive. As the ECJ has stated, "Community law does not impose any additional conditions for a person to be classifiable as a worker".[15]

(b) Services of Economic Value

7–09   The ECJ has put a gloss on the meaning of the requirement that the person must perform services of some economic value. In *Levin*[16] the ECJ stated that the rules on freedom of movement for workers "cover only the pursuit of effective and genuine activities, to the exclusion of activities on such a small scale as to be regarded as purely marginal and ancillary."[17] The ECJ plainly had in mind the application of a *de minimis* principle. The implication is that small-scale activities which are purely marginal and ancillary do not engage the free movement provisions because (in the words of the ECJ in *Levin*) these apply only to those "who pursue or are desirous of pursuing an economic activity."[18] This is readily explicable because the pursuance of an economic activity is the indispensable prerequisite of the free movement provisions for the economically active.[19] Unfortunately the application of this apparently straightforward *de minimis* principle has in one circumstance proved problematic to apply.[20]

7–10   The question of whether services have economic value should be analysed from the perspective of the employer. Assuming then that the activity has some economic value to someone else, if the scale of the activity is such that it is not so small as to be marginal and ancillary, the activity will be effective and genuine and the requirement satisfied.

7–11   As observed by the ECJ in *Lawrie-Blum*, in which the position of trainee teachers was considered, since they were required to give lessons to pupils, they provided a service of some economic value. Plainly without the trainee teachers the school would have been required to pay others to give lessons. See further paras 7–28 to 7–36 below.

---

[14] Case 53/81 *Levin v Staatssecretaris van Justitie* [1982] E.C.R. 1035.
[15] Case 197/86 *Brown v Secretary of State for Scotland* [1988] E.C.R. 3205, para.22.
[16] Case 53/81 *Levin v Staatssecretaris van Justitie* [1982] E.C.R. 1035.
[17] Case 53/81 *Levin v Staatssecretaris van Justitie* [1982] E.C.R. 1035, para.17.
[18] Case 53/81 *Levin v Staatssecretaris van Justitie* [1982] E.C.R. 1035.
[19] See Case 36/74 *Walrave and Koch v Association Union Cycliste Internationale, Koninklijke Nederlandsche Wielren Unie et Federación Española Ciclismo* [1974] E.C.R. 1405, para.4 and Case 13/76 *Dona v Mantaro* [1976] E.C.R. 1333, para.12: ". . . the practice of sport is subject to community law only in so far as it constitutes an economic activity within the meaning of Article 2 of the Treaty".
[20] See paras 7–37 *et seq*.

(c) *Services For and Under the Direction of Another Person*

The second requirement means that the services must be carried out in the con-   **7–12**
text of a relationship of subordination. Thus for example in *Asscher*,[21] Mr
Asscher, the director of a company of which he was also the sole shareholder
was not a worker since there was no subordination. However, although he was
found to be pursuing an activity as a self-employed person under Art.43 EC
Treaty and thus entitled to benefit from the free movement provisions in any
event. Indeed, in this respect, the question of whether a person who performs
services for remuneration does so under the direction of another person and
is thus a worker will be unlikely to cause much practical difficulty. As in
Asscher if the person is not a worker he or she will likely be self-employed and
this will benefit from free movement provisions in any event.

(d) *Remuneration*

Whilst remuneration is an essential element it is interpreted broadly.   **7–13**
Remuneration need not be at a particular level, nor even in the form of wages
as such . The "level" of wages was considered in *Levin*[22] in which the ECJ
rejected an argument that remuneration had to reach a particular level so as
to enable the person to be a worker (subject to the activity being effective and
genuine and not purely marginal and ancillary).[23]

Nor does the nature of the remuneration matter. In *Ex p. Agegate*[24] the ECJ   **7–14**
considered whether Spanish fishermen working on board British vessels were
workers when paid as "share fishermen" (namely on the basis of the proceeds
of sale of their catches). The ECJ emphasised that the identification of an
employment relationship was to be examined "on the basis of all the factors
and circumstances characterizing the arrangements between the parties, such
as, for example, the sharing of the commercial risks of the business, the freedom for a person to choose his own working hours and to engage his own
assistants". The sole fact that remuneration was on a collectively determined
paid "share" basis could not deprive the fishermen of their status as workers.

The breadth of approach taken to remuneration is well shown by the decision   **7–15**
of the ECJ in *Steymann*.[25] The case concerned a German national living in the
Netherlands as a member of the Bhagwan Community (which supplied its
material needs by means of commercial activities, which included running a
discothèque, a bar and a launderette). Mr Steymann contributed to the life of
the Bhagwan Community by doing plumbing work on its premises and general

---

[21] Case C-107/94 *Asscher v Staatssecretaris van Financiën* [1996] E.C.R. I–3089.

[22] See Case 53/81 *Levin v Staatssecretaris van Justitie* [1982] E.C.R. 1035.

[23] See also Case C-456/02 *Trojani v Centre public d'aide sociale de Bruxelles (CPAS)*, September 7, 2004.

[24] Case 3/87 *The Queen v Ministry of Agriculture, Fisheries and Food, Ex p. Agegate Ltd* [1989] E.C.R. 4459. The question referred related to the transitional arrangements contained in Arts 55 and 56 of the Act concerning the Accession of Spain and Portugal to the European Communities of 1985. These provisions introduced a derogation from the principle of the free movement of workers (excluding the application to Spanish workers of Arts 1 to 6 of Reg. 1612/68 until January 1, 1993).

[25] Case 196/87 *Steymann v Staatssecretaris van Justitie* [1988] E.C.R. 6159.

household duties. He also took part in the Bhagwan Community's commercial activity. For its part the Bhagwan Community provided for the material needs of its members (which included the payment of pocket money), irrespective of the nature and the extent of their activities. The ECJ considered that this was remuneration which was able to be regarded as "an indirect quid pro quo" for the work carried out by the members of the Bhagwan Community.[26]

(e) *Application of Principles*

(i) *Level of Productivity*

7–16   Services will still have some economic value even where the "productivity" of the person concerned is low, or indeed even if remuneration is largely provided by subsidies from public funds. As the ECJ stated in *Bettray* "neither the level of productivity nor the origin of the funds from which the remuneration is paid can have any consequence in regard to whether or not the person is to be regarded as a worker".[27]

(ii) *Part-time Work*

7–17   A consequence of the irrelevance of the level of productivity is that a person who works part-time can still be a worker. In *Levin*[28] the ECJ considered the position of a part-time British national worker resident in the Netherlands married to a third country national. It was argued by the Dutch (and Danish) Governments that the provisions of Art.39 EC Treaty could only be relied on by those in receipt of a wage "at least commensurate with the means of subsistence considered as necessary by the legislation of the member state in which they work, or who work at least for the number of hours considered as usual in respect of full-time employment in the sector in question".

7–18   These arguments were rejected robustly by the ECJ, not least since it is impermissible to define the Community concept of worker by reference to national laws.[29] Emphasising the fundamental nature of the freedom of movement for workers and the need for broad interpretation the ECJ noted the importance of part-time work for a large number of persons "as an effective means of improving their living conditions" and stated that "the effectiveness of community law would be impaired and the achievement of the objectives of the Treaty . . . . jeopardized if the enjoyment of rights conferred by the principle of freedom of movement for workers were reserved solely to persons engaged in full-time employment".[30]

---

[26] Case 196/87 *Steymann v Staatssecretaris van Justitie* [1988] E.C.R. 6159, para.14
[27] Case 344/87 *Bettray v Staatssecretaris van Justitie* [1989] E.C.R. 1621, para.15.
[28] See Case 53/81 *Levin v Staatssecretaris van Justitie* [1982] E.C.R. 1035.
[29] See Case 75/63 *Hoekstra v Netherlands* [1964] E.C.R. 117, para.11.
[30] See Case 75/63 *Hoekstra v Netherlands* [1964] E.C.R. 117, para.15.

The ECJ applied these principles in *Ruzius-Wilbrink* and *Rinner-Kühn* in 7–19
recognising women working part-time (respectively for 18 and 10 hours
a week) as workers.[31] In *Kempf*[32] a German national resident in the
Netherlands who worked as a part-time music teacher for 12 hours a week
was also a worker. Moreover it is to be emphasised that it is irrelevant
whether part-time work is the *principal* activity of the person concerned.
Such a person may for example undertake part-time work whilst a student.
Whether such person is a worker is answered by reference to the principles
here discussed: the relevant questions are not changed by reason only of the
person's status as a student.

(iii) *Contracts for Employment with Variable Conditions*

Those who undertake work for certain employers may perform services on an 7–20
irregular basis as and when required to do so by their employer. Such relationships are plainly of employment rather than self-employment since it is
the employer who dictates when and under what terms the person will work.
Thus for example an interpreter contracted to an agency supplying court
translators may work for a variable number of hours as and when required.
Are such persons workers?

The ECJ considered such contracts in *Raulin*[33] in which a French national liv- 7–21
ing in Holland signed an eight-month "on-call contract" (*oproepcontract*) to
provide services as an "on-call worker" (*oproepkracht*)[34] under which she had
worked for 60 hours as a waitress in a 16-day period. The ECJ considered
whether the nature of the activities of an on-call worker prevented such a
person from being a worker and whether the fact that such a person exercised
or sought to exercise an economic activity for only a short time was relevant
to the question of whether such activities are purely marginal and ancillary.

The ECJ held that the nature of the contract could not by reason of the con- 7–22
ditions of employment preclude the person's being a worker, nor could the
fact that the person had worked only for a short period of time. However, in
considering whether the activity was effective and genuine and not marginal
and ancillary the national court was entitled to take account of "the irregular

---

[31] Case 102/88 *Ruzius-Wilbrink v Bestuur van de Bedrijfsvereniging voor Overheidsdiensten*
[1989] E.C.R. 4311 (woman doing part time work of 18 no more than hours a week a worker);
Case 171/88 *Rinner-Kühn v FWW Spezial-Gebäudereinigung GmbH & Co. KG.* (woman doing
part-time work of 10 hours a week a worker); Case 171/88 *Rinner-Kühn v FWW Spezial-
Gebäudereinigung GmbH & Co KG* [1989] E.C.R. 2743 (woman doing part-time work of
10 hours a week a worker).
[32] Case 139/85 *Kempf v Staatssecretaris van Justitie* [1986] E.C.R. 1741.
[33] Case C-357/89 *Raulin v Minister van Onderwijs en Wetenschappen* [1992] E.C.R. I–1027.
[34] The ECJ describes the particular contract (para.9 of Case C-357/89 *Raulin v Minister van
Onderwijs en Wetenschappen* [1992] E.C.R. I–1027, above) in these terms: "It is apparent from
the reference for a preliminary ruling that under Netherlands law an oproepcontract is a means
of recruiting workers in sectors, such as the hotel trade, where the volume of work is subject to
seasonal variations. Under such a contract, no guarantee is given as to the hours to be worked
and, often, the person involved works only a very few days per week or hours per day. The
employer is liable to pay wages and grant social advantages only in so far as the worker has actually performed work. Furthermore, the Netherlands Government stated at the hearing that
under such an oproepcontract the employee is not obliged to heed the employer's call for him
to work".

nature and limited duration of the services actually performed under a contract for occasional employment." Furthermore, "the fact that the person concerned worked only a very limited number of hours in a labour relationship may be an indication that the activities exercised are purely marginal and ancillary".[35]

7–23 The answer to the question posed as to whether such person is a worker is that there is nothing in the nature of such contracts which prevents a person's being considered a worker for the purposes of the free movement provisions, subject always to the activities performed under such contracts being effective and genuine and not marginal and ancillary. In other words to be merely 'signed on' with an agency cannot make the person a worker if no meaningful activities are actually performed.

As regards fixed term contracts, the ECJ has made clear that "the fact that employment is of short duration cannot, in itself exclude that employment from the scope of Article 48 of the Treaty [now Art.39 EC Treaty]".[36]

(iv) *Receipt of Supplementary Funds Irrelevant*

7–24 The consequence of the rejection by the ECJ in *Levin* of the arguments that a worker is required to work for a minimum number of hours and to earn a minimum amount[37] is that the means used by part-time workers to supplement their income will not deprive them of their status as workers. Thus it was irrelevant in *Levin* that the part-time worker's funds were supplemented by the income from the employment of a member of her family. The position is the same where "public funds" are used to supplement income earned as a part-time worker. Thus in *Kempf* where the part-time music teacher supplemented his income with benefits payable from public funds available to workers the ECJ held that provided the effective and genuine nature of his work was established, it was irrelevant that his income was supplemented by assistance from public funds.[38] This approach reflects the decision in *Bettray*[39] in which remuneration financed largely by subsidies from public funds was held by the ECJ to be irrelevant to the question of whether the person concerned was a worker.

(v) *Nature of Activities Irrelevant*

7–25 The nature of the activities (for example whether they are said to offend public morality) is irrelevant to the question of whether a person may be a worker. This however does not mean that a worker could not face exclusion if the activities of the worker posed a genuine and sufficiently serious threat affecting one of the fundamental interests of society such that a Member

---

[35] Case C-357/89 *Raulin v Minister van Onderwijs en Wetenschappen* [1992] E.C.R. I-1027, paras 14–15.
[36] Case C-413/01 *Franca Ninni-Orasche v Bundesminister fur Wissenschaft*, November 6, 2003, para.25.
[37] See further paras 7–13 *et seq.*
[38] Case 139/85 *Kempf v Staatssecretaris van Justitie* [1986] E.C.R. 1741, para.14.
[39] Case 344/87 *Bettray v Staatssecretaris van Justitie* [1989] E.C.R. 1621, para.15.

State is able to invoke the public policy proviso.[40] Thus, in *Jany*,[41] the fact that the women were working as prostitutes could not affect the conclusion that the women were carrying out economic activities.

(vi) *Motives Irrelevant*

There is no requirement that a person who carries out economic activities 7–26 must have some subjective intention to do so in order to be defined as a worker. In *Levin*,[42] the ECJ robustly rejected an argument that free movement rights could be denied to a worker whose objectives were not the pursuit of an economic activity. The rights could be relied on only by those who "actually pursue or seriously wish to pursue activities as employed persons."[43] But this did not mean:

> "that the enjoyment of this freedom may be made to depend upon the aims pursued by a national of a Member State in applying for entry upon and residence in the territory of another member state, provided that he there pursues or wishes to pursue an activity which . . . is . . . an effective and genuine activity as an employed person".

Once this condition is satisfied the motives which may have prompted the 7–27 worker to seek employment in the Member State concerned are "of no account and must not be taken into consideration".[44] This will be the case even where it is alleged that the person has "sought abusively to create a situation enabling her to claim the status of worker". According to the ECJ, "the issue of abuse of rights can have no bearing".[45] The correctness of this principle was recently reaffirmed by the ECJ in *Akrich*.[46]

(vii) *Students, Trainees, Apprentices and Au-pairs*

Whether a person is a worker *whilst* a student is answered by reference to 7–28 whether genuine and effective services of some economic value are performed under the direction of another person for remuneration. The relevant questions are not changed by reason only of the person's status as a student. But is the position different where the activities relied on themselves constitute the studies (or training or apprenticeship)? For example is a student whose studies involve the performance of activities as a trainee teacher to be regarded as a worker?

---

[40] See Joined Cases 115 & 116/81 *Adoui and Cornuaille* [1982] E.C.R. 1665, para.8; Case C-348/96 *Calfa* [1999] E.C.R. I–11, para.21. See also Chapter 14.

[41] Case C-268/99 *Jany v Staatssecretaris van Justite* [2001] E.C.R. I–8615. The cases concerned Czech and Polish women working in the Netherlands who sought to benefit from the Association Agreements as self employed prostitutes.

[42] Case 53/81 *Levin v Staatssecretaris van Justitie* [1982] E.C.R. 1035.

[43] See Case 53/81 *Levin v Staatssecretaris van Justitie* [1982] E.C.R. 1035, paras 20–23. The ECJ refers to Art.39 EC Treaty and provisions of Reg. 1612/68 and Dir. 68/360.

[44] Case 53/81 *Levin v Staatssecretaris van Justitie* [1982] E.C.R. 1035.

[45] Case C-413/01 *Franca Ninni-Orasche v Bundesminister fur Wissenschaft*, November 6, 2003, para.31.

[46] Case C-109/01 *Secretary of State for the Home Department v Akrich*, judgment of September 23, 2003, paras 55–56.

7–29   The answer to such questions is provided by the decision of the ECJ in *Lawrie-Blum*[47] in which a British citizen who had passed exams to be a teacher at the University of Freiburg was subsequently refused admission (on the ground of her nationality) to do her teacher training ("a period of preparatory service" which would have qualified her for appointment as a teacher in a "Gymnasium"). The essential issue was whether the activities undertaken during the period of preparatory service as a trainee teacher were work (and Mrs Lawrie Blum ought thus to be regarded as a worker able to benefit from non-discrimination). The German Government argued that since a trainee teacher's activity was a matter of education policy it was not an "economic activity" within the meaning of Art.2 EC Treaty[48] and that the period of preparatory service should be regarded as the last stage of professional training (as opposed to work).

7–30   The ECJ robustly rejected such arguments. The broad Community concept of worker must be defined in accordance with the objective criteria to which reference has already been made. During the entire period of preparatory service the trainee teacher:

> "is under the direction and supervision of the school to which he is assigned. It is the school that determines the services to be performed by him and his working hours and it is the school's instructions that he must carry out and its rules that he must observe. During a substantial part of the preparatory service he is required to give lessons to the school's pupils and thus provides a service of some economic value to the school. The amounts which he receives may be regarded as remuneration for the services provided and for the duties involved in completing the period of preparatory service. Consequently, the three criteria for the existence of an employment relationship are fulfilled".[49]

7–31   Further, the fact that teachers' preparatory service ("like apprenticeships in other occupations") could be seen as practical preparation directly related to the actual pursuit of the occupation in point was not a bar to such a person's being a worker "if the service is performed under the conditions of an activity as an employed person". Nor indeed could the objection be sustained that "services performed in education do not fall within the scope of the EEC Treaty because they are not of an economic nature." As the ECJ stated, "all that is required for the application of Article 48 [now Art.39] is that the activity should be in the nature of work performed for remuneration, irrespective of the sphere in which it is carried out."[50] As the ECJ stated in answering the question "a trainee teacher who, under the direction and supervision of the school authorities, is undergoing a period of service in

[47] Case 66/85 *Lawrie-Blum v Land Baden-Württemberg* [1986] E.C.R. 2121.
[48] Art.2 EC Treaty refers to the implementation of common policies or activities referred to in Arts 3 and 4. Art.3(1)(q) refers to "a contribution to education and training of quality and to the flowering of the cultures of the Member States". Community policy in education is dealt with in Arts 149–150 EC Treaty.
[49] Case 66/85 *Lawrie-Blum v Land Baden-Württemberg* [1986] E.C.R. 2121, para.18.
[50] The ECJ further stated that "the nature of the legal relationship between employee and employer, whether involving public law status or a private law contract , is immaterial" as was the fact (by reference to Case 53/81 *Levin v Staatssecretaris van Justitie* [1982] E.C.R. 1035) that "trainee teachers give lessons for only a few hours a week and are paid remuneration below the starting salary of a qualified teacher" which did not prevent them from being regarded as workers.

preparation for the teaching profession during which he provides services by giving lessons and receives remuneration must be regarded as a worker."

In light of *Lawrie-Blum* it is clear that the activities undertaken by persons who are students, trainees or apprentices may be "work" and that such persons may be regarded as "workers". 7–32

Despite the clarity of the position established almost 20 years ago, the ECJ has been required to restate it on a number of occasions. For example in *USRAFF*[51] (which concerned the characterisation of a period of practical vocational training undertaken in France by an Irish national studying vocational training at a technical college in Ireland) the ECJ stated that "the fact that a person performs those services under a traineeship contract does not prevent him from being regarded as a worker, if he pursues an activity which is effective and genuine and if the essential characteristics of the employment relationship are fulfilled". The ECJ made the same point in relation to vocational training in *Kurz*[52] (albeit in the context of a Turkish Association Agreement case). Moreover in *Gunaydin*[53] (another Turkish Association Agreement case) the ECJ considered the position of a Turkish national being trained in Germany by Siemens for the specific purpose of taking up a post in a Siemens subsidiary in Turkey. The ECJ concluded that the mere fact that the employment had been designed solely to qualify Mr Gunaydin to work elsewhere did not deprive it of the character of employment on normal principles. 7–33

As regards au-pairs, their ability to be considered as workers is beyond doubt, both on normal principles and in light of *Watson and Belman*.[54] The case concerned an au pair employed as a family help who looked after children in return for board and lodging. Advocate General Trabucchi stated that the au-pair "would undoubtedly come into one of the categories of person upon whom the Treaty confers the right to move within the Community". The Advocate General continued: 7–34

"as this would in fact be work performed for a consideration (board and lodging), she could be classified as coming within a master and servant relationship or if this were not the case she would at least come under the alternative heading of provision of services".[55]

Although the ECJ did not specifically rule on the issue, the ECJ's decision was predicated on the au-pair falling within the scope of the Treaty. The only basis on which an au-pair could not be considered a worker would be if the au-pair was not genuine and effective in the activities undertaken. Certainly there is nothing intrinsic in the nature of the relationship, the activities carried out or the form of remuneration which could negate the possibility of an au-pair's being a worker. 7–35

---

[51] Case C-27/91 *Union de Recouvrement des Cotisations de Sécurité Sociale et d'Allocations Familiales de la Savoie (URSSAF) v Hostellerie Le Manoir SARL* [1991] E.C.R. I–5531.
[52] Case C-188/00 *Kurz v Land Baden-Württemberg* [2002] E.C.R. I–10691, para.34.
[53] Case C-36/96 *Gunaydin v Freistaat Bayern* [1997] E.C.R. I–5179.
[54] Case 118/75 *Watson and Belmann* [1976] E.C.R. 1185.
[55] Case 118/75 *Watson and Belmann* [1976] E.C.R. 1185, *per* A.G. Trabucchi, p.1202.

7–36   In sum it matters not whether the activities in question are characterised as studies, training, vocational training, an apprenticeship, work as an au-pair, or otherwise. Anyone carrying out such activities may be a worker if performing genuine and effective activities of some economic value under the direction of someone else for remuneration. Although such proposition might be considered somewhat trite, it is not always reflected by the practises of some Member States.[56]

(viii) *Rehabilitative Employment*

7–37   In *Bettray*,[57] the ECJ considered the position of a German national drug addict living in the Netherlands who worked in rehabilitative employment under a scheme which provided work "for maintaining, restoring or improving" the capacity for work of those who for an indefinite period are unable to work under normal conditions. Since Mr Bettray performed services under the direction of another person in return for which he received remuneration the ECJ concluded that the essential features of an employment relationship were present. However his work was not an effective and genuine economic activity if:

> "merely a means of rehabilitation or reintegration for the persons concerned and the purpose of the paid employment, which is adapted to the physical and mental possibilities of each person, is to enable those persons sooner or later to recover their capacity to take up ordinary employment or to lead as normal as possible a life".

7–38   A conceptual difficulty with such reasoning (focussing as it does on the benefit to the worker) is that it has nothing whatsoever to do with the "scale" of Mr Bettray's activities (namely whether so small as to be marginal and ancillary and thus not an economic activity within the meaning of Art.2 EC Treaty). Indeed, it is difficult to see how the rehabilitative nature of the activities and the fact that they are aimed at enabling those working under the scheme to "recover their capacity to take up ordinary employment" can deprive them of being economic activities where the criteria for determining the existence of an employment relationship are otherwise met.

7–39   The ECJ's focus on the benefit to the worker is inappropriate as a basis to conclude that the work is not genuine and effective. The motives which may have prompted a person to undertake activities are irrelevant to the question whether what is done is work. Moreover, such approach is, by implication at least, inconsistent with the approach taken by the ECJ in *Lawrie-Blum* where the fact that the trainee teacher gave lessons during the last stage of professional training which could be seen as "practical preparation directly related to the actual pursuit of the occupation in point" was not a bar to her being a worker if the service was performed "under the conditions of an activity as an employed person".[58]

---

[56] See in relation to the UK, Chapter 28.
[57] Case 344/87 *Bettray v Staatssecretaris van Justitie* [1989] E.C.R. 1621.
[58] Case 66/85 *Lawrie Blum v Land-Baden-Wurttemberg* [1986] E.C.R. 2121, para.19.

In fact *Bettray* is explicable because activities aimed "*merely* as a means of   **7–40**
rehabilitation or reintegration" of the person performing them which are of
no value to the employer will not be able to be characterised as work simply
because the person undertakes the task under the direction of someone else
and is remunerated. Although there may be *some* economic value in the activities undertaken, from the perspective of the employer they will likely be at
best marginal and ancillary. Rather the relationship is more akin to an act of
benevolence on the part of the employer.

Bettray has not been applied to preclude *any* activity of a rehabilitative nature   **7–41**
being considered as work. In *Birden*[59] the ECJ considered the position of a
Turkish national who worked as a semi-skilled odd-job man under a sponsored social assistance scheme which provided temporary work opportunities
to "improve the integration into working life of the person seeking assistance".[60] The fact that Mr Birden performed "as a subordinate, services for his
employer in return for which he receives remuneration, thus satisfying the
essential criteria of the employment relationship"[61] and that his work was not
marginal and ancillary[62] were not affected by *Bettray* which the ECJ in *Birden*
distinguished (this despite the rehabilitative nature of the employment).

The issue of rehabilitative employment was considered by the ECJ again in   **7–42**
Trojani[63] in which a French national carried out chores for some 30 hours a
week in a Salvation Army hostel in Brussels where he lived as part of a rehabilitation project. In return the hostel provided him with food, lodgings and
an allowance of €25 per week. In his opinion Advocate General Geelhoed[64]
interprets the decision in *Bettray* as based on the ECJ's view that the aim of
the activities was solely reintegration and not the carrying out of any real
economic activity. The Advocate General considered Mr Trojani's relationship with the Salvation Army to be one of care rather than work wherein a
service was being provided to Mr Trojani rather than to the Salvation Army.
Thus his activity had no (or virtually no) economic value.

It would be curious if the national court were to characterise 30 hours' work   **7–43**
doing chores as marginal and ancillary from the perspective of the Salvation
Army. The ECJ in its decision referred to *Bettray* as being particular on its
facts.[65] The ECJ confirmed that the nature of remuneration received by Mr
Trojani was not a bar to him being considered a worker. The ECJ left it to the
national court to determine if in the circumstances the nature of his activities
were real and genuine. Part of the national court's enquiry would require it to
ascertain "whether the services actually performed by Mr Trojani are capable

---

[59] Case C-1/97 *Birden v Stadtgemeinde Bremen* [1998] E.C.R. I–7447. The case arose in the context of the Turkish Association Agreement.
[60] The issue was whether he was "a duly registered member of the labour force" within the meaning of Art.6(1) of Dec. 1/80 of the EEC-Turkey Association Council.
[61] Case C-1/97 *Birden v Stadtgemeinde Bremen* [1998] E.C.R. I–7447, para.26.
[62] Case C-1/97 *Birden v Stadtgemeinde Bremen* [1998] E.C.R. I–7447, para.27. He worked for 38.5
hours a week receiving net pay of DM 2155.70.
[63] Case C-456/02 *Trojani v Centre public d'aide sociale de Bruxelles (CPAS)* not yet decided.
[64] A.G. Geelhoed's Opinion, February 19, 2004.
[65] Case C-456/02 *Trojani v centre public d'aide sociale de Bruxelles (CPAS)*, September 7, 2004,
para.19.

of being regarded as forming part of the normal labour market. For that purpose, account may be taken of the status and practices of the hostel, the content of the social reintegration programme, and the nature and details of performance of the services".[66] It is certainly clear that the ECJ does not regard the fact that activities are of a rehabilitative nature as being something which in itself will necessarily prevent them being effective and genuine

(f) Work Seekers

(i) Generally

7–44 Consideration has been given to persons whose activities may make them workers. But what of those who have never worked? Article 39 EC Treaty itself provides the right to move freely within Member States "to accept offers of employment actually made". However it would plainly undermine the fundamental freedom of movement for workers guaranteed by the EC Treaty were such a movement restricted to those who have sought and actually found work (thus requiring them to have job offers before moving to other Member States).

(ii) The Decision in Antonissen[67]

7–45 In Antonissen, the ECJ expressly rejected the argument that Art.39 EC Treaty limited the right to free movement solely to those accepting offers of employment actually made. Such interpretation could not be upheld since it would exclude the right of a national of a Member State to move freely and to stay in the territory of other Member States in order to seek employment there. It did so by reference to freedom of movement for workers as one of the foundations of the Community and the consequential need for a broad interpretation to be given to such freedom.[68] As made clear in Levin[69] the free movement rights may be enjoyed not only by those actually pursue activities as employed persons, but also those who "seriously wish" to pursue such activities.[70] And in Royer[71] the ECJ refers to the right to "look for" and pursue such activities.

---

[66] Case C-456/02 Trojani v centre public d'aide sociale de Bruxelles (CPAS), September 7, 2004, para.24.
[67] Case C-292/89 The Queen v Immigration Appeal Tribunal Ex p. Antonissen [1991] E.C.R. I–745.
[68] Case C-292/89 The Queen v Immigration Appeal Tribunal Ex p. Antonissen [1991] E.C.R. I–745, para.11.
[69] Case 53/81 Levin v Staatssecretaris van Justitie [1982] E.C.R. 1035.
[70] Case 53/81 Levin v Staatssecretaris van Justitie [1982] E.C.R. 1035, para.20.
[71] Case 48/75 Procureur de Roi v Royer [1976] E.C.R. 497, in which the ECJ described the right to enter the territory of other Member States and to reside there "for the purposes intended by the Treaty" as including the right "in particular to look for or pursue an occupation or activities as employed or self employed persons" (para.31).

(iii) *Scope of Right for Work Seekers*

In *Antonissen*, the domestic court had held that Mr Antonissen, who had **7–46** been seeking employment in the United Kingdom for more than six months, could no longer be treated as a Community worker.[72]

The UK Government and the Commission had argued that persons could **7–47** only be workseekers for three months. The ECJ rejected strict temporal limitations. The scope of the right of free movement for work seekers was expressed by the ECJ in these terms:

> "It is not contrary to the provisions of Community law governing the free movement of workers for the legislation of a Member State to provide that a national of another Member State who entered the first State in order to seek employment may be required to leave the territory of that State (subject to appeal) if he has not found employment there after six months, unless the person concerned provides evidence that he is continuing to seek employment and that he has genuine chances of being engaged".[73]

Antonissen thus identifies the scope of the right of freedom of movement for **7–48** work seekers. Member States may prescribe a period of six months within which work should be obtained, although not to be enforced if after such time evidence is provided that the person concerned continues to seek employment and has genuine chances of being engaged.[74]

(g) *Previous Employment*

(i) *Generally*

The position considered above of work seekers who have never worked for **7–49** whom the content of the right is about access to employment contrasts the position of persons who have worked previously but have ceased working. As a general rule (as stated by the ECJ in *Sala*[75]) "once the employment relationship has ended, the person concerned as a rule loses his status of worker".

However, there may be various reasons why a person ceases working (includ- **7–50** ing redundancy, retirement, retraining or the wish to embark on full-time

---

[72] Case C-292/89 *The Queen v Immigration Appeal Tribunal Ex p. Antonissen* [1991] E.C.R. I–745, para.5: The Immigration Appeal Tribunal based this part of its decision on para.143 of the Statement of Changes in Immigration Rules (HC 169), adopted pursuant to the Immigration Act 1971, under which "a national of a Member State may be deported if, after six months from admission to the United Kingdom, he has not yet found employment or is not carrying on any other occupation".

[73] Case C-292/89 *The Queen v Immigration Appeal Tribunal Ex p. Antonissen* [1991] E.C.R. I–745, para.22.

[74] This was confirmed by the ECJ in Case C-138/02 *Collins v Secretary of State for Work and Pensions*, [2004] 2 C.M.L.R. 8, para.37. However the principle could not avoid Mr. Tsiotras who remained unemployed for several years and "for whom it [was] objectively impossible to find employment": Case C-171/91 *Tsiotras v Landeshauptstadt Stuttgart* [1993] E.C.R. I-2925.

[75] Case C-85/96 *Martinez Sala v Freistat Bayern* [1998] E.C.R. I–2691, para.32.

studies). Some such situations are dealt with by expressly secondary legislation giving rights of residence in specific circumstances. Such rights derive from Art.39(3)(d) EC Treaty which identifies the scope of the right of freedom of movement as entailing the right to remain in a Member State "after having been employed in that State" and are considered in Chapter 12.

7–51 It is important to identify the circumstances in which the status of worker is able (in the words of the ECJ in *Sala*) to "produce certain effects after the relationship has ended". Are those circumstances limited to the specific instances in the secondary legislation where rights (principally of residence) are expressly given on cessation of employment (for example on retirement), or are such circumstances wider?

7–52 The answer to this question is undoubtedly that the secondary legislation does *not* represent the full extent of such circumstances. In a number of cases the ECJ has acknowledged that even although no longer employed, persons may nevertheless continue to be considered workers. By the same token it is not always easy to identify precisely *why* the ECJ has reached its conclusion, although in broad terms such situations have largely arisen where, despite cessation of employment, the person concerned can be regarded as having retained the objective status of worker.

(ii) *Status of Worker Not Lost Immediately*

7–53 The objective status of worker is obviously not lost *immediately* on cessation of employment. Just as Community law recognises the right of those who have never worked to be treated as workers whilst they seek employment, so where persons have worked previously they will always have a reasonable period within which to seek and obtain further employment by reference to the principles discussed above.[76] For such persons where national law provisions give benefits to own nationals, Community law will require workers of other Member States to be treated in the same way, even although not in an employment relationship. However, in this context the assessment of national authorities will determine whether the person can be said to retain the objective status of worker. It may be for instance that after a certain period of time a Member State does not characterise a person who has ceased economic activity as a worker. It would take extreme circumstances for Community law to characterise the national of another Member State as retaining the objective status of worker where national law no longer did, even in respect of its own nationals.

7–54 An example of a case in which someone retained the objective status of worker where the employment relationship had recently ended is *Meints*.[77] The case concerned an agricultural worker whose contract of employment was terminated as a result of the setting aside of land belonging to his former employer. The ECJ held Mr Meints was entitled to a payment made to

---

[76] See paras 7–44 *et seq.*
[77] Case C-57/96 *Meints v Minister van Landbouw, Natuurbeheer en Visserij* [1997] E.C.R. I–6689.

agricultural workers whose contract of employment was terminated because payment depended on the prior existence of his recently ended employment relationship which was thus intrinsically linked to his objective status as worker.[78]

(iii) *Those Previously Employed and Capable of Taking Further Employment*

More than 40 years ago in *Hoekstra*[79] the ECJ interpreted the concept of "wage earner or assimilated worker"[80] in a case involving a woman who had stopped working. The ECJ held that a protected worker was not exclusively someone in current employment, but extended logically "to the worker who, having left his job, is capable of taking another". Mrs Hoekstra was thus protected by Community law as a worker even though no longer in employment. National law provided the unemployed the possibility to participate in a social security system on the grounds of previous possession of the status of "worker" and capability of re-acquiring that status.

7–55

(iv) *Available for Work and Prepared to Take It Up*

The national legislation of some Member States would appear to treat own nationals as retaining the objective status of workers through the combination of being available for work and being prepared to take it up. In Belgium, for example, a general subsistence allowance known as the "minimex" is payable to all those in need who are prepared to accept work (unless prevented by the person's state of health or compelling social reasons[81]). In *Hoeckx*[82] and *Scrivner*[83] the ECJ stated the principle that migrant workers are entitled to all benefits:

7–56

> "generally granted to national workers primarily because of their objective status as workers or by virtue of the mere fact of their residence on the national territory and whose extension to workers who are nationals of other member states therefore seems likely to facilitate the mobility of such workers within the community".

The facts of *Hoeckx* are striking because the Dutch national had been unemployed for some two years and in receipt of unemployment benefits in both France and Belgium before the minimex was refused. However, *Hoeckx* does not help in identifying why a person unemployed for such a period retained the status of worker since the matter was not in dispute.

7–57

(v) *Workers Undertaking Retraining*

A further example of a situation in which the status of worker is retained arises where a person who has ceased employment undertakes some form of

7–58

---

[78] Case C-57/96 *Meints v Minister van Landbouw, Natuurbeheer en Visserij* [1997] E.C.R. I–6689, para.41.
[79] Case 75/63 *Hoekstra v The Netherlands* [1964] E.C.R. 177.
[80] Within the meaning of Council Reg. 3 concerning social security for migrant workers J.O. 58.
[81] Case 122/84 *Scrivner and Cole v Centre public d'aide sociale de Chastre* [1985] E.C.R. 1027, para.20.
[82] Case 249/83 *Hoeckx v Openbaar Centrum voor Maatschappelijk Welzijn, Kalmthout* [1985] E.C.R. 973, para.20.
[83] Case 122/84 *Scrivner and Cole v Centre public d'aide sociale de Chastre* [1985] E.C.R. 1027, para.24.

professional or vocational training. In *Lair*,[84] the ECJ stated that workers
who have exercised their freedom of movement are entitled in the same way
as national workers to all the advantages available to such workers "for
improving their professional qualifications and promoting their social
advancement." This will the position even although no longer in employment,
provided a relationship existed between the previous occupational activity
and the course of study.[85] Such a person will be regarded as having retained
the status of a worker.[86]

(vi) *Objective Status of Worker Must Be Linked to Previous Employment*

7–59   Although a person who has ceased to work may retain the status of worker
for the purpose of receipt of a particular benefit related to the past employment, such status may not be retained for all other purposes. In *Leclere*,[87] a
Belgian national who had been employed as a frontier worker in Luxembourg
until 1981 when he was a victim of an accident at work was in receipt of an
invalidity pension paid by the Luxembourg social services. As such he was
protected against any discrimination affecting rights acquired during his former employment relationship. However, since not currently engaged in an
employment relationship, he could not claim to acquire new rights having no
links with his former occupation. In particular, having had a child *after* he
had stopped working he could not claim the benefit of allowances provided
for workers on the birth of a child by the legislation of the Member State
responsible for paying his pension.

(vii) *Summary*

7–60   As the cases considered demonstrate despite cessation of an employment
relationship, Community law provides for the retention of the objective status of worker. The precise consequence of retention of the status of worker
may depend on the national law provisions of a Member State. At the heart
of most situations considered is the proposition that it would be discriminatory and contrary to Community law to treat own nationals and free movers
differently in terms of benefits and advantages given by national law to those
who have been in employment. This is discussed in detail in Chapter 9.

(h) *Frontier Workers*

7–61   Frontier workers are defined as those who reside in one Member State whilst
working in the territory of *another* Member State. The various provisions[88]

---

[84] Case 39/86 *Lair v Universität Hannover* [1988] E.C.R. 3161. See also Case C-197/86 *Brown v
Secretary of State for Scotland* [1988] E.C.R. 3205; Case C-357/89 *Raulin v Minister van
Onderwijs en Wetenschappen* [1992] E.C.R. I–1027; Case C-3/90 *Bernini v Netherlands Minstry of
Education and Science* [1992] E.C.R. I–1027.
[85] Although such link cannot be required where the migrant has involuntarily become unemployed and is obliged to undertake occupational retraining in another field of activity—Case
39/86 *Lair v Universität Hannover* [1988] E.C.R. 3161, para.37.
[86] Case 39/86 *Lair v Universität Hannover* [1988] E.C.R. 3161, para.39.
[87] Case C-43/99 *Leclere and Deaconescu v Caisse nationale des prestations familiales* [2001] E.C.R.
I–4265.
[88] Art.1(b) of Reg. 1408/71, Art.8 of Dir. 68/360, Art.2 of Reg. 1251/70, Art.2 of Dir. 75/34.

similarly define the necessary frequency of return from the state of employment to the state of residence as being "as a rule, each day or at least once a week". In *Bergemann*,[89] the ECJ refers to those who "return regularly and frequently, in other words 'daily or at least once a week' to their state of residence [as those who] may be regarded as having the status of frontier workers". This did not include a worker who "after having transferred his residence to a Member State other than the State of employment, no longer returns to that State".

(i) *The Public Service Exception*

(i) *Generally*

By Art.39(4) EC Treaty "the provisions of this article shall not apply to   **7–62**
employment in the public service". The exception protects the legitimate interest of Member States in reserving to their own nationals a range of posts connected with the exercise of powers conferred by public law and with the protection of general interests. However the scope of the exception is not so wide as to exclude *all* public service employment. Moreover, where those exercising free movement rights *are* admitted to the public service the provision cannot be used to justify discriminatory treatment (for example as regards remuneration or other conditions of employment[90]). As stated by the ECJ in *Sotgiu*[91] the very fact that they have been admitted shows that the interests which justify the exceptions to the principle of non-discrimination permitted by Art.39(4) "are not at issue".

(ii) *Scope of the Exception*

The importance of the principle that Community concepts in this field must   **7–63**
not be interpreted by reference to national concepts has already been underlined. This is particularly important in construing the scope of this exception. As stated by the ECJ in *Commission v Belgium*:[92]

"recourse to provisions of the domestic legal systems to restrict the scope of the provisions of community law would have the effect of impairing the unity and efficacy of that law and consequently cannot be accepted. That rule, which is fundamental to the existence of the community, must also apply in determining the scope and bounds of Article 48(4) of the Treaty [now Art.39(4)] ... It is necessary to ensure that the effectiveness and scope of the provisions of the Treaty on freedom of movement of workers and equality of treatment of nationals of all Member States shall not be restricted by interpretations of the concept of public service which are based on domestic law alone and which would obstruct the application of community rules".

---

[89] Case 236/87 *Bergemann v Bundesanstalt für Arbeit* [1988] E.C.R. 5125.
[90] See Case 225/85 *Commission v Italy* [1987] E.C.R. 2625.
[91] Case 152/73 *Sotgiu v Deutsche Bundespost* [1974] E.C.R. 153.
[92] Case 149/79 *Commission v Belgium No. 1* [1980] E.C.R. 3881, para.19. See similarly Case 307/84 *Commission v France* [1986] E.C.R. 1725, where the ECJ pointed out that access to certain posts may not be limited by reason of the fact that in a given Member State persons appointed to such posts have the status of civil servants since this would enable the Member States to determine at will the posts covered by the exception.

7–64 As to the actual posts removed from the ambit of Art.39(1) EC Treaty, the ECJ in *Commission v Belgium* defined them as those which involved "direct or indirect participation in the exercise of powers conferred by public law and duties designed to safeguard the general interests of the state or of other public authorities". Such posts were thought by the ECJ to presume on the part of those occupying them the existence of a "special relationship of allegiance" to the State and "reciprocity of rights and duties which form the foundation of the bond of nationality".[93]

7–65 In theory at least the application of such principles could strike a fair balance between the legitimate interest of Member States identified above and the requirement that the effectiveness and scope of the free movement provisions are not restricted by interpretations of public service based on national law. Unfortunately however the actual posts found to fall within Art.39(4) EC Treaty by the ECJ in *Commission v Belgium (No. 2)*[94] are so widely cast as to suggest that in practice the application of the principles is more difficult. Such posts are: "head technical office supervisor, principal supervisor, works supervisor, stock controller and night watchman with the municipality of Brussels and architect with the municipalities of Brussels and Auderghem". Whilst the ECJ also found that certain other jobs fell outside Art.39(4) EC Treaty (including railway shunters and signallers, drivers, plate-layers, various unskilled workers with the local railways as well as posts for hospital nurses, night-watchmen, plumbers, carpenters and electricians), it is difficult to see (for example) why a stock controller or night-watchman could be thought to be doing something which involved any special relationship of allegiance or reciprocity of rights and duties forming the foundation of the bond of nationality.

7–66 A more appropriate approach is shown by *Lawrie-Blum*[95] where the ECJ appeared concerned to limit the scope of application of Art.39(4) EC Treaty. By reference to the "fundamental principle that workers in the community should enjoy freedom of movement and not suffer discrimination" the ECJ cites the importance of construing the provision "in such a way as to limit its scope to what is strictly necessary for safeguarding the interests which that provision allows the member states to protect". Even if as argued by the German Government a trainee teacher exercises powers conferred by public law in the course of activities which contribute towards the safeguarding of the general interests of the State or of other public authorities, this did not mean that the "very strict conditions" were fulfilled in the case of a trainee teacher. In *Allue*,[96] the ECJ similarly held that employment as a foreign-language assistant at a university is not employment in the public service.

---

[93] Case 149/79 *Commission v Belgium, (No.1)* [1980] E.C.R. 3881, para.10.

[94] Case 149/79 *Commission v Belgium (No. 2)* [1982] E.C.R. 1845. When judgment was initially given on December 17, 1980 the ECJ stated (at paragraph 23) that it had insufficient information to enable "a sufficiently accurate appraisal to be made of the actual nature of the duties involved so as to make it possible to identify, in the light of the foregoing considerations , those of the posts which do not come within the concept of public service within the meaning of Article 48(4) of the Treaty [now Art.39(4)]".

[95] Case 66/85 *Lawrie-Blum v Land Baden-Württemberg* [1986] E.C.R. 2121.

[96] Case 33/88 *Alluè & Coonan v Università degli studi di Venzia* [1989] E.C.R. 1591.

CHAPTER 8

ESTABLISHMENT AND SERVICES

This chapter examines the Treaty provisions and subsidiary legislation on the freedom of establishment and the freedom to provide and receive services.

1. TREATY PROVISIONS AND SUBSIDIARY LEGISLATION ON ESTABLISHMENT

(a) *General Treaty Aims and Relationship with Provisions on Workers*

The EC Treaty contains a specific provision on the freedom of establish- **8–01**
ment in Art.43 consistent with the general aim of promoting free movement
of persons. The provision ensures that Member States accord to the nationals of other Member States the same treatment, as regards establishment, as
it accords to its own nationals:

Article 43 EC Treaty

Within the framework of the provisions set out below, restrictions on the freedom
of establishment of nationals of a Member State in the territory of another
Member State shall be prohibited. Such prohibition shall also apply to restrictions
on the setting-up of agencies, branches or subsidiaries by nationals of any Member
State established in the territory of any Member State.

Freedom of establishment shall include the right to take up and pursue activities as
self-employed persons and to set up and manage undertakings, in particular companies or firms within the meaning of the second paragraph of Article 48, under the
conditions laid down for its own nationals by the law of the country where such
establishment is effected, subject to the provisions of the chapter relating to capital.

Article 39 EC Treaty relating to workers and Art.43 EC Treaty are based on **8–02**
the same principles that the restrictions on the freedom of movement of
persons should be abolished. In this context entry into and residence in the
territory of Member States are covered by Community law.

The right of establishment contained in Art.43 EC Treaty applies to all nat- **8–03**
ural persons and to companies. The first paragraph of Art.43 EC Treaty prohibits restrictions on the freedom of establishment by nationals of a Member
State in the territory of another Member State, including the setting up of
agencies, branches or subsidiaries. The second paragraph of Art.43 EC
Treaty provides the direct right of establishment which includes the right to
take up and pursue activities as a self-employed person as well as the right to
set up and manage undertakings.

(b) *Secondary Legislation*

Directive 73/148 implements the right of establishment for nationals of **8–04**
the Member States.[1] It mirrors Regulation 1612/68 (implementing the free

---

[1] [1973] O.J. L172/14.

movement rights of workers). Regulation 73/148 also details the rights of those wish to provide services in another Member State[2] or indeed receive services in another Member State.[3] The rights of residence for the beneficiaries of Directive 73/148 are discussed in Chapter 12.

2. CONCEPT OF ESTABLISHMENT

8–05 Article 43 EC Treaty provides that the freedom of establishment includes, on the one hand, the right to take up and pursue activities as self-employed persons, and, on the other hand, the setting up and managing of undertakings. According to the ECJ:

> "The concept of establishment within the meaning of the Treaty is therefore a very broad one, allowing a Community national to participate, on a stable and continuous basis, in the economic life of a Member State other than his State of origin and to profit therefrom, so contributing to economic and social interpenetration within the Community in the sphere of activities as self-employed persons".[4]

(a) *Definition of Economic Activity*

8–06 In order to engage in the economic life of a Member State, a person or legal entity would plainly need to be engaged in economic activity within the meaning of Art.2 EC Treaty. As is the case with workers considered in Chapter 7 above, activities of those exercising the freedom of establishment must be genuine and effective rather than marginal and ancillary. Further the activities must include the provision of services in return for some form of remuneration.[5]

8–07 Consistent with the broad interpretation given to free movement rights, the ECJ has found persons to be engaged in "economic activity" in a wide variety of situations. They will include where they have been engaged in sports activities, provided that they are professional or semi-professional sportsmen in gainful employment or providing a remunerated service.[6] They will also include those who where they have carried out activities as members of a community based on religion or other form of philosophy where the services which the community provides to its members may be regarded as being an indirect remuneration for their work[7]. They will even include prostitutes, "satisfy[ing] a request by the beneficiary in return for consideration without producing or transferring material goods".[8]

---

[2] See paras 8–29 to 8–48 below.
[3] See paras 8–57 to 8–61 below. It is notable that recipient of services are not provided for in the Treaty itself.
[4] Case C-55/94 *Gebhard v Consiglio dell'Ordine degli Avvocati e Procuratori di Milano* [2001] E.C.R. I-4165, para.24.
[5] Case C-268/99 *Jany v Staatssecretaris van Justitie* [2001] E.C.R. I-8615.
[6] Case C-415/93 *Union Royal Belge des Societes de Football Association ASBL v Bosman* [1995] E.C.R. 4353, para.73.
[7] Case 196/87 *Steymann v Staatssecretaris van Justitie* [1988] E.C.R. 6159, para.13.
[8] Case C-268/99 *Jany v Staatssecretaris van Justitie* [2001] E.C.R. I-8615, para.48.

(b) *Cross-border Character*

In order to provide a Community law nexus to a situation, the activity can- **8-08**
not be purely internal, but must have a cross-border character. If there is no
element of the activity which goes beyond a purely national setting, the
provisions of Community law will not be applicable.[9]

Internal situations are discussed in Chapter 5 above. The two exceptions to **8-09**
the purely internal rule, namely those returning to their own Member State
and those with dual nationality, apply equally to establishment cases as they
do elsewhere.

In respect of returning nationals, the ECJ has confirmed that even where a **8-10**
national of a particular Member State acquires a vocational qualification in
another Member State which is recognised under Community law, that person is to be treated in accordance with the principles of Community law on
return to the state of origin.[10]

The EC Treaty provisions relating to freedom of establishment are directed **8-11**
mainly at ensuring that nationals and companies of other Member States are
not treated differently compared with own nationals and own companies in
the host Member State. However the provision are not limited to treatment
in a host Member State. Those provisions have also been interpreted as prohibiting the Member State of origin from hindering the establishment in
another Member State of one of its nationals or a company incorporated
under its legislation.[11]

(c) *Stable and Continuous Nature of Economic Activity*

According to the case law of the ECJ, the concept of establishment within the **8-12**
meaning of the EC Treaty requires the pursuit of an economic activity
through a fixed establishment in another Member State without a foreseeable
limit as to its duration.[12]

This is to be contrasted with the provision of services, which does not include **8-13**
an activity carried out on a permanent basis or, in any event, without a foreseeable limit to its duration.[13] It is thus the stable and continuous basis
on which the services are carried out in the other Member State which
distinguishes a situation of establishment from one concerned with the mere
provision of services.

However even where the activities are apparently temporary in nature, **8-14**
whether or not they constitute establishment has to be determined in the light
not only of the duration of the provision of the service, but also of its

---

[9] Case C-54/88 *Criminal Proceedings Against Eleonora Neno* [1990] E.C.R. I-3537, para.11.
[10] Case C-19/92 *Kraus v Land Baden-Wurttemberg* [1993] E.C.R. I-1663, para.15.
[11] Case C-415/93 *Union Royal Belge des Societes de Football Association ASBL v Bosman* [1995] E.C.R. 4353, para.97.
[12] Case C-221/89 *The Queen v Secretary of State for Transport Ex p. Factortame Ltd* [1991] E.C.R. I-3905, para.20.
[13] Case 196/87 *Steymann v Staatssecretaris van Justitie* [1988] E.C.R. 6159, para.16.

regularity and continuity. If carried out on a frequent basis or over a significant period of time, the provider of the services may need to obtain some form of infrastructure, such as office space, in the host Member State in order to carry out these services.[14] Obtaining permanent infrastructure would be thus regarded as establishment even if the provision of services is not continuous.

3. ESTABLISHMENT OF PERSONS

8–15 Establishment is granted to natural persons who are nationals of Member States as well as companies. The definition of an EU national for the purpose of benefiting from free movement rights is discussed in Chapter 5 above. Subject to the exceptions and conditions laid down in Art.43 EC Treaty, the Treaty provisions permit all types of self-employed activity to be taken up and pursued on the territory of any other Member State.

8–16 Self-employment is defined in Community law as existing where "economic activities are carried out by a person outside any relationship of subordination with regard to the conditions of work or remuneration and under his own personal responsibility".[15]

8–17 According to the case law of the ECJ there is nothing prevent an employee of a company in one Member State working in a self-employed capacity in another Member State.[16] Furthermore there is nothing to prevent a person being established as self-employed in two different Member States. This would be the case for example where a member of a profession establishes a second professional base in another Member State.[17]

8–18 Freedom of establishment is to be exercised under the conditions laid down for a host Member State's own nationals by the law of that Member State.[18] If own nationals do not have to have any specific qualifications in order to carry out a particular activity in a Member State, then nationals of other Member States cannot be required to comply with any additional rules or regulations in order to carry out these same activities.[19] The recognition of the qualifications obtained in other Member States is somewhat contentious and potentially stands in the way of the freedom of establishment of persons. As discussed in Chapter 12 below, it is for this reason that there are detailed Community law rules relating to the mutual recognition of qualifications and diplomas in a wide range of professional areas.

---

[14] Case C-55/94 *Gebhard v Consigol dell' Ordine degli Advocat AE Procuratori di Milano* [1995] E.C.R. I-4165, para.27.

[15] Case C-268/99 *Jany v Staatssecretaris van Justitie* [2001] E.C.R. I-8615, para.37.

[16] Case C-106/91 *Ramrath v Minister of Justice* [1992] E.C.R. I-3351, para.26.

[17] Case C-55/94 *Gebhard v Consigol dell' Ordine degli Advocat AE Procuratori di Milano* [1995] E.C.R. I-4165, para. 24.

[18] Case C-55/94 *Gebhard v Consigol dell' Ordine degli Advocat AE Procuratori di Milano* [1995] E.C.R. I-4165, para.33.

[19] Case C-55/94 *Gebhard v Consigol dell' Ordine degli Advocat AE Procuratori di Milano* [1995] E.C.R. I-4165, para.34.

As described in Chapter 7, work seekers in another Member State have free 8–19
movement rights which flow from Art.39 EC Treaty such that their right of
residence must be recognised for a reasonable period of time, and at least six
months. This principle must apply similarly to those who wish to establish
themselves in another Member State and require a period of time in order to
set themselves up.

4. ESTABLISHMENT OF COMPANIES

The right of establishment under the EC Treaty is equally provided to legal 8–20
persons, namely undertakings or companies. This is generally, although not
necessarily, exercised by the setting-up of agencies, branches or subsidiaries.
The ECJ tends to define the concept of establishment by reference to the
setting up of either undertakings or agencies somewhat interchangeably.[20]

(a) Primary Establishment—Head Office

A company's "primary establishment" is normally its head office where cen- 8–21
tralised decisions are made and where key management functions occur. In
the context of freedom of establishment a company may wish to move its
primary establishment to another Member State.

If a company is to make its primary establishment in another Member State 8–22
this would involve the transfer of central management and control of a company to another Member State. In the *Daily Mail* case, the ECJ considered
that the transfer of central management and control of a company to another
Member State could amount to establishment of the company in that second
Member State. This would be the case where the company locates its centre
of decision-making in the second Member State since this would constitute
genuine and effective economic activity.[21]

(b) Secondary Establishment—Branches, Subsidiaries and Agencies

As the ECJ has held on a number of occasions, freedom of establishment is 8–23
not confined to the right to create a single establishment within the
Community but includes the freedom to set up and maintain, subject to the
observance of professional rules of conduct, more than one place of work
within the territory of the Member States.[22]

The fact that the right of establishment for a company is capable of being 8–24
exercised by the setting up of agencies, branches or subsidiaries is supported
by the express provision to that effect in Art.43 EC Treaty. A company may

---

[20] See for instance Case 79/85 *Segers v Bestuur van de Bedrijfsvereniging voor Bank* [1986] E.C.R.
2375 and Case 270/53 *Commission v France* [1986] E.C.R. 273.
[21] Case 81/87 *The Queen v HM Treasury and Commissioners of Inland Revenue, Ex p. Daily Mail
and General Trust plc* [1988] E.C.R. 5483, para.12.
[22] See Case 107/83 *Ordre des avocats au barreau de Paris v Klopp* [1984] E.C.R. 2971; see also
Case C-53/95 *Inasti v Kemmler* [1996] E.C.R. I-703.

also exercise its right of establishment by taking part in the incorporation of a company in another Member State.[23]

(c) *Nationality of the Company*

8–25   The nationality of a company is determined by the law of the individual Member States. This is not a matter governed by Community law which at the present time does not include rules relating to the incorporation and functioning of companies. Such national laws vary greatly as regards the means of incorporation. The EC Treaty takes a flexible approach by treating all such factors which could be said to connect a company to that state as equal. Thus Community law draws no distinction between for example the registered office, central administration and principle place of business of a company. This flexibility is necessary to take account of the variety in national legislation.[24]

8–26   However there are problems which are yet to be resolved regarding the differences in national legislation concerning the factors connecting a company to a particular Member State. Such differences can result in difficulties. Where for example incorporation rules in one Member State treat the location of a company's head office as determinative of incorporation, that company might not able to establish itself in another Member State by simply moving its head office, if incorporation laws are different in that other Member State.

(d) *Nationality of the Employees*

8–28   The nationality of the employees is irrelevant to the question of the establishment of a legal person, whether it be a company or a subsidiary. However if the employees are third country nationals and the company wishes to transfer those employees on a permanent basis to a branch or subsidiary in another Member State, such transfer will be governed by national immigration laws as regards those third country nationals. As described below,[25] a company established in one Member State will have the right to 'post' a third country national employee on a temporary basis in order to perform services there. The Posted Workers Directive regulates the legal framework of such transfers as regards working conditions and applicable employment legislation to safeguard the rights of those employees.[26]

---

[23] Case 81/87 *The Queen v HM Treasury and Commissioners of Inland Revenue, Ex p. Daily Mail and General Trust plc* [1988] E.C.R. 5483, para.17.

[24] Case 81/87 *The Queen v HM Treasury and Commissioners of Inland Revenue, Ex p. Daily Mail and General Trust plc* [1988] E.C.R. 5483, para.21.

[25] At paras 8–51 to 8–57.

[26] Dir. 96/71 of the European Parliament and of the Council of December 16, 1996 concerning the posting of workers in the framework of the provision of services [1997] O.J. L18/1.

5. Treaty Provisions and Subsidiary Legislation on Service Provision and Recipients of Services

Article 49 EC Treaty

Within the framework of the provisions set out below, restrictions on freedom to provide services within the Community shall be prohibited in respect of nationals of Member States who are established in a State of the Community other than that of the person for whom the services are intended.

The Council may, acting by a qualified majority on a proposal from the Commission, extend the provisions of the Chapter to nationals of a third country who provide services and who are established within the Community.

Article 50 EC Treaty

Services shall be considered to be "services" within the meaning of this Treaty where they are normally provided for remuneration, in so far as they are not governed by the provisions relating to freedom of movement for goods, capital and persons. "Services" shall in particular include:

(a) activities of an industrial character;
(b) activities of a commercial character;
(c) activities of craftsmen;
(d) activities of the professions.

Without prejudice to the provisions of the chapter relating to the right of establishment, the person providing a service may, in order to do so, temporarily pursue his activity in the State where the service is provided, under the same conditions as are imposed by that State on its own nationals.

(a) *General Treaty Aims and Relationship with Establishment Provisions*

The situation of a Community national who moves to another Member State in order to pursue an economic activity there is governed by the Treaty provisions on free movement of workers, the right of establishment or the provision of services. The ECJ has described them as mutually exclusive.[27] The EC Treaty provides that persons or companies established in one Member State should be able to provide their services in other Member States.

8–29

The ECJ considers that the provisions in the EC Treaty relating to the provision of services are subordinate to those relating to the right of establishment.[28] The first paragraph of Art.50 EC Treaty makes clear that a person will only fall within the scope of the provisions relating to services if he is not governed by the provisions relating to freedom of movement for goods, capital and persons. According to the ECJ within the context of Title III of the EC Treaty ("free movement of persons, services and capital"), the free movement of persons includes the movement of workers within the Community and

8–30

---

[27] Case C-55/94 *Gebhard v Consigol dell' Ordine degli Advocat AE Procuratori di Milano* [1995] E.C.R. I-4165, para.20.
[28] Case C-55/94 *Gebhard v Consigol dell' Ordine degli Advocat AE Procuratori di Milano* [1995] E.C.R. I-4165, para.22.

freedom of establishment within the territory of the Member States.[29] If person falls within the scope of the Treaty provisions relating to establishment he will be precluded from benefiting from the provisions relating to the provision of services.[30]

8–31   It is often advantageous for persons providing services in another Member State to characterise their activities as "provision of services" as opposed to "establishment" since this might avoid professional rules of conduct which would be applicable if they were established within that state. Thus for example the architect travelling to another Member State to advise on the completion of a building project will likely avoid having to comply with the rules of any professional body governing the conduct of architects in that second Member State by merely providing services on a temporary basis. Community law does not prevent a Member State from adopting measures to ensure a person who is directing his services principally towards that Member State from circumventing its laws relating to establishment. In the case of dispute as to the legality of such measures, they fall to be determined in accordance with Art.43 EC Treaty relating to establishment.

8–32   There are four basic conditions to be met for a person or company to benefit from the Community law provisions relating to service provision. Firstly the service provision must be a form of economic activity. Secondly, there must be a cross-border element in that the service provider should be established in one Member State and providing services in another Member State. Thirdly, the service provision must be of a temporary nature. Finally the service provider, if a natural person, must be an EU national and, if a company, must be incorporated under the legislation of a Member State. These conditions are considered in detail below.[31]

(b) *Articles 49 to 55 EC Treaty*

8–33   Article 49 EC Treaty prohibits the restriction on the right of freedom of movement in order to provide services. The wording of Art.49 EC Treaty assumes that the provider and the recipient of the service are "established" in two different Member States.[32] Article 55 makes clear that the provisions of Art.45 to 48 EC Treaty are extended to the provisions on the provision of services. Through Art.48 EC Treaty the right to freedom of movement in order to provide services is extended to companies.

8–34   Article 50 EC Treaty provides that the person providing a service may temporarily pursue his activity in the host Member State, on the same conditions as own nationals are permitted to provide services.

---

[29] Joined Cases C-286/82 & 26/83 *Luisi and Carbone v Minstero del Tesoro* [1984] E.C.R. 377, para.9.
[30] Case C-55/94 *Gebhard v Consigol dell' Ordine degli Advocat AE Procuratori di Milano* [1995] E.C.R. I-4165, para.22.
[31] See paras 8–38 to 8–48.
[32] Case C-55/94 *Gebhard v Consigol dell' Ordine degli Advocat AE Procuratori di Milano* [1995] E.C.R. I-4165, para.22.

(c) *Secondary Legislation—Directive 73/148*

Directive 73/148[33] is the implementing directive for the EC Treaty provisions **8–35** relating to the free movement of persons for the purpose of establishment as well as free movement for the purposes of provision of services. As with the freedom of establishment, the Directive makes clear that the freedom to provide services in another Member State includes the right to leave the Member State of origin, to enter the other Member State and to reside there. However unlike establishment, where the right of residence is continuous and permanent, service providers only obtain the right of residence as long as they continue to provide those services.[34]

The Directive is significant because it takes the EC Treaty provisions a step further than the strict wording of those provisions might suggest. As the preamble **8–36** to the Directive makes clear the "freedom to provide services entails that persons provide and *receiving services* should have the right of residence for the time during which the services are being provided."[35] As discussed below[36] those who wish to receive services are given the right to enter the territory of another Member State and reside there for so long as there are receiving services.

Service providers and recipients are not defined by the Directive and thus the **8–37** general Community law definition of service provision applies.

The Directive only covers the situation of natural persons who are recipients and providers of services in another Member State. It does not cover the situation of employees of companies established in one Member State wishing to provide services in another Member State. The conditions relating to the entry and residence of those "posted" employees are discussed below.[37]

6. SERVICE PROVIDERS

(a) *Economic Activity*

The first paragraph of Art.50 EC Treaty provides that activities are to be considered "services" within the meaning of the chapter on services in the EC **8–38** Treaty where they are normally provided for remuneration. Whilst Art.50 EC Treaty expressly states that "services" include four types of activity this list is not exhaustive and indeed any activity which is economic in character would fulfil the requirements of Art.50.

---

[33] Council Dir. 73/148 of May 21, 1973 on the abolition of restrictions on movement and residence within the Community for nationals of Member States with regard to establishment and services [1973] O.J. L-172/14.
[34] See Chapter 12 on right of residence.
[35] Emphasis added.
[36] See paras 8–57 to 8–61.
[37] See paras 8–51 to 8–56.

Service provision will fall within the scope of the EC Treaty where the specific activity is one which is normally provided for remuneration. The essential characteristic of remuneration is that it constitutes consideration for the service in question, and is normally agreed upon between the provider and recipient of the service. Where there is no remuneration for the service, it will not fulfil the conditions in the EC Treaty. Thus provision of state education or state-provided health services would not constitute service provision within the meaning of the EC Treaty.

8–39   In *Humbel*,[38] the ECJ considered whether the position of state education constituted service provision. The ECJ held that the essential characteristic of economic activity was not fulfilled. This was because the state was not seeking to engage in gainful economic activity but it was fulfilling social and cultural obligations. Secondly, the state education system is in general funded from the public purse and not by the pupils or their carers. However state education is to be distinguished from private education, which is capable of fulfilling the economic activity condition since it is aimed at producing a commercial benefit.[39]

8–40   The fact that a service provides entertainment or recreation to the recipient does not deprive it of its economic character, nor does the fact that profits made are for charity or public benefit. In this context in the case of *Schindler*[40] the ECJ considered that running a lottery could constitute service provision within the meaning of the EC Treaty. It held that the entertainment or recreational nature of a lottery did not take it outside the scope of the provision of services, nor did the fact that in most Member States the profits made from lotteries could be used only for certain public interest purposes.

8–41   The condition that the service is normally provided for remuneration is not a requirement that the service is paid for by those for whom it is performed. For instance in *Bond van Adverteerders*[41] the ECJ considered that services provided by cable network operators were capable of falling within the EC Treaty provisions relating to services. This was despite the fact that the service that they provide to broadcasters, namely relaying their programmes, are not generally paid for by the broadcasters themselves but by their subscribers.

(b) *Cross-border Element*

8–42   The ECJ has consistently held that the provisions of the EC Treaty on freedom to provide services cannot apply to activities all of which are confined within one Member State. As with the EC Treaty provisions relating to free movement of persons and the freedom of establishment, those relating to the free movement of services do not apply to purely internal situations in a Member State.[42] Thus there must be a cross-border element to the provision of services.

---

[38] Case C-263/86 *Belgium v Humbel and Adele* [1988] E.C.R. 5365, paras 17–19.
[39] Case C-109/92 *Wirth v Landefhauptstadt Hannover* [1993] E.C.R. I-6447.
[40] Case C-275/92 *HM Customs and Excise v Schindler* [1994] E.C.R. I-1039.
[41] Case C-352/85 *Bond van Aderteerders v Netherlands State* [1988] E.C.R. 2085, para.16.
[42] Case C-3/95 *Reiseburo Broede v Sandke* [1996] E.C.R. I-6511; Case C-17/94 *Gervais* [1995] E.C.R. I-4353.

However the requirement of the cross-border element can be satisfied with-   **8–43**
out the person or company's physically moving across the border to provide
the service. The offer of services by telephone to potential recipients in other
Member States, for instance, and the provision of those services without
actually moving from the Member State in which the provider is established,
will fall within the scope of the EC Treaty.[43]

Further the condition of the cross-border element may be fulfilled by either   **8–44**
the provider or the recipient of the service moving across a border. Article 49
EC Treaty is aimed at abolishing restrictions on freedom to provide services
by nationals established in one Member State to persons established in other
Member States. It may be that in order for those services to be provided, the
provider of services would go to the Member State where the recipient of the
service is established or the recipient of the service would go to the Member
State where the provider of the service is established.[44]

(c) Temporary Character

Except where the person or company is established, service provision is con-   **8–45**
cerned with the *temporary* pursuit of economic activity in a state. The emphasis on temporary for the purposes of the service provisions in the EC Treaty
means that not every cross-border provision of services will fall within the
scope of Art.49 EC Treaty. Where a person has a stable and permanent establishment in both the Member States concerned, only Art.43 EC Treaty concerning the right of establishment is relevant.[45] An activity carried out on a
permanent basis, or in any event without a foreseeable limit to its duration
does not fall within the scope of the EC Treaty provisions relating to services.

The ECJ has held that the temporary nature of the provision of services   **8–46**
is to be determined in light of its "duration, regularity, periodicity and
continuity".[46]

(d) Nationality of Natural Persons

In order to benefit from the EC Treaty provisions relating to provision of   **8–47**
services and the secondary legislation giving effect those provisions, the service provider must be an EU national. The beneficiaries of free movement
provisions are considered in Chapter 5.

In *Svensson*,[47] the ECJ held the nationality of the intended recipient of the   **8–48**
services to be irrelevant to the application of the EC Treaty provisions on
services. According to Art.49 EC Treaty the requirement is only that the
recipient is established in another Member State. Although the judgment is

---

[43] Case C-384/93 *Alpine Investments BV v Minister van Financien* [1995] E.C.R. I-1141.
[44] Joined Cases C-286/82 & 26/83 *Luisi and Carbone v Minstero del Tesoro* [1984] E.C.R. 377.
[45] Case C-53/95 *Inasti v Kemmler* [1996] E.C.R. I-703, para.8.
[46] Case C-55/94 *Gebhard v Consigol dell' Ordine degli Advocat AE Procuratori di Milano* [1995]
E.C.R. I-4165, para.39.
[47] Case C-484/93 *Svensson and Gustavsson v Ministre du Logement et de L'Urganisme* [1995]
E.C.R. I-3955.

somewhat unclear, the nationality of the intended recipient is only relevant when examining the rights of the recipient. However this does not confer a free movement right on a third country national recipient of services since the beneficiaries of Directive 73/148 extending the right of entry and residence to recipients of services apply to EU nationals only.[48]

7. COMPANIES AS SERVICE PROVIDERS

(a) *Nationality of Company*

8–49   Article 55 EC Treaty applies the provisions relating to establishment contained in Arts 45 to 48 EC Treaty to service provision. This has the consequence that companies established in one Member State benefit from the freedom to provide services in another. The nationality of a company is discussed in detail above.[49] The essential requirement is that the company is established and incorporated in a Member State. Under the EC Treaty provisions on services as extended to companies it is the freedom to provide services in other Member States, in addition to setting up secondary establishments there,[50] which is of principal interest.

8–50   It can be difficult to distinguish between the provision of services by a company on the one hand and the creation of a secondary establishment by such company on the other. However it will be the temporary nature of the provision of services that will bring the company's activities within the scope of the EC Treaty provisions on services. Where a company obtains infrastructure such as office space in another Member State this will tend to suggest more permanent establishment with the consequence that the activity will likely fall within the scope of the establishment provisions in the EC Treaty rather than the service provisions.

(b) *Personnel of Company*

8–51   It is not a requirement of the EC Treaty provisions that the employees of the company providing the services are EU nationals. If they are EU nationals then they may benefit from a free movement right under Treaty provisions themselves and gain a right of entry and residence in other Member States as workers under Regulation 1612/68. However, the significance of the provisions relating to services under the EC Treaty is that companies which transfer employees who are third country nationals are entitled to do so as a matter of Community law.

8–52   Employees who are transferred to another Member State for the purpose of providing a service in that State on behalf of a company are known as "posted workers". In a landmark decision in the case of *Rush Portuguese*,[51]

---

[48] See below at para.8–58.
[49] See paras 8–25 to 8–27.
[50] See paras 8–23 to 8–24 on secondary establishments above.
[51] Case C-113/89 *Rush Portuguesa Lda v ONI* [1990] E.C.R. I-1417.

the ECJ held that a company established in one Member State is entitled to transfer its third country national workforce to another Member State for the duration of a project to be carried out there.

Rush Portuguese was a building works company with its registered office in **8-53** Portugal. It entered into a sub-contract with a French company for works to be carried out on several different sites in France. In order to carry out the contract *Rush Portuguese* transferred some of its Portuguese work force to France. The case occurred during the transitional period of Portuguese membership of the European Community and therefore Portuguese workers were not able to rely on free movement rights during that time.[52] The French authorities therefore required that *Rush Portuguese* employees obtained work permits. However *Rush Portuguese* could still rely on Art.49 EC Treaty because the transitional provisions applied only to derogation from Regulation 1612/68 relating to access to the labour force for workers.[53] The ECJ held that Arts 49 and 50 EC Treaty meant that a company established in Portugal and providing services in the construction industry in France must be able to move its own work force from Portugal for the duration of the contract. The French authorities were thus not permitted to impose conditions such as the obtaining of work permits on the *Rush Portuguese* work force.

Although *Rush Portuguese* occurred during the transitional period of **8-54** Portugal's entry to the Community, the principles established in it apply to any company registered in a Member State wishing to provide services in another Member State. This right to post workers belongs to the company and not the employee. It is dependent on the employee being posted by the company to another Member State to fulfil a contract.

The ECJ judgment in *Vander Elst*[54] makes clear that it is a condition precedent **8-55** to the application of the principle that the employee can move under the umbrella of the service providing company that the employee should have been lawfully and "habitually employed" by that company prior to being posted (although not necessarily in another Member State[55]). The nationality of the employee is irrelevant. In *Vander Elst* the employer was established in Belgium as a specialist demolition business. Some of his employees were Moroccan nationals who were legally resident and permitted to work in Belgium. The employer sent Belgian and Moroccan staff to fulfil a contract on a demolition

---

[52] For further discussion about transititional provisions on accession see Chapter 6.
[53] The same derogation applies as regards the 10 new Member States who joined the EU with effect from May 1, 2004. See Chapter 6.
[54] Case C-43/93 *Vander Elst v Office des Migrations Internationales*, judgment of August 9, 1994, not yet reported.
[55] On the facts of both *Vander Elst* and *Rush Portuguesa* the employees had been employed in the Member State in which their employers were established. However the test of "habitual employment" could be satisfied if the posted worker had been previously employed by the company in one of its branch in a non-E.U. Member State providing that the company itself is established in a Member State (other than the Member State to which the worker is to be posted). However more difficult is the question of how long an employee must work for the employer prior to posting in order to be regarded as being in "habitual employment". This will turn on the facts of each case and depend on various factors including importantly the terms of the employment contract and the length of time for the employee has been employed. It is suggested that the test could be satisfied in a matter of months.

site in France. The French authorities stated that the Moroccans required work permits. The ECJ held that the requirement to obtain a work permit in such situation went beyond the permissible restrictions on service provision under the EC Treaty. The ECJ considered that work permits are intended to regulate access to the French labour market and are not necessary therefore for employees of a company who would be temporarily present only and who would return to the home state of the company on completion of the work.

8–56 Following the ECJ's decisions in *Rush Portuguese* and *Vander Elst*, the Posted Workers Directive[56] was adopted in 1996. The objective of the Directive is to avoid social dumping between companies from the various Member States and to ensure that minimum rights are guaranteed for workers posted by their employers to work in another Member State. The basic principle is that working conditions and pay in a Member State should be applicable both to workers from that State, and those from other Member States posted to work there. The Directive covers undertakings established in a Member State which, in the framework of the trans-national provision of services, posts workers to the territory of another Member State. It does not, however, set out the rights of companies to move staff, or the entry or residence conditions that apply to such workers. These are taken from the guidelines of the ECJ in the two landmark cases.[57]

8. RECIPIENTS OF SERVICES

(a) *Concept of Recipients of Services*

8–57 As outlined above Directive 73/148 includes within its scope the recipients as well as the providers of services. EU nationals have the right to enter the territory of other Member States in the exercise of the freedom to provide services which "is enjoyed both by providers and by recipients of services".[58] In order to enable services to be provided, the person providing the service may go to the Member State where the recipient is established. Alternatively, the recipient may go to the Member State in which the provider of the service is established in order to receive the service. The movement of the service provider to another Member State is expressly provided for in Art.50 EC Treaty. However the ECJ has held that the movement of the recipient of services is a "necessary corollary" of the right contained in Art.50 EC Treaty "which fulfils the objective of liberalising all gainful activity not covered by the free movement of goods, person and capital".[59]

---

[56] Dir.96/71 concerning the posting of workers in the framework of the provision of services [1997] O.J. L18/1.
[57] See Chapter 12.
[58] Case C-43/93 *Vander Elst v Office des Migrations Internationales*, judgment of August 9, 1994, not yet reported, para.13.
[59] Joined Cases C-286/82 & 26/83 *Luisi and Carbone v Minstero del Tesoro* [1984] E.C.R. 377.

(b) *Personal Scope of Recipients of Services*

In order to obtain the right of entry and residence provided for in Directive   **8–58**
73/148 and the protection against discrimination envisaged by the Treaty, the
recipient of services must be an EU national or the family member of such a
person. The Directive itself is quite clear on this issue[60] and the ECJ has never
extended free movement rights to third country nationals (other than as
family members) under Title III.

The risk of ambiguity lies in the fact that the nationality of the recipient of   **8–59**
services is not relevant if it is the *provider's* rights that are under consideration, since those rights are only dependant on the provider of services
providing them to a person established in another Member State[61] (the
nationality of the recipient being irrelevant).

There is no restriction on the type of services that the recipient should be   **8–60**
travelling to receive in the other Member State. In the case of *Luisi and
Carbone*[62] the ECJ held that tourists, persons receiving medical treatment and
persons travelling for the purposes of education or business are to be
regarded as recipients of services. In *Bickel and Franz*[63] the ECJ reiterated
that a person visiting another Member State falls within the scope of Art.59
EC Treaty on the following grounds:

> "Article 59 [now Art.49] therefore covers all nationals of Member States who, inde-
> pendently of freedoms guaranteed by the Treaty, visit another Member State where
> they *intend or are likely to receive services*".

The ECJ's statement would appear to negate any need for a visitor to establish the particular services that will be received in the course of any visit.

Finally since an essential element of service provision is remuneration, a per-   **8–61**
son will not be regarded as a recipient of services unless the service which is
being received is paid for. Such payment need not be made by the recipient
directly. However, in *Humbel*, the ECJ held that state school education did
not fulfil the requirements of the EC Treaty since it was not "normally for
remuneration", even if parents do make some financial contribution to the
school.[64]

---

[60] Art. 1. See above at para. 8–48
[61] See paras 8–42 to 8–44 above.
[62] Joined Cases C-286/82 & 26/83 *Luisi and Carbone v Minstero del Tesoro* [1984] E.C.R. 377.
[63] Case C-274/96 *Bickel and Franz* [1998] E.C.R. I-7637.
[64] Case C-263/86 *Belgium v Humbel* [1988] E.C.R. 5365. See para. 8–39 above.

THE ECONOMICALLY INACTIVE

This chapter considers the position of those who exercise their right to free movement without engaging in economic activity. Three categories are considered: the self-sufficient person exercising a general right of residence; the retired person and the student. Each category is dealt with specifically in secondary legislation. Together these free movers are referred to as the economically inactive.

1. INTRODUCTION: BEYOND THE ECONOMICALLY ACTIVE

The foundations of the European Economic Community as reflected by the Treaty of Rome were principally concerned with the free movement of persons who wished to further the aim of the EEC through economic activity. Thus the Treaty itself only referred to free movement rights for workers and the self-employed. Secondary legislation gave effect those free movement rights.[1]   **9–01**

In 1979 the Commission first put forward a proposal to extend the right of residence to other categories of person who were not engaged in any economic activity.[2] Ten years later the original proposal culminated in the adoption by the European Council on June 28, 1990 of Directives 90/364 on the right of residence, 90/365 on the right of residence of employees and self-employed persons who have ceased their occupational activity and 90/366 on the right of residence for students.[3]   **9–02**

This extension in secondary legislation of the categories of persons entitled to the right of residence has been formally enshrined at EC Treaty level with the insertion of Art.8a into the Maastricht Treaty (now Art.18 EC Treaty), which states that "every citizen of the Union shall have the right to . . . reside freely within the territory of the Member States, subject to the limitations and conditions laid down in this Treaty and by the measures adopted to give it effect."   **9–03**

Indeed as the European Commission points out whilst the right of a national of a Member State to reside in the territory of another Member State of the European Community was originally subject to that person engaging in an economic activity in that State: **9–04**

> "such a state of affairs could not be allowed to continue indefinitely, because it did not fully comply with one of the objectives laid down in Article 3c of the Treaty of Rome ('the abolition, as between Member States, of obstacles to the free movement

---

[1] Reg. 1612/68, Dirs 68/360, 64/221, 73/148.
[2] The background is discussed further in Chapter 4.
[3] This was later replaced by Dir. 93/96.

of ... persons'), nor did it meet the political aspiration expressed at the Paris Summit in 1974 to move towards a 'citizens' Europe'".

9–05 Prior to the legislative extension of free movement rights to the economically inactive, the ECJ had in fact already begun to recognise their rights, particularly where students were concerned. In 1985 the ECJ considered that the mobility of students for vocational training was so important to the aims of the Treaty that, despite the fact that a student did not satisfy the requirements of existing free movement legislation in so far as she could not be considered a worker, such a person should fall within the scope of the Treaty.[4]

2. GENERAL REQUIREMENTS OF THE PROVISIONS RELATING TO THE ECONOMICALLY INACTIVE

9–06 As discussed in Chapter 4, Art.18 EU Treaty grants to all EU nationals the right to move and reside in other Member States. However the provision makes such right subject to the limitations and conditions laid down in the EC Treaty and secondary legislation. The secondary legislation concerning the economically inactive includes an express condition regarding self-sufficiency which makes clear that a person wishing to exercise the right to move as an economically inactive person must be self-sufficient. Furthermore such a person is required to obtain sickness insurance for all risks.

9–07 As discussed in Chapter 4 in detail the extent to which the limitations and conditions contained this secondary legislation can be maintained following inclusion of Art.18 in the EC Treaty is continually evolving.

9–08 The decisions of the ECJ in the cases of *Baumbast*[5] and *Grzelczy*[6] make clear that the limitations and conditions placed on the economically inactive remain relevant and have not been made entirely redundant by Art.18 EU Treaty. However, the ECJ has categorically rejected the suggestion that failure to meet all the conditions laid down in the legislation relating to the economically inactive should automatically lead to the end of the right of residence. The conditions laid down in the Directives therefore cannot be treated as absolutes that must be strictly met at all times by all beneficiaries of the Directives.

9–09 In *Grzelczyk*,[7] for instance, the ECJ recognised that a Member State could conclude that a student applying for social assistance no longer met the conditions to which his right of residence was subject and could accordingly require him to leave. However, the ECJ held that such a decision must be made "within the limits imposed by Community law" and that "in no case

---

[4] Case 293/83 *Gravier v City of Liege* [1985] E.C.R. 593.
[5] Case C–413/99 *Baumbast and R. v the Secretary of State for the Home Department* [2002] E.C.R. I–7091.
[6] Case C–184/99 *Grzelczyk v Centre Public d'Aide Sociale d'Ottignies-Louvain-la-Neuve* [2001] E.C.R. I-6193.
[7] Case C–184/99 *Grzelczyk v Centre Public d'Aide Sociale d'Ottignies-Louvain-la-Neuve* [2001] E.C.R. I-6193.

may such measures become the automatic consequence of a student who is a national of another Member State having recourse to the host Member State's social assistance system".

In *Baumbast*[8] the ECJ was referred a question by an English tribunal about the right of residence of an EU national who had not met the requirement in Directive 90/364 to have sickness insurance for all risks. The ECJ concluded that it would be a disproportionate interference with the exercise of the right of residence for the host Member State to withhold a residence permit on the ground that the healthcare insurance of the person concerned did not cover emergency treatment. The ECJ held that any decision about withholding a residence permit must be made in compliance with the limits imposed by Community law and in accordance with the general principles of Community law, in particular the proportionality principle.   **9–10**

At the present stage of development of Community law the inclusion of Art.18 EC Treaty has not abolished all limitations or conditions on the freedom of movement. However the application of any such limitations or conditions is subject to the general principles of Community law and furthermore to judicial review. The principle of proportionality and the language of the directives for the economically inactive permit Member States to ensure that the beneficiaries do not become "unreasonable burdens". However Member States must accept a "certain degree of financial solidarity between nationals of a host Member State and nationals of other Member States, particularly if the difficulties which a beneficiary of the right of residence encounters are temporary".[9]   **9–11**

(a) *The Concept of Self-sufficiency*

(i) *Directives 90/364 and 90/365*

The concept of self-sufficiency is to some extent explained in the relevant directives themselves. As Art.1(1) of Directive 90/365 on retired persons makes clear, persons are deemed to be self-sufficient if their resources are "higher than the level of resources below which the host Member State may grant social assistance to its nationals." This naturally makes the level of resources required variable from one Member State to another since levels at which social assistance is granted is not uniform across the Member States. This lack of uniformity is not surprising in the light of both the lack of social security harmonisation at EU level[10] and the variable cost of living across the Member States. The wording is exactly the same in Directive 90/364 on the general right of residence.   **9–12**

---

[8] Case C–413/99 *Baumbast and R. v the Secretary of State for the Home Department* [2002] E.C.R. I–7091.
[9] Case C–184/99 *Grzelczyk v Centre Public d'Aide Sociale d'Ottignies-Louvain-la-Neuve* [2001] E.C.R. I-6193, para.44.
[10] For further discussion see Chapter 13.

9–13   If a beneficiary of either Directive is accompanied by one or more family members, Member States have the right to require that the amount of family resources must be higher than where one person alone seeks the benefit of the directive.[11]

9–14   In *Commission v Italy*[12] the ECJ considered a situation where Italy granted more favourable treatment to persons who had previously been gainfully employed falling within the scope of Directive 90/365 (retired persons) than to beneficiaries of Directive 90/364 (the general right of residence). Italy had required the families of those falling within the general right of residence Directive to demonstrate that they had more resources than families falling within the retired persons Directive.[13] Overruling the Commission, the ECJ held that this differentiation was permissible since Member States have a degree of discretion in setting the amounts required. According to the ECJ the higher amount required for those falling within the general right of residence was not excessive. This is a surprising decision in view of the principle of equal treatment. Although considered by the ECJ to be justified, the decision is arguably wrong. The ECJ considered that the difference was permissible, based on its view that the Member State had not exceeded its "latitude" in having in place a regime that is more favourable to the family members of retired persons than to the beneficiaries of Directive 90/364. However, at issue under both Directives is the same question: are resources sufficient to avoid the person becoming a burden on the host Member State's social security system. It is impossible to see how the sufficiency of resources can vary as between different groups of people. The "latitude" to be given to a Member State must relate to that state's assessment of the necessary level of resources for anyone to survive in their state. There is no reason why that assessment should differ as between either Directive's beneficiaries.

9–15   The Commission remains of the view that there is no general principle that Member States are free to fix different amounts of sufficient resources for the beneficiaries of the two Directives.[14] This particular problem would appear presently to be purely theoretical, as the only Member State which provided for differentiation was Italy. Italy amended its legislation to abolish the differentiation before the ECJ gave judgment.

9–16   Neither Directive 90/364 nor Directive 90/365 specify what the source of the resources referred to therein might be. Indeed resources could come from the income of a spouse or child accompanying the EU national or indeed from any other family member, whether accompanying the EU national or not. The accompanying spouse and dependent children are entitled to take up employment or self-employment in the host Member State even where they

---

[11] This applies similarly to those seeking to benefit from Dir. 90/364
[12] Case C–424/98 *Commission v Italy* [2000] E.C.R. I-4001.
[13] The Commission has understood the different level of resources required to be one third more. According to the ECJ, this calculation by the Commission was wrong. Italian legislation in fact required resources three times higher in respect of beneficiaries of Dir. 90/364. See Case C-424/98 *Commission v Italy* [2000] E.C.R. I-4001, para.22.
[14] Second Commission Report to the Council and Parliament on the implementation of Directives 90/364, 90/365 and 93/96 (right of residence), COM (2003) 101 final, March 5, 2003.

are not EU nationals. The income derived from such activity can be included in considering the resources of the family as a whole.

The Commission has taken issue with a number of Member States which 9–17
have required that the EU national has sufficient resources of his own or originating only from a spouse or a child.[15] The Commission considers that this adds a supplementary condition to the Directives that does not exist on the face of the Directives. The Commission considers that this is contrary to those Directives which do not exclude the possibility of sufficient resources coming from a third person such as a parent or unmarried partner.

One Member State, Sweden, even went so far as to require that the sufficient 9–18
resources be personal to the EU national and that such requirement could not be satisfied by reference to the resources provided by any family member, whether a spouse or child, or any other third party. Following intervention by the Commission, Sweden removed this condition from its legislation.[16]

(ii) *Directive 93/96*

The concept of self-sufficiency for students is articulated differently in Art.1 9–19
of Directive 93/96. This provision, as with Directives 90/364 and 90/365, refers expressly to the requirement that resources are sufficient to avoid the student becoming a burden on the social assistance system of the host Member State during the period of residence. However there is no express reference to the level of resources which are deemed sufficient. Despite this it is difficult to imagine the application of a different test from that contained in Directives 90/364 and 90/365 could be justified.

There is a further difference between Directives 90/364, Directive 90/365 and 9–20
Directive 93/96. Whereas in the former Directives the beneficiaries are required to *have* the relevant resources, students need only *assure* the relevant authorities that they have sufficient resources by means "of a declaration or by such alternative means as the student may chose that are at least equivalent".[17]

(b) *Sickness Insurance*

All three Directives relating to the economically inactive refer to the require- 9–21
ment that the EU nationals themselves and their families are covered by sickness insurance in respect of *all* risks in the host Member State. Neither the exact form that this sickness insurance should take nor the meaning of "all" risks is specified. However, a form of sickness insurance which provides cover for *general* health risks should suffice, particularly when it is borne in mind that emergency treatment will be covered by Art.19 of Reg. 1408/71.[18] This interpretation is supported by the ECJ in *Baumbast*.[19]

---

[15] By issuing reasoned opinions, prior to taking action before the ECJ, Second Commission Report to the Council and Parliament on the implementation of Directives 90/364, 90/365 and 93/96 (right of residence), COM (2003) 101 final, p.12. See now decision of the ECJ in Case 200/02 *Man Lavette Chen and Kunqian Catherine Zhu v Secretary of State for the Home Department*, October 19, 2004.
[16] See Case C–424/98 *Commission v Italy* [2000] E.C.R. I–4001.
[17] See further Chapter 11.
[18] See Chapter 13.
[19] Case C–413/99 *Baumbast and R. v the Secretary of State for the Home Department* [2002] E.C.R. I–7091.

9–22   Under the reciprocal arrangements for the provision of health care contained in Reg. 1408/71, the beneficiaries of that Regulation are guaranteed the right to receive sickness benefits in kind provided by the institution of Member State of residence at the expense of the Member State of origin. The beneficiaries include workers and those who were in employment previously. In these circumstances it would be unnecessary for the beneficiaries of the Regulation to obtain the sickness insurance required by the Directives on economically inactive persons.[20]

For those who do not benefit from Reg. 1408/71, there would be a need to obtain sickness insurance. However, a failure to obtain a sickness insurance which covers *all* risks could not automatically result in the denial of the right of residence since such a result could "amount to a disproportional interference with the exercise of that right".[21]

3. DIRECTIVE 90/364 (THE GENERAL RIGHT OF RESIDENCE)

9–23   In order to enjoy the general right of residence as a self-sufficient economically inactive persons, Union citizens need only demonstrate that they have sufficient resources to avoid becoming a burden on the social assistance system of the host Member State and sickness insurance.

9–24   Directive 90/364, which introduced the general right of residence for the economically self-sufficient but inactive, was intended to provide those EU nationals who were not covered by the provisions of any other Treaty provision or secondary legislation with rights of residence. The Directive's implementation has been both largely successful in the Member States and non-contentious.

4. DIRECTIVE 90/365 (THE RETIRED PERSON)

9–25   There are two categories of retired person covered by Community law. The first category includes persons who have reached retirement age in a host Member State having been a worker or self-employed person in that state for the preceding 12 months having resided in that state continuously for at least three years. This category of retired person is dealt with in detail in Chapter 11.

9–26   The second category includes persons who have ceased their economic activity either as employed or self-employed persons, but who may not have resided in the territory of another Member State before retirement. Such persons are covered by Directive 90/365. In order to qualify for the right of

---

[20] Art. 19(1) of Reg. 1408/71 provides for the repayment of health care costs by the member State of origin to the host Member State. See Case C–413/99 *Baumbast and R. v the Secretary of State for the Home Department* [2002] E.C.R. I–7091.

[21] Case C-413/99 *Baumbast and R. v The Secretary for the Home Department* [2002] E.C.R. I-7091, para.93. See also discussion in paras 9–07 to 9–10 above.

residence they must be in receipt of an invalidity or early retirement pension, or old age benefit or of a pension in respect of an industrial accident or disease.

The amount such persons receive through these benefits must be sufficient to 9–27 avoid their becoming a burden on the social security system of the host Member State. They must also be covered by sickness insurance in respect of all risks in the host Member State.[22]

This right of residence is obviously very beneficial to those EU nationals and 9–28 their family members who have retired and who wish to enjoy their retirement away from their own Member State. It is most advantageous to those EU nationals in receipt of benefits from Member States where the rates of benefit are relatively high and who wish to move to a Member State where the cost of living is low. In contrast EU nationals in receipt of benefits from a Member State where such benefit rates are relatively low, may find it difficult to fulfil the requirements of the Directive if they move to a state where the cost of living is high.

However it is arguable that it would be entirely contrary to the aims of the 9–29 Directive, namely to encourage the free movement of the retired, if in such circumstances the difference in benefit levels was able to prevent the exercise of free movement rights by nationals of certain Member States, particularly if the difference is marginal or temporary. It is to be noted that the preamble to the Directive refers to the fact that beneficiaries of the right of residence under the Directive must not become "an unreasonable burden" on the public finances of the host Member State—a term that must be interpreted consistently with the principle of proportionality.[23]

5. STUDENTS

(a) *Generally*

Secondary legislation relating to workers provides for two categories of per- 9–30 sons who enjoy educational rights: children of workers[24] and workers themselves who enter into vocational training.[25] Furthermore Directive 93/96 provides the right of residence for students who fall outside the ambit of the two provisions relating to workers.[26] This section examines both those students falling under Directive 93/96 and those whose rights flow from other provisions of Community law.

Even before Directive 93/96 was adopted, the ECJ had recognised a right of 9–31 residence for students who wished to enter into vocational training in another

---

[22] As to the meaning of "all" risks, see paras 9–21 to 9–22.
[23] Case C–413/99 *Baumbast and R. v the Secretary of State for the Home Department* [2002] E.C.R. I–7091, para.91.
[24] Art. 12 of Reg. 1612/68.
[25] Art. 7(3) of Reg. 1612/68.
[26] See paras 9–43 to 9–48.

Member State more generally than in the circumstances provided for in Regulation 1612/68. In *Gravier*,[27] a French student in Belgium challenged the requirement of an enrolment fee for non-Belgians. She had no family members in Belgium and thus no rights of residence there, apart from her claim as a student to such a right. The ECJ stated:

"Article 128 of the Treaty [now Art.150] provides that the Council is to lay down general principles for implementing a common vocational training policy capable of contribution to the harmonious development both of the national economies and of the common market . . . It constitutes, moreover, an indispensable element of the activities of the Community, whose objectives include, *inter alia*, the free movement of persons, the mobility of labour, and the improvement of the living standards of workers. Access to vocational training is in particular likely to promote free movement of persons throughout the Community . . . It follows from all the foregoing that the conditions of access to vocational training fall within the scope of the Treaty".[28]

9–32   In *Raulin*,[29] the ECJ held that the principle of non-discrimination deriving from Arts 12 and 150 EC Treaty meant that an EU national who had been admitted to a vocational training course in another Member State must have a right of residence in that State for the duration of the course.

9–33   Furthermore as regards students the Maastricht Treaty introduced a new chapter into the Treaty concerning "social policy, education, vocational training and youth". Article 126 of the Maastricht Treaty[30] makes clear that Community action is to be aimed at "encouraging mobility of students and teachers". In order to contribute to the achievement of the objectives, the Council is called on to "adopt incentive measures".

(b) *Specific Provisions Relating to the Right of Residence of Students*

(i) *Children of Workers*

9–34   Article 12 of Reg. 1612/68 provides that where an EU national is or has been employed in the territory of another Member State the child of that EU national must be admitted to that State's general educational, apprenticeship and vocational training courses under the same conditions as the nationals of that state.

9–35   The ECJ has stated that this provision exists to ensure that a child of a worker has the possibility of going to school and pursuing further education in the host Member State and able to complete that education successfully.[31] This is consistent with the general aim of Reg. 1612/68, namely that free movement for workers requires "the best possible conditions for the integration of the Community worker's family in the society of the host Member State."[32]

---

[27] Case 293/83 *Gravier v City of Liege* [1985] E.C.R. 593.
[28] Case 293/83 *Gravier v City of Liege* [1985] E.C.R. 593, paras 19–25.
[29] Case 357/89 *Raulin v Minister for Education and Science* [1992] E.C.R. I–1071.
[30] Now Art. 149 EC Treaty.
[31] Joined Cases C-389–390/87 *Echternach and Moritz* [1989] E.C.R. 723, para.21
[32] Case C–308/89 *Di Leo v Land Berlin* [1990] E.C.R. I–4185, para.13

The corollary of the right to education for the children of workers is the right   **9–36**
of residence for those children. That right of residence continues even once
the worker ceases economic activity, or ceases to reside in the territory of the
host Member State.

Based on a narrow reading of the ECJ's judgment in the case of *Echternach*   **9–37**
and Moritz,[33] some Member States considered that the right to remain
beyond the worker was limited to circumstances where education could not
be continued in the Member State of origin of the worker because of lack of
co-ordination of diplomas or some other reason.[34] In *Baumbast* the ECJ
rejected this argument stating that the right of residence for children of
workers in education exists independently of the workers remaining in the
host Member State and irrespective as to whether education could be
continued elsewhere.[35]

Where a parent has ceased to work and reside in another Member State prior   **9–38**
to the birth of a child, the child derives no benefit from Art.12 of Reg.
1612/68 in that Member State.[36]

The right of residence for the children of an EU national worker exists irre-   **9–39**
spective of their nationality. Thus even where the children of an EU national
worker are nationals of third countries they will have independent rights of
residence. This is consistent with the fact that any descendents of an EU
national worker, irrespective of nationality, have the right to install themselves
with the worker.[37] The ECJ has held that the right to be admitted to the education system of the host Member State must apply to the same descendants.[38]

(ii) *Workers Undertaking Vocational Training*

Article 7(3) of Reg. 1612/68 provides that EU national workers in the territory   **9–40**
of another Member State shall have access to training in vocational schools
and retraining centres under the same conditions as national workers.

The ECJ has interpreted the term "vocational schools" relatively restrictively.   **9–41**
It has found that the fact that a teaching establishment provides some vocational training is not sufficient to enable it to be regarded as a vocational
school within the meaning of that provision. According to the ECJ the term
vocational school has a narrower meaning and refers solely to establishments
which provide only teaching between periods of employment or teaching
which is closely connected with employment, particularly during apprenticeship. It rejected a suggestion that universities could be regarded as "vocational
schools".[39]

---

[33] Joined Cases C-389–390/87 *Echternach and Moritz* [1989] E.C.R. 723, para.21
[34] See the German Government's argument recited at para.42 of Case C–413/99 *Baumbast and R. v Secretary of State for the Home Department* [2002] E.C.R. I–7091.
[35] Case C-413/99 *Baumbast and R. v Secretary of State for the Home Department* [2002] E.C.R. I–7091, para. 63.
[36] Case 197/86 *Brown v Secretary of State for Scotland* [1988] E.C.R. 3205.
[37] Art. 10(1) of Reg. 1612/68
[38] Case C-413/99 *Baumbast and R. v Secretary of State for the Home Department* [2002] E.C.R. I–7091, para.56.
[39] Case 197/86 *Brown v Secretary of State for Scotland* [1988] E.C.R. 3205, para.13.

9–42 This restrictive definition is somewhat surprising in light of the fact that the ECJ has acknowledged consistently that universities are capable of providing "studies which prepare for a qualification for a particular profession, trade or employment or which provide the necessary training and skills for such a profession, trade or employment" and that this would constitute "vocational training" for the purposes of Art.150 EC Treaty which applies to EU nationals generally as opposed to the narrower class of workers.[40]

(iii) Directive 93/96

9–43 Directive 93/96 provides that an EU national student, who has been accepted to attend a vocational training course in another Member State, has the right of residence in that Member State. The student must provide assurance by means of a declaration that he has sufficient resources to avoid becoming a burden on the social assistance system of the host Member State. The student must additionally be enrolled in a recognised educational establishment and be covered by sickness insurance in respect of all risks in the host Member State.

9–44 The difference between the requirement in this Directive to provide a declaration of means as opposed to having to prove means in the other two economically inactive categories is significant. It reflects a more flexible attitude towards students and the Commission has taken action against Member States which require more than a declaration from students. In *Commission v Italy*[41] the ECJ upheld the Commission's view that the system of Directive 93/96 on the right of residence for students differs from that of the two other Directives with regard to sufficient resources. The ECJ noted that Directive 93/96 contains no requirement regarding a given amount or moreover the furnishing of evidence thereof in the form of specific documents. In the circumstances the ECJ concluded that a Member State could not require a student benefiting from this Directive to provide evidence or a guarantee of a given amount of resources. The Member State must be satisfied with a declaration or equivalent, at the choice of the student, even where the student is accompanied by family members.

9–45 "Vocational training" is not defined in the Directive or in the EC Treaty itself. In relation to Art.150 EC Treaty the term has been interpreted as "studies which prepare for a qualification for a particular profession, trade or employment or which provide the necessary training and skills for such a profession, trade or employment" but excluding education with the aim of improving general knowledge.[42]

9–46 Whether students in general education fall outside the scope of Directive 93/96 is questionable. It is to be noted firstly that there is no need for the student to establish any link between the education and any occupational activity.[43]

---

[40] Case 293/93 *Gravier v City of Liege* [1985] E.C.R. 593.
[41] Case C–424/98 *Commission v Italy* [2000] E.C.R. I–4001.
[42] Case 39/86 *Lair v Universität Hanover* [1988] E.C.R. 3161.
[43] Which is different from those wishing as workers to benefit from the provisions of Art. 7(2) of Reg. 1612/68. See Case 39/86 *Lair v Universität Hanover* [1988] E.C.R. 3161.

Secondly the ECJ has considered even secondary school education to fall **9–47** within the scope of the EC Treaty. In *D'Hoop*,[44] the ECJ affirmed the importance of free movement of persons for educational purposes. As the ECJ observed in that case:

> "The objectives set for the activities of the Community include, in Article 3(p) of the Treaty (now, amendment Art. 3(1)(q) EC Treaty), a contribution to education and training of quality. That contribution must according to the second indent of Article 126(2) of the Treaty (now the second indent of Article 149(2) EC Treaty) be aimed, inter alia, at encouraging mobility of students and teachers".[45]

The judgment then makes quite clear that students who move in order to **9–48** enter secondary school education fall within the scope of Art.18 EC Treaty.[46] Since the case was not related to a worker or the child of the worker, the ECJ must have intended that Art.18 EC Treaty would be read to include all students. The right of students to move, however, will not be unconditional. It is likely that the conditions and limitations laid down in Directive 93/96 would apply by analogy to such other students.

---

[44] Case C–224/98 *D'Hoop v Office national de l'emploi* [2002] E.C.R. I–6191.
[45] Case C–224/98 *D'Hoop v Office national de l'emploi* [2002] E.C.R. I–6191, para.32.
[46] Case C–224/98 *D'Hoop v Office national de l'emploi* [2002] E.C.R. I–6191, para.33.

FAMILY MEMBERS

This chapter considers the right of EU national free movers to install family members and the interpretation that the ECJ has given to the principle of family unity.

1. INTRODUCTION

(a) General Community Law Principles

(i) Importance of Family Life

Community law has always respected the notion of family life within the context of free movement provisions.[1] It recognises that without the right to family reunion, EU nationals would be deterred from exercising free movement rights.[2]

10–01

The ECJ has recently re-confirmed the importance of ensuring protection for the family life of nationals of Member States in order to eliminate obstacles to the exercise of the fundamental freedoms guaranteed by the EC Treaty.[3] Furthermore the ECJ has made clear that the integration of EU nationals and their family members into the life of the Member State in which they are resident is a fundamental objective of Community law.[4]

10–02

In light of these principles the ECJ has even considered in *MRAX*[5] that it would be contrary to Community law to send back a third country national married to an EU national who arrives at the border of a Member State without the appropriate visa, where he is able to prove his identity and the conjugal ties and there is no evidence to establish that he represents a risk to the requirements of public policy, public security or public health.[6] The ECJ also considered that it would unlawful to refuse to recognise the right of residence of a third country national married to a national of a Member State where the third country national had entered the territory of the Member State unlawfully.[7]

10–03

---

[1] Council Reg. 1612/68, Art.10(1) includes the right of EC national workers to install their family members in the Member State in which they are residing.
[2] Case C-3709/90 *The Queen v the Immigration Appeal Tribunal Ex p. Surinder Singh* [1992] E.C.R. I–4265, para.20.
[3] Case 60-00 *Carpenter v Secretary of State for the Home Department* [2002] E.C.R. I–6279, para.38.
[4] Case C-308/89 *Di Leo v Land Berlin* [1990] E.C.R. I–4185: "the aim of Regulation 1612/68, namely freedom of movement for workers, requires for such freedom to be guaranteed in compliance with the principles of liberty and dignity, the best possible conditions or the integration of the Community worker's family in the society of the host country" (para.13).
[5] Case C-459/99 *Mouvement contre le racisme, l'antisémitisme et la xénophobie ASBL (MRAX) v Belgian State* [2002] E.C.R. I–6591.
[6] Case C-459/99 *Mouvement contre le racisme, l'antisémitisme et la xénophobie ASBL (MRAX) v Belgian State* [2002] E.C.R. I–6591, para.61.
[7] See further Chapter 11.

(ii) *Interpretation of Family Reunion Provisions*

10–04 In *Diatta*,[8] the ECJ made clear "having regard to its context and the objectives which it pursues, that provision [Art.10 of Reg. 1612/68] cannot be construed restrictively". Demonstrating its flexible attitude to the interpretation of family reunion provisions the ECJ held that in order to benefit from the right of residence family members wishing to install themselves with a worker were not required to live permanently with the worker.[9]

10–05 The Advocate General's opinion in the case of *Baumbast*[10] referred to a right of residence in favour of the "spouse and other members of the family of a migrant worker". He considered that the terms of the Regulation should not be defined *restrictively* in light of the principles identified and was of the view that the ECJ must have regard to both social and Community law developments: "If no account were taken of those developments the relevant rules of law risk losing their effectiveness".[11]

(b) *Inter-relationship with the Right to Family Life in Human Rights Law*

(i) *Generally*

10–06 In a series of cases decided since 2001 the ECJ has emphasised the importance of ensuring protection for the right to respect for family life of nationals of the Member States in order to eliminate obstacles to the exercise of the fundamental freedoms guaranteed by the EC Treaty.[12]

10–07 In Chapter 3 the inter-relationship between human rights law, in particular the European Convention on Human Rights (ECHR), and Community law was examined. Those principles have particular application in the field of the free movement of persons and the right to respect for family life in that context. The ECJ has consistently held that free movement provisions must be interpreted in conformity with Art.8 ECHR and the fundamental right to respect for family life contained in that provision.[13]

(ii) *The Scope of Protection Afforded by Article 8 ECHR*

10–08 It must be recalled that the right to respect for family life contained in Art.8(1) ECHR is not an absolute right and thus the right of non-nationals to enter a country is not guaranteed by the ECHR. However, the only permissible interferences with the Art.8(1) rights are those outlined in Art.8(2) which, although similar, are more extensive than the corresponding excep-

---

[8] Case 267/83 *Diatta v Land Berlin* [1985] E.C.R. 567, para.17.

[9] Case 267/83 *Diatta v Land Berlin* [1985] E.C.R. 567, para.18.

[10] A.G. Geelhoed in Case C-413/99 *Baumbast and R. v Secretary of State for the Home Department*, delivered on July 5, 2001, para.19.

[11] A.G. Geelhoed in Case C-413/99 *Baumbast and R. v Secretary of State for the Home Department*, delivered on July 5, 2001, para.19.

[12] Case 60-00 *Carpenter v Secretary of State for the Home Department* [2002] E.C.R. I–6279, para.38.

[13] Case 249/86 *Commission v Germany* [1989] E.C.R. 1263, para.10. See also A.G.'s opinion in Case C-459/99 *Mouvement contre le racisme, l'antisémitisme et la xénophobie ASBL (MRAX) v Belgian State* [2002] E.C.R. I–6591.

tions in Community law to the enjoyment of rights given by the EC Treaty.[14] Assuming there is family life under Art.8(2) ECHR the state must establish a legitimate aim for the interference with the individual's right which in the present context will likely be sought to be justified by reference to the need to have fair and firm immigration control in the context of the maintenance of public order. However, the state must establish also that any interference is proportionate when the state's interest in the interference in the family life is balanced against the effect that the measure would have on the individual's rights to respect for that family life.

Thus whether there is a breach of Art.8 ECHR will turn on the following issues: **10–09**

(i)   Is there family life?

(ii)   Has there been an interference or failure to respect family life?

(iii) Is the interference or failure to respect family life in accordance with the law?

(iv) Is the interference or failure to respect family life necessary in a democratic society and on what basis?

(v)   Is the interference or failure to respect family life proportionate to the legitimate aim pursued?

The state's negative obligations under Art.8 are well established and preclude a state from taking action, including expulsion or removals, which will disproportionately interfere with a person's right to the enjoyment of family life.[15] In assessing what is proportionate it will be necessary to examine whether there are obstacles to the family life being enjoyed outside the contracting state. In this context it is to be recalled that the European Court of Human Rights (ECtHR) has even considered language and cultural difficulties as impediments to family life being enjoyed elsewhere.[16] The ECHR thus imposes negative obligations on states to refrain from such interferences. **10–10**

Additionally however Art.1 also demands that states "secure" the rights protected by the ECHR. The European Court of Human Rights has therefore held in many cases that states are under a positive obligation to take steps to ensure that Convention rights are protected, not just to refrain from negative interferences. The state is obliged to have in place laws that grant individuals the legal status, rights and privileges required to ensure, for example, that their family life is properly respected.[17] **10–11**

Article 8 also carries positive obligations for the state to protect all aspects of family life.[18] The judgment of the European Court of Human Rights in *Sen* **10–12**

---

[14] As to which see Chapter 14.
[15] See most recently *Yildiz v Austria* (Application no. 37295/97), judgment of October 31, 2002, ECtHR.
[16] *Boultif v Switzerland* (Application no. 54273/00), judgment of August 2, 2001, ECtHR.
[17] *Marckx v Belgium* (1979) 2 E.H.R.R. 330, para.36.
[18] *Marckx v Belgium* (1979) 2 E.H.R.R. 330.

v Netherlands[19] suggests that the state has a positive obligation to facilitate family life which goes beyond protecting the family life that already exists in the territory of a state, but includes an obligation to permit the reunion of family members who have been living apart and to foster family life in the best possible environment. In this context the failure to meet this obligation must be weighed against the state's legitimate aims which will include immigration control.

(iii) *The ECJ's approach to Article 8 ECHR*

10–13   In a situation where an EU Member State denies entry to the family member of an EU national exercising EU free movement rights it is not difficult to argue that to exclude the family member would be a breach of Community law when read compatibly with the ECHR, irrespective of whether Community law alone would force that conclusion. For the EU national, it would constitute a breach of fundamental rights of free movement if the only way to enjoy family life is by leaving the host Member State. Similarly it would be a breach of Community law if the only way to enjoy free movement rights were without family members being present. In other words Community law would not force an EU national to choose between the enjoyment of family life and the continued exercise of EC Treaty rights to freedom of movement.

10–14   This approach has been affirmed by the ECJ in *Carpenter*[20] which concerned the spouse of a provider of services. The ECJ found that notwithstanding that the spouse had infringed the immigration laws of the United Kingdom she was entitled to reside in the territory with the provider of services. In doing so, the ECJ read Art.49 EC Treaty in light of the fundamental right to respect for family life so as to infer a right of residence for the family member.

10–15   Moreover in *MRAX*,[21] the ECJ ruled that a Member State could not refuse to issue a residence permit to a third country national married to a national of a Member State who entered the territory of that Member State lawfully on the sole ground that the visa expired before the application was made for a residence permit.[22]

10–16   The two cases illustrate the determination of the ECJ to ensure the protection of the family life of Member State nationals in order to eliminate obstacles to the exercise of the fundamental freedoms guaranteed by the Treaty, even in the face of contrary domestic legislation.

10–17   *Carpenter*[23] in particular is also indicative of the ECJ's willingness to interpret the EC Treaty obligations in light of the rights protected by the ECHR. In its judgment the ECJ explicitly relied on the right to respect for family life as guaranteed by Art.8(1) ECHR, recalling that it is one of the fundamental

---

[19] *Sen v Netherlands* (Application no. 31465/96), judgment of December 20, 2001.
[20] Case 60-00 *Carpenter v Secretary of State for the Home Department* [2002] E.C.R. I–6279, para.38.
[21] Case C-459/99 *Mouvement contre le racisme, l'antisémitisme et la xénophobie ASBL v Belgium* [2002] E.C.R. I–6591.
[22] The ECJ also held that a non-EU national spouse who had entered the territory of a Member State unlawfully was not grounds for exclusion or refusal of residents permit.
[23] Case 60/00 *Carpenter v Secretary of State for the Home Department* [2002] E.C.R. I–6279.

rights which are protected in Community law through the case law of the ECJ, the Single European Act and Art.6(2) EU Treaty.[24]

There has been some criticism of the ECJ's approach to the ECHR and sugges- **10–18** tion that it has given undue weight to the rights of the individuals as opposed to that of the state. However, such criticism is not warranted if the decisions of the ECJ are seen in light of the above observations and the fact that family members are seen in Community law as being capable of "facilitating" free movement in so far as they may offer support,[25] care[26] and in some cases financial ability to exercise that free movement right. In the words of the ECJ in *Carpenter*:

> "It is clear that the separation of Mr and Mrs Carpenter would be detrimental to their family life and, therefore, to the conditions under which Mr Carpenter exercises a fundamental freedom. That freedom could not be fully effective if Mr Carpenter were to be deterred from exercising it by obstacles raised in his country origin to the entry and residence of his spouse".[27]

(c) *Which Family Members can be Installed with the EU National?*

The right to install family members is set out in detail in secondary legisla- **10–19** tion relating to free movement. The different categories of person exercising free movement have the right to install different family members.[28] The respective rights of residence are considered in detail in Chapter 11. For present purposes the beneficiaries of the right to install family members for each category of free mover are listed below.

(i) *Workers*[29] *and the Self-employed* [30]

Workers and the self-employed have the right to install the following persons **10–20** (irrespective of nationality):

(a) spouse;

(b) descendants of the EU national and spouse who are under the age of 21 or are dependants;

(c) dependent relatives in the ascending line of the EU national and spouse.

Member States are further required to facilitate the admission of any mem- **10–21** ber of the family who does not fall into the above categories, and who is dependent on the EU national or living under the his roof in the country from where he comes.

---

[24] Art.6(2) EU Treaty provides "The Union shall respect fundamental rights, as guaranteed by the European Convention for the Protection of Human Rights and Fundamental Freedoms signed in Rome on 4 November 1950 and as they result from the constitutional traditions common to the Member States, as general principles of Community law".

[25] Case 60/00 *Carpenter v Secretary of State for the Home Department* [2002] E.C.R. I–6279.

[26] Case C-413/99 *Baumbast and R. v Secretary of State for the Home Department* [2002] E.C.R. I–7091.

[27] See Case 60/00 *Carpenter v Secretary of State for the Home Department* [2002] E.C.R. I–6279, para.39.

[28] See Chapter 11.

[29] Reg. 1612/68.

[30] Dir. 73/148.

(ii) *Directive 90/364 (General Right of Residence) and Directive 90/365 (Retired Persons)*

10–22   Those EU nationals exercising the general right of residence as self-sufficient persons or those EU nationals who are retired have the right to install:

(a)   spouse;

(b)   the EU national's and spouse's descendants who are dependants;

(c)   the ascendants of the EU national and spouse who are dependants.

(iii) *Directive 93/96 (Students)*

10–23   EU national students have the right to install their spouse and their dependent children.[31] For those students falling outsider the scope of Directive 93/96, there is no express right of residence conferred for family members. Their position is considered below.

2. Spouse

(a) *Legal Spouse*

(i) *Meaning of Spouse*

10–24   The ECJ case law suggests that the term "spouse" refers to "a marital relationship only". Thus relationships outside legal marriage cannot be regarded as "spouses" for the purposes of Community law.

10–25   *Reed*[32] is the most significant decision of the ECJ in which the meaning of the term "spouse" referred to in the free movement Directives and Regulations[33] has been considered. Ann Reed, a UK national, attempted to obtain a residence permit in the Netherlands on the grounds that she was cohabiting with a UK national who was working in the Netherlands. She had been living in a stable heterosexual relationship with her partner for more than five years. It was argued on her behalf that in view of legal and social developments since the late 1960s when Community law evolved, unmarried cohabiting partners should be treated as within the scope of the term "spouse".

10–26   The ECJ rejected this submission reasoning that the term "spouse" must be given a Community law meaning and that it should take into account legal and social developments in the whole of the Community and not just one Member State.

> "12. According to Article 189 of the EEC Treaty, Regulation No. 1612/68 has general application, is binding in its entirety and is directly applicable in all Member States.

---

[31] Note the use of the word 'children' instead of 'descendants', see below.

[32] Case 59/85 *Reed v the Netherlands* [1986] E.C.R. 1283.

[33] In the particular case Reg. 1612/68.

13. It follows that an interpretation given by the Court to a provision of that Regulation has effects in all of the Member States, and that any interpretation of a legal term on the basis of social developments must take into account the situation in the whole community, not merely in one Member State".[34]

The ECJ did not consider that social developments in the whole of the   **10–27**
Community could prompt the conclusion at that time that spouse could be construed so as to include unmarried co-habiting partners. Those in stable co-habiting relationships recognised by the national law of a Member State may nevertheless benefit from the provisions of Art.7(2) of Reg. 1612/68.[35]

(ii) *Divorce and Separation*

It is the corollary of the very narrow definition of the term "spouse" (relat-   **10–28**
ing to the technical legal status of a couple) that, for as long as they remain legally married, they should be regarded as spouses. This includes situations where the couple have separated and even intend to divorce. It is only when the marriage is finally dissolved in law that they can no longer be regarded as spouses for the purposes of Community law.

In *Diatta*,[36] the couple in question had separated and were living in different   **10–29**
accommodation. The German authorities sought to deport Ms Diatta, a Sengalese national, on the basis that she had no right of residence in Community law. The German authorities pointed to the fact that the couple intended to divorce and in that Art.10(3) of Reg. 1612/68 refers to the requirement that the EU national has adequate accommodation for his family members.

The ECJ held that a marriage could not be regarded as dissolved until it had   **10–30**
been terminated by the relevant authorities and that the requirement that the EU national has adequate accommodation on installing his family members could not be translated into a requirement that they remain living together.

(iii) *Sham Marriages*

Consistent with its jurisprudence in other areas, the ECJ has held that   **10–31**
Community law will not act as a front for fraudulent conduct. In the case of *Surinder Singh*[37] the ECJ recalled that Community law does not prevent national authorities from preventing abuse. More recently in *Akrich*[38] the ECJ held that:

> "there would be an abuse if the facilities afforded by Community law in favour of migrant workers and their spouses were invoked in the context of marriages of convenience entered into in order to circumvent the provisions relating to entry and residence of nationals of non-Member States".

---

[34] Case 59/85 *Reed v the Netherlands* [1986] E.C.R. 1283.
[35] See paras 10–32 to 10–34 below.
[36] Case 267/83 *Diatta v Land Berlin* [1985] E.C.R. 567.
[37] Case C-370/90 *R. v the IAT and the Secretary of State for the Home Department Ex p. Surinder Singh* [1992] E.C.R. I–4265.
[38] Case C-109/01 *Secretary of State for the Home Department v Akrich*, judgment of September 23, 2003, para.57.

The ECJ has not defined what would constitute a "marriage of convenience". However a marriage could only be seen as one of convenience if the *sole* purpose of the marriage were to circumvent the provisions of domestic law.[39]

(b) *Unmarried Partners*

(i) *The Established Position in Community Law—The Social Advantages Approach*

10–32 As discussed above the ECJ has resisted extending the term "spouse" to include a person in a stable unmarried relationship, whether heterosexual or homosexual. This would seemingly end any argument that EU nationals are entitled to install their unmarried partners in the territory of a host Member State.

10–33 However, the ECJ has used the concept of a "social advantage" to provide a partial solution to the problem faced by an EU national wishing to be accompanied by an unmarried partner when residing in another Member State. The concept of social advantages is discussed in Chapter 12 and is characterised as "all advantages, which, whether or not linked to a contract of employment are generally granted to national workers . . . and the extension of which to workers who are nationals of other member countries therefore seems suitable to facilitate their mobility within the Community".[40]

10–34 In *Reed*,[41] the ECJ held that the possibility of a migrant worker's obtaining permission for his unmarried partner to reside with him could fall within the concept of social advantage for the purposes of Art.7(2) of Reg. 1612/68. The ECJ considered that it would be discriminatory to allow own nationals residence permits for their cohabiting partners, but to refuse to grant the same advantage to EU nationals exercising Treaty rights.

(ii) *The Limitations of the Social Advantages Approach*

10–35 The "social advantages" approach to the rights of residence of unmarried partners is plainly only a partial and somewhat unsatisfactory solution to the problem. The deficiencies of such approach stem primarily from the fact that no Community law right to install an unmarried partner is created. This has a number of consequences.

10–36 Firstly, the right of an EU national to install an unmarried partner in another Member State is entirely dependant on recognition through domestic legislation of such right of residence for unmarried partners of that Member State's own nationals. Where no such right is afforded to own nationals, the EU national may not use this argument to assert a right of residence for an unmarried partner. This will cause an obvious disparity in rights for unmarried partners across the European Union, where the right to be accompanied

---

[39] This is to be contrasted with certain Member State's domestic interpretation of such concepts which question more deeply the motivation for marriage.
[40] Case 122/84 *Scrivener and Cole v Centre Public d'Aide Sociale de Chastre* [1985] E.C.R. 1027.
[41] Case 59/85 *Reed v the Netherlands* [1986] E.C.R. 1283

by an unmarried partner is recognised by some Member States but not others.[42]

Secondly, the reliance on "social advantages" will mean that Community **10–37** law rules do not govern the rights in question, even if they do exist in the Member States' domestic law. This means that there will be differences in interpretation between Member States as to what constitutes an unmarried partner or co-habitee and the rights attained will vary between Member States.

Thirdly, the reliance on social advantages means there is no obligation of **10–38** "mutual recognition" of unmarried partners who are recognised or legally registered in one Member State. Thus a couple who had been recognised in one Member State may not be so recognised or obtain any rights when they move to another Member State, creating an obstacle to free movement.

A final potential problem with the "social advantage" approach (based as it is **10–39** on the application of Art.7(2) of Reg. 1612/68 relating to *workers*) is that it is arguably restricted to workers since there is no comparable provision to Art.7(2) in subordinate Community legislation for other free movers. However, this would be an unnecessarily restrictive interpretation. The "social advantages" approach is clearly based on principles of non-discrimination on grounds of nationality and such non-discrimination extends through Art.12 EC Treaty to all EU citizens exercising their free movement rights pursuant to Art.18 EC Treaty.

In these circumstances a failure to grant an EU national exercising free move- **10–40** ment rights the same rights in relation to unmarried partners as workers enjoy in light of *Reed*[43] would be an unwarranted interference with free movement rights creating an impermissible obstacle to the enjoyment of a fundamental freedom guaranteed by the Treaty. It is unlikely that the ECJ would sanction a different result for a self-employed person as against a worker. Such discrimination would be contrary to Art.12 EC Treaty which provides that "within the scope of application of this Treaty, and without prejudice to any special provisions contained therein, any discrimination on grounds of nationality shall be prohibited".

However these arguments may still be limited by the fact that no Community **10–41** law right is created. Thus the potential success of such argument would remain dependent on establishing that a Member State does indeed grant such rights to its own nationals. Where no such national laws or practices exists, the EU national would appear to be precluded from installing an unmarried partner.

---

[42] Austria, Ireland, Luxembourg, Spain, Italy, Greece and most Accession States do not recognise unmarried partners in national laws; Finland, Sweden, Denmark, Netherlands, France, Germany, Belgium, United Kingdom, Portugal and Hungary do recognise unmarried partners in national laws, (2003)3(2) *ILGA-Europe Newsletter.*
[43] Case 59/85 *Reed v the Netherlands* [1986] E.C.R. 1283.

(iii) *Creating an EU Law Right to Install Unmarried Partners: the Future*

10–42   In light of the existence in many Member States since the ECJ's decision in *Reed* of a domestic law right to install an unmarried partner, the lack of a Community law right to install an unmarried partner will not in fact create significant problems. Thus the creation of such discrete Community law right may be unnecessary. For many EU nationals it will be sufficient to deploy non-discrimination arguments to be able to move to another Member State with an unmarried partner.

10–43   However, in those states where no such right exists it will clearly be necessary to deploy an argument beyond non-discrimination if those in unmarried partnerships are not to be disadvantaged. With increasing numbers of Member States recognising, registering and in one case (the Netherlands) even legally marrying same-sex partnerships, there is an ever-growing number of EU nationals and their partners who are disadvantaged as compared to their heterosexual, married equivalents. They will continue to be disadvantaged for so long as there are any states which refuse to recognise their partnerships and such disadvantage creates a real obstacle to free movement. At the present time for instance a couple, who may be legally recognised in Denmark, is immediately disadvantaged in states such as Spain where unmarried partnerships are not recognised. This may impact in a significant way upon the decision to move with the European Union.

10–44   It is necessary therefore to consider ways in which Community law solutions to these problems might be found. There are two ways in which the ECJ's restrictive definition of spouse and failure to recognise unmarried couples as equivalent to those legally married might be overcome. The first is for the ECJ to re-interpret the term "spouse"; the second is to employ an "obstacles to free movement" argument.

Re-interpreting the term spouse

10–45   It is arguable that the time has come for the ECJ to re-interpret the term "spouse" to include unmarried partners in a stable relationship, despite the Council's failure to do so.[44] The decision in Reed was given nearly 15 years ago and it is undoubtedly arguable that in the light of legal and social developments over the last 15 years, the term "spouse" should be given a more liberal meaning. The ECJ is mindful of such developments and has been prepared to make similar developments in relation to transsexuals.[45]

10–46   However there is undoubtedly a risk that the ECJ would reject that argument even today. As recently as 2001 the ECJ did not consider that legal and social developments could support the conclusion that a consensus had been reached amongst the Member States.[46]

---

[44] It is to be noted that Dir. 2004/38 on the rights of citizens does not include unmarried partners in the definition of a spouse, see Appendix 30.
[45] See paras 10–54 to 10–57 below.
[46] See Case C-122/99P *D. v Council* [2001] E.C.R. I–4319.

Even if the ECJ were not prepared to go so far as to interpret "spouse" to **10–47** include unmarried partnerships, it must surely at least recognise situations where same-sex partners have legally married. Although the question of whether a same-sex couple legally married in the Netherlands would have to be recognised as "spouses" as a matter of Community law by other Member States has not arisen before the ECJ, a positive answer would surely be required to be given to such question for the following reasons.

A married same-sex couple who could provide a legal document from the **10–48** Netherlands (or indeed anywhere else where same-sex couples can legally marry) confirming their status have fulfilled the only relevant requirements of Community law in order to obtain recognition in other Member States.[47] For that Member State to make any further enquiry or require any further documentation would be unlawful as a matter of Community law.[48] The only possible grounds for exclusion therefore would be those that apply generally, namely public policy, public security or public health. Given that the assessment of any of those grounds must be made on an individual basis,[49] a general finding that public policy reasons could justify the exclusion of any same-sex married couple would surely be an affront to Community law. Furthermore, in light of both the interference with private life that separation of the couple would involve (itself contrary to Art.8 ECHR) and societal developments in the European Union, is difficult to suggest that there could now be good public policy reasons for failing to recognise such a marriage.

Using "an obstacles to free movement" argument

Absent a redefinition of the term "spouse" it may be possible to develop an **10–49** argument based on "obstacles to free movement". The refusal to recognise a stable relationship is an obstacle to free movement and indeed such a relationship might feasibly facilitate the free movement of an EU national. The fact that an EU national exercising Treaty rights cannot take a partner to another Member State is an obstacle to free movement. This would be particularly so in the case where the couple were able to co-habit in the EU national's state of origin but apparently not in the host Member State.

As the ECJ held in the case of *Bosman*,[50] a provision does not need to be dis- **10–50** criminatory on grounds of nationality, in order to constitute an obstacle to the right of free movement. Thus it would not be necessary to establish that the EU national suffers any discrimination *vis-à-vis* the host Member State's own nationals.

It must be recognised that in the case of non-discriminatory rules which form **10–51** obstacles to free movement, Member States are entitled to justify such rules by reference to pressing reasons of public interest.[51] These justifications are

---

[47] Art.4 of Dir. 68/360.
[48] See Chapter 11.
[49] Extreme criminal activities apart, see Chapter 14.
[50] Case C-415/93 *Union Royal Belge des Societes de Football Association ASBL v Bosman* [1995] E.C.R. I–4921.
[51] Case C-415/93 *Union Royal Belge des Societes de Football Association ASBL v Bosman* [1995] E.C.R. I–4921, para.104.

subject to a strict proportionality test. However, it would be difficult for a Member State to justify the failure to give recognition to unmarried partnerships on grounds of public interest at the present stage of societal development in the European Union where discrimination on ground of sex or sexuality is not tolerated.[52]

10–52 The recent decisions of the ECJ in *Carpenter*[53] and in *Baumbast*[54] certainly lend support to an obstacle to free movement argument. In those cases the ECJ reinforced the view that family members may be necessary to facilitate the exercise of a free movement right and furthermore that Community law should be read in conformity with the ECHR and in particular the right to family life.

10–53 The only difficulty here is that whilst the ECHR has long given recognition to *de facto* relationships over and above *de jure* relationships, it has consistently avoided finding that a same-sex relationship amounts to "family life". Nevertheless it has been prepared to accept the application of Art.8 ECHR to same-sex relationships, and has recently found contracting states to be in breach of Art.14 taken together with Art.8 where they refuse treat same-sex couples in a discriminatory fashion, *vis-à-vis* their heterosexual equivalents.[55]

In the final analysis, this issue must be addressed and solved by Community law. It is wholly illogical that Community law is prepared to treat as a family member as the distant relative of a worker who happens to live under the worker's roof, but is not prepared to recognise the *de facto* relationship between unmarried partners living akin to spouses.

(c) *Transsexuals*

(i) *Community Law*

10–54 In *S v Cornwall County Council*[56] the ECJ held that the right not to be discriminated on grounds of sex constitutes a fundamental human right and must be extended to discrimination arising from gender reassignment. Such discrimination, in the ECJ's view, would constitute a failure to respect dignity and freedom. The ECJ did not determine whether a relationship involving a transsexual is equivalent to marriage for the purposes of Community law until recently.

10–55 The case of *KB*[57] concerned a British citizen who worked for the National Health Service (NHS) for 20 years, during which time she paid contributions to the NHS pension scheme. The scheme provided for a survivor's pension to be payable to a member's surviving spouse. "Spouse" meant the person to whom the scheme member had been married. KB argued that her partner, R, who had undergone female-to-male gender reassignment surgery, should be entitled to

---

[52] EU Charter on Fundamental Rights.
[53] Case 60/00 *Carpenter v Secretary of State for the Home Department* [2002] E.C.R. I–6279.
[54] Case C-413/99 *Baumbast and R. v Secretary of State for the Home Department* [2002] E.C.R. I–7091.
[55] *Karner v Austria*, July 23, 2003.
[56] Case C-13/94 *S v Cornwall County Council* [1996] E.C.R. I-2143, paras 21–22.
[57] Case C–117/01 *KB v (1) National Health Service Pensions Agency (2) Secretary of State for Health*, judgment of January 7, 2004.

receive the widower's pension. United Kingdom legislation, however, prevented transsexuals from marrying on the basis of their acquired gender.

The ECJ rejected an argument that restricting the widower's pensions to married couples only was contrary to Community law. The ECJ held that the decision to restrict certain benefits to married couples, while excluding all persons who lived together without being married from accessing such benefits, was either a matter for the legislature to decide or a matter of the interpretation of domestic legal rules for the national courts. Individuals affected could not claim that there was discrimination on grounds of sex, prohibited by Community law. There was however inequality of treatment which related to the couple's inability to marry. The ECJ relied on the decision of the European Court of Human Rights in *Goodwin*[58] to conclude that the legislation making it impossible for transsexuals to marry on the basis of their acquired gender was incompatible with the EC Treaty. In *Goodwin*, the European Court of Human Rights had held that since it was impossible for a transsexual to marry a person of the sex to which he or she belonged prior to gender reassignment surgery, the United Kingdom was in breach of the right to marry in Art.12 ECHR. Thus the pensions legislation was incompatible with the EC Treaty.   **10–56**

The consequence of this case would appear to be that it is contrary to Community law for Member States to prohibit transsexuals from marrying, whereas the failure to treat as equal married and unmarried couples is not in contradiction with EU law.   **10–57**

(ii) *Human Rights Law*

Article 8 ECHR protects the right to respect for private life. Article 12 ECHR protects the fundamental right of "men and women of marriageable age" to marry. The right to marry is guaranteed also by Art.9 of the Charter of Fundamental Rights of the European Union.[59] Of further relevance for transsexuals in this context is Art.13 EC Treaty which calls on European institutions to take measures to combat discrimination on grounds of sex.   **10–58**

In *Goodwin*,[60] the European Court of Human Rights considered the position of transsexuals in a landmark decision holding that the UK Government's failure to alter the birth certificates of transsexuals or to allow them to marry in their new gender role was a breach of the ECHR. The European Court of Human Rights observed that the very essence of the ECHR is respect for human dignity and human rights. Under Art.8 ECHR in particular, where the notion of personal autonomy is an important principle underlying the interpretation of its guarantees, protection is given to the personal sphere of each individual including the right to establish details of identity as individual human beings.[61] The European Court of Human Rights recalled the emphasis given in previous cases to the importance of keeping under review the need for appropriate legal measures having regard to scientific and   **10–59**

---

[58] *Goodwin v United Kingdom* [2002] 35 E.H.R.R. 18.
[59] It is notable that Art.9 of the EU Charter does not restrict the protection of the right to marry to "men and women"
[60] *Goodwin v United Kingdom* [2002] 35 E.H.R.R. 18.
[61] *Goodwin v United Kingdom* [2002] 35 E.H.R.R. 18, para.89.

societal developments. In light of such developments the European Court of Human Rights concluded that the treatment of transsexuals no longer fell within the state's margin of appreciation and that there were no significant factors of public interest to weigh against the interest of the individual in obtaining legal recognition of a gender reassignment. Moreover, as for the right to marry, the European Court of Human Rights found no justification for barring a transsexual from enjoying the right to marry under any circumstances and thus considered the failure to permit the applicant to marry was a breach of Art.12 ECHR.[62]

(iii) *The Future*

10–60 It is now established in Community EC law that the failure to permit transsexual couples to marry is contrary to the Treaty and in breach of human rights law. If Member States fail to legalise marriages of transsexuals on the basis of their acquired gender the consequence must be that they give legal recognition to relationships akin to marriage.

10–61 In most Member States there remains a legal bar to marriage of a transsexual on the basis of acquired gender. However, the failure of national laws to reflect societal changes should not prevent the couple's being regarded as spouses for the purposes of Community law when national law would be so clearly in conflict with Arts 8 and 12 ECHR.

10–62 In the context of free movement law, absent the ability of transsexuals to marry on the basis of their acquired gender, this would have to mean that the term "spouse" is interpreted as including the stable relationship of a transsexual and his or her partner, where on the basis of the acquired gender they are of the opposite sex. The failure to do so amounts to indirect discrimination on the grounds of sex and is a breach of the ECHR.

10–63 The ECJ's decision in *KB*[63] has made clear that such breach of the ECHR is incompatible with Community law. This is consistent with its other jurisprudence that Community law must be compatible with ECHR obligations.[64]

3. DESCENDANTS

(a) *Under the Age of 21*

10–64 There is no definition of descendants to be found in the case law of the ECJ. However it should include all blood children, whether legitimate or not. It includes grandchildren and great-grandchildren. It is notable that the age of 21

---

[62] *Goodwin v United Kingdom* [2002] 35 E.H.R.R. 18., para.104. In *Bellinger v Bellinger* [2003] UKHL 21 the House of Lords determined that UK law was now incompatible with the ECHR since the UK laws relating to matrimony does not make provision for the recognition of gender reassignment.
[63] Case C–117/01 *KB v (1) National Health Service Pensions Agency (2) Secretary of State for Health*, judgment of January 7, 2004.
[64] Case 60/00 *Carpenter v Secretary of State for the Home Department* [2002] E.C.R. I–6279.

is the relevant age for the purposes of Community law below which descendants are in effect treated automatically as dependants. This may differ from national rules which define children as under 18 (or in some cases as even younger). Community law will prevail in the case of conflict with national rules.

Secondary legislation always refers to the principal's right to install his spouse and *their* children or descendants. The ECJ has stated that this is to be interpreted as meaning that the right is extended to both the descendants of the EU national and to those of his spouse. To give a restrictive interpretation to that provision (that only the children common to the migrant worker and his spouse have the right to install themselves) would run counter to the aim of Community law. It is thus clear that the stepchildren of an EU national are to be considered as falling within the scope of "their children/descendants" referred to in the relevant legislation.[65]   **10–65**

(b) *Dependent on Parents*

The concept of dependency is one which has a Community law meaning. The established case law can be summarised by reference to *Lebon*[66] in which the ECJ held that the factors for assessing dependency are ". . . the provision of support by the worker, without there being any need to determine the reasons for recourse to the worker's support". Accordingly the assessment of whether there is a relationship of dependency is simply a factual one, namely whether the principal provides support to the dependant. A broad approach has been adopted by the ECJ in defining the status of dependants and the relationship of dependency will not be affected by the fact that the worker does not "wholly or largely support" the dependant.[67]   **10–66**

It is an assessment of the emotional and financial situation which determines the issue, although there is in fact no need for there to be financial dependency. As the ECJ held in the case of *Lebon*, it would be discriminatory and contrary to the aims of Community law if a person was automatically excluded from being considered as dependent on the principal if the dependant was in receipt of social security benefits. If the dependant was so automatically excluded, EU nationals might be disadvantaged *vis-à-vis* own nationals in that they might feel unable to claim social security benefits to which they are entitled.   **10–67**

(c) *Adopted and Foster Children*

Where the relevant provisions relating to family members refer to descendants[68] as opposed to children,[69] there is the potential problem that the latter could be read restrictively to exclude children who are not blood descendants of either the EU national or his spouse. This might arise in the case of adopted or foster children.   **10–68**

---

[65] Case C-413/99 *Baumbast and R. v Secretary of State for the Home Department* [2002] E.C.R. I–7091.
[66] Case 316/85 *Centre public d'aide sociale de Courcelles v Lebon* [1987] E.C.R. 2811.
[67] J. Handoll, *"Free Movement of Persons in the EU"* (John Wiley and Sons 1995), p.251. The Dutch Government in the case of *Lebon* argued that a worker would have show that they wholly or largely supported the dependant. The ECJ did not accept that argument and instead held that even where the worker was unable to provide financial support to the dependant, that did not undermine the relationship of dependency.
[68] *e.g.* Reg. 1612/68, Art.10(1).
[69] *e.g.* Dirs 73/148 and 93/96.

10–69 Interestingly even where the legislation refers to descendants, the ECJ often uses the term "children" as if they are were inter-changeable. However there is no guidance from the ECJ on adopted children. In *Diatta*,[70] the ECJ reiterated that the family provisions could not be interpreted restrictively. The Advocate General's opinion in the case of *Baumbast*[71] referred to a right of residence in favour of the "spouse and other members of the family of a migrant worker." He considered that the terms of the regulation should not be defined restrictively. He was of the view that the ECJ must be able to take into account social and legal developments, otherwise "the relevant rules of law risk losing their effectiveness".[72]

10–70 It is axiomatic that if Community law wishes to facilitate the free movement of workers and their families then adopted children must be included. The philosophy which invariably underlines judgments of the ECJ, in particular when interpreting the scope of EC Treaty provisions and subordinate legislation, is the recognition that at their core such provisions reflect fundamental principles and thus fall to be widely and purposively construed. Certainly the ECJ has tended to eschew a literal reading of provisions where to do so would conflict with the underlying principles which any such provisions are intended to implement.

10–71 However even if adoption or fostering was not to be equated with "descendancy" it nonetheless should be equated with dependency and thus at the very least the child should fall within the scope of Art.10(2) of Reg. 1612/68.

10–72 In interpreting these provisions the ECJ would have regard to the ECtHR jurisprudence regarding the right to respect for family life. The existence of family life between adoptive parents and their adopted child is well established under the ECHR.[73] Both actual and potential family relationships are covered by Art.8 ECHR.

4. RELATIVES IN THE ASCENDING LINE

10–73 The notion of relatives in the ascending line covers not only the father and mother of the worker and his spouse, but also grandparents and great-grandparents. It potentially includes step-parents and adoptive parents. The age of the relative in the ascending line is irrelevant.

10–74 It is to be recalled that the relevant directives and regulations refer to such relatives being "dependent" on the EU national or his spouse. The definition of dependency is the same as that attaching to descendants and thus may include emotional as well as financial dependency.

---

[70] Case 267/83 *Diatta v Land Berlin* [1985] E.C.R. 567, para.17.
[71] A.G. Geelhoed in Case C-413/99 *Baumbast and R. v Secretary of State for the Home Department* [2002] E.C.R. I–7091, para.19.
[72] A.G. Geelhoed in Case C-413/99 *Baumbast and R. v Secretary of State for the Home Department* [2002] E.C.R. I–7091, para.20.
[73] See most recently *Pini & Bertani and Manera & Atripaldi v Romania* (Application nos. 78028/01 and 78030/01) judgment of June 22, 2004, ECtHR.

5. OTHER FAMILY MEMBERS

(a) *Other Dependants*

Article 10(2) refers to other members of the family who are dependent on the **10–75**
EU national. For family members falling within the scope of Art.10(2) as
Advocate General Geelhoed recalls "under the Court's case law, the status of
dependent member of a worker's family is the result of a factual situation".[74]

The concept of family member is not defined in Community law and the ECJ **10–76**
has yet to make a substantive ruling on this provision. However if the concept is to be read in conformity with the ECHR it must include *de facto* relationships beyond the biological relationships. In such cases the nature and
stability of the relationship ought to be taken into account.[75]

(b) *Living as Part of the Household*

Alternative to the other family members, being dependent on the EU **10–77**
national, they may be living as part of the household. This provision has yet
to receive the attention of the ECJ.

(c) *Beyond the Scope of Regulations*

Although Community law would appear to grant to EU nationals exercising **10–78**
free movement rights the right to be accompanied by a broad range of family members, it is still possible to envisage circumstances where the family
member in question cannot be easily fitted into the scope of the particular
free movement provision in question, for instance the non-dependent descen-
dant over the age of 21. The question then arises of whether Community law
would nevertheless provide an ability for that family member to be installed.

The answer is to be found in the ECJ's decision in *Baumbast*, where the ECJ **10–79**
held that a family member might facilitate the exercise of a free movement
right and that to exclude that family member would constitute an obstacle to
free movement. In *Baumbast* the persons exercising free movement rights
were children in education.[76] The children were dependent on their non-EU
national mother. The ECJ accepted that the children's rights could found a
right of residence for their mother, an ascendant upon whom *they* were
dependent, during the exercise of their free movement rights. This was
despite the fact that they could point to no Regulation or Directive upon
which to found such a right. The ECJ stated:

"The right conferred by Article 12 of Regulation No 1612/68 on the child of a
migrant worker to pursue, under the best possible conditions, his education in the

---

[74] Case C-413/99 *Baumbast and R. v Secretary of State for the Home Department* [2002] E.C.R.
I–7091, para.39.
[75] *Olsson v Sweden No.2* (Application no. 13441/87) judgment of November 27, 1992, ECtHR.
[76] Pursuant to Art.12 of Reg. 1612/68. See now decision of the ECJ in Case C-200/02 *Man
Lavette Chen and Kunqian Catherine Zhu v Secretary of State for the Home Department*, October
19, 2004.

host Member State necessarily implies that that child has the right to be accompanied by the person who is his primary carer and, accordingly, that that person is able to reside with him in that Member State during his studies. To refuse to grant permission to remain to a parent who is the primary carer of the child exercising his right to pursue his studies in the host Member State infringes that right".

The ECJ made reference to the right to family life protected by Art.8 ECHR as being a fundamental right to which the Community law would give effect.

10–80   It is interesting in this context to consider whether an EU national is also entitled as a matter of Community law to install child-carers who may not be family members in any strict sense. It is certainly arguable that Community law would entitle the EU national to install such person, if to fail to do so would represent an obstacle to free movement rights. A single parent EU national, for instance, who requires a carer to look after the children whilst he is at work, might argue that failure by a Member State to grant the right of residence to that child-carer either prevents the EU national from exercising the free movement right, or interferes with the EU national's right to respect for family life, if the inability to be accompanied by the carer means that the children must be left with the carer in the state of origin. This is a choice which in *Carpenter* the ECJ considered unacceptable as a matter of Community law when read in conjunction with the ECHR.[77]

---

[77] Case C-60/00 *Carpenter v Secretary of State for the Home Department* [2002] E.C.R. I–6279.

CHAPTER 11

RIGHT OF RESIDENCE

This chapter examines the scope of the right of residence enjoyed by persons who exercise free movement rights, both those who are economically active (workers, those exercising the right of establishment and providers and recipients of services) and the economically inactive (students, the retired and those with a general right of residence).

1. INTRODUCTION

(a) *Right of Residence as a Corollary of Right to Move*

The right of residence in other Member States is the corollary of the funda-   **11–01**
mental principle contained in Arts 2 and 3(1)(c) EC Treaty that, for the purpose of establishing a common market and the promotion of the harmonious development of economic activities between Member States, obstacles to the free movement of persons between Member States shall be abolished.[1] Plainly this would be impossible without the right to enter into and reside in other Member States.

(b) *Deriving the Right of Residence from the Treaty*

The ECJ has constantly emphasised that it is the EC Treaty itself (or, depend-   **11–02**
ing on the case, by the provisions adopted to implement it) which is the source of the right to enter into and reside in the territory of another Member State. This has important ramifications, notably that breaches of formalities, whether of specific provisions of the relevant directives or the national law of Member States relating to entry and residence, will not justify denial of the right. This principle was firmly established in *Royer*[2] in which a French national faced criminal proceedings and expulsion arising from his illegal entry into and residence in Belgian territory where his wife, also a French national, ran a café and dance hall. As the ECJ stated, the regulations and directives determine "the scope and detailed rules for the exercise of rights conferred directly by the Treaty".[3] Since the right of residence is acquired independently of the issue of a residence permit, the grant of the permit itself does not give rise to rights at all but is simply a measure "to prove the individual position of a national of another Member State with

---

[1] See Case 118/75 *Watson and Belmann* [1976] E.C.R. 1185, para.16a.
[2] Case 48/75 *Procureur de Roi v Royer* [1976] E.C.R 497. See also for example Case 370/90 *R. v Immigration Appeal Tribunal and Surinder Singh Ex p. Secretary of State for Home Department* [1992] E.C.R. I-4265 where at para.17 the ECJ refers to the right to enter and reside in the territory of other Member States in order to pursue an economic activity there as envisaged by Arts 39 and 43 as a right which such persons "derive directly from . . . the Treaty".
[3] Case 48/75 *Procureur de Roi v Royer* [1976] E.C.R 497, para.28.

regard to provisions of Community law".[4] Further, the issue of the permit has merely declaratory effect.[5] Whilst the Treaty itself thus confers the right of residence directly on all those within its ambit, the various directives and regulations (to adopt the words of the ECJ in *Royer*[6]) give "closer articulation" to such right.

(c) *Human Rights and Proportionality*

11–03   Even where the Treaty and secondary legislation does not directly confer a right of residence, the ECJ has in recent years through the use of human rights and the principle of proportionality inferred a right of residence, particularly in relation to third country national family members. This is most apparent where not to recognise such right would create an obstacle to the exercise of fundamental freedoms under the Treaty.

11–04   For example in *Carpenter*[7] the ECJ held that Art.49 EC Treaty, read in the light of the fundamental right to respect for family life, gave the right of residence in the United Kingdom to a third country national spouse of a British citizen who was providing services to recipients established in *other* Member States.

11–05   Further in *Baumbast*[8] the ECJ held that by direct application of Art.18(1) EC Treaty a right of residence in the United Kingdom was conferred on a German national who no longer enjoyed a right of residence as a worker. Whilst the exercise of such right is subject to the limitations and conditions laid down by the EC Treaty and by the measures adopted to give it effect, "the competent authorities and, where necessary, the national courts must ensure that those limitations and conditions are applied in compliance with the general principles of Community law and, in particular, the principle of proportionality". Such limitations and conditions include the requirements that a person has sufficient resources to avoid becoming a burden on the social assistance system of the host Member State during their period of residence and that they are covered by sickness insurance in respect of all risks.[9] As to the latter condition, an adjudicator had found that Mr Baumbast was not covered for emergency treatment. However, in light of the circumstances of the case the ECJ held that:

> "to refuse to allow Mr Baumbast to exercise the right of residence which is conferred on him by Article 18(1) E.C. Treaty by virtue of the application of the provisions of Directive 90/364 on the ground that his sickness insurance does not cover the emergency treatment given in the host Member State would amount to a disproportionate interference with the exercise of that right".

---

[4] Case 48/75 *Procureur de Roi v Royer* [1976] E.C.R 497, para.33.
[5] See Case 8/77 *Sagulo, Brenca and Bakhouche* [1977] E.C.R. 1495 and see also Case 157/79 *R. v Pieck* [1980] E.C.R. 2171.
[6] Case 48/75 *Procureur de Roi v Royer* [1976] E.C.R 497, para.23.
[7] Case C–60/00 *Carpenter v Secretary of State for the Home Department* [2002] E.C.R. I-6279, para.46.
[8] Case C–413/99 *Baumbast and R. v Secretary of State for the Home Department* [2002] E.C.R. I-7091, paras 80–94.
[9] See Art.1(1) of Dir. 90/364.

2. FORMALITIES

Identified below for each free mover are the particular documents which are   **11–06**
required in order to establish the rights of entry and residence. In this section
consideration is given to the principles which have been developed by the ECJ
in the context of formalities, the possible consequences of failure to comply
with formalities, time limits, fees and visas.

It is to be noted at the outset that the formalities are the same in respect of   **11–07**
all free movers covered by the secondary legislation. For workers the relevant
provisions are those contained in Directive 68/360 on the abolition of restrictions on movement and residence. Substantially the same provisions are set
out in Directive 73/148 for those exercising their right to establishment and to
provide and receive services. For the three economically inactive categories of
free mover, each Directive establishing their rights[10] contains a recital in the
preamble providing that beneficiaries of the Directives should be covered by
administrative arrangements similar to those laid down in Directive 68/360.

(a) *Declaratory Effect of Residence Permits and Visas*

The principles established by the ECJ in *Royer*[11] about the right of residence   **11–08**
deriving from the EC Treaty itself and the declaratory effect of residence permits have already been emphasised. For Mr Royer, a French national who
had failed to comply with formalities concerning his entry and residence in
Belgium, these principles meant that neither his temporary imprisonment for
such failures nor his expulsion could be justified.

However these principles have much wider impact as shown by the recent   **11–09**
decision in *MRAX*[12] where the ECJ considered the position of a third country national marrying a worker in Belgium after having entered and remained
unlawfully in Belgium. The Belgian Government argued that it was entitled
both to refuse a residence permit to a third country national and to expel
such person, lest Art.3 of both Directives 68/360 and 73/148 (which as will be
seen enable visas to be required of third country national family members)
would be rendered "meaningless and entirely redundant". The ECJ dis-
agreed. Just as the issue of a residence permit to a national of a Member
State is simply a measure to prove the person's position with regard to provisions of Community law, so "the same finding must be made" in relation to
such third country national whose right of residence exists irrespective of the
issue of a residence permit.[13] Refusal of a permit and expulsion based solely
on failure to comply with legal formalities concerning the control of aliens
"would impair the very substance of the right of residence directly conferred
by Community law and would be manifestly disproportionate to the gravity

---

[10] Dir. 90/364 (general right of residence); Dir. 90/365 (retired persons) and Dir. 93/96 (students)
[11] Case 48/75 *Procureur de Roi v Royer* [1976] E.C.R 497.
[12] Case C–459/99 *Mouvement contre le racisme, l'antisémitisme et la xénophobie ASBL (MRAX)
v Belgian State* [2002] E.C.R. I–6591.
[13] Case 48/75 *Procureur de Roi v Royer* [1976] E.C.R 497, para.74.

of the infringement."[14] Thus where a third country national is able to provide proof of identity and marriage to a national of a Member State[15] neither refusal of a permit nor expulsion "on the sole ground that he has entered the territory of the Member State concerned *unlawfully*" is permitted.[16]

11–10   It might be considered difficult to square the decision in *MRAX*[17] with the decision of the ECJ in *Akrich*[18] in which the ECJ appeared to require the third country national family member to be lawfully resident in one Member State if intending to move to a second Member State with an EU national exercising free movement rights. Detailed analysis of the decision of the ECJ in *Akrich* is provided in Chapter 5. More important for present purposes *Akrich* did not consider at all either the decision in *MRAX* itself or the fundamental principles long established by the ECJ on which the *MRAX* decision was based. Further, in *Akrich* the ECJ did not consider the obligations on a Member State to admit a third country national family member of an EU free mover who arrives at the border. In all the circumstances, the ECJ's decision in *Akrich* cannot be regarded as having impacted on the Member States' obligations arising from the decision of the ECJ in *MRAX*.

(b) *Member States Cannot Ask for More than Permitted in Legislation*

11–11   Although the Directives are slightly differently cast, it is a fundamental principle that Member States cannot ask more of those exercising rights of entry and residence than is prescribed in the provisions themselves.

11–12   Thus for example in relation to the right of entry of workers referred to in Art.3 of Directive 68/360 Member States may require only the production of a valid identity document or passport.[19] Article 3(1) states "Member States shall allow the persons referred to in Article 1 to enter their territory simply on production of a valid identity card or passport". Article 3(1) of Directive 73/148 is in substantially the same terms.

11–13   In *Commission v Netherlands*[20] an action was brought by the Commission for a declaration that the Netherlands had failed to fulfil the obligations imposed by Directives 68/360 and 73/148 by maintaining in force legislation requiring citizens of Member States to answer questions posed by border officials about

---

[14] Case C–459/99 *Mouvement contre le racisme, l'antisémitisme et la xénophobie ASBL (MRAX) v Belgian State* [2002] E.C.R. I–6591, para.78.
[15] As effectively required (respectively) by Arts 4 and 6 of Dirs 68/360 and 73/148 (although the language of Dir. 68/360 contemplates marriages celebrated abroad since the reference is to documents issued by "the competent authority of the state of origin or the state whence they came").
[16] Case C–459/99 *Mouvement contre le racisme, l'antisémitisme et la xénophobie ASBL (MRAX) v Belgian State* [2002] E.C.R. I–6591, para.80.
[17] Case C–459/99 *Mouvement contre le racisme, l'antisémitisme et la xénophobie ASBL (MRAX) v Belgian State* [2002] E.C.R. I–6591.
[18] Case C–109/01 *Secretary of State for the Home Department v Akrich*, judgment of September 23, 2003.
[19] Case 321/87 *Commission v Belgium* [1989] E.C.R. 997.
[20] Case C–68/89 *Commission v Netherlands* [1991] E.C.R. I–2637.

the purpose and duration of their journey and the financial means at their disposal. The Dutch Government argued that the Directives applied only to those with a right of residence by virtue of the EC Treaty and that Member States were entitled to carry out spot checks at frontiers to investigate whether nationals have such right of residence. The ECJ granted the declaration, emphasising the general right to *enter* enjoyed by nationals of Member States in the exercise of the various freedoms. The condition that a valid identity document or passport be produced could not be supplemented by a requirement of proving inclusion in any particular category covered by the directives. Nor more generally could the obligation to answer questions put by frontier officials be a precondition for entry. The lawfulness of control on entry is limited to assessing whether the identity document produced is valid.

It is clear that Art.3 of both Directives 68/360 and 73/148 enables Member **11–14** States to require only the production of an identity card or passport. A Member State may not impose any further border checks or require any further documentation as a precondition to admission. This principle was confirmed in *Commission v Belgium*[21] although at first blush the decision might be thought to dilute the principle.

The case concerned the carrying out of checks at the border of a person's res- **11–15** idence permit in order to ensure compliance with the obligation imposed by *Belgian law* to carry such permit. The Belgian Government argued that inspection of residence permits was not a frontier control but part of a general system of police checks carried out habitually throughout Belgian territory to which all inhabitants are liable which may "incidentally" be carried out at the same time as the frontier control. The Commission on the other hand argued that the controls carried out at the time of entry added to the requirement of a production of an identity card. The ECJ did not consider the checks to be inconsistent with Art.3. In particular there was no dispute that the controls were carried out "sporadically and unsystematically" and further that they were part of a system of internal control exercised by Belgium over all its inhabitants. As regards such internal controls the ECJ held:

> "The controls at issue are not a condition for the exercise of the right of entry into Belgian territory and it is undisputed that Community law does not prevent Belgium from checking, within its territory, compliance with the obligation imposed on persons enjoying a right of residence under Community law to carry their residence or establishment permits at all times, where an identical obligation is imposed upon Belgian nationals as regards their identity card".[22]

It was crucial to the ECJ's decision that the checks were in fact part of a sys- **11–16** tem of internal control. Such checks if carried out at the border outside of such system of internal control would constitute a barrier to the free movement of persons and be unlawful if carried out in a systematic, arbitrary or unnecessarily restrictive manner.

---

[21] Case 321/87 *Commission v Belgium* [1989] E.C.R. 997.
[22] Case 321/87 *Commission v Belgium* [1989] E.C.R. 997, para.12.

(c) *Failure to Comply with Formalities*

11–17   As is clear from the decisions of the ECJ in *Royer*[23] and *MRAX*,[24] where the person concerned is able to fulfil the relevant conditions laid down failure to comply with formalities will not in itself justify interference with the rights of either entry or residence, whether by refusal and return at the border, or by expulsion thereafter (nor indeed could any such failure in itself constitute a threat to public policy). This is because such measures would negate the very rights conferred and guaranteed by the EC Treaty.[25] Furthermore, the corollary to the principle that Member States cannot ask for more than is permitted in the provisions themselves is that all forms of punishment will be prohibited for disregard of a provision which is incompatible with Community law. This was the position in the case of the national law provisions considered by the ECJ in *Sagulo*[26] which required workers to possess a general residence permit instead of the document provided for in Directive 68/360.

11–18   On the other hand this principle does not preclude the application of sanctions to those exercising free movement rights for infringement of national provisions which have been adopted in conformity with Community law provisions. And moreover, as stated by the ECJ in *Royer*:[27]

> "Community law does not prevent the member states from providing, for breaches of national provisions concerning the control of aliens, any appropriate sanctions—other than measures of expulsion from the territory—necessary in order to ensure the efficacy of those provisions".

11–19   What are the possible sanctions for breaches of formalities? In *Pieck*[28] the ECJ confirmed the entitlement of national authorities to impose penalties in respect of such breaches "comparable to those attaching to minor offences by nationals". However penalties would not be justified if so disproportionate to the gravity of the infringement that they become an obstacle to the free movement of persons. This would be especially so if the penalty included imprisonment. In practice this means that breaches of formalities may be punishable by fines, provided always that they are at a level which is proportionate to the gravity of the offence.

(d) *Time-Limits for Providing Visas and Residence Permits*

11–20   Directives 68/360 and 73/148 are silent as to the period of time within which Member States are required to issue visas, although Member States are obliged to afford third country national family members with "every facility for obtaining visas".

---

[23] Case 48/75 *Procureur de Roi v Royer* [1976] E.C.R. 497.
[24] Case C–459/99 *Mouvement contre le racisme, l'antisémitisme et la xénophobie ASBL (MRAX) v Belgian State* [2002] E.C.R. I–6591.
[25] See also Case 157/79 *R. v Pieck* [1980] E.C.R. 2171, particularly para.18.
[26] Case 8/77 *Sagula* [1977] E.C.R. 1495.
[27] Case 48/75 *Procureur de Roi v Royer* [1976] E.C.R. 497, para.42.
[28] Case 157/79 *R. v Pieck* [1980] E.C.R. 2171, para.19.

As to residence permits, Art.5 of Directive 64/221[29] provides that "a decision **11–21** to grant or to refuse a first residence permit shall be taken as soon as possible and in any event not later than six months from the date of application for the permit". The provisions of Directive 64/221 apply to each category of free mover.[30]

Neither affording "every facility for obtaining visas" nor the obligation to **11–22** issue a residence permit "as soon possible" are defined by reference to any period of time. However, it is clear that such documents must be issued promptly and without delay since delay could impair the very substance of rights given by Community law by hindering their exercise. Furthermore any unreasonable or excessive delay would be disproportionate and unlawful. None of the formalities raise particularly difficult questions: on the contrary, most are straightforward matters.

These propositions clearly reflect the views of the Commission which has **11–23** instituted proceedings against Spain for its failure to take a decision concerning a residence permit promptly.[31] As stated by the Commission:

"The Member State must adopt the decision concerning the residence permit as soon as possible and in any event not later than six months of the date of application, it being understood that this maximum period of six months is to be taken into account *only* in cases where examination of the application is interrupted on the grounds of public policy".[32]

In sum the question of what is prompt will depend on all relevant circum- **11–24** stances having regard to the factors here mentioned. Absent substantial justification residence permits or visas should be issued in terms of days or weeks, rather than months. Certainly if the 'facility' offered by a Member State to a third country national family member to obtain a visa was an interview with a consular official at an overseas embassy, in some six months' time, this would be contrary to Community law.

(i) *Time Limits Imposed on Applicants for Providing Necessary Documents to Obtain Residence Permit*

As discussed, Member States are obliged to act promptly in providing free **11–25** movers with visas and residence permits. However there is no corresponding obligation on the free movers themselves to obtain residence documents within a prescribed period. Thus it would be contrary to Community law for a Member State to make provision in its legislation for the giving of automatic notification of an order to leave the country to Union citizens who have not produced the documents necessary to obtain a residence permit within a

---

[29] Dir. 64/221 of February 15, 1964 on the co-ordination of special measures concerning the movement and residence of foreign nationals [1963–64] O.J Spec. Ed. 117.
[30] As extended in the preamble to Dirs 68/360; 73/148; 90/364; 90/365 and 93/96 and extended by Dir. 72/194 to beneficiaries of Reg.1251/70.
[31] Case C–157/03 *Commission v Spain* [2003] O.J. C135/23.
[32] Emphasis added.

prescribed period. As pointed out by the Commission in proceedings instituted against Belgium:[33]

> "[T]he fact that the administrative procedures for the grant of the residence permit have not been complied with may not lead to a penalty such as refusal to grant the right of residence or removal from the territory, which would effectively deny the actual right of residence conferred by the Treaty. The notification of an order to leave the territory may be based not on exclusively administrative grounds, but on facts leading to the conclusion that the person concerned does not fulfil the conditions set for his right of residence by one of the relevant directives".

(e) *Fees*

11–26 Directives 68/360 and 73/148 distinguish between fees for residence permits and visas.[34] The provisions contain a general prohibition on the payment of charges for residence permits (to be issued and renewed free of charge). However where a Member State charges its own nationals for the issue of identity cards the general prohibition against charging becomes a limitation to an amount not exceeding "the dues and taxes" charged for the issue of identity cards. In relation to visas on the other hand[35] these must be free of charge in all circumstances.

(f) *Visas*

(i) *EU Nationals*

11–27 As discussed, EU nationals exercising free movement rights must be allowed to enter the territory simply on production of a valid identity card or passport.[36] The provisions expressly provide further that no "entry visa or equivalent document" may be demanded of such EU nationals. In *Pieck*[37] the British Government argued that the phrase meant exclusively a document issued *before* the traveller arrives at the frontier in the form of an endorsement on a passport or of a separate document, but not an endorsement stamped on a passport at the time of *arrival* giving permission to enter. The ECJ rejected the argument. The phrase covers "any formality for the purpose of granting leave to enter the territory of a Member State which is coupled with a passport or identity card check at the frontier, whatever may be the

---

[33] Case C–408/03 *Commission v Belgium* pending before the ECJ.
[34] Art.9, Dir. 68/360 (residence permits and visas); Art.7 Dir. 73/148 (residence permits and visas: documents and certificates required for the issue and renewal of residence documents are treated in the same way as residence permits themselves); Art.6 Reg. 1251/70 (residence permits); Art.6, Dir. 75/34 (residence permits); Art.2 of Dirs 90/364, 90/365 and 93/96 (applying *mutatis mutandis* the provisions of Art.9, Dir. 68/360).
[35] In addition, in Dir. 68/360 as provided by Art.9.2 in relation to the 'stamp' placed on the contract of employment of a seasonal worker (as referred to in Art.8(2)).
[36] Art.3 Dirs 68/360 and 73/148, and Art.2, Dirs 90/364, 90/365 and 93/96 (applying *mutatis mutandis* the provisions of Art.3 of Dir. 68/360).
[37] Case 157/79 *R. v Pieck* [1980] E.C.R. 2171, in which case a Dutch national working in Wales whose passport on entry was stamped "given leave to enter the United Kingdom for six months" was prosecuted for having knowingly remained beyond the six months given.

place or time at which that leave is granted and in whatever form it may be granted."[38]

(ii) *Family Members*

The position for family members who are not nationals of Member States is **11–28** different. The provisions do enable entry visas or equivalent documents to be demanded of third country nationals, although Member States are obliged to afford to such persons "every facility for obtaining any necessary visas." Plainly this obligation falls to be broadly construed consistent with fundamental nature of the rights being exercised both by the EU national and his or her family members. It would certainly not be met by the offer of an interview at an embassy for consideration to be given to an application for a visa some months away. Following the decision of the ECJ in *MRAX*[39] however for the third country national family member who arrives at the border without a visa there is to all intents and purposes little practical difference, at least in terms of the right of entry, between his or her position and that of the EU national.

The first question considered by the ECJ in *MRAX* was whether the provi- **11–29** sions of the Directives, read in the light of the principles of proportionality and non-discrimination and the right to respect for family life, allowed a Member State at the border to send back a foreign national married to a Community national who seeks to enter without being in possession of either an identity document or a visa. The ECJ acknowledged that the exercise of the right of entry could be made conditional on possession of a visa. However the obligation to accord every facility would be denied its "full effect" unless visas were issued without delay and as far as possible at the place of entry into the national territory.[40] Further, in view of the importance attached to the protection of family life it would be disproportionate and prohibited:

> "to send back a third country national married to a national of a Member State where he is able to prove his identity and the conjugal ties and there is no evidence to establish that he represents a risk to the requirements of public policy, public security or public health within the meaning of Article 10 of Directive 68/360 and Article 8 of Directive 73/148".[41]

In sum the position is as follows. Member States *are* entitled to make the **11–30** exercise of the right of entry for family members conditional on possession of a visa. In practical terms this may mean that the third country national who tries to travel without a visa could face difficulties because of carrier

---

[38] Moreover to require such endorsement would offend the principle that Member States cannot ask for more than permitted in the legislation discussed above. Following *Pieck*, the UK's legislation was changed: by s.7, Immigration Act 1988 those exercising Treaty rights do not require "leave to enter or remain".

[39] C–459/99 *Mouvement contre le racisme, l'antisémitisme et la xénophobie ASBL (MRAX) v Belgium* [2002] E.C.R. I-6591.

[40] C–459/99 *Mouvement contre le racisme, l'antisémitisme et la xénophobie ASBL (MRAX) v Belgium* [2002] E.C.R. I-6591.

[41] C–459/99 *Mouvement contre le racisme, l'antisémitisme et la xénophobie ASBL (MRAX) v Belgium* [2002] E.C.R. I-6591.

sanctions. For those family members who do make it to the border without documents but are able to prove their identity and relationship this potential precondition is irrelevant since they will not (subject to the public policy proviso) be able to be returned. This does not mean, however, that they might not be liable to lesser sanctions than being returned for having failed to obtain necessary visas. The ECJ has suggested that such lesser sanctions could take the form of administrative fines.

11–31 Family members may be required to provide confirmation of the family relationship. However obtaining visas cannot be made subject to any requirements beyond such confirmation. Thus for example evidence of means of support must not be required of the third country national spouse of a worker or work seeker.

(g) Residence Permits

11–32 In respect of each category of free mover the documentation required to be produced by both principal and family member in order to obtain a residence permit is considered below. The documents themselves are issued as proof of the right of residence and are required to take a particular form (entitled "Residence permit for a national of a Member State of the EEC").

11–33 The corollary to the proposition that residence permits are declaratory of the underlying rights to which they relate is that possession of a residence permit cannot be taken to be proof positive of the existence of a right to remain. Thus for example the holder of a five-year residence permit who is the third country national spouse of a worker cannot rely on this document to avoid expulsion where the third country national and worker are not merely separated but divorced.[42] This is because the right to remain expires on divorce and possession of a residence permit is not proof to the contrary. Subject to such divorced spouse's having any independent right to remain (as for example in *Baumbast*[43] through her child), such a divorcee may face expulsion in accordance national laws and human rights obligations.

11–34 The right of entry is evidenced by production of a valid identity card or passport.[44] Article 4 of Directive 68/360 and Art.6 of Directive 73/148 lay down the requirements for obtaining residence permits. Member States may require production of the document with which the person entered the territory.[45] However the person might no longer have the *actual* identity card or passport with which he entered. In *Giagounidis*[46] the ECJ stated that the purpose of the Art.4 of Directive 68/360 requiring *only* production of the document with which the person entered for the issue of a residence permit was "to preclude the host Member State from imposing disproportionate conditions on the

---

[42] See Case 267/83 *Diatta v Land Berlin* [1985] E.C.R. 567.
[43] Case C–413/99 *Baumbast and R. v Secretary of State for the Home Department* [2002] E.C.R. I-7091. See Chapter 10.
[44] See for example Art.3(1), Dir. 68/360.
[45] See for example Art.4, Dir. 68/360 (such document will be the aforementioned identity card or passport.
[46] Case C–376/89 *Giagounidis v Stadt Reutlingen* [1991] E.C.R. I–1069.

exercise of the right of residence". Thus the ECJ held that it would be contrary to the principle of freedom of movement for workers if issue of the residence permit were to be made conditional "on production of that same document".

3. SPECIFIC RIGHTS OF RESIDENCE FOR EU NATIONALS AND THEIR FAMILY MEMBERS

(a) *The Rights of Residence for the Five Categories of Free Mover*

(i) *Workers*

The specific rights of residence for workers (and members of their families to whom Reg. 1612/68 applies) are set out in Directive 68/360.[47]   **11–35**

Obtaining residence permits

The Directive identifies two discrete rights for workers exercising free movement rights. Firstly, the right given by Art.3 to enter the territory of Member States simply on production of a valid identity card or passport. Secondly, the right of residence which by Art.4(1) Member States must grant to those workers able to produce certain specified documents (from the worker the document on which the worker entered the territory and confirmation of engagement from the employer or a certificate of employment). Article 4(2) obliges Member States to issue a "Residence permit for a national of a Member State of the EEC" (to take the form set out in the Annex to the Directive) as proof of the right of residence.   **11–36**

Validity

Article 6 deals with the residence permit itself. The article distinguishes between employment which will last for more than 12 months and employment of between 3 and 12 months. In the former case the residence permit must be valid throughout the territory of the issuing Member State for at least five years and be automatically renewable.   **11–37**

Validity of the residence permit is not affected by breaks in residence not exceeding six months or absence on military service. It is to be inferred that a break in residence of more than six months may provide grounds for withdrawal of the permit, at least until the Art.4 documents are obtainable.   **11–38**

In the case of employment which will last for between 3 and 12 months a "temporary residence permit" shall be issued. The validity of this document may be limited to the expected period of the employment. A seasonal worker with a contract of employment stamped by the competent authority of the relevant Member State[48] shall also be issued with a temporary residence permit of more than three months.   **11–39**

---

[47] Council Dir. 68/360 of October 15, 1968 on the abolition of restrictions on movement and residence within the Community for workers of Member States and their families [1968] O.J. L257/13.
[48] As provided for in Art.8(1)(c).

Renewal and withdrawal

11–40   The five-year residence permit is automatically renewable. However Art.7(2) provides for an exception in the case of renewal for the first time where the worker has been involuntarily unemployed in the Member State for more than 12 consecutive months in which case the period of the residence permit may be restricted to not less than 12 months. This applies only in relation to renewal for the first time. A temporary residence permit on the other hand is automatically renewable. On expiry such worker could obtain a further temporary permit on production of the documents referred to in Art.4.

11–41   Lengthy involuntary unemployment (even for example throughout a second five-year period of residence) would not justify refusal of further renewal. Beyond the specific Art.7(2) exception, Article 7(1) provides that a valid residence permit may not be withdrawn solely on the ground that the worker is no longer in employment either because of temporary incapacity (as a result of illness or accident) or because of involuntary unemployment.

Workers not issued residence permits

11–42   The right of residence is wholly discrete from the issue of a residence permit which has only declaratory effect. Article 8 makes specific provision for circumstances in which the right of residence is to be recognised by Member States without issuing a residence permit. These are workers whose activity is not expected to last for more than three months. For such persons (subject to one exception[49]), the document with which the person entered together with a statement by the employer on the expected duration of the employment are sufficient to cover his stay.

11–43   For frontier workers the competent authority of the State of employment may issue a special permit valid for five years and automatically renewable. However this is not a residence permit. For seasonal workers whose contract of employment is stamped by the competent authority the right of residence in the territory is also recognised without issuing a residence permit. In all cases the worker may be required by the competent authority of the Member State to report his presence in the territory.

Work seekers

11–44   The right of free movement extends not only to those pursuing economic activities as workers, but includes those who wish to pursue such activities.[50] As recognised by the ECJ in *Antonissen*[51] there is no Community provision prescribing the period during which Community nationals seeking employment in a Member State may stay there. Indeed work seekers are not dealt

---

[49] A statement by the employer is not required in the case of workers coming within the provisions of Dir. 64/224 on the attainment of freedom of establishment and freedom to provide services of the activities of intermediaries in commerce, industry and small craft industries.
[50] See Chap.7.
[51] Case C–292/89 *The Queen v Immigration Appeal Tribunal, Ex p. Antonissen* [1991] E.C.R. 745, para.21.

with at all in Community legislation,[52] even although free movement rights extend to them.

However the absence of such Community law provision cannot mean that the   **11–45**
right of residence enjoyed by work seekers is not required to be recognised by Member States. To the contrary, at the very least in Member States whose national laws require persons to register their presence within three months and where the absence of a residence permit may give rise to penalties (as is the case for example in Belgium), Community law would the require the issue of confirmation of the right to reside. Failure to so recognise the right of residence by such Member States would fundamentally undermine the right of free movement otherwise enjoyed. At the same time in Member States which would not so penalise work seekers (as would be the case for example in the United Kingdom) the right must still be recognised—even by analogy with Art.8 of Directive 68/360, without issuing a residence permit.

In these cases following *Antonissen*,[53] the right must be recognised (whether   **11–46**
by confirmation of the right to reside or without issuing such permit) in the first instance for six months. At the end of such period a person who has found work would be entitled to a residence permit on normal principles. Otherwise a further period of recognition should follow if the person concerned is able to provide evidence that he is continuing to seek employment and that he has genuine chances of being engaged. This is because, as stated in *Antonissen*, a person could not be required to leave the territory of the host Member State in such circumstances.

(ii) *The Self-employed and Service Providers and Recipients*

Obtaining the right of residence—self-employed

The specific rights of residence for the self-employed and service providers   **11–47**
and recipients are set out in Directive 73/148.[54] As recognised by the ECJ in *Royer*[55] the provisions of this Directive are substantially the same as those in Directive 68/360 for workers. Thus the jurisprudence in relation to one is equally applicable to the other.

---

[52] At para.17 in *Antonissen* the ECJ considered a declaration recorded in the Council minutes at the time of the adoption Reg. 1612/68 and Council Dir. 68/360 which referred to work seekers in the following terms: "Nationals of a Member State as referred to in Article 1 [of the directive] who move to another Member State in order to seek work there shall be allowed a minimum period of three months for the purpose; in the event of their not having found employment by the end of that period, their residence on the territory of this second State may be brought to an end". However, the ECJ declined to use such declaration "for the purpose of interpreting a provision of secondary legislation where, as in this case, no reference is made to the content of the declaration in the wording of the provision in question. The declaration therefore has no legal significance."
[53] Case C–292/89 *The Queen v Immigration Appeal Tribunal, Ex p. Antonissen* [1991] E.C.R. 745, paras 21–22.
[54] Council Dir. 73/148 of May 21, 1973 on the abolition of restrictions on movement and residence within the Community for nationals of Member States with regard to establishment and the provisions of services.
[55] Case 48/75 *Procureur de Roi v Royer* [1976] E.C.R. 497, para.15.

11–48   As with Directive 68/360, Directive 73/148 also deals with the discrete rights of entry and residence. As to the right of entry Art.3 is cast in the same terms as Art.3 of Directive 68/360. As to the right of residence, Directive 73/148 distinguishes between the right of residence for the self-employed on the one hand and service providers and recipients on the other.

11–49   Article 6 provides that an applicant for a residence permit is not to be required to produce anything other than the identity card or passport with which the person entered and proof that the person comes within the class of persons to whom the Directive applies.

Validity

11–50   In relation to the self-employed, Art.4(1) of Directive 73/148 deals with those who establish themselves in order to pursue activities as self-employed persons and provides (somewhat confusingly) that the right of "permanent residence" shall be granted to them "when the restrictions on these activities have been abolished pursuant to the Treaty". Quite apart from the fact that restrictions on such activities remain,[56] the word "permanent" should be read as *continuous* when compared with the position of service providers.[57] As in Directive 68/360, Art.4(1) of Directive 73/148 provides for the issue as proof of the right of residence of an automatically renewable five-year residence permit entitled "Residence Permit for a National of a Member State of the European Communities". Article 4(1) provides also that validity of the residence permit is not affected by breaks in residence not exceeding six months or absence on military service.

Renewal

11–51   In terms which reflect Art.7(1) of Directive 68/360, Art.4(1) also provides that a valid residence permit may not be withdrawn solely on the grounds that the person is no longer in employment because he is temporarily incapable of work as a result of illness or accident.

Obtaining residence permit—service providers and recipients

11–52   As to service providers and recipients, the right of residence is dealt with in Art.4(2) which provides that the right shall be of equal duration with the period during which the services are provided. Where such period exceeds three months the Member State in which the services are performed shall issue a right of abode as proof of the right of residence. In practice this means the issue of a five-year residence permit subject to the production of the Art.6 documents. Where the period does not exceed three months Art.4(2) provides that the identity card or passport with which the person

---

[56] Even the right of every citizen of the Union to move and reside freely in Art.18 EC Treaty is subject to the limitations and conditions laid down in the Treaty.

[57] Certainly such interpretation is consistent with the provision in Art.4(1) which requires that as proof of the right of residence a residence permit is issued which is both valid for not less than five years and automatically renewable. If permanent required the grant of a residence permit of indefinite duration Art.4(1) would not refer to a five-year minimum. Moreover, if not construed as suggested there would have been no reason for the adoption of Dir. 75/34 giving "the right to remain permanently" to the self-employed in certain circumstances.

entered is sufficient to cover his stay, but such person may be required to report his presence in the territory.

(iii) *Students*

Specific rights of residence for students are set out in Directive 93/96.[58] Article 1 of Directive 93/96 requires Member States to recognise the right of residence for students who are nationals of Member States not enjoying that right under other provisions of Community law.[59] The student must assure the Member State by means of declaration or by such alternative means as the student may choose that are at least equivalent, that he has sufficient resources to avoid becoming a burden on the social assistance system of the host Member State during their period of residence'. The student must be also enrolled in a recognised educational establishment and covered by sickness insurance "in respect of all risks in the host Member State". **11–53**

In *Commission v Italy*[60] proceedings were brought against Italy because students were being required to prove their ability to support themselves, rather than provide the relevant assurance by means of the declaration prescribed in Art.1. The ECJ stated that such practice was unlawful. It was evident from the wording of Art.1 that the conditions for obtaining the right of residence did not include any requirement to have resources of a specific amount, evidenced by specific documents. Member States cannot require more than is laid down by the Directive (here the assurance by declaration or alternative means of sufficiency of resources, rather than evidence of any such resources themselves). **11–54**

In practice students at the outset of their stay may find difficulties in *proving* their means; it is for this reason that the Directive requires only an assurance by way of declaration. It is to be noted, however, that neither enrolment nor sickness insurance is a matter in respect of which an assurance can be given. Rather the Directive refers to the establishment of the facts that the student *is* enrolled and *is* covered.[61] **11–55**

The right is expressly restricted in Art.2 of the Directive to the duration of the course of studies in question. Such limitation as to duration will apply to any person exercising free movement rights for the purposes of study.[62] Article 2 also provides that the right is evidenced by a residence permit[63] **11–56**

---

[58] Council Dir. 93/96 of October 29, 1993 on the right of residence for students (replacing Dir. 90/366 following successful challenge to the legal basis of the former directive in Case C–295/90 *Parliament v Council* [1992] E.C.R. I-4193).

[59] See Chapter 9.

[60] Case C–424/98 *Commission v Italy* [2000] E.C.R. I-4001.

[61] Case C–424/98 *Commission v Italy* [2000] E.C.R. I-4001, para.44.

[62] See Case C-357/89 *Raulin v Minister van Onderwijs en Wetenschappen* [1992] E.C.R. I-1027 where the ECJ considered the right of residence for students derived from [Art.7 and 128 EC Treaty] and stated (at para.34): "It follows that the principle of non-discrimination with regard to conditions of access to vocational training deriving from Articles 7 and 128 of the EEC Treaty implies that a national of a Member State who has been admitted to a vocational training course in another Member State enjoys, in this respect, a right of residence for the duration of the course".

[63] As in other provisions entitled "Residence permit for a national of a Member State of the EEC".

which may be limited to the duration of the course or to one year (renewable annually) where the course lasts longer. For the purpose of issuing the residence permit the Member State may require only the presentation of a valid identity card or passport and proof that the person meets the Art.1 conditions. Article 4 provides that the right of residence shall remain for as long as beneficiaries of that right fulfil the conditions laid down in Art.1.

(iv) *Retired Persons*

11–57 The specific rights of residence for employees and self-employed persons who have ceased their occupational activity are contained in Directive 90/365.[64]

11–58 The right of residence is provided by Art.1 of the Directive to nationals of Member States who have pursued an active as an employee or self-employed person provided that they are in receipt of sufficient pension or benefits so as not to become a burden on the social security system and provided they are covered by sickness insurance. These are matters of which proof will be required. The right (as in the case of all the economically inactive) is not linked in any way to the person's having previously exercised free movement rights.

11–59 Article 2 deals with the length of validity of the residence permit.[65] The permit is issued as evidence of the exercise of the right of residence for five years on a renewable basis. Article 2 however differs from other provisions making provision for five-year residence permits[66] since Member States are given the discretion to require revalidation of the permit at the end of the first two years of residence. This will mean that the persons concerned will again have to demonstrate satisfaction of the Art.1 conditions if required to do so. However this can happen only once, namely at the end of *the first* two years of residence. Thereafter a renewable five-year residence permit must be issued without the possibility of further revalidation. In practical terms there may be little difference between revalidation and renewal, since Member States require production of the same documents on renewal in any event.

11–60 In terms identical to those in Directive 93/96, Art.2 also provides that for the purpose of issuing the residence permit the Member State may require only the presentation of a valid identity card or passport and proof that the person meets the Art.1 conditions. Article 3 provides that the right of residence shall remain for as long as beneficiaries of that right fulfil the conditions laid down in Art.1.

(v) *Self-sufficient Persons*

11–61 The specific rights of residence for self-sufficient persons are contained in Directive 90/364.[67] Article 1 of the Directive provides that Member States

---

[64] Dir. 90/365 of June 28, 1990 on the right of residence for employees and self-employed persons who have ceased their occupational activity.

[65] As in other provisions entitled "Residence permit for a national of a Member State of the EEC".

[66] For example Art.6, Dir. 68/360 and Art.4, Dir. 73/148.

[67] Dir. 90/365 of June 28, 1990 on the right of residence.

shall grant the right of residence to nationals of Member States who do not enjoy such right under other provisions of Community law provided they are covered by sickness insurance and have sufficient resources to avoid becoming a burden on the social assistance system of the host Member State during their period of residence. As with retired persons these matters must to be proved.

Article 2 is identically worded to Art.2 of Directive 90/365 in providing for   **11–62** the issue of a five-year renewable residence permit[68] as evidence of the exercise of the right of residence, subject to the same revalidation discretion discussed above. It is similarly identical in providing that for the purpose of issuing the residence permit the Member State may require only the presentation of a valid identity card or passport and proof that the person meets the Art.1 conditions.

Article 3 (also similarly worded) provides that the right of residence shall   **11–63** remain for as long as beneficiaries of that right fulfil the conditions laid down in Art.1.

The Commission has sought a declaration from the ECJ that Belgium had   **11–64** failed in its obligation under Directive 90/364 by making the right of residence subject to the condition that persons have sufficient personal resources for the entirety of his stay.[69] The Commission emphasised the flexibility of the Directive which was intended to allow the citizen of the Union to move easily within the territory of the Member States without having to prove that he has means of subsistence for the entire duration of his stay. The Commission submited:

> "However, the system of the Belgian authorities seeks to introduce additional guarantees in order to avoid ab initio the citizen of the Union becoming a burden on the social assistance system, which is inherently contrary to the spirit of Directive 90/364/EEC".

(b) Permanent residence

(i) Introduction

Those who have been economically active by exercising free movement rights   **11–65** in other Member States (employees, the self-employed and service providers and recipients) have the right to remain permanently in such Member States in certain circumstances.

As regards workers, Art.39(3)(d) EC Treaty provides that the right of free   **11–66** movement for workers shall entail the "right to remain in the territory of a Member State having been employed in that State". The conditions under

---

[68] Again entitled "Residence permit for a national of a member State of the EEC".
[69] Case C–408/03 *Commission v Belgium* [OJ C257/37]. The case is pending before the ECJ.

which the right of permanent residence may be exercised for workers are contained in Reg. 1251/70.[70]

11–67   As regards the self-employed, the conditions under which the right of permanent residence may be exercised are contained in Directive 75/34.[71] As the Preamble to this Directive notes, EC Treaty provisions do not expressly provide a similar right for self-employed persons (as that contained in Art.39(3)(d) EC Treaty for workers). Nevertheless, as stated in the Preamble, "the nature of establishment, together with attachments formed to the countries in which they have pursued their activities, means that such persons have a definite interest in enjoying the same right to remain as that granted to workers". The provisions of the Directive are substantially the same as those contained in Reg. 1251/70.

(ii) *Retired Workers*

11–68   Article 2(1)(a) of Reg. 1251/70 provides the right to remain permanently for a worker who at the time of termination of activity has reached the age laid down by the law of the Member State for entitlement to an old-age pension. In addition such person must have been employed in the state for at least the last 12 months and have resided there continuously for more than three years. Article 2(2) provides that the additional conditions as to employment and residence shall not apply if the worker's spouse is either a national of the Member State concerned, or lost that nationality by marriage to the worker.

11–69   Article 4 provides that continuity of residence may be attested by any means of proof in use in the Member State and that such continuity of residence is not affected by temporary absences not exceeding three months a year, nor by longer absences due to military service obligations. Further, Art.4 also provides that periods of duly recorded involuntary unemployment and absences due to illness or accident are to be considered periods of employment within the meaning of Art.2(1).

11–70   Article 5 provides the possibility of delaying the exercise of the right for up to two years from the time at which entitlement under Art.2(1)(a) and (b)[72] arises.[73] During such period the person may leave the territory without adversely affecting such right. In other words, once the right has arisen continuity or residence (which was critical to the creation of the right) ceases to be relevant. By Article 5(2) no formality shall be required on the part of the persons concerned in respect of the exercise of the right to remain.

11–71   Article 6 provides[74] that those coming under the Regulation's provisions shall be entitled to a residence permit (issued and renewed free of charge or for no more than the dues and taxes payable by nationals for the issue or renewal of

---

[70] Commission Reg. 1251/70 of June 29, 1970 on the right of workers to remain in the territory of a Member State after having been employed in that state.

[71] Council Dir. 75/34 of December 17, 1974 concerning the right of nationals of a Member State to remain in the territory of another Member State.

[72] See para.11–72 below.

[73] See Case C–257/00 *Givane v Secretary of State for the Home Department* [2003] E.C.R. I 345.

[74] The terms of Art.6 reflect those in Art.6 of Dir. 68/360.

identity documents) which must be valid throughout the territory of the issuing state for at least five years and be renewable automatically. The validity of the residence permit is not affected by periods of non-residence of less than six months.

(iii) *Incapacitated Workers*

Article 2(1)(b) of Reg. 1251/70 provides the right to remain permanently for   **11–72** a worker who, having resided continuously in the territory of that state for more than two years, ceases to work there as an employed person as a result of permanent incapacity to work. However, if the incapacity is the result of an accident at work or an occupational disease entitling the person to a pension payable either wholly or in part by an institution of the relevant state, then there is no condition as to length of residence. Similarly Art.2(2) provides that the condition as to residence shall not apply if the worker's spouse is either a national of the Member State concerned, or lost that nationality by marriage to the worker.

Articles 4, 5 and 6 apply as in relation to retired workers considered above.   **11–73**

(iv) *Frontier Workers*

Article 2(1)(c) of Reg. 1251/70 provides the right to remain permanently   **11–74** for a worker who after three years' continuous employment and residence in the territory of the relevant state works as an employed person in the territory of *another* Member State while retaining his residence in the territory of the first state, to which he returns, as a rule, each day or at least once a week.

At the very least this provision protects the position of a person who becomes   **11–75** a frontier worker in the period prior to retirement or prior to becoming incapacitated. For such persons the final paragraph of Art.2(1) provides expressly that periods of employment in the territory of the other Member State as a frontier worker shall "for the purposes of entitlement to the rights referred to in sub-paragraph (a) and (b), be considered as having been completed in the territory of the State of residence." Without such provision frontier workers would not be able to satisfy the sub-para. (a) or (b) requirements of employment at time of retirement or incapacity in the state of residence.

However, Art.2(1)(c) can be read also as giving a discrete right of permanent   **11–76** residence to those who become frontier workers whilst exercising free movement rights where they have done so for three years. Although some texts interpret this provision differently,[75] there are a number of reasons why the provision falls to be so construed.

First, the right—which is unrelated to retirement or incapacity—arises on the   **11–77** plain language of sub-para. (c) (without reference to the last paragraph of Art.2(1)). Secondly, such interpretation gives meaning to the reference in

---

[75] See for example Wyatt and Dashwood, "European Union Law" (Sweet & Maxwell, 2000) which at p.413 limits the right to the saving discussed.

sub-para. (c) to 'three years' which would otherwise be otiose because the three-year period is surely irrelevant to the provision in the last paragraph of Art.2(1). It could hardly sensibly be suggested that the saving could be relied on only where a person had clocked up three years continuous residence before becoming a frontier worker (not least since in sub-para. (b) the right of permanent residence on incapacity arises after two years' continuous residence which in the case of an incapacitated frontier worker would mean that the provision would not apply for at least a further 12 months). It seems unlikely that Community law would so discriminate against frontier workers. Thirdly, it is difficult otherwise to make sense of the use of the present tense in Art.2(1)(c), which if to be construed as applicable *only* to the provision in the last paragraph of Art.2(1) would make no sense at all in light of the fact that retirement and incapacitation arises on cessation of work. Indeed, in this respect the use of the present tense in sub-para. (c) as against the use of the past tense in the context of the last paragraph of Art.2(1) only makes sense if construed as suggested. Finally, such interpretation is supported by the following recitation in the Preamble which clearly distinguishes between the right to remain on cessation of work on retirement or incapacitation on the one hand and the right to remain ("that right") for the frontier worker:

"Whereas it is important, in the first place, to guarantee to the worker residing in the territory of a Member State the right to remain in that territory when he ceases to be employed in that State because he has reached retirement age or by reason of permanent incapacity to work; whereas, however, it is equally important to ensure that right for the worker who, after a period of employment and residence in the territory of a Member State, works as an employed person in the territory of another Member State, while still retaining his residence in the territory of the first State; . . .".

11–78   This interpretation does not however make the minimum interpretation referred to above otiose. On the contrary, the provision treating periods of employment in the other Member State as if completed in the State of residence would appear to be intended to avoid the possibility of the frontier worker's acquiring the right of permanent residence in two Member States.[76]

11–79   Further, periods of employment completed working as a frontier worker in this way are—for the purposes of the rights of retired workers and incapacitated workers in Art.2(1)(a) and (b)—considered as having been completed in the territory of the state of residence.

11–80   Articles 4, 5(2) and 6 apply as in relation to retired and incapacitated workers considered above. There is however no ability to delay the time within which the right is to be exercised. The contrast with the retired or incapacitated person is made in the Preamble which acknowledges that such persons should be given a period of time in which to consider where permanently to reside.

---

[76] Although it might be said that the very definition of frontier worker would preclude an argument that the person resides in the territory of work, such argument (for the purposes at least of Arts 2(1)(a) and (b) of Dir. 1251/70) could well be sought to be advanced where the frontier worker returns to the state of residence only once a week.

(v) *Retired Self-employed Workers*

Article 2(1)(a) of Directive 75/34 requires that Member States recognise the   **11–81**
right to remain permanently of self-employed persons in exactly the same circumstances as retired workers attain the same right in Art.2(1)(a) of Reg.
1251/70. However, where the law of the Member State does not grant the
right to an old-age pension to certain categories of self-employed workers,
the age requirement is considered satisfied when the beneficiary reaches 65
years of age. The Art.2(2) caveat is similar, as are the provisions contained in
Arts 4, 5 and 6.

(vi) *Incapacitated Self-employed Workers*

Article 2(1)(b) of Directive 75/34 makes provision for incapacitated self-   **11–82**
employed persons. It mirrors the provision in Art.2(1)(b) of Reg. 1251/70 for
incapacitated workers. The same comments apply in relation to the Art.2(2)
caveat, and Arts 4, 5 and 6 as made in relation to self-employed retired
workers.

(vii) *Self-employed Frontier Workers*

The Art.2(1)(c) provision for self-employed frontier workers in Directive   **11–83**
75/34 mirrors that in Art.2(1)(c) of Reg. 1251/70 for frontier workers. In particular, the same detailed comments apply as those made above as to why the
provision should be read as giving a discrete right of permanent residence to
those who become frontier workers after three years' continuous residence
and activity in a second Member State. Although the Preamble recital is
differently worded it is to like effect.

Moreover, the same comments apply in relation to the Art.2(2) caveat, and   **11–84**
Arts 4, 5(2) and 6 as made in relation to retired and incapacitated workers.
For frontier workers there is again no possibility of delaying the exercise of
the right (see discussion above).

(c) *Family Members*

(i) *Generally*

The rights of residence identified above extend to family members. This is   **11–85**
entirely unsurprising in view of the importance given by Community law to
respect for family life in order to eliminate obstacles to the exercise of the
fundamental freedoms guaranteed by the EC Treaty. Importantly family
members not only have the right to reside, but also the right to take up
economic activity in the host Member State.[77]

---

[77] See Art.11 Reg. 1612/68; Art.2(2) Dir. 90/364; Art.2(2) Dir. 90/365 and Art.2(2) Dir. 93/96.
Although Dir. 73/148 is silent as to such right for the family of self-employed persons, the right
logically extends to them.

(ii) *The Economically Active*

11–86 For those who are economically active the provisions are largely the same. The scheme is as follows. Article 4 of Directive 68/360 requires that Member States shall grant the right of residence—to be evidenced by the issue of the aforementioned residence permit—to those referred to in Art.1 able to produce specified documents. Article 1 applies the provisions of the Directive to nationals and members of their families to whom Reg. 1612/68 applies. Article 10 of Reg. 1612/68 gives family members, *irrespective of their nationality*, the right to install themselves with a worker. Family members are defined as the spouse and their descendents who are under the age of 21 or are dependants, and dependent relatives in the ascending line of both worker and spouse.[78]

11–87 Further Art.10 also obliges Member States to facilitate the admission of any other family member "if dependent on the worker . . . or living under his roof in the country whence he comes."[79]

11–88 The document to be produced by family members[80] are the document with which they entered the Member State, a document issued by the competent authority of the state of origin or whence they came proving their relationship and (in cases referred to in Art.10(1) and (2) of Reg. 1612/68), a document testifying dependency on the worker or that they live under the worker's roof.

11–89 The requirement that the document proving the relationship is issued by the competent authority of the state of origin can cause real difficulties. Some Member States seem intent on questioning the competence of the authorities of certain third countries. The Netherlands, for example, routinely rejected marriage certificates issued by the Pakistani authorities (based on the perceived prevalence of the use of forgery). In such cases the Dutch authorities would insist on *themselves* confirming the underlying issue sought to be established by production of the document. Thus the Dutch would seek to go behind marriage certificates, for example requiring a Pakistani spouse to return to Pakistan to undergo some sort of marriage test at the Dutch Embassy there. It is difficult to see how such practice could be considered lawful in light of the decision of the ECJ in *MRAX*.[81]

11–90 Another problem relates to adoption, where some Member States do not recognise the adoption proceedings in certain non-EU countries.[82] Such Member States may not accept a child adopted as having complied with the

---

[78] Art.10(1)(a) and (b) of Reg.1612/68.
[79] Art.10(2) of Reg.1612/68.
[80] Art.4(3) LDir. 68/360.
[81] Case C–459/99 *Mouvement contre le racisme, l'antisémitisme et la xénophobie ASBL (MRAX) v Belgian State* [2002] E.C.R. I–6591.
[82] See for example in the UK para.310(vi)(a) of the Immigration Rules (HC 395) which require that an adoption was "in accordance with a decision taken by the competent administrative authority or court in his country of origin or the country in which he is resident, being a country whose adoption orders are recognised by the United Kingdom". Such countries are identified by statutory instrument: see the Adoption (Designation of Overseas Adoptions) Order 1973 (SI 1973/19) (as variously amended).

documentary requirements where the document is produced by a country whose adoption proceedings are not recognised. Such an approach is in contravention of Community law. The principles relating to formalities are dealt with above. It is a basic principle that Member States cannot ask for more than is prescribed.

The issue of dependency—in particular when it is not financial—can be difficult to demonstrate. The nature of such difficulties are discussed in Chapter 10. The requirement that the competent authority issue a "document testifying dependency" can also be hard to satisfy, not least in situations of emotional (as opposed to financial) dependency. Indeed, where there has not been court intervention in family matters there may be nothing able to be said by the competent authority going to the very issue about which the Directive demands documentation. In practice the fact that dependency is often sought to be established by declaration made by family members themselves is not treated by Member States as in itself a failure to comply, although this is doubtless a matter to which heightened scrutiny is given by Member States.

11–91

For the self-employed Art.1 of Directive 73/148 identifies the family members to whom the provisions of the Directive apply. They are broadly the same persons as those covered by Art.10 of Reg. 1612/68, subject to minor differences. As to documents required to be produced, the provisions of Art.6 apply.

11–92

The differences are as follows. Firstly, whereas Reg. 1612/68 refers to descendants under 21, Directive 73/148 refers to children under 21. The former would cover a grandchild, the latter would not. If dependent this may not matter (subject to the slight difference noted below); if not, then the under 21-year-old grandchild would benefit if the grandchild of a worker, but not someone self-employed (although such narrow construction may be inconsistent with the analysis, of the ECJ in *Baumbast*[83].

11–93

Secondly, whereas Reg. 1612/68 refers to "their" descendants, Directive 73/148 refers to "the spouse and *the* children . . . of such nationals". The use of "their" in the former case of workers would potentially exclude a stepchild; no such ambiguity arises on the face of Directive 73/148. As recently held by the ECJ in *Baumbast*[84] however the right in Reg. 1612/68 "must be interpreted as meaning that it is granted both to the descendants of that worker and to those of his spouse". To require the children to be common to both migrant worker and spouse would run counter to the aim of Reg. 1612/68 of guaranteeing "the best possible conditions for the integration of the Community worker's family in the society of the host Member State."[85]

11–94

---

[83] Case C–413/99 *Baumbast and R. v Secretary of State for the Home Department* [2002] E.C.R. I-7091.
[84] Case C–413/99 *Baumbast and R. v Secretary of State for the Home Department* [2002] E.C.R. I-7091, para.57.
[85] See Case C–308/89 *Di Leo v Land Berlin* para.13, quoted in *Baumbast and R. v Secretary of State for the Home Department* [2002] E.C.R. I-7091, para.50. See also Case C-275/02 *Ayaz v Land Baden-Württemberg*, September 30, 2004.

11–95   Thirdly, the other family members whose admission is to be "facilitated" in Reg. 1612/68 (or "favoured" in Directive 73/148), must in the former case be dependent on the worker, whereas in the latter dependency may be on the self-employed person or the spouse. It is important to emphasise that this provision must not be treated as if the admission of such other family members was entirely a matter for the discretion of the Member States. Such an approach would amount to an unwarranted dilution of the obligation to facilitate the entry of other family members.

11–96   The difference in language between Art.10(1) and Art.10(2) is acknowledged. It may be that a Member State would be entirely justified in seeking to scrutinise the claim of a distant relative to be dependent or living under the principal's roof closely. Nevertheless a failure to consider the admission of such family member or routinely to refuse applications from more distant relatives would plainly negate the very substance of the obligation otherwise imposed by Art.10(2). Moreover the importance ascribed by Community law to Art.8 ECHR in this context must always be borne in mind. The existence of family life is a question of fact which can be established between more distant relatives than those catered for by Art.10(1).

(iii) *The Economically Inactive*

Students

11–97   For students those family members covered are substantially more restricted than either the economically active or the other categories of economically inactive persons exercising free movement rights. Article 1 of Directive 93/96 extends only to the student's spouse and their dependent children. The use of the word "their" might be thought to exclude step children. However by analogy with the ECJ's reasoning in *Baumbast*[86] referred to above, to exclude a dependent step child would be contrary to Community law since it would create a disproportionate obstacle to the exercise of a Community law right. Third country national family members must be issued with a residence document of the same validity as the student on whom the person is dependent. Issue of the permit depends on production of a valid identity card or passport and proof of the relationship.

Retired persons and those exercising a general right of residence

11–98   For retired persons and those exercising a general right of residence the family members who have the right to install themselves with the holder of the right of residence are identical and are set out in Art.1(2) of each Directive.[87] These are the spouse and their descendants who are dependants and their dependent relatives in the ascending line. Although reflective of the provisions in Reg. 1612/68 dependency is required irrespective of age. The comment made above about the use of "their" in relation to students applies here. As with students, third country national family members of both retired persons and the self-sufficient must be issued with a residence document of the

---

[86] Case C–413/99 *Baumbast and R. v Secretary of State for the Home Department* [2002] E.C.R. I-7091.
[87] Dirs 90/365 and Dir. 90/364.

same validity as the national on whom the person is dependent; again, issue of the permit is subject to the same limitation as to documents able to be required of the principal (subject also to proof of the relationship).

(iv) *The Permanently Resident*

Regulation 1251/70 and Directive 75/34 recognise the right to remain perma-   **11–99**
nently for workers and the self-employed in the same circumstances. In each, Art.1 extends the scope to the same family members as covered before the activity ceased. Thus Art.1 of Reg. 1251/70 refers to family members as defined in Reg. 1612/68, whilst Art.1 of Directive 75/34 refers to family members as defined in Art.1 of Directive 73/148. Those covered are largely the same, subject to the two minor differences noted. No formalities are required in respect of the exercise of this right (whether by the principal or family members).

(d) *Remaining Beyond the Worker or Self-employed Person*

(i) *The Permanently Resident*

In the situations considered above the right of residence of family members   **11–100**
is derivative of the right of the Member State national exercising free movement rights.

As a general rule such rights will expire when the EU national ceases to exercise EC Treaty rights, ceases to reside in the territory of the host Member State or, in the case of spouses, the relationship is permanently dissolved.

Article 3(1) of each of Reg. 1251/70 and Directive 75/34 however give a right to family members to remain permanently if the worker or self-employed person has acquired the right to remain in the territory of that state in accordance with Art.2 of each. Thus the right for family members which is initially derived becomes personal. The right arises only where the family members are residing with the worker or self-employed person. As stated in Art.3(1) the right endures even after death of the worker or self-employed person. The reference to death however is potentially misleading: death is irrelevant to acquisition of the right which is triggered by the worker or self-employed person's having acquired the right to remain in accordance with Art.2. The right would be retained also in the event of divorce.

Specific provision is also made for the situation where the worker or self-   **11–101**
employed person dies before having acquired the right to remain in the territory concerned.[88] In such a situation members of the family have the right to remain permanently where the deceased on the date of death had resided continuously in the territory for at least two years, or the death resulted from an accident at work or an occupational disease, or the surviving spouse is a national of that state or lost nationality by marriage to the worker or self-employed person. In *Givane*[89] the ECJ considered an argument that the

---

[88] Art.3(2) of each Directive.
[89] Case C–257/00 *Givane v Secretary of State for the Home Department* [2003] E.C.R. I-345.

provision could be satisfied where Mr Givane had resided continuously in the United Kingdom for two years at any time prior to his death. Although there was some ambiguity in the different languages of the text of the Directive the ECJ held that "the period of two years' continuous residence required by [Art.3(2))] must immediately precede the worker's death."

(ii) *Children of Workers in Education*

11–102 Article 12 of Reg. 1612/68 makes specific provision for the education of the children of a national of a Member State who "is or has been employed" in the territory of another Member State. Such children shall be admitted to the state's "general educational, apprenticeship and vocational training courses under the same conditions as nationals of that state" if residing in the territory.

11–103 The scope of such right of residence for children where the worker is no longer employed in the other Member State (and in this sense the possibility of the child's right of residence "surviving" the cessation of the exercise of free movement rights by the worker) was considered by the ECJ in *Echternach and Moritz*.[90] The ECJ held that Art.12 of Reg. 1612/68 required the child "to be able to complete that education successfully." In Mr Moritz's case this meant that when he returned with his family to his father's state of origin, he could not continue his studies there because of the lack of co-ordination of school diplomas and had no choice but to return to the country where he attended school in order to continue studying. Mr Moritz retained the right of residence given by Art.12 as a child "of a national of a Member State who is or has been employed in the territory of another Member State".

11–104 This independent right of residence for children however is not limited to situations where education cannot be continued in the Member State of origin. Indeed, the ECJ specifically rejected such submission made by the German Government in *Baumbast*[91] in which a child's German father had ceased working in the United Kingdom and the issue referred to the ECJ was whether despite such cessation the children could nevertheless continue their education. The ECJ considered that to prevent a child of a citizen of the Union from continuing education in the host Member State by refusing permission to remain in such circumstances "might dissuade that citizen from exercising the rights to freedom of movement . . . and would therefore create an obstacle to the effective exercise of the freedom thus guaranteed by the EC Treaty".[92] Furthermore, to limit the scope of the right as argued by German Government would offend not only the letter of Art.12 of Reg. 1612/68 (children of a national who has been employed), but also its spirit.[93] Thus the ECJ held that:

---

[90] Joined Cases 389/87 and 390/87 *Echternach and Moritz v Minister van Onderwijs en Wetenschappen* [1989] E.C.R. 723.
[91] Case C-413/99 *Baumbast and R. v Secretary of State for the Home Department* [2002] E.C.R. I-7091, para.42 and 53–55.
[92] Case C-413/99 *Baumbast and R. v Secretary of State for the Home Department* [2002] E.C.R. I-7091, para.52.
[93] Case C-413/99 *Baumbast and R. v Secretary of State for the Home Department* [2002] E.C.R. I-7091, para.54.

"children of a citizen of the European Union who have installed themselves in a Member State during the exercise by their parent of rights of residence as a migrant worker in that Member State are entitled to reside there in order to attend general educational courses there, pursuant to Article 12 of Regulation No 1612/68. The fact that the parents of the children concerned have meanwhile divorced, the fact that only one parent is a citizen of the Union and that parent has ceased to be a migrant worker in the host Member State and the fact that the children are not themselves citizens of the Union are irrelevant in this regard".

(iii) *Carers of Children of Workers in Education*

The corollary of the right of children of workers to continue to reside in a Member State is a right for those children to be accompanied by their primary carers during the period of the children's education. As stated by the ECJ in *Baumbast*,[94] to refuse such right "might deprive those children of a right . . . granted to them by the Community legislature." Thus the Art.12 right necessarily implies "that the child has the right to be accompanied by the person who is his primary carer . . . [who] . . . is able to reside with him in that Member State during his studies".[95] Since the right is derived through the child it is irrelevant whether the mother/carer has divorced from the worker.[96] Furthermore, although in *Baumbast*[97] the ECJ was concerned with the position of carers who were in fact parents, it is clear that the right is one enjoyed by any person who is the primary carer. Not only does this reflect the language used by the ECJ itself, but it plainly also reflects the rationale of the ECJ's decision of ensuring that children are not deprived of the very essence of the right granted to them.

11–105

---

[94] Case C-413/99 *Baumbast and R. v Secretary of State for the Home Department* [2002] E.C.R. I-7091, para.71.
[95] Case C-413/99 *Baumbast and R. v Secretary of State for the Home Department* [2002] E.C.R. I-7091, para.73.
[96] As in the case of *R.* heard with *Baumbast and R. v Secretary of State for the Home Department* [2002] E.C.R. I-7091.
[97] Case C-413/99 *Baumbast and R. v Secretary of State for the Home Department* [2002] E.C.R. I-7091.

CHAPTER 12

DISCRIMINATION AND OTHER OBSTACLES TO FREEDOM OF MOVEMENT

The principal focus of this chapter is the examination of the principle of equal treatment as it applies to those benefiting from free movement rights in the EC Treaty and secondary legislation. Other obstacles to the exercise of free movement rights are also considered including the failure to recognise professional qualifications.

1. GENERAL PRINCIPLE OF NON-DISCRIMINATION IN THE COMMUNITY LAW CONTEXT

(a) *Introduction*

The general principle of non-discrimination in the context of Community law finds articulation in Art.12 EC Treaty which provides as follows: **12–01**

> "Within the scope of application of this Treaty, and without prejudice to any special provisions contained therein, any discrimination on grounds of nationality shall be prohibited".

The importance of the principle in the Community legal order is apparent   **12–02**
not only from its articulation in Art.12 EC Treaty, but also from the fact that it is repeated throughout the EC Treaty and secondary legislation. Thus for example in relation to workers, Art.39(2) EC Treaty provides expressly that the freedom of movement of workers shall entail "the abolition of any discrimination based on nationality between workers of the Member States as regards employment, remuneration and other conditions of work and employment".

Moreover, the principle is seen by the ECJ as one of the fundamental principles of Community law.[1] At its core the principle of equality requires that   **12–03**
similar situations shall not be treated differently unless differentiation is objectively justified.

---

[1] Case 117/76 *Albert Ruckdeschel & Co. et Hansa-Lagerhaus Ströh & Co. Contre Hauptzollamt Hamburg-St Annen; Diamalt AG v Hauptzollamt Itzehoe* [1977] E.C.R. 1753. The ECJ was considering the prohibition contained in Art. 34(2) EC Treaty on discrimination between producers or consumers in the context of the common organisation of agricultural markets. As the ECJ stated "This does not alter the fact that the prohibition of discrimination laid down in [Art. 34(2)] is merely a specific enunciation of the general principle of equality which is one of the fundamental principles of community law".

(b) *The Scope and Application of Article 12 EC Treaty*

(i) *Discrimination on Grounds of Nationality*

12–04　Immediately apparent from the text of Art.12 EC Treaty is that it is discrimination on grounds of *nationality* which is prohibited (rather than discrimination on *any* grounds such as those listed—albeit by way of example—in Arts 2 UDHR and 14 ECHR). This is unsurprising since it is the free movement rights of *nationals* of the Member States which is one of the four fundamental principles of the EC Treaty.

12–05　Moreover, the *nationality* limitation does not mean that discrimination on other grounds is of no interest in the context of the Community legal order. To the contrary, Art.13 EC Treaty makes provision for the Council to take "appropriate action to combat discrimination based on sex, racial or ethnic origin, religion or belief, disability, age or sexual orientation". As seen from Chapter 3, the wider non-discrimination obligations of the ECHR must be enjoyed not only by EU nationals but also third country nationals who find themselves within the territories of the Member States. Further, testament to the substantial interest taken by the Commission in discrimination is demonstrated by its activities undertaken in the context of the Action Programme to combat discrimination.[2]

(ii) *Discrimination Within the Scope of Application of the Treaty*

12–06　It must be emphasised that the prohibition on discrimination in Art.12 EC Treaty applies only "within the scope of application" of the EC Treaty. In order to determine whether discrimination falls within the scope (or as it is sometimes described the "sphere") of application of the Treaty there are two matters which must be established. First, that the circumstances of the individual fall within the personal scope of the provisions of the EC Treaty; second that the subject-matter of any dispute is one falling within the material scope of application of the EC Treaty. As frequently articulated in decisions of the ECJ the ability to invoke Art.12 depends on the relevant facts falling within the scope *ratione personae* and the scope *ratione materiae* of the Treaty.

12–07　Those falling within the personal scope of the Treaty include the free movers who are the subject-matter of the preceding chapters of this book. It will include also Union citizens lawfully residing in another Member State (see *Martinez-Sala*[3]) and EU nationals visiting another Member State (see *Bickel and Franz*[4]). The latter fall within the scope of the EC Treaty because they are recipients of services.

12–08　Since the inclusion of Art.17 in the EC Treaty establishing citizenship of the Union, all Union citizens residing in other Member States will benefit from the protection of Art.12 EC Treaty.[5] The detail is considered in Chapter 4. In

---

[2] See for example *www.stop-discrimination.info/index.php?english*.
[3] Case C–85/96 *Martinez Sala v Freistaat Bayern* [1998] E.C.R. I–2691.
[4] Case C–274/96 *Bickel and Franz* [1998] E.C.R. I–7637.
[5] Case C-456/02 *Trojani v Centre public d'aide sociale de Bruxelles (CPAS)*, September 7, 2004, paras 39–46.

short, a Union citizen need not establish that his residence in another Member State is founded on the exercise of a free movement right in Community Law in order to so benefit.[6]

Far more difficult however is the question of material scope, namely whether **12–09** the subject matter in dispute is something to which Community law principles should be applied. This will be dependant on various factors, including the nature of the activity of the Union citizen and the reason why the Union citizen is residing in another Member State. The Union citizen whose presence in another Member State arises because of the exercise of a free movement right must be accorded every facility to enjoy that free movement right. Such Union citizen must be treated on a par with own nationals in all respects. The scope of that obligation is considered in detail at paras 12.21 onwards.

In *Elsen*[7] the ECJ stated that Member States are required to act in manner **12–10** which is not "disadvantageous to Community nationals who have exercised their right to move and reside freely in the Member States as guaranteed in Art.8A of the EC Treaty [now Art.18 EC Treaty]". For those exercising free movement rights the material scope is by no means limited to access to financial benefits on a non-discriminatory basis. In *Bickel and Franz*[8] (following its earlier decision in *Mutsch*[9]) the ECJ held that measures which would enhance the exercise of the right to move and reside freely in another Member State fell within the material scope Art.12. The ECJ held that the use of a given language to communicate with the administrative and judicial authorities of a State on the same footing as nationals was a measure that would enhance the exercise of the right to move and freely reside in another Member State.

On the other hand, for the Union citizen whose residence is not derived from Community law material scope is more limited. The ECJ has been prepared to require Member States to provide all Union citizens with non discriminatory access to minimum forms of social assistance.[10] Further, in *Avello*[11] the ECJ held that the material scope of Art.12 EC Treaty included national rules governing the use of surnames for lawfully resident Union citizen children. To benefit from wider material scope Union citizens will likely need to establish more Community law nexus to their situation. For further discussion of material scope in these contexts see Chapter 4.

(c) *Inter-relationship with Other Non-discrimination Provisions*

As regards the economically active the Treaty provisions and secondary leg- **12–11** islation providing for their free movement include specific non-discrimination

---

[6] See paras 41–25 to 41–29 for discussion of the meaning of residence in this context.
[7] Case C-135/99 *Elsen v Bundesversicherungsandstalt für Angestellte* [2000] E.C.R. I-10409.
[8] Case C–274/96 *Bickel and Franz* [1998] E.C.R. I–7637.
[9] Case 137/84 *Ministere Public v Mutch* [1985] E.C.R. 2681.
[10] See Case C-85/96 *Martinez Sala v Freistaat Bayern* [1998] E.C.R. I-2691 (child raising allowance) and Case C-456/02 *Trojani v Centre public d'aide sociale de Bruxelles (CPAS)* September 7th, 2004 (minimex).
[11] Case C-148/02 *Avello v Etat Belge* [2004] 1 C.M.L.R. 1.

provisions. For instance, in relation to workers the combination of Art.39(2) EC and Reg. 1612/68 (considered in detail below) make comprehensive provision guaranteeing equality of treatment for workers. Where such provision is made Art.12 may be superfluous, or indeed only be necessary where the discrimination alleged falls outside the scope of Art.39(2) or Reg. 1612/68.

12–12   The potential overlap between Art.12 and specific Community law provisions dealing expressly with non-discrimination for particular free movers was recognised in *Ameyde*[12] where the ECJ stated in the context of the inter-relationship between Art.12 EC Treaty and Arts 43 and 49 EC Treaty that:

> "Article 7 of the Treaty [now Art.12] prohibits in general terms all discrimination based on nationality. In the respective spheres of the right of establishment and the freedom to provide services Articles 52 and 59 EC Treaty [now Art.43 and 49 EC Treaty] guarantee the application of the principle laid down by Article 7. It follows therefore that if rules are compatible with Articles 52 and 59 they are also compatible with Article 7".[13]

12–13   In *Kremlis*[14] the ECJ stated (without analysis) that Art.12 EC Treaty "applies independently *only* to situations governed by Community law in regard to which the Treaty lays down no specific prohibition of discrimination".[15] The same point was reiterated by the ECJ in *Scholz*[16] in which the ECJ considered an allegation of discrimination made relying on Arts 12 and 39 EC Treaty and Arts 1 and 3 of Reg. 1612/68. At para. 6 of its decision the ECJ stated:

> "It should be borne in mind, first of all, that Article 7 of the Treaty [now Art.12 EC Treaty], which prohibits any discrimination on grounds of nationality, does not apply independently where the Treaty lays down, as it does in Article 48(2) [now Art.39(2)] in relation to the free movement of workers, a specific prohibition of discrimination (see the judgment in Case 305/87 *Commission v Greece* [1989] ECR 1476, at paragraphs 12 and 13). In addition, Articles 1 and 3 of Regulation No 1612/68 merely clarify and give effect to the rights already conferred by Article 48 of the Treaty [now Art.39]. Accordingly, that provision alone is relevant to this case".

12–14   The breadth of the specific non-discrimination provisions in the EC Treaty for the economically active will mean that reliance on Art.12 EC Treaty may be unnecessary. Plainly such provisions must always be interpreted at least as broadly as Art.12 EC Treaty.

---

[12] Case 90/76 *S.r.l. Ufficio Henry van Ameyde v S.r.l. Ufficio centrale italiano di assistenza assicurativa automobilisti in circolazione internazionale (UCI)* [1977] E.C.R. 1091.
[13] Para.27.
[14] Case 305/87 *Kremlis v Greece* [1989] E.C.R. 1476 (a case in which proceedings were brought by the Commission against Greece for a declaration that, by maintaining in force and applying certain provisions of its legislation with regard to the conclusion, by nationals of other Member States, of legal acts in respect of immovable property the Hellenic Republic had failed to fulfil its obligations under Arts 12, 39, 43 and 49 EC Treaty).
[15] Para.13 (emphasis added).
[16] Case C–419/92 *Scholz v Opera Universitaria di Cagliari, Cinzia Porcedda* [1994] E.C.R. I–505.

(d) *Indirect Discrimination*

Community law does not just prohibit direct discrimination. As stated in **12–15** Art.12 EC Treaty itself, *any* discrimination is prohibited. Indirect discrimination arises where a provision is likely to affect EU nationals in the exercise of their Treaty rights disproportionately. It may arise where a condition is imposed which is sought to be justified on the basis that it applies both to those exercising Treaty rights and own nationals, but where the ability of those exercising Treaty rights to satisfy any such condition is intrinsically more difficult.

For example if a residence requirement is attached to the grant of a particular **12–16** benefit, whilst not impossible for EU nationals to satisfy such criterion, they are certainly more unlikely to be able to do so than own nationals, especially if they are "new" free movers, or have only recently exercised such rights.[17] As explained by the ECJ, such a residence requirement could be justified only if based on objective considerations independent of the nationality of the persons concerned and if proportionate to the legitimate aim of the national provisions. It is important to emphasise—as made clear by the ECJ in *Flynn*[18]—that it is not necessary to prove that the provision does in practice affect a substantially higher proportion of migrant workers. It will be enough that a provision is *liable* to have such an effect.

(e) *Justification*

A finding of discrimination on grounds of nationality however will not in **12–17** and of itself mean that Art.12 EC Treaty has been contravened. As is repeatedly stated by the ECJ discrimination may be justified. However, justification in practice is not a simple matter for a Member State to establish. To do so the Member State will have to demonstrate that any condition is:

"based on objective considerations independent of the nationality of the persons concerned and is proportionate to the legitimate aim of the national provisions (see, to that effect, Case C–15/96 *Schöning-Kougebetopoulou* [1998] E.C.R. I-47, para.21)".[19]

The importance of the principle of proportionality cannot be overstated. The **12–18** principle applies even where a measure justified on objective considerations must be proportionate to the legitimate aim of the national provisions. Thus in the case of *Bickel and Franz*[20] whilst the ECJ recognised that the protection of an ethno-cultural minority might constitute a legitimate aim, it did not consider that the aim would be undermined if the rules in issue, namely those concerned with the use of language in criminal proceedings, were extended to cover nationals of other Member States exercising their free movement rights.

---

[17] See for example Case C–237/94 *O'Flynn v Chief Adjudication Officer* [1996] E.C.R. I–2617, paras 20–21 and Case C–138/02 *Collins v Secretary of State for Work and Pensions*, judgment of March 23, 2004, not yet reported.
[18] Case C–237/94 *O'Flynn v Chief Adjudication Officer* [1996] E.C.R. I–2617
[19] See Case C-274/96 *Bickel and Franz* [1998] E.C.R. I-7637, para.27.
[20] Case C-274/96 *Bickel and Franz* [1998] E.C.R. I-7637.

12–19 The principles of objective justification and proportionality are well established in international human rights law. Under the ECHR, the effect of the discrimination is weighed against its aims to determine whether the two are proportionate. If the disadvantage suffered is excessive in relation to the legitimate aim pursued, then the discrimination is unjustified and thus illegal. Part of the analysis involves inquiring as to whether a less restrictive alternative exists: if it does, such alternative must be used.

12–20 This strict level of scrutiny has also been applied to discrimination on the grounds of nationality in Community law. Discrimination is only permissible if based on public policy, public security and public health grounds. Such grounds have been narrowly interpreted by the ECJ. The application of the principle is discussed in Chapter 14.

2. OBSTACLES TO THE FREE MOVEMENT OF WORKERS

(a) *Introduction*

12–21 Article 39(2) EC Treaty gives specific articulation of the principle of non-discrimination in relation to workers providing that the freedom of movement of workers "shall entail the abolition of any discrimination based on nationality between workers of the Member States as regards employment, remuneration and other conditions of work and employment". The principle is referred in provisions of secondary legislation, principally in Reg. 1612/68 which implements and facilitates the right of freedom of movement for workers laid down in Art.39 EC Treaty.

(b) *The Provisions of Regulation 1612/68*

12–22 The fundamental importance of the principle to Reg. 1612/68 is clear from its preamble in which more than half of the recitations deal expressly with the importance of non-discrimination.

12–23 Title I of Reg. 1612/68 (entitled "Eligibility for Employment") is concerned with the ability of EU national workers to access the work forces of other Member States. For example by Art.6(1) the engagement and recruitment of a national of one Member State for a post in another Member State must not depend on medical, vocational or other criteria which are discriminatory on grounds of nationality. It will be recalled that where the European Union has sought to prevent the nationals of *new* Member States from enjoying the right of free movement for workers from accession it has prevented access to the labour forces of existing Member States by suspending the Title I provisions.[21]

---

[21] See Chapter 6. In relation to the eight new Eastern European Member States who joined from May 1, 2004, Arts 1 and 2 of the Annex in respect of each such Member State requires the "present member States" to apply national law measures for a two year period "by way of derogation-from Articles 1 to 6 of Reg. 1612/68". A similar approach (as regards derogation from Arts 1 to 6 of Reg. 1612/68) was taken when Portugal joined (see Art. 216(1) of that Act of Accession). And

Title II of Regulation 1612/68 (entitled "Employment and Equality of   **12–24**
Treatment") identifies the specific rights in respect of which equality of treatment must be enjoyed. They include (in Art.7(1)) a statement of the references in Art.39(2) EC Treaty to the general prohibition of discrimination on
grounds of nationality as regards employment, remuneration and other conditions of work and employment. Article 7(1) provides as follows:

> "A worker who is a national of a Member State may not, in the territory of
> another Member State, be treated differently from national workers by reason of
> his nationality in respect of any conditions of employment and work, in particu-
> lar as regards remuneration, dismissal, and should he become unemployed,
> reinstatement or re-employment".

By Art.7(2) workers from other Member States must enjoy the same "social   **12–25**
and tax advantages" as national workers. This provision goes some way to
eliminating potential obstacles to the free movement of workers. In light of
both its importance and the extent of consideration given to it by the ECJ,
Art.7(2) is considered in detail below.

Article 7(3) makes similar provision as regards access to "training in voca-   **12–26**
tional schools and retraining centres". Article 7(4) provides that discriminatory conditions in collective or individual agreements or regulations
concerning "eligibility for employment, employment, remuneration and
other conditions of work or dismissal" will be null and void.

Article 8 deals with non-discriminatory treatment as regards trade union   **12–27**
membership, workers' representative bodies and such like (although with
"public law" exceptions reflecting Art.39(4) EC Treaty which states that
Art.39 does not apply to employment in the public services). Article 9 spells
out the non-discrimination obligation as regards "all the rights and benefits
accorded to national workers in matters of housing, including ownership of
the housing he needs", including benefits and priorities given in relation to
"housing lists".

(c) *Personal Scope*

(i) *Workers*

Workers are unambiguously within the personal scope of the EC Treaty. The   **12–28**
question "who *is* a worker" is considered in detail in Chapter 7. It is important to emphasise that whilst as a general rule a person loses the status as a
worker once the employment relationship has ended,[22] a person's status as a
worker may endure in various circumstances despite the fact that such person
is no longer in an employment relationship. Those circumstances are considered in Chapter 7 and include that:

---

also as regards the accession of Greece (the transitional provisions of Art 44 to 47 of the Act concerning the conditions of accession of the Hellenic Republic suspended, until December 31, 1987,
the operation of Arts 1 to 6 (and 13 to 23) of Reg. 1612/68).
[22] See Case–85/96 *Martinez Sala v Freistat Bayern* [1998] E.C.R. I–2691, para. 32.

(a)   the status of worker is not lost immediately on cessation of employment;

(b)   the status may be retained where the person has previously worked and remains capable of taking further employment;

(c)   the status may be retained where the person is available for work and capable of taking it up; and

(d)   the status may be retained where workers undertake retraining.

12–29   Where in spite of cessation of employment the person retains worker status such person remains within the personal scope of the Treaty for the purposes of the non-discrimination provisions.

(ii) *Work Seekers*

12–30   As regards work seekers, until *Collins*[23] a distinction was drawn between work seekers and workers in terms of their access to social and tax advantages on a non-discriminatory basis. In *Lebon*[24] the ECJ considered whether equal treatment with regard to social and tax advantages in Art.7(2) of Reg. 1612/68 applied to work seekers.[25] The ECJ held that the right did not apply to work seekers:

> "It must be pointed out that the right to equal treatment with regard to social and tax advantages applies only to workers. Those who move in search of employment qualify for equal treatment only as regards access to employment in accordance with Article 48 of the EEC Treaty [now Art.39 EC Treaty] and Articles 2 and 5 of Regulation No 1612/68".[26]

12–31   The ECJ reached the same conclusion in *Commission v Belgium*[27] which concerned the dependent children of workers living in Belgium seeking "tideover allowances".[28] The ECJ rejected the Commission's argument that tideover allowances fell within the scope of the rules on free access to employment (as provided for in Art.3(1) of Reg. 1612/68). The ECJ did so on the basis that the payment of the allowances constituted "active measures in the sphere of unemployment insurance" which were as such "linked to unemployment falling outside the field of access to employment in the strict sense".

---

[23] Case C–138/02 *Collins v Secretary of State for Work and Pensions*, judgment of March 23, 2004, not yet reported.

[24] Case 316/85 *Centre public d'aide sociale de Courcelles v Lebon* [1987] E.C.R. 2811.

[25] The position of work seekers is considered in Chapter 7.

[26] Case 316/85 *Centre public d'aide sociale de Courcelles v Lebon* [1987] E.C.R. 2811, para. 26.

[27] Case C–278/94 *Commission v Belgium* [1996] E.C.R. I–4307. See also Case 147/87 *Saada Zaoui v Caisse régionale d'assurance maladie de l'Ile-de-France (CRAMIF)* [1987] E.C.R. 5511, where the ECJ held that the Community rules on freedom of movement for workers would not apply to workers who have never exercised the right and that accordingly a member of the family of a worker cannot rely on Reg. 1612/68 to claim the same social advantages as workers who are nationals of that State when the worker has never exercised the right to freedom of movement within the Community.

[28] These are grants provided to young people who have just completed their studies and are seeking their first employment allowing recipients to be regarded as "wholly unemployed and on benefit" within the meaning of the rules on employment and unemployment.

However, these decisions are no longer good law following the decision of the **12–32**
ECJ in *Collins*[29] which concerned a dual Irish/American national who—after
an absence of 17 years from the United Kingdom—returned there in May
1998 in order to find work in the social services sector. As expressly acknowledged by the ECJ by reference to *Lebon*[30] and *Commission v Belgium*,[31] the
right to equal treatment enjoyed by work seekers seeking benefits of a financial nature applied only as regards *access* to employment, but not as regards
the social and tax advantages otherwise enjoyed by workers. Moreover, the
provisions of Reg. 1612/68 dealing with such access did not expressly refer to
benefits of a financial nature. Despite these facts ECJ stated:

> "in view of the establishment of citizenship of the Union and the interpretation in
> the case-law of the right to equal treatment enjoyed by citizens of the Union, it is
> no longer possible to exclude from the scope of Article 48(2) of the Treaty [now
> Art.39(2) EC Treaty]—which expresses the fundamental principle of equal treatment,
> guaranteed by Article 6 of the Treaty [now Art.12 EC Treaty]—a benefit of a financial
> nature intended to facilitate access to employment in the labour market of a Member
> State. [. . .] The interpretation of the scope of the principle of equal treatment in rela-
> tion to access to employment must reflect this development, as compared with the
> interpretation followed in *Lebon* and in Case C–278/94 *Commission v Belgium*."[32]

The position now is clear: the principle of equal treatment for work seekers **12–33**
applies both as regards matters relating to access to employment in Title I of
Reg. 1612/68 and to social and tax advantages contained in Title II. No
longer can any distinction be drawn between workers and work seekers.

(d) *Material Scope*

Plainly matters falling within the scope of Reg. 1612/68 are within the mate- **12–34**
rial scope of the EC Treaty of the purposes of the prohibition against discrimination. Identification of such matters is for the most part
straightforward. The provisions in Art.7(1), (3) and (4) of Reg. 1612/68 are
self-defining.[33] For example discriminatory conditions of employment as
regards remuneration prohibited by Art.7(1) need no further explanation.
The same however cannot be said for Art.7(2). In particular considerable
attention has been given by the ECJ to the meaning of the phrase "social
advantage" in Art.7(2). The Art.7(2) provision is considered below.

(i) *Article 7(2) Social Advantages*

Article 7(2) is a provision unique to workers and is important in the elimina- **12–35**
tion of obstacles to the right of free movement for workers. Generally the
provision has been interpreted by the ECJ in a broad manner, consistent with
the general aim of ensuring that EU national workers who move around the
European Union are not disadvantaged *vis-à-vis* own national workers. The

---

[29] Case 137/84 *Collins v Secretary of State for Work and Pensions*, judgment of March 23, 2004.
[30] Case 316/85 *Centre public d'aide sociale de Courcelles v Lebon* [1987] E.C.R. 2811.
[31] Case C–278/94 *Commission v Belgium* [1996] E.C.R. I-4307.
[32] Case 316/85 *Centre public d'aide sociale de Courcelles v Lebon* [1987] E.C.R. 2811, paras 63 and
64.
[33] As to Art. 7(3) see further Chapter 9.

failure to give EU national workers the same rights and benefits as own national workers would constitute an obstacle to free movement.

12–36 The concept of social advantage was considered by the ECJ in *Even*.[34] The case concerned the payment of a pension to a French national living in Belgium who sought to a benefit payable to Belgian workers who had fought in the Allied Forces during the Second World War and had suffered incapacity for work attributable to an act of war. He argued that the refusal of such a benefit constituted discrimination on the grounds of nationality. The ECJ described the concept as follows:

> "It follows from all its provisions and from the objective pursued that the advantages which this Regulation extends to workers who are nationals of other Member States are all those which, whether or not linked to a contract of employment, are generally granted to national workers primarily because of their objective status as workers or by virtue of the mere fact of their residence on the national territory and the extension of which to workers who are nationals of other member states therefore seems suitable to facilitate their mobility within the community."[35]

12–37 Further in *Lair*[36] the ECJ described social advantage in the following terms:

> "In addition to the specific right mentioned in Article 7 (1) of [Regulation 1612/68] not to be treated differently from national workers in respect of any conditions of employment and work, in particular as regards reinstatement or re-employment, 'social advantages' include all other advantages by means of which the migrant worker is guaranteed, in the words of the third recital in the preamble to the regulation, the possibility of improving his living and working conditions and promoting his social advancement."

12–38 There are many examples of rights or benefits which have been recognised as social advantages by the ECJ. These include:[37]

- benefits guaranteeing a minimum subsistence allowance dependent on residence qualification;[38]

---

[34] Case 207/78 *Even v Office National des Pensions pour Travailleurs Salariés* [1979] E.C.R. 2019.
[35] Para. 22. The definition has been consistently repeated ever since: see, *inter alia*, Case 65/81 *Reina and Reina v Landeskreditbank Baden-Württemberg* [1982] E.C.R. 33 and Case 137/84 *Mutsch* [1985] E.C.R. 2681. On the facts in *Even* the ECJ held that the benefit was not a social advantage: based on a scheme of national recognition it could not be considered as an advantage granted to a national worker by reason primarily of his status of worker or residence on the national territory.
[36] Case 39/86 *Lair v Univerität Hannover* [1988] E.C.R. 3161.
[37] The list is not intended to be exhaustive but gives a flavour of the breadth of what has been treated by the ECJ as social advantages.
[38] Case 249/83 *Hoeckx v Openbaar Centrum voor Maatschappelijk Welzijn* [1985] E.C.R. 973 and Case 122/84 *Scrivner and Cole v Centre Public d'aide Sociale de Chastre* [1985] E.C.R. 1027 in which the ECJ held that the minimum means of subsistence was a social advantage which could not be denied to a migrant worker or members of his family who were members of another Member State resident within the territory of the granting State, nor could it be subject to a residence qualification which was not imposed on nationals of the granting state.

- grants for training with a view to entry to university;[39]

- a scholarship to study in another Member State granted under a bilateral agreement reserving access for nationals of the two Member State Parties to the agreement;[40]

- benefit in the form of a single payment paid under a compensation scheme for agricultural workers whose contracts of employment have been terminated as a result of the setting aside of land;[41]

- child raising allowances;[42]

- childbirth loans given interest free by a credit institution incorporated under public law;[43]

- childbirth and maternity allowances;[44]

- provisions guaranteeing a minimum wage;[45]

- the right to require that legal proceedings take place in a specific language;[46]

- disability allowance in the form of a benefit for disabled adults for the assistance of a third person;[47] and

- the possibility of a migrant workers obtaining permission for an unmarried companion to reside.[48]

These cases show the breadth of the ECJ's approach, both to the interpretation of social advantages in general and the meaning of "facilitating mobility" in particular. **12–39**

In *Reina*[49] for example the ECJ held that interest-free childbirth loans were social advantages—the ECJ emphasised that the concept of social advantage encompassed not only benefits granted to own nationals as right, but also those granted on a discretionary basis.[50] Further in *Mutsch*[51] the ECJ had held that the right to require that criminal proceedings take place in a language other than the language normally used in proceedings before the Court **12–40**

---

[39] Case 39/86 *Lair v Univerität Hannover* [1988] E.C.R. 3161. The ECJ held also that Art. 12 EC Treaty applied only to that portion of State-given assistance which related to payment of registration and other fees, in particular tuition fees: see to the same effect Case 197/86 *Brown v Secretary of State for Scotland* [1998] E.C.R. 3205. In Case C–209/03 *The Queen on the application of Dany Bidar v London Borough of Ealing and the Secretary of State for Education* the ECJ will consider whether community competence in education has extended so as to enable grants for maintenance (in the form of student loans) fall within Art. 12 EC Treaty.
[40] Case 235/87 *Annunziata Matteucci v Communauté française of Belgium and Commissariat général aux relations internationals* [1988] E.C.R. 5589.
[41] Case C–57/96 *Meints v Minister van Landbouw, Natuurbeheer en Visserij* [1997] E.C.R. I–6689.
[42] Case C–85/96, *Martinez Sala v Freistaat Bayern* [1998] E.C.R. I–2691.
[43] Case 65/81 *Reina and Reina v Landeskreditbank Baden-Württemberg* [1982] E.C.R. 33.
[44] Case C–111/91 *Commission v Luxembourg* [1993] E.C.R. I–817.
[45] Case C–299/01 *Commission v Luxembourg* [2002] E.C.R. I–5899.
[46] Case 137/84 *Mutsch* [1985] E.C.R. 2681.
[47] Case C–310/91 *Schmid v Belgium State* [1993] E.C.R. I–3011.
[48] Case 59/85 *Reed v Netherlands* [1986] E.C.R. 1283.
[49] Case 65/81 *Reina and Reina v Landeskreditbank Baden-Württemberg* [1982] E.C.R. 33.
[50] Case 65/81 *Reina and Reina v Landeskreditbank Baden-Württemberg* [1982] E.C.R. 33, para.17. The German Government had tried to argue that the benefit was not a social advantage because it was payable only on a demographic basis to counteract the decline in birth rate.
[51] Case 137/84 *Mutsch* [1985] E.C.R. 2681.

which tries a worker was a social advantage—the ECJ reached its conclusion on the basis that:

> The right to use his own language in proceedings before the courts of the Member State in which he resides, under the same conditions as national workers, plays an important role in the integration of a migrant worker and his family into the host country, and thus in achieving the objective of free movement for workers".[52]

12–41   The non-discrimination provisions are enjoyed also by the family members of a worker, but only where those family members are dependent on the worker. In *Inzirillo*[53] the ECJ held that an allowance for disabled adults granted to own nationals must be granted to the worker's disabled adult dependants. The rationale for extending the availability of social advantages to family members dependent on the worker is that if a worker's dependent family member was to be deprived of a social benefit, the worker might be induced to leave the host Member State. In *Deak*[54] the ECJ explained the principles as follows:

> "The principle of equal treatment laid down in Article 7 of Reg. No 1612/68 is also intended to prevent discrimination against descendents of a worker who are dependent on him . . . A worker anxious to ensure for his children the enjoyment of the social benefits provided for by the legislation of the Member States for the support of young persons seeking employment would be induced not to remain in the Member State where he had established himself and found employment if that state could refuse to pay the benefits in question to his children because of their foreign nationality . . . That result would run counter to the objective of the principle of freedom of movement for workers within the community, bearing in mind *inter alia* the right granted under that principle to employed persons and to members of their families to remain within the territory of a Member State . . .".

12–42   It is however to be noted that the extension of the principle to family members is "indirect", that is the right is not a discrete one given to the family member as such. Rather it is one enjoyed only through the principal on whom the family member is dependent. This was stated expressly by the ECJ in *Deak*.

12–43   It is important to bear in mind that the right is restricted to one of equality of treatment. When relying on the Art.7(2), conditions that are imposed on own nationals in order to obtain a benefit might also be applied to EU national workers. A worker for instance who wishes to install a same-sex partner, claiming that this is a social advantage which is afforded to own nationals, will have to meet the conditions laid down in national legislation. This is of course entirely different from the position where an EU national worker wishes to install a member of the family covered by Art.10 of Reg. 1612/68 since only Community law provisions and conditions may be applied.

---

[52] Case 137/84 *Mutsch* [1985] E.C.R. 2681, para.16.
[53] Case C–63/76 *Inzirillo v Caisse d'allocations familiales de l'arrondissement de Lyon* [1976] E.C.R. 2057, paras 21–22
[54] Case 94/84 *Office national de l'emploi v Deak* [1985] E.C.R. 1873, paras 22–26.

(ii) *Article 7(2) Tax Advantages*

The non-discrimination provision in Art.7(2) includes "tax advantages".   **12–44**
However it has very rarely been used by individuals wishing to obtain any
such advantages. The ECJ has yet to explain the concept of tax advantages
or their application to a case in any detail. As with social advantages, the concept should however be broadly construed and would include any matter
relating to taxation,[55] direct or indirect, and social security contributions.[56]
European Union national workers must not be placed in a worse situation
than own nationals *vis-à-vis* the amount of tax they must pay or the conditions under which they must pay it. Furthermore they should be able to
access all the tax incentive and rebate schemes that own national workers
can. Since issues of taxation inter-relate with issues surrounding conditions
of remuneration, which is specifically provided for in the principal non-
discrimination provision relating to workers (Art.39(2) EC Treaty), it is
unsurprising that the ECJ has mainly considered alleged discrimination on
tax issues under Art.39 EC Treaty itself.[57]

(e) *Prohibited Forms of Discrimination*

The prohibition in Community law of discrimination against workers pro-   **12–45**
hibits direct discrimination such as where a Member State limits employment
in a particular sector (not covered by Art.39(4) EC Treaty) to own nationals.
However, the prohibition applies more widely and includes indirect forms of
discrimination by the application of other criteria which lead to the same
result.

The prohibition against indirect discrimination has been consistently restated   **12–46**
by the ECJ. In *Sotgiu*[58] one of the questions concerned whether Art.7(1) and
(4) of Reg. 1612/68 were to be interpreted as containing a prohibition not
only against treating a worker differently because he is a national of another
Member State, but also against treating him differently because he is resident
in another Member State. The ECJ held:

> "The rules regarding equality of treatment, both in the Treaty and in Article 7 of
> Regulation No 1612/68, forbid not only overt discrimination by reason of nation-
> ality but also all covert forms of discrimination which, by the application of other
> criteria of differentiation, lead in fact to the same result. This interpretation, which
> is necessary to ensure the effective working of one of the fundamental principles of
> the community, is explicitly recognized by the fifth recital of the preamble to
> Regulation No 1612/68 which requires that equality of treatment of workers shall
> be ensured 'in fact and in law'. It may therefore be that criteria such as place of ori-
> gin or residence of a worker may, according to circumstances, be tantamount, as
> regards their practical effect, to discrimination on the grounds of nationality, such
> as is prohibited by the Treaty and the Regulation".

---

[55] See for instance Case C–279/93 *Schumacker* [1995] E.C.R. I–225 and Case C–175/88 *Biehl*
[1990] E.C.R. I–1779.
[56] Case C–18/95 *FC Terhoeve v Inspecteur van der Belastingdienst Particulieren* [1999] E.C.R.
I–345.
[57] Case C–18/95 *FC Terhoeve v Inspecteur van der Belastingdienst Particulieren* [1999] E.C.R.
I–345.
[58] Case 152/73 *Sotgiu v Deutsche Bundespost* [1974] E.C.R. 153.

12–47   The principle of indirect discrimination was further described by the ECJ in *O'Flynn*[59] as follows:

> "[A] provision of national law must be regarded as indirectly discriminatory if it is intrinsically liable to affect migrant workers more than national workers and if there is a consequent risk that it will place the former at a particular disadvantage. . . . It is not necessary in this respect to find that the provision in question does in practice affect a substantially higher proportion of migrant workers. It is sufficient that it is liable to have such an effect. Further, the reasons why a migrant worker chooses to make use of his freedom of movement within the Community are not to be taken into account in assessing whether a national provision is discriminatory. The possibility of exercising so fundamental a freedom as the freedom of movement of persons cannot be limited by such considerations, which are purely subjective".

12–48   A form of indirect discrimination could be where national law imposes a residence condition for the payment of a particular benefit in respect of all applicants, both EU migrant workers and own nationals alike. Whilst perhaps not at first blush discriminatory such condition would generally be regarded as discriminatory by the ECJ if it was more difficult for a migrant worker to fulfil it than an own national. A similar a condition was considered by the ECJ in its decision in *Collins*[60] which concerned an application made for job seekers allowance where the national law provision which introduced a difference in treatment according to whether the person involved was "habitually resident" in the United Kingdom. Identifying whether such provision—which on its face applied equally to all nationals—was discriminatory the ECJ stated:

> "Since that requirement is capable of being met more easily by the State's own nationals, the 1996 Regulations place at a disadvantage Member State nationals who have exercised their right of movement in order to seek employment in the territory of another Member State (see, to this effect, Case C–237/94 *O'Flynn* [1996] E.C.R. I-2617, para. 18, and Case C–388/01 *Commission v Italy* [2003] E.C.R. I-721, paras 13 and 14)".[61]

(f) *Justification*

12–49   A finding of discrimination on grounds of nationality against a worker however will not in and of itself mean that the prohibition has been contravened. As discussed above discrimination may be justified if based on objective considerations independent of the nationality of the worker concerned and if proportionate to the legitimate aim of the national provisions.

---

[59] Case C–237/94 *O'Flynn v Chief Adjudication Officer* [1996] E.C.R. I–2617, paras 20–21.
[60] Case C–138/02 *Collins v Secretary of State for Work and Pensions*, judgment of March 23, 2004.
[61] Case C–138/02 *Collins v Secretary of State for Work and Pensions*, judgment of March 23, 2004, para. 65.

The ECJ's analysis in this respect in *Collins*[62] is instructive. Basing its decision   **12–50**
on *D'Hoop*[63] the ECJ stated that it was legitimate for the national legislature
to wish to ensure the existence of a genuine link between an applicant for an
allowance in the nature of a social advantage within the meaning of Art.7(2)
of Reg. 1612/68 and the geographic employment market in question (as was
the case with job-seekers' allowance). Moreover, the UK authorities could
seek to determine the existence of such a link by establishing that the person
concerned has, for a reasonable period, in fact genuinely sought work. The
ECJ continued:

> "However, while a residence requirement is, in principle, appropriate for the pur-
> pose of ensuring such a connection, if it is to be proportionate it cannot go beyond
> what is necessary in order to attain that objective. More specifically, its application
> by the national authorities must rest on clear criteria known in advance and provi-
> sion must be made for the possibility of a means of redress of a judicial nature. In
> any event, if compliance with the requirement demands a period of residence, the
> period must not exceed what is necessary in order for the national authorities to be
> able to satisfy themselves that the person concerned is genuinely seeking work in the
> employment market of the host Member State".[64]

3. OBSTACLES TO ESTABLISHMENT

(a) *Definition of Restrictions of Freedom of Establishment*

Article 43 EC Treaty precludes any national measure which is liable to   **12–51**
hamper or render less attractive the exercise of the right of establishment
by Community nationals.[65] That said Member States are entitled to regulate, within certain limits, the conditions for all traders or persons carrying
out a particular activity. However those who seek to establish themselves
from other Member States must not be placed at a disadvantage or treated
differently from the Member State's own nationals.[66]

Furthermore even where national measures are not applied in a discriminatory   **12–52**
way, they may still have the effect of hindering nationals of other Member
States in the exercise of their right of establishment. For instance national
rules which take no account of the knowledge and qualifications acquired by
a person in another Member State might represent such an obstacle to free
movement and would therefore be prohibited by Art.43 EC Treaty.[67]

The rights conferred by Art.43 EC Treaty are unconditional and a Member   **12–53**
State cannot make respect for them subject to a condition of reciprocity.[68]

---

[62] Case 138/02 *Collins v Secretary of State for Work and Pensions*, judgement of March 23, 2004.
[63] Case C–224/98 *D'Hoop v Office national de l'emploi* [2002] E.C.R. I–6191.
[64] para. 72.
[65] Case C–418/93 *Semeroro Casa Uno Srl v Sindaco del Comune di Erbusco*, [1996] E.C.R. I-2975.
para.32.
[66] Case C–19/92 *Kraus v Land Baden-Württemburg* [1993] E.C.R. 1663, para.32
[67] Case C–340/89 *Vlassopoulou v Ministerium vor Justiz Bundes und Europaangelgenheiten Baden-
Württemburg* [1991] ECR I–2357, para.15.
[68] Case C–58/90 *Commission v Italy* [1991] E.C.R. I–4193.

12-54 Although Art.43 EC Treaty is primarily aimed at ensuring that nationals and companies of other Member States are treated in the same way as own nationals and companies in the host Member State, it also prohibits the Member State of origin from hindering establishment in another Member State. The ECJ has considered that measures which prohibit undertakings from leaving the Member State of origin would render the rights guaranteed by Art.43 EC Treaty meaningless.[69] With respect to natural persons, the right to leave the Member State of origin is expressly provided for in Directive 73/148.[70]

12-55 A national of a Member State who acquires professional qualifications in another Member State which are recognised by Community law must be able to carry out professional services in the same way as any other Community national. Excluding own nationals from such benefit would constitute a restriction on establishment which is contrary to Art.43 EC Treaty.[71]

(b) *Prohibited Discrimination Based on Nationality*

12-56 Article 43 EC Treaty ensures that all EU nationals who establish themselves in another Member State, even where that establishment is only secondary, receive the same treatment as nationals of that Member State. The provision prohibits, as a restriction on the freedom of establishment, any discrimination on grounds of nationality.

12-57 According to the ECJ's case law the principle of equal treatment, of which Art.43 EC Treaty embodies specific instances, prohibits not only overt discrimination by reason of nationality but also more covert forms of discrimination through the application of other criteria of differentiation.[72]

12-58 For instance a requirement that the owners and charterers of a vessel and, in the case of a company, the shareholders and directors, be resident and domiciled in the Member State in which the vessel is to be registered results in discrimination on grounds of nationality. This is not justified by the rights and obligations which the Member State may claim are created by the grant of a national flag to a vessel. Plainly it is much easier for nationals of the Member State to satisfy the requirement of being domiciled in that State since the majority of them will be resident and domiciled there, whereas nationals of other Member States would, in most cases, have to move their residence in order to comply with the legislation.[73]

12-59 In certain instances the discriminatory treatment is very well disguised. The ECJ has held that the difference in treatment as regards access to sickness

---

[69] Case C–415/93 *Union Royal Belge des Societes de Football Association ASBL v Bosman* [1995] E.C.R. I–4353.
[70] Case 81/87 *The Queen v HM Treasury and Commissioners of Inland Revenue Ex p. Daily Mail and General Trust PLC* [1988] E.C.R. 5483.
[71] Case 115/78 *J Knoors v Secretary of State for Economic Affairs* [1979] E.C.R. 399, para.24.
[72] Case C–1/93 *Halliburton Services BV v Staatssecretaris van Financiën* [1994] E.C.R. I–1137, para.15.
[73] Case C–221/89 *The Queen v Secretary of State for Transport Ex p. Factortame Ltd* [1991] E.C.R. I–3905, para.32.

insurance between directors of a company formed under national law and those of a company formed under the law of another Member State, amounted to discrimination on grounds of nationality. The ECJ considered that such discrimination against employees of a company was contrary to the provision of Art.43 EC Treaty since it indirectly restricted the freedom of establishment of the company itself.[74]

The case of *Gebroeder Beentjes*[75] concerned a company which submitted a **12–60** tender for a public works contract in connection with a land consolidation operation. One of the conditions for tender required the tenderer to employ long-term unemployed persons. The ECJ held that an obligation to employ long-term unemployed persons could infringe the prohibition of discrimination if it became apparent that such a condition could be satisfied only by tenderers from the state concerned or that tenderers from other Member States would have difficulties in complying with it.

(c) *Non-prohibited Restrictions*

(i) *Non-discriminatory Measures*

Some restrictions on freedom of establishment may, in certain instances, be **12–61** justified. Such restrictions must, however, fulfil certain general conditions: they must be applied in a non-discriminatory manner (see exceptions below); they must be justified by imperative requirements in the general interest; they must be suitable for securing the attainment of the objective which they pursue; and they must not go beyond what is necessary in order to attain that objective.[76]

In *Kraus*[77] the ECJ considered that even though a measure was not discrimi- **12–62** natory it could still be contrary to Art.43 EC Treaty as it was liable to hamper or to render less attractive the exercise of fundamental freedoms guaranteed by the Treaty. The restriction would only be permissible if it pursued a legitimate objective compatible with the EC Treaty and was justified by pressing reasons of public interest.[78] It would also be necessary for the Member State to demonstrate that the national rules are both appropriate for ensuring the attainment of the objective and proportionate.[79]

In the *Commission v Italy*[80] the ECJ held that imposing a duty of secrecy on **12–63** the staff of companies which if breached would lead to criminal sanctions was not justified. The ECJ considered that the Italian Government had sufficient legal powers at its disposal to be able to adapt the performance of

---

[74] Case 79/85 *Serges* [1986] E.C.R. 2375.
[75] Case 31/87 *Gebroeders Beentjes* [1988] E.C.R. 4635.
[76] Case C–55/94 *Gebhard v Consigol dell' Ordine degli Advocat AE Procuratori di Milano* [1995] E.C.R. I–4165, para.37.
[77] Case C–19/92 *Kraus v Land Baden-Württemberg* [1993] E.C.R. 1663, para.32.
[78] Case 71/76 *Thieffry v Counseil de l'Ordre des Avocats a la Cour de Paris* [1977] E.C.R. 765, paras 12–15.
[79] Case C–19/92 *Kraus v Land Baden-Württemberg* [1993] E.C.R. 1663, para.32.
[80] Case 3/88 *Commission v Italy* [1989] E.C.R. 4035, para.11.

contracts to protect the confidential nature of the data in question in a manner which was less restrictive.

(ii) *Discriminatory Measures*

12–64 There are two exceptions to the general rule that restrictions on freedom of establishment should be exercised in a non-discriminatory manner: first in relation to participation in the exercise of official authority and secondly where public policy, public security or public health justifies such a discriminatory measure.

12–65 It is to be noted that the first paragraph of Art.45 EC Treaty excludes from the application of the provisions on freedom of establishment activities which in a Member State are connected, even occasionally, with the exercise of official authority. However the ECJ has made clear that the derogation provided for in Art.45 EC Treaty must be restricted to activities which in themselves are directly and specifically connected with the exercise of official authority.[81]

12–66 The ECJ does not consider that professional activities involving regular contact with national courts to be connected with the exercise of official authority.[82] Nor does it consider the function of an internal auditor to be connected with the exercise of official authority.[83]

12–67 Other than where activities are connected with official authority, discriminatory measures may only be justified on grounds of public policy, public security and public health. These are discussed in detail in Chapter 14. It is to be noted that these grounds do not include economic aims[84] and thus anti-competitive measures or those that protect a Member State's market will not be permissible.

4. MUTUAL RECOGNITION OF DIPLOMAS/TRAINING

(i) *General Treaty Provisions Relating to Mutual Recognition of Qualifications*

12–68 In order to make it easier for persons to take up and pursue activities as self-employed persons, Art.47 EC Treaty provides that the Council will issue directives concerning the mutual recognition of diplomas and other formal qualifications. Article 47 EC Treaty further provides that the Council shall issue directives for the "coordination of the provisions laid down by law, regulation or administrative action in Member States concerning the taking-up and pursuit of activities as self-employed persons".

12–69 The system of the Chapter in the Treaty relating to establishment thus provides a "general programme" and the directives provided for in Art.47 EC

---

[81] Case C–42/92 *Thijssen v Controledienst voor de verzekeringen* [1993] E.C.R. I–4047, para.8.
[82] Case 2/74 *Reyners v Belgium* [1974] E.C.R. 631, para.51.
[83] Case C–42/92 *Thijssen v Controledienst voor de verzekeringen* [1993] E.C.R. I–4047, para.18.
[84] Case 288/89 *Stichting Collective Antennevorrziening Gouda v Commissariaat voor de Media* [1991] E.C.R. I–4007, para.11.

Treaty are intended to accomplish two functions. The first is the elimination of obstacles to the freedom of establishment and the second is the introduction into the law of Member States of a set of provisions intended to facilitate the effective exercise of this freedom.[85]

The ECJ has held that that provision is directed towards reconciling freedom of establishment with the application of national professional rules justified by the general interest of states, in particular rules relating to organisation, qualifications, professional ethics, supervision and liability.   **12–70**

Where a directive has not been adopted for a particular profession under Art.47 EC Treaty, a person subject to Community law cannot be denied the practical benefit of the freedom of establishment.   **12–71**

There is no specific Treaty provision directing the Council to make legislation relating to the mutual recognition of professional qualifications for employed persons. However the system for mutual recognition of qualifications described below plainly benefits the employed as well as the self-employed. Indeed the failure to recognise the professional qualifications of EU national workers will act as an obstacle to the freedom of movement of such workers and would plainly nullify and impair the exercise of such rights, if not negate their very existence. Moreover the content of the directives themselves prompts the same conclusion. For example, the sector directives considered below cover seven professions, few if any of which are exclusively the domain of the self-employed.   **12–72**

(ii) *General System for Mutual Recognition in Secondary Legislation*

Three Directives have been adopted to provide a *general* system of mutual recognition of diplomas and education: Directives 86/48, 92/51 and 99/42. The Directives do not provide regulation in the areas in which there are specific directives relating to a particular profession.   **12–73**

Directive 86/48,[86] now amended by Directive 2001/19,[87] was adopted to enable higher-education professional diplomas gained in one Member State to be recognised in another Member State where the profession is regulated. The minimum period of higher education must be at least three years. A Member State which regulates a profession must recognise the qualifications obtained in another Member State and allow their holder to pursue his profession on the territory of the Member State on the same conditions as apply to its own nationals. The Directive applies to all the professions for which higher education is required and which are not covered by specific directives governing recognition.   **12–74**

Directive 86/48 permitted Member States to require a person to take an aptitude test or complete an adaptation period of up to three years where the training and education received substantially different from that required by   **12–75**

---

[85] Case 2/74 *Reyners v Belgium* [1974] E.C.R. 631.
[86] Council Dir. 89/48 of December 21, 1988 [1989] O.J. L19/16.
[87] Council Dir. 2001/19 [2001] O.J. L206/1.

the host Member State or where the person obtained qualifications in a Member State in which the particular profession is not regulated. However as a result of amendment by Directive 2001/19 Member States are not permitted systematically to require the applicant to take measures, such as aptitude tests or adaptation periods, but must simplify and if possible eliminate these measures.

12–76 Directive 92/51,[88] also amended by Directive 2001/19, was intended to supplement Directive 86/48, by extending the system of mutual recognition introduced by Directive 86/48 to those professions for which the required level of training is not as high or as long in duration.[89] The Directive covers a very wide range of qualifications including those obtained at a level corresponding to a secondary course or short post-secondary course. As with the Directive 86/48, amendment by Directive 2001/19 means that Member States can no longer systematically require aptitude tests or adaptation periods.

12–77 Directive 99/42[90] was intended to simplify and collate a whole range of transitional directives on the mutual recognition of diplomas in commerce, industry and craft trades and to supplement the two general system directives. A Member State is not permitted to refuse to permit a person to engage in activities specified in the Directive unless it has examined the skills and experience of the person concerned and satisfied itself that these are not equivalent to the skills and experience that own nationals would be expected to have achieved.

(iii) *Mutual Recognition in Specific Fields*

12–78 There now exist 12 sectoral Directives[91] covering the seven professions of doctor, nurse, dentist, veterinary surgeon, midwife, pharmacist and architect. Additionally there are two Directives[92] relating to the authorisation to practice as a lawyer.[93]

12–79 It is not proposed to examine the Directives relating to mutual recognition in specific fields in any detail. The basic aim of the Directives is to facilitate the free movement of professionals and to provide a scheme whereby their qualifications obtained in other Member States can be recognised. To that end the Directives harmonise the minimum criteria for certain types of training for those practising professionally in the particular field. Furthermore the Directives provide for the mutual recognition of their diplomas, certificates and other evidence of formal qualifications.

12–80 The Commission has proposed a Directive to replace all the sectoral Directives, as well as the three Directives relating to the general system for

---

[88] Council Dir. 92/51 of June 18, 1992 [1992] O.J. L209/25.
[89] The minimum period of study under this Directive is one year.
[90] Dir. 99/42 of the European Parliament and of the Council of June 7, 1999 [1999] O.J. L201/77.
[91] Council Dirs 93/16, 77/452, 77/453, 78/686, 78/687, 78/1026, 78/1027, 80/154, 80/155, 85/432, 85/433 and 85/384.
[92] Dirs 77/249 and 98/5.
[93] The mutual recognition of qualifications are covered by the general system set out in Dir. 89/48.

mutual recognition.[94] While maintaining the guarantees afforded by each of the existing recognition systems, this proposal aims to create a single, consistent legal framework which is based on further liberalisation of the provision of services, more automatic recognition of qualifications and greater flexibility in the procedures for updating the Directive. The Commission is aware that free movement of workers in an enlarged European Union requires a simpler and clearer system for the recognition of professional qualifications in order to increase labour market flexibility and to help improve public services. The proposed Directive is subject to a co-decision making procedure.[95]

5. OBSTACLES TO SERVICE PROVISION

As with the freedom of establishment, the EC Treaty provisions relating to the **12–81** freedom to provide services are aimed at the abolition of restrictions on that freedom. At the heart of Art.49 EC Treaty is the requirement that measures discriminating, directly or indirectly, between nationals of other Member States and the nationals of the host Member State are abolished.[96] Discrimination on grounds of nationality is discussed in detail in relation to establishment above. The same principles apply in relation to service provision.

In the context of service provision the ECJ has found that the requirement **12–82** that the service provider resides in the host Member State when this is not imposed on own nationals is discriminatory.[97] The ECJ has also found that rules which limit the right to play in football matches as professional or semi-professional players solely to the nationals of the Member State in question are discriminatory and incompatible with the Treaty, except where the rules exclude foreign players for sporting reasons as opposed to economic ones.[98] This would be the case for example in matches played between national teams from different countries where played in the words of the ECJ, for reasons of "sporting interest".[99]

Furthermore the ECJ has stated that Art.49 EC Treaty requires not only the **12–83** elimination of discrimination against a person providing services on grounds of nationality, but also the abolition of any restriction when its effect is liable to prohibit or otherwise impede the activities of a provider of services established in another Member State where he lawfully provides similar services. Such a restriction would be prohibited by Art.49 EC Treaty even if it is applied without distinction to national providers of services and those from other Member States.[1]

---

[94] Proposal for a Directive of the European Parliament and of the Council of March 7, 2002 on the recognition of professional qualifications, COM (2002) 119 final [2002] O. J. C181E.
[95] In February 2004 Parliament voted to adopt the proposal.
[96] Joined Cases C 330 & 331/90 *Criminal Proceedings against Lopez Brea and M Carlos Hidaglo Palacios* [1992] E.C.R. I–323.
[97] Case C–186/87 *Cowan v Trésor Public* [1989] E.C.R. 195.
[98] Case 13/76 *Dona v Mantero* [1976] E.C.R. 1333.
[99] Case 13/76 *Dona v Mantero* [1976] E.C.R. 1333, para.14.
[1] Case C–76/90 *Sager v Dennemeyer & Co Ltd* [1991] E.C.R. I–4221.

12–84   In *Seco*[2] for instance, the ECJ held that the obligation to pay the employer's share of social security contributions imposed on persons providing services within the national territory if extended to persons established in another Member State could create a barrier to free movement. Such persons might already be liable to pay social security contributions in their own Member State and thus the provision of services in another Member State might lead to a heavier social security contributions' burden than a person would be liable to if established in one Member State and providing services in that Member State alone.

12–85   As with any restriction on the free movement rights contained within the EC Treaty, a restriction on the provision of services by nationals or companies from other Member States will only be permissible if it falls within one of express exemptions laid down in Art.46 EC Treaty, namely public policy, public security or public health.[3]

6. OBSTACLES TO THE EXERCISE OF FREE MOVEMENT
BY THE ECONOMICALLY INACTIVE

(a) *Introduction*

12–86   Prior to the Maastricht Treaty there was no specific Treaty provision for the freedom of movement for the economically inactive. As outlined in Chapter 9 the rights of free movement for the economically inactive were created by secondary legislation. Article 18 EC Treaty now provides the Treaty basis for the free movement of the economically inactive. This right, which is one of the consequences of the creation through the Maastricht Treaty of Union Citizenship, is discussed in detail in Chapter 4.

12–87   The secondary legislation providing for the free movement of the economically inactive[4] contains no express non-discrimination provision, although the preambles to the Directives each identify in the first recitation by reference to Art.3 EC Treaty that the activities of the Community "shall include, as provided in the Treaty, the abolition, as between Member States, of obstacles to freedom of movement for persons".

12–88   The economically inactive whose free movement rights are founded upon the provisions of these Directives plainly fall within the personal scope of the EC Treaty and therefore will be able to rely on the non-discrimination provision contained in Art. 12 EC Treaty.[5] Even those E U nationals whose situation is not covered by any secondary legislation will nonetheless also benefit from the non-discrimination provision in Art.12 EC Treaty. They will do so

---

[2] Joined Cases 62 & 63/81 *Société anonyme de droit français Seco et société anonyme de droit francais Desquenne & Giral v Etablissement d'assurance contre la vieillesse et l'invalidite* [1982] E.C.R. 223.
[3] See Chapter 14.
[4] Dirs 90/364, 90/365 and 93/96.
[5] See for example Case C-224/98 *D'Hoop v Office national de l'emploi* [2002] E.C.R. I-6191.

through the application of Art.18 EC Treaty, although as acknowledged in Chapter 4 the precise parameters of Art.18 EC Treaty have yet to be set.

(b) Application to the Economically Inactive

The self-sufficient and the retired do not in practice appear to have faced **12–89** obstacles to their free movement or indeed discrimination.[6] Were they to do so since they plainly fall within the personal scope of the EC Treaty, the question of whether any such discrimination would be contrary to the prohibition contained in Art.12 EC Treaty would (subject to justification) depend on whether the subject-matter fell within the Treaty's material scope.

The position is different however as regards students in respect of whom **12–90** experience has shown that Member States can be less receptive. Doubtless such concern is founded on the fear that the student who is required by Directive 93/96 merely to declare his self-sufficiency will in fact cease to be able to maintain himself and become a burden on the public finances of host Member States. Thus in practice it has generally been the position of students which has exercised the ECJ in the context of non-discrimination.

In *Grzelczyk*[7] for example a student who had ceased fully to comply with the **12–91** requirements of Directive 93/96 was held by the ECJ to be entitled to receipt of "the minimex" (a non-contributory minimum subsistence allowance) without discrimination. However it is right to point out that his ability to do so— given that he no longer fulfilled the Directive 93/96 conditions in every respect—depended on the willingness of the ECJ to use Art.18 EC Treaty to interpret the conditions generously. Mr Grzelczyk had previously fulfilled the conditions of Directive 93/96 in that he supported himself through taking on various jobs and obtaining credit facilities. It was only at the beginning of his fourth and final year of study that he applied the minimex.

Moreover as regards students it has long been the position that Member States will be obliged—as the consequence of the prohibition on discrimination contained in Art.12 EC Treaty—to pay tuition fees for EU nationals where such fees are paid for own nationals. However this requirement does not extend to the payment of maintenance grants (as is expressly stated in Art.3 of Directive 93/96)—although the ECJ will consider whether such grants now fall within the scope of the EC Treaty in *Bidar*.[8] The answer to the question may depend on whether the student is newly arrived or is already integrated into the host Member State through the exercise of another free movement right.

---

[6] Case C-224/02 *Pusa v Osuuspankkien Keskinäinen Vakuutusyhtiö* April 29, 2004, however did concern discrimination against a retired Finnish national living in Spain in respect of taxation on his pension.
[7] Case C–184/99 *Grzelczyk v Centre Public d'aide sociale d'Ottignies-Louvain-la-Neuve* [2001] E.C.R. I–6193.
[8] Case C–209/03 *The Queen v London Borough of Ealing and Secretary of State for Education Ex p. Bidar*, pending before the ECJ. See Case C–39/86 *Lair v Universität Hannover* [1998] E.C.R. 316 and Case C–187/97 *Brown v Secretary of State for Scotland,* for earlier case law on student finance.

CHAPTER 13

ACCESS TO SOCIAL SECURITY

This chapter provides an outline and general guide to social security provisions in Community law.

1. INTRODUCTION

There are two basic mechanisms for EU nationals exercising their free **13–01** movement rights to access social security and other social and tax benefits in their host Member State. The first is through specific social security provisions laid down in Reg. 1408/71[1] which apply in the main to employed and self-employed persons. The second is through an application of non-discrimination provisions, both in the EC Treaty itself and in secondary legislation on free movement.

It is important to note that the Community provisions on social security do **13–02** not replace the different national social security systems with a single European system. This type of harmonisation has been seen as impossible given the divergence in social security systems across the Member States and the varying standards and costs of living within them. In general Community law therefore only attempts to co-ordinate these systems of social security. This chapter provides an outline and general guide to social security provisions. However in view of the detail and complexity of the provisions, a textbook such as this cannot provide an in-depth analysis of all the provisions or indeed how they are applied in the various Member States.

Secondary legislation relating to workers has also provided for non- **13–03** discrimination in respect of social and tax advantages, ensuring that EU national workers are not disadvantaged *vis-à-vis* own nationals in other Member States. Additionally Art.12 EC Treaty contains a general non-discrimination provision which might be employed if an EU national, lawfully resident in another Member State, needed to access social welfare or other tax benefits. The ECJ has begun to develop a line of case law supporting an assertion that Art.12 might oblige Member States to make social security provision for EU nationals resident in their territories, at least on a non-discriminatory basis. These principles are discussed in Chapter 12.

---

[1] Unless otherwise indicated, references in this Chapter to the 'Regulation' are to Reg. 1408/71.

2. Social Security Provisions

(a) *Introduction*

13–04   Regulation 1408/71 contains the principal provisions relating to social security for EU nationals.[2] It is extremely complex and provides detailed technical rules relating to social security across the European Union. These provisions have existed for more than 30 years although they have been amended on numerous occasions to keep pace with developments in national social security laws.[3]

13–05   The basic premise of the Regulation is to offer solutions to most of the cross-border problems arising in the field of social security and to ensure that those who exercise free movement rights have sufficient social security protection. Such persons should not be placed in a worse position than those who have resided and worked in one single Member State and never moved.

13–06   Community law aims to solve a number of problems that result from the differences in social security systems across the Member States. In some Member States, social security insurance is based on residence whereas in others it is based on exercise of economic activity. Community law aims to ensure that migrant workers are not insured twice or precluded from insurance altogether by making clear which Member State's legislation applies to a worker. Further problems exist as the result of national legislation often making the entitlement to benefits conditional upon the completion of certain periods of insurance, residence or employment the length of which varies according to the type of benefit and the Member State. The Community provisions provide for aggregation of periods of insurance, residence or employment completed under the legislation of one Member State to be taken into account for entitlement for benefit under the legislation of another Member State.

(b) *Who Benefits*

13–07   At present, the Community provisions on social security do not apply to all persons moving within the European Union. Art.2 of Reg. 1408/71 defines which persons are covered by the provisions of the Regulation. The following persons are protected:[4]

(a)   employed and self-employed persons who are nationals of the Member States (or the EEA) and who are insured or have been insured under the legislation of one of these States;

---

[2] This regulation is implemented through Reg. 574/72.

[3] An updated consolidated version of the Regulations which takes account of all amendments up to September 2001 was produced by the Office for Official Publications of the European Community, CONSLEG: 1971R1408–01/09/2001. This is not an official consolidation. The last of these was published in [1997] O.J. L28.

[4] As provided for in Art.2 of Reg. 1408/71 as amended by Council Reg. 307/1999 of February 8, 1999 L 38 1 12.2.1999.

(b) students who are nationals of the Member States, who study or receive vocational training leading to a qualification officially recognised by the authorities of a Member State, and who are insured under a general social security scheme or a special social security scheme applicable to students;

(c) members of the families and survivors of (a) and (b), regardless of their nationality;

(d) civil servants and members of their families, provided that they are not insured with a special scheme for civil servants; and

(e) refugees and stateless persons.

Frontier workers are treated similarly to employed persons although there are **13–08** special rules relating to them which are detailed below.[5]

Annex I details specific definitions for the individual Member States.

Each of the categories of beneficiary of the Regulation is examined below.

(i) *Employed and Self-employed Persons*[6]

An employed or self-employed person is defined in the Regulation as a per- **13–09** son who has social security insurance. In order to qualify the person may be insured, compulsorily or on an optional[7] continued basis:

(i) for one or more of the contingencies covered by the branches of a social security scheme for employed or self-employed persons or by a special scheme for civil servants,[8] or

(ii) a scheme that can be identified as a scheme for employed or self-employed persons by virtue of its characteristics,[9] or

(iii) a scheme ascribed according to national legislation laid down in Annex I to the Regulation.[10]

It should be noted that the term "worker" is not used for an "employed per- **13–10** son" although it is difficult to see how in real terms the two terms could be differently interpreted. Since the key to access to benefits under Reg. 1408/71 is the requirement that the person is insured in a social security scheme, greater deference is paid to the national legislation and definitions of employed and self-employed persons. This, however, will not necessarily be detrimental to the EU national legislation in various Member States continues to provide social security protection to those who have long since ceased work.[11]

---

[5] See para.13–53 below.
[6] Art.1(a) of Reg. 1408/71 defines 'employed person' and 'self-employed person' for the purposes of the Regulation.
[7] Art.1(a)(iv) of Reg. 1408/71.
[8] Art.1(a)(i) of Reg. 1408/71.
[9] Art.1(a)(ii) of Reg. 1408/71.
[10] Art.1(a)(ii) of Reg. 1408/71.
[11] See Case 249/83 *Hoeckx v Openbaar Centrum voor Maatschappelijk Welzijn, Kalmthout* (1985) E.C.R. 973.

13–11   The ECJ has examined the term "employed person" in contradistinction to "worker". The ECJ considered that there is no single definition of worker in Community law and that the definition varied according to its area of application. The ECJ stated expressly that the term "employed person" would not necessarily coincide with the term "worker". It is clear that a person will fall within the scope of Reg. 1408/71 if that person has the necessary insurance, regardless of whether or not the person is to be regarded as currently in an employment relationship.

13–12   It is notable that an employed or self-employed person may be insured in respect of one single risk only, and yet receive all the benefits relevant to the status of being employed or self-employed. The benefits of this are obvious since a person need not establish that he is insured in respect of the specific benefit which he seeks to obtain. However Member States may limit the receipt of a specific benefit to certain categories of insured person, provided they do so by entering a restriction in the Annex to the Regulation. However such restrictions are narrowly interpreted and if a Member State wishes to restrict access to a benefit to a particular class of insured person, then it must ensure that it does so specifically in respect of the particular benefit concerned.

13–13   In *Stöber and Piosa Pereira*[12] the proposition that being insured against only one risk (as provided for in Reg. 1408/71) was sufficient for a person to be classified as an employed person within the meaning of that Regulation was questioned. The ECJ stated that there was nothing to prevent Member States from restricting entitlement to family benefits to persons belonging to a particular insurance scheme, in that case an old-age insurance scheme for self-employed persons, providing it did so explicitly in the Annex to the Regulation.

13–14   The ECJ reiterated this principle in *Martinez Sala*.[13] The German Government had relied on its restriction in Annex I[14] which stipulated that only a person compulsorily insured against unemployment or who, as a result of such insurance, obtains cash benefits under sickness insurance or comparable benefits may be classified as an employed person for the purposes of receiving family benefits. However the ECJ pointed out that in fact the German restriction was only in respect of family benefits falling within Title III, Chapter 7, whereas the benefit which Ms Sala had sought to obtain was a family benefit falling within the scope of another provision of the Regulation, namely Art.4(1)(h). Since the German restriction did not apply to her, her status as an employed person was to be determined in the usual way, namely by reference to whether she was covered, even if only in respect of a single risk, by a general or special social security scheme. The ECJ had insufficient information to determine this for itself and therefore referred the matter back to the national court for consideration. The case shows the importance of identifying precisely the scope of any restriction entered in Annex I.

---

[12] Joined Cases C 4 & 5/95 *Stöber and Piosa Pereira* [1997] E.C.R. I–511.
[13] Case C–85/96 *Martinez Sala v Freistant Bayern* [1998] E.C.R. I–2691.
[14] Annex I, I, C ("Germany") of Reg. 1408/71.

Specific provision is made for unemployed, seasonal workers and frontier workers in the Regulation. However for such persons to benefit they must be insured within a social security system. **13–15**

(ii) *Students*[15]

Students were added to the scope of the Regulation in 1999 in order to provide better co-ordination of the social security systems which apply to students.[16] Whilst harmonisation of those social security systems is by no means achieved in the amended Reg. 1408/71, better co-ordination was seen as desirable to prevent the students concerned from being subject to a double levy of contributions, or acquiring dual rights to benefits. As with employed and self-employed persons it is necessary for students to establish that they are insured under the general social security system applicable to students. **13–16**

The Regulation makes explicit that the extension of its provisions to students is without prejudice to the application of Directive 93/96 on the free movement of students. This means that a student who arrives in another Member State in order to study must already be insured under a general social security system or become insured (normally through work) if the Regulation is to apply. Students who are not so insured will need to declare their self-sufficiency and will not have access to benefits by virtue of Reg. 1408/71. However they might obtain access to social security benefits through the operation of non-discrimination provisions and principles of Community law.[17] **13–17**

(iii) *Members of the Family*[18]

The Regulation defines "member of the family" as any person defined or recognised as a member of the family or designated as a member of the household by the legislation under which benefits are provided by the legislation of the Member State in whose territory such a person resides. Where such national legislation treats as a member of the family or a member of the household only a person living under the same roof as the employed or self-employed person or student, this condition shall be considered satisfied if the person in question is mainly dependent on that person. Where the legislation of a Member State does not make clear which members of the family to which it applies, the term "member of the family" shall have the meaning given to it by the relevant Member State in an annex to the Regulation.[19] **13–18**

It may seem surprising that Community law should pay deference to varying national concepts of the family and family members when in other areas such **13–19**

---

[15] Art.1(ca) of Reg. 1407/81 defines "student" for the purposes of the Regulation.

[16] Reg. 307/1999 of February 8, 1999 amending Reg. 1408/71 on the application of social security schemes to employed persons, to self-employed persons and to members of their families moving within the Reg. 574/72 laying down the procedure for implementing Reg. 1408/71 with a view to extending them to cover students.

[17] See Chapter 12.

[18] Art.1(f) of Reg. 1408/71 defines "member of the family" for the purposes of the Regulation.

[19] Annex I where for instance a Member State may describe the term member of the family for particular types of benefit falling within the scope of the Regulation.

concepts have strict Community law meanings. However it is to be recalled that social security legislation across the Member States varies greatly and Community law in this area does not attempt to *harmonise* those systems but simply to *co-ordinate* them. Community law in the area of social security is not sufficiently developed to require that social security benefits are provided to any particular family members.

13–20   Where the benefits concerned are benefits for disabled persons granted under the legislation of a Member State to all nationals of that State who fulfill the prescribed conditions, the term "member of the family" means at least the spouse of an employed or self-employed person or student and the children of such person who are either minors or dependent upon such person.

13–21   "Survivor" means any person defined or recognised as such by the legislation under which the benefits are granted. Where, however, the national legislation regards as a survivor only a person who was living under the same roof as the deceased, this condition shall be considered satisfied if such person was mainly dependent on the deceased.

(iv) *Civil Servants*[20]

13–22   Civil servants were added into the Regulation by amendment in 1998[21] to reflect the special insurance schemes that Member States may have in place for their civil servants and to provide rules of co-ordination for such schemes.[22] There is no definition of the term "civil servant" in the Regulation and thus national definitions of the term will apply.

(v) *Refugees and Stateless Persons*[23]

13–23   It is unusual for Community law relating to the free movement of EU nationals to extend to any third country national other than the family members of EU nationals. However the Regulation is explicitly extended to cover recognised refugees and stateless persons.

13–24   Refugees are defined as those falling within the scope of Art.1 of the Convention Relating to the Status of Refugees, done at Geneve on July 28, 1951. Stateless person are those falling within the scope of Art.1 of the Convention Relating to the Status of Stateless Persons, adopted in New York on September 28, 1954.

13–25   As yet there has been no case law concerning the application of this Regulation to refugees or stateless persons. However, given the general reference to the Conventions on Refugees and Statelessness, as opposed to domestic defini-

---

[20] Art.1(a)(i) of Reg. 1408/71 includes "civil servants" with the definition of"employed persons and self employed persons". Art.1(ja) defines "special scheme for civil servants" (referring to special insurance schemes for civil servants).

[21] Council Reg. 1606/98 of June 29, 1998.

[22] Art.14(e) and (f) of Reg. 1408/71 which in essence provide that a person employed as a civil servant in a Member State will be subject to that State's legislation. If they are so employed in two States then the civil servant will be subject to the legislation of both States.

[23] Art.1(d) and (e) of Reg. 1408/71 define "refugee" and "stateless person" for the purposes of the Regulation.

tions, there is certainly scope for disagreement between Member States as to the application of the Regulation to an individual. The lack of harmonisation in the definition of a refugee in particular could result in a persons being treated as a refugee in one Member State whilst not being recognised as such in another.[24] It would be for the ECJ to resolve a dispute regarding the definition of a refugee. Such a dispute might feasibly occur if a person had been recognised as a refugee in one Member State but another Member State, applying the exclusion clauses under Art.1F of the 1951 Convention,[25] considered that the person was not a refugee. The application of Art.1F is inconsistent across Member States although its use has undoubtedly increased in the post-September 11 era.

(c) *The Benefits covered by the Regulation*

Article 4 of Reg. 1408/71 provides that the Regulation will apply to all national legislation with regard to the following types of social security: **13–26**

(a) Sickness and maternity;

(b) Accidents at work;

(c) Occupational diseases;

(d) Invalidity benefits;

(e) Old-age pensions;

(f) Survivor's benefits;

(g) Death grants;

(h) Unemployment benefits; and

(i) Family benefits.

It is not relevant whether these benefits are financed by contributions, or whether they are paid by employers, social insurance institutions or public administrations.

A person will usually only be subject to the legislation of one Member State at a time. Generally speaking a person will be insured in the Member State where professional activity is exercised. Exceptions to this rule apply to those who are temporarily posted abroad by an employer. Persons who work in more than one Member State will be insured in the Member State in which they reside.   **13–27**

---

[24] Dir. 2004/83 On minimum standards for the qualification and status of third country nationals or stateless persons as refugees or as persons who otherwise need international protection and content of the protection granted of April 29, 2004 (O.J. September 30, 2004, L 304/12). This provides for harmonised minimum standards on the definition of a refugee and should go some way to eradicating any significant differences in the definition of who is a refugee amongst Member States.

[25] Art.1F of the 1951 Convention on the Status of Refugees provides that the provisions of the Convention will not apply to any person in respect of whom there are serious reasons for considering that he has committed a crime against peace or humanity, a serious non-political crime or has been guilty of acts contrary to the purposes and principles of the UN.

13–28   The principle of equality means that if a person is insured in one Member State such a person will be entitled to the same rights and obligations as nationals of that Member State. It does not matter for instance that the Member State of origin of the person concerned has a less generous system of benefits than the host Member State where the person is now insured.

(i) *Sickness or Maternity*[26]

13–29   Chapter I of Title III of Reg. 1408/71 contains detailed provisions on sickness and maternity benefits with special rules for workers, unemployed persons, pensioners, students and members of their family.

In order to ensure continuous entitlement to these particular benefits, whenever the completion of a waiting period is required for entitlement to benefits, the period of insurance, residence or employment completed in other Member States must be taken into account.

13–30   Sickness and maternity benefits are different in each of the Member States. There are two major categories of benefits: benefits in cash and benefits in kind.

Sickness benefits in cash are benefits normally intended to replace income which is lost through sickness. In some Member States national legislation provides that wages will be paid for a period of time once a person becomes incapacitated. The ECJ regards these payments as sickness benefits in cash. Sickness benefits in cash are paid according to the legislation of the Member State in which the person is insured, regardless of place of residence.

13–31   Sickness benefits in kind comprise medical and dental care. Sickness benefits in kind are provided according to the legislation of the Member State in which the person resides rather than place of insurance. If the person is resident in a Member State other than where he is insured, he is entitled to all the benefits in kind provided under the legislation of the Member State in which he resides, even where that might be more generous than that of the Member State in which he is insured.

13–32   In cases where a person is temporarily staying in a Member State other than where he is insured, he is entitled to all "immediately necessary benefits", which means all urgent medical treatment which is necessary with regard to the state of health of the person. Pensioners are entitled during a temporary stay to all benefits in kind which become necessary during their stay.

13–33   It is not unusual for EU nationals to move to other Member State specifically to obtain medical treatment there. In such cases the costs will only be covered by the relevant sickness insurance institution if permission is received in advance. Normally this is a matter of discretion for that sickness insurance institution. However, in cases where the treatment in question is among the benefits provided for by the legislation of the Member State of the person but not available within the time normally necessary with regard to the person's health, the permission may not be refused.

---

[26] Arts 18 to 35.

(ii) *Accidents at Work and Occupational Diseases*[27]

Chapter 4 of Title III of Reg. 1408/71 provides the rules relating to benefits paid following an accident at work or an occupational disease.   **13–34**

Where someone suffers from an accident at work or an occupational disease, such a person is entitled to benefits in kind according to the legislation in the Member State of residence. If the person resides in a Member State which is different from the one in which such a person is insured, the Member State of residence will provide the benefits in kind according to its legislation and will be reimbursed by the competent institution in the Member State in which the person is insured. A frontier worker can opt to get benefits in kind in the Member State in which the frontier worker is insured instead of the Member State of residence.

Cash benefits are paid according to the legislation of the Member State in which the person was insured at the time when the accident or disease occurred. If the amount of cash benefit depends on the number of members of the family there are, account will be taken of family members residing in another Member State.   **13–35**

(iii) *Invalidity*[28]

Chapter 2 of Title III of Reg. 1408/71 provides the detailed rules relating to invalidity pensions. Invalidity pensions are extremely variable across the Member States. In some Member States invalidity pensions are only paid to those who are actually insured at the time when the invalidity occurs, at a rate which is independent of the insurance period. In other Member States pensions are paid to those who were insured and the amount depends on the length of insurance period.   **13–36**

As a general rule, on becoming incapacitated a worker exercising free movement rights must not be in an inferior position when compared with someone who has always lived and worked in one single country. If a person has been insured in several Member States the calculation of the amount of pension payable is determined differently according to whether the person was insured in Member States where the amount of pension depends on the *length* of insurance periods or where the amount of pension is *independent of* the length of insurance periods. The result may be that the person ends up with two separate pensions on the basis of the payments being split between the two States according to the length of time spent in each Member State.   **13–37**

(iv) *Old-age Pensions*[29]

Chapter 3 of Title III of Reg. 1408/71 provides the detailed rules concerning old-age pensions. In an increasingly ageing Europe, old-age pensions are amongst the most important social security benefits. The following principles apply to a person who stops working in one country and continues activities in another: **13–38**

---

[27] Arts 52 to 63.
[28] Arts 37 to 43.
[29] Arts 44 to 51.

(a)   In every Member State where the person was insured the insurance record is preserved until the person reaches pensionable age. Contributions are not transferred to another Member State or paid out if the person is no longer insured in that Member State.

(b)   Every Member State where the person was insured for at least one year will have to pay an old-age pension when the person reaches pensionable age. If the person has worked in three Member States, the person will receive three separate pensions.

(c)   The pension will be calculated according the insurance record in the Member State in question.

13–39   The pension will be paid regardless of where the person resides within the European Union without reduction. This principle does not apply to some special benefits which are not contributions based. In most such special benefits are means-tested and only paid to persons who reside in the state concerned.

13–40   Pensionable ages are defined by Member State's domestic laws rather than by Community law. Member States are further permitted to have different pensionable ages for women and men.[30]

(v) *Survivors' Benefits and Death Grants*[31]

13–41   Chapter 5 of Title III of Reg. 1408/71 provides the detailed rules relating to the payment of death grants and survivors' benefits. In general the same rules apply to pensions for surviving spouses as to invalidity and old-age pensions. The pensions have to be paid without any reduction regardless of where surviving spouse resides in the European Union. If the deceased person was still an employed or self-employed person, the pension for the surviving spouse will be calculated according to the same principles which would have applied to the insured person. If the deceased person was already a pensioner, the pension of the surviving spouse will be calculated according to the national legislation concerned.

13–42   The orphan of a person who was insured under the legislation of a single Member State will be entitled to orphan's benefits according to the legislation of that state, regardless of where the orphan resides. The orphan of a person who was insured under the legislation of two or more Member States will be entitled to the highest benefit which is provided under the legislation of one of these states.

13–43   In the case of death grants, as with all other categories of benefits, Member States must take into account periods of insurance or residence completed under the legislation of any other Member State. The death grants will be paid by the Member State in which the deceased person was insured.

---

[30] Case C–196/98 *Hepple v Adjudication Officer* [2000] E.C.R. I–3701.
[31] Arts 64 to 66.

(vi) *Unemployment Benefit*[32]

Chapter 6 of Title III of Reg. 1408/71 makes detailed provision for the pay- **13–44**
ment of unemployment benefit. Compared with the provisions for other categories of benefits, unemployment benefit rules are relatively restrictive and
less generous.

If a person becomes unemployed, the Member State in which the person **13–45**
claims unemployment benefit is obliged to take account of periods of insurance or employment completed in any other Member State, if this is necessary for entitlement to unemployment benefit. This only applies, however, if
the person completes such periods immediately before becoming unemployed. In other words it is not possible for a person to claim unemployment
benefit in a Member State where that person was not insured immediately
before becoming unemployed.

If the person is insured in the Member State of residence, the person is enti- **13–46**
tled to unemployment benefits according to its legislation under the same
conditions as the nationals of this state.

If the calculation of unemployment benefit is based on the amount of previous wages or salaries, only wages or salaries which the person received in the
Member State where the person was most recently employed are taken into
account, providing the person was employed for at least four weeks there.

In order to obtain unemployment benefit whilst looking for work in another **13–47**
Member State, the person must satisfy certain conditions. The person must
have remained available to the unemployment services of the state which pay
the unemployment benefit for at least four weeks after becoming unemployed. This period may be shortened by the unemployment services concerned. Within seven days of departing, the person must register with the
unemployment services of the Member State in which he is looking for work.
Unemployment benefits will be retained for a maximum of three months. If
the person is unable to find a new job in that time period, such person will
continue to receive unemployment benefit only in the event of return to the
Member State in which the person was last employed. If the person returns
later than this, entitlement to all benefits is lost. Entitlement to the three-
months payment may only occur once between two periods of employment.

The clear scheme of these provisions is to provide only the transfer of enti- **13–48**
tlement to unemployment benefit when a work seeker moves from one
Member State to another. Thus those not entitled to unemployment benefit
in the first Member State will not obtain such entitlement in a second
Member State. A person who has not previously worked in any Member State
is unlikely to be able to obtain unemployment benefits in a second Member
State, unless the first Member State has generous provision in respect of
persons who have never worked.[33]

---

[32] Arts 67 to 71.
[33] Such as for instance young people having recently completed education.

The scheme outlined above is concerned with the ability of an EU national to move his unemployment benefit if he moves to seek work in another Member State. However, for those unable to benefit from the scheme, non-discrimination arguments maybe able to be deployed.[34] See further para. 13–57 below.

(vii) *Family Benefits*[35]

13–49   Chapter 7 of Title III of Reg. 1408/71 is concerned with the payment of family benefits. The nature and amounts of family benefits available in the different Member States vary greatly. As in the case of entitlement to other benefits, the Member State which has to pay family benefits is obliged to take into account periods of insurance or employment completed under the legislation of any other Member State.

13–50   If the members of the family reside in the same Member State under whose legislation the principal is insured as an employed or self-employed person, that Member State will be obliged to pay the benefits. The principal is entitled to the same amounts of benefits as nationals of that state. If the members of the family do not reside in the Member State under whose legislation the employed or self-employed principal is insured, as a rule the family will get the highest amount of benefit which is provided for in one of the Member States in which either the family or the principal resides or is insured.

13–51   Unemployed persons drawing unemployment benefit under the legislation of a Member State are entitled to family benefits according to the legislation of that State, and for members of their families residing in another Member State.

13–52   Pensioners normally receive family benefits from the state which pays their pension. However where the pensioner receives more than one pension, in most cases entitlement is to the highest benefits which are provided by one of the states concerned.

(d) *Frontier Workers*

13–53   Article 1(b) of Reg. 1408/71 defines a frontier worker. Generally such workers enjoy all benefits granted to migrant workers in the Member State of employment. However, frontier workers have an entitlement to unemployment benefits from the state of residence rather than the state of employment.[36] They are able to choose between either their state of residence or employment as regards health care.[37] Their family members, by contrast, have no such choice as regards health care: they are covered by the state of residence.

---

[34] Case C-138/02 *Collins v Secretary of State for Work and Pensions,* judgement of March 23, 2004, not yet reported.
[35] Arts 72 to 76.
[36] Art.71 of Reg. 1408/71.
[37] Art.20.

3. ACCESS TO SOCIAL SECURITY FOR THE "ECONOMICALLY INACTIVE"

The economically inactive are described in Chapter 9. It is a basic pre-   **13–54**
condition attached to those who are economically inactive that they are self-
sufficient. They might have acquired rights to certain social security benefits
under the provisions of national law or Reg. 1408/71 (*e.g.* as an old-age pensioner) and plainly they may be regarded as self-sufficient if they are in
receipt of such benefits by virtue of that Regulation. Thus a pensioner will be
able to rely on pension payments received in other Member States if moving
to the territory of a Member State. A person exercising a general right of residence under Directive 90/364 may be in receipt of invalidity benefit or a
death grant which can provide the resources necessary to establish that such
a person is self-sufficient.

However where the person does not acquire rights to benefits under social   **13–55**
security provisions of Reg. 1408/71, what entitlement is there to any form
of social assistance? The ECJ has now established that in certain circumstances, where the need for social assistance is temporary and where the
person previously fulfilled the conditions and limitations placed on residence, such access should not be denied. This is consistent with the principle of non-discrimination protected by Art.12 EC Treaty and with
Community principles of proportionality. These principles are discussed in
Chapter 12.

Thus in *Grzelczyk*[38] a student, who had studied for three years during which   **13–56**
time he had been self-sufficient in compliance with conditions placed on him
by Directive 93/96, could not be denied access to social assistance because it
was requested on a temporary basis. The ECJ recalled that the fourth recital
to the Directive (and indeed to Directives 90/365 and 90/364 on the self-
sufficient and retired persons) refers to the fact that beneficiaries of the
Directive should not become an "*unreasonable* burden" on the finances of the
host Member State. According to the ECJ this meant that Member States
accept "a certain degree of financial solidarity between nationals of a host
Member State and nationals of other Member States, particularly if the difficulties which a beneficiary of the right of residence encounters are temporary". The ECJ acknowledged the possibility for Member States to take the
view that a student who has recourse to social assistance no longer fulfils the
requirements of the Directive and thus withdraw the residence permit or
refuse to renew it. However, the ECJ emphasised that this should never be the
automatic consequence of recourse to social assistance. It is implicit in the
ECJ's judgment that the Member State must always act proportionately and,
as stated above, accept a certain degree of "financial solidarity".

---

[38] Case C-184/99 *Grzelczyk v Centre public d'aide sociale d'Ottignies-Louvain-la-Neuve* [2001]
E.C.R. I-4921.

4. Access to Social Security Flowing from Citizenship of the Union

13–57   There is no doubt that access to social security benefits is widening as a result of the inclusion in the EC Treaty of the provisions on Union citizenship contained in Arts 17 and 18 EC Treaty. Citizenship of the Union is considered in detail in Chapter 4, whilst in Chapter 12 the potential non discrimination arguments enabling EU nationals to access certain benefits are considered.

13–58   In summary, for those falling within the scope of Art.18 EC Treaty as free movers access to benefits on a non discriminatory basis will extend to those benefits that facilitate the exercise of the rights of free movement. This will mean for instance that a work seeker who falls outside the scope of Regulation 1408/71 may nonetheless be entitled to job seekers allowance on a non discriminatory basis where he seeks work in another Member State.[39]

13–59   More broadly, as Union citizens all EU nationals resident in other Member States, irrespective as to whether or not they are exercising EC Treaty rights, have the right to enjoy at the least non discriminatory access to minimum forms of non contributory means tested social assistance. Thus for instance in *Trojani*[40] the ECJ held that an EU national deriving no benefit from Art.18 EC Treaty nonetheless derived the right to be granted a social assistance benefit by relying on Arts 12 and 17 EC Treaty.

---

[39] Case C-138/02 *Collins v Secretary of State for Work and Pensions*, judgment of March 23, 2004, not yet reported.
[40] Case C-456/02 *Trojani v Centre public d'aide sociale de Bruxelles (CPAS)* September 7, 2004, not yet reported.

CHAPTER 14

EXCLUSION

This chapter examines the rights of free movers and other EU nationals when they face exclusion or expulsion from the territories of the Member States.

1. INTRODUCTION

Community law clearly provides the right of EU nationals and their family members to enter and reside in the territories of other Member States under certain conditions. This right plainly impacts on the sovereign right of Member States to control their borders. Where the EU nationals and their family members can demonstrate a Community law free movement right, their entry and stay can be interfered with only on very limited grounds of public policy, public security and public health and subject to strict provisions of Community law.[1] The meaning of these provisions and the protection enjoyed by such persons from exclusion and expulsion are considered in sections 2 to 4 below. Where on the other hand EU nationals and their family members can establish no Community law nexus to their situation in a host Member State, that Member State may be entitled to take expulsion or exclusion measures on a broader basis. Such measures are considered in section 5 below.

2. COMMUNITY LAW PROVISIONS ON THE EXPULSION AND EXCLUSION OF FREE MOVERS

Article 39(3) EC Treaty makes clear that the right to move within the **14–01** Member States and remain in other Member States for the purposes of employment is "subject to limitations justified on grounds of public policy, public security or public health". Likewise Art.46 permits Member States to have in place measures for the special treatment of self-employed nationals of other Member States on grounds of public policy, public security or public health.[2]

Directive 64/221,[3] which applies to both employed and self-employed per- **14–02** sons, contains provisions to ensure consistency in the application of the

---

[1] As from April 30, 2006, EU nationals who have resided in a host Member State for 10 years or more will face expulsion or exclusion only "on imperative national security grounds", Article 28 of the Dir. 2004/38/EC on the rights of citizens of the Union and their family members. See further Appendix 30.

[2] The ECJ has held that the slight difference in wording between the Arts 39(3) and 46 EC Treaty should not make any difference to the application of these provisions. See Case 48/75 *Procureur de Roiv Royer* [1976] E.C.R. 497.

[3] Dir. 64/221 of February 15, 1964 on the co-ordination of special measures concerning the movement and residence of foreign nationals: [1963–64] O.J. Spec. Ed. 117.

"public policy, public security and public health" provisos laid down in the EC Treaty and provides procedural safeguards to ensure proper application and co-ordination in this area. Directive 64/221 is extended by two further Directives to workers who remain in the territory of a Member State having been employed[4] and to persons who remain in a Member State after having pursued self-employed activity there.[5] The provisions of Directive 64/221 are finally extended to the economically self-sufficient categories by express reference to Directive 64/221 in the three Directives creating the rights of residence for the self-sufficient. All three Directives provide that derogation from the right of residence will only be on grounds of public policy, public security or public health and that Directive 64/221 shall apply.[6] The provisions of Directive 64/221 apply equally to the third country national family members of EU nationals exercising Treaty rights as to the EU nationals themselves.[7]

14–03 The EC Treaty provisions contemplate that Member States will be able to prevent a national of another Member State from entering their territory and remaining there on grounds of public policy, public security or public health. These measures are referred to both in the EC Treaty and secondary legislation as "special treatment" because they offend the basic principles of free movement and because they cannot be used against own nationals, making them discriminatory.

14–04 In view of their discriminatory application as well as the fact that they create obstacles to free movement these measures have to be justified by the Member State using them by reference to very restrictive definitions of all three grounds for such measures. As with any measure which restricts one of the fundamental freedoms guaranteed by the Treaty, measures taken pursuant to Arts 39(3) and 46 EC Treaty will be justified only if they comply with the principle of proportionality: "In that respect, such a measure must be appropriate for securing the attainment of the objective which it pursues and must not go beyond what is necessary in order to attain it".[8]

14–05 Apart from grounds of public policy, public security or public health, there are no other grounds for the exclusion or expulsion of either an EU national exercising Treaty rights or that EU national's family members, regardless of nationality. In other circumstances the right of states to exclude or expel non-nationals is both recognised by international law and jealously guarded by

---

[4] Council Dir. 72/194 of May 18, 1972 extending the scope of Dir. 64/221 to workers exercising the right to remain in the territory of a Member State after having been employed in that State within the meaning of Reg. 1251/70 [1972] O.J. L121/32.

[5] Council Dir. 75/35 of December 17, 1974 extending the scope of Dir. 64/221 to include nationals of a Member State who exercise the right to remain in the territory of another Member State after having pursued therein an activity in a self-employed capacity under Dir. 75/34 [1975] O.J. L14/14.

[6] See for instance Dir. 90/364 provides in its preamble "Whereas the beneficiaries of this Directive should be covered by administrative arrangements similar to those laid down in particular by Directive 68/360/EEC and Directive 64/221/EEC". Art.2(2) states "Member States shall not derogate from the provisions of this Directive save on grounds of public policy, public security or public health. In that event, Directive 64/221/EEC shall apply".

[7] Art.1(2) of Dir. 64/221.

[8] Case C-55/94 *Gebhard v Consigol dell' Ordine degli Advocat AE Procuratori di Milano* [1995] E.C.R. I–4165, para.37.

States. In the Community context, however, this right cannot be applied to EU nationals and their families unless the strict requirements of the Treaty and secondary legislation are met. The importance of the fundamental shift caused by the impact of Community law on the exercise by states of powers otherwise seen as reflective of their own sovereignty cannot be overstated. Indeed there is at times a tendency by national authorities and courts to fail properly to reflect the importance of the Community law context in this area. However antithetical to notions of national sovereignty, Member States' obligations properly to reflect principles of Community law in the context of exclusion and expulsion must always remain at the forefront of the minds of decision-makers.

Member States have not co-ordinated criminal legislation[9] and in principle   **14–06**
such legislation is a matter for individual Member States. Article 39(3) EC Treaty implies that Member States continue in principle to be free to determine their own public policy and public security needs. However Community law sets limits on the exercise by Member States of this power where such exercise interferes with the fundamental freedoms set down in the EC Treaty.[10]

3. GROUNDS FOR EXCLUSION/EXPULSION OF FREE MOVERS

(a) *General Observations*

(i) *Grounds for Taking Special Measures Against EU Nationals*

The secondary legislation implementing the EC Treaty provisions as well as   **14–07**
interpretation of this legislation by the ECJ have provided a number of principles to guide Member States on the application of the three grounds for taking special measures against EU nationals exercising free movement rights under the EC Treaty.

Firstly, a decision leading to the expulsion or exclusion of an EU national exercising or wishing to exercise a Treaty right in another Member State may only be made on grounds of public policy, public security or public health. These concepts are very narrowly defined.[11] Decisions based upon them must be both strictly justified, and proportionate to the objective which they pursue.[12]

Secondly, a decision to expel or exclude an EU national must be limited to   **14–08**
circumstances relating to the conduct of the individual concerned only[13] and not based on general considerations of public interest (such as the fight against drugs or organised crime).

---

[9] The EU Treaty does contain chapters on co-operation between Member States on criminal policing.
[10] Case 186/87 *Cowan v Trésor Public* [1989] E.C.R. 195.
[11] See for instance Case 41/74 *Van Duyn v Home Office* [1974] E.C.R. 1337.
[12] Case 36/75 *Rutili v Ministre de l'interieur* [1975] E.C.R. 1219.
[13] Art.3(1) of Dir. 64/221, see also Case 48/75 *Procureur de Roi v Royer* [1976] E.C.R. 497.

Thirdly, a Member State employing expulsion or exclusion measures would need to demonstrate that the use of such measures does not amount to the taking of arbitrary measures against nationals of other Member States. Thus it will be necessary for the Member State in question to demonstrate that it takes genuine and effective measures against its own nationals in order to combat the conduct justifying the expulsion or exclusion.[14]

(ii) *Economic Reasons for Expulsion*

14–09 As Art.2(2) of Directive 64/221 makes clear, the three grounds for expulsion or exclusion cannot be invoked "to service economic ends". In practice this will mean that the Member States will be unable to justify expulsion or exclusion against EU nationals and their family members simply on the basis that they are an economic burden on the Member State, if those persons have retained a right of residence under the EC Treaty or secondary legislation. Further the failure to meet administrative requirements laid down by Member States for registration or taxation of employment or self-employed activities will not constitute grounds for expulsion or exclusion.[15]

(iii) *Failure to Comply with Formalities*

14–10 As outlined in Chapter 11 above, the mere failure to comply with immigration formalities such as obtaining visas or residence permits is not a basis for exclusion or expulsion under the EC Treaty or Directive 64/221.[16]

(iv) *Restrictions on Free Movement Within a Member State*

14–11 Instead of expulsion or exclusion, a Member State may take administrative measures limiting an EU national's right of residence to a part of the territory. However there is no distinction in the principles that are applied to a measure restricting movement within the territory as against those explicable in expulsion cases. Such measures may only be taken if, by reason of the seriousness of the individual's conduct, he could otherwise be liable to expulsion or exclusion from the whole of the territory of that Member State.[17]

(b) *Public Policy*

(i) *General Test to be Applied in Public Policy Cases*

14–12 "Public policy" is the ground most frequently invoked against EU nationals and their family members when expulsion or exclusion measures are contemplated. However as the ECJ has made clear consistently, this ground is to be narrowly construed. The test for whether public policy grounds exist for such measures to be taken is that the individual poses a "genuine and sufficiently serious threat affecting one of the fundamental interests of society."[18]

---

[14] See for instance Case C-348/96 *Criminal Proceedings Against Calfa* [1999] E.C.R. I–11.
[15] Case C-363/89 *Roux v Belgium* [1991] E.C.R. I–273.
[16] Case 48/75 *Procureur de Roi v Royer* [1976] E.C.R. 497; Case C–459/99 *Mouvement contre le Racisme, l'antisemitisme et la xenophobie ASBL (MRAX) v Belgium State* [2002] E.C.R. I–6591.
[17] Case C-100/01 *Ministre de l'Intérieur v Olazabal* [2002] E.C.R. I–10981, para.45.
[18] See for instance Case 30/77 *R. v Bouchereau* [1977] E.C.R. 1999.

The ECJ has not imposed any minimum level of crime or offence which   **14–13**
might justify measures to be taken on public policy grounds and thus to some
extent an assessment of whether conduct is contrary to public policy is left to
Member States. However conduct can never be considered to be of a sufficiently serious nature to justify expulsion or exclusion of the national of
another Member State where the host Member States does not take genuine
and effective measures against its own nationals for that conduct.

In *Adoui and Cornuaille*[19] the EU nationals were "waitresses in a bar which   **14–14**
was 'suspect' from the point of view of morals".[20] The ECJ held that where
own nationals in engaging in similar activities were not subject to any repressive measures, the expulsion of EU nationals could not be justified on public
policy grounds.

(ii) *General Deterrence*

Article 3(1) of Directive 64/221 provides that any measures taken on grounds   **14–15**
of public policy must be based exclusively on the personal conduct of the individual concerned. Article 3(2) states that previous criminal convictions shall
not in themselves constitute grounds for expulsion or exclusion of EU nationals or their family members. The ECJ has read these two provisions together as
meaning that the expulsion of an EU national cannot be justified on the
grounds of general deterrence.

In *Bonsignore*,[21] an Italian national residing in Germany had purchased a gun   **14–16**
without a licence and had accidentally killed his own brother. He was found
guilty of illegal possession of a weapon as well as causing death by negli-
gence. The German authorities wanted to deport him for general deterrent
reasons and not because he was likely to re-offend. The ECJ ruled that
Art.3(1) read together with Art.3(2) barred Member States from expelling
EU nationals in order to deter others from committing similar offences.

(iii) *Serious Crime*

Even where in principle the offence committed is one which is so serious as   **14–17**
to entitle a Member State to regard the person's continued presence as constituting a danger to society, it is only the individual's own conduct which
may justify expulsion or exclusion. In *Calfa*[22] the ECJ considered a case
where the EU national had committed drugs offence which in Belgian law
automatically led to deportation with a three-year ban on re-entry. The ECJ
held that such automatic expulsion following a drugs offence, notwithstanding the danger to society that drugs represent, does not fulfil the requirements
of Directive 64/221 since it does not take into account the personal conduct
of the offender.

---

[19] Joined Cases 115 & 116/81 *Adoui and Cornuaille* [1982] E.C.R. 1665.
[20] Case 30/77 *R. v Bouchereau* [1977] E.C.R. 1999, para.2. The women concerned were French
nationals working in Belgium as prostitutes.
[21] Case C-67/74 *Bonsignore v Oberstadtdirector der Stadt Köln* [1975] E.C.R. 297.
[22] Case C-348/96 *Criminal Proceedings Against Calfa* [1999] E.C.R. I–11.

14-18   When examining the individual's conduct Member States must be satisfied that the individual constitutes a *present* threat to the fundamental interests of society. Past conduct alone will not justify expulsion or exclusion. The ECJ has held that a finding that such a threat exists implies the existence of a "propensity to act in the same way in the future".[23] Thus regardless of the public interest that Member States might have in combating a particular crime, any measure taken against an individual must be on the basis of that individual's posing a present threat.[24]

14-19   In the post-September 11 era when Member States are intent on combating terrorism, it might be tempting for them to invoke public policy reasons for expelling or excluding a person who has been convicted of a crime relating to terrorism. This is only be permissible if it can be demonstrated that there is a propensity to act in the same way in the future, regardless of any public sentiment towards those branded as terrorists or indeed any wish on the part of the Member State to deter others from engaging in terrorism.

This principle is shown by the decision of the ECJ in *Olazabal*[25] which concerned a member of ETA (whose activites constituted a threat to both public order and security). As regards Mr Olazabal himself who was convicted of conspiracy to disturb public order by "intimidation or terror", the ECJ applied exactly the same principles as with other public policy cases without dilution of such principles by reason of any reference to terrorism.

14-20   Furthermore, the ECJ took this approach to the fight against drugs, which since the 1980s has been a major concern of Member States, in *Nazli*.[26] The ECJ acknowledged the special measures which Member States may wish to employ to deal with this problem but held fast to the principle that an interference with the fundamental right of free movement can only be justified by reference to the individual's conduct and the threat that he poses:

> "While a Member State may consider that the use of drugs constitutes a danger for society such as to justify, in order to maintain public order, special measures against aliens who contravene its laws on drugs, the public policy exception, like all derogations from a fundamental principle of the Treaty, must nevertheless be interpreted restrictively, so that the existence of a criminal conviction can justify expulsion only in so far as the circumstances which gave rise to that conviction are evidence of personal conduct constituting a present threat to the requirements of public policy (see, most recently, Case C–348/96 *Calfa* [1999] E.C.R. I—11, paras 22, 23 and 24).
>
> The Court has thus concluded that Community law precludes the expulsion of a national of a Member State on general preventive grounds, that is to say an expulsion ordered for the purpose of deterring other aliens (see, in particular, Case 67/74 *Bonsignore v Stadt Köln* [1975] ECR 297, paragraph 7), especially where that meas-

---

[23] Case 67/74 *Bonsignore v Stadt Köln* [1975] E.C.R. 297.
[24] The Advocate General in the case of Case 30/77 *R. v Bouchereau* [1977] E.C.R. 1999, was of the opinion that in exceptional circumstances following a particularly heinous crime past conduct alone might constitute such a threat to the requirements of public policy. The ECJ has never applied such reasoning.
[25] Case C-100/01 *Ministre de l'Intérieur v Olazabal* [2002] E.C.R. I–10981.
[26] Case C-340/97 *Nazli v Stadt Nürnburg* [2000] E.C.R. I–957.

ure has automatically followed a criminal conviction, without any account being taken of the personal conduct of the offender or of the danger which that conduct represents for the requirements of public policy (*Calfa*, cited above, para. 27)".[27]

Member States which jealously guard their rights both to control the entry of non-nationals to their territories and to combat serious crime can find the application of these principles difficult, at odds with their own domestic law and even the application of international human rights instruments (where past conduct may be sufficient to justify expulsion).[28] However Member States have long since forgone their absolute right to control their borders, at least in respect of EU nationals and their family members who exercise the free movement rights conferred by the EC Treaty and secondary legislation. It is the exercise of such fundamental right of free movement which Community law protects in the present context by ensuring that derogation from the right is permitted only in very limited circumstances and where absolutely necessary. **14–21**

(c) *Public Security*

Article 3(1) of Directive 64/221 requires that measures taken on grounds of public security must be based exclusively on the personal conduct of the individual concerned. As with public policy, the concept of public security must be narrowly construed and must relate only to conduct of the individual which demonstrates a propensity to pose a public security threat in the future. **14–22**

There have been no cases where public security has been relied on alone as a basis for taking measures against an EU national since public policy and public security are often closely inter-related. However the principles outlined above would apply equally to any decisions based on the public security exception. **14–23**

(d) *Public Health*

Article 4 of Directive 64/221 states that only diseases or disabilities which are listed in the Annex to the Directive justify exclusion or the refusal to issue a first residence permit on grounds of public health. The diseases included in the Annex are those which are subject to quarantine listed in the International Health Regulation of the World Health Organization; tuberculosis and syphilis. Drug addiction and profound mental disturbance are listed as diseases or disabilities which might threaten public policy or public security. **14–24**

It is notable that AIDS/HIV is not included in the Annex. This means that the fact that a person is suffering from AIDS or is HIV positive cannot justify **14–25**

---

[27] Case C-340/97 *Nazli v Stadt Nürnburg* [2000] E.C.R. I–957, paras 58–59.
[28] See for example *Boultif v Switzerland* (2001) 33 E.H.R.R. 50 where the European Court of Human Rights held that the seriousness of the crime committed by the individual, rather than his propensity to re-offend is a factor to be taken into account in assessing his rights under Art.8 ECHR (right to respect for family and private life).

exclusion or refusal of a first residence permit. Member States are not entitled to introduce new provisions or practices in relation to diseases or disabilities which are more restrictive than those in force at the time the Directive was ratified. If Member States wish to include a new disease or disability on the list they would need to amend the Annex by agreement. This has not occurred since the Directive was adopted in 1964.

14–26   If the disease or disability occurs after the person has entered the territory of another Member State and obtained a first residence permit, this cannot justify the refusal to renew the permit or expulsion from the territory of the Member State.[29]

4. PROCEDURAL SAFEGUARDS AGAINST EXCLUSION OR EXPULSION OF FREE MOVERS

(a) *Notification of Decision to Expel or Exclude*

14–27   As discussed in Chapter 11, Art.5 of Directive 64/221 requires that a decision to grant or refuse a first residence permit must be taken within six months. The Commission considers this to be a maximum period of time for consideration of the application for a residence permit where there are possible public policy, public security or public health reasons for refusal of the residence permit.[30] Where essential, during this period Member States are permitted to obtain records from other Member States.[31] The person must be allowed to remain on the territory of the Member State pending consideration of an application for a residence permit.[32]

14–28   Persons refused a residence permit must be informed of the grounds of public policy, public security or public health of the Member State concerned on which the decision is taken, unless the interests of the security demand otherwise.[33] This requirement is aimed at ensuring that a person faced with such a decision may prepare his defence. According to the ECJ, the reasons given must be a "precise and comprehensive statement of the grounds for the decision, to enable him to prepare his defence".[34]

14–29   The person must be formally notified of the decision to refuse an application for a residence permit or to expel him from the territory. Where the person has not been granted a residence permit before he must be given 15 days to leave the territory, save in urgent cases. Where the person has previously held a residence permit he must be given a month to leave the territory of the Member States, save in urgent cases.[35]

---

[29] Art.4(2).
[30] Action brought on April 7, 2003 by Case C–157/03 *Commission v Spain*, Official Journal (2003/C 135/23).
[31] Art.5(2).
[32] Art.5(1).
[33] Art.6.
[34] Case 36/75 *Rutili v Ministre de l'interieur* [1975] E.C.R. 1219, para.39.
[35] Art.7.

(b) *Legal Remedies*

(i) *Article 8—General Remedies*

Directive 64/221 provides specific rights as regards legal remedies in respect   **14–30**
of any decision concerning entry, or refusing the issue or renewal of a residence permit, or ordering expulsion from the territory. Article 8 of the
Directive guarantees EU nationals the same legal remedies as are available to
nationals of the state concerned in respect of acts of the administration.

This means that Member States cannot organise "legal remedies governed by   **14–31**
special procedures affording lesser safeguards than those pertaining to remedies available to nationals in respect of acts of the administration".[36]
However this does not guarantee nationals of other Member States the right
to the same remedies that might be afforded to nationals in disputes concerning entry since they are not in comparable situations given the inability
of Member States to expel their own nationals. If national law affords a different remedy in respect of acts of the administration generally, it is this
remedy which the nationals of the Member States are granted.[37]

(ii) *Specific Procedural Requirements Following Refusal to Renew a Residence Permit or Expel a Person After the Grant of a Residence Permit*

Article 9 complements the provisions of Art.8 and is intended to mitigate the   **14–32**
deficiencies of any remedies contemplated by Art.8.[38] Article 9(1) provides
for a decision to refuse to renew a residence permit or to expel a person to be
referred to "a competent authority" of the host Member State before which
the person enjoys such rights of defence or representation as provided in
domestic law. In order to obtain this right of reference to a competent
authority the national law remedies must be defective in one of three ways:
where national law provides no right of appeal to a court of law; where such
an appeal may be made only about the legal validity of the decision; or where
the appeal cannot have suspensory effect.[39] The referral to a competent
authority must take place before a final decision to refuse the residence permit or to expel the person is made. Where the right of appeal is restricted to
consideration of the legal validity of the decision, the purpose of the
involvement of the competent authority referred to in Art.9(1) is to enable an
exhaustive examination of all the facts and circumstances to be carried out
before the decision is finally taken.[40]

---

[36] Joined Cases C65 & 111/95 *R. v Secretary of State for the Home Department, Ex p. Shingara and Radiom* [1997] 3 C.M.L.R. 703, para.25; see also Case *Dzodzi v Belgium* [1990] E.C.R. I–3763, para.58.
[37] Joined Cases C-65 & 111/95 *R. v Secretary of State for the Home Department, Ex p. Shingara and Radiom* [1997] 3 C.M.L.R. 703, para.30.
[38] Joined Cases C-65 & 111/95 *R. v Secretary of State for the Home Department, Ex p. Shingara and Radiom* [1997] 3 C.M.L.R. 703.
[39] Art.9(1) of Dir. 64/221.
[40] Case 131/79 *R. v Secretary of State for Home Affairs Ex p. Santillo* [1980] E.C.R. 1585, para.12; Joined Cases 115–116/81 *Adoui and Cornuaille* [1982] E.C.R. 1665, para.15, and Case C–175/94 *R. v Secretary of State for the Home Department, Ex p. Gallagher* [1995] E.C.R. I–4253, para.17.

14–33   The "competent authority" to which the matter is referred cannot be the same as the one making the decision to refuse the residence permit or order the expulsion of the person. However in *Gallagher*[41] the ECJ held that the body making the decision to expel or refuse the residence permit may appoint the competent authority, provided that this authority performs its duties independently. Thus a criminal court recommending deportation might be considered a competent authority, provided that the court is able to take into account the individual's circumstances and is not required to make decisions based on general public policy considerations such as the fight against drugs.[42]

(iii) *Specific Requirements Following Refusal of First Residence Permit*

14–34   Any decision refusing the issue of a first residence permit or ordering the expulsion of a person before the issue of that permit shall on request by the person concerned be referred to the competent authority.[43] The ECJ has held that the person concerned is only entitled to obtain the opinion of such competent authority on the basis of one of the three deficiencies in national law remedies listed in Art.9(1).[44]

(iv) *Refusal of Entry to the Territory*

14–35   By contrast Art.9 of the Directive does not lay down *any* particular requirement as regards legal remedies in respect of decisions refusing entry to the territory. A Community national who is the subject of such a decision is therefore granted the same legal remedies as are available to nationals of the state concerned in respect of acts of the administration.[45] The ECJ has justified this difference in treatment on the basis that as a general rule a person who is challenging a decision to refuse entry will not be physically present on the territory of the Member State and therefore will not be able to present his defence in person. However where the person *is* physically present on the territory he should be granted the same procedural safeguards as are laid down in Art.9.

(v) *Decisions on Re-entry*

14–36   Where a person seeks to re-enter a Member State from which he has been expelled, the ECJ has stated that providing a reasonable amount of time has elapsed, he is entitled to have a fresh application for entry or a residence permit examined. In those circumstances the person will be entitled to the legal remedies provided by Art.8 of the Directive and, if appropriate, to an opinion of the competent authority under Art.9. This is not altered by the fact that the person may not have availed himself of any appeal rights against expulsion at the time the original decision was made.[46] The ECJ has not

---

[41] Case C-17594 *R. v Secretary of State for the Home Department, Ex p. Gallagher* [1995] E.C.R. I–4253.
[42] Case C-17594 *R. v Secretary of State for the Home Department, Ex p. Gallagher* [1995] E.C.R. I–4253.
[43] Art.9(2).
[44] Joined Cases C-658 111/95 *R. v Secretary of State for the Home Deparment, Ex p. Shingara and Radiom* [1997] 3 C.M.L.R. 703, para.35, and see para.14–32 above.
[45] Case C-357/98 *R. v the Secretary of State for the Home Department Ex p. Nana Yaa Konadu Yiadom* E.C.R. I-9265.
[46] Joined Cases C-658 111/95 *R. v Secretary of State for the Home Department, Ex p. Shingara and Radiom* [1997] 3 C.M.L.R. 703.

explained what a "reasonable" amount of time would be before re-entry could be sought, but certainly following a change of circumstances the individual should be entitled to re-examination.[47]

5. THE EXCLUSION/EXPULSION OF OTHER EU NATIONALS

The position for the EU national resident in another Member State who is **14–37** not exercising a free movement right is different from that of the free mover. The host Member State is entitled to expel such EU national without reliance being able to be placed by that EU national on the protection provided by Directive 64/221 discussed above.

This means that the non-economically active EU national who is unambigu- **14–38** ously unable to support himself may face expulsion measures on the grounds that he no longer meets the conditions laid down in the secondary legislation applicable to his situation.[48] However, any such expulsion will be permissible only subject to other relevant international obligations (such as the Convention on Social and Medical Assistance and ECHR obligations). Further, such expulsion measure could be taken only within the limits imposed by Community law, namely the principles of proportionality and procedural safeguards.

Principles of proportionality if properly applied could have an important **14–39** impact on the exercise by a Member State of the power to expel an EU national who does not meet the limitations and conditions contained in secondary legislation. For instance, such principles would dictate that where an EU national was only *temporarily* unable to meet the conditions laid down in relevant secondary legislation, an automatic decision to expel would be contrary to Community law. The position would be the same where only a *minor* condition was unable to be met.

For example in *Grzelczyk*[49] a French national student who had been self- **14–40** sufficient for the first three years of his studies in Belgium applied to the Belgian authorities for payment of the minimex, a minimum form of social assistance. Although the ECJ acknowledged that Community law would not prevent a Member State from taking the view that a student having recourse to social assistance no longer fulfilled the conditions of his right of residence, or from taking measures either to withdraw his residence permit or not renew it, "in no case may such measures become the automatic consequence of a student . . . having recourse to the host Member State's social assistance system".[50] Further, in *Trojani*[51] the ECJ reiterated that it remains open to

---

[47] "A Community national against whom such a prohibition has been issued must therefore be entitled to apply to have his situation re-examined if he considers that the circumstances which justified prohibiting him from entering the country no longer exist", para.40.
[48] Art.1 of Directives 90/364 and 90/365 refer.
[49] Case C-184/99 *Grzelczyk v Centre public d'aide social d'Ottignies-Louvain-la-Neuve* [2001] E.C.R. I-6193.
[50] Case C-184/99 *Grzelczyk v Centre public d'aide social d'Ottignies-Louvain-la-Neuve* [2001] E.C.R. I-6193, para.43.
[51] Case C-456/02 *Trojani v Centre public d'aide social de Bruxelles (CPAS)*, September 7, 2004.

Member States to remove EU nationals who no longer fulfil the conditions of their right of residence. Again, however any such measures must be "within the limits imposed by Community law".[52]

14–41 In *Baumbast*[53] the ECJ took a similar approach where it appeared that Mr Baumbast did not have sickness insurance for *all* risks in compliance with the provisions of Directive 90/364. The ECJ considered that the fact that Mr Baumbast's sickness insurance did not cover emergency treatment could not result in a refusal to allow him to exercise his right of residence in the host Member State since such refusal would be disproportionate.

14–42 Although as stated EU nationals facing exclusion or expulsion measures in these circumstances cannot place reliance on the protection provided by Directive 64/221 identified above, this does not mean that they are without any form of procedural protection. An EU national against whom an expulsion decision is made must at least be accorded the same procedural safeguards that would be afforded to own nationals in respect of whom administrative decisions have been made. It would be absurd if a Member State could determine that an EU national had no right to reside in its territory and therefore could be expelled without any form of judicial supervision. This could lead to arbitrary decisions being taken against EU nationals as regards their continued status as free movers, thereby allowing the Member State to circumvent all protections otherwise given expressly by Directive 64/221.

---

[52] Case C-456/02 *Trojani v Centre public d'aide social de Bruxelles (CPAS)*, September 7, 2004 para.45.
[53] Case C-413/99 *Baumbast and R. v Secretary of State for the Home Department* [2002] E.C.R. I-7091, paras 91–93.

Part Three

ASSOCIATION AGREEMENTS WITH THIRD COUNTRIES

CHAPTER 15

AGREEMENTS WITH THIRD COUNTRIES

This chapter examines the powers of the European Union to negotiate and enter into agreements with third countries. The resulting agreements are considered and particular emphasis is placed on any provisions which might impact on the free movement of persons.

1. TREATY PROVISION FOR AGREEMENTS WITH THIRD COUNTRIES

Article 310 EC Treaty provides for the conclusion of agreements between the Community and third countries or international bodies. In this sense Member States act collectively to conclude agreements with third countries, notwithstanding any bilateral agreements they might have with those third countries: **15–01**

Article 310 EC Treaty

The Community may conclude with one or more States or international organisations agreements establishing an association involving reciprocal rights and obligations, common action and special procedure.

Article 300 EC Treaty sets out the procedure for the conclusion of such agreements, with particular rules relating to the conclusion of agreements under Art.310 EC Treaty. As Art.300(7) EC Treaty makes clear, agreements concluded in accordance with the procedures laid down under Art.300 are to be binding on all the institutions of the Community and on the Member States: **15–02**

Article 300 EC Treaty

1. Where this Treaty provides for the conclusion of agreements between the Community and one or more States or international organisations, the Commission shall make recommendations to the Council, which shall authorise the Commission to open the necessary negotiations. The Commission shall conduct these negotiations in consultation with special committees appointed by the Council to assist it in this task and within the framework of such directives as the Council may issue to it.

In exercising the powers conferred upon it by this paragraph, the Council shall act by a qualified majority, except in the cases where the first subparagraph of paragraph 2 provides that the Council shall act unanimously.

2. Subject to the powers vested in the Commission in this field, the signing, which may be accompanied by a decision on provisional application before entry into force, and the conclusion of the agreements shall be decided on by the Council, acting by a qualified majority on a proposal from the Commission. The Council shall act unanimously when the agreement covers a field for which unanimity is required for the adoption of internal rules and for the agreements referred to in Article 310.

[...]¹

7. Agreements concluded under the conditions set out in this Article shall be binding on the institutions of the Community and on Member States.

15–03   Historically a wide range of agreements with third countries have been concluded under Art.310 EC Treaty (or its predecessor Art.238 Treaty of Rome). Agreements tend to be regional to the extent that although they are concluded between the Community and an individual third state, the terms of such agreements tend to be replicated around the region reflective of the intentions of the Community as regards its relations with that particular region.

15–04   With increasing intensity since the early 1990s the European Union broadened its relations to include nearly all regions of the world and signed agreements and conventions with a wide range of partners. However, the content of these agreements varies enormously. Pre-Accession Agreements with countries like Turkey and Bulgaria confer considerable rights connected with the free movement of persons, whereas the EU-Central America Political Dialogue and Co-operation Agreements confer no rights at all in this field.

15–05   Of particular interest in the free movement field is the EEA Agreement which extends free movement provisions to nationals of Iceland, Norway and Liechtenstein and the Agreement with Switzerland which likewise extends free movement of person provisions to Swiss nationals. None of those countries has joined the European Union, although that prospect would be open to them. Legally therefore Iceland, Norway, Liechtenstein and Switzerland remain third countries to the European Union.

15–06   It is intended that in the future the five countries of the Western Balkans will become full Members of the European Union. As part of the process of stabilisation in the region and in preparation for such accession, Stabilisation and Association Agreements with these countries will be agreed. As yet the Agreement with Macedonia is the only agreement to be ratified. An Agreement with Croatia has been signed but not ratified. The Macedonian Agreement, like the Agreements with Bulgaria, Romania and Turkey, is a pre-accession agreement. There are no provisions granting the right of free movement of persons contained in that Agreement. The furthest that the Macedonian Agreement goes is to guarantee non-discrimination for workers from Macedonia lawfully working in the Member States and the right of establishment for companies which replicate provisions in the Agreements with Bulgaria and Romania.

15–07   Various other Association Agreements, such as the Euro-Mediterranean Agreements with the Maghreb countries and the EC Agreement with Russia, reflect a wish on the part of the European Union to have close economic relations with these countries although it is not intended that they will become full Member States in the foreseeable future. These agreements contain non-discrimination provisions relating to workers lawfully present in the Member States similar to those contained in the Bulgarian and Romanian Agreements.

---

¹ Art.300(3) to (6) EC Treaty covers procedure to be followed by the Community institutions in concluding an agreement under Art.300 EC Treaty.

Given the scope of this book it is not possible to discuss all the various agree-   **15–08**
ments with third countries. In the rest of Part Three it is Association
Agreements with Bulgaria, Romania and Turkey that are of principal interest. This chapter examines more generally agreements with third countries
which contain provisions relating to the free movement of persons.

2. EEA AGREEMENT

(a) *Background*

The European Economic Area Agreement was signed on May 2, 1990 by   **15–09**
seven countries: Austria, Iceland, Finland, Norway, Sweden, Switzerland and
Liechtenstein and the Community.[2] With the exception of Switzerland and
Liechtenstein the Agreement came into force on January 1, 1994. Austria,
Sweden and Finland joined the European Union as full Member States on
January 1, 1995.

The EEA was maintained because of the wish of the three remaining states—   **15–10**
Norway, Iceland and Liechtenstein—to participate in the single market,
while not assuming the full responsibilities of membership of the European
Union. The Agreement gives them the right to be consulted by the
Commission during the formulation of Community legislation, but not the
right to have any say in the decision-making, which is retained exclusively by
Member States. All new Community legislation in areas covered by the EEA
is integrated into the Agreement through a Joint Committee Decision. The
Agreement is concerned principally with "four freedoms"—freedom of
movement of goods (but agriculture and fisheries are included in the
Agreement only to a very limited extent), freedom of movement of persons,
of services and of capital. There are also provisions relevant to these four
freedoms in the areas of social policy, consumer protection, environment,
company law and statistics which complete the extended internal market.

The implementation of the Agreement is achieved through a set of special   **15–11**
institutional arrangements. The Agreement established a Joint Committee
whose main function is to take decisions extending Community Regulations
and Directives to the EEA states. In 2000 the Joint Committee made 114 such
Decisions. The Community is represented in the Joint Committee by the
Commission, and decisions are taken by agreement between the Community
and the EEA states, which have to "speak with one voice".

The EEA Council meets twice a year. Its members are the members of the   **15–12**
General Affairs Council and one member of the Government of each of the
EEA states and EU Member States. Its Presidency is held alternately for six
months by a member of the EU Council and a member of an EEA state
Government.

---

[2] The EEA Agreement (see below) refers to "EFTA". Iceland, Liechtenstein, Norway and
Switzerland are members of the European Free Trade Association (EFTA). The EFTA
Convention established a free trade area among its Member States in 1960. In addition, the
EFTA States have jointly concluded free trade agreements with a number of countries
worldwide.

15–13   In addition to the obligation to accept Community *acquis* in the fields of the four freedoms, the Agreement contains provisions to allow co-operation between the Community and the EEA states in a range of the Community's activities: in research and technological development, information services, the environment, education, social policy, consumer protection, small and medium-sized enterprises, tourism, the audio-visual sector and civil protection.

(b) *Free Movement of Persons*

15–14   Part III of the main EEA Agreement is entitled "Free movement of persons, services and capital". Article 28 of the Agreement provides for the free movement of workers from EEA states:

Article 28

1. Freedom of movement for workers shall be secured among EC Member States and EFTA States.

2. Such freedom of movement shall entail the abolition of any discrimination based on nationality between workers of EC Member States and EFTA States as regards employment, remuneration and other conditions of work and employment.

3. It shall entail the right, subject to limitations justified on grounds of public policy, public security or public health:

(a)   to accept offers of employment actually made;
(b)   to move freely within the territory of EC Member States and EFTA States for this purpose;
(c)   to stay in the territory of an EC Member State or an EFTA State for the purpose of employment in accordance with the provisions governing the employment of nationals of that State laid down by law, regulation or administrative action;
(d)   to remain in the territory of an EC Member State or an EFTA State after having been employed there.

15–15   Annex 8 extends the relevant secondary legislation on workers to EEA nationals.[3]

15–16   Article 31 of the Agreement abolishes all restrictions on the freedom of establishment for persons from EEA states:

Article 31

1. Within the framework of the provisions of this Agreement, there shall be no restrictions on the freedom of establishment of nationals of an EC Member State or an EFTA State in the territory of any other of these States. This shall also apply to the setting up of agencies, branches or subsidiaries by nationals of any EC Member State or EFTA State established in the territory of any of these States.

---

[3] Namely Dir.64/221 (except Art.4(3)); Reg.1612/68 (except Arts 41, 42 or 48); Dir.68/360 (except Arts 11 and 13); Reg.1250/71 (except Art.9) and Dir.72/194.

Freedom of establishment shall include the right to take up and pursue activities as self-employed persons and to set up and manage undertakings, in particular companies or firms within the meaning of Article 34, second paragraph, under the conditions laid down for its own nationals by the law of the country where such establishment is effected, subject to the provisions of Chapter 4.

Article 36 abolishes all restrictions on the freedom of EEA nationals to pro- **15–17**
vide services in the EU Member States. Annex 8 extends the relevant secondary legislation relating to establishment of persons and freedom to provide services to EEA nationals.[4] Finally, Annex 8 extends the three Directives relating to economically inactive self-sufficient persons to EEA nationals.[5]

All the free movement provisions are reciprocal thereby extending these free **15–18**
movement rights to EU nationals wishing to exercise them in the EEA states.[6] However, it should be noted that Art.18 EC Treaty (which refers to Citizens of the Union) is not extended to EEA states through the Agreement or any protocol to the Agreement. Thus whilst non-EU EEA state nationals benefit from all free movement provisions that flow from the relevant secondary Community legislation, those rights that are said to derive directly from Art.18 EC Treaty arguably are not extended to the three EEA states. In practice this will have very limited effect since the free movement rights contained in the relevant secondary legislation are extensive covering workers, self-employed, retired persons and students and even those economically inactive (albeit that the last three categories must be self-sufficient). It remains to be seen whether an EEA national child in secondary education would for instance derive the same free movement rights as an EU national child does as a result of Art.18 EC Treaty.[7]

3. AGREEMENT WITH SWITZERLAND

(a) *Background*

As the result of a referendum in 1992, Switzerland never became part of the **15–19**
EEA. However, negotiations for agreements in seven sectors began in 1994. These are Free Movement of Persons, Trade in Agricultural Products, Public Procurement, Conformity Assessments, Air Transport, Transport by Road and Rail and Swiss Participation in the 5th Framework Programme for Research. These were concluded and Agreements signed on June 21, 1999. On May 6, 2000 the Swiss approved the Agreements in a referendum. Ratification in all EU Member States was concluded in early 2002 and the seven Agreements entered into force on June 1, 2002.[8]

---

[4] Namely Dir.73/148 (except Article 10); Dir.75/34 and Dir.75/35.
[5] Dir.90/364 (right of residence); Dir.90/365 (retired persons) and Dir.93/96 (students).
[6] Art.5 of Protocol 15 provided transitional provisions relating to the free movement of workers between Liechtenstein and the EU permitting national rules relating to free movement to remain in place until 1998 and Liechtenstein to retain sectoral or quantative restrictions on the number of workers from the EU or indeed other EEA States that would be granted a right of residence until 1998.
[7] See Chapter 4.
[8] Decision of the Council, and of the Commission as regards the Agreement on Scientific and Technological Cooperation, of April 4, 2002 on the conclusion of seven Agreements with the Swiss Confederation [2002] O.J. L114/1.

(b) *Free Movement Rights*

15–20   One of the agreements entering into force on June 1, 2002 was the Agreement between the European Community and its Member States and the Swiss Confederation on the free movement of persons.[9] Article 1 states:

Article 1

The objective of this Agreement, for the benefit of nationals of the Member States of the European Community and Switzerland, is:

(a)   to accord a right of entry, residence, access to work as employed persons, establishment on a self-employed basis and the right to stay in the territory of the Contracting Parties;

(b)   to facilitate the provision of services in the territory of the Contracting Parties, and in particular to liberalise the provision of services of brief duration;

(c)   to accord a right of entry into, and residence in the territory of the Contracting Parties to persons without an economic activity in the host country;

(d)   to accord the same living, employment and working conditions as those accorded to nationals.

15–21   The purposes of this Agreement are gradually to introduce over a 12-year period the free movement of persons (both the economically active and inactive)[10] and to liberalise free cross-border trade in certain services.[11] The free movement of persons is supplemented by the mutual recognition of professional diplomas[12] and the co-ordination of the social insurance systems of the Contracting States.[13]

15–22   Since the coming into force of the Agreement nationals of E U or EEA States have enjoyed the right to stay in Switzerland and to engage in economic activity as a self-employed or as an employed person, although subject to significant restrictions. During the first five years these rights are linked to the conditions of the quota system, the priority of Swiss nationals and the control of working and wage conditions by the Labor Market Authority.[14] Additionally for the first two years after the entry into force of the Agreement all the Contracting Parties may retain "controls on the priority of workers integrated into the labour markets".[15] Thereafter, the absolute prohibition of discrimination enters into force. Subject to these transitional provisions from entry into force of the Agreement Swiss nationals enjoyed free movement rights in the E U Member States. In addition, the Agreement gives the right both to be joined by family members (irrespective of the nationality of the individual family members)[16] and the right to purchase immovable property

---

[9] [2002] O.J. L114/6.
[10] Art.4
[11] Art.5
[12] Art.9
[13] Art.9
[14] Art.10(1)
[15] Art.10(2)
[16] Art.8(d).

without a permit for those domiciled in Switzerland.[17] Further, the requirements for frontier workers are significantly relaxed.

The Agreement on the Free Movement of Persons provides for three cate- **15–23** gories of residence permit: the short-term residence permit (valid for a maximum of one year), the permanent residence permit (valid for five years) and the frontier worker permit.

4. AGREEMENT WITH TURKEY

(a) *Background*

The Association Agreement with Turkey ("the Ankara Agreement") was **15–24** signed in 1963 as a first step towards accession of Turkey to the European Economic Community. It replicated much of the Agreement with Greece and was only the second agreement that the Community had signed with a third country. It reflected the desire of the Community to be more closely linked economically with Turkey.

The Ankara Agreement established a customs union in stages. An Additional **15–25** Protocol to the Ankara Agreement was signed in 1970. It set down the timetable for the establishment of a full customs union of between 12 and 22 years. Free movement of persons was to be achieved in the same time.

Changing economic conditions and a military coup in Turkey in 1980 dam- **15–26** aged relations between Turkey and the Community. Although the timetable for the full free movement of persons has overrun, in 1987 Turkey made an application for full membership of the European Union. To date negotiations for Turkey's accession to the Union have not begun. Member States will revisit the question of Turkey's membership in December 2004.

(b) *Free Movement of Persons*

The provisions of the Ankara Agreement and its Protocol relating to the free **15–27** movement of persons are discussed in detail in Chapters 21 to 25 below. In short the Ankara Agreement and decisions of the Association Council con- fer rights on workers who are legally employed in the Member State to con- tinued employment and residence subject to the satisfaction of certain conditions[18] and rights for their family members.[19] Additionally Turkish nationals seeking to establish themselves in business or provide services ben- efit from a "standstill clause" which does not permit Member States to place greater restrictions on them than were in place at the time when the Member State became party to the Additional Protocol.[20]

---

[17] Art.8(e).
[18] See Chapter 7 on workers.
[19] See Chapter 10 on family members.
[20] See Chapter 9 on establishment.

5. AGREEMENTS WITH BULGARIA AND ROMANIA

(a) *Background*

15–28 Agreements have been concluded between the Community and a number of Central and Eastern European countries ("the Europe Agreements"). Like the Ankara Agreement the Europe Agreements were negotiated as "pre-accession" agreements. Plans to negotiate the first of the Europe Agreements were put in place as early as 1989 at the time of the fall of the Berlin Wall. The Community was keen to embrace these newly liberated states and integrate them within its midst as quickly as possible.

15–29 The Europe Agreements were concluded between the Community and 10 states: Bulgaria, Czech Republic, Estonia, Hungary, Latvia, Lithuania, Poland, Romania, Slovenia and Slovakia. The Agreements with Hungary and Poland entered into force on February 1, 1994, the Bulgaria, Czech, Romania and Slovak Agreements on February 1, 1995 and the Estonian, Latvian and Lithuania Agreements on February 2, 1998.

15–30 Chapter 6 discusses the accession of eight of these States to the European Union. The Accession Treaty replaces the Europe Agreements with all of those states. It is therefore only Bulgaria and Romania which remain outside the European Union and therefore party to the Europe Agreements. Accession talks between Bulgaria and Romania and the European Union commenced in March 2000. On December 13, 2002, the EU leaders at the Copenhagen summit reiterated the Union's intention to welcome Bulgaria and Romania as members in 2007: "depending on further progress in complying with the membership criteria". The process towards accession continues to progress with negotiations on certain crucial areas resulting in agreement in June 2004.[21]

(b) *Free Movement of Persons*

15–31 All of the Europe Agreements were very similar in structure and content. As regards the free movement of persons provisions, these were limited to freedom of establishment with a non-discrimination provision relating to workers legally resident in the EU Member States. These provisions are entirely different from those contained in the Ankara Agreement. The free movement provisions are discussed in greater detail in Chapters 17 to 20 below.

6. AGREEMENTS WITH WESTERN BALKAN STATES

(a) *Background*

15–32 After a period of violent conflict in the western Balkans, the European Union attempted through its "Regional Approach" to underpin the implementation

---

[21] Weekly Press Release of the European Commission "Enlargement Weekly", June 7, 2004. *http://europa.eu.int/comm/enlargement/docs/newsletter.*

of the Dayton/Paris and Erdut Agreements and bring basic stability and prosperity to the region. The prospect of the five Western Balkan countries—Albania, the former Yugoslav Republic of Macedonia, Bosnia and Herzegovina, Croatia and the Federal Republic of Yugoslavia—of eventually becoming full members of the European Union was offered explicitly at the Feira European Council in June 2000. The Commission and the Council recognised that such a prospect offered a real motivation for democratic, legal and economic reform in the region.

The November 24, 2000 Zagreb Summit initiated the Stabilisation and Association process by gaining the region's agreement to a clear set of objectives and conditions. In return for the European Union's offer of a prospect of accession on the basis of the Treaty on European Union and the 1993 Copenhagen criteria and an assistance programme to support that ambition, the countries of the region undertook to abide by the European Union's conditionality and use the Stabilisation and Association process, and in particular the Stabilisation and Association Agreements when signed, as the means to begin to prepare themselves for the demands of the perspective on accession to the European Union. **15–33**

The Stabilisation and Association Agreements are both the cornerstone of the stabilisation and association process and a key step to its completion. The conclusion of Stabilisation and Association Agreements represents the Contracting Parties' commitment to complete over a transition period a formal association with the European Union. Such an association has a high political value. It is based on the gradual implementation of a free trade area and both legislative and economic reforms aimed at ensuring that the western Balkan countries move towards EU standards. Just as with the Europe Agreements, the Stabilisation and Association Agreements are seen as preparatory steps to full EU membership. **15–34**

It is anticipated that each of the Stabilisation and Association Agreements will be tailored to the circumstances of each country. However, each Agreement is intended to have the common purpose of achieving formal association with the European Union. The Agreements set up Association Councils at Ministerial level, with committees and subcommittees, to assist with the implementation of the Agreements. **15–35**

Thus far a Stabilisation and Association Agreement has been signed with both the former Yugoslav Republic of Macedonia and Croatia. The Macedonian Agreement was signed in April 2001 and came into force on April 1, 2004. It is the first of the Stabilisation and Association Agreements with the western Balkan countries to come into force. Despite this progress, in a speech made in April 2004 the European Union's external relations Commissioner, Chris Patten, warned Macedonia of the amount of work it needed to do before consideration could be given to its accession to the European Union.[22] **15–36**

---

[22] Speech to German Bundestag, "European Affairs Committee", Berlin, April 28, 2004 (SPEECH/04/209)

15–37   The Croatian Agreement was signed in October 2001 but has not yet been ratified. An interim Agreement has been in force since March 2002 which relates to free trade between the European Union and Croatia.[23] Some issues between the Union and Croatia have hampered progress in the stabilisation and association process. The most difficult matter was the question of relations with the International Criminal Tribunal for the former Yugoslavia (ICTY). Croatia's record of compliance in the past had been far from perfect, although by the beginning of 2004 this had improved considerably. On April 20, 2004 the Commission adopted its opinion on Croatia's application for membership to the European Union.[24] It recommended that the Council open negotiations with Croatia for accession. It remains to be seen whether and when the Council will begin such negotiations.

(b) *Free Movement Provisions*

15–38   The content of both the Croatian and Macedonian Agreements is substantially the same for free movement purposes. The Macedonia Agreement is referred to in this chapter since at the time of writing it is the one in force. However, comments would apply equally to the Croatia Agreement.

15–39   There are no free movement provisions relating to workers in the Stabilisation and Association Agreement with Macedonia. However there is a non-discrimination provision relating to Macedonian workers who are legally employed in the Member States of the European Union. Article 44 states:

Article 44

1. Subject to the conditions and modalities applicable in each Member State:

– treatment accorded to workers who are nationals of the former Yugoslav Republic of Macedonia and who are legally employed in the territory of a Member State shall be free of any discrimination based on nationality, as regards working conditions, remuneration or dismissal, compared to its own nationals;

– the legally resident spouse and children of a worker legally employed in the territory of a Member State, with the exception of seasonal workers and of workers coming under bilateral agreements, within the meaning of Article 45, unless otherwise provided by such agreements, shall have access to the labour market of that Member State, during the period of that worker's authorised stay of employment.

15–40   Article 44 of the Macedonian Agreement replicates Art.38(1) of the Europe Agreements which is discussed in detail in Chapter 18 below. Bearing in mind the aim of the Macedonian Agreement and its clear and unambiguous nature, there is no reason why it would not be interpreted exactly as Art.38(1) of the Europe Agreements has been interpreted.

---

[23] Council Dec. of October 29, 2001 concerning the signing on behalf of the Community and the provisional application of the Interim Agreement on trade and trade-related matters between the European Community, of the one part, and the Republic of Croatia, of the other part [2001] O.J. L330.

[24] Commission of the European Communities, Brussels, April 20, 2004 COM (2004) 257 final, Croatia: Opinion on the application of Croatia for membership of the European Union.

In relation to establishment, the Macedonian Agreement is more conserva-   **15–41**
tive than the Europe Agreements. Establishment of Macedonian companies
is provided for in Art.48(3) of the Agreement:

Article 48

3. The Community and its Member States shall grant, from the entry into force of
this Agreement:

(i) as regards the establishment of companies from the former Yugoslav Republic of
Macedonia, treatment no less favourable than that accorded by Member States to
their own companies or to any company of any third country, whichever is the better;

(ii) as regards the operation of subsidiaries and branches of companies from the
former Yugoslav Republic of Macedonia, established in their territory, treatment
no less favourable than that accorded by Member States to their own companies
and branches, or to any subsidiary and branch of any third country company,
established in their territory, whichever is the better.

Article 48(1) provides reciprocal provisions for the establishment of compa-   **15–42**
nies from the Member States in Macedonia. The provision in Art.48(3) replicates the form of the establishment provision in Art.45(1) of the Europe
Agreements, although the Europe Agreement provision is clearly wider in
that it relates to the establishment of persons.[25]

In the Macedonian Agreement the establishment of persons is not provided   **15–43**
for from entry into force of the Agreement. Art.48(4) only provides that the
Stabilisation and Association Council will examine whether to extend the
establishment provisions contained in Art.48(3) to persons who wish to take
up activities as self-employed persons after five years from the entry into
force of the Agreement. That possibility will be examined "in the light of the
relevant European Court of Justice case law, and the situation of the labour
market." At the time when the Agreement was concluded and signed the
ECJ's first judgments on the establishment provision in the Europe
Agreements were not available[26] and this provision undoubtedly reflected
uncertainty as to the outcome of those proceedings. Nevertheless it is somewhat unusual for a provision to make reference to the judgments of the ECJ
in this way. It rather suggests that the parties to the Agreement were unsure
themselves as to the scope of such an establishment provision.

The right of establishment conferred on Macedonian companies in Art.48 is   **15–44**
enhanced by Art.53 which gives those companies the right to post key
personnel in the EU Member States:

Article 53

1. A Community company or a company from the former Yugoslav Republic of
Macedonia established in the territory of the former Yugoslav Republic of

---

[25] Art.45(1) of the Europe Agreements is discussed in detail in Chapter 19 below although that
chapter is focused on the establishment of persons. In the context of free movement of persons,
it is the key personnel provisions which give effect to the freedom of establishment discussed in
Chapter 18.
[26] e.g. in Case C-257/99 *R. v Secretary of State for the Home Department Ex. p. Barkoci and
Malik* [2001] E.C.R. I-6557 and Case C-235/99 *R. v Secretary of State for the Home Department
Ex. p. Kondova* [2001] E.C.R. I-6427.

Macedonia or the Community respectively shall be entitled to employ, or have employed by one of its subsidiaries or branches, in accordance with the legislation in force in the host country of establishment, in the territory of the former Yugoslav Republic of Macedonia and the Community respectively, employees who are nationals of the Community Member States and former Yugoslav Republic of Macedonia respectively, provided that such employees are key personnel as defined in paragraph 2 and that they are employed exclusively by companies, subsidiaries or branches. The residence and work permits of such employees shall only cover the period of such employment.

15–45   Paragraph 2 describes "key personnel" in terms which are very similar to those provided for in the Europe Agreements, which are discussed in Chapter 18. It should be noted that the main difference between the key personnel provision in the Macedonian Agreement and that in the Europe Agreements is that the latter provides that self-employed persons as well as companies have the right to deploy key personnel. As the Macedonian Agreement does not provide for the right of establishment for persons, it follows that persons can have no right to post key personnel.

15–46   Finally the Agreement provides for some co-ordination of social security systems for legally employed workers and their family members. Their periods of insurance in a Member State are to be taken into account when calculations of entitlement to old-age and invalidity pensions are made.[27]

7. AGREEMENTS WITH OTHER EUROPEAN AND CENTRAL ASIAN COUNTRIES

(a) *Background*

15–47   With the collapse of the former Soviet Union, the European Union decided to support the transition process towards market economies and democratic societies in countries of Eastern Europe and Central Asia. Thus, since the beginning of the nineties, the European Union has developed a much more formal and political relationship with 13 countries of the region: Armenia, Azerbaijan, Belarus, Georgia, Kazakhstan, Kyrgystan, Moldova, Mongolia, Russia, Tajikistan, Turkmenistan, Ukraine and Uzbekistan.

Building strong trading links is a major objective, but the overall aim is to foster enduring political, economic and cultural links, so as to ensure peace and security.

15–48   Furthermore, with the EU enlargement process moving eastwards, the number of EU countries sharing a border with the partner countries will indeed sharply increase. This certainly influences the dialogue between the European Union and countries from Eastern Europe and Central Asia.

15–49   The formalisation of bilateral relations between the European Union and individual partner countries has been achieved through the negotiation of Partnership and Co-operation Agreements now in force with all the Eastern

---

[27] Art.46 of the Macedonian Stabilisation and Association Agreement.

European and Central Asian countries (with the exception of Mongolia, Turkmenistan and Belarus[28]). These nearly all entered into force on July 1, 1999 with the exception of the Agreements with Russia,[29] Moldova[30] and Ukraine.[31]

These Partnership and Co-operation Agreements are legal frameworks, **15–50** based on the respect of democratic principles and human rights, setting out the political, economic and trade relationship between the European Union and its partner countries. Each Agreement is a 10-year bilateral Treaty signed and ratified by the European Union and the individual state.

(b) *Free Movement Provisions*

For free movement purposes all the Partnership and Co-operation **15–51** Agreements are substantially the same. The provisions of the Russian Agreement are used by way of example and comments made would apply equally to the agreements with the other countries.

It is perhaps unsurprising given the nature of the relationship between the European Union and these countries that there are no provisions granting any free movement rights for nationals of those countries.

There is a non-discrimination provision in relation to conditions of work, **15–52** remuneration and dismissal for those Russian nationals who are lawfully working in a Member State. Article 23 states:

Article 23

1. Subject to the laws, conditions and procedures applicable in each Member State, the Community and its Member States shall ensure[32] that the treatment accorded to Russian nationals, legally employed in the territory of a Member State shall be free from any discrimination based on nationality, as regards working conditions, remuneration or dismissal, as compared to its own nationals.

This is very similar in wording to the non-discrimination provision in the **15–53** Europe Agreements. A Spanish court has referred a question to the ECJ on the interpretation of Art.23 of the Russian Agreement in a case concerning a lawfully employed footballer. The Spanish court questions the compatibility of Spanish football club rules which limit the number of non-EEA national players that can be used in national level matches with Art.23.[33] The question is not dissimilar to that referred in the case of *Kolpak*[34] under the Slovakian

---

[28] An Agreement was in fact signed in March 1995 with Belarus but it is not yet in force as it has not been ratified.
[29] December 1, 1997.
[30] July 1, 1998.
[31] March 1, 1998.
[32] Other agreements (for example with the Ukraine and Moldavia) use the phrase "shall endeavour to ensure". This however should make no difference to the declaration.
[33] Case C-265/03 *Simutenkov v Abogado del Estado, Real Federación Española de Fútbol and Ministerio Fiscal* (2003/C 213/20).
[34] Case C-438/00 *Deutscher Handballbund eV v Kolpak* [2003] E.C.R. I-4135 (concerning a handball player).

Agreement. As in *Kolpak* the ECJ is likely to consider that rules relating to the ability of a player to play in certain matches do relate to "conditions of work" within the meaning of Art.23. The essential question will be whether there is any justification for the discrimination. The fact that the Russian Agreement is not a pre-accession agreement does not deprive it of the ability to be directly effective in situations falling within the scope of Art.23. The result should therefore be no different from that in *Kolpak* where the ECJ found rules limiting the number of third country nationals who could be fielded in national matches to be contrary to the non-discrimination provision in the Europe Agreements. It is to be acknowledged that the provision is of limited benefit. As the ECJ has stated in relation to a similar provision in the Maghreb Agreements it does not relate to conditions of entry or residence to a Member State.[35]

15–54   Article 24 provides for some degree of co-ordination to social security systems enabling periods of employment to be included in calculations of invalidity and old-age pensions.

15–55   Additionally there is an establishment provision in each of the Agreements. Article 28 of the Russian Agreement is typical of the establishment provision in the Partnership and Co-operation Agreements:

Article 28

1. The Community and its Member States of the one part and Russia of the other part, shall grant to each other treatment no less favourable than that accorded to any third country, with regard to conditions affecting the establishment of companies in their territories and this in conformity with the legislation and regulations applicable in each Party.

15–56   It should be noted that this provision relates to companies only. Even more limiting is the fact that the provision protects the companies against discrimination as compared with companies from "any third country" only, as opposed to companies from the Contracting States themselves. In other words the provisions in the Partnership and Co-operation Agreements only ensure that companies from the relevant partner countries are not placed in a worse position than companies from any other third country. It is thus significantly weaker than the establishment provision for companies in either the Europe Agreements or the Macedonian Agreement.

8. EURO-MEDITERRANEAN AGREEMENTS

(a) *Background*

15–57   The Barcelona Declaration adopted at the Conference of Euro-Mediterranean Foreign Ministers held in Barcelona in late November 1995 stated the agreement of the (then) 15 EU Member States and 12

---

[35] Case C-416/96 *Nour Eddline El-Yassini v Secretary of State for Home Department* [1999] E.C.R. I-1209.

Mediterranean Partners on the establishment of a free trade area by the target date of 2010. This is to be achieved by means of the Euro-Mediterranean Association Agreements negotiated between the European Union and individual Mediterranean partners, to be complemented by Agreements between the partners themselves. Negotiations for Agreements have been concluded between the European Union and Tunisia, Algeria and Morocco (Maghreb), Lebanon, Israel and Jordan. An interim Agreement has been concluded between the Union and the PLO for the benefit of the Palestinian Authority. As regards Egypt and Syria, negotiations are still under way.

The original Co-operation Agreements between Morocco, Tunisia and Algeria **15–58** (the Maghreb Agreements) were similar in terms. They have now been supplemented by Euro-Mediterranean Agreements. No specific free movement rights have been included in the Euro-Mediterranean Agreements. However, the Maghreb Agreements do contain non-discrimination provisions in the field of employment and social security. The purpose of the Maghreb and Euro-Mediterranean Agreements is to promote co-operation between the Maghreb countries. There is no intention on the part of the European Community that the Maghreb countries will join the European Union at any time in the future.

(b) *Free Movement Provisions*

The main provision of interest in the field of free movement of persons is **15–59** Art.67(1) of the EC-Algeria Euro-Mediterranean Agreement (replicated in all the Maghreb Agreements but not the other Euro-Mediterranean Agreements) which states:

Article 67(1)

Each Member State shall accord to workers of Algerian nationality employed in its territory treatment which is free from any discrimination based on nationality, as regards working conditions, remuneration and dismissal, relative to its own nationals.

The provision replicates the non-discrimination provision relating to workers **15–60** in the Europe Agreements, the Macedonian Agreement and the Russian Agreement. The other agreements (apart from the Russian Agreement) are, however, pre-accession agreements. The question is therefore whether Art.67(1) would be interpreted consistently with the provisions in those other agreements.

In *El-Yassine*,[36] a Moroccan national attempted to rely on the non- **15–61** discrimination provision in Art.40 of the Moroccan Agreement to derive a right to remain in the United Kingdom where he had been lawfully resident and working previously as the spouse of a British citizen. The ECJ found that the non-discrimination provision in the Agreement was capable of direct effect and thus individuals can rely upon it in national courts. However, the ECJ considered that the narrow scope of the non-discrimination provision

---

[36] Case C-416/96 *Nour Eddline El-Yassini v Secretary of State for Home Department* [1999] E.C.R. I-1209.

meant that it did not extend to rights of entry and stay in a Member State but only to the conditions under which a person is employed there. The Member State is thus not prohibited from refusing to extend a residence permit of a Moroccan national whom it previously authorised to enter its territory and to take up employment where the reason for granting entry and stay—in that case marriage—no longer exists.

15–62   The wording of Art.40 of the Moroccan Agreement is on its face restricted to conditions of work and remuneration. In *El Yassine*[37] the ECJ stated that, absent any provisions in the Agreement that equated to the provisions relating to workers in the Ankara Agreement or Decision 1/80 of the Council of Association to that Agreement, no such provisions could be inferred.[38] The decision is important for the interpretation of equivalent non-discrimination provisions in other agreements with non-accession countries. This is since the ECJ held that the fact that the Moroccan Agreement is not a pre-accession agreement did not prevent Art.40 from having direct effect. Indeed the narrow interpretation of the scope of Art.40 is not influenced by the fact that it is not a pre-accession agreement since none of the equivalent provisions in the pre-accession agreements have been interpreted to extend to conditions of entry and stay.[39] Such narrow interpretation does not deprive the non-discrimination provision of any purpose since the ECJ has interpreted conditions of work broadly.

15–63   The Maghreb Agreements further provide for non-discrimination of lawfully resident workers and their families in the social security field.[40] The ECJ has also held that these provisions are capable of direct effect.[41]

9. AGREEMENTS WITH AFRICAN, CARIBBEAN AND PACIFIC COUNTRIES

(a) *Background*

15–64   Relations between the European Union and the African, Caribbean and Pacific States ("ACP states") have developed as a combination of aid, trade and political co-operation. These special EU-ACP relations date back to the Treaty of Rome. At that time, the first of today's ACP states (mainly in Africa) were dependent countries and territories of some of the founding Member States. According to Art.131 of the Treaty their association with the Community was made in order "to promote (their) economic and social

---

[37] Case C-416/96 *Nour Eddline El-Yassini v Secretary of State for Home Department* [1999] E.C.R. I-1209.
[38] The ECJ did state that the situation would be different if the Member State had granted the person concerned a residence permit for a period shorter than their work permit and if, before the expiry of the work permit, it refused to extend the residence permit without reference to reasons of public policy, public security or public health.
   In the UK this would have little benefit given that it is usually the case that it is the person's immigration status which dictates their ability to work rather than other way round. It is very unlikely that the situation envisaged by the ECJ would therefore even arise.
[39] See for example Case C-438/00 *Deutscher Handballbund eV v Kolpak* [2003] E.C.R. I-4135.
[40] Art.68 of the Algerian Euro-Mediterrean Agreement.
[41] Case C-18/90 *Office National de l'Emploi v Kziber* [1991] E.C.R. I-199.

development . . . and to establish close economic relations between them and the Community as a whole".

Following independence in the 1960s, the first Yaoundé Convention was nego-   **15–65**
tiated with 18 of these former French dependent countries and territories
(1963). These states are referred to as the Associated African States and
Madagascar (AASMs). Yaoundé II followed in 1969 to include Kenya,
Tanzania and Uganda. Then, after the accession of the United Kingdom to
the Community, came the first Lomé Convention, signed in 1975 (with 46 ACP
states), Lomé II in 1979 (58 ACP states), Lomé III in 1984 (65 ACP states) and
Lomé IV in 1989 (68 ACP states, extended in 1995 to 70 ACP states).

The Lomé Conventions set out the principles and objectives to co-operation   **15–66**
between the European Union[42] and the ACP states. Their main characteristics were the partnership principle, the contractual nature of the relationship,
development of relations in matters of aid, trade and political co-operation.
Moreover the Conventions emphasise the objective of lasting partnership
between the European Union and the ACP states.

In February 2000 the expiration of the Lomé Conventions provided the   **15–67**
opportunity for a thorough review of the future of EU–ACP relations. The
new EU-ACP Agreement was signed on June 23, 2000 in Cotonou, Benin.[43]
At present, 77 ACP countries are signatories to the Cotonou Agreement.
These comprise 48 African states, covering all sub-Saharan Africa, 15 states
in the Caribbean and 14 states in the Pacific.[44] The Agreement entered into
force on April 1, 2003.

(b) *Free Movement Provisions*

Despite the extent and duration of co-operation between the European   **15–68**
Union and the ACP states reflected by the wide ranging scope of the
Conventions referred to above, these Agreements are all essentially trade and
development agreements only. There is nothing in the Agreements which
confers any rights relating to free movement of persons.

Article 13(3) of the Cotonou Agreement prohibits discrimination against   **15–69**
workers of ACP countries legally employed in their territory:

> "The treatment accorded by each Member State to workers of ACP countries
> legally employed in its territory, shall be free from any discrimination based on
> nationality, as regards working conditions, remuneration and dismissal, relative to
> its own nationals. Further in this regard, each ACP State shall accord comparable
> non-discriminatory treatment to workers who are nationals of a Member State."

---

[42] At the time the European Community.
[43] Partnership Agreement between the members of the African, Caribbean and Pacific Group of
States of the one part, and the European Community and its Member States, of the other part,
signed in Cotonou on June 23, 2000 [2000] O.J. L317/3.
[44] For a fuller description of the developments in EU-ACP relations see "From Lomé to
Cotonou: The new EU-ACP Agreement" by C. Bjørnskov Danish Institute of Agricultural and
Fisheries Economics and E. Krivonos, IFPRI and University of Maryland, *www.ictsd.org/
issarealag/resources/RegEU.pdf*.

15–70   Attempts have been made to derive benefits from the equivalent non-discrimination provision in the Lomé Conventions. However the ECJ has held in the past that the non-discrimination provisions in the Lomé Conventions for instance did not prohibit different treatment between EC and ACP nationals or even between different ACP nationals.[45] That said, the non-discrimination provision in the first Lomé Convention had an express reservation which provided that Member States and the ACP states were not bound to accord such equal treatment.[46] The non-discrimination provision in the Contonou Agreement has no such reservation attached and there is no reason in principle why it would not be considered in the same way as the non-discrimination provisions in other agreements, such as the Russian and Maghreb Agreements.[47]

10. ASSOCIATION AGREEMENT WITH CHILE

(a) *Background*

15–71   Two Political Dialogue and Cooperation Agreements have been negotiated between the European Community and countries in Central and Latin America (known collectively as MERCOSUR): one with the Andean Community and its member countries (Bolivia, Colombia, Ecuador, Peru and Venezuela); the other with Central American countries (the Republics of Costa Rica, El Salvador, Guatemala, Honduras, Nicaragua and Panama). These Agreements are not association agreements, although they are seen as an intermediate step towards better trade relations. They are primarily aimed at political and economic dialogue.

15–72   A separate Association Agreement exists however with Chile. The objective of establishing a political and economic Association Agreement between the European Union and Chile was formulated in the 1996 Framework Co-operation Agreement. This Agreement constituted the basis that allowed the Commission to present directives for negotiations to the Council in July 1998. At the first EU and Latin American and Caribbean Summit, which took place on June 28–29, 1999 in Rio de Janeiro, the Heads of State of MERCUSOR countries and Chile, as well as of the European Union, strongly reaffirmed the objective of establishing a political and economic association in their common declaration.

15–73   The bulk of the Agreement—namely provisions relating to the institutional framework, to the trade part and more specifically to the trade in goods, to government procurement, to competition and to the dispute settlement

---

[45] Case 65/77 *Ratzanatsimba* [1978] 1 CMLR 246. In Case C-206/91 *Poirrez v CAF de la Seine-Saint-Denis* [1992] E.C.R. I-6685, which concerned access to disability benefits for the adoptive son from the Ivory Coast) of a French national. The ECJ did not refer to the Lomé Conventions and considered that as the French national adoptive father had not exercised his free movement rights anywhere in the Community, his situation was purely internal and therefore not covered by Community law.

[46] Art.65 of the first Lomé Covention signed in 1975.

[47] See comments above in relation to the Maghreb Agreements and Case C-416/96 *Nour Eddline El-Yassini v Secretary of State for Home Department* [1999] E.C.R. I-1209.

mechanism, and to the co-operation part—has been in force since February 1, 2003. The remaining provisions (political dialogue part, some titles of the trade part such as services, establishment, current payments and capital movements, intellectual property rights, and the bulk of the co-operation part) will enter into force following the ratification of the Agreement by national parliaments. The European Parliament gave its assent at its plenary session of February 12, 2003.

(b) *Free Movement Provisions*

Of principal interest in the Chilean Agreement is the inclusion of an establishment provision contained in Chapter III of Title III (Trade in Services and Establishment). Article 132 states: **15–74**

Article 132

In the sectors inscribed in Annex X, and subject to any conditions and qualifications set out therein, with respect to establishment, each Party shall grant to legal and natural persons of the other Party treatment no less favourable than that it accords to its own legal and natural persons performing a like economic activity.

Annex X contains various limitations on establishment in certain industries or sectors in different Member States.

Article 134 (Final Provisions) contains a provision affirming the right of Contracting Parties to have in place their own laws relating to entry, stay, working conditions and establishment providing that such laws do not "nullify or impair" the rights contained in the Agreement. **15–75**

The language of Arts 132 and 134 is very similar to that contained in the establishment provisions in the Europe Agreements. To that extent the provisions in the Chilean Agreement must said to be "clear and precise" just as they are in the Europe Agreements. However, there is a vital difference between the Chilean Agreement and the Europe Agreements which relates to the future intentions of the European Union. Whilst the Chilean Agreement is intended as an instrument to forge better economic relations with the Union; the Europe Agreements are a tool to accession. This aspect of the Europe Agreements has influenced considerably the manner in which their provisions have been interpreted by the ECJ. It remains to be seen whether for instance the ECJ would be prepared even to afford a provision in the Chilean Agreement direct effect. But even if it did, it is inevitable that the interpretation of the scope of any such provision would be bound to be circumscribed by the Agreement's limited objectives. **15–76**

ASSOCIATION AGREEMENTS IN COMMUNITY LAW

This chapter examines the Community law context of Association Agreements with third countries as an overview to both the Ankara Agreement and the Europe Agreements.

1. INTRODUCTION

The Ankara Agreement and the Europe Agreements are referred to collec- **16–01**
tively in this chapter as "the Association Agreements". Focus is placed on
these Association Agreements because of the rights of free movement that
are specifically conferred on the nationals of Turkey, Bulgaria and Romania
in the Agreements and the intention that these states will eventually accede to
the European Union. Other association and co-operation agreements are
founded on different aims and therefore interpretation of their provisions
may be different.[1] Furthermore other association agreements appear not to
make specific provisions regarding the free movement of persons and at best
include a non-discrimination provision relating to conditions of work.[2]

2. MIXED AGREEMENTS

The Association Agreements are mixed agreements. European Union law **16–02**
recognises three types of international agreement: firstly where obligations
and fulfilment of the agreement lie exclusively with the Community, secondly
where competence falls exclusively to the Member States,[3] and thirdly where
competence is shared between the Community and the Member States. The
Association Agreements fall into this third category since the Agreements are
concluded between the Community, the Member States and a third non-
member country.

The ECJ first ruled that an association agreement could be a mixed agree- **16–03**
ment in *Demirel*.[4] That case concerned the interpretation of specific provisions of the Ankara Agreement. It considered that an agreement concluded
by the Council under Arts 300 and 310 EC Treaty is an act of one of the institutions of the Community and "from its entry into force, the provisions of
such an agreement form an integral part of the Community legal system".

---

[1] See for example in relation to the Moroccan Agreement, Case C-416/96 *Nour Eddline El-Yassini
v Secretary of State for Home Department* [1999] E.C.R. I-1209.
[2] Which in the context of the Maghreb Agreements has already been held by the ECJ to confer
no rights as regards entry and residence of persons, see Case C-416/96 *Nour Eddline El-Yassini
v Secretary of State for Home Department* [1999] E.C.R. I-1209.
[3] The Dublin Convention, June 14, 1990 [30 ILM 425 (1991)].
[4] Case 12/86 *Demirel v Stadt Schwäbisch Gmünd* [1987] E.C.R. 3719.

16–04   The United Kingdom and German Governments had argued in *Demirel*[5] that in the case of mixed agreements the delineation between Community and Member State competence was clear, and that in areas where the Member State has entered into specific commitments with regard to the third country, the Member State had exclusive competence.

16–05   The ECJ rejected this delineation and stated that any matter which generally falls within the scope of the EC Treaty, would fall within "Community competence" since the Community would guarantee the commitment towards non-Member States in all the fields covered by the EC Treaty. The ECJ emphasised that the need for a common approach to the interpretation of obligations under an agreement to ensure uniformity.[6] The ECJ has in effect described this relationship as one in which the Member States act as if agents for the Community in the fulfilment of obligations towards the third country:

> "in ensuring respect for commitments arising from an agreement concluded by the Community institutions, the Member States fulfil, within the Community system, an obligation in relation to the Community, which has assumed responsibility for the due performance of the agreement".[7]

16–06   Given this general approach it is unsurprising that, where issues of competence arise regarding any aspect of free movement of persons, the ECJ has maintained a firm grip on competence for the Community institutions.[8] This is regardless of the fact that the Association Agreements do not explicitly grant unfettered free movement rights for persons but refer to the ability of Member States to have in place national rules on conditions of entry and stay.[9]

16–07   The fact that a matter is said to fall within "Community competence" does not mean that Community rules will automatically replace national rules. If an agreement stipulates that national rules may be applied, the ECJ will not stand in the way of the application and implementation of those national rules. However the ECJ retains for itself and the Commission the role of supervising the implementation of the substantive provisions of the Agreements and ensuring uniformity and general adherence to Community standards.

16–08   As is discussed in detail in Chapter 19 below, the Europe Agreements provide a right of establishment for Bulgarian and Romanian nationals and companies.[10] However the Europe Agreements refer to the fact that Member States may retain their own laws as regards entry and stay creating an inherent ten-

---

[5] Case 12/86 *Demirel v Stadt Schwäbisch Gmünd* [1987] E.C.R. 3719.

[6] Case 12/86 *Demirel v Stadt Schwäbisch Gmünd* [1987] E.C.R. 3719, para.9.

[7] Case C-13/00 *Commission v Ireland* [2002] E.C.R. I-2943, para.15.

[8] See Case C-192/89 *Sevince v Staatssecretaris van Justitie* [1990] E.C.R. I-3461 which relates to interpretation of Member State obligations towards Turkish workers under the Ankara Agreement; see also Case C-235/99 *R. v Secretary of State for the Home Department Ex p. Kondova* [2001] E.C.R. I-6427 relating to the interpretation of Member State obligations towards Polish self-employed national under the Europe Agreements.

[9] *e.g.* Art.59 of the EC-Bulgaria Association Agreement.

[10] Art.45 of the EC-Bulgaria Association Agreement.

sion in the Agreements.[11] The task of the ECJ has been to reconcile that tension and ensure that Member States' legislation is compatible with the Agreements. The judgments of the ECJ on the Europe Agreements even in areas concerned with national laws are replete with references to Community law concepts and principles such as proportionality, non-discrimination and adherence to human rights.[12]

The ECJ has taken a very similar approach in other fields outside the free   **16–09** movement of persons in relation to agreements with third countries. In *Commission v Ireland*[13] the Irish authorities had failed to give effect to the Berne Convention, relating to the protection of literary and artistic works, the provisions of which Member States must adhere to under Protocol 28 of the EEA Agreement. The ECJ considered that since Community legislation touches upon broad areas of intellectual property and protection of databases and copyright, there was sufficient overlap such that there would be "a Community interest in ensuring that all Contracting Parties to the EEA Agreement adhere to that Convention". The ECJ held that as a consequence the Commission was charged with assessing compliance with the Berne Convention, subject to review by the ECJ.[14]

3. THE AGREEMENTS AS A TOOL TO ACCESSION

The Ankara Agreement and the Europe Agreements are "pre-accession"   **16–10** agreements. The intention that the third countries (namely Turkey, Bulgaria and Romania) will eventually become full Member States of the European Union is clearly stated in the Preambles to the Association Agreements although framed in terms of the third countries' desires to be part of the European Union.

The use of an association agreement as a tool towards accession was first   **16–11** employed with Greece. The Community entered into an Association agreement in 1961. Two years later the Ankara Agreement was signed with Turkey. Article 28 contained a specific provision stating that parties to the Agreement would "examine the possibility of the accession of Turkey to the Community".[15] The Additional Protocol signed in 1970 sets out a specific programme of 12 to 22 years for the completion of a customs union and full free movement rights for workers.[16] If such progression had been made within the timetable set, Turkey would have secured a substantial proportion of the core benefits of full EU membership. As it is, progression has been hampered by civil and economic problems that have plagued Turkey since the early 1980s.

---

[11] Art.59 of the Bulgaria Agreement.
[12] See for instance judgment in Case C-63/99 *R. v Secretary of State for the Home Department Ex p. Gloszczuk and Gloszczuk* [2001] E.C.R. I-6369, paras 41, 84 and 85.
[13] Case C-13/00 *Commission v Ireland* [2002] E.C.R. I-2943, para.15.
[14] Case C-13/00 *Commission v Ireland* [2002] E.C.R. I-2943, para.21.
[15] Art.28 of the Ankara Agreement.
[16] Art.36 of the Additional Protocol to the Ankara Agreement, see Chapter 22.

16–12   The accession to the European Union of the Central and Eastern European countries had been rumoured ever since the fall of the Berlin Wall in 1989. Mandates to negotiate association agreements to prepare those countries to accede to the European Union were issued in 1989 and by 1994 the first two Association Agreements with Poland and Hungary were signed.[17] At the 1995 Madrid Council meeting a timetable for the accession of Central and Eastern European countries was laid down with the possibility of the first wave of applicant countries, being admitted as early as 2000. In fact the first wave did not take place until May 1, 2004 with eight of the countries, (together with Malta and Cyprus) becoming full members. Bulgaria and Romania will be the last of the Central and Eastern European countries to join the European Union and until that time the Europe Agreements set out the legal relationship between the European Union and those countries.

16–13   Whilst the Europe Agreements do not contain a similar provision to Art.28 of the Ankara Agreement which specifically requires parties to examine the question of accession, their Preambles make reference to the third countries' "ultimate objective" of becoming a member of the Community. The Europe Agreements are thus intended to provide a framework to prepare the way for the Community and the partner countries to converge economically, politically, socially and culturally. They cover political co-operation, favourable trade relations, economic activities and cultural co-operation.

16–14   The importance of an association agreement being employed as a tool to accession is that it represents a statement of future intentions of the parties and an instrument to facilitate the gradual movement towards the objective of eventual accession. It is with this in mind that the ECJ will give provisions contained in such an agreement a purposive interpretation and so far as is possible construe provisions consistently with similar Community law provisions.[18]

4. JURISDICTION OF THE ECJ

16–15   Article 234 EC Treaty provides:

> The Court of Justice shall have jurisdiction to give preliminary rulings concerning:
>
> (a)   the interpretation of this Treaty;
> (b)   the validity and interpretation of acts of the institutions of the Community and of the ECB;
> (c)   the interpretation of the statutes of bodies established by an act of the Council, where those statutes so provide.

---

[17] These were followed in 1995 with Association Agreements signed with Bulgaria, Czech Republic, Romania and Slovakia and in 1998 with Agreements signed with Estonia, Latvia and Lithuania.

[18] See for instance Case C-268/99 *Jany v Staatssecretaris van Justitite* [2001] E.C.R. I-8615, where the ECJ interpreted provisions relating to exclusion on public policy, public security and public health in the Europe Agreements consistently with interpretation given to such provisions in Community law.

Where such a question is raised before any court or tribunal of a Member State, that court or tribunal may, if it considers that a decision on the question is necessary to enable it to give judgment, request the Court of Justice to give a ruling thereon.

Where any such question is raised in a case pending before a court or tribunal of a Member State against whose decisions there is no judicial remedy under national law, that court or tribunal shall bring the matter before the Court of Justice.

The ECJ clearly regards any Agreement concluded under Arts 300 and 310 **16–16** Treaty as "an act of one of the institutions of the Community" and it provisions form "an integral part of the Community legal system".[19] This gives the ECJ jurisdiction to give preliminary rulings under Art.234(b) EC Treaty concerning the validity and interpretation of an agreement concluded under Arts 300 and 310.

The ECJ first considered its jurisdiction in relation to an association agree- **16–17** ment in the case of *Haegeman*[20] which concerned the interpretation of the Association Agreement with Greece. The ECJ was of the unequivocal view that the Agreement, concluded under Art.310 EC Treaty, was "an act of one of the institutions of the Community" within the meaning of Art.234 EC Treaty. In fact Belgium had not questioned the ability of the ECJ to give a preliminary ruling and the ECJ appears to have affirmed its own jurisdiction unprompted.

When the first case was referred to the ECJ on the interpretation of the **16–18** Ankara Agreement some Member States were less convinced of the ECJ's jurisdiction, at least when it came to issues relating to the exercise of the Member States' own powers under the Ankara Agreement.[21] The United Kingdom and Germany argued that the provisions on freedom of movement for workers were dependant on the exercise of the Member States' own powers to permit entry and residence in the first instance.

The ECJ recalled its decision in *Haegeman* regarding the integral part in the **16–19** Community legal order that such agreements played. The ECJ rejected the suggestion that its jurisdiction could be ousted on the basis that it was for Member States to lay down the rules necessary to give effect in their territory to the provisions of the Agreement. The ECJ reached its decision on the basis that in fact Member States fulfil an obligation under the Agreement on behalf of the Community, since it is the Community which assumes "responsibility for the due performance of the agreement."[22]

In the next case referred to the ECJ regarding the Ankara Agreement, the **16–20** question arose concerning the ECJ's jurisdiction to interpret decisions of the Council of Association. The Council of Association is a body established under each of the Association Agreements with the power to take decisions in order to attain the objectives laid down under the Agreements. The

---

[19] See Case 12/86 *Demirel v Stadt Schwäbisch Gmünd* [1987] E.C.R. 3719, para.7.
[20] Case 181/73 *Haegeman v Belgium* [1974] E.C.R. 449.
[21] Case 12/86 *Demirel v Stadt Schwäbisch Gmünd* [1987] E.C.R. 3719, para.6.
[22] Case 12/86 *Demirel v Stadt Schwäbisch Gmünd* [1987] E.C.R. 3719, para.12.

Council of Association established under Arts 22 and 23 of the Ankara Agreement for instance has taken a number of decisions relating to the implementation of provisions in the Agreement on free movement of workers. In the context of these decisions the ECJ repeated its opinion (previously stated in respect of the Association Agreement with Greece and decisions of the Council of Association[23] established under it) that: "since they are directly connected with the Agreement to which they give effect, the decisions of the Council of Association, in the same way as the Agreement itself, form an integral part, as from their entry into force, of the Community legal system".[24]

16–21   It is apparent the ECJ considers that since it has jurisdiction to give preliminary rulings under Art.234 EC Treaty on the Ankara Agreement itself, it must have jurisdiction to give rulings on the decisions of the body entrusted under the Agreement with the responsibility of giving effect to its provisions. Decisions of the Council of Association are in that sense akin to secondary legislation, such as Regulation 1612/68 giving effect to provisions of the EC Treaty.

16–22   The concern of Member States to retain within their preserve the interpretation of the Association Agreements did not stop there. In 1992 in the case of *Kus*[25] the German Government requested the ECJ to reconsider its jurisdiction to give preliminary rulings on the interpretation of decisions of the Council of Association. The ECJ refused to do so on the basis that the German Government had failed to put forward any new reasons why its jurisdiction should be limited.

16–23   In relation to the Europe Agreements, the Member States appear to have accepted more readily the ECJ's jurisdiction to interpret the Agreements. This may have reflected their confidence that the ECJ would not be able to confer any directly effective rights on individuals from the provisions of the Europe Agreements and therefore that the ECJ's interference would do little to obstruct their sovereign rights to control the entry and stay of non-EU nationals.[26] As far as Council of Association decisions are concerned, none relevant to the free movement of persons has been made under the Europe Agreements and therefore the jurisdiction of the ECJ in relation to such decisions has not arisen as an issue. Undoubtedly, however, the result would have to be the same as that under the Greek Association Agreement and the Ankara Agreement.

5. Direct Effect

16–24   The relationship between domestic and Community law is discussed in detail in Chapter 2. The concept of direct effect is integral to that relationship. A detailed analysis of the concept of direct effect is contained in Chapter 2.

---

[23] Case 30/88 *Greece v Commission* [1989] E.C.R. 449.
[24] Case C-192/89 *Sevince v Staatsecretaris Van Justitite* [1990] E.C.R. I-3461, para.9.
[25] Case C-237/91 *Kuz Landeshauptstadt* [1992] E.C.R. I-6781,
[26] See paras 16–24 *et seq.* below for a discussion about direct effect.

Shortly stated, the concept, established by the ECJ in *Van Gend en Loos*,[27] means that a provision of Community law can be relied on directly by an individual before national authorities and courts.

In essence the criteria laid down in *Van Geed en Loos* identify whether a provision is capable as it stands of judicial enforcement. Provisions which lay down general objectives for instance will not be directly effective.

The ECJ has held that provisions of the Association Agreements are capable **16–25**
of being directly effective, although many will not be due to their programmatic or imprecise nature. As the ECJ has pointed out in relation to the Ankara Agreement, Association Agreements often set out aims of the association without establishing the detailed rules for the attainment of those aims.

In order to establish whether a provision has a direct effect the general **16–26**
approach of the ECJ is first to examine the provision in question to establish its precision and clarity; then to consider whether further implementation would be required in order for the provision to be able to be *relied* upon; and finally to consider whether there is anything in the general structure of an agreement or the general aims of an agreement which would prevent it from being capable of direct effect.

Very few of the provisions of the Ankara Agreement itself for instance have **16–27**
been held to be directly effective because of their structure and lack of specific rules. Article 12 of the Agreement (relating to free movement of workers)[28] was described by the ECJ as being essentially programmatic and lacking in sufficient precision to be capable of conferring directly effective rights on individuals.[29] By contrast Art.41(1) of the Additional Protocol,[30] a standstill provision relating to establishment of persons, was held to be sufficiently precise and "unequivocal".[31] The ECJ noted its similarity in wording to Art.53 Treaty of Rome (a provision now repealed by Amsterdam Treaty) which it had already held to have direct effect.

The ECJ has found that many of the decisions of the Council of Association, **16–28**
which give effect to the programmes set out in the Ankara Agreement, are capable of direct effect. In *Sevince*[32] the ECJ stated:

"Decisions 2/76 and 1/80 were adopted by the Council of Association in order to implement Article 12 of the Agreement and Article 36 of the Additional Protocol

---

27 Case 26/62 *Van Gend en Loos v Nederlandse Administratie der Berlastingen* [1963] E.C.R. 1.
28 "The Contracting Parties agree to be guided by Articles 48, 49 and 50 of the Treaty establishing the Community for the propose of progressively securing freedom of movement for workers between them".
29 Case 12/86 *Meryem Demirel v Stadt Schwäbisch Gmünd* [1987] E.C.R. 3719, para.23.
30 "The Contracting Parties shall refrain from introducing between themselves any new restrictions on the freedom of establishment and the freedom to provide services."
31 Case C-37/98 *The Queen v Secretary of State for the Home Department, Ex p. Savas* [2000] E.C.R. I-2927.
32 Case C-192/89 *Sevince v Staatsecretaris Van Justitite* [1990] E.C.R. I-3461, para.21.

which, in its judgment in *Demirel* the Court recognised as being intended essentially to set out a programme ... The fact that the above mentioned provisions of the Agreement and the Additional Protocol essentially set out a programme does not prevent the decisions of the Council of Association which give effect in specific respects to the programmes envisaged in the Agreement from having direct effect."

16–29   This conclusion is not altered by the fact that the decisions of the Association Council provide that the procedures for applying the rights conferred on Turkish workers are to be established under national rules. According to the ECJ this is simply to clarify that Member States are obliged to take the necessary administrative measures for the implementation of the provisions. However Member States are not permitted to restrict the application of the rights which the decisions of the Council of Association grant to Turkish workers.[33]

16–30   Furthermore the ECJ has held that the fact that a decision of the Association Council is not officially published in the *Official Journal of the European Communities* does not deprive the individual of the rights contained within it.

16–31   In relation to the Europe Agreements, the ECJ has found that some of its provisions are capable of direct effect. In the context of free movement of persons, the most significant provision relating to the freedom of establishment contained in the Europe Agreements has been held to have direct effect.[34] The ECJ held that the establishment provision lays down in clear, precise and unconditional terms the prohibition against discrimination against those wishing to establish themselves from the third countries. No further implementation is required in order for a person to rely upon it in a national court.

16–32   From the ECJ's perspective, the purpose of the Europe Agreements, namely to promote the expansion of trade and economic relations between the Contracting Parties with a view to facilitating accession of the third country to the Community, is compatible with the establishment provision having direct effect. The fact that the Central and Eastern European country in question requires the Agreement to assist with its own economic development and the fact that there is somewhat of an imbalance in the obligations assumed by the Community towards the third country concerned do not prevent it from being capable of direct effect.[35]

16–33   The conclusion that a provision of an association agreement and indeed of a decision of a Council of Association has direct effect is highly significant. It means that individuals can rely upon the provision to create rights for themselves before national authorities without there being any need for national legislation to give effect to the provision. Given the variable approach that

---

[33] Case C-192/89 *Sevince v Staatsecretaris Van Justitie* [1990] E.C.R. I-3461, para.22.
[34] Art.45(1) of the E.C.-Bulgaria Association Agreement for instance.
[35] Case C-257/99 *R. v Secretary of State for the Home Department Ex p. Barkoci and Malik* [2001] E.C.R. I-6557, para.37.

Member States have taken to the implementation of the Association Agreements, this is very important to ensure that Community law rights created by such Association Agreements are not denied to individuals altogether.[36]

---

[36] No provision of the Ankara Agreement or the decisions of the Council of Association established under the Ankara Agreement have been transposed into UK immigration laws for instance. For detailed analysis of the implementation of the Europe Agreements in various Member States, see *Implementation of the Europe Agreements in France, Germany, the Netherlands and the UK: Movement of Persons*, A. Böcker and E. Guild, London, Platinium, 2002.

CENTRAL AND EASTERN EUROPEAN AGREEMENTS

INTRODUCTION TO THE EUROPE AGREEMENTS

This chapter provides an introduction to the pre-Accession Agreements with Bulgaria and Romania, the remaining two Central and Eastern European countries which did not join the European Union on May 1, 2004.

1. BACKGROUND TO THE AGREEMENTS

As discussed in Chapter 15 above, following the fall of the Berlin Wall the European Community was keen to strike formal relationships with the Central and Eastern European countries extremely quickly. For eight such countries those relationships culminated on May 1, 2004 with accession to the European Union. This chapter provides an introduction to the pre-accession agreements with the remaining two countries.   **17–01**

The provisions of the Bulgarian and Romanian Association Agreements[1]— themselves based largely on the agreements originally negotiated with other Central and Eastern European Accession States such as Hungary and Poland[2]—are substantially the same. Negotiations with Bulgaria and Romania were hampered somewhat by political problems in each country resulting in the Agreements, being signed after those agreed with Poland and Hungary. Of the two, the Agreement with Romania[3] was signed first (on February 1, 1993); signature of the agreement with Bulgaria[4] followed some five weeks later (on March 8, 1993). Each came into force on October 1, 1995.   **17–02**

2. THE STRUCTURE AND CONTENT OF THE EUROPE AGREEMENTS

The Europe Agreements follow the same structure: a core agreement with six Annexes appended to the agreement, largely relating to the movement of goods. Further, each Agreement has eight Protocols attached to it which again are mainly concerned with the free movement of goods. Finally there are joint and unilateral declarations attached to each agreement on the interpretation of various provisions in the Agreement and Protocols.[5] The political   **17–03**

---

[1] The Bulgarian and Romanian Association Agreements are referred to here collectively as "the Europe Agreements".
[2] See generally Chapter 15.
[3] Europe Agreement establishing an association between the European Economic Communities and their Member States, of the one part, and Romania, of the other part [1994] O.J. L357.
[4] Europe Agreement establishing an association between the European Communities and their Member States, of the one part, and the Republic of Bulgaria, of the other part [1994] O.J. L358.
[5] The Joint Declaration relating to visas is discussed in Chapter 19 below. Other declarations of interest are the Joint Declarations on the meaning of "children" and "families" for the purposes of the non-discrimination provisions in Art.38 which are defined by reference to national laws rather than Community law.

background and objectives of the Agreements are set out in full in lengthy preambles and Art.1 of the Agreements. These are discussed in more detail below.

17–04   The core Agreements are divided into nine titles:

17–05   *Title I* relates to "Political Dialogue" which sets out the framework in which future political negotiation between Bulgaria and Romania on the one hand, and the European Community on the other, should take place.

17–06   *Title II* sets out the "General Principles" of the Agreements. Both Agreements contain a human rights protection clause which stipulates that democracy and human rights constitute "an essential element of the present association".

17–07   *Title III* contains provisions relating to the free movement of goods which forms a principal part of the Europe Agreements. Detailed aspects of the free movement of goods, particularly relating to trade and product descriptions, are provided for in the Annexes and Protocols to the Agreements.

17–08   *Title IV* is entitled "Movement of Workers, Establishment, Supply of Services". The provisions under this title are the main focus of Chapters 18 to 20 since they form the principal provisions relating to the free movement of persons. Article 38 provides for non-discrimination of workers as regards conditions of work, remuneration and dismissal. Article 45 provides a right of establishment for persons and companies. Article 53 provides for the transfer of key personnel. Article 54 contains a public policy proviso that replicates the public policy exceptions in the EC Treaty. Article 59 makes clear that Contracting Parties are not prevented from applying their laws as regards entry, stay, labour conditions and conditions of establishment providing that they do not nullify or impair the rights contained in the Agreement.[6]

17–09   *Titles V to VIII* relate to issues of capital, competition law, economic, financial and cultural co-operation reflecting the objectives of the Europe Agreements and principal aim of harmonious economic relations and ever-greater financial union between the parties. Of particular significance is the aim of facilitating the tourist trade and reducing relevant formalities.[7]

17–10   *Title IX* entitled "Institutions, General and Final Provisions" creates three separate bodies under each of the Agreements:

---

[6] This provision has been the cause of considerable controversy since its language is unfamiliar to the Community lawyer. It is discussed in detail in Chapter 19 below.

[7] Art.90 of the Europe Agreements. It is significant in this regard that it was not until 2001 that Bulgarian and Romanian nationals were exempt from visa requirements to enter the Member States by virtue of Council Reg. 539/2001 [2001] O.J. L81/1 ("the Common Visa List"). The inclusion of Romania in the exempted list at the time was highly controversial despite the existence of the Association Agreement with the European Community. The UK and Ireland exercised their opt-out under Art.1 of the Protocol to the Treaty on the European Union and did not participate in this Regulation. To date the UK maintains a visa regime for Bulgarian and Romanian nationals wishing to enter the UK, even for the purpose of tourist visits.

- *The Association Council.* This consist of the Ministers from members of the Council of the European Communities (*i.e.* the Member States) and Members of the Commission of the European Communities, on the one hand, and of Ministers appointed by the Governments of Romania or Bulgaria on the other. All areas of approximation towards the European Union may be discussed at meetings of the Association Council.

- *The Association Committee.* The Committee consists of senior-level officials from all parties which review in more detail all areas covered by the Europe Agreements. The Association Committee will generally be complemented by a series of sub-committees, which provide for regular in-depth technical discussions on all areas covered by the Agreements. The Association Council may delegate tasks and areas of discussion to the Association Committee.

- *The Association Parliamentary Committee.* This brings together members of the national parliaments of the relevant associated country and members of the European Parliament.

3. THE OBJECTIVES OF THE EUROPE AGREEMENTS

As is discussed in Chapter 16, an appreciation of the objectives of an **17–11** association agreement is very important as an aid to interpretation of the agreement. Examination of the Preamble to the Europe Agreements as well as the first provisions in the Agreements reveals clear objectives, essentially that of eventual accession of the associated countries to the European Community.

(a) *Preamble to the Agreements*

The Preamble to each Agreement contains recitations which reflect (and **17–12** indeed culminate with a recitation *recognizing*) the "ultimate objective" of each state of becoming a member of the Community. Thus, for example, the Preamble refers to the importance of the traditional links existing between Community Member States on the one hand and Bulgaria and Romania on the other. Shared common values are also referred to, as is the wish of both Bulgaria and Romania to strengthen such links and to establish close and long lasting relations with the Community. Reference is made to the opportunities for relationships of "a new quality" offered by the emergence of the new democracies in both Bulgaria and Romania.

In relation to Bulgaria, recognition is given to "the fundamental character of **17–13** the democratic changes" which are taking place in a peaceful manner in the country and which are aimed at building "a new political and economic system, based on the rule of law and human rights, political pluralism, and a pluralist multi-party system involving free and democratic elections and the creation of the legislative and economic conditions, necessary for the development of a market economy". In relation to Romania, recognition is given to the need to continue and complete the country's transition towards "a new political and economic system which respects the rule of law and human rights, including the rights of persons belonging to minorities, operates a multi-party system with free and democratic elections, and provides for economic liberalization in order to establish a market economy."[8]

17–14   The Preamble also states the Parties' belief that "a link should be made between full implementation of association, on the one hand, and continuation of the actual accomplishment of [Bulgaria's/Romania's] political, economic and legal reforms on the other hand." The Parties' desire of establishing regular political dialogue is stated, as is the Community's willingness to provide "decisive support" (in relation to Bulgaria) for the "completion of the transition towards a market economy" and (in relation to Romania) "the implementation of reform". For each country decisive support is to help the country to "cope with the economic and social consequences of structural readjustment". To that end each Preamble states that the parties are "convinced" that each Agreement will "create a new climate for their economic relations and in particular for the development of trade and investment, instruments which are indispensable for economic restructuring and technological modernization".

(b) *Article 1*

17–15   Whilst the Preamble provides the political flavour of the Agreements, culminating (as stated above) in recognition of the "ultimate objective" of each state becoming members of the European Union, the "objectives" of the association established by each Agreement are stated expressly by Art.1. Subject to minor variations (and with one additional objective listed in the Bulgarian Agreement), the objectives listed in Art.1 are the same in each Agreement. Using the text of the Bulgarian Agreement by way of example the objectives are stated as follows:[9]

> – to provide an appropriate framework for the political dialogue between the parties allowing the development of close political relations;
>
> – *to establish gradually a free trade area between the Community and Bulgaria covering substantially all trade between them*;
>
> – to promote the expansion of trade and the harmonious economic relations between the Parties and so to foster the *dynamic* economic development *and prosperity* in Bulgaria;

---

[8] It is not only in relation to Romania that the importance of the human rights of minorities is emphasised. Both Agreements contain the following recitation, although the italicised words appear only in the Bulgarian Agreement: "Considering the firm commitment of the Community and its Member States and of Bulgaria/of Romania *to the rule of law and human rights, including those of persons belonging to minorities, and* to the full implementation of all other principles and provisions contained in the Final Act of the Conference on Security and Cooperation in Europe (CSCE), the concluding documents of Vienna and Madrid, the Charter of Paris for a new Europe, the CSCE Helsinki document 'The Challenges of Change'".

[9] Words in italics appear only in the Bulgarian Agreement; words in square brackets appear only in the Romanian Agreement.

– to provide a basis for economic, financial, cultural and social co-operation, *as well as for the Community's assistance to Bulgaria*;

– to support Bulgaria's efforts to develop its economy and to complete the *transition* [conversion] into a market economy, [and consolidate its democracy];

– to provide an appropriate framework for [Romania's] *the* gradual integration of Bulgaria into the Community. To this end *new rules, policies and practices will be established in compliance with market mechanisms, and* Bulgaria shall work towards fulfilling the necessary *requirements* [conditions] *in this respect*;

– to set up institutions suitable to make the association effective.

In interpreting provisions under the Europe Agreements the ECJ has made   **17–16**
extensive reference to the preamble and the objectives set out above. It is clearly important to keep in mind these objectives since they ensure that the broadest interpretation is given to provisions in these Agreements and, wherever possible, the provisions read compatibly with Community law.[10]

---

[10] See for instance Case C-268/99 *Jany v Staatssecretaris van Justitie* [2001] E.C.R. I–8615.

CHAPTER 18

WORKERS UNDER THE EUROPE AGREEMENTS

This chapter examines the two principal provisions contained in the Europe Agreements relating to workers. These are a non-discrimination provision contained in Art.38 of the Agreements and the provisions relating to key personnel in Art.53. The provisions are limited and do not grant the right of free movement for workers.

1. INTRODUCTION

Title IV to the Europe Agreements is headed: "Movement of workers, estab- **18–01** lishment, supply of services". Chapter 1 of Title IV refers to "Movement of workers". Despite the misleading title of Title IV, it is notable that there are no free movement provisions specifically relating to workers.[1] The provisions contained in the Ankara Agreement relating to the free movement of workers and the specific aim of gradual progression towards the attainment of that goal are not replicated in any provisions of the Europe Agreements. Initial access to the labour force is left firmly in the hands of the Member States. The principal rights relating to the free movement of persons under the Europe Agreements are derived from the right of establishment discussed in Chapters 19 and 20. It is only the right of establishment contained in Art.45(1) from which a right of entry and residence can be inferred.

This obvious limitation of the Europe Agreements is perhaps indicative of **18–02** the differences in the economic and social climates in which the Europe Agreements were negotiated when compared with the Ankara Agreement. During the 1960s and 1970s when the negotiations between Turkey and the European Community were taking place the Member States were experiencing a significant economic boom which relied at least to some extent upon a large migrant labour force. By the early 1990s when the Europe Agreements were under negotiation, the Member States' economies were less buoyant and the political climate was one of protectionism, particularly where employment and migrant labour forces were concerned.

This protectionism of labour markets has flowed through even to the acces- **18–03** sion of those Europe Agreement countries which have now joined the European Union to the extent that free movement of workers (as opposed to any other persons) may be delayed during the transitional period.[2]

Indeed under the Europe Agreements the Council of Association is only **18–04** charged with examining further ways of improving the movement of workers

---

[1] The Advocate General's Opinion in Case C-162/00 *Land Nordrhein-Westfalen v Beata Pokrzeptowicz-Meyer* [2002] E.C.R. I–149, is unquestioning in the assertion that there are no rights of entry or residence for workers contained in the Europe Agreements.
[2] See Chapter 6.

during the second stage of the transitional period prescribed by Art.7 of the Agreements (*i.e.* five years after the Agreements came into force).[3] When doing so it is to take into account the social and economic situation and requirements in Romania and Bulgaria and the employment situation in the Community. To this end the Council of Association is to make recommendations (as opposed to decisions), although in fact no such recommendations appear to have been made in the cases of either Bulgaria or Romania.

18–05   There are only two provisions that might benefit workers from Bulgaria and Romania in the Europe Agreements: one relating to non-discrimination and the second relating to the movement of key personnel by companies registered in either of those countries.

2. Non-Discrimination of Workers

(a) *Introduction*

18–06   Article 38 of both the Bulgaria and Romania Agreements is precisely the same: they contain a non-discrimination provision relating to Bulgarian and Romanian workers.

Article 38

1. Subject to the conditions and modalities applicable in each Member State:

– the treatment accorded to workers of Bulgarian nationality, legally employed in the territory of a Member State shall be free from any discrimination based on nationality, as regards working conditions, remuneration or dismissal, as compared to its own nationals.

It is to be noted this non-discrimination provision relates to those workers of Bulgarian or Romanian nationality who are "legally employed" within a Member State. Moreover the non-discrimination provision is restricted in its scope in so far as it relates to conditions of work, remuneration and dismissal only.[4] There is no reference to conditions of entry or stay and indeed the reference to those "legally employed" makes clear that workers wishing to benefit from the provision must have been granted permission to enter and work in the Member State already.[5]

(b) *Direct Effect*

18–07   Article 38 has been held by the ECJ to be directly effective in Community law. The ECJ noted that it is clear and precise and is not subject in its implementation to the adoption of any subsequent measure. According to the ECJ:

---

[3] See Art.43 of the Romanian Agreement for instance.

[4] In this respect the non-discrimination provision relating to workers should be compared with the non-discrimination provision relating to establishment in Art.45(1) of the Bulgarian Agreement for instance which is not so limited in scope.

[5] Case C-162/00 *Land Nordrhein-Westfalen v Pokrzeptowicz-Meyer* [2002] E.C.R. I–1049, para.20.

"This rule of equal treatment lays down a precise obligation to produce a specific result and, by its nature, can be relied on by an individual to apply to a national court to set aside the discriminatory provisions of a Member State's legislation, without any further implementing measures being required for that purpose".[6]

The German Government had argued that the equivalent provision in the **18–08** Polish Agreement was not unconditional since the provision is put into effect "subject to the conditions and modalities applicable in each Member State". The ECJ held that this proviso cannot be interpreted in a way that permits the Member States to make the principle of non-discrimination dependent on certain condition, being met or being diluted in anyway.

In concluding that the provision was capable of direct effect, the ECJ had **18–09** regard to the nature and purpose of the Europe Agreements which are aimed at promoting the expansion of trade and economic relations with a view to accession. The implications of a provision having direct effect are discussed in Chapters 2 and 16.

(c) *Relationship with National Laws Permitted by Article 59*

Article 59 of each Europe Agreement contains general provisions on the **18–10** operation of national laws and regulations which must be applied when examining the rights of workers and those wishing to exercise their right of establishment under the Agreements. Article 59 provides:

Article 59

1. For the purposes of Title IV of this Agreement, nothing in the Agreement shall prevent the Parties from applying their laws and regulations regarding entry and stay, work, labour conditions and establishment of natural persons and supply of services, provided that, in so doing, they do not apply them in a manner as to nullify or impair the benefits accruing to any Party under the terms of a specific provision of the Agreement. The above provision does not prejudice the application of Article 54.

At first sight the inclusion of Art.59 in the Agreements might suggest that **18–11** the non-discrimination provision contained in Art.38(1) (or indeed Art.45(1)) can be diluted in some way by Member States since Art.59 provides that they may have in place national laws concerning conditions of entry, stay, employment and working conditions. However, as the ECJ has made clear all that follows from Art.59 is that whilst the authorities of the Member States remain competent to apply their own national laws and regulations regarding entry, stay, employment and working conditions of Romanian or Bulgarian nationals, they do so subject to the conditions in the Europe Agreements.[7]

---

[6] Case C-162/00 *Land Nordrhein-Westfalen v Pokrzeptowicz-Meyer* [2002] E.C.R. I–1049, para.22.
[7] See for instance Case C-257/99 *R. v Secretary of State for the Home Department Ex p. Barkoci and Malik* [2001] E.C.R. I–6557.

18–12   The fundamental obligation in the Europe Agreements is that of non-discrimination in particular fields. Article 38(1) is concerned with non-discrimination in relation to conditions of work for those lawfully employed in the Member States whilst Art.45(1) is concerned with non-discrimination in relation to the right of establishment (which is broader in scope since it relates to rights of entry and stay as well as conditions of establishment[8]).

18–13   It is plain that Art.59(1) is not intended to make implementation or the effects of the principle of non-discrimination laid down in the first indent of Art.38(1) of the Europe Agreements subject to the adoption of further national measures.[9] Both Arts 38(1) and 45(1) would be rendered meaningless if Member States could have in place national measures which permitted discrimination against Bulgarian or Romanian nationals *vis-à-vis* their EU national equivalents.

(d) *Meaning of the Non-discrimination Provision*

18–14   The ECJ has held that Art.38 of the Europe Agreements has the same meaning as Art.39(2) EC Treaty which prohibits discrimination against non-Member State nationals. The importance of this comparison between the Europe Agreements and the EC Treaty itself is that it extends the ECJ's case law on discrimination under Art.39(2) EC Treaty to the interpretation of the Europe Agreements. The case law of the ECJ makes clear that the *scope* of the non-discrimination provision in the Europe Agreements is the same as that contained in Art.39(2) EC Treaty in that discrimination which relates to any condition of employment will be prohibited unless objectively justified. Conditions of employment are broadly interpreted and will include the type of activities that are carried out by the employee, as well as conditions of remuneration, other benefits and rewards.

18–15   In the contested area of sports rules, the ECJ held in *Bosman*[10] that rules governing the extent to which football clubs field their players for participation in official matches fell within the scope of Art.39(2) EC Treaty. Such rules were said to concern "conditions of work" since participation in such matches is the essential purpose of a professional sportsman's activities. The ECJ thus held that Art.39(2) EC Treaty must be read so as to prohibit sports rules which restrict the number of EU national players able to be fielded in an official match.

18–16   In *Kolpak*[11] the ECJ applied the same reasoning to a case concerning the application of rules restricting the number of non-EEA national handball players who could be chosen to play in an official match in Germany in

---

[8] See Chapters 19 & 20.
[9] See Case C-162/00 *Land Nordrhein-Westfalen v Pokrzeptowicz-Meyer* [2002] E.C.R. I–1049, para.23. See, as regards the provisions of the Europe Agreement concerning establishment, the judgment in Case C-63/99 *R. v Secretary of State for the Home Department Ex p. Gloszczuk and Gloszczuk* [2001] E.C.R. I–6369, para.37.
[10] Case C-415/93 *Union royale belge des sociétés de football association ASBL v Bosman* [1995] E.C.R. I–4921.
[11] Case C-438/00 *Deutscher Handballbund eV v Kolpak* [2003] E.C.R. I–4135.

relation to a Slovakian player lawfully employed in Germany. The ECJ considered that such rules had no objective justification and were thus discriminatory contrary to the Europe Agreements. If the rules had applied to matches between national teams there would have been objective justification for the discrimination. However these rules applied to all official matches between clubs. As the ECJ had pointed out in *Bosman*, a club's links with the Member State in which it is established cannot be regarded as any more essential than are its links with its locality, town or region. The ECJ noted that there were no rules relating to the locality within the country that the player had to come from.

The principle of non-discrimination in Community law protects individuals **18–17** from both direct and indirect forms of discrimination. The ECJ has interpreted the principle of non-discrimination under Art.39(2) EC Treaty as extending to situations of *indirect* discrimination. In *Spotti*[12] for instance the ECJ had held that Art.39(2) EC Treaty precludes the application of a provision of national law imposing a limit on the duration of the employment relationship between universities and foreign-language assistants where there is, in principle, no such limit with regard to other workers. The ECJ based its finding on the fact that the great majority of foreign-language assistants were foreign nationals. The difference in treatment between them and other teachers with special duties, placed the foreign nationals at a disadvantage compared with German nationals. This constituted indirect discrimination, prohibited by Art.39(2) EC Treaty, unless it was justified by objective reasons.

In *Pokrzeptowicz-Meyer*[13] the ECJ applied its interpretation of Art.39(2) EC **18–18** Treaty in *Spotti* to the Europe Agreements. The ECJ stated that there was no reason to give a more restrictive interpretation and thus, limitations on the duration of contracts for foreign language assistants constituted indirect discrimination against Polish nationals.

Whilst a broad interpretation is given to the non-discrimination provision, **18–19** it is plainly limited in scope to conditions of work, remuneration and dismissal for those in legal employment. The concept of "legal employment" is discussed below. However, it is plain that the provision does not extend to conditions of entry or residence or access to the labour market. Decisions about whether to admit a Bulgarian or Romanian national to the labour force remains the sole preserve of the Member States, unaffected by Community law. Likewise decisions regarding conditions of entry to the territory and continued residence fall within the jurisdiction of the Member States alone. A comparison with the Ankara Agreement and the decisions of its Council of Association demonstrates what measures could be taken to progress towards the free movement of workers. However no such steps have been taken by the Council of Association under either of the Europe

---

[12] Case C-272/92 *Chiara Spotti v Freistaat Bayern* [1993] E.C.R. I–5185.
[13] Case C-162/00 *Land Nordrhein-Westfalen v Beata Pokrzeptowicz-Meyer* [2002] E.C.R. I–1049, para.39.

Agreements and thus no progress towards the free movement of workers can be inferred.[14]

18–20 An example of the sort of question which might arise in the context of the non-discrimination provision is whether a Bulgarian national who obtained permission to work on the basis of an employment contract which excluded the Bulgarian national from access to maternity leave, could rely on Art.38(1) of the Europe Agreements in order subsequently to obtain maternity benefits or leave. The answer would have to be that such a Bulgarian national must be afforded the same conditions of work as a national of the Member State in question and thus obtain maternity leave and benefits on the same basis as the own-national worker. Moreover in the context of the Ankara Agreement the ECJ has found that the reasons for admitting a Turkish national to the labour force or the conditions under which such a worker is admitted are irrelevant for the purposes of obtaining the benefits of the provisions of the Ankara Agreement or decisions of the Council of Association.[15] There is no reason why the same approach would not be taken under the Europe Agreements.

(e) The Meaning of "Legally Employed"

18–21 Only those who are legally employed in a Member State obtain the benefits of Art.38(1) of the Europe Agreements. Legal employment is not defined anywhere in the Europe Agreements. Since E.U. nationals have the right to work in other Member States the term has little relevance to E.U. nationals and therefore has not had to be interpreted by the ECJ in the context of the EC Treaty. However "legal employment" is a term referred to in Decision 1/80 of the Council of Association established under the Ankara Agreement[16] and has been the subject of interpretation by the ECJ.

18–22 Legal working is discussed in greater detail in Chapter 22 in relation to workers under the Ankara Agreement. It must be appropriate to apply the ECJ's case law by analogy to Bulgarian and Romanian workers lawfully working in the Member States.[17] In short the worker must be in a *"stable and secure position"* as regards the legality of his residence in the Member State. The worker would need to have an undisputed right of residence since any dispute as to

---

[14] See for instance Case C-416/96 *Nour Eddline El-Yassini v Secretary of State for Home Department* [1999] E.C.R. I–1209, where the ECJ examined a similar non-discrimination provision in the Moroccan Agreement and concluded the lack of provisions equivalent to those under the Ankara Agreement and the plain wording of the provision meant that its scope could not extend to conditions of entry or stay. It might be thought that since the Europe Agreements have different objectives than the Moroccan Agreement in so far as the latter is not a pre-accession agreement, this will generally affect the method of interpretation of a provision and that the Europe Agreements should be more generously interpreted. In fact the plain wording of the provision in the Europe Agreements and the lack of any other provisions setting out any rights in relation to the free movement of workers must preclude a different interpretation.
[15] See for instance Case C-36/96 *Günaydin v Freistaat Bayern* [1997] E.C.R. I–5197.
[16] For more detailed discussion, see Chapter 22.
[17] Although Art.6(1) of Dec. 1/80 of the Council of Association under the Ankara Agreement additionally refers to the fact that Turkish workers who wish to benefit from that particular provision must be "duly registered as belonging to the labour force" as well as legally employed the ECJ has stated that the phrases are synonymous: see Case C-1/97 *Birden v Stadtgemeinde Bremen* [1998] E.C.R. I–7747.

the right of residence could lead to insecurity in the worker's situation. Thus a person who is working in a Member State with the permission of the authorities whilst awaiting the outcome of an application to remain[18] or of an appeal against the refusal of a residence permit would not fulfil the requirements of legal employment.[19]

The reasons why the worker is permitted to work, however, are not relevant to the question of whether the employment is "legal". If for instance work and residence permits were granted to a Bulgarian national by virtue of his being the spouse of a national of the relevant Member State, rather than because of a desire to have him admitted to the labour force, this would not affect the worker's rights under Art.38(1), even if the marriage subsequently dissolved.[20]   **18–23**

(f) *The Meaning of "Worker"*

Just as the notion of legal employment is nowhere defined in the Europe Agreements, so there is no definition of workers to be found in those Agreements. However, the meaning of "worker" has been comprehensively considered by the ECJ and in relation to the Ankara Agreement the ECJ has repeatedly emphasised that the concept of Turkish worker should take on the Community law definition. The same approach should be taken to the interpretation of the term worker in the Europe Agreements (not least given the fact that these are association agreements with the same underlying objective of accession to the European Union).   **18–24**

The Community concept of worker is considered in Chapter 7 and, in the context of the Ankara Agreement, in Chapter 22. For present purposes it suffices to emphasise that the concept must be interpreted broadly and that the person must pursue an activity which is genuine and effective, to the exclusion of activities on such a small scale as to be regarded as purely marginal and ancillary. The essential feature of an employment relationship is that for a certain period of time a person performs services for and under the direction of another person in return for which remuneration is received.   **18–25**

(g) *Temporal Effect of the Non-discrimination Provision for Workers*

The question has arisen as to the temporal effect of the non-discrimination provision. Does the provision have any affect on conditions of work for instance where a contract for employment was entered into prior to the coming into force of the relevant Europe Agreement?   **18–26**

The ECJ has answered this question by reference to general principles of Community law applied in accession cases and where new legislation is   **18–27**

---

[18] *e.g.* an application for asylum.
[19] Case C-237/91 *Kuz v Landeshauptstadt Wiesbaden* [1992] E.C.R. I–6781.
[20] Although of course the dissolving of the marriage might affect the right of residence itself.

brought into force. In *Pokrzeptowicz-Meyer*[21] it held that the non-discrimination provision contained in the Europe Agreements was a new rule which would apply with immediate effect from the date of coming into force of the relevant agreement to a fixed-term contract for employment. Thus it would apply to any situation arising after the date on which the Agreement comes into force.[22] It would not, however, apply to situations which arose prior to the coming into force of the Agreement. The ECJ dismissed arguments about legal certainty and the protection of the legitimate expectations of the persons concerned on the grounds that it was only the matters of law and fact which existed at the time of the conclusion of such contract which were to be applied to its operation. The ECJ held that such arguments had no application in the context of a non-discrimination provision which individuals should be able to rely upon immediately, regardless of when they entered into contracts of employment.

3. FAMILY MEMBERS

18–28   In addition to making provision for non-discrimination in relation to workers, Art.38 of the Bulgaria and Romania Agreements also makes specific provision for the legally resident spouse and children of workers legally employed in Member States who are given a right of access to the labour market. The relevant part of Art.38(1) provides as follows:

"1. Subject to the conditions and modalities applicable in each Member State:

– the legally resident spouse and children of a worker legally employed in the territory of a Member State, with the exception of seasonal workers and of workers coming under bilateral agreements in the sense of Article 42, unless otherwise provided by such agreements, shall have access to the labour market of that Member State, during the period of that worker's authorized stay of employment."

18–29   This provision is predicated expressly on the legal residence of family members. However, the existence of a right of access to the labour market for family members at least implies that some national law provision must be made so as to enable workers legally employed in a Member State to be joined by such family members. Just as the existence of free movement rights generally implies as a corollary the right to enter and reside, so a right in certain circumstances to access the labour market ought similarly to imply at least the possibility of entry, lest the right given be rendered entirely meaningless. Such an interpretation is mandated also by human rights obligations, in particular the right to respect for family life contained in Art.8 ECHR. As discussed in Chapters 3 and 10, the fundamental importance of Art.8 ECHR in the context of free movement rights in has recent years has been given particular prominence.

---

[21] Case C-162/00 *Land Nordrhein-Westfalen v Pokrzeptowicz-Meyer* [2002] E.C.R. I–1049, para.39.
[22] In a Community law context see Case 278/84 *Germany v Commission* [1987] E.C.R. 1, para.36, and Case C-60/98 *Butterfly Music Srl v Carosello Edizioni Musicali e Discografiche Srl* [1999] E.C.R. I–3939, para.25.

The ECJ has not considered the position of the family members of workers in   **18–30**
the context of the Europe Agreements. By contrast, the ECJ has considered
the limited provision made for the family members of Turkish nationals exercising their rights under the Ankara Agreement. The provision in Art.38(1) of
the Europe Agreements is not dissimilar to that contained in Art.7 of Decision
1/80 under the Ankara Agreement. It is acknowledged that the context is different because the Turkish worker attains rights of residence under the Ankara
Agreement whereas the Bulgarian and Romanian workers do not attain any
such comparable rights. However, to the extent that both family member provisions provide a right of access to the labour market the analysis of the ECJ
in the context of the Ankara Agreement provides a useful benchmark for the
assertion of the right to family unity in the present context. The family unity
provisions under the Ankara Agreement are discussed in Chapter 24.

4. KEY PERSONNEL

The right of establishment contained in Art.45(1) of the Europe Agreements   **18–31**
is extended by Art.53 of the Agreements which provides that the beneficiaries of the right of establishment are entitled to employ, or have employed by
a subsidiary, key personnel. In this way Art.53 provides an additional right to
the right of establishment making it more effective in practice since the
transfer of key personnel may be vital to that establishment:

Article 53

1. Notwithstanding the provisions of Chapter I of this Title, the beneficiaries of the
rights of establishment granted by Bulgaria and the Community respectively shall
be entitled to employ, or have employed by one of their subsidiaries, in accordance
with the legislation in force in the host country of establishment, in the territory of
Bulgaria and the Community respectively, employees who are nationals of
Community Member States and Bulgaria respectively, provided that such employees are key personnel as defined in paragraph 2, and that they are employed exclusively by such beneficiaries or their subsidiaries. The residence and work permits of
such employees shall only cover the period of such employment.

2. Key personnel of the beneficiaries of the rights of establishment herein referred
to as 'organization' are:

(a)   senior employees of an organization who primarily direct the management of
      the organization, receiving general supervision or direction principally from
      the board of directors or shareholders of the business, including:

      – directing the organization or a department or sub-division of the
        organization,
      – supervising and controlling the work of other supervisory, professional or
        managerial employees,
      – having the authority personally to engage and dismiss or recommend
        engaging, dismissing or other personnel actions;

(b)   persons employed by an organization who possess high or uncommon:

      – qualifications referring to a type of work or trade requiring specific
        technical knowledge,

– knowledge essential to the organization's service, research equipment, techniques or management.

These may include, but are not limited to, members of accredited professions. Each such employee must have been employed by the organization concerned for at least one year preceding the detachment by the organization.

18–32   The key personnel provision applies to both nationals and companies establishing themselves in the territory of a Member State who wish to employ key personnel in that Member State.[23] However, in practice it is more likely that companies will use this provision, particularly given the nature of the personnel that are transferable and the conditions for transfer.

18–33   Key personnel are defined as those involved in senior management of the organisation (normally directly answerable to the board of the company) or those with special technical knowledge or skills essential to the business. The employee must be exclusively employed by that company or one of its subsidiaries (not a branch or agency).

18–34   The key personnel employee must be a national of one of the Contracting Parties, not a third country national. The employee must have been employed by the beneficiary or its subsidiaries for at least one year before transfer. The employee cannot therefore have been employed by another company or person in the year before transfer. Finally the employee may not be employed by anyone else in the host Member State, although there would be nothing to prevent that employee engaging in self-employed activity in the exercise of his own right of establishment.[24]

18–35   The employment of key personnel under the Europe Agreements must be in accordance with national rules of the Member State concerned. Residence and work permits may be restricted in duration to that of the activity for which the employee is required.

18–36   The ability of Member States to regulate conditions relating to entry, work and residence permits is not unfettered. The key personnel provision is subject to Art.59 of the Europe Agreements which provides that national legal requirements must not nullify or impair the rights contained in the Agreements.[25] Thus if an employee satisfied the definition of key personnel, the Member State could not refuse entry or stay to that employee other than on grounds of public policy.[26] The Member State could however require that the person obtains a visa prior to entering its territory.

18–37   There have been no cases to date on the interpretation of the key personnel provisions in the Europe Agreements which may be reflective of their underutilisation, or perhaps the detail contained in the provision.

---

[23] Other Europe Agreements, such as the Slovakian Agreement confined the benefit of the key personnel provision to companies alone and did not entitle self-employed nationals to employ key personnel.

[24] For detailed discussion of the right of establishment, see Chapter 19.

[25] For further discussion of "nullify or impair", see Chapter 20.

[26] Art.54(1) of the Bulgarian or Romanian Agreements. For discussion see Chapter 20.

ESTABLISHMENT UNDER THE EUROPE AGREEMENTS

This chapter examines the provisions contained in the Bulgaria and Romania Agreements conferring the right of establishment for both persons and companies.

1. Basic Provisions

The principal provision on establishment is contained in Art.45 of each **19–01** Agreement which is substantially the same in each and subject only to minor variations. The relevant extracts of Art.45 of the Bulgaria Agreement are as follows:

Article 45

1. Each Member State shall grant, from entry into force of the Agreement, for the establishment of Bulgarian companies and nationals and for the operation of Bulgarian companies and nationals established in its territory, a treatment no less favourable than that accorded to its own companies and nationals, save for matters referred to in Annex XVa.
[. . .]

5. For the purposes of this Agreement

(a) 'establishment' shall mean

    (i) as regards nationals, the right to take up and pursue economic activities as self-employed persons and to set up and manage undertakings, in particular companies, which they effectively control. Self-employment and business undertakings by nationals shall not extend to seeking or taking employment in the labour market or confer a right of access to the labour market of the other Party. The provisions of this chapter do not apply to those who are not exclusively self-employed;
    (ii) as regards companies, the right to take up and pursue economic activities by means of the setting up and management of subsidiaries, branches and agencies;

(b) 'subsidiary' of a company shall mean a company which is effectively controlled by the first company;

(c) 'economic activities' shall in particular include activities of an industrial character, activities of a commercial character, activities of craftsmen and activities of the professions.

6. The Association Council shall, during the transitional period referred to in paragraph 2 (i), examine regularly the possibility of accelerating the granting of national treatment in the sectors referred to in Annexes XVb and XVc and the inclusion of areas or matters listed in Annex XVd within the scope of application of the provisions of paragraph 2 (i) of this Article. Amendments may be made to these Annexes by decision of the Association Council. Following the expiration of the transitional period referred to in paragraph 2 (i), the Association Council may

exceptionally, upon request by Bulgaria, and if the necessity arises, decide to prolong the duration of exclusion of certain areas or matters listed in Annexes XVb
and XVc for a limited period of time.

19–02   The benefit of the non-discrimination provision is to be granted by Member
States "for the establishment of Bulgarian companies and nationals and for
the operation of Bulgarian companies and nationals established in its territory". The provision requires that Member States give such companies and
nationals "a treatment no less favourable than that accorded to its own
companies and nationals".

19–03   Although not set out above, Art.45(2) contains the same non-discrimination
provision, both for the establishment of Community companies and for the
operation of Community companies and nationals established in Bulgaria
and Romania. However, some sectors are excluded altogether.[1]

19–04   Transitional savings apply also in relation to financial services which include
insurance and insurance-related services and banking and other financial
services (excluding insurance).[2] Further, in the Bulgaria Agreement transitional savings apply also in relation to other sectors.[3] Such savings are not
open-ended and, although differently worded in each Agreement, last for 10
years in the case of Bulgaria and five years in the case of Romania. Since
each Agreement came into force on February 1, 1995 in relation to Romania
the transitional period expired on February 1, 2000; in relation to Bulgaria
the period will end on February 1, 2005.

19–05   Each Agreement contains an identically worded "standstill" clause[4] which
provides that during the transitional period neither state is to adopt any new
regulations or measures which introduce discrimination as regards the establishment of Community companies and nationals in its territory in comparison to its own companies and nationals.

19–06   Article 45(6) of each Agreement makes similar provisions enabling the
Association Council to amend either the transitional periods or the list of
"excluded" matters and, following the expiration of the transitional period
exceptionally upon request by Bulgaria or Romania, to prolong the duration
of exclusion of certain areas or matters for a limited period of time.

---

[1] In relation to Bulgaria (Art.45(3), by reference to Annex XVd) excluded sectors include the
acquisition of land and dwellings in certain locations and in relation to Romania (Art.45.2, by
reference to Annex XVII) the purchase, ownership and sale of land, forestry and residence buildings (not related to foreign investments in Romania), cultural and historic monuments and buildings, the organisation of gambling, betting, lotteries and other similar activities and the
provision of legal services (excluding legal advisory services).

[2] Annex XVb of Bulgaria Agreement and Annex XVII of Romania Agreement.

[3] Including in certain circumstances companies engaged in the activities of manufacturing or
trading with weapons, munitions or military equipment, prospecting, development or extraction
of natural resources from the territorial sea, the provision of certain legal services and the
arrangement of gambling games and lotteries: Annex XVc of Bulgaria Agreement.

[4] Art.45(4) of each Agreement.

2. RELATIONSHIP WITH COMMUNITY LAW

(a) *Similarities to EC Treaty Provisions on Establishment*

The Community Law provisions on establishment are contained in Art.43 EC   **19–07**
Treaty which, as well as prohibiting restrictions on the freedom of establishment, provides that such freedom is to include "the right to take up and pursue activities as self-employed persons and to set up and manage
undertakings, in particular companies or firms". The Community law provisions are discussed in detail in Chapter 8. As has been held by the ECJ, the
Community concept of establishment is a very broad one, allowing
Community nationals "to participate, on a stable and continuous basis, in the
economic life of a Member State other than his State of origin and to profit
therefrom, so contributing to economic and social interpenetration within
the Community in the sphere of activities as self-employed persons".[5]

As can immediately be seen the definition of establishment contained in the   **19–08**
Bulgaria and Romania Agreements is all but identical to that contained in the
EC Treaty. In *Jany*,[6] the ECJ considered the identically worded definition of
establishment contained in the Czech and Polish Association Agreements[7] in
the context of Polish and Czech nationals carrying out economic activities as
prostitutes in the Netherlands. The national court asked whether under the
Czech and Polish Agreements the economic activities as self-employed persons there referred to were "different in meaning and scope from the activities as self-employed persons referred to in Art.52 of the Treaty [now Art.43
EC Treaty], so that the activity of prostitution carried on in a self-employed
capacity falls within the latter expression but not the former".[8]

In concluding that there was no difference in meaning between the two, the ECJ   **19–09**
emphasised that there was nothing in the context or purpose of the Agreements
to suggest any intention to give the expression "economic activities as self-
employed persons" any meaning other than its ordinary meaning in
Community law.[9] Nor was there anything in the agreements to suggest any
intention to limit the freedom of establishment conferred to one or more categories of self- employed activity. Thus the Agreements were to be construed "to
the effect that the economic activities as self-employed persons referred to in [the
Agreements] have the same meaning and scope as the activities as self-employed
persons referred to in Art.52 of the Treaty [now Art.43 EC Treaty]".

Although the concept of establishment in the Agreements and the EC Treaty   **19–10**
is thus the same, this does not mean that the interpretation of Art.43 EC
Treaty can in all respects be extended to the Europe Agreements. This is clear

---

[5] Case C-55/94 *Gebhard v Consiglio dell'Ordine degli Avvocati e Procuratori di Milano* [1995]
E.C.R. I-4165, para.24.
[6] Case C-268/99 *Jany v Staatssecretaris van Justitie* [2001] E.C.R. I-8615.
[7] See Art.44.4 of each Agreement.
[8] Case C-268/99 *Jany v Staatssecretaris van Justitie* [2001] E.C.R. I-8615, para.32.
[9] See Case C-268/99 *Jany v Staatssecretaris van Justitie* [2001] E.C.R. I-8615, para.37. Namely,
economic activities carried on by a person outside any relationship of sub-ordination with
regard to the conditions of work or remuneration and under his own personal responsibility.

from the decisions of the ECJ in *Kondova*,[10] *Gloszczuk*[11] and *Barkoci and Malik*[12] in which the ECJ interpreted the scope of the non-discrimination provision in the Europe Agreements.[13] In particular as regards the conferral of rights of entry and residence as corollaries of the right of establishment. The rights of entry and residence are considered in detail below in Chapter 20. For present purposes, it suffices to note that the ECJ did not accept the argument, based on the equivalence of the establishment rights in each of the Agreements and the EC Treaty, that the application of national immigration measures was in itself liable to render ineffective the rights granted to the beneficiaries of the Agreements.

(b) *Direct Effect of the Establishment Provision*

19–11   The principal effect of Art.45(1) of the Bulgaria and Romania Agreements (read together with Art.45(5) defining establishment), is to prohibit discrimination on grounds of nationality by Member States against Bulgarian and Romanian nationals who wish to pursue economic activities as self employed persons in Member States or to set up and manage undertakings there.

19–12   The ECJ first considered whether such provisions have direct effect in *Kondova*,[14] *Gloszczuk*[15] and *Barkoci and Malik*.[16] The ECJ held that the provisions did indeed have direct effect. The provisions contained a clear and precise obligation, notwithstanding the fact that in accordance with the provisions of each Agreement Member States remain competent to apply national laws regarding (for example) entry, stay and establishment.[17] The ECJ gave two reasons for its conclusion on direct effect. Firstly assisted in *Kondova*:[18]

> "Article 44(3) lays down, in clear, precise and unconditional terms, a prohibition preventing Member States from discriminating, on grounds of their nationality, against, inter alia, Bulgarian nationals wishing to pursue, within the territory of those States, economic activities as self-employed persons or to set up and manage undertakings there which they would effectively control".

---

[10] Case C-235/99 *R. v Secretary of State for the Home Department Ex p. Kondova* [2001] E.C.R. I-6427.

[11] Case C-63/99 *R. v Secretary of State for the Home Department Ex p. Gloszczuk and Gloszczuk* [2001] E.C.R. I-6369.

[12] Case C-257/99 *R. v Secretary of State for the Home Department, Ex p. Barkoci and Malik* [2001] E.C.R. I-6557.

[13] Although the ECJ examined the Bulgarian, Polish and Czech Agreements, they are in all material respects the same as the right given to Bulgarian and Romanian nationals by Art.45(1) of the Bulgaria and Romania Agreements.

[14] Case C-235/99 *R. v Secretary of State for the Home Department Ex p. Kondova* [2001] E.C.R. I-6427.

[15] Case C-63/99 *R. v Secretary of State for the Home Department Ex p. Gloszczuk and Gloszczuk* [2001] E.C.R. I-6369.

[16] Case C-257/99 *R. v Secretary of State for the Home Department, Ex p. Barkoci and Malik* [2001] E.C.R. I-6557.

[17] Art.59(1) of each Agreement refers.

[18] Case C-235/99 *R. v Secretary of State for the Home Department Ex p. Kondova* [2001] E.C.R. I-6427, para.33. See to like effect para.32 in Case C-63/99 *R. v Secretary of State for the Home Department Ex p. Gloszczuk and Gloszczuk* [2001] E.C.R. I-6369 and para.34 of Case C-257/99 *R. v Secretary of State for the Home Department, Ex p. Barkoci and Malik* [2001] E.C.R. I-6557.

Secondly, the discrimination prohibition was not subject to any need for fur-   **19–13**
ther implementing measures in order for it to be relied on. Thus the rule of
equal treatment could be relied on by individuals before national courts
which could be requested to set aside discriminatory provisions making the
establishment of Europe Agreement' nationals subject to conditions not
imposed by Member States on their own nationals.

The ECJ's finding was not invalidated by examination of the purpose and   **19–14**
nature of the Association Agreement,[19] nor by the fact that the Agreement
involves "an imbalance in the obligations assumed by the Community
towards the non-member country concerned."[20]

(c) Consequences of the Provisions Having Direct Effect

As is made clear in Chapter 2, the consequence of a provision's, having direct   **19–15**
effect is that it grants rights to natural and legal persons that can be relied
upon before the national courts and authorities of the Member States regardless of any other provisions in domestic law. In the present context this is the
case notwithstanding the fact that the authorities of Member States remain
competent to apply to Bulgarian and Romanian nationals their own national
laws ands regulations regarding entry, stay and establishment in accordance
with Art.59(1) of each Agreement. This means that even if a Member State
has failed to transpose the terms of the Agreements into domestic law (or has
done so incorrectly), an individual Bulgarian or Romanian national could
not be deprived of the rights given under the Agreements. Thus a Bulgarian
national who seeks to enter a Member State in order to set up a business but
who is refused entry to that Member State at a port or border can seek to
challenge relying on his directly effective right of establishment. Indeed, failure to give effect to a directly effective right could lead to a claim against the
Member State in damages.[21]

---

[19] See Case C-235/99 *R. v Secretary of State for the Home Department Ex p. Kondova* [2001]
E.C.R. I-6427, paras 35–36; Case C-63/99 *R. v Secretary of State for the Home Department Ex p.
Gloszczuk and Gloszczuk* [2001] E.C.R. I-6369 paras 34–35; and Case C-257/99 *R. v Secretary of
State for the Home Department, Ex p. Barkoci and Malik* [2001] E.C.R. I-6557, paras 35–36. By
reference to the 17th preamble recital and Art.1(2) the ECJ described the purpose as "to establish
an association designed to promote the expansion of trade and harmonious economic relations
between the Contracting Parties, in order to foster dynamic economic development and prosperity in the Republic of Bulgaria, with a view to facilitating its accession to the Community".
[20] Case C-235/99 *R. v Secretary of State for the Home Department Ex p. Kondova* [2001] E.C.R. I-
6427, para.37; Case C-63/99 *R. v Secretary of State for the Home Department Ex p. Gloszczuk and
Gloszczuk* [2001] E.C.R. I-6369, para.36; and Case C-257/99 *R. v Secretary of State for the Home
Department, Ex p. Barkoci and Malik* [2001] E.C.R. I-6557, para.37. As for the provision contained
Art.59(1) by which Member States retain competence in certain areas, in the words of the ECJ this
provides "only that the authorities of the Member States remain competent to apply, while respecting the limits laid down by the Association Agreement, their own national laws and regulations
regarding entry, stay and establishment". In particular, the provision does not concern the implementation of the provisions of the Agreement by Member States nor was it intended "to make
implementation or the effects of the obligation of equal treatment . . .. subject to the adoption of
further national measures". Case C-235/99 *R. v Secretary of State for the Home Department Ex p.
Kondova* [2001] E.C.R. I-6427, para.38; Case C-63/99 *R. v Secretary of State for the Home
Department Ex p. Gloszczuk and Gloszczuk* [2001] E.C.R. I-6369 para.37 and Case C-257/99 *R. v
Secretary of State for the Home Department, Ex p. Barkoci and Malik* [2001] E.C.R. I-6557, para.38.
[21] Joined Cases C 6&9/90 *Francovich and Bonifaci v Italy* [1991] E.C.R. I-5357.

(d) *Non-discrimination vis-à-vis Own Nationals*

19–16   For those established in a Member State under the provisions of Europe Agreements it is discrimination *vis-à-vis* own nationals which is prohibited. As much is provided in Art.45(1) which requires that Member States grant in the context of establishment "a treatment no less favourable than that accorded to its own companies and nationals".

19–17   However, as with EU nationals, there will be a difference in treatment between a Member States own nationals and those of other Member States regarding the right to enter and remain. This derives from the principle of international law which precludes a Member State from refusing the rights of entry and stay to its own nationals which the EC Treaty cannot be assumed to disregard in the context of relations between Member States. It is for this reason that a difference in treatment as compared with that of own host nationals is not incompatible with Art.45(1) of the Agreement as regards entry and stay.

19–18   Article 59(1) provides that Member States are entitled to have in place national rules regarding conditions of "entry and stay, work, labour conditions and establishment of natural persons and supply of services" (although not such as to nullify or impair the basic right of establishment[22]). However, it is important to understand that the provision does not permit discrimination in such fields, save as regards entry and stay which for reasons indicated above by their very nature will inevitably be discriminatory. To the contrary, as regards other matters, any requirement not demanded of own nationals would be discriminatory in the context of Art.45(1) since it would be treatment less favourable than that accorded to own nationals. Thus for example a condition requiring the presentation of audited accounts to the authorities of a Member State by Bulgarian and Romanian nationals irrespective as to the size of an undertaking would be unlawful and discriminatory if not demanded of own nationals.

3. THE RIGHT OF ESTABLISHMENT FOR PERSONS

(a) *Establishment Through Self-employed Activities*

19–19   The right of establishment given by Art.45(1) of each Agreement allows Bulgarian and Romanian nationals to establish themselves in EU Member States by taking up and pursuing economic activities as self-employed persons. This is clear from Art.45(5)(a)(i) of each Agreement which defines "establishment" as meaning "the right to take up and pursue economic activities as self employed persons". As stated above, the ECJ has noted that there is nothing in the context or purpose of the Agreements to suggest that there was any intention that the expression "economic activities" be given anything other than its ordinary meaning.

---

[22] See further Chapter 20.

This has important ramifications. In particular, there is no limitation on the   **19–20**
type of activity which Bulgarian or Romanian nationals, nor on the duration
for which it is required to be undertaken, nor as regards the qualifications of
the individual concerned, nor even as to the level of remuneration which can
be required by Member States of Bulgarian and Romanian nationals exercising rights of establishment. This means that subject to the requirement that
activity is effective and genuine and not marginal and ancillary, a self-
employed Bulgarian window cleaner is just as able to qualify under the
Agreements as a graduate IT consultant. However it is to be emphasised that
a Bulgarian or Romanian national wishing to establish himself will be
required to comply with any obligations placed by the host Member State on
self-employed own nationals.

Moreover, although by Art.45(5)(c) "economic activities" is defined as   **19–21**
including "activities of an industrial character, activities of a commercial
character, activities of craftsmen and activities of the professions", the
notion of economic activities is not limited to those there listed. As observed
by the ECJ in *Jany*,[23] in all except the Spanish and French versions of the
texts there are words signifying (as in the English version) *in particular, inter
alia* or *especially* which, according to the ECJ in *Jany*[24] "express the unequivocal intention of the Contracting Parties not to limit the notion of economic
activities solely to the activities listed."

(b) *Establishment Through Companies or Undertakings*

Alternatively to establishment as self-employed persons, nationals of   **19–22**
Bulgaria and Romania can establish themselves in Member States by setting
up and managing companies or undertakings. Express provision is made for
this in Art.45(5)(a)(i) which identifies the right of establishment as meaning
the right "to set up and manage undertakings, in particular companies, which
they effectively control." This means that the individual must be a majority
shareholder in the company with real and effective control of its assets.
However, it should be borne in mind that there is no requirement whatsoever
that such a company provides services of a particular kind. To use the same
example given above, the window cleaner can choose to establish himself
through the vehicle of a window-cleaning company.

It should be recalled that those seeking to establish companies or undertak-   **19–23**
ings will have to comply with all company law requirements in any particular
Member State (assuming that these are requirements demanded of own
nationals). These could include requirements as to the filing of accounts, the
filing of company returns, the honouring of legal obligations by directors,
etc. Such requirements may be extremely onerous for the individual who
might more simply set up in self-employment.

For some the vehicle of a company may provide useful tax or other   **19–24**
advantages. Any such potential benefits of utilising this alternative means of
establishment are beyond the scope of this book. However, the vehicle of a

---

[23] Case C-268/99 *Jany v Staatssecretaris van Justitie* [2001] E.C.R. I-8615.
[24] Case C-268/99 *Jany v Staatssecretaris van Justitie* [2001] E.C.R. I-8615, para.46.

company cannot be used (subject to the key personnel provisions considered in Chapter 18) to provide employment for Bulgarian or Romanian nationals under the Europe Agreements since access to the labour market is specifically excluded. It is only the position of the individual with the controlling interest in the company who stands to benefit from this alternative means of establishment.

(c) *Conditions on the Exercise of the Right*

19–25   As stated expressly in the Art.45(5)(a)(i) definition of establishment, self-employment and business undertakings "shall not extend to seeking or taking employment in the labour market or confer a right of access to the labour market of another Party". Moreover, the establishment provisions contained in the Europe Agreements do not apply to those who are not exclusively self-employed. Thus for example a self-employed Bulgarian music teacher could not supplement his income by being employed in a bar in the evenings.

19–26   In light of such limitations it is important to keep in mind the essential differences between employment and self-employment in Community law. Such differences were emphasised by the ECJ in its decision in *Jany*.[25] The Netherlands and Belgian Governments argued that prostitution could not be treated as an activity performed in a self-employed capacity under the Polish and Czech Agreements because of the impossibility of determining whether a prostitute has voluntarily moved to the host Member State or pursues her activities there freely. Although prostitution gave an appearance of independence (because the criminal prohibition of procuring means that any employment relationships must be organised illegally), it was argued that prostitutes are normally in a subordinate position in relation to a pimp.[26]

19–27   The essential characteristic of an *employment* relationship is that for a certain period of time a person performs services for and under the direction of another person in return for remuneration.[27] Thus, as emphasised in *Jany*, "any activity which a person performs outside a relationship of subordination must be classified as an activity pursued in a *self-employed* capacity".[28] The ECJ in *Jany* recognised the difficulties faced by the Netherlands' authorities when carrying out checks on Polish and Czech nationals wishing to become established for the purpose of engaging in the activity of prostitution. However, it could not be assumed that all such activity implies that the person concerned is in a disguised employment relationship thereby justifying rejection of an application for establishment solely on the ground that the activity is generally exercised in an employed capacity. The Netherlands Government had not provided support for the presumption that a person engaged in prostitution whose freedom was restricted by her pimp was to be treated as a person in an employment relationship. Since nothing in the

---

[25] Case C-268/99 *Jany v Staatssecretaris van Justitie* [2001] E.C.R. I-8615.
[26] Case C-268/99 *Jany v Staatssecretaris van Justitie* [2001] E.C.R. I-8615, para.54.
[27] See Chapter 7.
[28] See para.34 (referring also to Case C-107/94 *Asscher v Staatssecretaris van Financiën* [1996] E.C.R. I-3089, paras 25 and 26).

Agreements suggests any intended limit on the freedom of establishment to one or more categories of activities, such a result "would be at variance with the intention of the Contracting Parties to [the] Agreements."[29]

In *Jany*,[30] the ECJ did not decide whether the prostitutes were carrying out activities in a self-employed capacity. This would be a matter for the national court to determine, dependent on whether in each case prostitution was being carried on: **19–28**

(a)   outside any relationship of subordination concerning the choice of that activity, working conditions and conditions of remuneration;

(b)   under that person's own responsibility; and

(c)   in return for remuneration paid to that person directly and in full.

It is to be stressed, however, that in determining these matters the national court is considering whether a person is carrying out activity in a self-employed capacity through the eyes of Community law. National definitions or distinctions between employment and self-employment may not necessarily coincide with Community ones. In the United Kingdom, for example, attempts have been made by the tax authorities to define builders as employees for tax purposes, and the same is true for mini-cab drivers. However, whether such a builder or mini-cab driver is in fact an employee or self-employed for the purposes of the Europe Agreements is a matter to be determined by reference to Community law and to the individual's specific circumstances. It is certainly not answered on the basis of the characterisation by the tax authorities of a Member State of a particular class of person as an employee. Thus a Member State could not treat every Bulgarian builder as an employee just because this suited its tax rules to do so.   **19–29**

(d) *Nature of Activities*

As shown by *Jany*, there is no limitation on the nature or scope of activities which can (at least potentially) constitute self-employment. However, as in the case of work in a relationship of employment, the economic activity undertaken must be "genuine and effective and not such as to be regarded as purely marginal and ancillary."[31] The meaning of these phrases is discussed in detail in Chapter 7. Certainly activities cannot be excluded from the sphere of self-employment for the purposes of the Agreements merely for reasons of public morality. This is clear from *Jany* where the ECJ rejected the argument that prostitution could not be regarded as self-employment for reasons of public morality or because it would be difficult to control whether prostitutes are acting freely and not parties to disguised employment relationships.   **19–30**

---

[29] Case C-268/99 *Jany v Staatssecretaris van Justitie* [2001] E.C.R. I-8615, para.69.
[30] Case C-268/99 *Jany v Staatssecretaris van Justitie* [2001] E.C.R. I-8615, para.70.
[31] Case C-268/99 *Jany v Staatssecretaris van Justitie* [2001] E.C.R. I-8615, para.33.

19–31   Although the national court asked whether the illegal nature of activity took it outside the scope of the Agreement, the ECJ did not have to answer that question as it found prostitution in the Netherlands was not illegal. Community law would not recognise a free movement right for persons to engage in criminal activities. In this respect the most important feature of *Jany* was that the Netherlands both regulates prostitution and permits it to be carried out without sanction. Where own nationals are thus permitted to perform an activity, Community law will (in the context of the Europe Agreements) protect the rights of Bulgarian and Romanian nationals to be treated in the same way.

19–32   The ECJ rejected the absolute proposition that prostitutes could not fall within the Agreements. As to *immorality*, the ECJ emphasised both that it was not for the Court to substitute its own assessment for that of the legislatures of the Member States where an allegedly immoral activity is practised legally.[32] Further, far from being prohibited in all Member States, prostitution is "tolerated, even regulated, by most of those States, notably the Member State concerned in the present case".[33]

19–33   The ECJ acknowledged the possibility of derogation from the application of the provisions of the Agreements governing establishment "on grounds of, *inter alia*, public policy".[34] However, use of a public-policy derogation presupposes a genuine and sufficiently serious threat affecting one of the fundamental interests of society. Moreover, whilst Community law does not impose "a uniform scale of values" as regards the assessment of conduct which may be considered to be contrary to public policy, conduct cannot be considered to be sufficiently serious so as to justify restrictions on entry or residence in a Member State if such state "does not adopt, with respect to the same conduct on the part of its own nationals, repressive measures or other genuine and effective measures intended to combat such conduct".[35]

(e) *The Right of Establishment of Companies*

19–34   Article 45(1) also provides a right of establishment for Bulgarian or Romanian companies wishing to establish themselves in the territory of the Member States. Just as with Bulgarian and Romanian nationals wishing to establish themselves, they are to be treated in a non-discriminatory manner and no worse than companies of the Member States themselves.

19–35   Article 45(5)(a)(i) defines the right of establishment for companies as being the right to take up and pursue economic activities by means of the setting up and management of subsidiaries, branches and agencies. Establishment of

---

[32] At para.56 (referring, with regard to abortion, to Case C-159/90 *Society for the Protection of Unborn Children Ireland* [1991] E.C.R. I-4685, para.20, and, with regard to lotteries, Case C-275/92 *HM Customs and Excise v Schindler* [1994] E.C.R. I-1039, para.32).
[33] Case C-268/99 *Jany v Staatssecretaris van Justitie* [2001] E.C.R. I-8615, para.57.
[34] Case C-268/99 *Jany v Staatssecretaris van Justitie* [2001] E.C.R. I-8615, para.58.
[35] Case C-268/99 *Jany v Staatssecretaris van Justitie* [2001] E.C.R. I-8615, para.60.

companies in Community law is described in more detail in Chapter 8. As with nationals, there is no restriction on the type of economic activity that may be undertaken. The same limitations that apply to persons wishing to establish themselves apply equally to companies.[36] In order to give effect to the right of establishment for companies there are provisions on the deployment of key personnel by the company. Such provisions are considered in Chapter 18.

(f) Limitations on the Exercise of the Right of Establishment

(i) Sectoral and Transitional Limitations

The establishment provision does not apply at all in certain sectors, whilst in others the provision does not apply during a transitional period (now over in relation to Romania and in relation to Bulgaria to expire in February 2005). With the exception of the provisions "relating to real-estate property"[37] it is the reciprocal right enjoyed by Community nationals and companies to establish themselves *in Bulgaria and Romania* which is subject to the greatest limitations. This is reflective of the fact that the Agreements are intended essentially to promote the economic development of Bulgaria and Romania and that each "therefore involves an imbalance in the obligations assumed by the Community towards the non-member country concerned".[38]   **19–36**

However, Art.52 of each Agreement provides that the establishment provisions shall not apply "to air transport services, inland-waterways transport services and maritime cabotage transport services." This limitation on the right of establishment applies in the services specified whether in Bulgaria, Romania or Member States. In terms of its applicability to all parties of the Agreements a similar limitation is to be found in Art.54(2) of each Agreement which provides that the establishment provisions shall not apply "to activities which in the territory of each Party are connected, even occasionally, with the exercise of official authority".   **19–37**

(ii) Derogation by Bulgaria and Romania

A further example of the imbalance in the obligations assumed by the Community towards Bulgaria and Romania is the ability of both countries   **19–38**

---

[36] See paras 19–25 to 19–33 above.
[37] Annex XVa of Bulgaria Agreement and Annex XVI of Romania Agreement.
[38] Case C-235/99 *R. v Secretary of State for the Home Department Ex p. Kondova* [2001] E.C.R. I-6427, para.37. See also in relation to the Poland Case C-63/99, *R. v Secretary of State for the Home Department Ex p. Gloszczuk* [2001] E.C.R. I-6369 and in relation to the Czech Republic Case 257/99 *R. v Secretary of State for the Home Department, Ex p. Barksci and Malik* [2001] E.C.R. I-6557.

to derogate (albeit in specified circumstances and for limited periods) from the provisions of Chapter II on establishment contained in Art.51 of each Agreement as regards Community nationals and companies.[39] There is no corresponding provision enabling even limited derogation given to Member States.

---

[39] Such derogations apply if certain industries:
  - are undergoing restructuring, or
  - are facing serious difficulties, particularly where these entail serious social problems in [Bulgaria or Romania], or
  - face the elimination or a drastic reduction of the total market share held by [Bulgarian or Romanian] companies or nationals in a given sector or industry in [Bulgaria or Romania], or
  - are newly emerging industries in [Bulgaria or Romania].

CHAPTER 20

RIGHT OF ENTRY AND STAY UNDER THE EUROPE AGREEMENTS

This chapter examines the scope of the right of entry and stay for Bulgarian and Romanian nationals who seek to establish themselves in Member States under the Europe Agreements.

1. BASIC PROVISIONS

(a) *Article 59(1)*

For Bulgarian and Romanian nationals wishing to exercise establishment rights under the Agreements the most significant limitation to the exercise of such a right is that contained in Art.59(1) of each Agreement which provides as follows: **20–01**

Article 59(1)

For the purpose of Title IV, nothing in the Agreement shall prevent the Parties from applying their laws and regulations regarding entry and stay, work, labour conditions and establishment of natural persons and supply of services, provided that, in so doing, they do not apply them in a manner as to nullify or impair the benefits accruing to any Party under the terms of a specific provision of the Agreement. The above provision does not prejudice the application of Article 54.

It is this provision which is the main focus of this chapter.

(b) *The Public Policy Proviso*

Application of the establishment provisions is made subject to the public policy proviso by Art.54(1) of each Agreement which provides that "The provisions of this Chapter shall be applied subject to limitations justified on grounds of public policy, public security or public health". This is a concept well known to Community law and is considered in detail in Chapter 14 and at para. 20–44 in this Chapter   **20–02**

2. RIGHT OF ENTRY AND STAY AS A COROLLARY OF RIGHT OF ESTABLISHMENT

(a) *In General in Community Law*

It is the EC Treaty itself which is the source of the right for EU nationals to enter into and reside in the territory of other Member States.[1] In relation to   **20–03**

---

[1] The right of residence in other Member States is the corollary of the fundamental principle contained in Arts 2 and 3(1)(c) EC Treaty that, for the purpose of establishing a common market and the promotion of the harmonious development of economic activities between Member States,

workers, Art.39(3) EC Treaty refers *expressly* to the rights to move freely within and to stay in Member States for employment. By contrast Art.43 EC Treaty dealing with establishment is *silent* as to a right of residence as such. However, the ECJ recognises the right of entry and stay as corollary of right of establishment under the EC Treaty despite the absence of express reference to those rights.

20–04 There are important ramifications of such general propositions of Community law, notably that breaches of formalities, whether of specific provisions of the relevant directives or the national law of Member States relating to entry and stay, will not justify denial of the right of residence.[2]

(b) *Under the Europe Agreements*

(i) *Introduction*

20–05 How then does the general Community law principle identified above translate into the Bulgaria and Romania Agreements? As provided in Art.59(1) of each Agreement, Member States may apply their own national laws and regulations regarding, *inter alia*, the "entry and stay" of those exercising establishment rights under the Agreements. However this is subject to the caveat that Member States do not apply their national laws in a manner such as to "nullify or impair" the benefits accruing under the Agreements. There is no parallel or similar provision in Community law although that is not to say that Member States cannot, for example, require visas of third country family members of those exercising Treaty rights.[3]

20–06 In fact Art.59(1) is on its face a somewhat curious provision since it gives with the one hand (namely the right of Member States to control by provisions of national law the entry and stay of Bulgarian and Romanian nationals) what it apparently takes away with the other (namely the caveat that such controls must not nullify or impair the rights being relied on).

---

obstacles to the free movement of persons between Member States shall be abolished. Plainly this would be impossible without the right to enter into and reside in other Member States.
[2] Case 48/75 *Procureur de Roi v Royer* [1976] E.C.R. 497. See also for example Case C-370/90 *Queen v Immigration Appeal Tribunal Ex p. Surinder Singh* [1992] E.C.R. I-4265 where (at para.17) the ECJ refers to the right to enter and reside in the territory of other Member States in order to pursue an economic activity there as envisaged by Arts 39 and 43 as a right which such persons "derive directly from ... the Treaty".
[3] See generally Dir. 68/360, Art.3 and Chapter 11 above.

(ii) *Rights of Entry and Stay as a Corollary of Right of Establishment Under the Europe Agreements*

Kondova,[4] *Gloszczuk*[5] and *Barkoci and Malik*[6] were the first cases brought **20–07** before the ECJ on the Europe Agreements. It was argued that the right of establishment in the Europe Agreements was equivalent to that contained in the EC Treaty, and in particular that the absence of any reference to a right of residence in the wording of Art.52 EC Treaty (now Art.43 EC Treaty) had not prevented the ECJ from ruling that such provision conferred directly on the nationals of a Member State the right to enter the territory of another Member State and to remain there, irrespective of whether leave to remain has been granted by the host Member State.[7]

The ECJ agreed with the submission—but only up to a point. The ECJ stated **20–08** that, in the context of the interpretation of the establishment right in the provisions of both the EC Treaty and the Association Agreements, the similarity of wording did indeed mean that:

> "rights of entry and residence, as corollaries of the right of establishment, are conferred on [Association Agreement] nationals wishing to pursue activities of an industrial or commercial character, activities of craftsmen, or activities of the professions in a Member State."[8]

---

[4] Case C-235/99 *R. v Secretary of State for the Home Department Ex p. Kondova* [2001] E.C.R. I–6427. Ms Kondova was a Bulgarian national who initially entered the UK as an agricultural worker, then claimed asylum and thereafter applied under the provisions of the Bulgaria Agreement to remain to establish herself in a business offering general household care having started to work as a self-employed cleaner. However she was treated as an illegal entrant (having misled the authorities when she obtained her agricultural visa in Bulgaria and when she was questioned by an immigration officer on arrival in the UK since she had always intended to seek asylum) and was therefore in the UK unlawfully when she sought to invoke her establishment rights.

[5] Case C-63/99 *R. v Secretary of State for the Home Department, Ex p. Gloszczuk and Gloszczuk* [2001] E.C.R. I–6369. Mr and Mrs Gloszczuk were a Polish couple given entry to the UK as tourists in 1989 and 1991 who remained beyond the six months originally given and were therefore in the UK unlawfully when Mr Gloszczuk claimed to have become established as a self-employed building contractor and applied in January 1996 to regularise their stay under the establishment provisions of the Polish Agreement.

[6] Case C-257/99 *R. v Secretary of State for the Home Department Ex p. Barkoci and Malik* [2001] E.C.R. I–6557. These cases concerned Czech nationals, each refused asylum seekers who applied thereafter to establish themselves under the Czech Agreements (respectively as a gardener and domestic cleaner). At time of application each was lawfully present in the UK. The UK immigration officers—in deciding whether to *waive* the UK's mandatory prior entry clearance requirement—considered whether each "clearly and manifestly" satisfied the other conditions laid down in the immigration rules but refused both applications. Each was refused: the immigration officers were not satisfied as to the financial viability of the businesses or that each intended to carry them on in a genuinely self-employed capacity.

[7] Case C-235/99 *R. v Secretary of State for the Home Department Ex p. Kondova* [2001] E.C.R. I–6427, para.44; *R. v Secretary of State for the Home Department, Ex p. Gloszczuk and Gloszczuk* [2001] E.C.R. I–6369, para.43; *R. v Secretary of State for the Home Department Ex p. Barkoci and Malik* [2001] E.C.R. I–6557, para.45.

[8] Case C-235/99 *R. v Secretary of State for the Home Department Ex p. Kondova* [2001] E.C.R. I–6427, para.50; *R. v Secretary of State for the Home Department, Ex p. Gloszczuk and Gloszczuk* [2001] E.C.R. I–6369, para.43; and *R. v Secretary of State for the Home Department Ex p. Barkoci and Malik* [2001] E.C.R. I–6557, para.45. It is noteworthy that the ECJ's conclusion in this respect (namely that the right of establishment entails a right to enter and reside in the Member States) did not follow A.G. Mischo or A.G. Alber who had argued that nationals from the States party to the Association Agreements could not derive any right of entry and residence from those Agreements (Opinion of A.G. Mischo in *Barkoci and Malik*, paras 64 and 115 and the Opinion of A.G. Alber in *Gloszczuk*, paras 85 and 94).

20–09 According to the ECJ[9] the right "to take up and pursue economic activities not coming within the labour market presupposes that that person has a right to enter and remain in the host Member State." However, the rights of entry and residence are not absolute privileges. As the ECJ made clear, the rights of entry and residence flowing from the rights of establishment under the Europe Agreements were not equivalent to those flowing from the establishment provision in the Treaty. The reasons for this view were as follows.

20–10 Firstly, a mere similarity in wording was not sufficient to give the wording in the Europe Agreements the same meaning as it has in the Treaties. Of considerable importance is the aim pursued by each provision in its own particular context. Whereas the Association Agreements are designed "simply to create an appropriate framework for ... gradual integration into the Community, with a view to ... possible accession", the purpose of the EC Treaty by contrast is "to create an internal market, establishment of which involves the abolition, as between Member States, of obstacles to the free movement of goods, persons, services and capital."[10]

20–11 Secondly, Art.59(1) of the Europe Agreements makes clear that the rights of entry and residence as corollaries of the right of establishment are not "absolute privileges". As stated by the ECJ in *Kondova*:[11]

> "It also follows from the wording of Article 59(1) of the Association Agreement that the rights of entry and residence conferred on Bulgarian nationals as corollaries of the right of establishment are not absolute privileges, inasmuch as their exercise may, where appropriate, be limited by the rules of the host Member State concerning entry, stay and establishment of Bulgarian nationals".

20–12 A third possible justification for the conclusion that the rights under the Europe Agreements are not equivalent to those flowing from the EC Treaty potentially arises from the Joint Declaration on Art.59 annexed to the Final Act of each of the Europe Agreements.[12] However the ECJ has never relied upon it despite being referred to it by at least one Advocate General.[13] It is inappropriate to treat such a declaration as having more than interpretative value.[14]

---

[9] Case C-235/99 *R. v Secretary of State for the Home Department Ex p. Kondova* [2001] E.C.R. I–6427, para.43; Case C-63/99 *R. v Secretary of State for the Home Department, Ex p. Gloszczuk and Gloszczuk* [2001] E.C.R. I–6369, para.42; and Case C-257/99 *R. v Secretary of State for the Home Department Ex p. Barkoci and Malik* [2001] E.C.R. I–6557, para.43.

[10] Case C-235/99 *R. v Secretary of State for the Home Department Ex p. Kondova* [2001] E.C.R. I–6427, para.53; Case C-63/99 *R. v Secretary of State for the Home Department, Ex p. Gloszczuk and Gloszczuk* [2001] E.C.R. I–6369, para.50; and Case C-257/99 *R. v Secretary of State for the Home Department Ex p. Barkoci and Malik* Case C-257/99 [2001] E.C.R. I–6557, para.53.

[11] Case C-235/99 *R. v Secretary of State for the Home Department Ex p. Kondova* [2001] E.C.R. I–6427, para.54. See to like effect Case C-63/99 *R. v Secretary of State for the Home Department, Ex p. Gloszczuk and Gloszczuk* [2001] E.C.R. I–6369, para.51; and Case C-257/99 *R. v Secretary of State for the Home Department Ex p. Barkoci and Malik* [2001] E.C.R. I–6557, para.54.

[12] The Declaration states "The sole fact of requiring a visa for natural persons of certain Parties and not for those of others shall not be regarded as nullifying or impairing benefits under a specific commitment".

[13] Advocate General Alba in his Opinion in Case C-235/99 *R. v Secretary of State for the Home Department Ex p. Kondova* [2001] E.C.R. I–6427 relied on the declaration which he says forms part of the Agreement. The ECJ however do not refer to the declaration and certainly did not accept the A.G.'s analysis on rights of entry and residence.

[14] Reference is made to the Joint Declaration by the Advocate General in his Opinion in Case C-327/02 *Panayatova v Minister voor Vreemdelingenzaken en Integratie*, February 19, 2004, (at

(iii) Consequences of Conditional Nature of Rights of Entry and Stay

Since the rights of entry and stay are *not* absolute privileges, an individual   20–13
who seeks to rely on the right of establishment under a Europe Agreement
may be required to comply with national law provisions laid down by
Member States as a condition precedent to the exercise of such rights. There
are plainly competing tensions at issue. The decisions in *Kondova*,[15]
Gloszczuk[16] and *Barkoci and Malik*[17] make clear that the right of establishment be used to circumvent national law provisions, not enable entry for purposes other than establishment. On the other hand, any such national
provisions must not become an instrument to prevent the enjoyment of the
right of establishment by Bulgarian and Romanian nationals. There are limitations on the scope of any national law provisions which may be imposed
by Member States which are considered below.

(iv) Limitations Applied to National Law Provisions

National Law provisions are subject to the following limitations. Firstly,   20–14
national law provisions must not nullify or impair the benefits accruing under
the Agreements. Secondly, any such provisions must be susceptible to review
and procedures adopted must not impair the effectiveness of the rights arising under the Europe Agreements. Finally, any such measures must be consistent with the fundamental rights and general provisions of law to which
Member States are subject when acting within the scope of Community law.

Measures Must Not Nullify or Impair Rights Given

The limitation that measures must be applied so as not to nullify or impair   20–15
the benefits under the Europe Agreements is to be found in Art.59(1) itself.
The ECJ has interpreted the phrase as meaning that any such provisions must
be "appropriate for achieving the objective in view" and must not, in the
context of such objective, strike at the very substance of the rights given by
making their exercise "impossible or excessively difficult."[18]

---

paras 7 and 51) as something which should be taken into account in the interpretation of the
Europe Agreements. It would inappropriate to give it more than interpretative value and even
then any interpretation could not have the effect of negating the very rights conferred by the
Europe Agreements themselves. Moreover, two things should be stressed about the Declaration.
First, the word "sole"—which it is suggested conveys the notion "without more" or "in and of
itself"—should be seen merely as emphasising the obvious, namely that the imposition of a visa
requirement will not without more nullify or impair the rights given under the Europe
Agreements. Indeed, as much is clear from Art.59(1) itself. Second, the declaration should be
read as if it included the caveat "in principle". In other words, whilst the sole fact of requiring a
visa will not in principle nullify or impair rights, this does not mean this could never happen.
[15] Case C-235/99 *R. v Secretary of State for the Home Department Ex p. Kondova* [2001] E.C.R.
I–6427.
[16] Case C-63/99 *R. v Secretary of State for the Home Department, Ex p. Gloszczuk and Gloszczuk*
[2001] E.C.R. I–6369.
[17] Case C-257/99 *R. v Secretary of State for the Home Department Ex p. Barkoci and Malik* [2001]
E.C.R. I–6557.
[18] Case C-235/99 *R. v Secretary of State for the Home Department Ex p. Kondova* [2001] E.C.R.
I–6427, para.59; Case C-63/99 *R. v Secretary of State for the Home Department, Ex p. Gloszczuk
and Gloszczuk* [2001] E.C.R. I–6369, para.56; and Case C-257/99 *R. v Secretary of State for the
Home Department Ex p. Barkoci and Malik* [2001] E.C.R. I–6557, para.59.

20–16 The precise meaning of this limitation was considered by the Advocate General in *Panayatova*.[19] As stated by the Advocate General "the test to be applied requires . . . that the national measures capable of hindering the exercise of the right of establishment provided for in the Association Agreements should not affect the very substance of the right". The impact on the substance of the right will be assessed in light of the objectives pursued by the national measures. An assessment will be required to be made as to the appropriateness of any measures or their adequacy in terms of means and ends.

Measures to be Susceptible to Review Without Impairing Effectiveness

20–17 Any national law measures must be susceptible to review by the courts and not impair the effectiveness of the right of establishment. This flows from the fact that the rights of establishment under the European Agreements have direct effect. As stated by the Advocate General "inherent in the recognition of direct effect is an idea of effectiveness and judicial protection of the individual rights granted to individuals".[20]

Measures to be Consistent with Fundamental Rights and General Principles of Law

20–18 Any national measures must be consistent with the fundamental rights and general principles of law to which Member States are subject when acting within the scope of Community law. It is a general principle of Community law that when applying or derogating from the rules provided for in agreements between the Community and third countries, Member States must act in accordance with the principles of Community law.[21] Thus Member States and their national courts must observe (and not simply take into account) the fundamental rights applicable in the Community legal order, such as the right to respect for family life or the right to effective judicial protection. Indeed, in *Kondova*[22] and *Gloszczuk*[23] (although surprisingly not in *Barkoci and Malik*[24]) the ECJ recognised expressly that any measures adopted would be:

> "without prejudice to the obligation to respect that national's fundamental rights, such as the right to respect for his family life and the right to respect for his property, which follow, for the Member State concerned, from the European Convention for the Protection of Human Rights and Fundamental Freedoms of 4 November 1950 or from other international instruments to which that State may have acceded".[25]

---

[19] Case C-327/02 *Panayatova v Minister vopor Vreemdelinmgenzaken en Integratie* February 19, 2004, paras 40–44.

[20] Case C-327/02 *Panayatova v Minister vopor Vreemdelinmgenzaken en Integratie* February 19, 2004, paras 36–38.

[21] See for example Case C-2/92 *The Queen v Ministry of Agriculture, Fisheries and Food, Ex p. Bostock* [1994] E.C.R. I–955.

[22] Case C-235/99 *R. v Secretary of State for the Home Department Ex p. Kondova* [2001] E.C.R. I–6427.

[23] Case C-63/99 *R. v Secretary of State for the Home Department Ex p. Gloszczuk and Gloszczuk* [2001] E.C.R. I–6369.

[24] Case C-257/99 *R. v Secretary of State for the Home Department Ex p. Barkoci and Malik* [2001] E.C.R. I–6557.

[25] Case C-235/99 *R. v Secretary of State for the Home Department Ex p. Kondova* [2001] E.C.R. I–6427, para.90 and Case C-63/99 *R. v Secretary of State for the Home Department, Ex p. Gloszczuk and Gloszczuk* [2001] E.C.R. I–6369, para.85.

Although plainly an important principle, it is unclear how this would be   **20–19**
applied in practice. The ECJ's approach to human rights has been generous
(see for example *Carpenter*[26]) and the reference by the ECJ in *Kondova* and
Gloszczuk to the rights to respect for family life and property (particularly the
latter) reflect such generosity.[27] However, there is no explanation as to how this
might work in practice—and indeed in *Barkoci and Malik* where it was apparently argued (at least in effect) that expulsion would be a disproportionate
interference with the right to respect for property which had been accumulated
during their stay,[28] the ECJ fails even to mention such human rights caveat, let
alone explain how the interference with the running of an already established
business would have effected their right to respect for their property.

Furthermore, such a caveat is difficult to reconcile with the ECJ's endorse-   **20–20**
ment of expulsion without any prior consideration of the merits of an individual's application made when unlawfully present. The ECJ must plainly
have intended Member States to be under some obligation to give consideration to claims that the implementation of any national law measure infringes
an individual's human rights.

(v) *The Use of Systems of Prior Entry Control*

To date the national law provision which has most exercised the ECJ is the   **20–21**
imposition of a mandatory visa requirement for those wishing to exercise
establishment rights under the Europe Agreements. This provides a useful
example for an examination of the compatibility of national laws with the
requirements of the Europe Agreements.

Kondova,[29] *Gloszczuk*[30] and *Barkoci and Malik*[31] concerned the United   **20–22**
Kingdom's system of prior entry control which requires those seeking to
exercise rights under the Europe Agreements to produce a visa issued to them
for entry in such capacity. Ms Kondova and Mr and Mrs Gloszczuk were
each in the United Kingdom unlawfully at the time they applied to remain
whereas Mr Bakoci and Mr Malik were lawfully present. The visa requirement is mandatory save that discretion is exercised where an application
"clearly and manifestly" satisfies the substantive establishment conditions.[32]

---

[26] Case C-60/00 *Carpenter v Secretary of State for the Home Department* [2002] E.C.R. I–6279
and Chapter 3.
[27] Case C-235/99 *R. v Secretary of State for the Home Department Ex p. Kondova* [2001] E.C.R.
I–6427, para.90 and Case C-63/99 *R. v Secretary of State for the Home Department Ex p. Barkoci
and Malik* [2001] E.C.R. I–6557, para.89.
[28] See para.75: "Mr Barkoci and Mr Malik argue further that the measure of 'expulsion from the
territory of the host Member State threatened against them in this case, despite their actual presence in the United Kingdom, is liable to interfere dramatically with their ability to run an already
established business, something which could not be said of any measure that could be imposed
on United Kingdom nationals running a similar business."
[29] Case C-235/99 *R. v Secretary of State for the Home Department Ex p. Kondova* [2001] E.C.R.
I–6427.
[30] Case C-63/99 *R. v Secretary of State for the Home Department Ex p. Gloszczuk and Gloszczuk*
[2001] E.C.R. I–6369.
[31] Case C-257/99 *R. v Secretary of State for the Home Department Ex p. Barkoci and Malik* [2001]
E.C.R. I–6557.
[32] This approach was said by the ECJ to be in accordance with the "flexible practice demonstrated by the United Kingdom authorities in this area". Moreover, the ECJ was informed at the
hearing by the UK Government that the Secretary of State "normally exercises his discretion in
regard to applications for admission for purposes of establishment, submitted pursuant to the
Association Agreement, at the point of entry to the United Kingdom".

20–23   The ECJ's principal conclusions can be summarised as follows. Firstly, the use of a mandatory visa regime is not in principle incompatible with the Europe Agreements. Secondly, where an applicant is unlawfully present in a Member State an application can be rejected solely in reliance on such person's unlawful presence. Thirdly, the same applies where a person is lawfully present, although *provided* discretion may be exercised so as to admit such person without visa who clearly and manifestly satisfies the establishment requirements.

Compatibility of the visa requirement with the Europe Agreements

20–24   It is plain that a mandatory visa requirement is a measure falling within the scope of Art.59(1) since it relates squarely to the entry and stay of those seeing to invoke the Europe Agreements. The essential question by which compatibility was determined was whether the provision nullifies or impairs the exercise of the right of establishment. This depends on whether it is appropriate for achieving the objective in view and whether in the context of such objective it strikes at the very substance of the rights given by making their exercise impossible or excessively difficult.

20–25   The ECJ held that in principle a system of prior entry control such as a mandatory visa did not nullify or impair the right of establishment. Its reasons were as follows. Given that the establishment right applies only to the exclusively self-employed, a system of prior control so as to enable the Member State to check the exact nature of the activity to be undertaken was seen by the ECJ as a legitimate aim.[33] As for the substantive requirements laid down by the United Kingdom's Immigration Rules[34] these were similarly aimed at a legitimate objective and were appropriate to ensure the achievement of such objective. Moreover in *Barkoci and Malik* the ECJ relied also on the fact that the detailed investigations required to be carried out, particularly on grounds of language, would be difficult for an immigration officer at the point of entry.[35] The ECJ held that the Immigration Rules facilitated those wishing to establish themselves and were compatible with the Agreements.[36]

Illegality and systems of prior entry control

20–26   The ECJ considered it compatible with Art.59(1) to reject an application on the sole ground that when made the applicant was residing illegally. This

---

[33] Case C-235/99 *R. v Secretary of State for the Home Department Ex p. Kondova* [2001] E.C.R. I–6427, para.61; Case C-63/99 *R. v Secretary of State for the Home Department, Ex p. Gloszczuk and Gloszczuk* [2001] E.C.R. I–6369, para.58 and Case C-257/99 *R. v Secretary of State for the Home Department Ex p. Barkoci and Malik* [2001] E.C.R. I–6557, para.62.
[34] The Immigration Rules include provisions requiring that the person "genuinely intends to take up an activity as a self-employed person without at the same time entering into employment or having recourse to public funds, and that he possesses, from the outset, sufficient financial resources and has reasonable chances of success."
[35] At para.65. The ECJ continued: "Consequently, the requirement that verification of the substantive conditions be carried out in the Czech Republic allows easier access to information concerning the situation of Czech nationals wishing to become established in the United Kingdom." This is a curious justification in light of the wide availability of interpreters at ports of entry.
[36] Case C-235/99 *R. v Secretary of State for the Home Department Ex p. Kondova* [2001] E.C.R. I–6427, para.66 and Case C-63/99 *R. v Secretary of State for the Home Department, Ex p. Gloszczuk and Gloszczuk* [2001] E.C.R. I–6369, para.63.

would be the case whether the illegality arose by reason of the making of false representations or the non-disclosure of material facts for the purpose of obtaining initial entry to that Member State on a different basis. In reaching this view the ECJ was influenced by a number of related factors. Firstly, that the effectiveness of a system of prior control rests in very large measure on the correctness of the representations made by the persons concerned when they apply for entry visas or when they arrive in the host Member State. Secondly, an applicant should not be able to rely on the clientele, business assets or funds accrued during a period of unlawful stay in order to present himself to the national authorities as a self-employed person whose rights ought to be recognised. The ECJ stated:

> "such an interpretation would risk depriving Article 59(1) of the Association Agreement of its effectiveness and opening the way to abuse through endorsement of infringements of national legislation on admission and residence of foreigners."[37]

Thus the conduct of both Ms Kondova and Mr and Mrs Gloszczuk (each   **20–27** having "got around" national controls by making false declarations) placed them "outside the sphere of protection afforded ... under the Association Agreement".[38] In their cases it was not unjustified to require them to submit fresh applications abroad without first giving *any* consideration before expulsion to the merits of their applications.[39] According to the ECJ an approach which would allow illegalities to be regularised because the substantive conditions were met would "compromise the effectiveness and reliability of the national system of prior control".[40]

The unlawfulness of an applicant's presence will in principle thus be a suffi-   **20–28** cient ground to reject an application and require the person to return to apply from abroad. At the same time, however, expulsion in these circumstances must not have the effect of nullifying or impairing the rights. In *Panayotova*,[41] for example, the Advocate General postulated the possibility of a restrictive visa policy of a Member State working as an absolute barrier to entry and residence for the purposes of establishment.[42] Further, as the ECJ itself emphasised in *Kondova* and *Gloszczuk*, the actions of a Member State must have "neither the purpose nor the effect" of striking at the very substance of the rights of entry, residence and establishment under the Europe Agreements.[43] A good example of this would be if the previous unlawful

---

[37] Case C-235/99 *R. v Secretary of State for the Home Department Ex p. Kondova* [2001] E.C.R. I-6427, paras 76–79; Case C-63/99 *R. v Secretary of State for the Home Department, Ex p. Gloszczuk and Gloszczuk* [2001] E.C.R. I-6369, paras 71–74.

[38] Case C-235/99 *R. v Secretary of State for the Home Department Ex p. Kondova* [2001] E.C.R. I-6427, para.80; Case C-63/99 *R. v Secretary of State for the Home Department, Ex p. Gloszczuk and Gloszczuk* [2001] E.C.R. I-6369, para.75.

[39] See discussion of human rights caveat.

[40] Case C-235/99 *R. v Secretary of State for the Home Department Ex p. Kondova* [2001] E.C.R. I-6427, paras 87–88 and Case C-63/99 *R. v Secretary of State for the Home Department, Ex p. Gloszczuk and Gloszczuk* [2001] E.C.R. I-6369 paras 82–83.

[41] Case C-327/02 *Panayatova v Minister vopor Vreemdelinmgenzaken en Integratie* February 19, 2004..

[42] Paras 52–53.

[43] Case C-235/99 *R. v Secretary of State for the Home Department Ex p. Kondova* [2001] E.C.R. I-6427, para.89 and Case C-63/99 *R. v Secretary of State for the Home Department, Ex p. Gloszczuk and Gloszczuk* [2001] E.C.R. I-6369, para.84.

presence in a Member State could have the effect of preventing such person from having his situation reviewed at a later time when submitting a new application.[44] Finally, any such measures must always respect human rights.

Legality and systems of prior entry control

20–29   Where by contrast a person has lawfully entered the territory of a Member State, albeit not under the Europe Agreements, the position is different. Such person must be able to make an application to remain in the host Member State which must be considered by the host Member State, as opposed to being rejected solely in reliance on the absence of a visa obtained for the specific purpose of establishment under the Europe Agreements. This ability to apply when lawfully present in a Member State was an important part of the reasoning for the ECJ's conclusion that the mandatory visa requirement was otherwise generally compatible with the Europe Agreements. As the ECJ stated in *Kondova*:[45]

> "In addition, the national legislation at issue in the main proceedings includes rules allowing a person intending to become established in the host Member State under the provisions of a Europe association agreement to request leave to remain in that State as a self-employed worker notwithstanding the fact that the person had originally been admitted for a different purpose. Consequently, provisions such as those contained in paragraphs 217 and 219 of the Immigration Rules facilitate the establishment of Bulgarian nationals in the host Member State and must be regarded as being compatible with the Association Agreements".

The ECJ however did not give the benefit of such principle to Mr Barkoci and Mr Malik. Rather the ECJ treated them in effect as illegally present. This is somewhat surprising because it could not be said of either that their application was tainted with any illegality. Each was a refused asylum seeker whose presence in the host Member State had been authorised, albeit not having been given formal entry into the territory.

20–30   The ECJ appeared unimpressed with the argument made that expulsion would interfere dramatically with their ability to run an already established business. The ECJ referred to the fiction created by a provision of the United Kingdom's domestic immigration law which meant that each were deemed not to have entered the United Kingdom and stated that in the context of a national system based on a system of prior control "temporary physical admission of that person, where he does not have entry clearance for the territory of that State, is in no way equivalent to actual leave to enter that State."[46]

20–31   For at least two reasons this is unsatisfactory. Firstly, the ECJ has in other contexts been disparaging of such fiction.[47] Secondly, although only granted

---

[44] The UK's immigration rules would certainly admit such possibility since an application for an entry clearance "should normally be refused" where an applicant has failed to observe a time limit on conditions attached to any leave or has obtained a pervious leave by deception (para.320(1) and (12) of HC 395).

[45] Case C-235/99 *R. v Secretary of State for the Home Department Ex p. Kondova* [2001] E.C.R. I–6427, para.65.

[46] Section 11(1) Immigration Act 1971. See para.77 of judgment.

[47] See for example Case C-357/98 *R. v Secretary of State for the Home Department Ex p. Yiadom* [2000] E.C.R. I–9265 in which the ECJ (at para.37) the legal fiction under national law, according to

"temporary admission", in Mr Barkoci's case this was only made subject to a prohibition on his taking employment and/or on his becoming self-employed after refusal of his establishment application. In Mr Malik's case he had *never* been subjected to such a condition. Both therefore, at least for some time, had been able during their physical presence in the United Kingdom to work and establish themselves in business lawfully.

The need for flexibility in systems of prior entry control

A system of prior control, whilst permissible under the Agreements, must have some degree of flexibility. This proposition is clear from the decision of the ECJ in *Barkoci and Malik*.[48]   **20–32**

In *Barkoci and Malik*,[49] the ECJ did not directly address the question of whether Art.59(1) would allow refusal *solely* on the ground that the applicant did not hold a current entry clearance.[50] Instead the ECJ examined whether the United Kingdom's approach appeared "on the whole" to nullify or impair the benefits accruing under the agreements. The essential question was whether the need in such cases to demonstrate that an application clearly and manifestly satisfied the substantive criteria rendered it impossible or excessively difficult for the nationals of Europe Agreement countries to exercise their establishment rights. The ECJ did not consider the United Kingdom's approach to be so flawed: **20–33**

> "Articles 45(3) and 59(1) of the [Czech] Agreement do not preclude the competent immigration authorities of the host Member State from requiring a Czech national, prior to his departure to that State, to obtain entry clearance, grant of which is subject to verification of substantive requirements relating to establishment, such as those set out in paragraph 212 of the Immigration Rules, provided that those authorities exercise their discretion in regard to applications for leave to enter for the purpose of becoming established, submitted pursuant to that Agreement at the point of entry into that State, in such a way that leave to enter can be granted to a Czech national, on a basis other than that of the Immigration Rules, if that person's application clearly and manifestly satisfies the same substantive requirements as those which would have been applied had he sought entry clearance in the Czech Republic".

In the case of applications made by persons lawfully present the necessary flexibility within any system of prior entry control must mean as a minimum that such applications are not automatically rejected but are actually examined.   **20–34**

---

which the national who is physically present in the territory of the host Member State is regarded as not yet having been the subject of a decision concerning entry" with the result that such national does not qualify for the procedural safeguards granted under Article 9 of . . . Directive [64/221] to nationals regarded as lawfully present in the territory who are the subject, of a decision refusing the issue or renewal of a residence permit, or ordering expulsion from the territory".

[48] Case C-257/99 *R. v Secretary of State for the Home Department Ex p. Barkoci and Malik* [2001] E.C.R. I–6557.

[49] Case C-257/99 *R. v Secretary of State for the Home Department Ex p. Barkoci and Malik* [2001] E.C.R. I–6557

[50] It will however have to answer this question directly in Case C-327/02 *Panayatova v Minister vopor Vreemdelinmgenzaken en Integratie* February 19, 2004, since the Dutch provision has no flexibility enabling even summary consideration to be given to applications made by those lawfully present but who do not hold visas.

The decision of the Advocate General in Panayatova

20–35   *Panayotova*[51] involved Bulgarian, Slovak and Polish women present in the Netherlands who sought to establish themselves there as self-employed prostitutes. The Bulgarians were unlawfully present since at time of entry they did not have visas as required; the Slovak and Polish nationals on the other hand were lawfully present because they did not require visas. But under Dutch law such applications would be examined *only* if the alien has a valid temporary residence permit applied for abroad. According to the Advocate General neither the provisions, nor any administrative arrangements under which they were applied, allowed for the possibility of waiver.

20–36   *Panayatova* deals directly with the question not answered by the ECJ in *Barkoci and Malik*[52] because, according to the Advocate General, the Dutch system of prior control has no such flexibility. However, the Netherlands Government argued that automatic refusal was essential in order to guarantee the effectiveness of the system. As pointed out by the Advocate General a measure, such a system of prior control, must be appropriate and not excessive as regards the cost imposed on those seeking to exercise their right of establishment. Moreover a relationship had to exist between the alleged purpose of the measure and the means it establishes to pursue it.

20–37   The Advocate General did not consider these tests satisfied. The means used by the Netherlands imposed a substantial burden on applicants: though lawfully present they are forced to leave and to initiate a new process of application in their country of origin or residence without any consideration of their individual circumstances. The Netherlands authorities had failed to put forward convincing grounds to justify their system of automatic rejection beyond the presentation of automatic refusal as necessary to guarantee the effectiveness of a system of prior control recognised by the ECJ as permissible in *Barkoci and Malik*. But this failed to appreciate both that the ECJ's acceptance of a system of prior control in *Barkoci and Malik* was only acceptance "in principle" and that it was linked to the need for flexibility. The Advocate General stated:

> "I cannot find any legitimate purpose for a system such as that under the Netherlands rules which refuses to assess any application that is not preceded by a temporary residence permit to be obtained in the country of origin or residence. The Netherlands has not demonstrated why a system that imposes such a high burden on applicants for establishment from the Associated States lawfully present in the Union is appropriate to pursue a distinct legitimate aim recognised by the Association Agreements."

---

[51] Case C-327/02 *Panayatova v Minister vopor Vreemdelinmgenzaken en Integratie* February 19, 2004.
[52] Case C-257/99 *R. v Secretary of State for the Home Department Ex p. Barkoci and Malik* [2001] E.C.R. I-6557.

3. FORMALITIES

There are no formalities laid down in the Europe Agreements themselves   **20–38**
equivalent to those laid down in secondary legislation relating to the free
movement of EU nationals (such as those contained in Directive 68/360).
Article 59(1) of the Europe Agreements plainly permits Member States to
have in place laws and procedures regarding entry and residence for those
establishing themselves under the Agreements. However as the discussion on
visa requirements demonstrates, Member States do not have *carte blanche* to
impose any conditions that they wish on potential applicants. Whilst the
reviewing the UK Immigration Rules, the ECJ indicated that rules designed
to enable the Member State to verify that "the applicant genuinely intends to
pursue in that Member State a viable activity as a self-employed person" will
be compatible with the Europe Agreements.[53]

Europe Agreement nationals are not permitted to seek employment and will
have no right flowing from Community law to obtain social security benefits.
Further in order to satisfy the Community test of "establishment", such
nationals must demonstrate that they will be engaged in genuine and effective
economic activities (which are not marginal or ancillary). In view of these
requirements, it will be legitimate for Member States to require evidence from
applicants demonstrating matters, including that their businesses are viable,
that in the interim they have sufficient funds to avoid becoming burdens on
the social security system of the host Member State and that they will not
seek employment.

Delay in processing applications made abroad

In Chapter 11 consideration was given to the time limits within which both   **20–39**
visas and residence permits should be issued to EU nationals exercising
Treaty rights and their family members. A similar approach should be taken
to Bulgarian and Romanian nationals seeking to exercise establishments
rights under the Europe Agreements. Doubtless Member States would argue
that the processing of applications can be a complicated and time consuming
matter. However a delay of a time period approaching six months could,
depending on the circumstances and in the absence of substantial
justification on the part of a Member State, nullify or impair the right.

Albeit in the context of residence permits, Art. 5 of Directive 64/221[54] pro-   **20–40**
vides that "a decision to grant or to refuse a first residence permit shall be
taken as soon as possible and in any event not later than six months from the
date of application for the permit." This is an appropriate benchmark for the
time period within applications under the Europe Agreements should be
considered bearing in mind the equivalence of the right of establishment
under the Europe Agreements and the right contained in the EC Treaty as
expressly recognised by the ECJ in *Kondova*.

---

[53] Case C-235/99 *R v Secretary of State for the Home Department Ex p. Kondova* [2001] E.C.R.
I–6427, para.73.
[54] Dir. 64/221 of February 15, 1964 on the co-ordination of special measures concerning the
movement and residence of foreign nationals [1963–64] O.J. Spec. Ed. 117.

Refusal to consider applications

20-41 Refusal to consider applications could undoubtedly nullify or impair the right of establishment. Take for example the situation where a person's previous illegality in a Member State is treated as the ground for refusal of a later application made to that Member State. Any such refusal, especially if automatic and taken without substantive consideration of the merits of the application, would be unlawful. As the ECJ stated in *Kondova*:[55]

> "It follows that the decision by the competent authorities of the host Member State to reject an application for establishment submitted by a Bulgarian national ... because of false representations made to them or non-disclosure of relevant facts for the purpose of obtaining initial leave to enter, and the requirement that he submit, in due and proper form, a new application for establishment on the basis of that Agreement, by applying for an entry visa to the competent authorities in his state of origin or, as the case may be, in another country, can *never* have the effect of preventing that national from having his situation reviewed at a later time when he submits that new application".

4. Family Members in the Europe Agreement

20-42 Unlike the position relating to workers, for whom express provision is made as regards family members, the establishment provisions make no mention of family members. Such silence is not necessarily surprising. The right of establishment contained in the EC Treaty itself does not refer to the right of those establishing themselves to be accompanied by family members. However the constant jurisprudence of the ECJ demonstrates the extent to which Community law recognises the importance of family life. Indeed the failure to allow family members to join the free mover will act as an obstacle to the enjoyment of the free movement right itself.

20-43 Thus in *Carpenter*[56] the ECJ stated:

> "It should be remembered that the Community legislature has recognised the importance of ensuring the protection of the family life of nationals of the Member States in order to eliminate obstacles to the exercise of the fundamental freedoms guaranteed by the Treaty ...".

Bearing in mind both the directly effective nature of the right of establishment and that as pre-accession agreements the Europe Agreements must be interpreted purposively and as closely as possible to the EC Treaty, the principle enunciated in *Carpenter* falls to be applied equally in the present context.

---

[55] Case C-235/99 *R v Secretary of State for the Home Department Ex p. Kondova* [2001] E.C.R. I–6427, para.90.
[56] Case C-60/00 *Carpenter v Secretary of State for the Home Department* [2002] E.C.R. I–6279, para.38.

5. EXCLUSION UNDER THE AGREEMENTS

(a) *Expulsion on Limited Grounds*

Application of the establishment provisions is made subject to the public pol-　**20–44**
icy proviso by Art.54(1) of each Agreement. This is a concept well known to
Community law and is considered in detail in Chapter 14. For present purposes it suffices to stress that the concepts (public policy, public security or
public health) are narrowly defined and that decisions taken on this basis
must be both strictly justified and proportionate to the objective which they
pursue.[57] Moreover, any expulsion decision must be limited to circumstances
relating to the conduct of the individual concerned.[58] This means that expulsion cannot be based on general "public interest" considerations such as the
fight against drugs or organised crime. Further any expulsion must not be
arbitrary. The most commonly used ground to justify expulsion is "public
policy". The test for whether public policy grounds exist for such measures to
be taken is that the individual poses a "genuine and sufficiently serious threat
affecting one of the fundamental interests of society."[59]

(b) *Prohibited Activities*

There is no limitation on the nature or scope of activities which can consti-　**20–45**
tute self-employment. As made clear by *Jany*[60] (in which the ECJ considered
the position of women seeking to establish themselves in self-employment in
the Netherlands as prostitutes), activities cannot be excluded from the sphere
of self-employment under the Europe Agreements for reasons of public
morality. As noted in Chapter 19 the right does not extend to establishment
to pursue criminal activities. As to public morality, the ECJ emphasised that
far from being prohibited in all Member States prostitution is "tolerated,
even regulated, by most of those States, notably the Member State concerned
in the present case."[61]

Moreover, the Art.54(1) public policy proviso could not be engaged in cir-　**20–46**
cumstances where, in respect of the same conduct on the part of its own
nationals, the Member State does not adopt repressive measures or other
genuine and effective measures intended to combat such conduct.[62] Since
window and street prostitution are both permitted in the Netherlands and
regulated there at communal level, such condition was not met in *Jany*.[63]

---

[57] Case 36/75 *Rutili v Minister of the Interior* [1975] E.C.R. 1219.
[58] Art.3(1) of Dir. 64/221, see also Case 48/75 *Royer v Belgium* [1976] E.C.R. 497.
[59] See for instance Case 30/77 *R. v Bouchereau* [1977] E.C.R. 1999.
[60] Case C-268/99 *Jany v Staatssecretaris van Justitie* [2001] E.C.R. I-8615.
[61] Case 30/77 *R. v Bouchereau* [1977] E.C.R. 1999, para.57.
[62] Case 30/77 *R. v Bouchereau* [1977] E.C.R. 1999, para.60.
[63] Case C-268/99 *Jany v Staatssecretaris van Justitie* [2001] E.C.R. I-8615.

(c) *Appeals*

20–47 It is a requirement under the Agreements that measures taken against Bulgarian and Romanian nationals must be susceptible to review by the courts so as not to impair the effectiveness of the protected rights. This flows from fact that the rights given under the Europe Agreements have direct effect.

20–48 It follows that where national law measures are taken by a Member State against a Bulgarian or Romanian national as regards matters relating to entry and stay (as would plainly be the position were a visa application refused by a post abroad, or were a decision taken at a port to refuse entry and return a person, or after entry to deport or expel a person), such person must be able to appeal against any such decision. Failure to provide such an appeal mechanism would impair the rights given under the Europe Agreements.

ASSOCIATION AGREEMENT WITH TURKEY

CHAPTER 21

INTRODUCTION TO THE ANKARA AGREEMENT

This chapter provides the background to and identifies the key provisions of the EC-Turkey Association Agreement ("the Ankara Agreement") relating to the free movement of Turkish nationals.

1. BACKGROUND TO THE AGREEMENT

As discussed in Chapter 15 above, the Ankara Agreement is one of the oldest Association Agreements. The beginning of Turkey's relations with the European Union dates to that country's application for European Community membership of July 31, 1959 immediately after Greece's application made on June 8 of the same year. After the rejection of that application the Ankara Agreement itself was signed on September 12, 1963[1] and the Additional Protocol on November 23, 1970.[2] Eventual accession of Turkey to the European Community was envisaged by the Agreement and indeed the Additional Protocol detailed a timescale of between 12 and 22 years for the establishment of the customs union and the free movement of workers.   **21–01**

However in 1987 Turkey's application to join the European Community was rejected. The timetable for the free movement of workers has long overrun. Decision 1/95 of the EC-Turkey Association Council[3] implemented the final phase of the Customs Union but makes no reference to the free movement of persons.   **21–02**

At the December 2002 Copenhagen European Council meeting it was resolved that a decision would be made in December 2004 to open accession negotiations with Turkey "without delay" if recommended by the Commission that Turkey fulfils the Copenhagen political criteria. In the meantime, EU leaders undertook to extend and to deepen co-operation on the EC-Turkey Customs Union and to provide Turkey with increased pre-accession financial assistance.   **21–03**

Large-scale Turkish labour emigration to Europe started with an agreement signed by the Turkish and West German Governments in 1961. This agreement was made at a time of economic boom in West Germany. It aimed to provide the German economy with temporary unskilled labour (known as "guest workers"), while thinning the ranks of Turkey's unemployed. It was anticipated that these workers would return to Turkey with new skills and help the development of the Turkish economy from one based on agriculture to one based on industry. Turkey signed similar agreements with other European countries, including Austria, Belgium, the Netherlands, France,   **21–04**

---

[1] [1977] O.J. L361/29 and [1973] O.J. C113/2.
[2] [1977] O.J. L361/59 and [1973] O.J. C113/17.
[3] [1996] O.J. L35/1.

and Sweden. Many of these guest workers chose instead to settle in their host Member States and to bring their families to join them. Furthermore, it was often skilled labourers who took advantage of such agreements.

21–05   Today, it is estimated that there are approximately 3.6 million Turkish nationals living abroad, of whom about 3.2 million are in European countries—a substantial increase from 600,000 in 1972.[4]

2. THE STRUCTURE AND CONTENT OF THE ANKARA AGREEMENT AND THE ADDITIONAL PROTOCOL

(a) *The Ankara Agreement*

The Ankara Agreement is divided into three Titles.

21–06   *Title I* sets out the principles of the Agreement. Articles 2 to 5 lay down three stages of the Association: a preparatory, a transitional and a final stage. Article 7 provides that the Contracting Parties should take all protective measures, whether general or particular, to ensure the fulfilment of the obligations arising under the Agreement and should refrain from any measure liable to jeopardise the attainment of the objectives of the Agreement.

21–07   *Title II* lays down the framework for the transitional stage of the Association. Under this title Art.12 provides that the Contracting Parties agree to be guided by the relevant EC Treaty provisions relating to workers. Article 13 provides similarly that the contracting parties are to be guided by the relevant EC Treaty provisions relating to the freedom of establishment and Art.14 contains the corresponding provision with regard to abolition of restrictions on freedom to provide services.

21–08   *Title III* contains the final provisions to the Agreement. Articles 22 and 23 provide for the establishment of a Council of Association comprising members of the governments of the Member States of the Community, members of the Council and the Commission and members of the Turkish Government. The Association Council has the power to take decisions in order to attain the objectives laid down by the Agreement. Article 30 provides that the Protocols annexed to the Agreement should form an integral part of it. There are financial protocols annexed to the Agreement and one additional protocol outlined below.

---

[4] Taken from Turkey: A Transformation from Emigration to Immigration By Kemal Kirisci Center for European Studies, Bogaziçi University; *www.migrationinformation.com/Profiles/ display.cfm?ID=176.*

(b) *The Additional Protocol*

The Additional Protocol is divided into four titles, relating to specific free movement areas. **21–09**

Title I relates to the free movement of goods. It contains detailed provisions regarding the transitional phase of the customs union between the European Union and Turkey.

Title II is entitled "Movement of Persons and Services". Chapter I is concerned with workers and provides a programme for the progressive implementation of the free movement of workers between Turkey and the Member States of the Community.[5] The Council of Association is empowered to decide on the rules necessary to achieve this aim. Article 39 provides that the Council of Association should adopt social security measures for Turkish workers moving within the Community and for their family members who are resident within the Community. Chapter II is concerned with the right of establishment, services and transport. Of particular importance is Art.41(1) which contains a standstill provision relating to establishment and the freedom to provide services. Article 41(2) empowers the Council of Association to adopt rules and a timetable for the progressive abolition of restrictions on freedom of establishment and the freedom to provide services. **21–10**

Title III contains provisions relating to the closer alignment of economic policies, underlining the essentially economic relationship that is formed through the Association Agreement between Turkey and the Community. **21–11**

Title IV contains the final provisions of the Protocol. Of particular interest is Art.50 which provides that in fields covered by the Protocol, the arrangements applied by the Community in respect of Turkey shall not give rise to "any discrimination between Turkish nationals or its companies". This non-discrimination provision is however extremely weak. It relates only to the equal treatment of Turkish nationals and Turkish companies. Rather than discrimination as between Turkish nationals and Turkish companies on the one hand and nationals of the host Member State on the other. Article 60 permits Turkey to take economic protective measures in the case of serious disturbances to its economy. **21–12**

3. The Objectives of the Ankara Agreement and its Protocol

As discussed in Chapter 16 above, an examination of objectives of an association agreement is very important as an aid to interpretation of the agreement. The preamble to the Ankara Agreement and indeed some of the substantive provisions of both the Agreement and its protocol demonstrate **21–13**

---

[5] Art.36.

very clear objectives, essentially that of eventual accession of Turkey to the European Community.

(a) *Preamble to the Agreement*

21–14   The preamble to the Ankara Agreement provides for the establishment of "ever closer bonds between the Turkish people and the peoples brought together in the European Economic Community." Further the Contracting Parties resolved to ensure a continuous improvement in living conditions in Turkey and in the Community through "accelerated economic progress and the harmonious expansion of trade and to reduce the disparity between the Turkish economy and the economies of the Member States of the Community". The preamble also makes reference to the objective of facilitating the accession of Turkey to the Community at a later date.

21–15   As the ECJ has itself observed by reference to the fourth recital in the preamble and Art.28 of the Ankara Agreement, the:

> "purpose of that Agreement is to establish an association designed to promote the development of trade and economic relations between the Contracting Parties, including in the area of self-employment, the progressive abolition of restrictions on freedom of establishment, so as to improve the living conditions of the Turkish people and facilitate the accession of the Republic of Turkey to the Community at a later date".[6]

These aims of the Ankara Agreement influence the manner in which the substantive provisions of the Agreement are interpreted in so far as the clear intentions of the Contracting Parties of both the economic development of Turkey and the ultimate accession to the European Union ensure that where possible provisions are given direct effect.[7]

(b) *Other Provisions in the Agreement and its Protocol*

21–16   Articles 12, 13 and 14 of the Ankara Agreement provide that the Contracting Parties agree to be guided by the relevant EC Treaty provisions relating to the free movement of the workers, freedom of establishment and the freedom to provide services. These provisions are discussed in more detail in Chapters 22 and 23 below. However they demonstrate the clear aim of the parties that Community law concepts should apply to the Agreement and that eventually full free movement of persons as provided for in the EC Treaty will be secured as between Turkey and the Member States of the Community.

21–17   Article 36 of the Additional Protocol provides a specific timetable in which the full free movement of workers was to have been achieved, although the detailed rules are left to the Council of Association to make. Although the

---

[6] Case C-37/98 *R. v the Secretary of State for the Home Department Ex p. Savas* [2000] E.C.R. 1–2927, para.53.
[7] See for instance, *R. v the Secretary of State for the Home Department Ex p. Savas* [2000] E.C.R. 1–2927.

timetable has overrun this does not undermine the general aims of the Contracting Parties to achieve that objective but rather illustrates the difficulties in negotiating and implementing international agreements with long-term aims.

No such specific timetable is provided for the abolition of restrictions on **21–18** freedom of establishment or the freedom to provide services since this is left to the Council of Association. The lack of time table itself does not undermine the general aims of the Contracting Parties to secure those freedoms between Turkey and the Community.

4. DECISIONS OF THE ASSOCIATION COUNCIL

(a) *Decisions Relating to Free Movement*

There have been a number of decisions made by the Council of Association **21–19** which relate to the implementation of objectives of the Ankara Agreement and the Additional Protocol.[8] Of principal importance in the field of free movement of persons are Council of Association Decisions 2/76, 1/80 and 3/80.

(i) *Decision 2/76*

Decision 2/76 was the first decision relevant to the question of free movement **21–20** of workers. Article 2 provided for continued employment for a Turkish worker in the same occupation after three years and free access to any paid employment after five years. Article 5 provided for priority to be accorded to Turkish nationals in the offering of employment to non-EC nationals. Article 7 provided a standstill clause, prohibiting Member States from introducing new restrictions on the conditions of access to employment for workers legally resident and employed in their territory. However the Association Council adopted this Decision as a first step for a period of four years beginning on December 1, 1976. In light of its four-year duration the provisions contained in Decision 2/76 are of historic interest, except for the standstill clause which may continue to be of relevance.[9]

(ii) *Decision 1/80*

In contrast to Decision 2/76, Decision 1/80 has no time-limit on its applicabil- **21–21** ity. Decision 1/80 entered into force on December 1, 1980. The provisions contained Decision 1/80 have been said by the ECJ to constitute "one stage further, guided by Arts 48, 49 and 50 of the Treaty, towards securing freedom of movement for workers".[10] In order to ensure compliance with that

---

[8] See for instance Dec.2/2000 of the EC-Turkey Association Council of April 11, 2000 on the opening of negotiations aimed at the liberalisation of services and the mutual opening of procurement markets between the Community and Turkey [2000] O.J. L138/28; Dec.3/2000 of the EC-Turkey Association Council of April 11, 2000 on the establishment of Association Committee subcommittees [2000] O.J. L138/28.

[9] See para. 25–10 below.

[10] Case C-434/93 *Bozkurt v Staatssecretaris van Justitie* [1995] E.C.R. I-1475.

objective, the ECJ has held that it is "essential to transpose, so far as is possible, the principles enshrined in those articles to Turkish workers who enjoy the rights conferred by Decision 1/80."[11]

21–22   The ECJ has consistently held that the specific provisions of Decision 1/80 are capable of having direct effect. In *Sevince*,[12] the ECJ held that the fact that relevant provisions of the Ankara Agreement and the Additional Protocol essentially set out a programme "does not prevent the decisions of the Council of Association which give effect in specific respects to the programmes envisaged in the Agreement from having direct effect".[13] It is not surprising that the decisions of the Association Council, and in particular Decision 1/80, have been the subject of the most litigation to date.

21–23   Of specific interest with regard to the free movement of workers is Art.6(1) of Decision 1/80 which creates rights for Turkish workers legally employed in the territory of the Member States. The ECJ has repeatedly held that Art.6(1) has direct effect. However the rights provided for in Art.6(1) only benefit those workers who fulfil the requirements in terms of legal employment, belonging to the labour force and duration of employment. This provision is discussed in detail in Chapter 22.

21–24   Article 7 provides rights for members of the worker's family who may respond to offers of employment after three years subject to the priority of EU national workers and enjoy free access to the labour market after five years. Children who have completed vocational training are able to respond to an offer of employment irrespective of the length of time for which they have been resident in the Member State. This provision is discussed in detail in Chapter 24 on family members.

21–25   Article 13 contains a standstill clause regarding the introduction of new restrictions on access to the labour market for workers legally resident and employed in the territory of the Contracting States.

(iii) *Decision 3/80*

21–26   Decision 3/80[14] aims to co-ordinate Member States' social security schemes with a view to enabling Turkish workers employed or formerly employed in the Community, members of their families and their survivors to qualify for benefits in the traditional branches of social security. Decision 3/80 refers specifically to Reg. 1408/71 on the application of social security schemes to employed persons and their families moving within the Community.

---

[11] Case C-434/93 *Bozkurt v Staatssecretaris van Justitie* [1995] E.C.R. I-1475, para.20.
[12] Case C-192/89 *Sevince v Staatssecretaris van Justitite* [1990] E.C.R. I-3461.
[13] Case C-192/89 *Sevince v Staatssecretaris van Justitite* [1990] E.C.R. I-3461, para.21.
[14] [1983] O.J. C110/60.

There is no specified date of entry into force of Decision 3/80 (unlike in **21–27**
Decision 1/80). However the ECJ has held that the date of entry into force is
the date on which it was adopted, namely September 19, 1980.

Whilst Decision 3/80 refers specifically to Reg. 1408/71, the former lacks the **21–28**
cumbersome implementing measures set out in Reg. 574/72[15] which were
deemed necessary for the implementation of Reg. 1408/71. It is for this reason that the ECJ has held that the provisions of Decision 3/80 that refer to
further implementing measures[16] do not have direct effect.

In its judgment in the case of *Taflan-Met*[17] the ECJ referred to the fact that **21–29**
the Commission had submitted a proposal for a Council Regulation implementing Decision 3/80 in 1983, which was based to a large extent on Reg.
574/72.[18] That proposal however has not yet been adopted by the Council
depriving Decision 3/80 of much of its impact.

In *Kocak*[19] the ECJ held that the non-discrimination provision Art.3(1) of **21–30**
Decision 3/80 was however capable of direct effect. Under Art.3(1), Turkish
nationals who reside in one of the Member States and to whom Decision 3/80
applies are to enjoy in that Member State the same social security benefits
under the legislation of that Member State as the nationals of that state.
According to Art.2, Decision 3/80 applies to Turkish nationals who are or
have been subject to the legislation of one of the Member States and their
family members resident in that Member State, as well as the survivors of
these workers.

The detail of the social security provisions contained in Decision 3/80 is **21–31**
beyond the scope of this book. However it is to be noted that the Council of
Association has attempted through this decision to give effect to Art.39(1) of
the Additional Protocol which directs the Council to adopt social security
measures for Turkish workers.

(b) *The Direct Effect of Decisions of the Council of Association*

Whether a provision in the decisions of the Council of Association is capa- **21–32**
ble of creating directly effective rights in Community law is of importance.
The Council of Association is specifically charged with responsibility for
making rules in relation to the progressive securing of the free movement of
persons and if those rules were not held to be directly effective, that aim
might be undermined.

---

[15] Council Reg. (EEC) No 574/72 of March 21, 1972 laying down the procedure for implementing
Reg. (EEC) 1408/71.
[16] Arts 12 and 13 of Dec.3/80 which consist of co-ordinating provisions relating to sickness and
maternity benefits, invalidity benefits, old-age benefits and death benefits (pensions).
[17] Case C-277/94 *Talfan-Met, Altun-Baser, Andal-Bugdayci v Bestuur van de Sociale
Verzekeringsbank* [1996] E.C.R. I-4085.
[18] [1972] O.J. Spec. Ed.159.
[19] Case C-102/98 *Kocak v Landesversicherungsanstalt Overfranken und Mittelfranken* and Case
C-211/98 *Ramazan v Bundesknappschaft* [2000] E.C.R. I-1287.

21–33   In principle there is no reason why a body created by an association agreement with representatives from all the Contracting Parties involved could not make decisions that are directly effective in Community law. In the context of the Ankara Agreement the ECJ has repeated the view [previously held in respect of the Greek Association Agreement] that:

> "since they are directly connected with the Agreement to which they give effect, the decisions of the Council of Association, in the same way as the Agreement itself, form an integral part, as from their entry into force, of the Community legal system".[20]

21–34   The ECJ considers that since it has jurisdiction to give preliminary rulings on the Ankara Agreement itself, it must also have jurisdiction to give rulings on the interpretation of the decisions adopted by the authority established by the Agreement and entrusted with responsibility for its implementation.[21]

21–35   It is a function of the Art.234 EC Treaty to ensure uniform application of all the provisions forming part of the Community legal system, which would include decisions by the Association Council. The ECJ's jurisdiction is thereby fortified.

21–36   Despite the clarity with which the ECJ has declared its jurisdiction both in relation to the Ankara Agreement and to the decisions of the Association Council, Member States persisted until 1992[22] in requesting the ECJ to reconsider its jurisdiction to give rulings pursuant to Art.234. The ECJ has not been prepared to relinquish its jurisdiction.

21–37   In its case law the ECJ has held Arts 6(1), 6(2), 7(1), 7(2) and 13 of Decision 1/80 to have direct effect. There is in principle no reason why any other provision of a decision of the Council of Association which is sufficiently precise and unconditional would not be capable of conferring direct effective rights on individuals.

---

[20] Case C-192/89 *Sevince v Staatssecretaris van Justitite* [1990] E.C.R. I-3461, para.9.
[21] This is of course comparable with the situation under the EC Treaty itself where provisions need specifying through regulations and directives.
[22] Case C-237/91 *Kus v Landeshauptstadt Wiesbaden* [1992] E.C.R. I-6781.

WORKERS UNDER THE ANKARA AGREEMENT

This chapter examines the rights given by the Ankara Agreement to Turkish nationals legally employed in Member States. Although Member States retain control of the entry into their labour force of Turkish nationals, once admitted to the labour force the provisions confer significant rights.

1. INTRODUCTION: THE PROVISIONS

(a) *The Ankara Agreement and Additional Protocol*

Of principal importance in the context of the free movement of workers are **22–01** Art.12 of the Ankara Agreement and Art.36 of the Additional Protocol.

Article 12

The Contracting Parties agree to be guided by Articles 48, 49 and 50 of the Treaty establishing the Community for the purpose of progressively securing freedom of movement for workers between them.

Article 36

Freedom of movement for workers ... shall be secured by progressive stages in accordance with the principles set out in Article 12 of the Agreement of Association between the end of the twelfth and the twenty-second year after the entry into force of that Agreement.
    The Council of Association shall decide on the rules necessary to that end.

Article 12 follows from the general aim of the Ankara Agreement to promote **22–02** economic relations between Turkey and the Community and the eventual accession of Turkey to the Community. It outlines an objective of the Contracting Parties to the Agreement and lays the foundation stone for the free movement of workers. The ECJ has held however that the general nature of the provision deprives it of direct effect.[1] Under Art.36 of the Additional Protocol the aim of the free movement of workers was to be achieved between November 30, 1974 and November 30, 1986.

In *Demirel*,[2] ECJ held that Art.12 of the Ankara Agreement, together with **22–03** Art.36 of the Additional Protocol, were essentially programmatic and not sufficiently precise and unconditional to be capable of governing directly the

---

[1] Case 12/86 *Demirel v Stadt Schwäbisch Gmünd* [1987] E.C.R. 3719, para.23.
[2] Case 12/86 *Demirel v Stadt Schwäbisch Gmünd* [1987] E.C.R. 3719.

movement of workers. This is partly justified by the exclusive powers conferred on the Association Council to lay down the detailed rules to achieve the aims of the provisions. The fact that the time framework set out in Art.36 of the Protocol has now long overrun has not resulted in any legal measure making the provisions of Art.12 directly effective. This is to be contrasted with the provisions of Art.48 of the Treaty of Rome where the ECJ held that the end of the transitional period set out in the Treaty did confer rights on Community workers upon which they could rely directly.[3] Whilst the ECJ has not yet examined the specific question of the implication of the expiry of the time framework for the transitional stage, Advocate General Darmon suggested in his Opinion in *Demirel*[4] that the expiry of that time framework did not create any binding effect:

> "The passage of time, has no legal implications here. Progressive implementation depends on decisions of the Council of Association. The absence of such decisions in this field, reflecting the difficulties experienced by the Contracting Parties in reaching a consensus, precludes the application of provisions without a clearly circumscribed content. Any other solution would, indeed, be incompatible with the consensual nature of an international convention".

(b) *Relevant Provisions of the Decisions of the Council of Association*

22–04 Of specific interest with regard to the free movement of workers is Art.6(1) of Decision 1/80, which provides:

> "1. Subject to Article 7 on free access to employment for members of his family, a Turkish worker duly registered as belonging to the labour force of a Member State:
>
> > –shall be entitled in that Member State, after one year's legal employment, to renewal of his permit to work for the same employer, if a job is available;
> > –shall be entitled in that Member State, after three years of legal employment and subject to the priority to be given to workers of Member States of the Community, to respond to another offer of employment, with an employer of his choice, made under normal conditions and registered with the employment services of that State, for the same occupation;
> > –shall enjoy free access in that Member State to any paid employment of his choice, after four years of legal employment."

22–05 The ECJ has repeatedly held that Art.6(1) has direct effect.[5] As stated in *Kurz*,[6] Turkish nationals who satisfy its conditions are able therefore to rely directly "on the rights which the three indents of that provision confer on them progressively, according to the duration of their employment in the host Member State." However, the rights provided for in Art.6(1) only benefit those Turkish workers who fulfil the requirements in terms of legal employ-

---

[3] Case 41/74 *Van Duyn v Home Office* [1974] E.C.R. 1337.
[4] Case 12/86 *Demirel v Stadt Schwäbisch Gmünd* [1987] E.C.R. 3719, para.23.
[5] The ECJ has consistently so held since its decision in Case C-192/89 *Sevince v Staatssecretaris van Justitite* [1990] E.C.R. I–3461 (see for example Case C-1/97 *Birden v Stadtgemeinde Bremen* [1998] E.C.R. I-7747 and Case C-188/00 *Kurz v Land Baden-Württemberg* [2002] E.C.R. I–691).
[6] Case C-188/00 *Kurz v Land Baden-Württemberg* [2002] E.C.R. I–691, para.26.

ment, belonging to the labour force and time. The full implication of the provision is discussed below.

Article 6(2) makes provision for certain absences being incorporated into **22–06** periods of legal employment (annual holidays, short periods of sickness, etc.) and for other longer absences which, although not able to be incorporated into periods of legal employment, do not affect rights already acquired. Article 6(3) provides that the procedures for applying Arts 6(1) and (2) are those established under national law.

Article 7 makes provision for members of the worker's family to be able to **22–07** respond to offers of employment after three years and to access the labour market freely after five years. Provision is also made for children who have completed vocational training to be able to respond to offers of employment, irrespective of the length of time they have been resident in the Member State.

Article 13 contains a standstill clause regarding the introduction of new **22–08** restrictions on access to the employment of workers legally resident and employed in the territory of the Contracting States.

2. The Worker's Right to Continued Employment

(a) *Introduction*

Nothing in the Ankara Agreement itself or the decisions of the Council of **22–09** Association confers rights of free movement on workers not already part of the labour force. However Art.6(1) of Decision 1/80 does provide some rights for Turkish workers. In order to benefit from those rights Turkish nationals must satisfy three conditions, namely:

(a)   they must be workers;

(b)   they must be in legal employment and duly registered as belonging to the labour force of the host Member State; and

(c)   they must fulfil the requisite time periods.

Whilst the concept of worker is one familiar to Community law, the other requirements are imposed only on Turkish nationals in the context of Art.6 of Decision 1/80.

The conditions are interconnected and overlapping. This can be potentially **22–10** confusing. For instance in *Birden*[7] the ECJ treated the condition of legal employment and being duly registered as belonging to the labour force as synonymous.[8] Despite this the test of legal employment does indeed raise discrete questions from those considered when assessing whether a person is

---

[7] Case C-1/97 *Birden v Stadtgemeinde Bremen* [1998] E.C.R. I-7747.
[8] See para.22–17 below.

duly registered as belonging to the labour force. The overlap is reflected also in the fact that since its decision in *Sevince*,[9] the ECJ has consistently stated that legal employment presupposes a stable and secure situation as a member of the labour force, thereby merging the conditions treated as synonymous by the ECJ in *Birden*. Moreover, analysis of the relevant conditions is not helped by the fact that on occasions the ECJ has conflated its consideration of the various questions. Thus for example in *Günaydin*[10] having stated that the Turkish national was "undeniably" a worker duly registered as belonging to the labour force, the ECJ then examined whether the worker was "bound by an employment relationship covering a genuine and effective economic activity pursued for the benefit and under the direction of another person for remuneration" (thereby apparently considering again questions going to whether the person was a worker).

22–11   At the heart of such confusion is the tension between, on the one hand, the wishes of certain Member States to recruit Turkish nationals to the labour force for finite periods under potentially strict conditions, and, on the other hand, the practical consequences of such recruitment giving rights to those Turkish nationals in the circumstances laid down in Art.6. This is a tension because there is no doubt that the Art.6 rights go far beyond what will have been contemplated by the Member States when granting entry and permission to work to such Turkish nationals. The tension referred to is well shown by *Günaydin* in which the German Government sought to argue that a Turkish worker was not duly registered as belonging to Germany's labour force since his employment was both temporary and for a specific employer for the purpose of preparing him to work in Turkey.

22–12   In many cases it has not been in dispute whether the Turkish national was a "worker", but only whether or not the second condition had been fulfilled. Despite such overlap each condition raises specific questions and it is therefore necessary to examine each term.

(b) *The Concept of "Worker"*

22–13   Just as in the EC Treaty there is no definition of a Community "worker", so there is no definition of a "Turkish worker" in the Ankara Agreement, its Protocol or the decisions of the Council of Association. However, the references to various EC Treaty provisions and the general commitment in the Ankara Agreement towards eventual accession of Turkey to the Community indicate that the concept of "Turkish worker" should take on the Community law definition. Such approach is further indicated by the ECJ's commitment to providing uniform and objective application of the provisions contained within the Ankara Agreement and the decisions adopted by the Council of Association and the ECJ's attempts to interpret the decisions of the Council, as far as possible, in the light of EC Treaty provisions on the freedom of movement of workers.

---

[9] Case C-192/89 *Sevince v Staatssecretaris van Justitite* [1990] E.C.R. I–3461, para.30.
[10] Case C-36/96 *Güaydin v Freistaat Bayern* [1997] E.C.R. I–5143.

In fact the ECJ has repeatedly concluded from the wording of Art.12 of the   **22–14**
Agreement and Art.36 of the Protocol, as well as from the objective of
Decision 1/80, that the principles enshrined in Arts 39, 40 and 41 EC Treaty
must be extended, so far as possible, to Turkish nationals who enjoy the
rights conferred by Decision 1/80.[11] This has meant that reference *is* made to
the interpretation of the concept of worker under Community law for the
purposes of determining the scope of the same concept employed in Art.6(1)
of Decision 1/80.

The Community concept of worker is considered in detail in Chapter 7. The   **22–15**
concept must be interpreted broadly. In order to be treated as a worker, a person must pursue an activity which is genuine and effective, to the exclusion of
activities on such a small scale as to be regarded as purely marginal and ancillary. The essential feature of an employment relationship is that for a certain
period of time a person performs services for and under the direction of
another person in return for which remuneration is received. Neither the
nature of the employment relationship under national law, nor the level of
productivity of the person concerned, the origin of the funds from which the
remuneration is paid or the limited amount of the remuneration can have any
consequence in regard to whether or not the person is a worker for the purposes of Community law.[12] The term "worker" includes trainees and apprentices, part-time workers, au-pairs and those engaged in employment schemes.
Thus any person who pursues a genuine and effective economic activity for
and under the direction of an employer and receives remuneration (whether
in cash or kind) for that activity must be regarded as a worker for the purposes
of Community law.

In line with its case law on Art.39 EC Treaty the ECJ stated in *Birden*[13] that: **22–16**

> "A Turkish national such as Mr Birden, who is employed on the basis of a law such
> as the BSHG, performs, as a subordinate, services for his employer in return for
> which he receives remuneration, thus satisfying the essential criteria of the employ-
> ment relationship . . . That interpretation is not altered by the fact that the remu-
> neration of the person concerned is provided using public funds since, by analogy
> with the case-law relating to Article 48 of the Treaty [now Art.39 EC Treaty] nei-
> ther the origin of the funds from which the remuneration is paid, nor the 'sui
> generis' nature of the employment relationship under national law and the level of

---

[11] See to that effect, *inter alia*, Case C-434/93 *Bozkurt v Staatssecretaris van Justitie* [1995] E.C.R.
I–1475, paras 14, 19 and 20; Case C-171/95 *Tetik v Land Berlin* [1997] E.C.R. I–329, paras 20
and 28; Case C-1/97 *Birden v Stadtgemeinde Bremen* para.23; Case C-340/97 *Nazli* [2000] E.C.R.
I–957, paras 50 to 55 and Case C-188/00 *Kurz v Land Baden-Württemberg* [2002] E.C.R. I–691,
para.30.
[12] See in particular Case 66/85 *Lawrie-Blum* [1986] E.C.R. 2121, paras 16 and 17; Case 197/86
Brown [1988] E.C.R. 3205, para.21; Case 344/87 *Bettray v Staatssecretaris van Justitite* [1989]
E.C.R. 1621, paras 15 and 16; Case C-357/89 *Raulin v Minnster van Onderwijs en Wetenschappen*
[1992] E.C.R. I–1027, para.10; and Case C-3/90 *Bernini v Netherlands Ministry of Education and
Science* [1992] E.C.R. I–1071, paras 14 to 17; and, as regards Art.6(1) of Dec. 1/80, Case C-36/96
Günaydin v Freistaat Bayern [1997] E.C.R. I–5143, para.31; Case C-98/96 *Ertanir v Land Hessen*
[1997] E.C.R. I–5179, para.43, Case C-1/97 *Birden v Stadtgemeinde Bremen* [1998] E.C.R. I-7747,
paras 25 and 28 and Case C-188/00 *Kurz v Land Baden-Württemberg* [2002] E.C.R. I–691,
para.32.
[13] Case C-1/97 *Birden v Stadtgemeinde Bremen* [1998] E.C.R. I-7747, paras 26 and 28.

productivity of the person concerned can have any consequence in regard to whether or not the person is to be regarded as a worker".

(c) *The Concepts of "Legal Employment" and Being "Duly Registered as Belonging to the Labour Force"*

(i) *Introduction*

22–17   At the core of the concepts of legal employment and being duly registered as belonging to the labour force are the following matters which must be established by the worker that:

(i)   His situation as a member of the labour force is stable and secure ("legal employment");

(ii)   Formal requirements have been complied with ("duly registered");

(iii) He is a member of the "labour force"; and

(iv)   The employment can be located within the territory of the Member State or retains a sufficiently close link with that territory.

(ii) *Stable and Secure Situation*

22–18   Since its decision in *Sevince*[14] the ECJ has repeatedly stated that the legality of employment (the phrase "legal employment" being repeated in each indent of Art.6(1) of Decision 1/80) presupposes a stable and secure situation as a member of the labour force. Such requirement of legal employment does not *necessarily* presuppose the possession of residence documents or even a work permit.[15] However legality of employment must be determined in the light of the legislation of the Member State governing the conditions under which the Turkish worker entered the national territory and is employed there. The worker must not, therefore, be working in breach of any legal conditions of stay or have entered on false documentation and thereby entered into employment as the result of fraudulent conduct.[16]

22–19   The requirement of stability and security means that there must be an *undisputed* right of residence: plainly any dispute as to the existence of such right would lead to instability and lack of security in the worker's situation. Thus, a Turkish worker who is only able to work by virtue of making an appeal against the refusal of a residence permit will not be considered to fulfil the requirements of legal employment. This is equally the case where a first instance judgment upholds the right of residence, but where there is retroactive suspension of the residence permit ordered by a court through the exer-

---

[14] Case C-192/89 *Sevince v Staatssecretaris van Justitite* [1990] E.C.R. I–3461, para.30.
[15] See Case C-434/93 *Bozkurtz v Staatssecretaris van Justitite* [1995] E.C.R. I–1475, paras 14, 19 and 20. The case concerned the position of a Turkish worker employed as an international lorry driver by a company incorporated under Netherlands law with its head office in the Netherlands where, in periods between journeys and during his leave, Mr Bozkurt lived. As an international lorry driver under Netherlands law Mr Bozkurt did not require either a work permit or residence permit.
[16] Case C-285/95 *Kol v Land Berlin* [1997] E.C.R. I–3069.

cise of an appeal against such first instance judgment. Further, the same would apply to a period of temporary residence given whilst an asylum claim is considered where during such period the Turkish national is permitted to work.

In *Sevince*,[17] the ECJ considered the position of a Turkish national refused a **22–20** residence permit by the Dutch authorities who sought subsequently to rely— as periods of legal employment—on time spent working whilst he benefited from the suspensive effect of his appeal against refusal of the residence permit. The ECJ refused to treat such time as periods of legal employment for the purposes of Art.6. The ECJ justified its decision refusing to recognise as periods of legal employment those periods during which the worker was legally able to continue in employment *only* because of the suspensory effect of an appeal on the basis that it was "inconceivable" that a Turkish worker should be able to "contrive to fulfil" the condition of legal employment in this manner, provided always that the court dismisses such an appeal.[18]

However, the decision of the ECJ in *Kus*[19] was undoubtedly harsher than the **22–21** decision in *Sevince*[20] since in *Kus* it was the authorities which appealed against a first instance decision to grant the residence permit. The ECJ justi- fied the decision on the basis that if the national court subsequently refused the residence permit such refusal would have "no effect whatever and the per- son in question will be enabled to contrive to obtain the rights provided by ... Article 6(1) during a period when he did not fulfil the requisite condi- tions".[21] The ECJ did however acknowledge that if the right of residence was finally granted, then the worker must be deemed retrospectively to have had during the period in question a right of residence which was not provisional but fulfilled the requirement of being "stable and secure".[22]

The reasons for a Member State allowing a Turkish national to work and **22–22** reside in its territory are not relevant to the question of whether employment is legal. As the ECJ has repeatedly stated, Art.6(1) cannot be construed so as to allow a Member State to modify unilaterally the scope of the system of gradual integration of Turkish workers which is at the heart of the Ankara Agreement and Additional Protocol. Where a Turkish worker's employment is stable and secure the legality of such employment cannot be undermined by the terms on which the right of entry was first given. This is the case not withstanding the exclusive competence of Member States to regulate both the entry of Turkish nationals into their territory and the circumstances in which they are permitted to take up first employment. This reflects the ten- sion identified at para.22–11 above. Member States may suggest that the ECJ's interpretation of Art.6 does encroach upon such competence since initial restrictions can become meaningless where after a year the Turkish

---

[17] Case C-192/89 *Sevince v Staatssecretaris van Justitite* [1990] E.C.R. I–3461, para.30.
[18] See paras 31 and 32. See also Case C-237/9 *Kus v Landeshauptstadt Wiesbaden* [1992] E.C.R. I–6781.
[19] Case C-23/91 *Kus v Landeshauptstadt Wisbaden* [1992] E.C.R. I–6781.
[20] Case C-192/89 *Sevince v Staatssecretaris van Justitite* [1990] E.C.R. I–3461, para.30.
[21] Case C-23/91 *Kus v Landeshauptstadt Wisbaden* [1992] E.C.R. I–6781, para.16
[22] Case C-23/91 *Kus v Landeshauptstadt Wisbaden* [1992] E.C.R. I–6781, para.17.

worker begins to accumulate the rights given in Art.6(1) *irrespective* of any initial limitations.

22–23   The foregoing means, for instance, that the fact that work and residence permits were granted to a worker only after his marriage to a German national does not affect the worker's rights under Art.6(1), even where the marriage is subsequently dissolved.[23] Neither does the fact that the worker was allowed to enter into the Member State to fulfil a specific labour requirement there, for example as a specialist chef, deprive the worker of his rights derived from Art.6(1).[24] Even the fact that a Turkish worker expressly accepted restrictions on his length of stay does not deprive the worker of the rights acquired under Art.6(1). The ECJ has held that the fact that a Turkish worker declared his intention of returning to Turkey after having been employed in the Member State for the purpose of perfecting his vocational skills does not deprive him of the rights deriving from Art.6(1) unless it is established by a national court that he made that declaration with the sole intention of deceiving the national authorities.[25]

(iii) *Formal Requirements*

22–24   The Turkish worker must comply with any applicable formalities required by the national law of the Member State concerned. There is obvious overlap with the concept of legal employment which as already indicated requires compliance with the national law provisions governing the conditions under which the Turkish worker enters the national territory and is employed there. In *Birden*[26] however the ECJ distinguished between the requirements of compliance with legislation governing entry into the territory and pursuit of employment there. On the facts in *Birden* the ECJ considered there to be no doubt that Mr Birden satisfied the requirements since he both legally entered and occupied a post "organised and financed by public authorities" of the Member State. The ECJ stated that being duly registered as belonging to the labour force applied "to all workers who have complied with the requirements laid down by law and regulation in the Member State concerned and are thus entitled to pursue an occupation in its territory."[27] Examples of requirements relating to the pursuit of employment could include the payment of income tax, contributions for health, pension and unemployment insurance.

(iv) *The Meaning of "Labour Force"*

22–25   Turkish nationals workers are additionally required to be members of the labour force. It is perhaps difficult to conceive of a situation in which a Turkish national who is working in a Member State in a situation which is both stable and secure and who has complied with all formalities might nev-

---

[23] As in the case of Case C-23/91 *Kus v Landeshauptstadt Wisbaden* [1992] E.C.R. I–6781.
[24] Case C-98/96 *Ertanir v Land Hessen* [1997] E.C.R. I–5179.
[25] Case C-36/96 *Gunaydin v Freistaat Bayern* [1997] E.C.R. I–5179.
[26] Case C-1/97 *Birden v Stadtgemeinde Bremen* [1998] E.C.R. I-7747, paras 48–51.
[27] Case C-1/97 *Birden v Stadtgemeinde Bremen* [1998] E.C.R. I-7747, para.51.

ertheless be able to be said *not* to be part of the labour force. The facts of *Birden*[28] however provide a useful example in this respect. Mr Birden's work as a semi skilled odd-job man with a cultural centre (which was work of a kind offered to a limited group of persons) was sponsored by the German authorities with public funds, required the payment of social security contributions and was intended to enable him to enter or re-enter working life. It was argued by the German Government that the employment—which was essentially social in nature consisting of public utility work which in other circumstances would not be carried out—was intended to improve the integration into working life of a limited group of persons unable to compete with most other job seekers. Such persons were said to be distinguishable from workers as a whole and did not belong to the Germany's general labour force. The Commission similarly argued that being duly registered as belonging to the labour force referred only to the pursuit of "a normal economic activity on the labour market, as opposed to employment created artificially and financed by the public authorities such as that undertaken by Mr Birden".

The ECJ rejected the submission in these terms:[29]   **22–26**

"Consequently, the concept of 'being duly registered as belonging to the labour force' must be regarded as applying to all workers who have complied with the requirements laid down by law and regulation in the Member State concerned and are thus entitled to pursue an occupation in its territory. By contrast, contrary to the assertions of the German Government and the Commission, it cannot be interpreted as applying to the labour market in general as opposed to a specific market with a social objective supported by the public authorities".

The "labour force" to which the Turkish worker must belong is therefore   **22–27** broadly interpreted. It matters not whether the Turkish worker can be said to be part of the general workforce, or as in *Birden*, whether the Turkish worker is part of a specific sector labour force defined by specific objectives.[30] This approach chimes with that taken in relation to legal employment whereby, as discussed above, the ECJ has made clear that the reasons for a Member State's allowing a Turkish national to work and reside in its territory are not relevant to the question of whether the employment was legal.

Whether examined as an aspect of legal employment or being a duly regis-   **22–28** tered member of the labour force the ECJ has consistently refused to accept interpretations urged upon them by some Member States which would limit access to the rights contained in Art.6(1) by reference to the nature of the employment or the original conditions on which it was given.

---

[28] Case C-1/97 *Birden v Stadtgemeinde Bremen* [1998] E.C.R. I-7747, para.51.
[29] Case C-1/97 *Birden v Stadtgemeinde Bremen* [1998] E.C.R. I-7747, para.51.
[30] See also Case C-23/91 *Kus v Landeshauptstadt Wisbaden* [1992] E.C.R. I-6781, para.43 (". . . [T]he concept of being 'duly registered as belonging to the labour force of a Member State' cannot be interpreted as applying to the labour market in general as opposed to a restricted market with a specific objective").

22–29　　In *Kurz*,[31] the ECJ again examined a submission by the German Government seeking to limit the application of Art.6(1) rights to certain types of worker (on the facts an apprentice pursuing an activity of a purely temporary and specific nature). The ECJ rejected the submission that the worker was not duly registered as belonging to the labour force since his was not a "normal employment relationship" intended to bring about his future inclusion in the labour market in general. According to the ECJ there was no doubt that Mr Kurz (who was in legal employment in Germany for four years) was a Turkish worker who had complied with Germany's legislation governing entry into its territory and pursuit of employment. An interpretation limiting the applicability of Art.6(1) to such a person (who on the facts was "just as integrated in the host Member State as a worker who has carried out comparable work for an equivalent period"[32]) would be inconsistent with the aim and broad logic of Decision 1/80.

(v) *Employment Located Within Territory or Retaining Sufficiently Close Link With That Territory*

22–30　　The ECJ has repeatedly stated[33] that being duly registered as belonging to the labour force requires that the employment relationship:

> "can be located within the territory of a Member State or retains a sufficiently close link with that territory, taking account in particular of the place where the Turkish national was hired, the territory on or from which the paid activity is pursued and the applicable national legislation in the field of labour and social security law".[34]

22–31　　The requirement has been regarded by the ECJ as invariably met in a number of decisions and, subject to the example of persons whose work is not performed *in* the Member State concerned (as in the case of for example sailors or international lorry drivers considered below), rarely causes difficulty. In *Kurz*[35] for example the ECJ described the condition as "undoubtedly satisfied" where the worker had been hired and had pursued in the course of his apprenticeship a paid activity on the territory of the host Member State and his employment had been subject to the legislation of that state.[36]

22–32　　One example of potential dispute in relation to this condition is provided by *Bozkurt*[37] in which the principle identified above was first laid down. The case concerned a Turkish worker who—without the need to possess either a work or residence permit—lived in the Netherlands employed as an international lorry driver. One question considered by the ECJ was what criteria were to be

---

[31] Case C-188/00 *Kurz v Land Baden-Württemberg* [2002] E.C.R. I–691.
[32] Case C-188/00 *Kurz v Land Baden-Württemberg* [2002] E.C.R. I–691, para.45.
[33] See for instance Case C-434/93 *Bozkurt v Staatssecretaris van Justitie* [1995] E.C.R. I–1475, paras 22 and 23; Case C-36/96 *Günaydin* [1997] E.C.R. I-5143 para.29; Case C-98/96 *Ertanir v Land Hessen* [1997] E.C.R. I–5179, para.39; Case C-1/97 *Birden v Stadtgemeinde Bremen* [1998] E.C.R. I-7747, para.33 and Case C-188/00 *Kurz v Land Baden-Württemberg* [2002] E.C.R. I–691, para.37.
[34] Case C-188/00 *Kurz v Land Baden-Württemberg* [2002] E.C.R. I–691, para.37.
[35] Case C-188/00 *Kurz v Land Baden-Württemberg* [2002] E.C.R. I–691.
[36] See for example to like effect Case C-1/97 *Birden v Stadtgemeinde Bremen* [1998] E.C.R. I-7747, para.34.
[37] Case C-434/93 *Bozkurt v Staatssecretaris van Justitie* [1995] E.C.R. I–1475.

used to determine whether Mr Bozkurt belonged to the labour force. The ECJ accepted that the same criteria should be applied to his situation as an international lorry driver as were applied by the ECJ in *Lopes de Veiga*[38] to the position of a Member State national seaman employed on board a ship flying the flag of another Member State. The intervening Governments had argued that such interpretation, applicable in the context of full free movement rights conferred by the EC Treaty, would not be consistent with the modest objectives of an association agreement. The ECJ held that, so far as possible, it was essential to transpose the principles enshrined in the EC Treaty to Turkish workers enjoying the rights conferred by Decision 1/80.

The ECJ held that in deciding whether Mr Bozkurt's employment retained a   **22–33**
sufficiently close link with the territory of the Netherlands the national court would be required to take account in particular where he was hired, where his paid employment was based and the applicable national legislation in the field of employment and social security law.

(d) *Employment for One of Three Requisite Time Periods*

(i) *The Specified Time Periods*

In order to qualify under Art.6(1) of Decision 1/80 specific time periods of   **22–34**
legal employment must have been fulfilled.

The first indent of Art.6(1) provides that after one year's legal employment   **22–35**
the worker is entitled to a renewal of his work permit "for the same employer". The aim of the first indent is to ensure continuity of employment with the same employer and is therefore only applicable where the worker requests an extension of his work permit in order to continue working for the same employer after the initial year.[39] Furthermore, the ECJ has stated that even where the Turkish worker has worked for one year without interruption but for different employers, he does not qualify under the first indent of Art.6(1) and will only qualify when he has completed a full year's employment with one employer.[40] This is the case even where the national authorities have themselves authorised such changes of employment. Once a worker

---

[38] Case C-9/88 *Lopes da Veiga v Staatsecretaris van Justitite* [1989] E.C.R. 2989. The ECJ ruled that in the case of a worker who is a national of a Member State and who is permanently employed on board a ship flying the flag of another Member State, in that instance the Netherlands, in deciding whether the legal relationship of employment could be located within the territory of the Community or retained a sufficiently close link with that territory, for the purposes of the application of Reg. 1612/68, it was for the national court to take into account the following: the fact that the applicant worked on board a vessel registered in the Netherlands in the employment of a shipping company established in the Netherlands, that he was hired in the Netherlands, that the employment relationship between him and his employer was subject to Netherlands law and, finally, that he was insured under the social security system of the Netherlands and paid income tax there.

[39] See Dir. 2001/23 on the approximation of laws of the Member States relating to the safeguarding of employees' rights in the event of transfer of undertakings, businesses or parts of undertakings or businesses [2001] O.J. L82/16). The Directive would indicate that where there has been a transfer of undertakings, for these purposes the employer remains the same even if the legal entity has changed.

[40] See Case C-386/95 *Eker* [1997] E.C.R. I–2697.

has fulfilled the first year's legal employment with one employer any attempts by the national authorities to limit renewal of a work permit would be incompatible with Decision 1/80.

22–36   The second indent provides that the Turkish worker may after three years, legal employment, change employers and respond to any other offer of employment "for the same occupation".[41]

22–37   The third indent provides that after four years, legal employment the worker enjoys free access to any paid employment. This will include the right to seek employment for a "reasonable period".

(ii) *Annual Holidays, Absences, Accidents, Sickness and Involuntary Unemployment*

22–38   Article 6(2) specifically states that "annual holidays and absences for reasons of maternity or accident at work or short periods of sickness shall be treated as legal employment." The ECJ has not defined what periods of time are envisaged by Art.6(2) in precise terms and therefore it will be a question of fact and degree as to whether time taken off for illness constitutes "short periods of sickness". In *Ertanir*[42] the ECJ further clarified that short periods without a valid residence or work permit do not affect the periods of legal employment referred to in Art.6(1).

22–39   In the case of involuntary unemployment ("duly certified by the relevant authorities"[43]), Art.6(2) provides—as in the case of long periods of absence due to sickness—that the inactive periods cannot be treated as periods of legal employment for the purposes of Art.6(1). However such periods of unemployment do not affect the rights which the worker has acquired as the result of preceding employment. Thus a worker who had been employed for three years and is made involuntarily unemployed for three months, will not have the three months taken into account when calculating periods of legal employment, but will not have to recommence the periods of employment under Art.6(1) as if he had never previously been employed. The ECJ has not defined what periods of time are envisaged by Art.6(2) in precise terms and so "long absences on account of sickness" will be a question of fact and degree.

22–40   In *Tetik*,[44] the ECJ described the second sentence in Art.6(2) as relating to periods of inactivity due on the one to hand long-term sickness or, on the other, to involuntary unemployment when the failure to work was "not attributable to any misbehaviour on the part of the worker". Making the behaviour of the worker a relevant factor in this context was said by the ECJ to follow from the use of the adjective *"unverschuldet"* in the German version of Decision 1/80.[45] According to the ECJ:

---

[41] As yet there is no ECJ guidance on the meaning of "same occupation".
[42] Case C-98/96 *Ertanir v Land Hessen* [1997] E.C.R. I–5179, paras 63–69.
[43] The impact of failure to have involuntary absences certified is pending consideration by the ECJ in Case C-230/03 *Sedef v Freie und Hansestadt Hamburg* [2003] O.J. C200/11.
[44] Case C-171/95 *Tetik v Land Berlin* [1997] E.C.R. I–329.
[45] Case C-171/95 *Tetik v Land Berlin* [1997] E.C.R. I–329, para.38.

"The sole purpose of this latter provision is therefore to prevent a Turkish worker who recommences employment after having been forced to stop working because of long-term illness or unemployment through no fault of his own from being required, in the same way as a Turkish national who has never previously been in paid employment in the Member State in question, to recommence the periods of legal employment envisaged by the three indents of Article 6(1)."[46]

This aspect of the decision in *Tetik* is concerned with the circumstances in which a worker will have to have to reset the clock for the purposes of establishing one, three or four years' legal employment following a period of involuntary unemployment (or sickness). Where that unemployment is not the fault of the worker, the ECJ has stated in effect that the worker should not be penalised by being treated as if he had never worked. The implication is at the very least that for the worker whose period of unemployment *is* attributable to misbehaviour the clock will have to be reset and previous periods of employment will count for nothing. The notion that fault on the part of the worker can have such a consequence is extremely problematic for a number of reasons considered below. At the very least any assessment of "fault" must be determined in a manner which is fair and any decision taken must be proportionate.   **22–41**

If this were not the case, the consequences could be absurd. Firstly, would wholly disproportionate, for example, were a worker who was made unemployed as the result of a failure to pay an administrative fine resulting in a two-day prison sentence to be treated as being in the same position as someone who had never worked. Such person could have completed three years and 11 months of legal employment leaving him short by only one month of obtaining the right of free access to the labour market contained in the third indent of Art.6(1). Plainly there must be scope for the application of some form of *de minimis* principle. Secondly, it will always be only too easy for an employer to attribute fault at the feet of an employee. This could have the draconian consequence of the employee's entire record of legal employment being discounted without any opportunity for the employee to counter the allegation, or any assessment at all being able to be made of the gravity of any alleged misconduct. The latter matter is particularly important since even if the conduct alleged has been carried out by the employee, its gravity must surely be such as to justify the consequence. Again this would call for the application of some form of *de minimis* principle. By contrast with the foregoing, however, the position as regards misbehaviour is different where rights are already enjoyed on completion of such time periods.[47]   **22–42**

(iii) *Voluntary Unemployment*

In *Tetik*,[48] the ECJ made specific reference to its own jurisprudence under Art.39 EC Treaty in relation to those seeking employment. By reference to its   **22–43**

---

[46] Case C-171/95 *Tetik v Land Berlin* [1997] E.C.R. I–329, para.39.
[47] See discussion paras 22–52 to 22–55 below of Case C-340/97 *Nazli v Stadt Nürnberg* [2000] E.C.R. I–957.
[48] Case C-171/95 *Tetik v Land Berlin* [1997] E.C.R. I–329.

decision in *Antonissen*[49] (a case concerning work seekers in the context of Art.39 EC Treaty) the ECJ noted that:

"Article 48. . . [now Art.39 EC Treaty] requires that the person concerned be given a reasonable time in which to appraise himself, in the territory of the Member State which he has entered, of offers of employment corresponding to his occupational qualifications and to take, where appropriate, the necessary steps in order to be engaged."[50]

22-44 The ECJ went on reiterate the relationship between Decision 1/80 and the EC Treaty. Whilst Decision 1/80 does not confer a right of entry into a Member State and thus cannot confer the right to enter and seek employment analogous to the situation under Art.39 EC Treaty, the ECJ has held that a Turkish worker must be able, for a reasonable period, to seek new employment in the Member State and have a corresponding right of residence. The ECJ left it to the discretion of the Member State to determine how long a reasonable period for seeking employment would be but it may not deprive Art.6 of its substance by "jeopardising in fact the Turkish worker's prospects of finding new employment".[51]

22-45 *Antonissen* provides an appropriate benchmark of what would be a reasonable period without jeopardising the prospects of finding new employment. As pointed out by the ECJ in *Tetik*,[52] the principles enshrined in the EC Treaty worker provisions must so far as possible "inform the treatment of Turkish workers" in the context of Decision 1/80. In *Antonissen*, the ECJ held that Member States may prescribe a period of six months within which work should be obtained, although this should not to be enforced if after such time evidence is provided that the person concerned continues to seek employment and has genuine chances of being engaged. The same approach should be taken in the interpretation of the rights of residence of Turkish workers under Art.6(1).

22-46 It makes no material difference that voluntary unemployment is not specifically envisaged by Art.6(2). Where the time period in question is short, the worker cannot be deemed to have left the labour force, certainly where the Turkish national is available for work.

(iv) *Incapacity and Retirement*

22-47 In *Bozkurt*,[53] the ECJ stated that underlying Art.6 was the prerequisite that the worker is able to work. The ECJ pointed out that whilst Art.6(2) envisages temporary breaks in employment and therefore periods of legal employment will include annual holidays, absences for reason of maternity or an accident at work or short periods of sickness, the provisions of Art.6 presuppose fitness to continue working.

---

[49] C-292/89 *The Queen v Immigration Appeal Tribunal Ex p. Antonissen* [1991] E.C.R. I–745, paras 13, 15 and 16.
[50] Case C-171/95 *Tetik v Land Berlin* [1997] E.C.R. I–329, para.27.
[51] Case C-171/95 *Tetik v Land Berlin* [1997] E.C.R. I–329, para.32.
[52] C-292/89 *The Queen v Immigration Appeal Tribunal Ex p. Antonissen* [1991] E.C.R. I–745, paras 20 and 28.
[53] Case C-434/93 *Bozkurt v Staatssecretaris van Justitie* [1995] E.C.R. I–1475.

As stated above, where a worker is absent from work for long periods on **22–48** account of sickness, the second sentence of Art.6(2) stipulates that the "inactive" period cannot be treated as a period of legal employment, although the rights of the worker acquired as a result of previous employment cannot be affected. The ECJ has stated that this prevents a worker, who recommences work after a long period of illness, from having to reset the clock in terms of time periods fulfilled under Art.6(1) as a new arrival would.[54] However, in the case of permanent incapacity, the worker can no longer be considered as available for work and there is no reason to guarantee such worker the right of access to the labour force and an ancillary right of residence.

Turkish workers will not be able to benefit from the provisions of Art.6 where **22–49** they have "definitely ceased to belong to the labour force of a Member State"[55] whether by reason of reaching retirement age or becoming totally or permanently incapacitated for work. In the absence of any other right, the worker thus loses the right of residence.

(e) *The Right of Residence*

The ECJ has repeatedly held that the rights which Art.6(1) of Decision 1/80 **22–50** confers on Turkish workers in regard to employment "necessarily imply the existence of a corresponding right of residence for the person concerned, since otherwise the right of access to the labour market and the right to work as an employed person would be deprived of all effect".[56] Thus a worker qualifying under Art.6(1) for extensions of employment in the Member State will have a corresponding right to remain in that Member State. Furthermore, as is clear from the decision of the ECJ in *Tetik*[57] such corresponding right of residence will exist for a reasonable period where the worker concerned becomes a work seeker. Indeed, the right of residence will continue to exist until a Turkish national has definitely ceased to belong to the labour force.

There is no requirement in Art.6(1) that Turkish nationals must establish the **22–51** legality of their employment by possession of any specific administrative document (such as a work permit or residence permit) in order to have their right of residence recognised. The ECJ has made it clear that:

"the fact that (the worker's) residence permit was issued to him only for a fixed period is not relevant, since it is settled case-law that the rights conferred on Turkish workers by Article 6(1) of Decision 1/80 are accorded irrespective of whether or not the authorities of the host Member State have issued a specific administrative document, such as a work permit or residence permit."[58]

---

[54] Case C-171/95 *Tetik v Land Berlin* [1997] E.C.R. I–329, para.39.
[55] Case C-434/93 *Bozkurt v Staatssecretaris van Justitie* [1995] E.C.R. I–1475, para.39.
[56] See most recently Case C-1/97 *Birden v Stadtgemeinde Bremen* [1998] E.C.R. I-7747, para.20; C-36/96 *Günaydin v Freistaat Bayern* [1997] E.C.R. I–5179. para.26 and Case C-98/96 *Ertanir v Land Hessen* [1997] E.C.R. I–5179, para.26.
[57] Case C-171/95 *Tetik v Land Berlin* [1997] E.C.R. I–329.
[58] Case C-36/96 *Günaydin v Freistaat Bayern* [1997] E.C.R. I–5179, para.26.

In this context such administrative documents are only "declaratory" of the existence of the worker's rights and do not constitute a condition their existence. This is consistent with the position for workers in Community law in general.

22–52   It is clear from the decision of the ECJ in *Nazli*[59] that rights accrued under Art.6(1) will not be forfeited simply because of acts which are attributable to the worker's misbehaviour[60]. In *Nazli*, the ECJ considered the position of a Turkish worker who had been in legal employment in Germany for almost 10 years without interruption who on this basis enjoyed the right of "free access" in Germany to "any paid employment of his choice".[61] The question arose whether the worker retroactively forfeited the right because after such period of lawful work he was detained pending trial for more than a year in connection with an offence (being an accomplice to the trafficking of 1,500 grammes of heroin) for which he was ultimately sentenced to a term of imprisonment, albeit suspended in full. In particular the national court was uncertain whether Mr Nazli continued, while he was detained pending trial, to be duly registered as belonging to Germany's labour force, notwithstanding that he was neither working nor available for work whilst detained.

22–53   The ECJ characterised the unconditional right enjoyed by Mr Nazli to seek and take up any employment freely chosen by him as one which implied the right to give up one job in order to seek another. Moreover, the ECJ emphasised that the absence of a Turkish worker from the labour force of a Member State did not automatically lead to the loss of the rights acquired under Art.6(1). Whilst the right of residence as a corollary of the right to join the labour force and to be actually employed was not unlimited, the rights granted by Art.6(1) of Decision 1/80 are necessarily lost *only* if the worker's inactive status is permanent. Thus Art.6(1) implies also the right to take a temporary break from work without causing such worker to cease to be duly registered as belonging to the labour force. However this is subject to the caveat that the worker actually finds another job within a reasonable period. In these circumstances the ECJ held that:

> "the temporary break in the period of active employment of a Turkish worker such as Mr Nazli while he is detained pending trial is not in itself capable of causing him to forfeit the rights which he derives directly from the third indent of Article 6(1) of Decision No 1/80, provided that he finds a new job within a reasonable period after his release . . . A person's temporary absence as a result of detention of that kind does not in any way call into question his subsequent participation in working life, as is moreover demonstrated by the main proceedings, where Mr Nazli looked for work and indeed found a steady job after his release."[62]

22–54   Thus the German authorities could not deny Mr Nazli his right of residence. They could have done so only had Mr Nazli either "definitively ceased to be

---

[59] Case C-340/97 *Nazli v Stadt Nurnberg* [2000] E.C.R. I–957.
[60] The position is to be contrasted with that where rights have yet to be accrued; see paras. 22–40 to 22–42.
[61] Dec. 1/80, Art.6(1), third indent.
[62] Paras. 41 and 42.

duly registered as belonging to the labour force" or "exceeded a reasonable time-limit for entering into a new employment relationship."[63] The question of what is a reasonable period of time is discussed above.

In two references which are pending consideration by the ECJ questions are raised about the impact of imprisonment on rights accrued under Art.6(1).[64] In *Aydinli*[65] (where the worker had accrued the right of free access as a result of his many years of employment in the Member State) one of the questions referred is whether enforcement of a fixed-term prison sentence causes him "to have ceased to belong to that labour force, thereby leading to the forfeiture of rights . . . acquired under the to third indent of Article 6(1)?" The answer must surely be "no". It is clear from *Nazli*[66] that a term of imprisonment cannot in itself cause Mr Aydinli to forfeit his rights, provided only that he finds new employment within a reasonable period of release. Whilst the right of residence might in practice be lost for a person sentenced to a substantial period of imprisonment, this could be only be because of the invocation by a Member State of the public policy proviso,[67] rather than any view that temporary absence from the labour force whilst incarcerated must lead to forfeiture of rights.   **22–55**

(f) *The Right of Non-discrimination*

Equality of treatment is a fundamental principle of Community law which lies at the heart of the exercise of free movement rights. The principle and its application is considered in Chapter 12.   **22–56**

For Turkish national workers the principle is articulated in Art.10(1) of Decision 1/80 which provides as follows: **22–57**

> "The Member States of the Community shall as regards remuneration and other conditions of work grant Turkish workers duly registered as belonging to their labour forces treatment involving no discrimination on the basis of nationality between them and Community workers".

This non-discrimination provision was considered by the ECJ for the first time in *Wählergruppe Gemeinsam*[68]. The case concerned annulment of elections to a general assembly of workers because five Turkish workers fulfilled all the conditions in the third indent of Art.6(1) of Decision 1/80 had their names deleted from a candidate list for elections to the general assembly of   **22–58**

---

[63] Para.44. Subject also to the application of Art.14(1) of Dec. 1/80 (the 'public policy, public security or public health' proviso which was the subject matter of the second question referred in Case C-340/97 *Nazli v Stadt Nurnberg* [2000] E.C.R. I–957—see further below).
[64] Case C-373/03 *Aydinli v Land Baden-Württemberg* (OJ 2004/C 21/15) and Case C-383/03 *Dogan* (OJ 2004/C 35/03).
[65] Case C-373/03 *Aydinli v Land Baden-Wurttemberg* (OJ 2004/C 21/15); the facts of Case C-383/03 *Dogan* (OJ 2004/C 35/03) are unclear from the short report (in particular what rights he had accrued under Art.6(1)), although it concerned a three year sentence of imprisonment.
[66] Case C-340/97 *Nazli v Stadt Nurnberg* [2000] E.C.R. I–957.
[67] Art.14(1) of Dec. 1/80.
[68] Case C-171/01 *Wählergruppe "Gemeinsam Zajedno/Birlikte Alternative und Grüne GewerkschafterInnen/UG"* [2003] E.C.R. 4301.

workers because they were not Austrian nationals.[69] Two questions were referred. The first concerned the scope of the prohibition of discrimination laid down by Art.10(1), in particular whether "other conditions of work" in Art.10(1) encompassed the right to stand as a candidate in elections to the bodies legally representing the interests of workers; the second whether the provision had direct effect in Community law.

22–59   The ECJ dealt first with the direct effect. As pointed out in Chapter 16, a provision in an agreement concluded by the Community with a non-member has direct effect where, in light of its wording and the purpose and nature of the agreement, the provision contains a clear and precise obligation which is not subject to the adoption of any subsequent measure. The ECJ held that Art.10(1) satisfied the test.[70]

22–60   In considering the scope of Art.10(1) the ECJ reiterated the interpretative principle requiring the scope of rights in Decision 1/80 to be defined as far as possible by reference to the EC Treaty provisions relating to free movement of workers.[71] The ECJ stated that application of the principle was all the more justified because Art.10(1) is formulated in terms "almost identical" to those in Art.39(2) EC Treaty.[72] The ECJ held that:

> "in the context of Community law and, in particular, Article 48(2) of the Treaty [now Art.39(2)], the Court has consistently held that national legislation which denies workers who are nationals of other Member States the right to vote and/or the right to stand as a candidate in elections held by bodies such as occupational guilds to which those workers are compulsorily affiliated, to which they must pay contributions, which are responsible for defending and representing workers' interests and which perform a consultative function in the legislative field is contrary to the fundamental principle of non-discrimination on the grounds of nationality (see ASTI I and ASTI II)".[73]

22–61   Thus the ECJ held that national legislation which required candidates to hold Austrian nationality in order to be eligible for election to a body representing and defending the interests of workers was incompatible with Art.10(1). According to the ECJ this interpretation was the only one consistent with the aims of Decision 1/80 to secure progressively freedom of movement for Turkish workers and to promote their integration into host Member States. In such a context granting Turkish workers entitlement to the same conditions of work as those enjoyed by national workers was "an important step towards creating an appropriate framework for the gradual integration of

---

[69] According to Art.26(4) of Austria's Federal Constitution Law "All persons possessing Austrian nationality on the relevant date who have reached the age of 19 before 1 January of the year of the election shall be eligible for election".
[70] Case C-171/01 *Wählergruppe "Gemeinsam Zajedno/Birlikte Alternative und Grüne GewerkschafterInnen/UG"* [2003] E.C.R. 4301, para.57.
[71] Para.72; see also Case C-340/97 *Nazli v Stadt Nurnberg* [2000] E.C.R. I–957, paras 50 to 55 and references therein.
[72] Para.74. *ASTI I* is Case C-213/90 *ASTI* [1991] E.C.R. I–3507 and *ASTI II* is Case C-118/92 *Commission v Luxembourg* [1994] E.C.R. I–1891.
[73] Case C-171/01 *Wählergruppe "Gemeinsam Zajedno/Birlikte Alternative und Grüne GewerkschafterInnen/UG"* [2003] E.C.R. 4301, para.75.

migrant Turkish worker's"[74] As with the same phrase in Art.39(2) EC Treaty, the Art.10(1) reference to "conditions of work" was to be interpreted as having a broad scope providing for equal treatment "in all matters directly or indirectly related to the exercise of activity as an employee in the host Member State."[75]

This non-discrimination provision thus replicates those both in the EC   **22–62**
Treaty itself and the Europe Agreements. In the context of those provisions their application has been most contested in relation to rules governing the number of foreign players fielded in national sporting events.[76] The non-discrimination provision in the Europe Agreements is discussed in Chapter 18.

(g) *The Standstill Clause*

Article 13 of Decision 1/80 contains the only provision dealing with *access* to   **22–63**
employment for Turkish nationals (and thereby indicates the only limitation on the competence of Member States to regulate entry into their territories and access to first employment). Article 13 provides as follows:

> "The Member States of the Community and Turkey may not introduce new restrictions on the conditions of access to employment applicable to workers and members of their families legally resident and employed in their respective territories".

The provision in Decision 1/80 replaces that contained in Art.7 of Association Council Decision 2/76 which provided a standstill clause in relation to workers and employment, but did not include family members.

In *Sevince*,[77] the ECJ described the standstill clauses contained within   **22–64**
Decisions 2/76 and 1/80 as "unequivocal" and to have direct effect in the Member States. As indicated the Art.13 provision reproduced that made in Decision 2/76 as regards workers. Decision 2/76 had entered into force on December 20, 1976 and remained in force until the entry into force of Decision 1/80. Thus the relevant date for the purposes of "standstill" is December 20, 1976. Turkish workers must enjoy the conditions of access to employment which existed at that time in Member States. It is not open to Member States to apply more restrictive conditions than were in force on

---

[74] Case C-171/01 *Wählergruppe "Gemeinsam Zajedno/Birlikte Alternative und Grüne GewerkschafterInnen/UG"* [2003] E.C.R. 4301, para.79. Note that the ECJ rejected expressly a submission made by the Austrian Government that Art.10(1) was narrower in scope than the same term used in Art.48(2) EC Treaty because the latter was clarified in specific terms by Reg. 1612/68, the first paragraph of Art.8 of which expressly refers to trade-union and similar rights, whereas no such specific terms are used in the EC-Turkey Association Agreement, and because the aims of that Agreement were less ambitious than those of the Treaty. See judgment at paras 81–94.
[75] Case C-171/01 *Wählergruppe "Gemeinsam Zajedno/Birlikte Alternative und Grüne GewerkschafterInnen/UG"* [2003] E.C.R. 4301, paras 85–88.
[76] See for example Case C-415/93 *Union Royal Belge des Societes de Football Association ASBL v Bosman* [1995] E.C.R. 4353, para.73 and Case C-438/00 *Deutscher Handballbund eV v Kolpak*, May 8, 2003.
[77] Case C-192/89 *Sevince v Staatssecretaris Van Justitite* [1990] E.C.R. 3461, para.30.

December 20, 1976 as regards workers. However, the standstill clause relating to the family members was not part of Decision 2/76 and therefore family members may only enjoy conditions of access to employment which existed on the date of entry into force of Decision 1/80 (December 1, 1980).

22–65 The standstill clauses refer specifically to persons "legally resident and employed" in the Member States. The ECJ has repeatedly stated in relation to Art.6(1) of Decision 1/80 that reference to persons already in legal employment means that Member States are able to control both entry into their territory of Turkish nationals and conditions of initial employment. It would appear from the wording of the standstill clauses that similar provisos exist. Member States are therefore able to apply whatever conditions of entry to the territory and first access to employment they wish.

22–66 The benefit of the standstill clause is that Turkish nationals who are granted entry and access to the labour force by a Member State must have their subsequent stay and further access to employment regulated by the national laws in place at the time when Decision 2/76 came into force in the Member State. For the original Member States this was December 1976. Where those national laws are no more favourable than the provisions of Art.6 of Decision 1/80, the clause will be of no practical benefit. If however the national laws contained more favourable conditions, then such a Turkish worker must obtain the benefit of them. For example, if in 1976 national law gave the right of permanent residence after two years' legal employment, but such national law provision had been changed in 1981 so as to require four years' legal employment to qualify for permanent residence, the more favourable provision could benefit a Turkish worker who had completed two years' legal employment.

CHAPTER 23

ESTABLISHMENT UNDER THE ANKARA AGREEMENT

This chapter examines the scope of the establishment provisions contained in the Ankara Agreement and its Protocol. The provision of principal importance is the standstill clause relating to establishment in the Additional Protocol.

1. PROVISIONS IN THE ANKARA AGREEMENT AND ADDITIONAL PROTOCOL

(a) *Ankara Agreement Provisions Relating to Establishment and Services*

Article 13 of the Ankara Agreement states "The Contracting Parties agree to be guided by Arts 52 to 56 and Art.58[1] of the Treaty establishing the Community for the purpose of abolishing restrictions on the freedom of establishment between them".   **23–01**

Article 14 of the Agreement states "The Contracting Parties agree to be guided by Arts 55, 56 and 58 to 65[2] of the Treaty establishing the Community for the purpose of abolishing restrictions on freedom to provide services between them."   **23–02**

Articles 13 and 14 of the Ankara Agreement provide the foundation stone for freedom of establishment and the freedom to provide services, in much the same way as the foundation stone for the freedom of movement of workers is laid down by Art.12 of the Agreement. The provisions of Arts 13 and 14 are further developed in Art.41 of the Additional Protocol.   **23–03**

The similarities between Art.12, in relation to workers, and Arts 13 and 14 would suggest that the decisions of the ECJ relating to Art.12[3] of the Agreement are of interpretative value for Arts 13 and 14. Certainly those provisions provide guidance as to the general aims of the Contracting Parties and to the interpretation of various concepts including the meaning of "establishment".   **23–04**

(b) *Additional Protocol Relating to Establishment and Services*

Article 41 of the Additional Protocol states: **23–05**

"(1) The Contracting Parties shall refrain from introducing between themselves any new restrictions on the freedom of establishment and the freedom to provide services.

(2) The Council of Association shall, in accordance with the principles set out in Articles 13 and 14 of the Agreement of Association, determine the timetable and

---

[1] Now Arts 43 to 46 and 48 EC Treaty.
[2] Now Arts 45, 46 and 48 to 55 EC Treaty.
[3] Particularly Case 12/86 *Demirel v Stadt Schwäbish Gmünd* [1987] E.C.R. 3719.

rules for the progressive abolition by the Contracting Parties, between themselves, of restrictions on freedom of establishment and on freedom to provide services.

The Council of Association shall, when determining such timetable and rules for the various classes of activity, take into account corresponding measures already adopted by the Community in these fields and also the special economic and social circumstances of Turkey. Priority shall be given to activities making a particular contribution to the development of production and trade."

23–06 The provision in Art.41(1) is known as a "standstill clause", prohibiting Member States from changing their legislation to make exercising freedom to establish or provide services more difficult. The effect of this provision is discussed below.

23–07 The remainder of Art.41 is concerned with the progressive abolition of restrictions on freedom of establishment and on freedom to provide services under rules laid down by the Council of Association. It is notable that unlike the position in relation to workers, there have been no decisions of the Council of Association relating to establishment.

2. RIGHT OF ESTABLISHMENT AND RIGHT TO PROVIDE SERVICES UNDER THE AGREEMENT

(a) *Entry and Establishment*

23–08 As with workers, there is no express right contained within the Ankara Agreement or its Additional Protocol for Turkish nationals to establish themselves or to provide services in the territory of the Member States. Whilst Arts 13 and 14 of the Ankara Agreement make reference to Treaty provisions in order to "guide" Contracting Parties on the abolition of restrictions in those areas, neither provision creates any directly effective right.

23–09 Indeed as observed above the wording of Arts 13 and 14 is very similar to that contained in Art.12 of the Ankara Agreement. In *Demirel*,[4] the ECJ expressly rejected a suggestion that Art.12 was capable of directly governing the movement of workers or that any rights are created by the provision.[5]

23–10 Article 41(2) of the Additional Protocol charges the Council of Association with setting the timetable for the progressive abolition of restrictions on establishment and provision of services. Again this mirrors the provision relating to workers in Art.36 of the Additional Protocol which charges the Council of Association with responsibility for securing the free movement of workers in progressive stages. The ECJ has stated that Art.36 "essentially serves to set out a programme" which does not create directly effective rights which individuals can rely upon.

---

[4] Case 12/86 *Demirel v Stadt Schwäbish Gmünd* [1987] E.C.R. 3719, para.23.
[5] Case 12/86 *Demirel v Stadt Schwäbish Gmünd* [1987] E.C.R. 3719, para.25.

The rights of Turkish workers are discussed in Chapter 22. It is apparent that   **23–11**
the rights of Turkish workers flow from decisions of the Council of
Association (which are to be treated like secondary legislation). In relation to
Turkish workers the Council of Association has passed a number of decisions setting out in some detail the rights that they achieve. However, such
rights do not include the right of entry to the Member States in order to take
up employment. Member States retain the right to make decisions regarding
first entry and thereby prevent the free movement of Turkish workers into
their territory if they so choose.

The provisions in the Agreement relating to establishment (and services) of   **23–12**
those relating to workers. In light of the approach taken to workers it would be
impossible to suggest that the Agreement creates any right for Turkish nationals to enter the territory of a Member State the purposes of establishment.
The lack of any decisions of the Council of Association on establishment or
the provision of services only reinforces that position.

(b) *Lawful Residence and Establishment*

The case law relating to Turkish workers, demonstrates that those lawfully   **23–13**
resident and working in the territory of a Member State accumulate rights in
relation to their continued employment and residence once they have been in
legal employment for a specific period. Such rights are contained in Art.6 of
Decision 1/80 of the Council of Association.

The ECJ has stated that these provisions and the principles flowing from   **23–14**
them are established in the context of the interpretation of the provisions of
the Ankara Agreement for the progressive achievement of free movement of
Turkish workers. These principles must apply by analogy in the context of the
provisions of the Agreement concerning the right of establishment.

Thus whilst Art.13 of the Ankara Agreement and Art.41(2) of the Protocol   **23–15**
are not capable of creating a directly effective right of establishment, they
nevertheless create "certain rights under Community law in relation to . . .
exercising self-employed activity, and, correlatively, in relation to residence,
. . . in so far as [the Turkish national's] position in a Member State concerned
is regular".[6]

The ECJ has yet to examine what those rights might be. Moreover, the   **23–16**
Council of Association has not provided interpretation through its decisions.
However it is implicit from the ECJ's judgment in *Savas*[7] that a Turkish
national lawfully resident and lawfully carrying out a genuine and effective
self-employed activity in the territory of a Member State would have the right
in Community law to continue in that self-employed activity and, as a corollary, extend his residence.[8] Anything less would render the ECJ's statement

---

[6] Case C-37/98 *The Queen v Secretary of State for the Home Department Ex p. Savas* [2000]
E.C.R. I–2927, para.65.
[7] Case C-37/98 *The Queen v Secretary of State for the Home Department Ex p. Savas* [2000]
E.C.R. I–2927.
[8] At least one commentator has suggested that the analogy made by the ECJ between the position of Turkish workers and Turkish nationals in self-employed activity is very limited and that

that a Turkish national can claim "certain rights in Community law in relation to exercising self-employed activity" otiose since it is difficult to envisage that rights in Community law could have any real meaning if at the very least the position of the lawfully established person were not protected.

3. THE STANDSTILL PROVISION

(a) *The Concept of a Standstill Provision*

23–17   Community law has long recognised the concept of a standstill provision. Indeed, Art.53 Treaty of Rome[9] contained such a standstill clause as a first step in the transitional period towards the progressive abolition of restrictions on establishment provided for in Art.52 of the same Treaty [now Art.43 EC Treaty]. Whilst national laws still had some application to the situation of those wishing to establish themselves in other Member States, the Member States were directed to ensure that they did not make their national laws any more restrictive than those in existence at the time when the Treaty came into force.[10] Indeed, the provision also prevents a Member State from reverting back to less liberal measures than have been imposed during the transitional period by Community law. As stated by the ECJ in *Royer*:

> "Article 53 . . . of the Treaty prohibit[s] the introduction by a Member State of new restrictions on the establishment of nationals of other Member States and the freedom to provide services which has in fact been attained and that they prevent the Member States from reverting to less liberal provisions or practices in so far as the liberalization measures already adopted constitute the implementation of obligations arising from the provisions and objectives of the Treaty".[11]

23–18   In other words a standstill clause has the effect of preventing a Member State from reversing the progression imposed by Community law on domestic law at

---

the rights pertaining to workers cannot be applied to the self employed. This is because in the case of the self-employed the Council of Association has failed to implement any decision setting in motion the program towards progressive abolition of restrictions on establishment or freedom to provide services and furthermore there are distinctions made as a matter of policy between employed and self-employed persons (see A. Ott, *European Journal of Migration and Law* 2: 445–458, 2000). Such factors were also pointed to by the Advocate General in *Savas*. However valid these observations, the conclusion that the "rights" pertaining to self-employed persons are limited to the reliance on the standstill provision must be unsustainable in the light of the clear reference by the ECJ to "rights in Community law". A standstill clause does not create any rights *per se* in Community law. It must be arguable that the failure by the Council of Association to progress the abolition of restrictions on freedom of establishment does not render the provisions in Arts 13 and 14 nugatory and that if they are to have any meaning then at the very least a Turkish national who is lawfully resident and engaged in self-employed activity in a Member State can expect to be afforded stability and security in so doing. That would represent a first step towards the abolition of restrictions on freedom of establishment. It would be surprising if no progression had been made towards that goal in the forty or more years since the Ankara Agreement was agreed.

[9] Treaty of Rome 1957 "Member States shall not introduce any new restrictions on the right of establishment in their territories of nationals of other Member States, save as otherwise provided in the Treaty". The provision was transititional and is not replicated in the EC Treaty.

[10] See for instance Case C-48/75 *Procureur de Roi v Royer* [1976] E.C.R. 497, paras 65 to 74.

[11] Case C-48/75 *Procureur de Roi v Royer* [1976] E.C.R. 497, para.74.

the same time as preventing the imposition of any greater controls or restrictions in domestic law. The situation of nationals of other Member States in the relevant field can thereby only improve over time (or at worse remain static).

The standstill provision contained in Art.41(1) of the Additional Protocol to **23–19** the Ankara Agreement is very similarly worded to Art.53 of the Treaty of Rome. The provision has been interpreted by the ECJ in such as way as to give it the same effect as Art.53.[12] A Member State is thus prevented from imposing any new measure having the "object or effect" of making the establishment of a Turkish national in its territory subject to stricter conditions than those which applied at the time when the Additional Protocol entered into force for the particular Member State in question.

(b) *Applicability of the Standstill Clause*

The question of whether a provision of Community law has direct effect is of **23–20** significance in terms of its applicability and consequences. If a provision has direct effect then all those falling within its scope are able to rely upon it before national courts and authorities without need for any transposition into domestic law.

In *Savas*,[13] the ECJ had no difficulty in accepting the direct effect of **23–21** Art.41(1) of the Additional Protocol which "confers on individuals individual rights which national courts must safeguard". In *Abatay*,[14] the second judgment concerning Art.41(1) of the Additional Protocol, the ECJ confirmed that the provision has direct effect resulting from the fact that the provision, as with other standstill provisions under the Ankara Agreement,[15] lays down "clearly, precisely and unconditionally, unequivocal standstill clauses, which contain an obligation entered into by the Contracting Parties which amounts in law to a duty not to act".

This conclusion is reinforced when the purpose and subject-matter of the **23–22** Ankara Agreement is examined. As with other provisions in the Ankara Agreement the ECJ affirmed that the essential object of the Agreement, namely to promote the development of Turkey, trade and economic relations between the Contracting Parties, lends support to the conclusion that this provision has direct effect in Community law.[16]

(c) *The Scope of the Standstill Clause*

The ECJ has applied the provision in Art.41(1) to *any* measure having the **23–23** object or purpose of making the establishment, and as a corollary, the

---

[12] See Case C-37/98 *The Queen v Secretary of State for the Home Department Ex p. Savas* [2000] E.C.R. I–2927, para.69.

[13] See Case C-37/98 *The Queen v Secretary of State for the Home Department Ex p. Savas* [2000] E.C.R. I-2927.

[14] Case C-317/01 *Abatay v Bundesanstalt für Arbeit* and Case C-369/01 *Sahin v Bundesanstalt für Arbei.*

[15] Art.13 of Dec.1/80, see Chapter 22 above.

[16] See Case C-37/98 *The Queen v Secretary of State for the Home Department Ex p. Savas* [2000] E.C.R. I-2927, paras 52 to 53.

residence of a Turkish national in its territory subject to stricter conditions than those which applied at the time when the Member State become party to the Additional Protocol.

23–24   It is plain from the facts of *Savas*[17] that such a Turkish national does not have to be lawfully resident in the Member State in question in order to obtain the benefit of the standstill provision in Art.41(1). Mr Savas had obtained lawful entry to the United Kingdom as a visitor for one month with his wife. By the time of his application to remain in the United Kingdom as a self-employed person he had overstayed that visa by some 11 years and was plainly unlawfully resident in the United Kingdom. Nevertheless the ECJ held that it was the task of the national court to determine whether domestic rules applied to Mr Savas were stricter than those rules that were applicable to self-employed persons at the time the United Kingdom became a party to the Additional Protocol.

23–25   The scope of the standstill provision in Art.41(1) therefore extends to all Turkish nationals, whatever their legal status in the Member State in which they wish to establish themselves. No distinction in the application of the standstill clause can be made on the basis of whether the Turkish national is lawfully resident, unlawfully resident or only a prospective resident wishing to obtain entry to a particular Member State. The effect of the provision is to ensure that any immigration laws or laws relating to conditions of establishment to which the Turkish national is made subject are no stricter than those that would have been applicable to a Turkish national in the same position at the time when the Additional Protocol came into force in the Member State in question.[17] The benefit of the provision extends to both substantive and procedural provisions, as well as any policies or practises in existence at the relevant time.[18]

23–26   The benefits of such a provision can be significant. At the time at which the Additional Protocol came into force in a large number of the original Member States or those which joined in the 1960s and 1970s, Member States'

---

[17] The UK Government has attempted to restrict the scope of the standstill provision to conditions of residence and establishment for those who at some stage have already obtained lawful entry to the UK, regardless of their current immigration status, thereby excluding from the scope of the standstill provision conditions of entry. The Court of Appeal rejected such limitation on the scope in the case of *The Queen on the application of Tum and Dari v Secretary of State for the Home Department* (May 25, 2004) [2004] 1 C.M.L.R. 33. Plainly such restriction is unsustainable since the ECJ has repeatedly held that the concept of "freedom of establishment" in Community law in general includes conditions of entry, stay and establishment (see for instance Case C–106/91 *Ramrath v Minister of Justice* [1992] E.C.R. I-3351) where the ECJ affirmed that the "freedom of establishment" was concerned with "both the entry into and residence in the territory of the Member States" para.17). If conditions of entry were not within the scope of the provision, a Member State could effectively nullify the effect of the provision altogether and deprive all Turkish nationals from being able to establish themselves in the territory of that Member State by imposing on those nationals extremely restrictive immigration legislation. Neither the wording of the provision in Art.41(1) nor the aims of the Ankara Agreement support such limitation in its scope. In this regard the standstill provision in Art.41(1) of the Additional Protocol is wider in scope that the standstill provision in Art.13 of Decision 1/80 which is plainly restricted those already "legally resident" in the Member State.
[18] Case C–317/01 *Abatay v Bundesanstalt für Arbeit* and Case C–369/01 *Sahin v Bundesanstalt für Arbei*.

immigration regimes were extremely liberal. In a quest to stimulate post-war economies in Western Europe, non-EU nationals who could bring skills and economic benefit to a Member State were encouraged to migrate. Domestic immigration laws and policies have undoubtedly become far harsher in the last two decades. The Turkish national who wishes to establish himself in the territory of a Member State will likely be in a better position if able to rely on the liberal immigration regimes of the 1960s and 1970s than current immigration laws.

The scope of the standstill provision extends to "any new measure" which has   **23–27** the object or effect of making establishment more difficult for Turkish nationals. Such measures would include the imposition of new procedures, for instance a requirement to obtain certain permits,[19] as well as substantive provisions, such as the imposition of a new requirement to invest a certain sum of money in the Member State in question.

---

[19] See for instance Case C-317/01 *Abatay v Bundesanstalt für Arbeit* and Case C-369/01 *Sahin v Bundesanstalt für Arbeit* where the ECJ concluded that: "Article 41(1) precludes the introduction into the national legislation of a Member State of a requirement of a work permit in order for an undertaking established in Turkey to provide services in the territory of that State, if such a permit was not already required at the time of the entry into force of the Additional Protocol", para.117.

FAMILY MEMBERS UNDER THE ANKARA AGREEMENT

This chapter examines the extent to which Turkish nationals exercising rights under the Ankara Agreement enjoy the right of family unity. Although specific provision is limited, the ECJ has recognised the right of family unity for such Turkish nationals.

1. PROVISION FOR FAMILY MEMBERS IN THE ANKARA AGREEMENT AND THE DECISIONS OF THE COUNCIL OF ASSOCIATION

(a) *The Agreement*

There is no reference to rights of family reunification for Turkish nationals in the Ankara Agreement or the Additional Protocol. The question whether the rights of workers under the Ankara Agreement include the right to bring with them their spouse and children was included in the questions for reference in the case of *Demirel*.[1] The ECJ did not specifically answer the question, although it stated "There is at present no provision of Community law defining the conditions in which Member States must permit the family reunification of Turkish workers lawfully settled in the Community".[2]   **24–01**

Advocate General Darmon had stated in his Opinion that: **24–02**

"Although family reunification is certainly a necessary element in giving effect to the freedom of movement of workers, it does not become a right until the freedom which it presupposes has taken effect and a special provision on the matter has been adopted".[3]

Neither of these observations is particularly surprising since the Ankara Agreement does not confer any directly effective rights on Turkish workers itself. However the reference in Art.12 of the Agreement to the fact that Contracting Parties are to be guided by the provisions relating to workers in the EC Treaty is significant. Bearing in mind the importance that the ECJ places on the right to family unity in the context of free movement rights under the EC Treaty and the fact that lack of family reunification rights is seen by the ECJ as an unacceptable obstacle to the exercise of free movement rights, family unity must at least constitute an aim of the Agreement, even if it does not give rise to a right itself.[4]   **24–03**

---

[1] Case 12/86 *Demirel v Stadt Schwäbisch Gmünd* [1987] E.C.R. 3719, para.23.
[2] Case 12/86 *Demirel v Stadt Schwäbisch Gmünd* [1987] E.C.R. 3719,para.28.
[3] Case 12/86 *Demirel v Stadt Schwäbisch Gmünd* [1987] E.C.R. 3719, p.3745.
[4] See Chapter 10 and Case C-60/00 *Carpenter v Secretary of State for the Home Department* [2002] E.C.R. I-6279.

24–04   In respect of the free movement of workers and the freedom of establishment the Council of Association is charged under the Agreement with responsibility for deciding rules to give effect to the aim of gradually securing free movement in these areas. The absence of any specific reference to family unity in either the Agreement or the Additional Protocol means that there is no specific direction given to the Council of Association in this area. However, given the importance of family unity in the context of free movement rights, the Council of Association could be expected to decide rules in relation to this question in the context of effecting progression towards the free movement of workers and the freedom of establishment.

(b) *Decisions of the Council of Association*

24–05   In fact the Council of Association has only made decisions in relation to workers and their family members. Consistent with the guidance provided by secondary legislation relating to the free movement of EU national workers in the context of the EC Treaty, the Council of Association has made decisions relating to family unity. These provisions largely mirror the gradual progression towards free movement of workers contained in decisions of Council of Association, providing for access to the labour market only after certain conditions are fulfilled and retaining the right of Member States to control first entry to their territories.

24–07   It is Art.7 of Decision 1/80 which is of principal interest in the context of free movement, although family members of Turkish workers additionally fall within the scope of Decision 3/80 relating to social security.

There are no provisions in the decisions of the Association Council relating to the family members of those established in business.

2. THE RIGHTS OF FAMILY MEMBERS OF TURKISH WORKERS

The first paragraph of Art.7 of Decision 1/80 provides:

> "The members of the family of a Turkish worker duly registered as belonging to the labour force of a Member State, who have been authorised to join him:
>
> – shall be entitled—subject to the priority to be given to workers of Member States of the Community—to respond to any offer of employment after they have been legally resident for at least three years in that Member State;
> – shall enjoy free access to any paid employment of their choice provided they have been legally resident there for at least five years.

(a) *Direct Effect of Article 7 of Decision 1/80*

The ECJ has confirmed the direct effect of Art.7 of Decision 1/80 on several   **24–08**
occasions[5] which means that it can be directly relied upon by individuals
before national courts and authorities. In conferring direct effect on the provision the ECJ has emphasised that Art.7 contains social provision which
constitute a further stage in securing freedom of movement for workers on
the basis of the relevant provisions in the EC Treaty. Having regard to the
general aim of Art.7 the ECJ in *Kadiman*[6] stated:

> "it must be emphasised that the purpose of that provision is to favour employment
> and residence of Turkish workers duly registered as belonging to the labour force
> of a Member State by ensuring that their family links are maintained there".[7]

The extent of the obligations placed on the Member States by the provision   **24–09**
are discussed below, but at the heart of Art.7 is a system "designed to create
conditions conducive to family unity".[8] Such provision constitutes a very
important stage in securing freedom of movement of workers, guided by the
EC Treaty itself, and it is for this reason that the ECJ has held that it is essential to transpose as far as possible the principles enshrined in the EC Treaty[9].
Whilst this might not result in full rights of family unity at the present stage
of development in the relationship between Turkey and the Community, the
provisions contained in Art.7 must be interpreted as consistently as possible
with Community law.

(b) *Right of Entry for Family Members of Workers*

As with Turkish workers, Decision 1/80 confers no explicit right of entry into   **24–10**
the Member States for family members of Turkish workers. Indeed the ECJ
has confirmed on a number of occasions that the power to lay down conditions of first entry of a family member into the territories of the Member
States is retained by the Member States.[10] As the ECJ reiterated in *Ergat*:[11]

> "under Community law as it now stands, the Member States have retained the
> power to regulate both the entry into their territory of a member of the family of a
> Turkish worker and the conditions of his residence during the initial three-year
> period before he has the right to respond to any offer of employment."[12]

However the clear principle of family unity that underpins the provision in
the first paragraph of Art.7 of Decision 1/80 means that the Member States'
powers in this regard are not unfettered by Community law.

---

[5] See Case C-355/93 *Eroglu v Land Baden-Württemberg* [1994] E.C.R. I-5113 and Case C-351/97
Kadiman v State of Bavaria [1997] E.C.R. I-2133, see most recently Case C-329/97 *Ergat v Stadt
Ulm* [2000] E.C.R. I-1487.
[6] Case C-351/97 *Kadiman v State of Bavaria* [1997] E.C.R. I-2133.
[7] Case C-351/97 *Kadiman v State of Bavaria* [1997] E.C.R. I-2133, para.35.
[8] Case C-351/97 *Kadiman v State of Bavaria* [1997] E.C.R. I-2133, para.37.
[9] Case C-351/97 *Kadiman v State of Bavaria* [1997] E.C.R. I-2133, para.31.
[10] Case C-351/97 *Kadiman v State of Bavaria* [1997] E.C.R. I-2133, para.33.
[11] Case C-329/97 *Ergat v Stadt Ulm* [2000] E.C.R. I-1487.
[12] Case C-329/97 *Ergat v Stadt Ulm* [2000] E.C.R. I-1487, para.42.

24–11   Although it is clearly for Member States to lay down the conditions under which family members may enter their territories to join Turkish workers duly registered as belonging to the labour force, the inclusion of Art.7 does presume that Member States will in fact permit family unity of such workers. The ECJ held in *Kadiman*[13] that the system under Art.7 was "designed to create conditions conducive to family unity in the host Member State, first by enabling family members to be with a migrant worker."[14]

24–12   Plainly apart from any obligations that may be created by Community law, Member States retain the competence to determine which third country nationals can enter their territories. Seen in this context, it is curious that Member States would need such an "enabling" provision to permit family unity if the first indent of Art.7 only leaves open the possibility for Member States to permit first entry. It must be implicit from the inclusion of Art.7 in Decision 1/80 that it is anticipated that in view of the general objective of family unity that Member States would, subject to conditions of national law, *facilitate* family reunification in some form for Turkish workers lawfully resident in their territories.

24–13   Indeed it can be inferred from the ECJ's judgment in *Kadiman* that Member States should be facilitating entry to family members of workers integrated in their labour forces.

> "In view of its meaning and purpose, that provision cannot therefore be interpreted as *merely* requiring the host Member State to have authorised a family member to enter its territory to join a Turkish worker without at the same requiring the person concerned to continue actually to reside there with the migrant worker until he or she becomes entitled to enter the labour market".[15]

24–14   The Turkish worker can therefore claim no right in Community law to be joined by his family member under any particular conditions. However, an absolute bar to the entry of *any* family member of a Turkish national legally employed in the territory of a Member State would arguably contradict the general aims of the Ankara Agreement, the decisions of the Council of Association and the understanding of the position by the ECJ as reflected by its statements in *Kadiman*.

(c) *Right of Residence for Family Members During the First Three Years*

24–15   The first indent of Art.7 of Decision 1/80 provides that the family members of Turkish workers have the right to respond, subject to priority being given to own national workers, to any offer of employment after three years legal residence. What rights then pertain to family members who have been granted entry to a Member State but who have not been legally resident for three years?

---

[13] Case C-351/97 *Kadiman v State of Bavaria* [1997] E.C.R. I-2133.
[14] Case C-351/97 *Kadiman v State of Bavaria* [1997] E.C.R. I-2133, para.37.
[15] Case C-351/97 *Kadiman v State of Bavaria* [1997] E.C.R. I-2133, para.38. (emphasis added).

The ECJ has held that nothing in Decision 1/80 affects the power of Member   **24–16**
States to attach conditions to the stay of family members of Turkish workers
until they become entitled to respond to offers of employment after the initial period of three years' residence.[16] The ECJ has stated that the first paragraph of Art.7 of Decision 1/80 does not preclude Member States from
requiring that the family members of a Turkish worker live together for the
period of three years prescribed by the first indent of that provision. Other
conditions might equally be applied to those family members during the first
three years, such as a maintenance requirement to avoid the family member's
becoming a burden on the social security system of the host Member State.

As observed in relation to the right of entry of family members, the compe-   **24–17**
tence retained by Member States to permit family members to reside on their
territories during the three-year period is not unfettered. The provisions of
Art.7 exist to consolidate the family member's position in the Member State
and "deepen the integration" of the family unit in the Member State.[17] The
spirit and purpose of Art.7 would be entirely undermined by a Member
State's refusing under any conditions to countenance the continued residence
of the family members of Turkish workers. Any conditions that are applied
to such family members must be of the kind that are consistent with the general aims of Decision 1/80. For example, since Art.7 is aimed at family unity
a national law condition that the family reside together would be consistent
with that provision.[18]

(d) Right of Residence of Family Members of Workers After Three Years' Residence

(i) Right of Residence as a Corollary of Right to Take up Employment

Once the family member of a Turkish worker fulfils the conditions of Art.7   **24–18**
there is an implied right of residence as a corollary of the right to respond to
offers of employment since the right of residence is "essential to access to and
the pursuit of any paid employment".[19] This position consistently taken by
the ECJ in relation to Art.7 is in line with its jurisprudence in relation to
Art.39 of the EC Treaty and Art.6 of Decision 1/80.[20]

---

[16] Case C-351/97 *Kadiman v State of Bavaria* [1997] E.C.R. I-2133, para.33.
[17] Case C-351/97 *Kadiman v State of Bavaria* [1997] E.C.R. I-2133, para.36.
[18] Whilst at first blush inconsistent with the ECJ's judgment in relation to separated couples
under provisions of Community law (see Case C-267/83 *Diatta v Land Berlin* [1985] E.C.R. 567),
it is to be recalled that conditions such as one of co-habitation can only be applied by national
authorities during the first three year period when Community law does not provide an unequivocal right of residence for the family member. Once the family member has acquired the right of
residence under that provision, her residence cannot be made conditional on cohabitation with
the Turkish worker.
[19] Case C-355/93 *Eroglu v Land Baden-Württemberg* [1994] E.C.R. I-5113, para.20.
[20] Case C-210/97 *Akman v Oberkreisdirektor des Rheinisch-Bergischen-Kreises* [1998] E.C.R. I-7519.

24–19   This right of residence will also include a reasonable period of grace when the person concerned is looking for employment in the Member State.[21] The length of such period is a matter for the host Member State, although it should not so short as to impair the right.[22] The ECJ has referred to its case law in relation to EU nationals who are seeking work pursuant to Treaty rights when considering the position of family members of Turkish workers. The ECJ considers it appropriate to treat such family members in an equivalent way to EU nationals who have the right to seek work in the territory of other Member States.[23]

(ii) *Calculation of the Three-year or Five-year Period*

24–20   The first indent of the first paragraph of Art.7 refers to lawful residence for three years and the second indent to lawful residence for five years. The ECJ has stated that whilst the family member must in principle reside "uninterruptedly" during those three (or five) years with the Turkish worker, the notion is one which must be interpreted flexibly.[24] Accordingly absences from the family home for a reasonable period and for legitimate reasons such as to take holidays, are permissible and will not break continuity of residence.

24–21   Consistent with provisions in secondary legislation relating to EU national workers, breaks in residence of no longer than six months will not affect the right of residence.[25] So far as the calculation of the time periods under the first paragraph of Art.7 is concerned, absences of up to six months must be treated as periods in which the family member concerned actually lived with the Turkish worker, provided that there is a legitimate reason for such absence.[26]

24–22   Furthermore, although the first paragraph of Art.7 refers to "lawful residence", short periods when the family member is not in possession of a valid residence document cannot affect the running of time for the purposes of the three-year period. In *Kadiman*[27] the former spouse of a Turkish worker was without a valid residence permit for a period of four months after her first residence permit was curtailed on the grounds that the couple were separated and a second permit issued to her four months later when her husband declared that they would resume living together.[28] Although the ECJ concluded that the lack of residence permit during that period did not affect the calculation of the three-year time period under Art.7.[29]

---

[21] Case C-355/93 *Eroglu v Land Baden-Württemberg* [1994] E.C.R. I-5113, para.21.

[22] Case C-237/91 *Kus v Landehauptstadt Wiesbaden* [1992] E.C.R I-6781.

[23] See Chapter 10 and see Case C-210/97 *Akman v Oberkreisdirektor des Rheinisch-Bergischen-Kreises* [1998] E.C.R. I-7519

[24] Case C-351/95 *Kadiman v State of Bavaria* [1997] E.C.R. I-2133, paras 48–49. *Kadiman* was a case concerned with the first indent.

[25] *cf.* Art.6 of Dir.68/360 discussed in Chapter 11 in relation to EU nationals.

[26] Case C-351/95 *Kadiman v State of Bavaria* [1997] E.C.R. I-2133, paras 49 and 50.

[27] Case C-351/95 *Kadiman v State of Bavaria* [1997] E.C.R. I-2133.

[28] Case C-351/95 *Kadiman v State of Bavaria* [1997] E.C.R. I-2133, paras 15, 16 and 22.

[29] In fact the German authorities had not sought to argue that she was unlawfully resident during that period despite the lack of residence permit.

In the event of dispute as to the entitlement to rights under Art.7 of Decision **24–23** 1/80, and if the individual is unable to produce a valid residence permit for the relevant period, the ECJ has stated that he must prove by any other means that he was *present* on the territory of the Member State or that he only left it for *legitimate* reasons. This implies that emphasis is not to be placed on the legality of residence, but instead on the fact of residence for the relevant period (since presence on a territory cannot be equated in national laws with legal residence). This is at odds with the emphasis placed on legality of residence and employment under Art.6(1) of Decision 1/80. However, it can be explained by the fact that in giving effect to principles of family unity protection is given to families that have in fact resided together for three years, even if their situation was not at all times regularised by the host Member State and even if that Member State did not intend to create conditions conducive to family unity.

(iii) *Retaining the Right to Take up Employment and Residence*

Once a family member has remained in the territory of a Member State for **24–24** three years and thereby satisfied the requirements of the first indent of the first paragraph of Art.7, that family member acquires a Community law right to take up offers of employment, subject to the priority given to EU nationals in the labour market. After five years of residence (as provided in the second indent of the first paragraph of Art.7), the family member of the Turkish worker attains unfettered access to the labour market.

On satisfaction of the initial three-year period, a break in residence should **24–25** not in principle affect the right under Art.7 to take up offers of employment (and as a corollary to reside in the relevant Member State) since this is a right which has already been acquired. However the ECJ has made clear that a family member of a Turkish worker who leaves the territory of the relevant Member State for a "significant" length of time without legitimate reason, generally loses the legal rights acquired under the first paragraph of Art.7.[30] In such instance the family member concerned can be expected to make a fresh application to re-join the Turkish worker in the relevant Member State.

The ECJ's interpretation of these principles is generous to the absent family **24–26** member. In *Ergat*[31] the ECJ found a period of absence from Germany of one year to be irrelevant to the acquisition of rights under Art.7 of Decision 1/80. This was because Mr Ergat had made an application for residence before departing based on his acquired rights under the provision. The ECJ did not consider it necessary to consider why he remained away from Germany for that year.[32] It was of some significance that the German authorities had not made his re-admission to Germany conditional upon the issue of a fresh authorisation to enter.

Further, the fact that a person applies for recognition of his right of residence **24–27** acquired under Art.7 of Decision 1/80 after the expiry of his previous

---

[30] Case C-329/97 *Sezgin Ergat v Stadt Ulm* [2000] E.C.R. I-1487, para.48.
[31] Case C-329/97 *Sezgin Ergat v Stadt Ulm* [2000] E.C.R. I-1487.
[32] Case C-329/97 *Sezgin Ergat v Stadt Ulm* [2000] E.C.R. I-1487, para.51.

residence permit does not affect the right of residence. This is consistent with general principles of Community law that residence permits issued pursuant to rights under Community law do not themselves confer the rights and that the lack of residence permits does not affect the right of residence itself. As the ECJ stated in *Ergat*:

> "the issue of a residence permit does not constitute the basis of the right of residence which is conferred directly by Decision No 1/80, and that is so irrespective of whether the authorities of the host Member State have issued that particular document, which is merely evidence of the existence of that right".[33]

(iv) *Definition of the "Family Member"*

24-28   There is no definition of family member in the Agreement or any of the Council of Association decisions. The ECJ in Ayaz[34] described the scope of family members in the context of Art.7 of Decision 1/80 as follows:

> "[I]n the determination of the scope of 'member of the family' for the purposes of the first paragraph of Article 7 of Decision No 1/80, reference should be made to the interpretation given to that concept in the field of freedom of movement for workers who are nationals of the Member States of the Community and, more specifically, to the scope given to Article 10(1) of Regulation No 1612/68"

Family members at the very least must include:

(a)   spouses, their descendants under the age of 21 years or their dependants;

(b)   dependent relatives in the ascending line of the worker and his spouse.[35]

24-29   Beyond such relationships the ECJ has given a broad interpretation to the concept of "member of the family" in the context of Art.7 of Decision 1/80. In *Eyüp*,[36] for example, the ECJ treated a divorcee who co-habited with her ex-husband as a "member of the family" with the result her residence during that period of co-habitation could be included in calculating her period of stay Austria and determining her Art.7 rights. The interpretation of family members in Community law is discussed in Chapter 10 above. Undoubtedly the ECJ's decision in *Eyüp* represents a significant move forward in recognizing *de facto* family relationships. Furthermore in *Ayuz*,[37] the ECJ interpreted family members to include those who are not blood relations such as step-children.

---

[33] Case C-329/97 *Sezgin Ergat v Stadt Ulm* [2000] E.C.R. I-1487, para.61.

[34] Case C-275/02 *Ayuz v Land Baden-Wurttemberg*, September 30, 2004, para.45.

[35] Art.10 of Reg.1612/68. See Case C-179/98 *Mesbah* [1999] E.C.R. I-7955, in which the ECJ held that the term 'member of the family' of a Moroccan migrant worker, within the meaning of Art.41(1) of the Moroccan Cooperation Agreement, extends to relatives in the ascending line of that worker and of his spouse who live with him in the host Member State. As the ECJ observed in *Ayaz* "that interpretation, given in respect of a cooperation agreement, must apply a fortiori with respect to an association agreement, which pursues a more ambitious objective" (para.47)

[36] Case C-65/98 *Eyüp v Landesgeschäftsstelle des Arbeitsmarktservice Vorarlberg* [2000] E.C.R. I-4747.

[37] Case C-275/02 *Ayuz v Land Baden-Wurttemberg*, September 30, 2004, para.46.

3. CHILDREN

(a) *Provisions in Decision 1/80 Relating to Children*

In addition to the rights acquired by family members of Turkish workers **24–30** after certain periods of residence, the second paragraph of Art.7 of Decision 1/80 confers specific rights on the children of Turkish workers to respond to offers of employment following completion of a course of vocational training.

The second paragraph of Art.7 of Decision 1/80 provides:

Children of Turkish workers who have completed a course of vocational training in the host country may respond to any offer of employment there, irrespective of the length of time they have been resident in that Member State, provided one of their parents has been legally employed in the Member State concerned for at least three years."

Further, Art.9 of Decision 1/80 provides: **24–31**

"Turkish children residing legally with their parents, who are or have been legally employed in a Member State of the Community, will be admitted to courses of general education, apprenticeship and vocational training under the same educational entry qualifications as the children of nationals of the Member States. They may in that Member State be eligible to benefit from the advantages provided for under the national legislation in this area".

(b) *Children Who Have Completed Vocational Training*

The right contained in Art.7 to respond to employment offers which is con- **24–32** ferred on children who have undertaken vocational training is silent as to the length of time for which any such vocational training must be undertaken. The second paragraph of Art.7 extends the right to take up employment and as a corollary the right of residence to all children, whatever nationality, of Turkish workers. At least one parent must have been legally employed in the Member State for at least three years.

(i) *Reasons for Granting Entry to the Child*

It is clear from the ECJ's decision in *Eroglu*[38] that the fact that the child of a **24–33** Turkish worker was originally granted a right to enter and stay for the purposes of vocational training only cannot preclude that child from benefiting from his rights under the second paragraph of Art.7. Regardless of his conditions of entry and stay, if a Turkish national satisfies the conditions set out in the second paragraph of Art.7, he may respond to any offer of employment in the Member State concerned and, by the same token, rely on that provision to obtain the extension of his residence permit:

---

[38] Case C-355/93 *Eroglu v Land Baden-Württemberg* [1994] E.C.R. I-5113.

"The fact that the right was not given to [children of Turkish workers] with a view to reuniting the family but, for example, for the purpose of study does not, therefore, deprive the child of a Turkish worker who satisfies the conditions of the second paragraph of Article 7 of the enjoyment of the rights conferred thereunder".[39]

24–34   This is consistent with the ECJ's view expressed in the context of Turkish workers benefitting from Art.6 of Decision 1/80 that the intentions of the Member State in admitting a person are unimportant once the individual has acquired rights in Community law. Thus the operation of Art.7 cannot be hindered by a lack of motivation of the part on the Member States to encourage family unity.

(ii) *Limitations on Exercise of the Right to Take up Employment*

24–35   There is no indication in Art.7 that the temporal conditions of Art.6(1) of Decision 1/80 have any relevance to children benefitting from Art.7. Thus a child qualifying under the second paragraph of Art.7 should be able to change occupation at any time of Art.6(1), since there is no limitation on changes in employer or occupation contained in Art.7.

24–36   It is not clear whether there is a time-limit within which the Turkish child qualifying under the second paragraph of Art.7 has to take up employment. However, in view of the general aims of achieving the free movement of workers in progressive stages, it must not be restrictively interpreted and thus a reasonable amount of time should be given to seek employment and commence that employment.[40]

(iii) *Remaining Beyond Worker*

24–37   Whilst the second paragraph of Art.7 stipulates that at least one parent of the child must have been legally employed in the relevant Member State for at least three years, it does not exclude the possibility of the child's remaining beyond the worker.

24–38   In the case of *Akman*[41] the ECJ held that in order to benefit from the provisions of the second paragraph of Art.7, it is not necessary for the parent still to work or be resident in the Member State when his child wishes to gain access to the employment market there.

24–39   The rationale for this is that the second paragraph of Art.7 is intended to provide specific treatment for children with a view to facilitating their entry into the employment market following completion of a course of vocational training, the objective being the achievement by progressive stages of freedom of movement for workers. The ECJ considered that the second paragraph of Art.7 is not aimed at providing the conditions for family unity and

---

[39] Case C-355/93 *Eroglu v Land Baden-Württemberg* [1994] E.C.R. I-5113, para.22.
[40] Case C-210/97 *Akman v Oberkreisdirektor des Rheinisch-Bergischen-Kreises* [1998] E.C.R. I-7519, paras 38 and 39.
[41] Case C-210/97 *Akman v Oberkreisdirektor des Rheinisch-Bergischen-Kreises* [1998] E.C.R. I-7519.

it would thus be unreasonable to require that the Turkish migrant worker should continue to reside in the host Member State even after his employment relationship there has ceased in order to secure his child's position, when that child has already completed training and wishes to respond to an offer of employment.

In *Akman*[42] the German Government had argued that the child should only **24–40** be allowed to take up employment under the strict restrictions of Art.6(1) of Decision 1/80. The ECJ rejected this argument stating that such an interpretation of Art.7 would negate the effectiveness of Art.7.[43] Clearly Art.6(1) applies to a child who has been legally employed in the Member State for a year and wishes to extend his contract with that employer but the second paragraph of Art.7 goes further. In the ECJ's words it is a "special provision specifically conferring on [children of Turkish workers] more favourable conditions as regards employment" in Member States.[44]

(c) *Children and Education*

The provision in Art.9 of Decision 1/80 reflects the right of access to general **24–41** education conferred on the children of EU national workers by Art.12 Reg. 1612/68. Such access is seen as part of the integration of a worker and his family to the host Member State.

The clear and unambiguous nature of the provision means that it has direct **24–42** effect. The ECJ has observed that Art.9 does not require the parents of the child to be legally employed when the children wish to exercise the rights thus conferred on them.[45] This is consistent with the interpretation of the equivalent provision relating to EU nationals.[46]

A child who has benefited from the provisions of Art.9 may thereafter bene- **24–43** fit from the provisions of the second paragraph of Art.7 by responding to any offer of employment having completed vocational training. In order to benefit from the right given by Art.9 of entry to the education system, children must be resident with their parents in the Member State (although the parents need not still be employed). Thereafter it would appear unnecessary for the parents to even reside in the Member State.

---

[42] Case C-210/97 *Akman v Oberkreisdirektor des Rheinisch-Bergischen-Kreises* [1998] E.C.R. I-7519.
[43] Case C-210/97 *Akman v Oberkreisdirektor des Rheinisch-Bergischen-Kreises* [1998] E.C.R. I-7519, para.49.
[44] Case C-210/97 *Akman v Oberkreisdirektor des Rheinisch-Bergischen-Kreises* [1998] E.C.R. I-7519.
[45] Case C-210/97 *Akman v Oberkreisdirektor des Rheinisch-Bergischen-Kreises* [1998] E.C.R. I-7519, para.41.
[46] See Case C-413/99 *Baumbast and R. v Secretary of State for the Home Department.* E.C.R. I–709. See discussion in Chapter 10.

4. FAMILY MEMBERS OF THOSE ESTABLISHED IN BUSINESS

24–44   Given the lack of specific rights of establishment conferred on Turkish nationals beyond the standstill clause provided for in Art.41(1) of the Additional Protocol, the lack of any detailed rights relating to family unity for those established in the territory of the Member States is unsurprising.

24–45   However, Art.13 of the Agreement refers to the guidance given by EC Treaty provisions relating to establishment of EU citizens and further the ECJ has placed emphasis that the ECJ has placed on family unity as being fundamental to EC Treaty provisions. This must mean that the scope of the standstill clause in Art.41(1) of the Additional Protocol extends to rights of family reunification for those seeking to establish in the territory of the Member States.[47]

24–46   Thus although as a Turkish national established or seeking to establish himself in a Member State does not have the unequivocal right to be accompanied by family members conferred by the Ankara Agreement any application for family reunification must be considered at least under conditions which are no more stringent than those reflected in national laws in place in the relevant Member State at the time when the Agreement came into force in that particular Member State.

---

[47] For further discussion of the standstill provision in Art.41(1) of Additional Protocol, see Chapter 23.

CHAPTER 25

EXPULSION UNDER THE ANKARA AGREEMENT

This chapter considers the application of the "public policy proviso" to Turkish nationals and their family members exercising rights under the Ankara Agreement. The rights enjoyed by workers in relation to expulsion are distinguishable from those enjoyed by Turkish nationals established in the Member States.

1. WORKERS AND THEIR FAMILY MEMBERS

(a) *Workers and their Family Members with Accrued Rights under Articles 6 and 7 of Decision 1/80*

(i) *Measures Taken on Grounds of Public Policy, Public Security or Public Health*

Article 14(1) of Decision 1/80 provides in relation to workers that "the provisions of this section shall be applied subject to limitations justified on grounds of public policy, public security or public health". The public policy proviso is a concept well known to Community law which is considered in detail in Chapter 14. Article 14(1) is identical to that contained in Art.39(3) EC Treaty, and indeed to that contained in Art.54(1) of each of the Europe Agreements.

25–01

The interpretative principle requiring the scope of rights in Decision 1/80 to be defined as far as possible by reference to the EC Treaty provisions relating to free movement of workers[1] provides ample justification for applying the Community law meaning given to such identically worded proviso where expulsion is faced by Turkish workers exercising rights under Decision 1/80. Nevertheless in *Nazli*[2] one of these questions referred to the ECJ was whether the expulsion of a Turkish worker on general preventive grounds as a deterrent to other aliens was compatible with Art.14(1) of Decision 1/80. The German Government argued that the prohibition of recourse to expulsion on general preventive grounds could not be derived from Art.39 EC Treaty and was introduced for EU nationals *only* by Directive 64/221.

25–02

The ECJ in *Nazli* robustly rejected such approach. The ECJ had no difficulty whatsoever in applying the interpretative principle identified[3] and stated:

25–03

"It follows that, when determining the scope of the public policy exception provided for by Article 14(1) of Decision No 1/80, reference should be made to the interpretation given to that exception in the field of freedom of movement for

---

[1] Case C-340/97 *Nazli v Stadt Nürnberg* [2000] E.C.R. I–957, paras 50–55 and references therein.
[2] Case C-340/97 *Nazli v Stadt Nürnberg* [2000] E.C.R. I–957.
[3] Case C-340/97 *Nazli v Stadt Nürnberg* [2000] E.C.R. I–957, paras 50–55.

workers who are nationals of a Member State of the Community. Such an approach is all the more justified because Article 14(1) is formulated in almost identical terms to Article 48(3) of the Treaty [now Art.39(3) EC Treaty]".[4]

25–04   The ECJ did not find it necessary to refer at all to Directive 64/221. The ECJ held that Art.14(1) precluded the expulsion of a Turkish national enjoying a right granted by Decision 1/80 following a criminal conviction as a deterrent to other aliens where there was no reason to consider that he would commit other serious offences prejudicial to the requirements of public policy in the host Member State. The ECJ did so on the basis of the following principles which in light of *Nazli* must be applied to Turkish workers facing expulsion:[5]

(a)   the concept of public policy presupposes the existence of a genuine and sufficiently serious threat to one of the fundamental interests of society;

(b)   although Member States may consider the use of drugs to constitute a danger for society justifying special measures against aliens who contravene its laws on drugs, the public policy exception must nevertheless be interpreted restrictively so that the existence of a criminal conviction could justify expulsion only in so far as the circumstances which gave rise to that conviction are evidence of personal conduct constituting a present threat to the requirements of public policy[6]; and

(c)   expulsion on general preventive grounds for the purpose of deterring others is not permitted, especially where applied automatically following a criminal conviction without any account being taken of the personal conduct of the offender or of the danger which that conduct represents for the requirements of public policy.

25–05   The importance of these principles cannot be overstated. They mean that a Turkish national can be denied the rights derived from Decision 1/80 only if expulsion is justified because of personal conduct indicating a specific risk of new and serious prejudice to the requirements of public policy.[7]

Moreover in response to such specific question raised by the Berlin Administrative Court in *Bicakci*[8] the ECJ made an order on September 19, 2000 in which it ruled—without hearing argument[9]—that:

"Article 14(1) . . . is to be interpreted as precluding the expulsion of a Turkish national who enjoys a right granted directly by [Decision 1/80] when it is ordered, following a criminal conviction, as a deterrent to other aliens without the personal conduct of the person concerned giving reason to consider that he will commit

---

[4] Case C-340/97 *Nazli v Stadt Nürnberg* [2000] E.C.R. I–957, para.56.
[5] Case C-340/97 *Nazli v Stadt Nürnberg* [2000] E.C.R. I–957, paras 57–59 and references there given.
[6] As acknowledged by the German national court in making the references to the ECJ in Case C-275/02 *Ayuz v Land Baden-Wurttemberg,* September 30, 2004, where personal contact did not indicate a specific risk "of new and serious prejudice to the requirements of public policy" expulsion of a person falling within the scope of Decision 1/80 would not be justified ; see para. 29.
[7] Case C-340/97 *Nazli v Stadt Nürnberg* [2000] E.C.R. I–957, para.61.
[8] Case C-89/00 *Bulent Recep Bicakci* (OJ 2000/C 149/41).
[9] The ECJ invoked Art.104(3) of the rules of procedure relating to identical questions.

other serious offences prejudicial to the requirements of public policy in the host Member State."

The same approach taken to Turkish workers facing expulsion applies to members of the worker's family who enjoy rights of residence under Art.7 of Decision 1/80. This is clear because Art.14(1) applies both to Arts 6 and 7 of Decision 1/80.

The question of whether the expulsion of a Turkish worker who had **25–06** obtained a residence permit by fraud would be compatible with Art.14(1) of Decision 1/80 was raised, although not answered, in the earlier case of *Kol*.[10] In that case the Turkish worker had obtained his residence permit only by means of inaccurate declarations for which he was convicted of fraud. Expulsion was sought as a preventative measure with a view to deterring others. In light of *Nazli*[11] the answer to the question about the compatibility with Decision 1/80 of a measure taken on such grounds must be that such expulsion would be prohibited. This does not mean however that a Turkish worker who obtains a residence permit by fraud cannot be expelled. To the contrary, such person will not have any accrued rights under Art.6(1) of Decision 1/80 since—as held by the ECJ in *Kus*[12]—periods of employment in reliance on a fraudulently obtained residence permit cannot be regarded as legal employment for the purposes of Art.6(1). In these circumstances the narrow interpretation to be given to the public policy proviso contained in Art.14(1) is irrelevant to such person.

(ii) *Appeals*

The corollary to the proposition that Turkish national workers enjoying **25–08** rights of residence under Arts 6 and 7 of Decision 1/80 may not be expelled save in the circumstances identified by the ECJ in *Nazli*[13] must be the existence of some procedural guarantees to protect the individual from the arbitrary interference by a Member State of rights derived from Community law.

In the Community context Directive 64/221 provides procedural guarantees **25–09** for persons exercising free movement rights—together with members of their families—who face expulsion. The provisions of Directive 64/221 are considered in Chapter 14. These should be regarded as the minimum guarantees to be afforded to Turkish workers in these circumstances. The reach of Arts 8 and 9 of Directive 64/221 in cases where Turkish workers enjoy rights under Arts 6 and 7 of Decision 1/80 is the subject of a reference to the ECJ by the Austrian Higher Administrative Court in *Dorr*.[14] Although in Austria it appears that there is an appeal available in respect of expulsion decisions such an appeal is not necessarily suspensive and is limited in scope. The gravity of any interference with a Community law right enjoyed by Turkish nationals in the present context should lead to the conclusion that any appeal

---

[10] Case C-285/95 *Kol v Land Berlin* [1997] E.C.R. I–3069.
[11] Case C-340/97 *Nazli v Stadt Nürnberg* [2000] E.C.R. I–957.
[12] Case C-237/91 *Kus v Landeshauptstadt Wiesbaden* [1992] E.C.R. I–6781, para.26.
[13] Case C-340/97 *Nazli v Stadt Nürnberg* [2000] E.C.R. I–957.
[14] Case C-136/03 *Dorr and Unal* (OJ 2003/C 135/18).

must be both suspensive and capable of a subjecting the merits of the underlying expulsion decision to proper scrutiny.

(b) *Workers and their Family Members without Accrued Rights*

25–10 Workers and their family members who have yet to accrue rights otherwise contained in Arts 6 and 7 will nevertheless potentially benefit from the standstill provision in Art.13 of Decision 1/80 if legally resident (for example a legally resident worker who has only worked for six months in the host Member State). Although Art.13 prevents the introduction of new restrictions on the conditions of access to employment for both workers and their family members, *access* must plainly be interpreted broadly so as to include expulsion which by definition would prevent any access to employment.

2. SELF-EMPLOYED TURKISH NATIONALS

(a) *The Self-employed in a Regular Position*

25–11 If expulsion measures are taken against the six month legally resident worker, he can be subject to measures that are no more stringent than were in place at the time when Decision 2/76 came into force in the host Member State. This is because the standstill provision in relation to workers was first introduced by Art.7 of Decision 2/76, which as regards workers was repeated in identical terms in Art.13 of Decision 1/80. The position for family members on the other hand is different. They can be subject to measures that are no more stringent than were in place at the time when Decision 1/80 came into force in the host Member State. This is because Art.7 of Decision 2/76 made no mention whatsoever of family members. National law and practices in many Member States are likely to have been more benevolent in 1976 or 1980 (whichever applies) than they are today.

25–12 In this context Turkish nationals in self-employment in Member States should be accorded the same protections and guarantees as are accorded to workers and their families when expulsion measures are taken against them. According to the ECJ in *Savas*,[15] Turkish nationals who are lawfully resident and lawfully carrying out a genuine and effective self-employed activity in the territory of a Member State have the Community law rights to continue in that self-employed activity and, as a corollary, extend their residence. Such persons must similarly enjoy the same protections against expulsion as are enjoyed by workers or indeed any EU national enjoying Community law rights of free movement.

---

[15] Case C-37/98 *The Queen v Secretary of State for the Home Department Ex p. Savas* [2000] E.C.R. I-2927.

(b) *Self-employed Covered by the Standstill Provision*

As explained in Chapter 23, all Turkish nationals who wish to establish them- **25–13**
selves in business are protected by the standstill provision in Art.41(1) of the
Additional Protocol. Whilst those in a regular position will have the right of
continued residence and the corresponding protection against expulsion
other self-employed Turkish nationals attain only the right not to be subjected to any new restrictions on the freedom of establishment and the
freedom to provide services.

Turkish nationals who are unlawfully present (which will include both those **25–14**
who have been admitted and remained beyond their permission and those
who entered irregularly) cannot be subject to expulsion measures that are any
more stringent than those in place when the Additional Protocol came into
force in the host Member State.[16] Finally Turkish nationals who seek entry in
order to establish themselves must likewise receive at least such procedural
guarantees as were afforded to business applicants at the time when the
Additional Protocol came into force in the host Member State.

---

[16] Namely 1972 for the original Member States, the date of accession for the others.

Part Four
UK LAW AND PRACTICE

INTRODUCTION TO UK LAW AND PRACTICE

This Part provides information and analysis on UK law and practice and the 26–01
implementation of Community law provisions on the free movement of persons. It is intended to mirror the scheme of the book and be used alongside
the main parts of this book which describe the position in Community law.
It is divided into three parts:

• *Chapter 27* examines in brief the general implementation of Community
law into UK legislation and the relationship between the UK courts and
the ECJ.

• *Chapter 28* examines the United Kingdom's implementation of
Community law relating to the free movement of EU citizens and their
family members covered in Part Two.

• *Chapter 29* examines the United Kingdom's implementation of free
movement provisions contained in the Association Agreements covered
in Part Three.

It is not necessary or intended to describe in detail legal provisions and prac- 26–02
tices in the United Kingdom which conform properly with Community law
provisions. The aim of this part of the book therefore is to focus on contentious areas where UK law and practice would appear to diverge from
Community law standards. In addition areas are examined where UK law
and practice is relevant to the actual application of Community law provisions (for instance under the Association Agreements where national authorities may have in place their own laws regarding entry and stay).

The supremacy of Community law in the area of free movement must always 26–03
be kept in mind as must the fact that most concepts, procedures and rights
are spelt out in detail by Community law itself. In the case of divergence
between Community law and UK law and practice, the former will always
prevail. As a matter of good practice readers should always firstly have
regard to the substantive Community law provisions applicable in any given
situation. Certainly it must never be assumed that UK law and practice
accurately reflect Community law provisions or standards. Reading the decisions of some national courts at times gives the impression that national law
standards have been applied at the expense of the dilution of Community law
principles.

Finally detailed explanation in this Part of Community law principles is nec- 26–04
essarily extremely limited. It will always be important therefore to refer for
substantive discussion of Community law matters to Parts One to Three of
this book.

INCORPORATION OF COMMUNITY LAW INTO UK LAW

For the European Union law on the relationship between domestic law and Community law readers are referred to Chapter 2 in Part One of this book.

1. Relevant Legislation

European Communities Act 1972   **27–01**

European Communities (Spanish and Portuguese Accession) Act 1985

European Communities (Amendment) Act 1986

European Communities (Amendment) Act 1993

European Economic Area Act 1993

European Union Accessions Act 1994

European Communities (Amendment) Act 1998

European Communities (Amendment) Act 2002

European Union (Accessions) Act 2003

2. The Legal Framework for Community Law in the United Kingdom

(a) *Introduction*

In UK law the foundation of the United Kingdom's relationship with the   **27–02**
European Union is the European Communities Act 1972 ("the 1972 Act").
On January 1, 1973 the United Kingdom became a member of the European
Communities (the EEC, Euratom and ECSC) pursuant to the EEC Treaty of
Accession 1972. Politically the United Kingdom's membership of the
European Communities has not been easy. Despite the passing of the 1972
Act, membership has remained controversial. In 1975 a new Labour govern-
ment recommended that the United Kingdom remained in the European
Communities but that the matter be put to a referendum. In the only UK
national referendum to be held to date on the United Kindom's participation
in the European project, the electorate voted to remain in the European
Union.[1]

The 1972 Act makes it possible for the United Kingdom to comply with its   **27–03**
obligations arising from the Community Treaties. Section 1 of the Act defines

---

[1] 67.2 per cent of the electorate voted to remain in the European Communities; 32.8 per cent voted to leave. E.C.S. Wade and A.W Bradley, *Constitutional and Administrative Law* (10ᵗʰ ed.)

the Community Treaties to which the Act relates. They originally included the Treaty of Rome and the Euratom Treaty, the Treaty of Accession, the Council decision relating to the United Kingdom's accession to the ECSC and certain other treaties entered into by the Communities prior to Act.

(b) *Main Provisions of the European Communities' Act 1972*

(i) *Treaties Included in the Act*

27–04   Section 1 has been subsequently amended by a series of Acts where Treaty amendments have occurred:

(a)   European Communities (Spanish and Portuguese Accession) Act 1985 amends the 1972 Act to include Spain and Portugal in the Member States of the European Economic Community (as it was then known);

(b)   European Communities (Amendment) Act 1986 was passed to incorporate the provisions of the Single European Act 1986 into the 1972 Act;

(c)   European Communities (Amendment) Act 1993 was enacted following the Maastricht Treaty signed on February 7, 1992. Section 1 of the 1972 Act is amended to include the provisions of the Maastricht Treaty within its scope;

(d)   European Economic Area Act 1993 incorporated the provisions of the European Economic Area Agreement signed in Oporto on May 2, 1992 such that the 1972 Act will apply to the EEA where appropriate;[2]

(e)   European Union Accessions Act 1994 amended the definition of Treaties in s.1 of the 1972 Act so as to include the Treaty concerning the accession of Norway, Austria, Finland and Sweden to the European Union;

(f)   European Communities (Amendment) Act 1998 makes consequential provisions following the amendments to the EU and EC Treaties made by the Amsterdam Treaty signed on October 2, 1997;

(g)   European Communities (Amendment) Act 2002 amends the 1972 Act following amendments to the EU and EC Treaties by the Treaty of Nice signed on February 26, 2001;

(h)   European Union (Accessions) Act 2003 makes consequential provisions following the accession of the Czech Republic, Estonia, Cyprus, the Republic of Latvia, Lithuania, Hungary, Malta, Poland, Slovenia and the Slovak Republic to the European Union, signed at Athens on April 16, 2003. The 2003 Act additionally makes special provision in relation to the entitlement of nationals of certain acceding states to enter or reside in the United Kingdom as workers.

---

[2] See Chapter 15 para.15–18 on EEA Agreement.

(ii) *Operation of Community Law in the United Kingdom*

Section 2 of the 1972 Act is of paramount importance in ensuring the effective   **27–05**
operation of Community law in the United Kingdom. Section 2(1) provides:

> "All such rights, powers, liabilities, obligations and restrictions from time to time
> created or arising by or under the Treaties, and all such remedies and procedures
> from time to time provided for by or under the Treaties, as in accordance with the
> Treaties are without further enactment to be given legal effect or used in the United
> Kingdom shall be recognised and available in law, and be enforced, allowed and fol-
> lowed accordingly; and the expression 'enforceable Community rights' and similar
> expressions shall be read as referring to one to which this subsection applies".

Section 2(1) thus provides that all those provisions that under Community   **27–06**
law are directly effective,[3] shall be directly effective in United Kingdom and
given the force of law. The provision has both retroactive and prospective
effect in that it applies to Community law made both before and after the
coming into force of the 1972 Act. This provision gives effect to the doctrine
of primacy of Community law over national law.

Those Community law provisions which do not have direct effect require   **27–07**
implementation by the Member States[4]. Section 2(2) and (4) of the 1972 Act
give broad powers for the passing of delegated legislation to implement
Community legislation.

(iii) *Obligation on UK Courts*

Section 3 of the 1972 Act relates to the use of Community law in UK courts.   **27–08**
Section 3(1) provides that any question as to the interpretation or validity of
a Community law provision shall be treated as a question of law. If to not be
referred to the European Court of Justice such questions of law are to be
decided in accordance with the principles laid down by the relevant decisions
of the ECJ. Section 3(2) provides that all UK courts are to take judicial notice
of the Community Treaties, the *Official Journal of the European Communities*
and any decisions of the ECJ.

3. REFERENCE TO THE ECJ FROM UK COURTS

(a) *Circumstances in which a Case Will Be Referred from a UK Court*

The circumstances in which a court should refer a question for preliminary   **27–09**
ruling to the ECJ are discussed in Chapter 2 above. The UK courts, other
than the House of Lords which will for most cases be the final court of
appeal for the purposes of Art.234 EC Treaty are guided by the case of *Else*[5]
in which Sir Thomas Bingham, M.R. stated:

---

[3] See Chapter 2.
[4] See Chapter 2 for discussion about which provisions of Community law have direct effect.
[5] *R. v International Stock Exchange Ex p. Else Ltd* [1993] 1 All E.R. 420.

"I understand the correct approach in principle of a national court (other than a final court of appeal) to be quite clear: if the facts have been found and the Community law issue is critical to the court's final decision, the appropriate course is ordinarily to refer the issue to the Court of Justice unless the national court can with complete confidence resolve the issue itself. In considering whether it can with complete confidence resolve the issue itself the national court must be fully mindful of the differences between national and Community legislation, of the pitfalls which face a national court venturing into what may be an unfamiliar field, of the need for uniform interpretation throughout the Community and of the great advantages enjoyed by the Court of Justice in construing Community instruments. If the national court has any real doubt, it should ordinarily refer. I am not here attempting to summarise comprehensively the effect of such leading cases as *H P Bulmer Ltd v J Bollinger* ([1973] 2 All ER 1226) *Srl CILFIT v Ministry of Health* (Case C-283/81) and *R v Pharmaceutical Society of GB, Ex p. Association of Pharmaceutical Importers* ([1987] 3 CMLR 951), but I hope I am fairly expressing their essential point."

27–10   Paragraph 32 of the House of Lords' *The Blue Book*[6] sets out the circumstances in which the House of Lords will refer a question to the ECJ. As the final court of appeal. In many instances, Art.234(3) EC Treaty obliges the House of Lords to refer a question for reference in accordance with the ECJ's guidance in the case of *CILFIT*.[7] This obligation is reflected by para.32.3 of *The Blue Book*:

"32.2 When the House refuses leave to appeal on a petition which includes a contention that a question of Community law is involved, the House will give reasons for its decision not to grant leave to appeal. These reasons will reflect the decision of the Court of Justice in *CILFIT v. Ministry of Health* (Case C–283/81) which laid down the categories of case where the Court of Justice considered that no reference should be made to it, namely (a) where the question raised is irrelevant; (b) where the Community provision in question has already been interpreted by the Court of Justice; (c) where the question raised is materially identical with a question which has already been the subject of a preliminary ruling in a similar case; and (d) where the correct application of Community law is so obvious as to leave no scope for any reasonable doubt."

Such guidance would also apply to any other court from which there was no other judicial remedy.

(b) *Which English Courts or Tribunals are Entitled to Refer Questions to the ECJ*

27–11   Article 234(2) EC Treaty provides that any court or tribunal may make a reference to the ECJ. The question of whether a referring body is a "court or tribunal" for the purposes of Art.234(2) is a matter of Community law, not national law.[8] In *Dorsch Consult*[9] the ECJ laid down the following criteria for determining whether a body is a court or tribunal for these purposes:

---

[6] *The Blue Book* is published by the House of Lords judicial office and outlines procedures before the House of Lords.
[7] Case 283/81 *CILFIT v Ministry of Health* [1982] E.C.R. 3415.
[8] Case 246/80 *Broekmeulen v Huisarts Regstratie Commissie* [1981] E.C.R. 2311.
[9] Case C-54/96 *Dorsch Consult Ingenieurgesellshaft mbH v Bundesbaugesellschaft Berlin mbH* [1997] E.C.R. I-4961.

- whether the body concerned is established in law;
- whether it is permanent;
- whether it is independent;
- whether its jurisdiction is compulsory;
- whether its procedure is *inter partes*;
- whether it applies rules of law;
- whether it is called upon to give judgment in proceedings intended to lead to a decision of a judicial nature.

In the immigration jurisdiction the ECJ has found that an adjudicator satisfies these requirements and thus can refer questions for reference to the ECJ.[10] Similarly questions for reference have been accepted from the Immigration Appeal Tribunal.[11] Indeed there is no reason for an Adjudicator or the Immigration on Appeal Tribunal (IAT)[12] indeed established (or/when established and operational the Asylum and Immigration Tribunal) to refrain from referring a question for reference if there are issues that are determinative of an appeal that cannot be answered by reference to the ECJ's existing case law. No practice directions exist for adjudicators or the IAT on referring questions for the ECJ which may be indicative of the infrequency with which this occurs. **27–12**

On a judicial review the High Court may make an order for reference providing the hearing is *inter partes*. Part 68 of the Civil Procedure Rules (CPR) sets out the rules in relation to the making of an order for reference by a court in England and Wales. A court may make the order of its own initiative or on an application by a party. An order may not however be made by a Master or district judge in the High Court or a district judge in the County Court. The CPR make clear that where an order for reference is made, unless the court orders otherwise the proceedings will be stayed until the ECJ has given a preliminary ruling on the question referred. **27–13**

(c) *The Final Court*

In most civil matters, the House of Lords will be the final court of appeal for the purposes of Art.234(3) EC Treaty. However with the introduction of "statutory review" to the immigration jurisdiction by s.101 Nationality, Immigration and Asylum Act 2002 (the 2002 Act), the final court in an immigration case may well be the High Court on a statutory review since the decision by the High Court on a statutory review is not subject to any further form of review. Statutory review is available where any party to an appeal to **27–14**

---

[10] Case C-416/96 *Nour Eddline El-Yassine v the Secretary of State for the Home Department* [1999] E.C.R. I-1209.
[11] Case C-109/01 S*ecretary of State for the Home Department v Akrich*, judgment of September 23, 2003.
[12] See s.26 Asylum and Immigration (Treatment of Claimants, etc.) Act 2004, amending s.82(1) Nationality Immigration and Asylum Act 2002 substituting the previous two tier system with the single Asylum and Immigration Tribunal. The single tribunal will likely be operational from April 2005.

an adjudicator seeks permission to appeal to the IAT and is refused permission. The party may then apply by way of paper application to the High Court for a statutory review of the refusal of the IAT of permission to appeal. The position will be the same with respect to applications made to the High Court under s.103A of the 2002 Act (as amended by the Asylum and Immigration (Treatment of Claimants, etc.) Act 2004).

27–15 However the statutory review proceedings are not *inter partes* and for this reason do not satisfy the *Dorsch Consult*[13] requirements. This means that the High Court on a statutory review could not refer a matter to the ECJ. The position is extremely unsatisfactory because the High Court is the final appeal court but is unable to refer. In a case where there is any doubt as to the application of Community law it appears that the only possible approach would be for the High Court to grant the statutory review—with the result that the permission is granted to appeal to the IAT—so as to enable the IAT itself then to refer questions to the ECJ. The situation is not improved by the Asylum and Immigration (Treatment of Claimants, etc.) Act 2004.

(d) *Appeals Against the Making of a Reference*

27–16 It is often agreed (or at least conceded) between the parties that a question should be referred by the court or tribunal in question to the ECJ. However where a party is aggrieved by a questions being referred that party may appeal, although such appeals rarely succeed.[14]

(e) *Costs*

27–17 No order for costs is generally made by the ECJ in a preliminary reference. All ECJ judgments have a standard formula in the final paragraph of the reasoning in which the ECJ states that since the preliminary reference proceedings are, for the parties to the main proceedings, a step in the proceedings pending before the national court, the decision on costs is a matter for that court. In the English courts the decision in *Fish Producers' Organisation*[15] makes clear that costs in respect of the reference generally follow the event.

27–18 Since in the immigration jurisdiction there are no provisions for the award of costs before adjudicators or the IAT, it is often beneficial for parties to seek references from these tribunals rather than waiting until the matter reaches the Court of Appeal or House of Lords.

---

[13] Case C-54/96 *Dorsch Consult Ingenieurgesellshaft mbH v Bundesbaugesellschaft Berlin mbH* [1997] E.C.R. I-4961.

[14] An appeal to the Court of Appeal against the decision by Scott Baker J. in the Administrative Court to refer two questions to the ECJ in Case C-37/98 *The Queen (on the Application of "A") v Secretary of State for the Home Department* [2002] EWCH Civ 1008, was successful. The Court of Appeal considered that the ECJ had already determined the question of law central to the case in Case C-37/98 *R. v Secretary of State for the Home Department Ex p. Savas* [2000] 3 C.M.L.R. 729.

[15] *R. v Intervention Board for Agricultural Produce Ex p. Fish Producers' Organisation Ltd* [1993] 1 C.M.L.R. 707.

FREE MOVEMENT OF UNION CITIZENS AND THEIR FAMILY MEMBERS

For the Community law provisions and practice relating to the free movement of EU nationals and their family members readers are referred to Part Two (Chapters 5 to 14) of this book.

1. RELEVANT PRIMARY AND SECONDARY LEGISLATION

Immigration Act 1971   **28–01**

Immigration Act 1988

Immigration and Asylum Act 1999

Immigration (European Economic Area) Regulations 2000 (SI 2000/2326)

Immigration (European Economic Area) (Amendment) Regulations 2001 (SI 2001/865)

Immigration (Swiss Free Movement of Persons) (No.3) Regulations 2002 (SI 2002/1241)

Nationality, Immigration and Asylum Act 2002

Immigration (European Economic Area) (Amendment) Regulations 2003 (SI 2003/549)

Nationality, Immigration and Asylum Act 2002 (Juxtaposed Controls) Order 2003

The Accession (Immigration and Worker Registration) Regulations 2004 (SI 2004/121)

Social Security (Habitual Residence) Amendment Regulation 2004 (SI 2004/1232)

The Immigration (European Economic Area) and Accession (Amendment) Regulations 2004 (SI 2004/1236)

2. UK NATIONALS FOR THE PURPOSES OF EU LAW

In Chapter 5 the beneficiaries of Community law are outlined. It is permissi-   **28–02**
ble for Member States to define which of their nationals are EU citizens for
the purposes of EU law. For most Member States this has no relevance and
all their nationals are treated as EU citizens and accordingly acquire full free
movement rights within the European Union. However for the United
Kingdom some of the categories of national are precluded from obtaining

the benefits of EU law. In the United Kingdom, the Declaration accompanying the United Kingdom's Treaty of Accession, the Government defined the meaning of national for the purposes of the Treaties. A new declaration was made at the time of the British Nationality Act 1981 when much of British nationality law was changed.

28–03 The United Kingdom's Declaration means that the following are to be considered as "nationals" for the purposes of EU law:

(a) British citizens;

(b) British subjects with the right of abode in the United Kingdom;

(c) British Dependent Territories citizens who acquire that citizenship as a result of a connection to Gibraltar.[1]

28–04 In *Kaur*[2] the ECJ was referred questions on the validity of the UK declaration[3] and whether Art.17 EC Treaty conferred any rights on persons who were not defined as "nationals" under the terms of such a declaration. The ECJ was categorical in its response that EU citizenship was conferred only on "nationals of Member States" and the declarations entered by the United Kingdom defining who its "nationals" are for the purposes of EU citizenship were valid and unchallengeable.

3. GENERAL SCHEME FOR EEA NATIONALS AND THEIR FAMILY MEMBERS

(a) *Introduction*

28–05 As will be apparent from the discussion of the free movement of persons in Community law, Member States of the European Union, by being party to the EC Treaty, forego their sovereign right to control the entry and stay of nationals of other Member States who are exercising free movement rights contained within the EC Treaty and secondary legislation.[4] The only exception is where exclusion or expulsion is justified on grounds of public policy, public security and public health.[5]

28–06 This is reflected in UK law by the Immigration Act 1988 (the 1988 Act). Unlike other non-UK citizens, a person entitled to enter or remain in the United Kingdom "by virtue of an enforceable Community right or of any provision made under section 2(2) of the European Communities Act 1972"[6] does not require leave to enter or remain under the Immigration Act 1971 (the 1971 Act).

---

[1] January 28, 1983 [1983] O.J. C23/1, (Cmnd 9062 1983). The term 'British Dependent Territories Citizen' is now a reference to British Overseas Territories Citizens (with effect from February 26, 2003, on passing of the British Overseas Territories Act 2002).

[2] Case C-192/99 *The Queen v Secretary of State for the Home Department Exp. Kaur* [2001] All E.R. (EC) 250.

[3] The validity of the 1982 Declaration was questioned as it was made without any statutory authority or parliamentary approval.

[4] See Chapters 5 and 14.

[5] See Chapter 14.

[6] Section 7(1) of the Immigration Act 1988.

Thus the control by immigration officers and other agents of the Secretary of **28–07**
State on the movement of persons exercising Treaty rights is removed.[7]
Section 7(2) of the 1988 Act provides that where EU nationals are not enti-
tled to enter or remain in the United Kingdom pursuant to the Treaties, the
Secretary of State may make an order giving them leave to enter for a limited
period.

European Union free movement law is for the most part adequately repre- **28–08**
sented the Immigration (European Economic Area) Regulations 2000 (the
EEA Regulations). These Regulations replaced the Immigration (EEA)
Order 1994 which had been regarded as an unsatisfactory and inaccurate
reflection of free movement rights. The EEA Regulations are an attempt to
consolidate within one statutory instrument the rights and procedures applicable to both EU nationals exercising Treaty rights flowing from the relevant
Regulations and Directives[8] and EEA nationals who benefit from the EEA
Treaty.[9] In most respects the EEA Regulations are consistent with those
Regulations and Directives. However caution must be used in approaching
the EEA Regulations since they are not the ultimate source of rights. In the
case of Community law Regulations, the provisions of those Regulations are
directly effective. In the case of Community law directives, where there is conflict between the EEA Regulations and the relevant Community law
Directive, the provisions of the Community law directive will prevail.[10]

The general scheme of the EEA Regulations is considered below. National **28–09**
regulations relating to the accession of 10 new Member States on May 1,
2004 are considered separately below.[11]

(b) *Beneficiaries of Free Movement Rights*

The EEA Regulations refer to the beneficiaries of rights of free movement as **28–10**
"qualified persons". Regulation 5 of the EEA Regulations defines which
EEA nationals are exercising free movement rights and are thus "qualified
persons". They are a worker, a self-employed person, a provider of services,
a recipient of services, a self-sufficient person, a retired person, a student, a
self-employed person who has ceased activity and the family member of a
self-employed person (both active and one who has ceased activity) and who
has died whether that person was active or had ceased activity prior to death.

---

[7] As regards third country national family members, however, they will be subject to Sch.2 to
the Immigration Act 1971 examination powers in order to establish whether they *are* in fact entitled to enter or remain by virtue of an enforceable Community law right.
[8] Namely Regs 1612/68 (workers) and 1251/70 (permanent residence for workers); Dirs 64/221
(exclusion), 68/360 (abolition of restrictions on movement and residence), 73/148 (establishment
and services); 75/34 (permanent residence of those established); 90/364 (general right of residence); 90/365 (retired persons) and 93/96 (students).
[9] See Chapter 15. Whilst there is in principle nothing impermissible about including EU and EEA
nationals within the same regulation, the wider rights enjoyed by EU nationals flowing from the
EC Treaty (principally Arts 17 and 18 EC Treaty) will not be adequately reflected in regulations
which fail to distinguish between EU and EEA nationals when the scope of their rights is in fact
different.
[10] See Chapter 2.
[11] See paras 28–61 *et seq.* below.

28–11   The terms "worker", "self-employed person", "provider of services" and "recipients of services" are defined in Reg.3 of the EEA Regulations. These concepts are all defined by reference to the EC Treaty. Thus for example "worker" means a worker within the meaning of Art.39 EC Treaty.

28–12   As a result of an amendment to the EEA Regulations[12] the definitions of the "self-sufficient person" and "retired person" include a reference to the fact the resources of the principal must be sufficient to avoid him and his family members from becoming a burden on the social security system of the United Kingdom. Students must be enrolled at a recognised education establishment in the United Kingdom for the principal purpose of following a vocational training course. Students must assure the Secretary of State that their resources and those of family members are sufficient to avoid the student and any family members becoming such a burden.[13]

28–13   In terms of the identification of qualified persons the EEA Regulations fall short in two specific respects. Firstly there is no provision made in the EEA Regulations (or indeed in the Immigration Rules) for posted workers who are performing services in the United Kingdom for an employer established in another Member State.[14]

28–14   Secondly there is no residual discretion contained in the EEA Regulations to treat any other EU national falling outside for these categories as a "qualified person". This results in mandatory refusals of those who fall outside the definition of a qualified person. Chapter 4 deals with the right of Union citizens to move and reside freely given by Art.18 EC Treaty. Although the scope of the Art.18 EC Treaty right is continuing to evolve, the provision has had impact and has been held by the ECJ to extend to circumstances beyond the scope of specific provisions in the EC Treaty and secondary legislation. Domestic law makes no attempt to reflect this possibility.

28–15   Thirdly, the EEA Regulations are silent as to work seekers who fall unambiguously within Art.398 EC Treaty.[15] Mention should also be made of the fact the EEA Regulations are silent as to frontier workers. Although they are "workers", they nevertheless in certain specific circumstances may qualify for a discrete Community law right of permanent residence not given generally to workers.[16]

(c) *Family Members*

(i) *General*

28–16   The family members who may accompany the qualified person are provided for in Reg.6. This provision defines the family members of qualified persons

---

[12] The Immigration (European Economic Area) and Accession (Amendment) Regulations 2004, SI 2004/1236.
[13] Reg.3 of the EEA Regulations as amended properly reflects the difference in evidential requirements between those exercising a general right of residence and retired persons on the one hand and students on the other. See Chapter 11.
[14] See Chapter 8.
[15] Case C-292/89 *R. v IAT Ex. p. Antonissen* [1991] E.C.R. I-745.
[16] Reg.1251/70 and Dir. 75/34; see Chapter 11.

as the spouse, their descendants who are under 21 or dependent, dependent relatives in the ascending line of both the qualified person and his spouse. The definition of family members for a student is more limited and only includes the student's spouse and dependent children.[17]

Other family members[18] are provided for in Reg.10. This regulation makes   **28–17** provision for the grant of an EEA family permit or residence permit for the "relatives"[19] of the EEA national or his spouse who are dependent on the EEA national or spouse, are living as part of the EEA national's household outside the United Kingdom or were living as part of the EEA national's household before he came to the United Kingdom. Reflective of the relevant Community law Directives, EEA Reg.10 does not extend to the relatives of EEA nationals who are in the United Kingdom as self-sufficient persons, retired persons or students.

These provisions identifying family members generally conform with   **28–18** Community law. However there are a number of areas where UK definitions of family members present a potential conflict with the provisions of Community law.

(ii) *Spouses*

The EEA Regulations specifically exclude from the meaning of spouses "a party   **28–19** to a marriage of convenience".[20] The meaning of the term "marriage of convenience" is not defined in the Regulations or the Immigration Directorate's Instructions (IDIs). The Community law definitions of this phrase must be applied.[21] It would not be legitimate for any requirements of cohabitation to be imposed on EU nationals following the ECJ's decision in *Diatta*.[22]

(iii) *Family Member of Returning UK Nationals*

As is discussed in Chapter 5 the case of *Surinder Singh*[23] provides an excep-   **28–20** tion to the general rule that own nationals do not benefit from Community law in their own Member State. The ECJ's decision on returning residents in the case of *Surinder Singh* is reflected in Reg.11 of the EEA Regulations which states that if the UK national resides in another Member State and is either employed or self-employed there and resided with his family member there, then that family member will be treated on return to the United Kingdom as if that person were a family member of an EEA national.

However Reg.11(2)(b) of the EEA Regulations provides that such family   **28–21** member only obtains the benefit of being treated as the family member of an EEA national if "the United Kingdom national did not leave the United

---

[17] This reflects Community law: see Dir. 93/96 on students.

[18] As provided for in Art.10(2) of Reg.1612/68.

[19] The term in Art.10(2) of Reg. 1612/68 is "any member of the family". Both relative and member of the family should be interpreted purposively to include a broad range of family members. See Chapter 11.

[20] Reg.2 of the EEA Regulations state "spouse does not include a party to a marriage of convenience".

[21] See Chapter 10.

[22] Case 267/83 *Diatta v Land Berlin* [1985] E.C.R. 567.

[23] Case C-370/90 *The Queen v Immigration Appeal Tribunal Ex p. Surinder Singh* [1992] E.C.R. I–4265.

Kingdom in order to enable his family member to acquire rights under these Regulations and thereby to evade the application of United Kingdom immigration law".

28–22 In *Akrich*[24] the ECJ confirmed that the intention of the parties exercising Treaty rights was irrelevant to the application of the *Surinder Singh* principle. In light of this Reg.11(2)(b) must be incompatible with Community law. Furthermore the requirement that the UK national actually resides in another Member State and must either have been employed or self-employed there does not accord with the ECJ's decision in *Carpenter*.[25]

(iv) *Unmarried Partners*

28–23 As a matter of current Community law the unmarried partners of EEA nationals exercising free movement rights in the United Kingdom are entitled to be treated at least as favourably as the unmarried partners of British citizens.[26] Provision for unmarried partners to be permitted to join persons present and settled in the United Kingdom is included in the Immigration Rules at para.295(d). The unmarried partner of an EEA national would therefore be expected to meet the requirements set out in that paragraph. Unlike family members of EEA nationals who fall within the scope of EC regulations and directives, the unmarried partners will need to meet all the requirements of domestic law which includes for instance a maintenance and accommodation requirement. The non-EEA national partner is normally given a residence permit with no restriction on employment or self-employment.

28–24 However, unlike the unmarried partners of British nationals, those of EEA nationals are not eligible after the 24-month period for indefinite leave to remain. Instead he or she must wait until the EEA national is eligible for settlement after four years' residence.

(v) *Transsexuals*

28–25 An obvious lacuna in UK law is that no provision has been made to reflect the cases of *Goodwin* (ECtHR),[27] *Bellinger and Bellinger* (House of Lords)[28] or *KB* (ECJ).[29] These cases have established the proposition that the inability of post-operative transsexuals to marry a person of the opposite sex is incompatible with the requirements of Arts 12 and 14 ECHR,[30] which Community Law should reflect.

---

[24] Case C-109/01 *Secretary of State for the Home Department v Akrich*, judgment of September 23, 2003.

[25] Case C-60/00 *Carpenter v Secretary of State for the Home Department* [2002] E.C.R. I-6279, discussed in Chapter 5. It will be recalled that Mr Carpenter resided continuously in the UK whilst exercising his free movement right to provide and receive services in other Member States.

[26] In *R. v Secretary of State of the Home Department Ex p. McCollum* the Administrative Court refused to construe a stable same-sex relationship as falling within the meaning of "member of family" for the purpose of Community law. This does not affect reliance on the "social advantages" argument. See further Chapter 10.

[27] *Goodwin v United Kingdom* [2002] 35 E.H.R.R. 18.

[28] *Bellinger v Bellinger* [2003] UKHL 21.

[29] Case C-117/01 *KB v (1) National Health Service Pensions Agency (2) Secretary of State for Health*, judgment of January 7, 2004.

[30] In *Silvo Londono Ruben Marlon v Secretary of State* (HR/15244/2003), July 23, 2003, an adjudicator allowed an appeal against the refusal by the Secretary of State to grant an EEA residence document to post-operative female transsexual in a long-term relationship with an EEA national who was running his own business in the UK. The Secretary of State did not appeal this decision.

(vi) *Children*

UK law raises two specific issues relating to children. Firstly, Reg.6(2)(b) of the EEA Regulations defining the family members of students refer to the dependent children of the student only. This does not reflect Directive 93/96, which refers to the dependent children of both the student and his spouse. This Community law definition covers the step-children of the student, whereas the UK provision does not.

As discussed in Chapter 11, adopted children must be regarded as children   **28–26** for the purposes of Community law. However in the United Kingdom the adoption of children from outside the European Union can be a contentious issue. A child who is adopted under a procedure which is not recognised under the Adoption Act 1976 will not be treated as the legitimate child of the adoptive parents for the purposes of UK immigration law. The application of this principle to the adoptive child of an EEA national residing in the United Kingdom might unlawfully result in the refusal of a residence permit or EEA family permit. A Member State would need to justify on public policy grounds why a particular adoption could not be recognised under provisions of Community law. Even if the adoptive child were not to be considered as a child within the meaning of Community law, that child should surely be considered as a dependent.[31] A more restrictive interpretation would be incompatible with the right to respect for family life.[32]

(vii) *Primary Carers of Children*

The United Kingdom has given effect to the *Baumbast*[33] judgement through   **28–27** an amendment to the EEA Regulations.[34] Regulation 6 now provides the primary carer of a child in education will be granted a residence permit subject to certain conditions. A child over the age of four in nursery school education would qualify as a child in education. The EEA national can have exercised any Treaty right in the United Kingdom.[35]

It is not entirely clear why the Regulations refer to the child being under the   **28–28** age of 19 since there is nothing in the ECJ's judgement in *Baumbast* which restricts the age of the child. In Community law children under the age of 21 do not need to prove dependency. There must be situations in which a child in education might still require the support and presence of a parent to continue (e.g. a disabled child). The decision of the ECJ in *Chen*,[35A] relating to "self-sufficient" children and their carers, will require an amendment to the Regulations.

---

[31] Under Art.10(2) of Reg.1612/68 for instance.

[32] See further Chapter 11 on family members.

[33] Case C-413/99 *Baumbast and R. v Secretary of State for the Home Department* [2002] E.C.R. I-7091.

[34] For discussion of Case C-413/99 *Baumbast and R. v Secretary of State for the Home Department* [2002] E.C.R. I-7091, see Chapter 11.

[35] Letter dated November 14, 2003 from IND to Philip Barth of Mishcon de Reya.

[35A] Case C-200/02 *Man Lavette Chen and Kunqian Catherine Zhu v Secretary of State for the Home Department*, October 19, 2004. See further Chapter 4, paras 4–60 to 4–63.

(d) *Admission of EU Nationals and Their Family Members*

(i) *EU Nationals*

28–29   By virtue of s.7(1) Immigration Act 1988 persons exercising rights under Community law do not require leave to enter or remain in the United Kingdom. It follows that nationals of Member States not exercising Treaty rights will therefore require leave to enter or remain under immigration controls normally applicable to non-EU nationals.

28–30   In compliance with Art.3 of Directive 68/360, EEA nationals are admitted to the United Kingdom freely on production of a valid identity card or passport issued by an EEA State by virtue of Reg.12(1) and (2) of the EEA Regulations without enquiry as to the precise basis in Community law on which the person seeks to enter.[36] The Home Office Immigration Directorates' Instructions (IDIs) remind immigration officers that they may not examine an EEA national beyond the production of his identity card unless there are reasons to believe that there may be grounds for exclusion for reasons of public policy, public security or public health.

28–31   Where there is reason to believe that an EEA national may be liable to be excluded on grounds of public policy, public security or public health he will be subject to immigration controls under the 1971 Act. More particularly such EEA national will be subject also to the administrative provisions which permit his detention, temporary admission or release pending a decision to give or refuse him leave to enter.

(ii) *Family Members*

28–32   Under the EEA Regulations third country national family members of EEA nationals exercising Treaty rights in the United Kingdom must obtain an EEA family permit before travelling to the United Kingdom to join the EEA principal.[37] An EEA family permit is equivalent to a visa. The EEA family permit must be issued free of charge. Regulation 29 provides a right of appeal against the refusal to issue an EEA family permit. This must be exercised outside the United Kingdom except where there is an allegation that the refusal would breach human rights.

28–33   The IDIs state that there is a discretion to grant entry to the family member of an EEA national who does not hold a valid EEA family permit.[38] Where discretion is exercised and the family permit requirement is waived, the family member will be admitted for 12 months and advised to apply for a residence document. The discretionary power to admit an EEA national without an

---

[36] The Nationality, Immigration and Asylum Act 2002 (Juxtaposed Controls) Order 2003 gives effect to the Treaty between UK and France providing for the exercise of immigration control by the authorities of each State in the sea ports of the other State, the sea ports being Dover, Calais, Boulogne and Dunkirk. Reg.5 of the Order amends the EEA Regulations by amending reg.12(2) and enabling immigration officers to request authorised passports, identity cards, family permits, residence permits or documents proving family relationships (which may be required to be produced under the EEA Regulations as a condition for admission to the UK) to be produced in a control zone.

[37] Regs. 12 and 13 of the EEA Regulations.

[38] Annex E to Chapter 7, section 3 refers.

EEA family permit is plainly required for the United Kingdom to act compatibly with the ECJ's decision in *MRAX*.[39] A lengthy wait for admission or grant of an EEA family permit will not conform with Art.3 of Directive 68/360 which provides that family members must be accorded every facility to obtain any necessary visas.[40]

(e) *Residence Permits*

(i) *EU Nationals*

Part IV of the Regulations makes provisions regarding the issue of residence permits. Qualified persons are to be granted "residence permits" save in circumstances where the duration of stay is short, normally less than three months. Residence permits are granted for five years' duration save in certain cases (such as for the provider or recipients of services) where the residence permit will be limited to the period of service provision.

28–34

Unlike other Member States the United Kingdom does not require EEA Nationals to obtain residence permits. They are able to reside and take up employment without the need for residence permits. Regulation 15 of the EEA Regulations provides for the issuing of residence permits to EEA nationals on production of "proof that [the EEA national] is a qualified person". Regulation 16 provides for the circumstances in which there is no requirement to issue a residence permit such as where the qualified person is a worker whose employment is limited to three months. Regulations 15 and 16 would appear to comply with the requirements of Directive 68/360.[41]

28–35

(ii) *Family Members*

Regulation 15(2) provides for the issue of a residence document to the family member of a qualified person under the EEA Regulations. This will take the form of a stamp in the person's passport.[42] The duration of the family member's residence document will be equivalent to the duration of the EEA principal's residence permit.[43] The family member of a qualified person is entitled to reside in the United Kingdom without the requirement for leave to remain under the 1971 Act for as long as he remains the family member of a qualified person.[44] The family member may however be removed from the United Kingdom if he ceases to be the family member of a qualified person. As with EEA nationals, their family members may appeal against the refusal to issue a residence document. However the same limitations to the exercise of this right of appeal were inserted for family members in so far as they also must have valid identity documents.

28–36

---

[39] See further Chapter 11.
[40] In *Jimale, Re (For Costs)* (2003) (Case No. CO/2289/2003), October 15, 2003. The applicant applied for judicial review against an entry clearance officer for breach of Community law where the ECO had refused to provide an interview for the spouse of an EEA national in respect of her application for an EEA in less than nine months. After permission to apply for judicial review was granted on the papers the ECO offered an interview within weeks but refused to pay costs in respect of the judicial review proceedings. Costs were awarded by Bellamy J.
[41] For further discussion on residence permits under Community law, see Chapter 11.
[42] Reg.17(2).
[43] Reg.20.
[44] Reg.14.

(iii) *Indefinite Leave to Remain*

28–37   Paragraphs 255 and 256 of the Immigration Rules HC 395 make provision for the grant of indefinite leave to remain to certain EEA nationals and their family members.

28–38   Any person who has resided in the United Kingdom in compliance with the EEA Regulations for four years is eligible to apply for the national status of indefinite leave to remain under para.255 of the Immigration Rules HC 395.

> "255. Any person (other than a student) who under, either the Immigration (European Economic Area) Order 1994, or the 2000 EEA Regulations has been issued with a residence permit or residence document valid for 5 years, and who has remained in the United Kingdom in accordance with the provisions of that Order or those Regulations (as the case may be) for 4 years and continues to do so may, on application, have his residence permit or residence document (as the case may be) endorsed to show permission to remain in the United Kingdom indefinitely".

28–39   Although para.255 refers to the applicant already having a residence permit it is possible to apply simultaneously for a residence permit and indefinite leave to remain if the EEA national is a qualified person and can evidence the fact that he has been a qualified person for the past four years. The EEA national does not need to have been "qualified" in the same capacity for four years. For example, there is nothing in the wording of para.255 of the Immigration Rules that would prevent a worker who after two years working in the United Kingdom then retired and remained as a retired person for a further two years from applying for indefinite leave to remain. There is no right of appeal against the refusal to grant indefinite leave to remain to EEA nationals.

28–40   The possibility of applying for indefinite leave to remain is usually of most interest to the third country national family members of EU nationals. This is because once granted, their status is no longer dependent on the exercise of EC Treaty rights by their principal, or their continued relationship with such principal. The Secretary of State's normal practice is to grant indefinite leave to remain to a third country national spouse of an EU national where the couple are in the process of divorcing.[45]

28–41   Paragraph 257 of the Immigration Rules HC 395 provides for the grant of indefinite leave to remain to all those entitled to permanent residence under Reg.1251/70[46] with two exceptions. Firstly, and rather inexplicably, the provision in Art.3(2) for family members of a deceased worker were the surviving spouse is a UK national or has lost UK nationality by virtue of marriage is not replicated in para.257. Secondly the provision is silent as to frontier workers for whom specific provision is made in Art.2(1)(c) of Reg.1251/70.

---

[45] Letter dated December 8, 2003 from IND to Philip Barth of Mishcon de Reya Solicitors.
[46] Reg.1251/70 provides for the grant of permanent residence for workers and their family members under certain circumstances following the termination of employment or death of the worker. See Chapter 11.

Those who obtain the right to permanent residence under Directive 75/34[47] **28–42**
are entitled to obtain indefinite leave to remain by virtue of Reg.8 of the EEA
Regulations. Again the regulation does not properly reflect the provisions of
Directive 75/34 as the surviving spouse (of a self-employed person) who lost
UK nationality by virtue of marriage is not provided for. Further those
"frontier" self-employed persons referred to in Art.2(1)(c) of Directive 75/34
are again not provided for.

It is important to recall that "indefinite leave to remain" is created by domes- **28–43**
tic law and not Community law. Only those entitled to permanent residence
under Reg.1251/70 and Directive 75/34 could claim a Community law right
to indefinite leave to remain.[48] It will not be a breach of Community law to
refuse to grant indefinite leave to remain unless the EEA nationals and their
family members are being treated in a discriminatory manner.

In *Kaba*,[49] the ECJ found that it was permissible and not discriminatory for **28–44**
the UK Government to make applicants choose whether they wanted to
pursue all their immigration applications under national provisions or under
Community law. It is thus not necessary for the UK authorities to allow
applicants to rely on the provision which is more favourable to them
depending on what application they are making at the time.

(f) *Exclusion and Expulsion*

Part VI of the Regulations deals with the inter-relationship between the **28–45**
Regulations and the 1971 Act. Where a person seeks admission as the family
member of an EEA national or where the person is an EEA national but
there is reason to believe he may be excluded on grounds of public policy,
public security or public health, that person is to be treated "as if he were a
person seeking leave to enter the United Kingdom under the 1971 Act". This
means that the person may be detained, temporarily admitted or released
whilst liable to detention in accordance with the provisions of the 1971 Act.

---

[47] Dir. 75/34 replicates the provisions for the grant of permanent residence set out in Reg.1251/70
in respect of self-employed persons. See further Chapter 11.
[48] For such persons enjoying a Community law right to permanent residence the grant of the
domestic law creation of indefinite leave to remain might be thought to be otiose, quite apart
from the fact that such person would, by virtue of s.7(1) of the 1988 Act not be subject to immigration control. However there are substantial benefits for those granted indefinite leave to
remain including most obviously the possibility of applying for citizenship.
[49] Case C-356/98 *Arben Kaba v Secretary of State for the Home Department* [2000] E.C.R. I-2623.
The facts were that in May 1994 Mr Kaba married a French national who was working in the
UK and was permitted to remain the UK. In January 1996, Mr Kaba applied for indefinite leave
to remain. This request was refused as Mr Kaba did not fulfil the requirements of the
Immigration Rules as his wife had only been in the UK for one year and 10 months as the spouse
of a qualified person. Mr Kaba appealed to an adjudicator contending that the provisions of the
Immigration Rules applicable to persons present and settled in the UK were more favourable
than those applicable to him and his wife. One question referred to the ECJ by the adjudicator
asked if the right to apply for indefinite leave to remain in the UK, and the right to have that
application considered, constituted a "social advantage" within the meaning of Art.7(2) of
Reg.1612/68. The adjudicator also asked if the requirement imposed on the spouses of EU
nationals, to have been resident in the UK for four years before such an application might be
made and considered as compared to a requirement of 12 months' residence as was applied to
spouses of UK nationals and spouses of those present and settled in the UK (para.287 of the
Immigration Rules), constituted unlawful discrimination.

28–46 Regulation 21 of the EEA Regulations makes provision for the exclusion and removal from the United Kingdom of EEA nationals in certain circumstances. Regulation 21(3) provides that an EEA national may be removed from the United Kingdom if he is not a qualified person within the meaning of the EEA Regulations. By Reg.26 of the EEA Regulations, a person who ceases to be a qualified person will be liable to administrative removal under s.10 Immigration and Asylum Act 1999.

28–49 Concerns arise because the definition of a qualified person is restricted to certain categories of free mover (namely to the economically active and non-active free movers specifically provided for in secondary legislation, *i.e.* workers, self-employed, students, retired persons and self-sufficient persons). This does not reflect the more extensive interpretation of the scope of free movement rights contained in Art.18 EC Treaty.[50] Children for instance who might be exercising free movement rights pursuant to Art.18 EC Treaty are not provided for in the EEA Regulations.[51] This is a clear example of a situation where readers must emphasise the primacy of Community law provisions.

28–50 The EEA Regulations allow the Secretary of State to refuse to renew or revoke a residence permit or document on the grounds that the individual is a threat to public policy, public security or public health. Regulation 23 sets out the circumstances on which a decision can be made public policy grounds to exclude or expel a person. These are reflective of the provisions in Directive 64/221.

28–51 Guidance given to Immigration Officers on the refusal of admission of EEA nationals and their family members on grounds of policy, public security or public health are set out in the IDIs at Annex E which states:

"A person must present a serious threat to the fundamental interests of Society by his personal conduct. Whether or not such a threat exists is a matter for judgement in the individual circumstances of each case. However, it should be borne in mind that:

- Previous criminal convictions would not in themselves be sufficient grounds, unless the offence(s) was particularly serious (e.g. rape, murder, drug smuggling) or it was likely that the person would re-offend.
- Person charged with minor Customs offences should not be refused admission on this basis alone.
- A person who was the leader of an extreme political party might present such a threat.
- Facilitation of illegal entry may in itself be sufficient grounds to refuse admission to EEA Nationals.
- National security can fall under this heading.

---

[50] See further Chapter 4 on Union Citizenship.
[51] Classically a situation where initial reliance will be placed on the EEA Regulations without reference to such wider Community law obligations.

Although this is guidance, as regards serious criminal convictions it plainly   **28–52**
purports to reflect the Court of Appeal's decision in *Marchon*.[52] This
approach is not easy to reconcile with the ECJ's case law which is discussed
in Chapter 14. It is notable that the ECJ has never accepted that past conduct
alone constitutes grounds for expulsion but rather that there must be
"propensity" to re-offend, indicating a risk higher than the smallest risk of re-
offending. The Court of Appeal's decision in *Marchon* is an example of a case
which leaves the impression that Community law principles have been diluted
by the application of national law principles.

A more recent example is the decision of the Court of Appeal in *Schmelz*[53] in   **28–53**
which an adjudicator had found that although there was a low risk of the
appellant re-offending, his offence was nevertheless serious enough to justify
expulsion. Schmelz was a German national who had been granted indefinite
leave to remain in 1985. He claimed to have worked in his uncle's business
since 1979 although no records of work or payment of tax or national insurance was available. Schmelz was convicted of conspiracy to rob, having been
found to be the main organiser of the hijacking of an armoured Securicor
van and was sentenced to 12 years' imprisonment. The Secretary of State
decided to make a deportation order against him. In the appeal against this
decision, Schmelz relied on probation officer's report which put the chance of
his re-offending as low.

On a judicial review the Court of Appeal stated its view that "There were   **28–54**
some exceptional cases in which past criminal conduct itself justified
deportation of an EC citizen. The present case fell into that category".[54]

(g) *Appeals*

Part VII of the Regulations makes provision for appeals in respect of deci-   **28–55**
sions concerning removals, entitlement to be admitted and entitlement to be
issued with a residence permit in accordance with the Regulations. Sections
82 and 84 of the Nationality, Immigration and Asylum Act 2002 (the NIA
2002) also makes provision for appeals against immigration decisions on the
grounds that the decision is not in accordance with Community law.

(i) *Appeals Against Refusal of Admission*

An EEA national refused admission to the United Kingdom has a right of   **28–56**
appeal under Reg.29 of the EEA Regulations. The right of appeal can be
invoked in-country. Regulation 30 makes clear that the right of appeal is generally exercisable from abroad. Where a ground of the appeal is the decision
matter acted in breach of the person's human rights (Reg. 30(3)(b)). The right
of appeal is also in country where on arrival the person held an EEA family
permit or a residence permit or residence document (Reg.30(3)(c)).[55]

---

[52] *R. v the Secretary of State for the Home Department Ex p. Marchon* [1993] 2 C.M.L.R. 132.
[53] *R. (on the application of Schmelz) v Immigration Appeal Tribunal* [2004] EWCA Civ 29, CA,
January 15, 2004.
[54] *R. (on the application of Schmelz) v Immigration Appeal Tribunal* [2004] EWCA Civ 29, CA,
January 15, 2004 *per* Buxton L.J., para.15.
[55] Also appeals to the Special Immigration Appeals Commission are in-country (Reg.30(3)(a)).

Subsequently however the appeal rights of EEA Nationals were further restricted by the Immigration (EEA) (Amendment) Regulations 2003 (the 2003 Amendment Regulations), which amend Reg.29 and excludes a right of appeal unless a person claiming to be an EEA national produces a valid national identity card or a valid passport issued by an EEA state. The 2003 Amendment Regulations also state that, for the purposes of the appeal regulations, a document is to be regarded as being what it purports to be provided that this is "reasonably apparent" and it is to be regarded as being related to the person using it unless it is reasonably apparent that it relates to another person.

28–57 The 2003 Amendment Regulations also amend Reg.29(5) by preventing multiple appeals by those who claim to have rights under the EEA Regulations where the Secretary of State or an immigration officer has certified that an EEA ground in respect of an appeal was previously considered in connection with an appeal brought under the regulation or under s.82(1) of the NIA 2002.

28–58 Where the Secretary of State refuses to revoke a deportation order, an out-of-country right of appeal also exists under Reg.29 of the EEA Regulations.

28–59 The 2003 Amendment Regulations also amend the 2000 Regulations by inserting new provisions on appeals to the Special Immigration Appeals Commission (SIAC) where a decision to exclude or remove a person from the United Kingdom is taken in the interests of national security or in the interests of the relationship between the United Kingdom and another country.

(ii) *Right of Appeal Against Refusal of Residence Permit*

28–60 A person refused a residence permit or served with a decision to remove him from the United Kingdom has a right of appeal under Reg.29 of the EEA Regulations. The appeal lies to an adjudicator (except in national interest cases[56]). An EEA national may only appeal under Reg.29 (as amended by the 2003 Amendment Regulations) if he produces a valid national identity card or a valid passport, issued by an EEA state.

4. Accession

(a) *Relevant Legislation*

28–61 The Accession (Immigration and Worker Registration) Regulations 2004 (SI 2004/121)

Social Security (Habitual Residence) Amendment Regulation 2004 (SI 2004/1232)

---

[56] In which case the appeal lies to the Special Immigration Appeals Commission. The grounds for exclusion or removal must be that the person's exclusion or removal from the UK is (a) in the interests of national security, or (b) in the interests of the relationship between the UK and another country.

The Immigration (European Economic Area) and Accession (Amendment) Regulations 2004 (SI 2004/1236)

(b) *General Provisions*

The Accession (Immigration and Worker Registration) Regulations 2004 (the   **28–62**
Accession Regulations) amended the EEA Regulations to include within
their scope the 10 new Member States as from May 1, 2004. In compliance
with the Treaty of Accession the EEA Regulations reflect the fact that free
movement rights are generally extended to the nationals of the 10 new
Member States and their family members.

In accordance with the Treaty of Accession national laws were put in place to   **28–63**
provide for the situation of workers from eight of the 10 new Member States'
(A8)[57] workers. As is set out in more detail below the right of residence for
workers and work-seekers from the A8 countries is limited in the following ways:

(a)   A8 workers will only be lawfully resident in the United Kingdom during
their first year of employment if they have registered their employment
and are working for authorised employers;

(b)   A8 workers who cease to work during their first year of employment
will only be lawfully resident for the remainder of the month in which
they worked;

(c)   work-seekers from the A8 countries are not "entitled to reside in the
UK";

(d)   the family members of A8 workers during the first year of employment
will not be granted residence permits

Regulations 4 and 7 of the Accession Regulations refer to derogation from   **28–64**
Art.39 EC Treaty as well as Arts 1 to 6 of Reg.1612/68. Whilst doubtless this
reflects the Secretary of State's view of the scope of permissible derogation,
derogation from Art.39 EC Treaty is not permitted by the terms of the Annexes
to the Treaty of Accession. Paragraph 1 of the Annex V (Czech Republic) to the
Treaty of Accession for instance makes quite clear that Art.39 EC Treaty and
Reg.1612/68 will apply in full from the date of accession save where derogation
is permitted. Paragraph 2 of the Annex permits derogation only from Arts 1 to
6 of Reg.1612/68. This reflects the fact that it is only conditions of *access* to the
labour market that can be limited in the transition period.

This apparent conflict with the Treaty of Accession is not simply academic. It   **28–65**
is reflective of a fundamental flaw in the United Kingdom's post-accession
regime. It would appear that the underlying motivation of the UK Government
in implementing the Accession Regulations and changes to social security legislation discussed below was to respond to the media frenzy that occurred
immediately prior to accession of the 10 new Member States about the potential for exploitation of the United Kingdom's benefits regime. Many of the

---

[57] Nationals of Czech Republic, Hungary, Poland, Slovak Republic, Slovenia, Estonia, Latvia
and Lithuania.

changes implemented at the time of accession were therefore aimed at preventing new Member State nationals from obtaining any form of welfare benefits.[58]

28–66 However, the very specific derogation permitted by the Treaty of Accession, which is not reflected in the UK legislation, is aimed at permitting Member States to protect their labour markets. It might be suggested that Member States that do open up their labour markets are acting generously and ought not to have the detail of the regime put in place analysed too critically. However lest any regime be exploitative such Member State cannot provide *less* protection or afford *less* social rights to A8 nationals than would be afforded to any other EU national. Non-discrimination is a fundamental principle of Community law and it is extremely unlikely that the Community would turn its back on decades of progress and permit Member States to benefit from labour migration without acquiring at least some social responsibilities for the migrants. In other words if Member States wish to enjoy the benefits of labour migration, Community law will expect them to take on the attendant social responsibilities involved.[59]

(c) *Workers and their Family Members*

28–67 The Accession Regulations create a legal requirement that A8 nationals register their employment during the first 12 months of employment in the United Kingdom (except those subject to exemption from the regime who are considered below). Failure to register will result in the person working in breach of immigration laws and an offence being committed by the employer.[60] There is no requirement for the nationals of Malta or Cyprus to register their work.[61]

28–68 During the first 12 months of employment, an A8 national requiring registration will not be granted a residence permit although he is a "qualified person" for the purpose of the EEA Regulations.[62] Thus an A8 national who properly registers his employment will be lawfully resident but will not be able to evidence that lawful residence by obtaining a residence permit.

28–69 After the first 12 months of working, the A8 national may apply for an EEA Residence Permit in accordance with the EEA Regulations 2000.[63]

28–70 An A8 national is exempt from the worker registration scheme if he:

---

[58] See paras 28–86 to 28–88 *et seq.* on social security below.
[59] Shortly after the UK announced its accession regime, European Commission President, Romano Prodi, expressed concern at the UK regime, *http://news.bbc.co.uk/1/hi/uk_politics/3518047.stm.*
[60] Section 9 of the EEA Regulations.
[61] Indeed such requirement would be contrary to the Treaty of Accession which does not permit any derogation from Reg.1612/68 in respect of citizens from Malta or Cyprus.
[62] Regs 5(2) and 5(6) of the Accession (Immigration and Worker Registration) Regulations 2004.
[63] It should be recalled that this residence permit will not give Community law rights in other Member States during the transitional period if that Member State retains derogations to free movement provisions on workers: see Chapter 6.

- had leave to enter/remain in the United Kingdom on April 30, 2004 with no restriction on employment[64] (for instance those with probationary leave as a spouse);

- had leave to enter or remain in the United Kingdom on April 30, 2004 with a condition restricting employment and had worked in accordance with that condition in the United Kingdom without interruption up to April 30, 2004[65] (for instance a work permit holder);

- worked legally in the United Kingdom for a period of at least 12 months ending after April 30, 2004 without interruption;[66]

- has dual nationality and is a national of the United Kingdom, an EEA State (except an A8 Member State) or Switzerland;[67]

- is a posted worker;[68]

- is the family member of a Swiss or EEA national, who is in the United Kingdom as

  (i)   a worker, other than an A8 national requiring registration;
  (ii)   a self sufficient person;
  (iii) a retired person;
  (iv)   a self-employed person;
  (v)   a student.[69]

Furthermore the Accession Regulations provide that during the period when **28–71** the A8 national is required to register his employment, his spouse or other relatives may not obtain a residence permit.[70] However since Reg.14 of the EEA Regulations (giving the right of residence to qualified persons) is not disapplied by anything in the Accession Regulations:

(a) the A8 national who is registered is entitled to reside in the United Kingdom without the requirement for leave to remain (as he is a qualified person according to Reg.5(2) of the Accession Regulations); and

(b) the spouse of that A8 national is entitled to reside in the United Kingdom without the requirement for leave to remain under the 1971 Act for as long as the spouse remains a family member (as the spouse is a family member of a qualified person according to both Reg.2(9)(c) of the Accession Regulations and Reg.6 of the EEA Regulations 2000).

Thus the A8 national and any family members will be lawfully resident in the United Kingdom providing that the A8 national is properly registered, but they will not be given residence permits as evidence of their right of residence.

---

[64] Reg.2(2).
[65] Reg.2(3).
[66] Reg.2(4).
[67] Reg.2(5).
[68] Reg.2(6)(a).
[69] Reg.2(6)(b) as amended by the Immigration (European Economic Area) and Accession (Amendment) Regulations 2004 (SI 2004/1236).
[70] Reg.5(5).

28–72   The family member of the A8 national worker however can obtain a stamp in the passport which will state:

> "In accordance with the Immigration (European Economic Area) Regulations 2000 [name] has a right to reside in the United Kingdom as the family member of [name] who is working in the United Kingdom for an authorised employer in accordance with the Accession (Immigration and Worker Registration) Regulations 2004".[71]

28–73   Removal directions given for the removal of a qualified person or the family member of a qualified person ceased to have effect on or after May 1, 2004.[72]

Finally the family members of an A8 national required to register under the Accession Regulations are also required to register their employment. However the family members of other A8 nationals (including those workers who are not required to register) are not required to register their employment.[73]

28–74   The Accession Regulations define "family member" of a worker as " his spouse and his children who are under 21 or dependent on him".[74] Article 10 of Reg.1612/68 which defines a family member of a worker for the purposes of EU law is considerably broader and includes dependants in the ascending line as well as other dependent relatives. Furthermore the reference to the worker's children ("his children") would apparently exclude the child of the spouse in contradiction with Art.10(1) of the Reg.1612/68 (which refers to "their descendants"). Since no derogation from Art.10 of Reg.1612/68 is permitted under the Treaty of Accession, the limited definition of family member under the Accession Regulations is impermissible.

28–75   Registration of work in the United Kingdom or acquisition of a residence permit as a worker in the United Kingdom will have no effect on the status of the individual in other Member States. During the transition period, the situation of workers in this context is purely a question of national law.

(d) *Work Seekers*

28–76   Regulation 4 of the Accession Regulations purports to deprive work-seekers from the A8 countries of any right of residence in the United Kingdom unless they are self-sufficient and can meet the conditions laid down in Directive 90/364.

28–77   Access to the labour market during the transitional period is a matter of national law. In the case of the United Kingdom access to the labour market *is* given to A8 nationals. Yet at the same time the United Kingdom's treat-

---

[71] See the IDI's Chapter 7, Section 3. Reg.33 of the Accession Regulations as amended by the Immigration (European Economic Area) and Accession (Amendment) Regulations 2004 refer to a "family member residence stamp". Applicants are advised by the IND website to use form EEC3 for obtaining this stamp.
[72] Reg.6 of the Accession (Immigration and Worker Registration) Regulations 2004.
[73] Reg.2.
[74] Reg.2(9)(c).

ment of work seekers has the practical effect of undermining such right of access otherwise granted. This is because of the undesirable consequence that the United Kingdom fails to grant a right of lawful residence to those otherwise encouraged to enter the territory to seek work. Undoubtedly the denial of a right of residence to work seekers was aimed at ensuring their exclusion from access to benefits. However, the failure to provide any legal framework within which such work seekers exist in the territory is both somewhat difficult to understand and regrettable.

A8 nationals who have worked in the United Kingdom but who lose their **28–78** jobs or cease work, perhaps through no fault of their own, during the first year of residence in the United Kingdom become unlawfully resident if they have not obtained alternative employment within one month. Community law requires that Member States grant work seekers at least six months in order to find work.[75] Provision requiring that alternative employment is found within only a month would appear to fly in the face of Community law.[76]

(e) *Students*

The requirement for A8 nationals to register their employment is not **28–79** restricted to workers but to any "national of the relevant accession State working in the UK during the accession period".[77] In principle this could mean that an A8 national student who works part-time during the course of his studies is required to register his work. This does not accord with the Treaty of Accession which only permits derogation from Arts 1 to 6 of Reg.1612/68 relating to workers. Furthermore it seems that A8 students are in the worst of all situations since they are apparently required to register their work (at least for the first 12 months of work) but are not entitled to count periods of stay in the United Kingdom towards obtaining indefinite leave to remain under para.255 of the Immigration Rules since that provision specifically excludes periods spent in the United Kingdom as a student.

(f) *Indefinite Leave to Remain*

Accession state nationals can apply for indefinite leave to remain under **28–80** para.255B of the Immigration Rules HC 395. Their periods of stay prior to May 1, 2004 can in certain circumstances be taken into account for calculating the necessary four-year period prior to obtaining indefinite leave to remain.

> "255B. This paragraph applies where an Accession State national has been issued with a residence permit under the 2000 EEA Regulations and, prior to 1st May 2004, remained in the United Kingdom in accordance with the provisions of these Rules and in a capacity which would have entitled that Accession State national to apply for indefinite leave to remain after a continuous period of 4 years in that capacity in the United Kingdom.

---

[75] See Chapter 11.
[76] Reg.5(4)(b).
[77] Reg.2(1).

Where this paragraph applies, the period during which the Accession State national remained in the United Kingdom prior to 1st May 2004 shall be treated as a period during which he remained in the United Kingdom in accordance with the 2000 EEA Regulations for the purpose of calculating the 4 year period referred to in paragraph 255."

5. SOCIAL SECURITY AND STUDENT FINANCE

(a) *Relevant Legislation*

28–81   The body of statutes and regulations on social security generally is very large. Some of the most significant are listed below:

Social Security Contributions and Benefit Act 1992

Social Security Benefit (Persons) Abroad Amendment (No.2) Regulations 1994

Income-related Benefits Schemes (Miscellaneous Amendments) (No.3) Regulations 1994

Social Security (Persons from Abroad) (Miscellaneous Amendments) Regulations 1995

Job Seekers Act 1995

Immigration and Asylum Act 1999

National Asylum Support Service

Nationality Immigration and Asylum Act 2002, Sch.3

Withholding and Withdrawal of Support (Travel Assistance and Temporary Accommodation) Regulations 2002

European Union (Accessions) Act 2003

Accession (Immigration and Worker Registration) Regulations 2004

Social Security (Habitual Residence) Amendment Regulations 2004

Immigration (European Economic Area) and Accession (Amendment) 2004

Regulations 2004

Education (Student Support) Regulations

Allocation of Housing and Homelessness (Amendment) Regulations 2004

(b) *Social Security Law Overview*

28–82   Detailed analysis of the United Kingdom's social security system is beyond the scope of this book.[78] However in summary in the United Kingdom there are three main categories of public funds available:

---

[78] For a more detailed analysis of social security legislation in the UK, see *Migration and Social Security Handbook* (3rd ed., CPAG) and *Welfare Benefits & Tax Credits Handbook 2004/2005* (6th ed., CPAG).

1.   contributory social security benefits;

2.   non-contributory family and disability benefits;

3.   means-tested benefits.

Section 54 of and Sch. 3 to the Nationality Immigration and Asylum Act   **28–83**
2002 are aimed at preventing local authorities from providing support to
EEA nationals unless to withhold support would breach Community law or
the ECHR. These provisions were enacted to meet government concerns
that EEA nationals were travelling to the United Kingdom in order to obtain
benefits to which they were not entitled.

Further concerns about such "benefit tourists" post-accession led to the pass-   **28–84**
ing of the Social Security (Habitual Residence) Amendment Regulations.
These Regulations impose a new requirement to the habitual residence test
for the obtaining of certain benefits namely that claimants are "lawfully
resident" in the United Kingdom.

The Social Security Advisory Committee published its report in April 2004   **28–85**
on the Social Security (Habitual Residence) Amendment Regulations.[79] The
Committee's Report is extremely critical of the changes to the habitual
residence test. The report recommended that the Government did not proceed with the proposals which the Committee considered unnecessary to prevent benefit tourism since new arrivals were unlikely to meet the existing
requirements of the habitual residence test.[80] The Committee's views however
did not prompt any change of policy.

(c) *Access to Social Security for A8 Nationals*

The Social Security (Habitual Residence) Amendment Regulations when   **28–86**
read together with the Accession Regulations, makes clear that the intention
is clearly that the following categories of A8 national will not be eligible for
income support, income-based job-seekers allowance, housing benefit,
council tax benefit and pension credit[81] which are dependent on satisfaction
of the habitual residence test:

(a)   A8 work-seekers;

(b)   A8 workers who cease employment during the first year of employment;

(c)   The family members of A8 workers during the first year of the workers'
      employment.

Regulation 5 of the Accession Regulations seeks to make unlawful the   **28–87**
residence of an A8 national if he ceases work during the first year of

---

[79] Report by the Social Security Advisory Committee under s.174(1) of the Social Security
Administration Act and the statement by the Secretary of State for work and Pensions in accordance of s.174(2) of that Act, Cm 6181.
[80] The Government proceeded with the legislative changes. No amendments to the habitual residence test have been made to reflect the ECJ's judgment in *Collins*.
[81] Exclusion from homelessness assistance is provided for through the Allocation of Housing
and Homelessness (Amendment) Regulation 2004.

employment thus depriving him of access to social security benefits (or any other social and tax advantages that he might otherwise have obtained as a worker). This is in apparent contradiction with Community law since EU national workers, regardless of the length of time they have worked (provided the work was "genuine and effective") are entitled to be treated in the same way as the host Member State's own nationals with regards access to income based benefits. This is made clear by Art.7(2) of Reg.1612/68[82] as interpreted by the ECJ, which has treated access to benefits for those who have become unemployed as falling within the scope of this provision.[83]

28–88   Furthermore, the co-ordination of certain social security benefits is provided for in Reg.1408/71 and EU national workers are entitled to unemployment benefits on the same basis as own nationals. The United Kingdom is not permitted to derogate from either Art.7(2) of Reg.1612/68 or any provision of Reg.1408/71 under the Accession Treaty. To deprive A8 workers of access to benefits simply on the basis that they have not worked for a full 12 months is plainly discriminatory and incompatible with the Treaty of Accession.

(d) *Students*

28–89   Under current regulations EU students undertaking first degrees are charged tuition fees in the same way as home students and are eligible for the same assistance (means-tested whole or partial remission of fees) but are generally not eligible for the subsidised loans provided for living costs under the Education (Student Support) Regulations.[84] The case of *Bidar*[85] was referred to the ECJ in February 2003. The questions referred concern the legality of excluding EU students arriving from other Member States from obtaining student maintenance grants and/or subsidised loans. An essential question that the ECJ will have to grapple with is whether maintenance grants or loans remain outside the scope of the Treaty as held by the ECJ in *Brown*[86] and *Lair*.[87]

(e) *EU Nationals not Covered by the EEA Regulations*

The consequence of the change to the habitual residence test is that EU nationals who are not qualified persons for the purpose of the EEA Regulations are not entitled to the benefits listed in para.28–26. Denial of access to job seekers' allowance for work seekers is in plain contradiction of the decision in *Collins*.[88] Denial of minimum forms of social assistance such as homelessness assistance and income support to EU citizens residence in the UK is potentially contrary to Art.12 and 17 EC Treaty. These principles are discussed in Chapters 4 and 12.

---

[82] Such benefits are social advantages within the meaning of Art.7(2) of Reg.1612/68.

[83] Case C-85/96 *Martinez Sala v Freistat Bayern* [1998] E.C.R. I–2691.

[84] SI 2002/195. The regulations however make provision amongst others EEA migrant workers, their spouses of such migrant workers and their children to access student loans.

[85] Case C-209/03 *The Queen (on the application of Dany Bidar) v the London Borough of Ealing and 2) the Secretary of State for Education.*

[86] Case 197/86 *Brown v Secretary of State for Scotland* [1988] E.C.R. 3205.

[87] Case 39/86 *Lair v Universität Hannover* [1988] E.C.R. 3161.

[88] Case C-138/02 *Collins v Secretary of State for Work and Pensions*, judgment of March 23, 2004.

AGREEMENTS WITH THIRD COUNTRIES

For detailed discussion on the free movement provisions contained in Agreements between the European Communities and third countries readers are referred to Part Three (Chapters 15 to 25) of this book.

1. SWISS AGREEMENT

(a) *Relevant Legislation*

Immigration (Swiss Free Movement of Persons) (No.3) Regulations 2002.   **29–01**

(b) *General Provisions*

The provisions of the EEA Regulations have generally been extended to   **29–02**
Swiss nationals by the Agreement between the European Community and the Swiss Confederation on the Free Movement of Persons. The Immigration (Swiss Free Movement of Persons) (No.3) Regulations 2002 (the Swiss Regulations) replace two previous statutory instruments which gave effect to the Swiss Agreement. As a result of this extension of the EEA Regulations to Swiss nationals those who are exercising free movement rights under the Swiss Agreement are able to obtain confirmation of their right of residence, as can their family members. Paragraph 255A provides that after four years of exercising free movement rights, Swiss nationals may apply for indefinite leave to remain.

(c) *Posted Workers*

In the Swiss Regulations modifications are made to the EEA Regulations to   **29–03**
reflect the terms of Swiss Agreement. In particular provision for the "posted worker" is made in the Swiss Regulations. A posted worker is defined as a non-EEA national who comes to the United Kingdom for the purpose of providing services on behalf of his employer, who must be a Swiss national or company. Posted workers must be able to demonstrate that they have been integrated into the Swiss labour market or the labour market of another EEA State. A posted worker will only be permitted to work in the United Kingdom for 90 days in any calendar year.[1]

---

[1] It is peculiar that special provisions on posted workers are implemented in respect of the Swiss Agreement only when in fact the right to post workers exists for all EU nationals or companies pursuant to the ECJ's case law and this right is not reflected in the EEA Regulations. See posted workers in Chapter 8.

2. THE EUROPE AGREEMENTS[2]

(a) *Relevant Legislation*

29–04   Immigration Rules HC 395

(b) *Provision in the Immigration Rules*

29–05   The Immigration Rules HC 395 set out in detail at paras 211–223 the requirements for those seeking to establish businesses in the United Kingdom either
by applying for visas abroad or by applying to switch their status in the
United Kingdom. The ECJ has examined the UK Immigration Rules and
stated that they generally give effect to the establishment provisions
contained in the Europe Agreements.[3] The ECJ's examination of the
Immigration Rules in the past has focused on the mandatory entry clearance
requirement.

29–06   In basic terms a prospective applicant will need to show the ability adequately
to maintain and accommodate himself and any dependents from profits of
the business. The applicant will have to stop receiving any social security
benefits that are means-tested and are available only to those who are entitled
to be employed in the United Kingdom. Additionally the applicant will need
to cease any employment (even if it is only part-time). This is because the
applicant may only be engaged in self-employed activities.

29–07   Those making such applications must ensure that it is obvious from the documents submitted to the immigration authorities with the application that
the applicant will be able to make enough money to provide for himself and
any dependants. If the applicant is not able to make enough money from the
outset, the applicant will need to show the availability of an independent
source of funds until such time as the activities become sufficiently profitable
that the applicant can live off them.

29–08   The Immigration Rules require that the applicant submits audited accounts.
Whilst this requirement has not always been strictly applied, practice varies.
This is a discriminatory requirement as it does not apply to British business
persons who are established in business and if the applicant is able to provide

---

[2] The Europe Agreements are at present confined to the Association Agreements with Bulgaria
and Romania. In this part however reference is made additionally to CEEC nationals and busi-
nessmen since when substantively considered by the ECJ the Agreements under consideration
included all Agreements with Central and Eastern European countries, most of which are now
full Member States of the European Union.
[3] See further Chapters 18 and 19. The first cases referred to the ECJ on the Europe Agreements
emanated from the UK: Case C-257/99 *R. v Secretary of State for the Home Department Ex p.
Barkoci and Malik* [2001] E.C.R. I–6557, Case 235/99 *R. v Secretary of State for the Home
Department Ex p. Kondova* [2001] E.C.R. I–6427 and Case C-63/99 *R. v Secretary of State for the
Home Department Ex p. Gloszczuk and Gloszczuk* [2001] E.C.R. I–6369. All three cases concerned the application of the Immigration Rules to applicants for leave to enter or remain
pursuant to their right of establishment under the Europe Agreements.

a reasonable explanation for not complying with this requirement it would arguably be discriminatory to enforce it against him.

If the application is successful the applicant and any dependants will be granted leave to remain for one year, renewable for up to four years (after which time the applicant will be able to apply for permanent settlement). The applicant's spouse will be able to enter into employment after leave is granted. The applicant's spouse will not require additional work permission. **29–09**

There are additional requirements if the applicant wishes to set up a company. These are that the applicant has a controlling interest in the company, that the company is registered in the United Kingdom and trading or providing services in the United Kingdom, that the applicant is actively involved in the company and that the company is the owner of the assets of the business. **29–10**

(c) Visas

Romanian or Bulgarian nationals applying for entry clearance abroad in order to come to the United Kingdom to establish a business must demonstrate that they meet all the requirements of paras 212 and 213 of the Immigration Rules. **29–11**

The procedure for applications from abroad underwent considerable change in 2003 and 2004. Until April 2003 all applicants were interviewed by UK Embassy officials and decisions were made by those officials. However following complaints by representatives about delay the interview was removed from the procedure and all applications were sent directly by the UK Embassy overseas to the Home Office for decision. During March 2004 a new procedure was put in place whereby applications for "assessment" were made directly by the Bulgarian or Romanian business applicant to the Business Case Work Unit in the Home Office in the United Kingdom. The aim was to speed up the process further. If the application was approved by the Home Office, the applicant would then apply for entry clearance at a British Embassy abroad. **29–12**

However following recommendations made by Ken Sutton[4], a new procedure was put in place in August 2004. From that time applications must be made to the entry clearance officers in Bulgaria and Romania directly. Those applications are processed by the entry clearance officer on the basis of guidance in the Diplomatic Service Procedure[5]. Broadly stated emphasis in the guidance is placed on close scrutiny of evidence to ensure that the application for entry clearance is credible and that the applicant "really will be able to comply with the requirements in practice". Evidence required to demonstrate compliance with the Immigration Rules is substantial and will include bank statements, information about "extraordinary payments" into a bank **29–13**

---

[4] See further below at para.29–24.
[5] Chapter 18.7 of Diplomatic Services Procedure. Website: *www.ukvisas.gov.uk/*. Guidance does change periodically.

account, a detailed break-down of set costs, and projected profit and loss accounts. Entry clearance officers are further instructed that previous immigration history, proficiency in English and the general circumstances in which the application is made are to be taken into account in assessing the "credibility" of the application[6].

(d) *On Entry*

29–14   Before the ECJ in *Barkoci and Malik*,[7] the UK Government had sought to defend the mandatory entry clearance requirement by giving the impression that in practice the Immigration Rules were applied in a reasonable manner. The Government pointed to the practice of waiving the mandatory entry clearance requirement in cases which "clearly and manifestly" met the requirements of the Rules.

29–15   Following the ECJ's decision in *Barkoci and Malik*,[8] CEEC nationals arriving without entry clearance at a port should have applications made for leave to enter under the Europe Agreements approved if they "clearly and manifestly" meet the requirements of the Immigration Rules. Applications will be treated as "clearly and manifestly" meeting such requirements if:

     "i.   from a brief perusal;
     ii.   of the documents provided together with any information;
     iii.   it is readily apparent that there is;
     iv.   an established and viable business that meets the immigration criteria"[9].

29–16   However the reality is that an immigration officer is highly unlikely to approve a port application from a person who has arrived without entry clearance. In practice the failure to provide adequate documentation to satisfy the 'clearly and manifestly' test if often a ground of refusal.

(e) *In-country applications*

29–17   In August 2004, para. 217 of the Immigration Rules was amended to impose a mandatory entry clearance requirement on Bulgarian and Romanian nationals who wish to switch their status if they are lawfully in the United Kingdom when they apply.

29–18   The Immigration Directorates' Instructions state that an applicant seeking to switch into status as a self-employed person under the Europe Agreement should therefore be refused if they do not have entry clearance for the purpose. However the guidance states that it is necessary for decision-makers to consider the proportionality of the such refusal[10]. There is a lack of clarity as to which cases will be considered suitable for in-country switching. However

---

[6] Evidential requirements are discussed further at paras 29–24 to 29–26 below.
[7] Case C-257/99 *R. v Secretary of State for the Home Department Ex P Barkoci & Malik* [2001] E.C.R. I-6557.
[8] Case C-257/99 *R. v Secretary of State for the Home Department Ex P Barkoci & Malik* [2001] E.C.R. I-6557.
[9] Chapter 6, Section 2, Immigration Directorates' Instructions, website *www.ind.homeoffice.gov.uk*.
[10] Chapter 6, Section 2, Immigration Directorates' Instructions, website *www.ind.homeoffice.gov.uk*.

it is likely that those applicants who have only been granted leave to enter or remain for short periods will be unable to switch. Particular categories of applicant, such as students and visitors, may face mandatory refusal. The guidance instructs decision-makers to apply the "clear and manifest" test to persons lawfully in the UK seeking to switch to remain under the Europe Agreements.

It is noteworthy that when the ECJ considered the mandatory entry clearance **29–19** requirement in the UK Immigration Rules, such requirement was not placed on those lawfully in the UK seeking to switch status to remain under the Europe Agreements. Indeed the fact that there was no mandatory entry clearance requirement placed on those who were lawfully in the UK applying to switch status was one reason why the ECJ considered the imposition of a mandatory entry clearance requirement in other situations, such as persons unlawfully in the UK, to be reasonable[11].

(f) *The position of overstayers and illegal entrants*

The United Kingdom government has taken a hard line on the position of **29–20** overstayers and illegal entrants since the decisions of the ECJ in *Kondova*[12] and *Gloczszuck*.[13] Any individual who is an overstayer and who established a business after the expiry of leave to remain, or who entered the United Kingdom illegally, cannot benefit from the provisions of the Europe Agreements. Such persons will be expected to return to their country of origin to apply for entry clearance. Accordingly illegal entrants and overstayers will likely be forced return to their country of origin unless they benefit from, for example, the long residence provision of the Immigration Rules[14] or such other concessions as may exist at any particular time.

By virtue of s.82 of the Nationality, Immigration and Asylum Act 2002 **29–21** Bulgarian and Romanian nationals facing removal will be able to appeal specified 'immigration decisions'.

It is important to bear in mind that at the time the ECJ considered the UK's **29–22** mandatory entry clearance requirement the queues in the relevant Embassies were not long as there were very few applications for entry clearance made under the Europe Agreements and applications were taking no more than 3 months to process. However, that situation has changed: queues are longer and delay is considerably longer than 3 months. A wait of over 6 months for instance may have a particularly adverse impact on a small business. Such lengthy delay would arguably be a disproportionate interference with rights given by Community law which has the effect of nullifying and impairing the

---

[11] Case C-235/99 *R. v Secretary of State for the Home Department ex parte Kondova* [2001] E.C.R. I-6427. See further Chapter 20.

[12] Case C-235/99 *R. v Secretary of State for the Home Department ex parte Kondova* [2001] E.C.R. I-6427.

[13] Case C-63/99 *R. v Secretary of State for the Home Department, ex parte Gloszczuk and Gloszczuk* [2001] E.C.R. I-6369.

[14] Immigration Rules HC 395 paras. 276A and 276B and concessions relating to families with children who have remained in the UK for 7 years or more.

right of establishment. The Immigration Directorates' Instructions recognise that it will be necessary to consider whether it would be disproportionate in the circumstances of a particular case for the applicant to be made to return to his country of origin to apply for entry clearance[15]. The seriousness of the breach of immigration laws will be one of the key factors in determining the question of proportionality in such cases.

(g) *Family Members*

29–23   The Immigration Rules permit spouses and children under 18 to accompany or join the Bulgarian or Romanian applicant in the UK[16]. Where an application for leave to enter or remain by a family member is refused arguments concerning the right to respect for family life provided by Art. 8 ECHR as protected by the ECJ will need to be employed since the Europe Agreements themselves do not refer to family members in the context of the right of establishment at all. In *Baumbast*[17] the ECJ considered that the refusal to permit close family members to remain with those exercising EU free movement rights, might have the effect of depriving them of those rights.

(h) *Compatibility of the regime for Bulgarian and Romanian nationals with Community law*

29–24   It was allegations that fraudulent applications had been approved by the Home Office in Sheffield which had resulted in the establishment by the Government of an inquiry into the processing of all Europe Agreement applications. Between March and August 2004 Ken Sutton led the inquiry into the processing of these applications. The enquiry found little actual evidence of abuse within IND.[18] However the Sutton report recommended *inter alia* "a more robust process" for deciding applications, the re-instatement of interviews and a tightening of the approach taken to in-country applications[19]. Following the publication of the Sutton report, both UK visas and the Immigration and Nationality Directorate substantially amended guidance to caseworkers on the processing of applications under the Europe Agreements.

29–25   There is no doubt that the evidential burden placed on applicants for entry clearance or leave to remain under the Europe Agreements has been heightened considerably. The emphasis on the "credibility" of applications demonstrates a conceptual misunderstanding of the nature of the rights in play which at their core are dependant on the satisfaction of objective criteria testing whether or not an applicant intends to establish himself in business, rather than the satisfaction of subjective criteria which assess the qualitative nature of the business.

---

[15] Chapter 6, Section 2, Immigration Directorates' Instructions, website *www.ind.homeoffice. gov.uk.*
[16] Para. 243 of Immigration Rules HC 395.
[17] Case C-413/99 *Baumbast and R. v the Secretary of State for the Home Department*, [2002] E.C.R. I-7091.
[18] Para. 1.18 of summary refers.
[19] Para. 1.17 summary refers.

There are serious reasons to question to the compatibility of the current **29–26** regime with Community law. It would appear from the guidance to case-workers[20] that the evidential burden placed on applicants far exceeds what could reasonably be expected from the substantive requirements of the Immigration Rules. Whilst the Immigration Rules reasonably require that applicants demonstrate their businesses will be sufficiently profitable to maintain and accommodate themselves in the UK, entry clearance officers are encouraged to require evidence that goes well beyond establishment of that requirement. For example, the guidance refers to the requirement to produce bank statement dating back six months and to give a credible explanation of any "extraordinary payments". It is difficult to see how such evidence is relevant to the viability of a business. Moreover, such requirements will amount to an unreasonably heavy burden on applicants, particularly where the customary practice in some countries is not the routine use of bank accounts.

Further, the emphasis placed in the guidance on knowledge of English raises the very real question whether these applications are being viewed in a discriminatory way. National immigration law does not impose a requirement that business applicants must demonstrate any knowledge of English, whether such applications are made by EU nationals exercising the EC Treaty right of establishment, or other nationals in accordance with Immigration Rule provisions relating to the establishment of businesses[21]. The guidance may have the effect of encouraging the unwarranted refusal of applications and arbitrary decision making. This is because the extensive requirements in the guidance are not reflected by the Immigration Rules. Seen in the context of domestic law, it is questionable whether the guidance satisfies the requirement that it must be "not inconsistent with the immigration rules"[22]. By far the most worrying aspect of this guidance, however, is the fact that it goes far beyond what is laid down in the Europe Agreements themselves and the legitimate enquiry that Community law would permit[23].

3. EC-TURKEY ASSOCIATION AGREEMENT

(a) *Residence of Turkish Workers Under Article 6 of Decision 1/80*

The provisions of Art.6 of Decision 1/80 are not incorporated into the **29–27** Immigration Rules. The provisions are mentioned in the IDIs in Chapter 5, s.10. There is no possibility in UK immigration law of making an application for entry clearance to first enter the UK as a worker under the Ankara Agreement. This is reflective of Art.6 of Decision 1/80 itself. All applicants will be applying to switch status in country, having entered the UK as a spouse, a work permit holder or in some other capacity and been granted at least one year leave to remain with permission to work. Successful applicants under Art.6 of Decision 1/80 are granted a further year's leave to remain,

---

[20] Para. 29–13 refers.
[21] Paras 200–203 of HC 395 refer.
[22] See para.1(3) of Sch.2 Immigration Act 1971.
[23] See further Chapters 11 and 20.

extendable for successive 12-month periods only. The IDI's make reference to the fact that trainees, students and au-pairs do not benefit from the Agreement, despite the clear jurisprudence of the ECJ in *Birden*,[24] as reaffirmed by *Kurz*.[25]

29–28 Despite such clear jurisprudence the IAT appears to have accepted the Home Office position on this issue in *K v Secretary of State for the Home Department*.[26] The appellant, a Turkish national, entered the United Kingdom as an au-pair and was given two years' permission to stay for leave to continue her employment pursuant to her rights under Art.6(1) of Decision 1/80. The appellant worked for a family two days a week for a total of 15 hours, receiving £30 per week and had previously worked until her marriage for 22–25 hours per week. The IAT accepted the Home Office's argument that the appellant was not a worker because she was pursuing activity as an au-pair within the specific provisions of the Immigration Rules. The IAT found that as an au-pair she would not be regarded as belonging to the labour force since the au-pair placement is an arrangement primarily for the purpose of learning English.

The decision is contrary to the ECJ's definition of worker in *Birden*[27]. See further Chapter 7 and the discussion of the decision of the ECJ in *Watson and Belman*.[28]

29–29 The IDIs refer to the Home Office's view that there is no obligation to grant indefinite leave to remain to Turkish nationals who have worked in the UK for four years. Although indefinite leave to remain is not referred to specifically in Decision 1/80 (and indeed it would not be as it is a creature of domestic law), Art. 6 does refer to "free access to any paid employment". The ECJ has consistently treated the right of residence as a direct corollary of the right to access the labour market. If this access to the labour market is to be truly "free", the requirement to apply for leave to remain on an annual basis could interfere with that right. This is particularly the case if the applicant's passport (containing the endorsement confirming permission to work) is retained by the Home Office during consideration of the application for months at a time making it difficult for the applicant to be able to prove to prospective employers that any employment would be lawful. Moreover, since non-EU national work permit holders can apply for indefinite leave to remain after four years residence in the UK it is clearly discriminatory and contrary to the spirit of the Ankara Agreement for Turkish nationals to be treated in a manner which is plainly less favourable.

29–30 The absence of provision for Turkish national workers in the Immigration Rules has a further important consequence. Where a Turkish national seeks to vary leave in-country by relying on Decision 1/80 there will be no appeal

---

[24] Case C-1/97 *Birden v Stadtgemeinde Bremen* [1998] E.C.R. I–7747.
[25] Case C-188/00 *Kurz v Land Baden-Württemberg* [2002] E.C.R. I–10691.
[26] [2003 UKIATOOO33] Immigration Appeal Tribunal, July 22, 2003.
[27] Case C-1/97 *Birden v Stadtgemeinde Bremen* [1998] E.C.R. I–7747.
[28] Case 118/75 *Watson and Belmann* [1976] E.C.R. 1185.

against refusal of such application because of s.88(2)(d) Nationality, Immigration and Asylum Act 2002 which prevents an appeal where the application was for a purpose not covered by the Immigration Rules. Such blatantly discriminatory consequence of the failure incorporate the obligations arising under Decision 1/80 into the Immigration Rules cannot be justified.

(b) *Self-employed Turkish Nationals*

(i) *General*

The Additional Protocol entered into force in the United Kingdom on January 1, 1973 when the United Kingdom entered the European Community as a full Member State and become party to all international agreements concluded by the Community under the Treaty. **29–31**

Those wishing to establish themselves in business in the United Kingdom will therefore need to rely on the immigration laws and practice that were in place on January 1, 1973. This was primarily the Immigration Act 1971 and the Immigration Rules HC 509 (control on entry) and Immigration Rules HC 510 (control after entry). **29–32**

Compared with the current immigration rules applicable to business persons (HC 395) the 1973 Immigration Rules HC 509 and 510 were extremely flexible and generous. In brief the principal differences are: **29–33**

(a) there was no minimum level of investment under HC 510 or 509;

(b) there was no requirement to offer employment to a minimum number of people under HC 510 or 509;

(c) there was no mandatory entry clearance requirement under HC 509 and passengers arriving without entry clearance would be given a period of leave to enter to have their application examined by the Home Office

The ECJ in *Savas*[29] confirmed that this provision applied to all Turkish nationals resident in the Member States, whether or not that residence had become unlawful by virtue of the Turkish national overstaying a visa. In the case of Mr Savas, he had in fact been an overstayer for 11 years before seeking to rely on the standstill provision in the Additional Protocol. Despite so many years overstaying he was still entitled to be treated in accordance with rules that are no more stringent than those that were in place on January 1, 1973. **29–34**

After *Savas* the Home Office issued guidance in January 2003 stating that the standstill clause only applied to those who sought to lawfully switch **29–35**

---

[29] Case C-37/98 *The Queen v Secretary of State for the Home Department Ex p. Savas* [2000] E.C.R. I-2927.

in-country or overstayers[30], but not to port applicant asylum seekers on temporary admission, illegal entrants or persons applying for entry clearance. Applicants on temporary admission, illegal entrants or those applying for entry clearance would have their applications considered under the *current* Immigration Rules (HC 395) and not the 1973 Rules. Thus the United Kingdom did not accept that the standstill provision could benefit anyone who had at one stage been given leave to enter or remain. Since only those few Turkish nationals obtain visas or leave to enter in other capacities, the Government was substantially limiting the benefit of the standstill provisions.

29–36   Whether the standstill provision (and therefore the 1973 Rules) could apply to on-entry and temporary admission cases was challenged in an action for judicial review in the two joined cases of *Tum and Dari*.[31] At first instance Davies J. found that the standstill provision must apply to all Turkish nationals, whether or not they had been granted leave to enter in some other capacity. He therefore quashed decision letters which had refused business applications on the basis of the current immigration rules and held that the SSHD was obliged to apply the 1973 Rules to the applications.

29–37   The Secretary of State appealed. By judgment dated May 25, 2004 the Court of Appeal dismissed the Secretary of State's appeal. In the leading judgment the Lord Chief Justice held that all Turkish nationals could obtain the benefit of the standstill clause, whether in the United Kingdom or outside (and including asylum seekers on temporary admission). All such Turkish nationals should have their applications considered under the 1973 Rules. The only Turkish nationals excluded from the benefit of the standstill provision are those who had committed fraud. The Court of Appeal refused Secretary of State permission to appeal to the House of Lords.[32]

29–38   Subject to any further appeal to the House of Lords, analysis of the Court of Appeal's judgment identifies the following categories of Turkish national potentially benefiting from the standstill provisions:

(a)   port applicants and persons on temporary admission;

(b)   out of country applicants for entry clearance;

(c)   illegal entrants;

(d)   those with leave to enter or remain;

(e)   overstayers.

Each category is dealt with below in turn.

---

[30] Remarkably, in spite of the fact that Mr Savas had overstayed for 11 years, the IDIs (as at September 2004) state (at para. 7 in s.10 of Chapter 5) that applications for overstayers can be rejected since such persons "do not have any right to remain" Such approach is plainly unlawful. Any application from an overstayer must be considered under the 1973 Rules.

[31] *R. (on the Application of Tum) and R. (on the application of Dari v Secretary of State* [2003] EWHC 2745 (Admin) (Davies J.); [2004] EWCA Civ 788 (CA).

[32] A petition to the House of Lords itself is pending consideration.

(ii) *Port Applicants and Persons on Temporary Admission*

Those who arrive at port or who are asylum seekers on temporary admission **29–39**
must be treated as if they are applying for leave to enter for business purposes. For those asylum seekers granted temporary admission this is the position regardless of the stage they have reached in the asylum procedure. It is
to be noted that both Mr Tum and Mr Dari were asylum seekers subject to
the third country procedure who would otherwise have been sent to Germany
to have their asylum claims determined. Mr Tum had in fact obtained an
injunction against removal.

Paragraph 30 of the 1973 Immigration Rules: control on entry (HC 509) pro- **29–40**
vides that persons who are unable to provide entry clearance but who "nevertheless seem likely to be able to satisfy the requirements" should be
admitted for a period of two months and advised to present their case to the
Home Office. Thus there is no mandatory entry clearance requirement. Since
however the question whether the requirements are likely to be satisfied will
be judged by reference to those requirements set out in the Rules for the issue
of entry clearance it is to those Rules (considered below) that reference
should be made.

(iii) *Applicants for Entry Clearance*

The requirements for obtaining entry clearance are set out in paras 31 and 32 **29–41**
of the Rules which provide as follows:

A business person who is joining an established business must show that:

(a) he will be bringing money of his own to put into the business;

(b) he will be able to bear his share of the liabilities;

(c) that his share of the profits will be sufficient to support him and any
dependants without recourse to employment;

(d) he will be actively concerned in the running of the business;

(e) there is a genuine need for his services and investment;

(f) audited accounts of the business of the previous years must be produced;

(g) the partnership or directorship does not amount to disguised employment.

If the person wishes to establish a new business in the United Kingdom he
must show that:

(a) he will be bringing into country sufficient funds to establish a business;

(b) the business can realistically be expected to support him and any dependants without recourse to employment.

It is of particular importance to note that past immigration history is not a **29–43**
matter that can be taken into account by the entry clearance officer under to

the 1973 control on entry Rules (HC 509). This is because—unlike the position under para.320 of the current Rules (HC 395)—the general considerations under which entry clearance could be refused in 1973 did not include provisions requiring that applications should be normally be refused on grounds of overstay, breach of conditions or the obtaining of leave by deception.[33]

29–44 Persons who obtain entry clearance will be granted leave to enter for 12 months with a prohibition on employment.

(iv) *Illegal Entrants*

29–45 Those who have entered illegally probably do not stand to benefit immediately from the standstill clause save that they could leave the United Kingdom and apply to re-enter on the basis of the 1973 Immigration Rules (control on entry). This is because even in 1973 illegal entrants could be removed pursuant to the Immigration Act 1971, Sch.2, para.8.

29–46 The Court of Appeal held that those who had been fraudulent would not benefit from the standstill provision. This would appear to have which probably has the same effect as an immigration officer treating someone who entered by fraud as an illegal entrant and effecting removal. Whilst tempting to suggest that the category of persons who perpetrate "fraud" is (or may be) narrower than illegal entrants and therefore there might be a category of illegal entrant who could benefit from the standstill provisions, such argument would unlikely prevail. This is because all illegal entrants—whether or not they have perpetrated fraud—were removable as such in 1973.

29–47 Since the 1973 Rules make no reference to refusals of entry clearance on the basis of past immigration history,[34] a person formerly in the United Kingdom illegally could leave the United Kingdom and re-apply to enter without that person's immigration history acting as a barrier to entry.

(v) *Those with Leave to Enter or Remain*

29–48 Those present in the United Kingdom with leave to enter or remain may apply to switch to remain on the basis of their business. The Home Office has long accepted this to be the position. Their application for in-country switching should be considered on the basis of the 1973 Immigration Rules: control after entry (HC 510).

29–49 Paragraph 21 of the HC 510 sets out the requirements for leave to remain as business persons. These are in fact very similar to the requirements relating to entry (HC 509). A person must demonstrate that:

(a) he is devoting assets of his own to the business proportionate to his interest in the business;

---

[33] *cf.* para.320(11) and (12) of the current Immigration Rules HC 395.
[34] *cf.* para.320 of the current Immigration Rules HC 395.

(b) he will be able to bear his share of any liabilities the business may incur;

(c) his share of the profits will be sufficient to support him and any dependants;

(d) his part in the business does not amount to disguised employment and that he will not need to supplement his business activities with employment.

Where the applicant intends to join an existing business he will need to produce: **29–50**

(a) audited accounts for the business to establish its financial position;

(b) a written statement of the terms on which he entered into the business;

(c) evidence that he will be actively concerned with the running of the business;

(d) evidence that there is a genuine need for his services and investment.

Successful applicants will be granted an extension of leave to remain for 12 months with a prohibition on employment.

(vi) *Overstayers*

Turkish nationals granted leave to enter but who have overstayed their lawful residence may apply for leave to remain as business persons. Their applications should be considered on the basis of the 1973 Immigration Rules: control after entry (HC 510) and they need to meet the same requirements as those applying to switch in-country. **29–51**

Under s.3(5)(a) of the Immigration Act 1971 (as then in force) the Secretary of State was entitled to make a decision to make a deportation order on the basis that the person had failed to comply with a condition attached to his leave or has remained beyond the time limited by such leave. **29–52**

However if a decision to make a deportation order was taken, an in-country merits appeal was given by s.15(1)(a) of the Immigration Act 1971 (as then in force). At such an appeal (unencumbered by the provisions of the Immigration Act 1988 which in broad terms limited such an appeal to persons who had been in the United Kingdom for more than seven years) the adjudicator would have been able to balance all the factors, such as good character, business and personal contacts and length of stay against the gravity of the breach of conditions or the overstaying. **29–53**

Since these were the appeal provisions in force at the time, self-employed Turkish nationals facing removal at the present time for overstay or breach of conditions (as provided for by s.10(1)(a) of the Immigration and Asylum Act 1999) must benefit from the previously existing appeals regime. **29–54**

Part Five
APPENDICES

CONTENTS OF APPENDICES

CONTENTS

PRIMARY LEGISLATION

TREATY ESTABLISHING THE EUROPEAN UNION (EXCERPTS): ARTICLES 1–7

TITLE I

COMMON PROVISIONS

Article 1

By this Treaty, the HIGH CONTRACTING PARTIES establish among themselves a **A1–01** EUROPEAN UNION, hereinafter called "the Union".

This Treaty marks a new stage in the process of creating an ever closer union among the peoples of Europe, in which decisions are taken as openly as possible and as closely as possible to the citizen.

The Union shall be founded on the European Communities, supplemented by the policies and forms of cooperation established by this Treaty. Its task shall be to organise, in a manner demonstrating consistency and solidarity, relations between the Member States and between their peoples.

Article 2

The Union shall set itself the following objectives:

–   to promote economic and social progress and a high level of employment and to achieve balanced and sustainable development, in particular through the creation of an area without internal frontiers, through the strengthening of economic and social cohesion and through the establishment of economic and monetary union, ultimately including a single currency in accordance with the provisions of this Treaty,

–   to assert its identity on the international scene, in particular through the implementation of a common foreign and security policy including the progressive framing of a common defence policy, which might lead to a common defence, in accordance with the provisions of Article 17,

–   to strengthen the protection of the rights and interests of the nationals of its Member States through the introduction of a citizenship of the Union,

–   to maintain and develop the Union as an area of freedom, security and justice, in which the free movement of persons is assured in conjunction with appropriate measures with respect to external border controls, asylum, immigration and the prevention and combating of crime,

     –   to maintain in full the acquis communautaire and build on it with a view to con-
sidering to what extent the policies and forms of cooperation introduced by this
Treaty may need to be revised with the aim of ensuring the effectiveness of the
mechanisms and the institutions of the Community.

The objectives of the Union shall be achieved as provided in this Treaty and in accordance with the conditions and the timetable set out therein while respecting the principle of subsidiarity as defined in Article 5 of the Treaty establishing the European
Community.

Article 3

The Union shall be served by a single institutional framework which shall ensure the
consistency and the continuity of the activities carried out in order to attain its
objectives while respecting and building upon the acquis communautaire.

The Union shall in particular ensure the consistency of its external activities as a
whole in the context of its external relations, security, economic and development
policies. The Council and the Commission shall be responsible for ensuring such consistency and shall cooperate to this end. They shall ensure the implementation of
these policies, each in accordance with its respective powers.

Article 4

The European Council shall provide the Union with the necessary impetus for its
development and shall define the general political guidelines thereof.

The European Council shall bring together the Heads of State or Government of the
Member States and the President of the Commission. They shall be assisted by
the Ministers for Foreign Affairs of the Member States and by a Member of the
Commission. The European Council shall meet at least twice a year, under the chair-
manship of the Head of State or Government of the Member State which holds the
Presidency of the Council.

The European Council shall submit to the European Parliament a report after each
of its meetings and a yearly written report on the progress achieved by the Union.

Article 5

The European Parliament, the Council, the Commission, the Court of Justice and the
Court of Auditors shall exercise their powers under the conditions and for the purposes provided for, on the one hand, by the provisions of the Treaties establishing the
European Communities and of the subsequent Treaties and Acts modifying and
supplementing them and, on the other hand, by the other provisions of this Treaty.

Article 6

1. The Union is founded on the principles of liberty, democracy, respect for human rights and fundamental freedoms, and the rule of law, principles which are common to the Member States.

2. The Union shall respect fundamental rights, as guaranteed by the European Convention for the Protection of Human Rights and Fundamental Freedoms signed in Rome on 4 November 1950 and as they result from the constitutional traditions common to the Member States, as general principles of Community law.

3. The Union shall respect the national identities of its Member States.

4. The Union shall provide itself with the means necessary to attain its objectives and carry through its policies.

Article 7(2)

1. On a reasoned proposal by one third of the Member States, by the European Parliament or by the Commission, the Council, acting by a majority of four fifths of its members after obtaining the assent of the European Parliament, may determine that there is a clear risk of a serious breach by a Member State of principles mentioned in Article 6(1), and address appropriate recommendations to that State. Before making such a determination, the Council shall hear the Member State in question and, acting in accordance with the same procedure, may call on independent persons to submit within a reasonable time limit a report on the situation in the Member State in question.

The Council shall regularly verify that the grounds on which such a determination was made continue to apply.

2. The Council, meeting in the composition of the Heads of State or Government and acting by unanimity on a proposal by one third of the Member States or by the Commission and after obtaining the assent of the European Parliament, may determine the existence of a serious and persistent breach by a Member State of principles mentioned in Article 6(1), after inviting the government of the Member State in question to submit its observations.

3. Where a determination under paragraph 2 has been made, the Council, acting by a qualified majority, may decide to suspend certain of the rights deriving from the application of this Treaty to the Member State in question, including the voting rights of the representative of the government of that Member State in the Council. In doing so, the Council shall take into account the possible consequences of such a suspension on the rights and obligations of natural and legal persons.

The obligations of the Member State in question under this Treaty shall in any case continue to be binding on that State.

4. The Council, acting by a qualified majority, may decide subsequently to vary or revoke measures taken under paragraph 3 in response to changes in the situation which led to their being imposed.

5. For the purposes of this Article, the Council shall act without taking into account the vote of the representative of the government of the Member State in question. Abstentions by members present in person or represented shall not prevent the adoption of decisions referred to in paragraph 2. A qualified majority shall be defined as the same proportion of the weighted votes of the members of the Council concerned as laid down in Article 205(2) of the Treaty establishing the European Community.

This paragraph shall also apply in the event of voting rights being suspended pursuant to paragraph 3.

6. For the purposes of paragraphs 1 and 2, the European Parliament shall act by a two-thirds majority of the votes cast, representing a majority of its Members.

TREATY ESTABLISHING THE EUROPEAN COMMUNITY (EXCERPTS): ARTICLES 2, 3, 5, 12, 13, 17,18, 39–55, 149, 150, 234, 249, 251–255, 300, 310

Article 2

The Community shall have as its task, by establishing a common market and an eco-   **A2–01**
nomic and monetary union and by implementing common policies or activities
referred to in Articles 3 and 4, to promote throughout the Community a harmonious,
balanced and sustainable development of economic activities, a high level of employment and of social protection, equality between men and women, sustainable and
non-inflationary growth, a high degree of competitiveness and convergence of economic performance, a high level of protection and improvement of the quality of the
environment, the raising of the standard of living and quality of life, and economic
and social cohesion and solidarity among Member States.

Article 3

1. For the purposes set out in Article 2, the activities of the Community shall include,
as provided in this Treaty and in accordance with the timetable set out therein:

(a) the prohibition, as between Member States, of customs duties and quantitative
restrictions on the import and export of goods, and of all other measures having
equivalent effect;

(b) a common commercial policy;

(c) an internal market characterised by the abolition, as between Member States, of
obstacles to the free movement of goods, persons, services and capital;

(d) measures concerning the entry and movement of persons as provided for in Title
IV;

(e) a common policy in the sphere of agriculture and fisheries;

(f) a common policy in the sphere of transport;

(g) a system ensuring that competition in the internal market is not distorted;

(h) the approximation of the laws of Member States to the extent required for the
functioning of the common market;

(i) the promotion of coordination between employment policies of the Member
States with a view to enhancing their effectiveness by developing a coordinated
strategy for employment;

(j) a policy in the social sphere comprising a European Social Fund;

(k) the strengthening of economic and social cohesion;

(l)   a policy in the sphere of the environment;

(m) the strengthening of the competitiveness of Community industry;

(n) the promotion of research and technological development;

(o) encouragement for the establishment and development of trans-European networks;

(p) a contribution to the attainment of a high level of health protection;

(q) a contribution to education and training of quality and to the flowering of the cultures of the Member States;

(r) a policy in the sphere of development cooperation;

(s) the association of the overseas countries and territories in order to increase trade and promote jointly economic and social development;

(t) a contribution to the strengthening of consumer protection;

(u) measures in the spheres of energy, civil protection and tourism.

2. In all the activities referred to in this Article, the Community shall aim to eliminate inequalities, and to promote equality, between men and women.

Article 5

The Community shall act within the limits of the powers conferred upon it by this Treaty and of the objectives assigned to it therein.

In areas which do not fall within its exclusive competence, the Community shall take action, in accordance with the principle of subsidiarity, only if and in so far as the objectives of the proposed action cannot be sufficiently achieved by the Member States and can therefore, by reason of the scale or effects of the proposed action, be better achieved by the Community.

Any action by the Community shall not go beyond what is necessary to achieve the objectives of this Treaty.

Article 12

Within the scope of application of this Treaty, and without prejudice to any special provisions contained therein, any discrimination on grounds of nationality shall be prohibited.

The Council, acting in accordance with the procedure referred to in Article 251, may adopt rules designed to prohibit such discrimination.

Article 13

1. Without prejudice to the other provisions of this Treaty and within the limits of the powers conferred by it upon the Community, the Council, acting unanimously on a proposal from the Commission and after consulting the European Parliament, may take appropriate action to combat discrimination based on sex, racial or ethnic origin, religion or belief, disability, age or sexual orientation.

2. By way of derogation from paragraph 1, when the Council adopts Community incentive measures, excluding any harmonisation of the laws and regulations of the Member States, to support action taken by the Member States in order to contribute to the achievement of the objectives referred to in paragraph 1, it shall act in accordance with the procedure referred to in Article 251.

PART TWO

CITIZENSHIP OF THE UNION

Article 17

1. Citizenship of the Union is hereby established. Every person holding the nationality of a Member State shall be a citizen of the Union. Citizenship of the Union shall complement and not replace national citizenship.

2. Citizens of the Union shall enjoy the rights conferred by this Treaty and shall be subject to the duties imposed thereby.

Article 18

1. Every citizen of the Union shall have the right to move and reside freely within the territory of the Member States, subject to the limitations and conditions laid down in this Treaty and by the measures adopted to give it effect.

2. If action by the Community should prove necessary to attain this objective and this Treaty has not provided the necessary powers, the Council may adopt provisions with a view to facilitating the exercise of the rights referred to in paragraph 1. The Council shall act in accordance with the procedure referred to in Article 251.

3. Paragraph 2 shall not apply to provisions on passports, identity cards, residence permits or any other such document or to provisions on social security or social protection.

TITLE III

FREE MOVEMENT OF PERSONS, SERVICES AND CAPITAL

CHAPTER 1

WORKERS

Article 39

1. Freedom of movement for workers shall be secured within the Community.

2. Such freedom of movement shall entail the abolition of any discrimination based on nationality between workers of the Member States as regards employment, remuneration and other conditions of work and employment.

3. It shall entail the right, subject to limitations justified on grounds of public policy, public security or public health:

(a)   to accept offers of employment actually made;

(b)   to move freely within the territory of Member States for this purpose;

(c)   to stay in a Member State for the purpose of employment in accordance with the provisions governing the employment of nationals of that State laid down by law, regulation or administrative action;

(d)   to remain in the territory of a Member State after having been employed in that State, subject to conditions which shall be embodied in implementing regulations to be drawn up by the Commission.

4. The provisions of this article shall not apply to employment in the public service.

Article 40

The Council shall, acting in accordance with the procedure referred to in Article 251 and after consulting the Economic and Social Committee, issue directives or make regulations setting out the measures required to bring about freedom of movement for workers, as defined in Article 39, in particular:

(a)   by ensuring close cooperation between national employment services;

(b)   by abolishing those administrative procedures and practices and those qualifying periods in respect of eligibility for available employment, whether resulting from national legislation or from agreements previously concluded between Member States, the maintenance of which would form an obstacle to liberalisation of the movement of workers;

(c)   by abolishing all such qualifying periods and other restrictions provided for either under national legislation or under agreements previously concluded between Member States as imposed on workers of other Member States conditions regarding the free choice of employment other than those imposed on workers of the State concerned;

(d) by setting up appropriate machinery to bring offers of employment into touch with applications for employment and to facilitate the achievement of a balance between supply and demand in the employment market in such a way as to avoid serious threats to the standard of living and level of employment in the various regions and industries.

Article 41

Member States shall, within the framework of a joint programme, encourage the exchange of young workers.

Article 42

The Council shall, acting in accordance with the procedure referred to in Article 251, adopt such measures in the field of social security as are necessary to provide freedom of movement for workers; to this end, it shall make arrangements to secure for migrant workers and their dependants:

(a) aggregation, for the purpose of acquiring and retaining the right to benefit and of calculating the amount of benefit, of all periods taken into account under the laws of the several countries;

(b) payment of benefits to persons resident in the territories of Member States.

The Council shall act unanimously throughout the procedure referred to in Article 251.

Chapter 2

Right of Establishment

Article 43

Within the framework of the provisions set out below, restrictions on the freedom of establishment of nationals of a Member State in the territory of another Member State shall be prohibited. Such prohibition shall also apply to restrictions on the setting-up of agencies, branches or subsidiaries by nationals of any Member State established in the territory of any Member State.

Freedom of establishment shall include the right to take up and pursue activities as self-employed persons and to set up and manage undertakings, in particular companies or firms within the meaning of the second paragraph of Article 48, under the conditions laid down for its own nationals by the law of the country where such establishment is effected, subject to the provisions of the chapter relating to capital.

Article 44

1. In order to attain freedom of establishment as regards a particular activity, the Council, acting in accordance with the procedure referred to in Article 251 and after consulting the Economic and Social Committee, shall act by means of directives.

2. The Council and the Commission shall carry out the duties devolving upon them under the preceding provisions, in particular:

(a)   by according, as a general rule, priority treatment to activities where freedom of establishment makes a particularly valuable contribution to the development of production and trade;

(b)   by ensuring close cooperation between the competent authorities in the Member States in order to ascertain the particular situation within the Community of the various activities concerned;

(c)   by abolishing those administrative procedures and practices, whether resulting from national legislation or from agreements previously concluded between Member States, the maintenance of which would form an obstacle to freedom of establishment;

(d)   by ensuring that workers of one Member State employed in the territory of another Member State may remain in that territory for the purpose of taking up activities therein as self-employed persons, where they satisfy the conditions which they would be required to satisfy if they were entering that State at the time when they intended to take up such activities;

(e)   by enabling a national of one Member State to acquire and use land and buildings situated in the territory of another Member State, in so far as this does not conflict with the principles laid down in Article 33(2);

(f)   by effecting the progressive abolition of restrictions on freedom of establishment in every branch of activity under consideration, both as regards the conditions for setting up agencies, branches or subsidiaries in the territory of a Member State and as regards the subsidiaries in the territory of a Member State and as regards the conditions governing the entry of personnel belonging to the main establishment into managerial or supervisory posts in such agencies, branches or subsidiaries;

(g)   by coordinating to the necessary extent the safeguards which, for the protection of the interests of members and other, are required by Member States of companies or firms within the meaning of the second paragraph of Article 48 with a view to making such safeguards equivalent throughout the Community;

(h)   by satisfying themselves that the conditions of establishment are not distorted by aids granted by Member States.

Article 45

The provisions of this chapter shall not apply, so far as any given Member State is concerned, to activities which in that State are connected, even occasionally, with the exercise of official authority.

The Council may, acting by a qualified majority on a proposal from the Commission, rule that the provisions of this chapter shall not apply to certain activities.

Article 46

1. The provisions of this chapter and measures taken in pursuance thereof shall not prejudice the applicability of provisions laid down by law, regulation or administrative action providing for special treatment for foreign nationals on grounds of public policy, public security or public health.

2. The Council shall, acting in accordance with the procedure referred to in Article 251, issue directives for the coordination of the abovementioned provisions.

Article 47

1. In order to make it easier for persons to take up and pursue activities as self-employed persons, the Council shall, acting in accordance with the procedure referred to in Article 251, issue directives for the mutual recognition of diplomas, certificates and other evidence of formal qualifications.

2. For the same purpose, the Council shall, acting in accordance with the procedure referred to in Article 251, issue directives for the coordination of the provisions laid down by law, regulation or administrative action in Member States concerning the taking-up and pursuit of activities as self-employed persons. The Council, acting unanimously throughout the procedure referred to in Article 251, shall decide on directives the implementation of which involves in at least one Member State amendment of the existing principles laid down by law governing the professions with respect to training and conditions of access for natural persons. In other cases the Council shall act by qualified majority.

3. In the case of the medical and allied and pharmaceutical professions, the progressive abolition of restrictions shall be dependent upon coordination of the conditions for their exercise in the various Member States.

Article 48

Companies or firms formed in accordance with the law of a Member State and having their registered office, central administration or principal place of business within the Community shall, for the purposes of this Chapter, be treated in the same way as natural persons who are nationals of Member States.

"Companies or firms" means companies or firms constituted under civil or commercial law, including cooperative societies, and other legal persons governed by public or private law, save for those which are non-profit-making.

CHAPTER 3

SERVICES

Article 49

Within the framework of the provisions set out below, restrictions on freedom to provide services within the Community shall be prohibited in respect of nationals of Member States who are established in a State of the Community other than that of the person for whom the services are intended.

The Council may, acting by a qualified majority on a proposal from the Commission, extend the provisions of the Chapter to nationals of a third country who provide services and who are established within the Community.

Article 50

Services shall be considered to be "services" within the meaning of this Treaty where they are normally provided for remuneration, in so far as they are not governed by the provisions relating to freedom of movement for goods, capital and persons.

"Services" shall in particular include:

(a) activities of an industrial character;

(b) activities of a commercial character;

(c) activities of craftsmen;

(d) activities of the professions.

Without prejudice to the provisions of the chapter relating to the right of establishment, the person providing a service may, in order to do so, temporarily pursue his activity in the State where the service is provided, under the same conditions as are imposed by that State on its own nationals.

Article 51

1. Freedom to provide services in the field of transport shall be governed by the provisions of the title relating to transport.

2. The liberalisation of banking and insurance services connected with movements of capital shall be effected in step with the liberalisation of movement of capital.

Article 52

1. In order to achieve the liberalisation of a specific service, the Council shall, on a proposal from the Commission and after consulting the Economic and Social

Committee and the European Parliament, issue directives acting by a qualified majority.

2. As regards the directives referred to in paragraph 1, priority shall as a general rule be given to those services which directly affect production costs or the liberalisation of which helps to promote trade in goods.

Article 53

The Member States declare their readiness to undertake the liberalisation of services beyond the extent required by the directives issued pursuant to Article 52(1), if their general economic situation and the situation of the economic sector concerned so permit.

To this end, the Commission shall make recommendations to the Member States concerned.

Article 54

As long as restrictions on freedom to provide services have not been abolished, each Member State shall apply such restrictions without distinction on grounds of nationality or residence to all persons providing services within the meaning of the first paragraph of Article 49.

Article 55

The provisions of Articles 45 to 48 shall apply to the matters covered by this chapter.

CHAPTER 3

EDUCATION, VOCATIONAL TRAINING AND YOUTH

Article 149

1. The Community shall contribute to the development of quality education by encouraging cooperation between Member States and, if necessary, by supporting and supplementing their action, while fully respecting the responsibility of the Member States for the content of teaching and the organisation of education systems and their cultural and linguistic diversity.

2. Community action shall be aimed at:

–   developing the European dimension in education, particularly through the teaching and dissemination of the languages of the Member States,

- encouraging mobility of students and teachers, by encouraging inter alia, the academic recognition of diplomas and periods of study,
- promoting cooperation between educational establishments,
- developing exchanges of information and experience on issues common to the education systems of the Member States,
- encouraging the development of youth exchanges and of exchanges of socioeducational instructors,
- encouraging the development of distance education.

3. The Community and the Member States shall foster cooperation with third countries and the competent international organisations in the field of education, in particular the Council of Europe.

4. In order to contribute to the achievement of the objectives referred to in this Article, the Council:

- acting in accordance with the procedure referred to in Article 251, after consulting the Economic and Social Committee and the Committee of the Regions, shall adopt incentive measures, excluding any harmonisation of the laws and regulations of the Member States,
- acting by a qualified majority on a proposal from the Commission, shall adopt recommendations.

Article 150

1. The Community shall implement a vocational training policy which shall support and supplement the action of the Member States, while fully respecting the responsibility of the Member States for the content and organisation of vocational training.

2. Community action shall aim to:

- facilitate adaptation to industrial changes, in particular through vocational training and retraining,
- improve initial and continuing vocational training in order to facilitate vocational integration and reintegration into the labour market,
- facilitate access to vocational training and encourage mobility of instructors and trainees and particularly young people,
- stimulate cooperation on training between educational or training establishments and firms,
- develop exchanges of information and experience on issues common to the training systems of the Member States.

3. The Community and the Member States shall foster cooperation with third countries and the competent international organisations in the sphere of vocational training.

4. The Council, acting in accordance with the procedure referred to in Article 251 and after consulting the Economic and Social Committee and the Committee of the Regions, shall adopt measures to contribute to the achievement of the objectives

referred to in this article, excluding any harmonisation of the laws and regulations of the Member States.

Article 234

The Court of Justice shall have jurisdiction to give preliminary rulings concerning:

(a) the interpretation of this Treaty;

(b) the validity and interpretation of acts of the institutions of the Community and of the ECB;

(c) the interpretation of the statutes of bodies established by an act of the Council, where those statutes so provide.

Where such a question is raised before any court or tribunal of a Member State, that court or tribunal may, if it considers that a decision on the question is necessary to enable it to give judgment, request the Court of Justice to give a ruling thereon.

Where any such question is raised in a case pending before a court or tribunal of a Member State against whose decisions there is no judicial remedy under national law, that court or tribunal shall bring the matter before the Court of Justice.

CHAPTER 2

PROVISIONS COMMON TO SEVERAL INSTITUTIONS

Article 249

In order to carry out their task and in accordance with the provisions of this Treaty, the European Parliament acting jointly with the Council, the Council and the Commission shall make regulations and issue directives, take decisions, make recommendations or deliver opinions.

A regulation shall have general application. It shall be binding in its entirety and directly applicable in all Member States.

A directive shall be binding, as to the result to be achieved, upon each Member State to which it is addressed, but shall leave to the national authorities the choice of form and methods.

A decision shall be binding in its entirety upon those to whom it is addressed.

Recommendations and opinions shall have no binding force.

Article 300(52)

1. Where this Treaty provides for the conclusion of agreements between the Community and one or more States or international organisations, the Commission

shall make recommendations to the Council, which shall authorise the Commission to open the necessary negotiations. The Commission shall conduct these negotiations in consultation with special committees appointed by the Council to assist it in this task and within the framework of such directives as the Council may issue to it.

In exercising the powers conferred upon it by this paragraph, the Council shall act by a qualified majority, except in the cases where the first subparagraph of paragraph 2 provides that the Council shall act unanimously.

2. Subject to the powers vested in the Commission in this field, the signing, which may be accompanied by a decision on provisional application before entry into force, and the conclusion of the agreements shall be decided on by the Council, acting by a qualified majority on a proposal from the Commission. The Council shall act unanimously when the agreement covers a field for which unanimity is required for the adoption of internal rules and for the agreements referred to in Article 310.

By way of derogation from the rules laid down in paragraph 3, the same procedures shall apply for a decision to suspend the application of an agreement, and for the purpose of establishing the positions to be adopted on behalf of the Community in a body set up by an agreement, when that body is called upon to adopt decisions having legal effects, with the exception of decisions supplementing or amending the institutional framework of the agreement.

The European Parliament shall be immediately and fully informed of any decision under this paragraph concerning the provisional application or the suspension of agreements, or the establishment of the Community position in a body set up by an agreement.

3. The Council shall conclude agreements after consulting the European Parliament, except for the agreements referred to in Article 133(3), including cases where the agreement covers a field for which the procedure referred to in Article 251 or that referred to in Article 252 is required for the adoption of internal rules. The European Parliament shall deliver its opinion within a time limit which the Council may lay down according to the urgency of the matter. In the absence of an opinion within that time limit, the Council may act.

By way of derogation from the previous subparagraph, agreements referred to in Article 310, other agreements establishing a specific institutional framework by organising cooperation procedures, agreements having important budgetary implications for the Community and agreements entailing amendment of an act adopted under the procedure referred to in Article 251 shall be concluded after the assent of the European Parliament has been obtained.

The Council and the European Parliament may, in an urgent situation, agree upon a time limit for the assent.

4. When concluding an agreement, the Council may, by way of derogation from paragraph 2, authorise the Commission to approve modifications on behalf of the Community where the agreement provides for them to be adopted by a simplified procedure or by a body set up by the agreement; it may attach specific conditions to such authorisation.

5. When the Council envisages concluding an agreement which calls for amendments to this Treaty, the amendments must first be adopted in accordance with the procedure laid down in Article 48 of the Treaty on European Union.

6. The European Parliament, the Council, the Commission or a Member State may obtain the opinion of the Court of Justice as to whether an agreement envisaged is compatible with the provisions of this Treaty. Where the opinion of the Court of Justice is adverse, the agreement may enter into force only in accordance with Article 48 of the Treaty on European Union.

7. Agreements concluded under the conditions set out in this Article shall be binding on the institutions of the Community and on Member States.

Article 310

The Community may conclude with one or more States or international organisations agreements establishing an association involving reciprocal rights and obligations, common action and special procedure.

TREATY ON ACCESSION

[2003] O.J. L236

Treaty Between The Kingdom of Belgium, The Kingdom of Denmark,
The Federal Republic of Germany, The Hellenic Republic,
The Kingdom of Spain, The French Republic, Ireland
The Italian Republic, The Grand Duchy of Luxembourg,
The Kingdom of the Netherlands, The Republic of Austria,
The Portuguese Republic, The Republic of Finland, The Kingdom of Sweden,
The United Kingdom of Great Britain and Northern Ireland
(Member States of the European Union)
AND
The Czech Republic, The Republic of Estonia, The Republic of Cyprus,
The Republic of Latvia, The Republic of Lithuania, The Republic of Hungary,
The Republic of Malta, The Republic of Poland,
The Republic of Slovenia, The Slovak Republic
Concerning the Accession of The Czech Republic, The Republic of Estonia,
The Republic of Cyprus, The Republic of Latvia, The Republic of Lithuania,
The Republic of Hungary, The Republic of Malta, The Republic of Poland,
The Republic of Slovenia, The Slovak Republic
to The European Union

UNITED in their desire to pursue the attainment of the objectives of the Treaties on **A3–01**
which the European Union is founded,

DETERMINED in the spirit of those Treaties to continue the process of creating an
ever closer union among the peoples of Europe on the foundations already laid,

CONSIDERING that Article 49 of the Treaty on European Union affords European
States the opportunity of becoming members of the Union,

CONSIDERING that the Czech Republic, the Republic of Estonia, the Republic of
Cyprus, the Republic of Latvia, the Republic of Lithuania, the Republic of Hungary,
the Republic of Malta, the Republic of Poland, the Republic of Slovenia and the
Slovak Republic have applied to become members of the Union,

CONSIDERING that the Council of the European Union, after having obtained the
opinion of the Commission and the assent of the European Parliament, has declared
itself in favour of the admission of these States,

HAVE DECIDED to establish by common agreement the conditions of admission
and the adjustments to be made to the Treaties on which the European Union is
founded, and to this end have designated as their Plenipotentiaries:

WHO, having exchanged their full powers found in good and due form,

HAVE AGREED AS FOLLOWS:

Article 1

1. The Czech Republic, the Republic of Estonia, the Republic of Cyprus, the Republic of Latvia, the Republic of Lithuania, the Republic of Hungary, the Republic of Malta, the Republic of Poland, the Republic of Slovenia and the Slovak Republic hereby become members of the European Union and Parties to the Treaties on which the Union is founded as amended or supplemented.

2. The conditions of admission and the adjustments to the Treaties on which the Union is founded, entailed by such admission, are set out in the Act annexed to this Treaty. The provisions of that Act shall form an integral part of this Treaty.

3. The provisions concerning the rights and obligations of the Member States and the powers and jurisdiction of the institutions of the Union as set out in the Treaties referred to in paragraph 1 shall apply in respect of this Treaty.

Article 2

1. This Treaty shall be ratified by the High Contracting Parties in accordance with their respective constitutional requirements. The instruments of ratification shall be deposited with the Government of the Italian Republic by 30 April 2004 at the latest.

2. This Treaty shall enter into force on 1 May 2004 provided that all the instruments of ratification have been deposited before that date.

If, however, the States referred to in Article 1(1) have not all deposited their instruments of ratification in due time, the Treaty shall enter into force for those States which have deposited their instruments. In this case, the Council of the European Union, acting unanimously, shall decide immediately upon such adjustments as have become indispensable to Article 3 of this Treaty, to Articles 1, 6(6), 11 to 15, 18, 19, 25, 26, 29 to 31, 33 to 35, 46 to 49, 58 and 61 of the Act of Accession, to Annexes II to XV and their Appendices to that Act and to Protocols 1 to 10 annexed thereto; acting unanimously, it may also declare that those provisions of the aforementioned Act, including its Annexes, Appendices and Protocols, which refer expressly to a State which has not deposited its instrument of ratification have lapsed, or it may adjust them.

3. Notwithstanding paragraph 2, the institutions of the Union may adopt before accession the measures referred to in Articles 6(2) second subparagraph, 6(6) second subparagraph, 6(7) second and third subparagraphs, 6(8) second and third subparagraphs, 6(9) third subparagraph, 21, 23, 28(1), 32(5), 33(1), 33(4), 33(5), 38, 39, 41, 42 and 55 to 57 of the Act of Accession, Annexes III to XIV to that Act, and Protocol 2, Article 6 of Protocol 3, Article 2(2) of Protocol 4, Protocol 8 and Articles 1, 2 and 4 of Protocol 10 annexed thereto. These measures shall enter into force only subject to and on the date of the entry into force of this Treaty.

II. DECLARATIONS ADOPTED BY THE PLENIPOTENTIARIES
(Excerpts)

(ANNEXED TO THE FINAL ACT)

Furthermore, the Plenipotentiaries have adopted the Declarations listed below, **A4–01** annexed to this Final Act.

1. Joint Declaration: One Europe
2. Joint Declaration on the Court of Justice of the European Communities

1. JOINT DECLARATION: ONE EUROPE

Today is a great moment for Europe. We have today concluded accession negotiations between the European Union and Cyprus, the Czech Republic, Estonia, Hungary, Latvia, Lithuania, Malta, Poland, Slovakia and Slovenia. 75 million people will be welcomed as new citizens of the European Union.

We, the current and acceding Member States, declare our full support for the continuous, inclusive and irreversible enlargement process. The accession negotiations with Bulgaria and Romania will continue on the basis of the same principles that have guided the negotiations so far. The results already achieved in these negotiations will not be brought into question. Depending on further progress in complying with the membership criteria, the objective is to welcome Bulgaria and Romania as new members of the European Union in 2007. We also welcome the important decisions taken today concerning the next stage of Turkey's candidature for membership of the European Union.

Our common wish is to make Europe a continent of democracy, freedom, peace and progress. The Union will remain determined to avoid new dividing lines in Europe and to promote stability and prosperity within and beyond the new borders of the Union. We are looking forward to working together in our joint endeavour to accomplish these goals.

Our aim is One Europe.

Belgium	Czech Republic	Denmark
Germany	Estonia	Greece
Spain	France	Ireland
Italy	Cyprus	Latvia
Lithuania	Luxembourg	Hungary
Malta	Netherlands	Austria
Poland	Portugal	Slovenia
Slovakia	Finland	Sweden
United Kingdom		

2. JOINT DECLARATION ON THE COURT OF JUSTICE OF THE EUROPEAN COMMUNITIES

Should the Court of Justice so request, the Council, acting unanimously, may increase the number of Advocates-General in accordance with Article 222 of the E.C. Treaty and Article 138 of the Euratom Treaty. Otherwise, the new Member States will be integrated into the existing system for their appointment.

6. DECLARATION ON THE FREE MOVEMENT OF WORKERS: CZECH REPUBLIC

The E.U. stresses the strong elements of differentiation and flexibility in the arrangement for the free movement of workers. Member States shall endeavour to grant increased labour market access to Czech nationals under national law, with a view to speeding up the approximation to the acquis. As a consequence, the employment opportunities in the E.U. for Czech nationals should improve substantially upon the Czech Republic's accession. Moreover, the E.U. Member States will make best use of the proposed arrangement to move as quickly as possible to the full application of the acquis in the area of free movement of workers.

7. DECLARATION ON THE FREE MOVEMENT OF WORKERS: ESTONIA

The E.U. stresses the strong elements of differentiation and flexibility in the arrangement for the free movement of workers. Member States shall endeavour to grant increased labour market access to Estonian nationals under national law, with a view to speeding up the approximation to the acquis. As a consequence, the employment opportunities in the E.U. for Estonian nationals should improve substantially upon Estonia's accession. Moreover, the E.U. Member States will make best use of the proposed arrangement to move as quickly as possible to the full application of the acquis in the area of free movement of workers.

10. DECLARATION ON THE FREE MOVEMENT OF WORKERS: LATVIA

The E.U. stresses the strong elements of differentiation and flexibility in the arrangement for the free movement of workers. Member States shall endeavour to grant increased labour market access to Latvian nationals under national law, with a view to speeding up the approximation to the acquis. As a consequence, the employment opportunities in the E.U. for Latvian nationals should improve substantially upon Latvia's accession. Moreover, the E.U. Member States will make best use of the proposed arrangement to move as quickly as possible to the full application of the acquis in the area of free movement of workers.

11. DECLARATION ON THE FREE MOVEMENT OF WORKERS: LITHUANIA

The E.U. stresses the strong elements of differentiation and flexibility in the arrangement for the free movement of workers. Member States shall endeavour to grant increased labour market access to Lithuanian nationals under national law, with a view to speeding up the approximation to the acquis. As a consequence, the employment opportunities in the E.U. for Lithuanian nationals should improve substantially upon Lithuania's accession. Moreover, the E.U. Member States will make best use of the proposed arrangement to move as quickly as possible to the full application of the acquis in the area of free movement of workers.

13. Declaration on the Free Movement of Workers: Hungary

The E.U. stresses the strong elements of differentiation and flexibility in the arrangement for the free movement of workers. Member States shall endeavour to grant increased labour market access to Hungarian nationals under national law, with a view to speeding up the approximation to the acquis. As a consequence, the employment opportunities in the E.U. for Hungarian nationals should improve substantially upon Hungary's accession. Moreover, the E.U. Member States will make best use of the proposed arrangement to move as quickly as possible to the full application of the acquis in the area of free movement of workers.

14. Declaration on the Free Movement of Workers: Malta

Should the accession of Malta give rise to difficulties relating to the free movement of workers, the matter may be brought before the institutions of the Union in order to obtain a solution to this problem. This solution will be in strict accordance with the provisions of the Treaties (including those of the Treaty on European Union) and the provisions adopted in application thereof, in particular those relating to the free movement of workers.

15. Declaration on the Free Movement of Workers: Poland

The E.U. stresses the strong elements of differentiation and flexibility in the arrangement for the free movement of workers. Member States shall endeavour to grant increased labour market access to Polish nationals under national law, with a view to speeding up the approximation to the acquis. As a consequence, the employment opportunities in the E.U. for Polish nationals should improve substantially upon Poland's accession. Moreover, the E.U. Member States will make best use of the proposed arrangement to move as quickly as possible to the full application of the acquis in the area of free movement of workers.

16. Declaration on the Free Movement of Workers: Slovenia

The E.U. stresses the strong elements of differentiation and flexibility in the arrangement for the free movement of workers. Member States shall endeavour to grant increased labour market access to Slovenian nationals under national law, with a view to speeding up the approximation to the acquis. As a consequence, the employment opportunities in the E.U. for Slovenian nationals should improve substantially upon Slovenia's accession. Moreover, the E.U. Member States will make best use of the proposed arrangement to move as quickly as possible to the full application of the acquis in the area of free movement of workers.

18. DECLARATION ON THE FREE MOVEMENT OF WORKERS: SLOVAKIA

The E.U. stresses the strong elements of differentiation and flexibility in the arrangement for the free movement of workers. Member States shall endeavour to grant increased labour market access to Slovak nationals under national law, with a view to speeding up the approximation to the acquis. As a consequence, the employment opportunities in the E.U. for Slovak nationals should improve substantially upon Slovakia's accession. Moreover, the E.U. Member States will make best use of the proposed arrangement to move as quickly as possible to the full application of the acquis in the area of free movement of workers.

D. JOINT DECLARATIONS BY VARIOUS PRESENT MEMBER STATES

19. JOINT DECLARATION BY THE FEDERAL REPUBLIC OF GERMANY AND THE REPUBLIC OF AUSTRIA ON THE FREE MOVEMENT OF WORKERS: CZECH REPUBLIC, ESTONIA, HUNGARY, LATVIA, LITHUANIA, POLAND, SLOVENIA AND SLOVAKIA

The wording of point number 13 of the transitional measures on the free movement of workers under Directive 96/71/EC in Annexes V, VI, VIII, IX, X, XII, XIII and XIV is understood by the Federal Republic of Germany and the Republic of Austria in agreement with the Commission as meaning that "certain regions" may, where appropriate, also comprise the entire national territory.

E. GENERAL JOINT DECLARATIONS BY THE PRESENT MEMBER STATES

21. GENERAL JOINT DECLARATION

The present Member States underline that the Declarations attached to this Final Act cannot be interpreted or applied in a way contrary to the obligations of the Member States arising from the Treaty and Act of Accession.

The present Member States note that the Commission subscribes fully to the above.

25. DECLARATION BY THE CZECH REPUBLIC ON WORKERS

The Czech Republic declares that it expects that the intentins of a present Member State to liberalise the access of Czech workers to its labour market based on individual sectors and professions will be subject to bilateral consultations between the Member State concerned and the Czech Republic.

Act of Accession
(Excerpts)

Article 24

The measures listed in **Annexes V, VI, VII, VIII, IX, X, XI, XII, XIII, XIV** to this Act   **A5–01**
shall apply in respect of the new Member States under the conditions laid down in
those Annexes.

ANNEX V TO THE TREATY ON ACCESSION (EXCERPTS):
CHAPTER 1 (FREE MOVEMENT OF PERSONS)

ANNEX V

LIST REFERRED TO IN ARTICLE 24 OF THE ACT OF ACCESSION: CZECH REPUBLIC

1. Freedom of Movement for Persons

Treaty establishing the European Community;

31968 L 0360: Council Directive 68/360/EEC of 15 October 1968 on the abolition of
restrictions on movement and residence within the Community for workers of
Member States and their families (OJ L 257, 19.10.1968, p. 13), as last amended by:

–   11994 N: Act concerning the conditions of accession and the adjustments to the
    Treaties—Accession of the Republic of Austria, the Republic of Finland and the
    Kingdom of Sweden (OJ C 241, 29.8.1994, p. 21);

31968 R 1612: Council Regulation (EEC) No 1612/68 of 15 October 1968 on freedom
of movement for workers within the Community (OJ L 257, 19.10.1968, p. 2), as last
amended by:

–   31992 R 2434: Council Regulation (EEC) No 2434/92 of 27.7.1992 (OJ L 245,
    26.8.1992, p. 1);

31996 L 0071: Directive 96/71/EC of the European Parliament and of the Council of
16 December 1996 concerning the posting of workers in the framework of the provision of services (OJ L 18, 21.1.1997, p. 1).

1.   Article 39 and the first paragraph of Article 49 of the E.C. Treaty shall fully
    apply only, in relation to the freedom of movement of workers and the freedom
    to provide services involving temporary movement of workers as defined in
    Article 1 of Directive 96/71/EC between the Czech Republic on the one hand, and
    Belgium, Denmark, Germany, Estonia, Greece, Spain, France, Ireland, Italy,
    Latvia, Lithuania, Luxembourg, Hungary, the Netherlands, Austria, Poland,

Portugal, Slovenia, Slovakia, Finland, Sweden and the United Kingdom on the other hand, subject to the transitional provisions laid down in paragraphs 2 to 14.

2.   By way of derogation from Articles 1 to 6 of Regulation (EEC) No 1612/68 and until the end of the two year period following the date of accession, the present Member States will apply national measures, or those resulting from bilateral agreements, regulating access to their labour markets by Czech nationals. The present Member States may continue to apply such measures until the end of the five year period following the date of accession.

Czech nationals legally working in a present Member State at the date of accession and admitted to the labour market of that Member State for an uninterrupted period of 12 months or longer will enjoy access to the labour market of that Member State but not to the labour market of other Member States applying national measures.

Czech nationals admitted to the labour market of a present Member State following accession for an uninterrupted period of 12 months or longer shall also enjoy the same rights.

The Czech nationals mentioned in the second and third subparagraphs above shall cease to enjoy the rights contained in those subparagraphs if they voluntarily leave the labour market of the present Member State in question.

Czech nationals legally working in a present Member State at the date of accession, or during a period when national measures are applied, and who were admitted to the labour market of that Member State for a period of less than 12 months shall not enjoy these rights.

3.   Before the end of the two year period following the date of accession, the Council shall review the functioning of the transitional provisions laid down in paragraph 2, on the basis of a report from the Commission.

On completion of this review, and no later than at the end of the two year period following the date of accession, the present Member States shall notify the Commission whether they will continue applying national measures or measures resulting from bilateral agreements, or whether they will apply Articles 1 to 6 of Regulation (EEC) No 1612/68 henceforth. In the absence of such notification, Articles 1 to 6 of Regulation (EEC) No 1612/68 shall apply.

4.   Upon the request of the Czech Republic, one further review may be held. The procedure referred to in paragraph 3 shall apply and shall be completed within six months of receipt of the request from the Czech Republic.

5.   A Member State maintaining national measures or measures resulting from bilateral agreements at the end of the five year period indicated in paragraph 2 may, in case of serious disturbances of its labour market or threat thereof and after notifying the Commission, continue to apply these measures until the end of the seven year period following the date of accession. In the absence of such notification, Articles 1 to 6 of Regulation (EEC) No 1612/68 shall apply.

6.   During the seven year period following the date of accession, those Member States in which, by virtue of paragraphs 3, 4 or 5, Articles 1 to 6 of Regulation (EEC) No 1612/68 apply as regards Czech nationals, and which are issuing work permits to nationals of the Czech Republic for monitoring purposes during this period, will do so automatically.

7.   Those Member States in which, by virtue of paragraphs 3, 4 or 5, Articles 1 to 6 of Regulation (EEC) No 1612/68 apply as regards Czech nationals, may resort to the procedures set out in the subparagraphs below until the end of the seven year period following the date of accession.

When a Member State referred to in the first subparagraph undergoes or foresees disturbances on its labour market which could seriously threaten the standard of living or level of employment in a given region or occupation, that Member State shall inform the Commission and the other Member States thereof and shall supply them with all relevant particulars. On the basis of this information, the Member State may request the Commission to state that the application of Articles 1 to 6 of Regulation (EEC) No 1612/68 be wholly or partially suspended in order to restore to normal the situation in that region or occupation. The Commission shall decide on the suspension and on the duration and scope thereof not later than two weeks after receiving such a request and shall notify the Council of such a decision. Any Member State may, within two weeks from the date of the Commission's Decision, request the Council to annul or amend the Decision. The Council shall act on such a request within two weeks, by qualified majority.

A Member State referred to in the first subparagraph may, in urgent and exceptional cases, suspend the application of Articles 1 to 6 of Regulation (EEC) No 1612/68, followed by a reasoned ex-post notification to the Commission.

8. As long as the application of Articles 1 to 6 of Regulation (EEC) No 1612/68 is suspended by virtue of paragraphs 2 to 5 and 7 above, Article 11 of the Regulation shall apply in the Czech Republic with regard to nationals of the present Member States, and in the present Member States with regard to Czech nationals under the following conditions:

   – the members of a worker's family referred to in Article 10(1)(a) of the Regulation, legally residing with the worker in the territory of a Member State at the date of accession, shall have, upon accession, immediate access to the labour market of that Member State. This does not apply to family members of a worker legally admitted to the labour market of that Member State for a period of less than 12 months;

   – the members of a worker's family referred to in Article 10(1)(a) of the Regulation, legally residing with the worker in the territory of a Member State from a date later than the date of accession, but during the period of application of the transitional provisions laid down above, shall have access to the labour market of the Member State concerned once they have been resident in the Member State concerned for at least eighteen months or from the third year following the date of accession, whichever is the earlier.

These provisions shall be without prejudice to more favourable measures whether national or resulting from bilateral agreements.

9. Insofar as certain provisions of Directive 68/360/EEC may not be dissociated from those of Regulation (EEC) No 1612/68 whose application is deferred pursuant to paragraphs 2 to 5 and 7 and 8, the Czech Republic and the present Member States may derogate from those provisions to the extent necessary for the application of paragraphs 2 to 5 and 7 and 8.

10. Whenever national measures, or those resulting from bilateral agreements, are applied by the present Member States by virtue of the transitional provisions laid down above, the Czech Republic may maintain in force equivalent measures with regard to the nationals of the Member State or States in question.

11. If the application of Articles 1 to 6 of Regulation (EEC) No 1612/68 is suspended by any of the present Member States, the Czech Republic may resort to the procedures laid down in paragraph 7 with respect to Estonia, Latvia, Lithuania, Hungary, Poland, Slovenia or Slovakia. During any such period work permits issued by the Czech Republic for monitoring purposes to nationals of Estonia, Latvia, Lithuania, Hungary, Poland, Slovenia or Slovakia shall be issued automatically.

12. Any present Member State applying national measures in accordance with paragraphs 2 to 5 and 7 to 9, may introduce, under national law, greater freedom of movement than that existing at the date of accession, including full labour market access. From the third year following the date of accession, any present Member State applying national measures may at any time decide to apply Articles 1 to 6 of Regulation (EEC) No 1612/68 instead. The Commission shall be informed of any such decision.

13. In order to address serious disturbances or the threat thereof in specific sensitive service sectors on their labour markets, which could arise in certain regions from the transnational provision of services, as defined in Article 1 of Directive 96/71/EC, and as long as they apply, by virtue of the transitional provisions laid down above, national measures or those resulting from bilateral agreements to the free movement of Czech workers, Germany and Austria may, after notifying the Commission, derogate from the first paragraph of Article 49 of the E.C. Treaty with a view to limit in the context of the provision of services by companies established in the Czech Republic, the temporary movement of workers whose right to take up work in Germany and Austria is subject to national measures.

The list of service sectors which may be covered by this derogation is as follows:

– in Germany:

Sector	NACE[1] code, unless otherwise specified
Construction, including related branches	45.1 to 4;
Industrial cleaning	74.70 Industrial cleaning
Other services	74.87 Only activities of interior decorators

– in Austria:

Social work and activities without accommodations	85.32

To the extent that Germany or Austria derogate from the first paragraph of Article 49 of the E.C. Treaty in accordance with the preceding subparagraphs, the Czech Republic may, after notifying the Commission, take equivalent measures.

The effect of the application of this paragraph shall not result in conditions for the temporary movement of workers in the context of the transnational provision of services between Germany or Austria and the Czech Republic which are more restrictive than those prevailing on the date of signature of the Treaty of Accession.

14. The effect of the application of paragraphs 2 to 5 and 7 to 12 shall not result in conditions for access of Czech nationals to the labour markets of the present Member States which are more restrictive than those prevailing on the date of signature of the Treaty of Accession.

Notwithstanding the application of the provisions laid down in paragraphs 1 to 13, the present Member States shall, during any period when national measures or those resulting from bilateral agreements are applied, give preference to workers who are nationals of the Member States over workers who are nationals of third countries as regards access to their labour market.

---

[1] NACE: see 31990 R 3037: Council Regulation (EEC) No 3037/90 of 9 October 1990 on the statistical classification of economic activities in the European Community (OJ L 293, 24.10.1990, p. 1), as last amended by 32002 R 0029: Commission Regulation (E.C.) No 29/2002 of 19.12.2001 (OJ L 6, 10.1.2002, p. 3).

Czech migrant workers and their families legally resident and working in another Member State or migrant workers from other Member States and their families legally resident and working in the Czech Republic shall not be treated in a more restrictive way than those from third countries resident and working in that Member State or the Czech Republic respectively. Furthermore, in application of the principle of Community preference, migrant workers from third countries resident and working in the Czech Republic shall not be treated more favourably than nationals of the Czech Republic.

SECONDARY LEGISLATION

SECONDARY LEGISLATION

COUNCIL DIRECTIVE 64/221 OF 25 FEBRUARY 1964 ON THE COORDINATION OF SPECIAL MEASURES CONCERNING THE MOVEMENT AND RESIDENCE OF FOREIGN NATIONALS WHICH ARE JUSTIFIED ON GROUNDS OF PUBLIC POLICY, PUBLIC SECURITY OR PUBLIC HEALTH

Article 1

1. The provisions of this Directive shall apply to any national of a Member State who resides in or travels to another Member State of the Community, either in order to pursue an activity as an employed or self-employed person, or as a recipient of services.:

A6–01

2. These provisions shall apply also to the spouse and to members of the family who come within the provisions of the regulations and directives adopted in this field in pursuance of the Treaty.

Article 2

1. This Directive relates to all measures concerning entry into their territory, issue or renewal of residence permits, or expulsion from their territory, taken by Member States on grounds of public policy, public security or public health.:

2. Such grounds shall not be invoked to service economic ends.

Article 3

1. Measures taken on grounds of public policy or of public security shall be based exclusively on the personal conduct of the individual concerned.

2. Previous criminal convictions shall not in themselves constitute grounds for the taking of such measures.

3. Expiry of the identity card or passport used by the person concerned to enter the host country and to obtain a residence permit shall not justify expulsion from the territory.

4. The State which issued the identity card or passport shall allow the holder of such document to re-enter its territory without any formality even if the document is no longer valid or the nationality of the holder is in dispute.

Article 4

1. The only diseases or disabilities justifying refusal of entry into a territory or refusal to issue a first residence permit shall be those listed in the Annex to this Directive.

2. Diseases or disabilities occurring after a first residence permit has been issued shall not justify refusal to renew the residence permit or expulsion from the territory.

3. Member States shall not introduce new provisions or practices which are more restrictive than those in force at the date of notification of this Directive.

Article 5

A decision to grant or to refuse a first residence permit shall be taken as soon as possible and in any event not later than six months from the date of application for the permit.

The person concerned shall be allowed to remain temporarily in the territory pending a decision either to grant or to refuse a residence permit.

2. The host country may, in cases where this is considered essential, request the Member State of origin of the applicant, and if need be other Member States, to provide information concerning any previous police record. Such enquiries shall not be made as a matter of routine. The Member State consulted shall give its reply within two months.

Article 6

The person concerned shall be informed of the grounds of public policy, public security, or public health upon which the decision taken in his case is based, unless this is contrary to the interests of the security of the State involved.

Article 7

The person concerned shall be officially notified of any decision to refuse the issue or renewal of a residence permit or to expel him from the territory. The period allowed for leaving the territory shall be stated in this notification. Save in cases of urgency, this period shall be not less than fifteen days if the person concerned has not yet been granted a residence permit and not less than one month in all other cases.

Article 8

The person concerned shall have the same legal remedies in respect of any decision concerning entry, or refusing the issue or renewal of a residence permit, or ordering expulsion from the territory, as are available to nationals of the State concerned in respect of acts of the administration.

Article 9

1. Where there is no right of appeal to a court of law, or where such appeal may be only in respect of the legal validity of the decision, or where the appeal cannot have suspensory effect, a decision refusing renewal of a residence permit or ordering the expulsion of the holder of a residence permit from the territory shall not be taken by the administrative authority, save in cases of urgency, until an opinion has been obtained from a competent authority of the host country before which the person concerned enjoys such rights of defence and of assistance or representation as the domestic law of that country provides for.

This authority shall not be the same as that empowered to take the decision refusing renewal of the residence permit or ordering expulsion.

2. Any decision refusing the issue of a first residence permit or ordering expulsion of the person concerned before the issue of the permit shall, where that person so requests, be referred for consideration to the authority whose prior opinion is required under paragraph 1. The person concerned shall then be entitled to submit his defence in person, except where this would be contrary to the interests of national security.

Article 10

1. Member States shall within six months of notification of this Directive put into force the measures necessary to comply with its provisions and shall forthwith inform the Commission thereof.

2. Member States shall ensure that the texts of the main provisions of national law which they adopt in the field governed by this Directive are communicated to the Commission.

Article 11

This Directive is addressed to the Member States.

ANNEX

A. Diseases which might endanger public health:

1. Diseases subject to quarantine listed in International Health Regulation No 2 of the World Health Organisation of 25 May 1951;

2. Tuberculoses of the respiratory system in an active state showing a tendency to develop;

3. Syphilis;

4. Other infectious diseases or contagious parasitic diseases if they are the subject of provisions for the protection of nationals of the host country.

B. Diseases and disabilities which might threaten public policy or public security:

1. Drug addiction;

2. Profound mental disturbance; manifest conditions of psychotic disturbance with agitation, delirium, hallucination or confusion.

REGULATION (EEC) NO 1612/68 OF THE COUNCIL OF 15 OCTOBER 1968 ON FREEDOM OF MOVEMENT FOR WORKERS WITHIN THE COMMUNITY
(Excerpts)

THE COUNCIL OF THE EUROPEAN COMMUNITIES,   A7–01

Having regard to the Treaty establishing the European Economic Community, and in particular Article 49 thereof;

Having regard to the proposal from the Commission;

Having regard to the Opinion of the European Parliament;[1]

Having regard to the Opinion of the Economic and Social Committee;[2]

Whereas freedom of movement for workers should be secured within the Community by the end of the transitional period at the latest ; whereas the attainment of this objective entails the abolition of any discrimination based on nationality between workers of the Member States as regards employment, remuneration and other conditions of work and employment, as well as the right of such workers to move freely within the Community in order to pursue activities as employed persons subject to any limitations justified on grounds of public policy, public security or public health;

Whereas by reason in particular of the early establishment of the customs union and in order to ensure the simultaneous completion of the principal foundations of the Community, provisions should be adopted to enable the objectives laid down in Articles 48 and 49 of the Treaty in the field of freedom of movement to be achieved and to perfect measures adopted successively under Regulation No 15[3] on the first steps for attainment of freedom of movement and under Council Regulation No 38/54/EEC[4] of 25 March 1964 on freedom of movement for workers within the Community;

Whereas freedom of movement constitutes a fundamental right of workers and their families ; whereas mobility of labour within the Community must be one of the means by which the worker is guaranteed the possibility of improving his living and working conditions and promoting his social advancement, while helping to satisfy the requirements of the economies of the Member States

Whereas the right of all workers in the Member States to pursue the activity of their choice within the Community should be affirmed;

Whereas such right must be enjoyed without discrimination by permanent, seasonal and frontier workers and by those who pursue their activities for the purpose of providing services;

---

[1] OJ No 268, 6.11.1967, p. 9.
[2] OJ No 298, 7.12.1967, p. 10.
[3] OJ No 57, 26.8.1961, p. 1073/61.
[4] OJ No 62, 17.4.1964, p. 965/64.

Whereas the right of freedom of movement, in order that it may be exercised, by objective standards, in freedom and dignity, requires that equality of treatment shall be ensured in fact and in law in respect of all matters relating to the actual pursuit of activities as employed persons and to eligibility for housing, and also that obstacles to the mobility of workers shall be eliminated, in particular as regards the worker's right to be joined by his family and the conditions for the integration of that family into the host country;

Whereas the principle of non-discrimination between Community workers entails that all nationals of Member States have the same priority as regards employment as is enjoyed by national workers;

Whereas it is necessary to strengthen the machinery for vacancy clearance, in particular by developing direct co-operation between the central employment services and also between the regional services, as well as by increasing and co-ordinating the exchange of information in order to ensure in a general way a clearer picture of the labour market;

Whereas workers wishing to move should also be regularly informed of living and working conditions ;

Whereas, furthermore, measures should be provided for the case where a Member State undergoes or foresees disturbances on its labour market which may seriously threaten the standard of living and level of employment in a region or an industry;

Whereas for this purpose the exchange of information, aimed at discouraging workers from moving to such a region or industry, constitutes the method to be applied in the first place but, where necessary, it should be possible to strengthen the results of such exchange of information by temporarily suspending the abovementioned machinery, any such decision to be taken at Community level;

Whereas close links exist between freedom of movement for workers, employment and vocational training, particularly where the latter aims at putting workers in a position to take up offers of employment from other regions of the Community ; whereas such links make it necessary that the problems arising in this connection should no longer be studied in isolation but viewed as inter-dependent, account also being taken of the problems of employment at the regional level ; and whereas it is therefore necessary to direct the efforts of Member States toward co-ordinating their employment policies at Community level;

Whereas the Council, by its Decision of 15 October 1968[5] made Articles 48 and 49 of the Treaty and also the measures taken in implementation thereof applicable to the French overseas departments;

HAS ADOPTED THIS REGULATION:

---

[5] OJ No L 257, 19.10.1968, p. 1.

PART I

EMPLOYMENT AND WORKERS' FAMILIES

TITLE I

ELIGIBILITY FOR EMPLOYMENT

Article 1

1. Any national of a Member State, shall, irrespective of his place of residence, have the right to take up an activity as an employed person, and to pursue such activity, within the territory of another Member State in accordance with the provisions laid down by law, regulation or administrative action governing the employment of nationals of that State.

2. He shall, in particular, have the right to take up available employment in the territory of another Member State with the same priority as nationals of that State.

Article 2

Any national of a Member State and any employer pursuing an activity in the territory of a Member State may exchange their applications for and offers of employment, and may conclude and perform contracts of employment in accordance with the provisions in force laid down by law, regulation or administrative action, without any discrimination resulting therefrom.

Article 3

1. Under this Regulation, provisions laid down by law, regulation or administrative action or administrative practices of a Member State shall not apply:—where they limit application for and offers of employment, or the right of foreign nationals to take up and pursue employment or subject these to conditions not applicable in respect of their own nationals ; or—where, though applicable irrespective of nationality, their exclusive or principal aim or effect is to keep nationals of other Member States away from the employment offered.

This provision shall not apply to conditions relating to linguistic knowledge required by reason of the nature of the post to be filled.

2. There shall be included in particular among the provisions or practices of a Member State referred to in the first subparagraph of paragraph 1 those which:

(a) prescribe a special recruitment procedure for foreign nationals;

(b) limit or restrict the advertising of vacancies in the press or through any other

medium or subject it to conditions other than those applicable in respect of
employers pursuing their activities in the territory of that Member State;

(c) subject eligibility for employment to conditions of registration with employment
offices or impede recruitment of individual workers, where persons who do not
reside in the territory of that State are concerned.

Article 4

1. Provisions laid down by law, regulation or administrative action of the Member
States which restrict by number or percentage the employment of foreign nationals in
any undertaking, branch of activity or region, or at a national level, shall not apply
to nationals of the other Member States.

2. When in a Member State the granting of any benefit to undertakings is subject to
a minimum percentage of national workers being employed, nationals of the other
Member States shall be counted as national workers, subject to the provisions of the
Council Directive of 15 October 1963.[6]

Article 5

A national of a Member State who seeks employment in the territory of another
Member State shall receive the same assistance there as that afforded by the
employment offices in that State to their own nationals seeking employment.

Article 6

1. The engagement and recruitment of a national of one Member State for a post in
another Member State shall not depend on medical, vocational or other criteria which
are discriminatory on grounds of nationality by comparison with those applied to
nationals of the other Member State who wish to pursue the same activity.

2. Nevertheless, a national who holds an offer in his name from an employer in a Member
State other than that of which he is a national may have to undergo a vocational test, if
the employer expressly requests this when making his offer of employment.

---

[6] OJ No 159, 2.11.1963, p. 2661/63.

TITLE II

EMPLOYMENT AND EQUALITY OF TREATMENT

Article 7

1. A worker who is a national of a Member State may not, in the territory of another Member State, be treated differently from national workers by reason of his nationality in respect of any conditions of employment and work, in particular as regards remuneration, dismissal, and should he become unemployed, reinstatement or re-employment;

2. He shall enjoy the same social and tax advantages as national workers.

3. He shall also, by virtue of the same right and under the same conditions as national workers, have access to training in vocational schools and retraining centres.

4. Any clause of a collective or individual agreement or of any other collective regulation concerning eligibility for employment, employment, remuneration and other conditions of work or dismissal shall be null and void in so far as it lays down or authorises discriminatory conditions in respect of workers who are nationals of the other Member States.

Article 8

1. A worker who is a national of a Member State and who is employed in the territory of another Member State shall enjoy equality of treatment as regards membership of trade unions and the exercise of rights attaching thereto, including the right to vote ; he may be excluded from taking part in the management of bodies governed by public law and from holding an office governed by public law. Furthermore, he shall have the right of eligibility for workers' representative bodies in the undertaking. The provisions of this Article shall not affect laws or regulations in certain Member States which grant more extensive rights to workers coming from the other Member States.

2. This Article shall be reviewed by the Council on the basis of a proposal from the Commission which shall be submitted within not more than two years.

Article 9

1. A worker who is a national of a Member State and who is employed in the territory of another Member State shall enjoy all the rights and benefits accorded to national workers in matters of housing, including ownership of the housing he needs.

2. Such worker may, with the same right as nationals, put his name down on the housing lists in the region in which he is employed, where such lists exist ; he shall enjoy the resultant benefits and priorities.

If his family has remained in the country whence he came, they shall be considered for this purpose as residing in the said region, where national workers benefit from a similar presumption.

TITLE III

WORKERS' FAMILIES

Article 10

1. The following shall, irrespective of their nationality, have the right to install themselves with a worker who is a national of one Member State and who is employed in the territory of another Member State:

(a)   his spouse and their descendants who are under the age of 21 years or are dependants;

(b)   dependent relatives in the ascending line of the worker and his spouse.

2. Member States shall facilitate the admission of any member of the family not coming within the provisions of paragraph 1 if dependent on the worker referred to above or living under his roof in the country whence he comes.

3. For the purposes of paragraphs 1 and 2, the worker must have available for his family housing considered as normal for national workers in the region where he is employed ; this provision, however must not give rise to discrimination between national workers and workers from the other Member States.

Article 11

Where a national of a Member State is pursuing an activity as an employed or self-employed person in the territory of another Member State, his spouse and those of the children who are under the age of 21 years or dependent on him shall have the right to take up any activity as an employed person throughout the territory of that same State, even if they are not nationals of any Member State.

Article 12

The children of a national of a Member State who is or has been employed in the territory of another Member State shall be admitted to that State's general educational, apprenticeship and vocational training courses under the same conditions as the nationals of that State, if such children are residing in its territory.

Member States shall encourage all efforts to enable such children to attend these courses under the best possible conditions.

Part II

Clearance of Vacancies and Applications for Employment

Title I

Co-operation Between the Member States and With the Commission

Article 13

1. The Member States or the Commission shall instigate or together undertake any study of employment or unemployment which they consider necessary for securing freedom of movement for workers within the Community.

The central employment services of the Member States shall co-operate closely with each other and with the Commission with a view to acting jointly as regards the clearing of vacancies and applications for employment within the Community and the resultant placing of workers in employment.

2. To this end the Member States shall designate specialist services which shall be entrusted with organising work in the fields referred to above and co-operating with each other and with the departments of the Commission.

The Member States shall notify the Commission of any change in the designation of such services; the Commission shall publish details thereof for information in the Official Journal of the European Communities.

Article 14

1. The Member States shall send to the Commission information on problems arising in connection with the freedom of movement and employment of workers and particulars of the state and development of employment by region and by branch of activity.

2. In co-operation with the Technical Committee, the Commission shall determine the manner in which the information referred to in paragraph 1 shall be drawn up and the intervals at which it shall be communicated. To assess the state of their labour markets, the Member States shall use uniform criteria established by the Commission in accordance with the results of the work of the Technical Committee carried out in pursuance of Article 33 (d), after having obtained the Opinion of the Advisory Committee.

3. In accordance with the procedure laid down by the Commission in agreement with the Technical Committee, the specialist service of each Member State shall send to the specialist services of the other Member States and to the European Co-ordination Office such information concerning living and working conditions and the state of the labour market as is likely to be of guidance to workers from the other Member States. Such information shall be brought up to date regularly.

The specialist services of the other Member States shall ensure that wide publicity is given to such information, in particular by circulating it among the appropriate employment services and by all suitable means of communication for informing the workers concerned.

APPENDIX 8

COUNCIL DIRECTIVE 68/360/EEC OF 15 OCTOBER 1968 ON THE ABOLITION OF RESTRICTIONS ON MOVEMENT AND RESIDENCE WITHIN THE COMMUNITY FOR WORKERS OF MEMBER STATES AND THEIR FAMILIES

THE COUNCIL OF THE EUROPEAN COMMUNITIES,   A8–01

Having regard to the Treaty establishing the European Economic Community, and in particular Article 49 thereof;

Having regard to the proposal from the Commission;

Having regard to the Opinion of the European Parliament;[1]

Having regard to the Opinion of the Economic and Social Committee;[2]

Whereas Council Regulation (EEC) No 1612/68[3] fixed the provisions governing freedom of movement for workers within the Community ; whereas, consequently, measures should be adopted for the abolition of restrictions which still exist concerning movement and residence within the Community, which conform to the rights and privileges accorded by the said Regulation to nationals of any Member State who move in order to pursue activities as employed persons and to members of their families;

Whereas the rules applicable to residence should, as far as possible, bring the position of workers from other Member States and members of their families into line with that of nationals;

Whereas the co-ordination of special measures relating to the movement and residence of foreign nationals, justified on grounds of public policy, public security of public health, is the subject of the Council Directive of 25 February 1964,[4] adopted in application of Article 56(2) of the Treaty;

HAS ADOPTED THIS DIRECTIVE:

Article 1

Member States shall, acting as provided in this Directive, abolish restrictions on the movement and residence of nationals of the said States and of members of their families to whom Regulation (EEC) No 1612/68 applies.

---

[1] OJ No 268, 6.11.1967, p. 10.
[2] OJ No 298, 7.12.1967, p. 10.
[3] OJ No L 257, 19.10.1968, p. 2.
[4] OJ No 56, 4.4.1964, p. 850/64.

Article 2

1. Member States shall grant the nationals referred to in Article 1 the right to leave their territory in order to take up activities as employed persons and to pursue such activities in the territory of another Member State. Such right shall be exercised simply on production of a valid identity card or passport. Members of the family shall enjoy the same right as the national on whom they are dependent.

2. Member States shall, acting in accordance with their laws, issue to such nationals, or renew, an identity card or passport, which shall state in particular the holder's nationality.

3. The passport must be valid at least for all Member States and for countries through which the holder must pass when travelling between Member States. Where a passport is the only document on which the holder may lawfully leave the country, its period of validity shall be not less than five years.

4. Member States may not demand from the nationals referred to in Article 1 any exit visa or any equivalent document.

Article 3

1. Member States shall allow the persons referred to in Article 1 to enter their territory simply on production of a valid identity card or passport.

2. No entry visa or equivalent document may be demanded save from members of the family who are not nationals of a Member State. Member States shall accord to such persons every facility for obtaining any necessary visas.

Article 4

1. Member States shall grant the right of residence in their territory to the persons referred to in Article 1 who are able to produce the documents listed in paragraph 3.

2. As proof of the right of residence, a document entitled "Residence Permit for a National of a Member State of the EEC" shall be issued. This document must include a statement that it has been issued pursuant to Regulation (EEC) No 1612/68 and to the measures taken by the Member States for the implementation of the present Directive. The text of such statement is given in the Annex to this Directive.

3. For the issue of a Residence Permit for a National of a Member State of the EEC, Member States may require only the production of the following documents;—by the worker: (a) the document with which he entered their territory; (b) a confirmation of engagement from the employer or a certificate of employment;

– by the members of the worker's family: (c) the document with which they entered the territory; (d) a document issued by the competent authority of the State of origin or the State whence they came, proving their relationship; (e) in the cases referred to in Article 10 (1) and (2) of Regulation (EEC) No 1612/68, a document issued by the competent authority of the State of origin or the State whence they came, testifying that they are dependent on the worker or that they live under his roof in such country.

4. A member of the family who is not a national of a Member State shall be issued with a residence document which shall have the same validity as that issued to the worker on whom he is dependent.

Article 5

Completion of the formalities for obtaining a residence permit shall not hinder the immediate beginning of employment under a contract concluded by the applicants.

Article 6

1. The residence permit: (a) must be valid throughout the territory of the Member State which issued it; (b) must be valid for at least five years from the date of issue and be automatically renewable.

2. Breaks in residence not exceeding six consecutive months and absence on military service shall not affect the validity of a residence permit.

3. Where a worker is employed for a period exceeding three months but not exceeding a year in the service of an employer in the host State or in the employ of a person providing services, the host Member State shall issue him a temporary residence permit, the validity of which may be limited to the expected period of the employment.

Subject to the provisions of Article 8 (1) (c), a temporary residence permit shall be issued also to a seasonal worker employed for a period of more than three months. The period of employment must be shown in the documents referred to in paragraph 4 (3) (b).

Article 7

1. A valid residence permit may not be withdrawn from a worker solely on the grounds that he is no longer in employment, either because he is temporarily incapable of work as a result of illness or accident, or because he is involuntarily unemployed, this being duly confirmed by the competent employment office.

2. When the residence permit is renewed for the first time, the period of residence may be restricted, but not to less than twelve months, where the worker has been involuntarily unemployed in the Member State for more than twelve consecutive months.

Article 8

1. Member States shall, without issuing a residence permit, recognise the right of residence in their territory of: (a) a worker pursuing an activity as an employed person, where the activity is not expected to last for more than three months. The document with which the person concerned entered the territory and a statement by the employer on the expected duration of the employment shall be sufficient to cover his stay ; a statement by the employer shall not, however, be required in the case of workers coming within the provisions of the Council Directive of 25 February 19641 on

the attainment of freedom of establishment and freedom to provide services in respect of the activities of intermediaries in commerce, industry and small craft industries.

(b) a worker who, while having his residence in the territory of a Member State to which he returns as a rule, each day or at least once a week, is employed in the territory of another Member State. The competent authority of the State where he is employed may issue such worker with a special permit valid for five years and automatically renewable;

(c) a seasonal worker who holds a contract of employment stamped by the competent authority of the Member State on whose territory he has come to pursue his activity.

2. In all cases referred to in paragraph 1, the competent authorities of the host Member State may require the worker to report his presence in the territory.

Article 9

1. The residence documents granted to nationals of a Member State of the EEC referred to in this Directive shall be issued and renewed free of charge or on payment of an amount not exceeding the dues and taxes charged for the issue of identity cards to nationals.

2. The visa referred to in Article 3 (2) and the stamp referred to in Article 8 (1) (c) shall be free of charge.

3. Member States shall take the necessary steps to simplify as much as possible the formalities and procedure for obtaining the documents mentioned in paragraph 1.

Article 10

Member States shall not derogate from the provisions of this Directive save on grounds of public policy, public security or public health.

Article 11

1. This Directive shall not affect the provisions of the Treaty establishing the European Coal and Steel Community which relate to workers with recognised skills in coal mining and steel making, or the provisions of the Treaty establishing the European Atomic Energy Community which deal with the right to take up skilled employment in the field of nuclear energy, or any measures taken in implementation of those Treaties.

2. Nevertheless, this Directive shall apply to the categories of workers referred to in paragraph 1, and to members of their families, in so far as their legal position is not governed by the abovementioned Treaties or measures.

Article 12

1. Member States shall, within nine months of notification of this Directive, bring into force the measures necessary to comply with its provisions and shall forthwith inform the Commission thereof.
2. They shall notify the Commission of amendments made to provisions imposed by law, regulation or administrative action for the simplification of the formalities and procedure for issuing such documents as are still necessary for the entry, exit and residence of workers and members of their families.

Article 13

1. The Council Directive of 25 March 19642 on the abolition of restrictions on movement and on residence within the Community of workers and their families shall continue to have effect until this Directive is implemented by the Member States.

2. Residence permits issued pursuant to the Directive referred to in Paragraph 1 shall remain valid until the date on which they next expire.

Article 14

This Directive is addressed to the Member States.

ANNEX

Text of the statement referred to in Article 4 (2):

"This permit is issued pursuant to Regulation (EEC) No 1612/68 of the Council of the European Communities of 15 October 1968 and to the measures taken in implementation of the Council Directive of 15 October 1968.

In accordance with the provisions of the above-mentioned Regulation, the holder of this permit has the right to take up and pursue an activity as an employed person in . . .[6] territory under the same conditions as . . .[6] workers."

---

[5] OJ No 56, 4.4.1964, p. 869/64. 2 OJ No 62, 17.4.1964, p. 981/64.
[6] Belgian, German, French, Italian, Luxembourg, Netherlands, according to the country issuing the permit.

REGULATION (EEC) NO 1251/70 OF THE COMMISSION OF 29 JUNE 1970 ON THE RIGHT OF WORKERS TO REMAIN IN THE TERRITORY OF A MEMBER STATE AFTER HAVING BEEN EMPLOYED IN THAT STATE

THE COMMISSION OF THE EUROPEAN COMMUNITIES, **A9–01**

Having regard to the Treaty establishing the European Economic Community, and in particular Article 48 (3) (d) thereof, and Article 2 of the Protocol on the Grand Duchy of Luxembourg;

Having regard to the Opinion of the European Parliament;[1]

Whereas Council Regulation (EEC) No 1612/68[2] of 15 October 1968 and Council Directive No 68/360/EEC of 15 October 1968[3] enabled freedom of movement for workers to be secured at the end of a series of measures to be achieved progressively ; whereas the right of residence acquired by workers in active employment has as a corollary the right, granted by the Treaty to such workers, to remain in the territory of a Member State after having been employed in that State ; whereas it is important to lay down the conditions for the exercise of such right;

Whereas the said Council Regulation and Council Directive contain the appropriate provisions concerning the right of workers to reside in the territory of a Member State for the purposes of employment ; whereas the right to remain, referred to in Article 48 (3) (d) of the Treaty ; is interpreted therefore as the right of the worker to maintain his residence in the territory of a Member State when he ceases to be employed there;

Whereas the mobility of labour in the Community requires that workers may be employed successively in several Member States without thereby being placed at a disadvantage;

Whereas it is important, in the first place, to guarantee to the worker residing in the territory of a Member State the right to remain in that territory when he ceases to be employed in that State because he has reached retirement age or by reason of permanent incapacity to work ; whereas, however, it is equally important to ensure that right for the worker who, after a period of employment and residence in the territory of a Member State, works as an employed person in the territory of another Member State, while still retaining his residence in the territory of the first State;

Whereas, to determine the conditions under which the right to remain arises, account should be taken of the reasons which have led to the termination of employment in the territory of the Member State concerned and, in particular, of the difference between retirement, the normal and foreseeable end of working life, and incapacity to work which leads to a premature and unforeseeable termination of activity ; whereas

---

[1] OJ No C 65, 5.6.1970, p. 16.
[2] OJ No L 257, 19.10.1968, p. 2.
[3] OJ No L 257, 19.10.1968, p. 13.

special conditions must be laid down where termination of activity is the result of an accident at work or occupational disease, or where the worker's spouse is or was a national of the Member State concerned;

Whereas the worker who has reached the end of his working life should have sufficient time in which to decide where he wishes to establish his final residence;

Whereas the exercise by the worker of the right to remain entails that such right shall be extended to members of his family ; whereas in the case of the death of the worker during his working life, maintenance of the right of residence of the members of his family must also be recognised and be the subject of special conditions;

Whereas persons to whom the right to remain applies must enjoy equality of treatment with national workers who have ceased their working lives;

HAS ADOPTED THIS REGULATION:

Article 1

The provisions of this Regulation shall apply to nationals of a Member State who have worked as employed persons in the territory of another Member State and to members of their families, as defined in Article 10 of Council Regulation (EEC) No 1612/68 on freedom of movement for workers within the Community.

Article 2

1. The following shall have the right to remain permanently in the territory of a Member State: (a) a worker who, at the time of termination of his activity, has reached the age laid down by the law of that Member State for entitlement to an old-age pension and who has been employed in that State for at least the last twelve months and has resided there continuously for more than three years;

(b) a worker who, having resided continuously in the territory of that State for more than two years, ceases to work there as an employed person as a result of permanent incapacity to work. If such incapacity is the result of an accident at work or an occupational disease entitling him to a pension for which an institution of that State is entirely or partially responsible, no condition shall be imposed as to length of residence;

(c) a worker who, after three years "continuous employment and residence in the territory of that State, works as an employed person in the territory of another Member State, while retaining his residence in the territory of the first State, to which he returns, as a rule, each day or at least once a week.

Periods of employment completed in this way in the territory of the other Member State shall, for the purposes of entitlement to the rights referred to in subparagraphs (a) and (b), be considered as having been completed in the territory of the State of residence.

2. The conditions as to length of residence and employment laid down in paragraph 1 (a) and the condition as to length of residence laid down in paragraph 1 (b) shall

not apply if the worker's spouse is a national of the Member State concerned or has lost the nationality of that State by marriage to that worker.

Article 3

1. The members of a worker's family referred to in Article 1 of this Regulation who are residing with him in the territory of a Member State shall be entitled to remain there permanently if the worker has acquired the right to remain in the territory of that State in accordance with Article 2, and to do so even after his death.

2. If, however, the worker dies during his working life and before having acquired the right to remain in the territory of the State concerned, members of his family shall be entitled to remain there permanently on condition that:—the worker, on the date of his decease, had resided continuously in the territory of that Member State for at least 2 years ; or

− his death resulted from an accident at work or an occupational disease ; or

− the surviving spouse is a national of the State of residence or lost the nationality of that State by marriage to that worker.

Article 4

1. Continuity of residence as provided for in Articles 2 (1) and 3 (2) may be attested by any means of proof in use in the country of residence. It shall not be affected by temporary absences not exceeding a total of three months per year, nor by longer absences due to compliance with the obligations of military service.

2. Periods of involuntary unemployment, duly recorded by the competent employment office, and absences due to illness or accident shall be considered as periods of employment within the meaning of Article 2 (1).

Article 5

1. The person entitled to the right to remain shall be allowed to exercise it within two years from the time of becoming entitled to such right pursuant to Article 2 (1) (a) and (b) and Article 3. During such period he may leave the territory of the Member State without adversely affecting such right.

2. No formality shall be required on the part of the person concerned in respect of the exercise of the right to remain.

Article 6

1. Persons coming under the provisions of this Regulation shall be entitled to a residence permit which: (a) shall be issued and renewed free of charge or on payment of

a sum not exceeding the dues and taxes payable by nationals for the issue or renewal identity documents;

(b) must be valid throughout the territory of the Member State issuing it;

(c) must be valid for at least five years and be renewable automatically.

2. Periods of non-residence not exceeding six consecutive months shall not affect the validity of the residence permit.

Article 7

The right to equality of treatment, established by Council Regulation (EEC) No 1612/68, shall apply also to persons coming under the provisions of this Regulation.

Article 8

1. This Regulation shall not affect any provisions laid down by law, regulation or administrative action of one Member State which would be more favourable to nationals of other Member States.

2. Member States shall facilitate re-admission to their territories of workers who have left those territories after having resided there permanently for a long period and having been employed there and who wish to return there when they have reached retirement age or are permanently incapacitated for work.

Article 9

1. The Commission may, taking account of developments in the demographic situation of the Grand Duchy of Luxembourg, lay down, at the request of that State, different conditions from those provided for in this Regulation, in respect of the exercise of the right to remain in Luxembourg territory.

2. Within two months after the request supplying all appropriate details has been put before it, the Commission shall take a decision, stating the reasons on which it is based.

It shall notify the Grand Duchy of Luxembourg of such decision and inform the other Member States thereof;

This Regulation shall be binding in its entirety and directly applicable in all Member States.

COUNCIL DIRECTIVE 72/194/EEC OF 18 MAY 1972 EXTENDING TO WORKERS EXERCISING THE RIGHT TO REMAIN IN THE TERRITORY OF A MEMBER STATE AFTER HAVING BEEN EMPLOYED IN THAT STATE THE SCOPE OF THE DIRECTIVE OF 25 FEBRUARY 1964 ON COORDINATION OF SPECIAL MEASURES CONCERNING THE MOVEMENT AND RESIDENCE OF FOREIGN NATIONALS WHICH ARE JUSTIFIED ON GROUNDS OF PUBLIC POLICY, PUBLIC SECURITY OR PUBLIC HEALTH

THE COUNCIL OF THE EUROPEAN COMMUNITIES,   **A10–01**

Having regard to the Treaty establishing the European Economic Community, and in particular Articles 49 and 56 (2) thereof;

Having regard to the proposal from the Commission;

Having regard to the Opinion of the European Parliament;

Having regard to the Opinion of the Economic and Social Committee;

Whereas the Council Directive of 25 February 1964[1] coordinated special measures concerning the movement and residence of foreign nationals which are justified on grounds of public policy, public security or public health and whereas Commission Regulation (EEC) No 1251/70[2] of 29 June 1970 on the right of workers to remain in the territory of a Member State after having been employed in that State laid down conditions for the exercise of such right;

Whereas the Directive of 25 February 1964 should continue to apply to persons to whom that Regulation applies;

HAS ADOPTED THE FOLLOWING DIRECTIVE:

Article 1

The Council Directive of 25 February 1964 on coordination of special measures concerning the movement and residence of foreign nationals which are justified on grounds of public policy, public security or public health shall apply to nationals of Member States and members of their families who pursuant to Regulation (EEC) No 1251/70, exercise the right to remain in the territory of a Member State.

---

[1] OJ No 56, 4.4.1964, p. 850/64.
[2] OJ No L 142, 30.6.1970, p. 24.

APPENDIX 10

Article 2

Member States shall put into force the measures necessary to comply with this Directive within six months of its notification and shall forthwith inform the Commission thereof.

Article 3

This Directive is addressed to the Member States.

COUNCIL DIRECTIVE 73/148/EEC OF 21 MAY 1973 ON THE ABOLITION OF RESTRICTIONS ON MOVEMENT AND RESIDENCE WITHIN THE COMMUNITY FOR NATIONALS OF MEMBER STATES WITH REGARD TO ESTABLISHMENT AND THE PROVISION OF SERVICES

THE COUNCIL OF THE EUROPEAN COMMUNITIES   A11–01

Having regard to the Treaty establishing the European Economic Community, and in particular Article 54 (2) and Article 63 (2) thereof;

Having regard to the General Programmes for the abolition of restrictions on freedom of establishment and freedom to provide services,[1] and in particular Title II thereof;

Having regard to the proposal from the Commission;

Having regard to the Opinion of the European Parliament;[2]

Having regard to the Opinion of the Economic and Social Committee;[3]

Whereas freedom of movement of persons as provided for in the Treaty and the General Programmes for the abolition of restrictions on freedom of establishment and on freedom to provide services entails the abolition of restrictions on movement and residence within the Community for nationals of Member States wishing to establish themselves or to provide services within the territory of another Member State;

Whereas freedom of establishment can be fully attained only if a right of permanent residence is granted to the persons who are to enjoy freedom of establishment ; whereas freedom to provide services entails that persons providing and receiving services should have the right of residence for the time during which the services are being provided;

Whereas Council Directive of 25 February 1964[4] on the abolition of restrictions on movement and residence within the Community for nationals of Member States with regard to establishment and the provision of services laid down the rules applicable in this area to activities as self-employed persons;

Whereas Council Directive of 15 October 1968[5] on the abolition of restrictions on movement and residence within the Community for workers of Member States and their families, which replaced the Directive of 25 March 1964[6] bearing the same title, has in the meantime amended the rules applicable to employed persons;

---

[1] OJ No 2, 15.1.1962, p. 32/62 and 36/62.
[2] OJ No C 19, 28.2.1972, p. 5.
[3] OJ No C 67, 24.6.1972, p. 7.
[4] OJ No 56, 4.4.1964, p. 845/64.
[5] OJ No L 257, 19.10.1968, p. 13.
[6] OJ No 62, 17.4.1964, p. 981/64.

Whereas the provisions concerning movement and residence within the Community of self-employed persons and their families should likewise be improved;

Whereas the coordination of special measures concerning the movement and residence of foreign nationals, justified on grounds of public policy, public security or public health, is already the subject of the Council Directive of 25 February 1964;[7]

AS ADOPTED THIS DIRECTIVE:

Article 1

1. The Member States shall, acting as provided in this Directive, abolish restrictions on the movement and residence of:

(a) nationals of a Member State who are established or who wish to establish themselves in another Member State in order to pursue activities as self-employed persons, or who wish to provide services in that State;

(b) nationals of Member States wishing to go to another Member State as recipients of services;

(c) the spouse and the children under twenty-one years of age of such nationals, irrespective of their nationality;

(d) the relatives in the ascending and descending lines of such nationals and of the spouse of such nationals, which relatives are dependent on them, irrespective of their nationality.

2. Member States shall favour the admission of any other member of the family of a national referred to in paragraph 1 (a) or (b) or of the spouse of that national, which member is dependent on that national or spouse of that national or who in the country of origin was living under the same roof.

Article 2

1. Member States shall grant the persons referred to in Article 1 the right to leave their territory. Such right shall be exercised simply on production of a valid identity card or passport. Members of the family shall enjoy the same right as the national on whom they are dependent.

2. Member States shall, acting in accordance with their laws, issue to their nationals, or renew, an identity card or passport, which shall state in particular the holder's nationality.

3. The passport must be valid at least for all Member States and for countries through which the holder must pass when travelling between Member States. Where a passport is the only document on which the holder may lawfully leave the country, its period of validity shall be not less than five years.

4. Member States may not demand from the persons referred to in Article 1 any exit visa or any equivalent requirement.

---

[7] OJ No 56, 4.4.1964, p. 850/64.

Article 3

1. Member States shall grant to the persons referred to in Article 1 right to enter their territory merely on production of a valid identity card or passport.

2. No entry visa or equivalent requirement may be demanded save in respect of members of the family who do have the nationality of a Member State. Member States shall afford to such persons every facility for obtaining any necessary visas.

Article 4

1. Each Member State shall grant the right of permanent residence to nationals of other Member States who establish themselves within its territory in order to pursue activities as self-employed persons, when the restrictions on these activities have been abolished pursuant to the Treaty.

As proof of the right of residence, a document entitled "Residence Permit for a National of a Member State of the European Communities" shall be issued. This document shall be valid for not less than five years from the date of issue and shall be automatically renewable.

Breaks in residence not exceeding six consecutive months and absence on military service shall not affect the validity of a residence permit.

A valid residence permit may not be withdrawn from a national referred to in Article 1(1) (a) solely on the grounds that he is no longer in employment because he is temporarily incapable of work as a result of illness or accident.

Any national of a Member State who is not specified in the first subparagraph but who is authorized under the laws of another Member State to pursue an activity within its territory shall be granted a right of abode for a period not less than that of the authorization granted for the pursuit of the activity in question.

However, any national referred to in subparagraph 1 and to whom the provisions of the preceding subparagraph apply as a result of a change of employment shall retain his residence permit until the date on which it expires.

2. The right of residence for persons providing and receiving services shall be of equal duration with the period during which the services are provided.

Where such period exceeds three months, the Member State in the territory of which the services are performed shall issue a right of abode as proof of the right of residence.

Where the period does not exceed three months, the identity card or passport with which the person concerned entered the territory shall be sufficient to cover his stay. The Member State may, however, require the person concerned to report his presence in the territory.

3. A member of the family who is not a national of a Member State shall be issued with a residence document which shall have the same validity as that issued to the national on whom he is dependent.

Article 5

The right of residence shall be effective throughout the territory of the Member State concerned.

Article 6

An applicant for a residence permit or right of abode shall not be required by a Member State to produce anything other than the following, namely:

(a) the identity card or passport with which he or she entered its territory;

(b) proof that he or she comes within one of the classes of person referred to in Articles 1 and 4.

Article 7

1. The residence documents granted to nationals of a Member State shall be issued and renewed free of charge or on payment of an amount not exceeding the dues and taxes charged for the issue of identity cards to nationals. These provisions shall also apply to documents and certificates required for the issue and renewal of such residence documents.

2. The visas referred to in Article 3 (2) shall be free of charge.

3. Member States shall take the necessary steps to simplify as much as possible the formalities and the procedure for obtaining the documents mentioned in paragraph 1.

Article 8

Member States shall not derogate from the provisions of this Directive save on grounds of public policy, public security or public health.

Article 9

1. Member States shall, within six months of notification of this Directive, bring into force the measures necessary to comply with its provisions and shall forthwith inform the Commission thereof.

2. They shall notify the Commission of amendments made to provisions imposed by law, regulation or administrative action for the simplification with regard to establishment and the provision of services of the formalities and procedure for issuing such documents as are still necessary for the movement and residence of persons referred to in Article 1.

Article 10

1. The Council Directive of 25 February 1964 on the abolition of restrictions on movement and residence within the Community for nationals of Member States with regard to establishment and the provision of services shall remain applicable until this Directive is implemented by the Member States.

2. Residence documents issued pursuant to the Directive referred to in paragraph 1 shall remain valid until the date on which they next expire.

Article 11

This Directive is addressed to the Member States.

COUNCIL DIRECTIVE 75/34/EEC OF 17 DECEMBER 1974 CONCERNING THE RIGHT OF NATIONALS OF A MEMBER STATE TO REMAIN IN THE TERRITORY OF ANOTHER MEMBER STATE AFTER HAVING PURSUED THEREIN AN ACTIVITY IN A SELF-EMPLOYED CAPACITY

THE COUNCIL OF THE EUROPEAN COMMUNITIES,   **A12–01**

Having regard to the Treaty establishing the European Economic Community, and in particular Article 235 thereof;

Having regard to the General Programme for the abolition of restrictions on freedom of establishment[1], and in particular Title II thereof;

Having regard to the proposal from the Commission;

Having regard to the Opinion of the European Parliament[2];

Having regard to the Opinion of the Economic and Social Committee[3];

Whereas pursuant to Council Directive No 73/148/EEC[4] of 21 May 1973 on the abolition of restrictions on movement and residence within the Community for nationals of Member States with regard to establishment and the provision of services, each Member State grants the right of permanent residence to nationals of other Member States who establish themselves within its territory in order to pursue activities as self-employed persons, when the restrictions on these activities have been abolished pursuant to the Treaty;

Whereas it is normal for a person to prolong a period of permanent residence in the territory of a Member State by remaining there after having pursued an activity there ; whereas the absence of a right so to remain in such circumstances is an obstacle to the attainment of freedom of establishment ; whereas, as regards employed persons, the conditions under which such a right may be exercised have already been laid down by Regulation (EEC) No 1251/70[5];

Whereas Article 48 (3) (d) of the Treaty recognizes the right of workers to remain in the territory of a Member State after having been employed in that State ; whereas Article 54 (2) does not expressly provide a similar right for self-employed persons ; whereas, nevertheless, the nature of establishment, together with attachments formed to the countries in which they have pursued their activities, means that such persons have a definite interest in enjoying the same right to remain as that granted to workers;

---

[1] OJ No 2, 15.1.1962, p. 36/62.
[2] OJ No C 14, 27.3.1973, p. 20.
[3] OJ No C 142, 31.12.1972, p. 12.
[4] OJ No L 172, 28.6.1973, p. 14.
[5] OJ No L 142, 30.6.1970, p. 24.

whereas in justification of this measure reference should be made to the Treaty provision enabling it to be taken;

Whereas freedom of establishment within the Community requires that nationals of Member States may pursue self-employed activities in several Member States in succession without thereby being placed at a disadvantage;

Whereas a national of a Member State residing in the territory of another Member State should be guaranteed the right to remain in that territory when he ceases to pursue an activity as a self-employed person in that State because he has reached retirement age or by reason of permanent incapacity to work ; whereas such a right should also be guaranteed to the national of a Member State who, after a period of activity in a self-employed capacity and residence in the territory of a second Member State, pursues an activity in the territory of a third Member State, while still retaining his residence in the territory of the second State;

Whereas, to determine the conditions under which the right to remain arises, account should be taken of the reasons which have led to the termination of activity in the territory of the Member State concerned and, in particular, of the difference between retirement, the normal and foreseeable end of working life, and permanent incapacity to work which leads to a premature and unforeseeable termination of activity; whereas special conditions must be laid down where the spouse is or was a national of the Member State concerned, or where termination of activity is the result of an accident at work or occupational illness;

Whereas a national of a Member State who has reached the end of his working life, after working in a self-employed capacity in the territory of another Member State, should have sufficient time in which to decide where he wishes to establish his final residence;

Whereas the exercise of the right to remain by a national of a Member State working in a self-employed capacity entails extension of such right to the members of his family; whereas in the case of the death of a national of a Member State working in a self-employed capacity during his working life the right of residence of the members of his family must also be recognized and be the subject of special conditions;

Whereas persons to whom the right to remain applies must enjoy equality of treatment with nationals of the State concerned who have reached the end of their working lives,

HAS ADOPTED THIS DIRECTIVE:

Article 1

Member States shall, under the conditions laid down in this Directive, abolish restrictions on the right to remain in their territory in favour of nationals of another Member State who have pursued activities as self-employed persons in their territory, and members of their families, as defined in Article 1 of Directive No 73/148/EEC.

Article 2

1. Each Member State shall recognize the right to remain permanently in its territory of: (a) any person who, at the time of termination of his activity, has reached the age laid down by the law of that State for entitlement to an old-age pension and who has pursued his activity in that State for at least the previous twelve months and has resided there continuously for more than three years.

Where the law of that Member State does not grant the right to an old-age pension to certain categories of self-employed workers, the age requirement shall be considered as satisfied when the beneficiary reaches 65 years of age;

(b) any person who, having resided continuously in the territory of that State for more than two years, ceases to pursue his activity there as a result of permanent incapacity to work. If such incapacity is the result of an accident at work or an occupational illness entitling him to a pension which is payable in whole or in part by an institution of that State no condition shall be imposed as to length of residence;

(c) any person who, after three years' continuous activity and residence in the territory of that State, pursues his activity in the territory of another Member State, while retaining his residence in the territory of the first State, to which he returns, as a rule, each day or at least once a week.

Periods of activity so completed in the territory of the other Member State shall, for the purposes of entitlement to the rights referred to in (a) and (b), be considered as having been completed in the territory of the State of residence.

2. The conditions as to length of residence and activity laid down in paragraph 1 (a) and the condition as to length of residence laid down in paragraph 1 (b) shall not apply if the spouse of the self-employed person is a national of the Member State concerned or has lost the nationality of that State by marriage to that person.

Article 3

1. Each Member State shall recognize the right of the members of the self-employed person's family referred to in Article 1 who are residing with him in the territory of that State to remain there permanently, if the person concerned has acquired the right to remain in the territory of that State in accordance with Article 2. This provision shall continue to apply even after the death of the person concerned.

2. If, however, the self-employed person dies during his working life and before having acquired the right to remain in the territory of the State concerned, that State shall recognize the right of the members of his family to remain there permanently on condition that:—the person concerned, on the date of his decease, had resided continuously in its territory for at least two years ; or

–   his death resulted from an accident at work or an occupational illness ; or

–   the surviving spouse is a national of that State or lost such nationality by marriage to the person concerned.

Article 4

1. Continuity of residence as provided for in Articles 2 (1) and 3 (2) may be attested by any means of proof in use in the country of residence. It may not be affected by temporary absences not exceeding a total of three months per year, nor by longer absences due to compliance with the obligations of military service.

2. Periods of inactivity due to circumstances outside the control of the person concerned or of inactivity owing to illness or accident must be considered as periods of activity within the meaning of Article 2 (1).

Article 5

1. Member States shall allow the person entitled to the right to remain to exercise such right within two years from the time of becoming entitled thereto pursuant to Article 2 (1) (a) and (b) and Article 3. During this period the beneficiary must be able to leave the territory of the Member State without adversely affecting such right.

2. Member States shall not require the person concerned to comply with any particular formality in order to exercise the right to remain.

Article 6

1. Member States shall recognize the right of persons having the right to remain in their territory to a residence permit, which must: (a) be issued and renewed free of charge or on payment of a sum not exceeding the dues and taxes payable by nationals for the issue or renewal of identity cards;

(b) by valid throughout the territory of the Member State issuing it;

(c) be valid for five years and renewable automatically.

2. Periods of non-residence not exceeding six consecutive months and longer absences due to compliance with the obligations of military service may not affect the validity of a residence permit.

Article 7

Member States shall apply to persons having the right to remain in their territory the right of equality of treatment recognized by the Council Directives on the abolition of restrictions on freedom of establishment pursuant to Title III of the General Programme which provides for such abolition.

Article 8

1. This Directive shall not affect any provisions laid down by law, regulation or administrative action of any Member State which would be more favourable to nationals of other Member States.

2. Member States shall facilitate re-admission to their territories of self-employed persons who left those territories after having resided there permanently for a long period while pursuing an activity there and who wish to return when they have reached retirement age as defined in Article 2 (1) (a) or are permanently incapacitated for work.

Article 9

Member States may not derogate from the provisions of this Directive save on grounds of public policy, public security or public health.

Article 10

1. Member States shall, within twelve months of notification of this Directive, bring into force the measures necessary to comply with its provisions and shall forthwith inform the Commission thereof.

2. Following notification of this Directive, Member States shall further ensure that the Commission is informed, in sufficient time for it to submit its comments, of all proposed laws, regulations or administrative provisions which they intend to adopt in the field covered by this Directive.

Article 11

This Directive is addressed to the Member States.

COUNCIL DIRECTIVE 75/35/EEC OF 17 DECEMBER 1974 EXTENDING THE SCOPE OF DIRECTIVE NO 64/221/EEC ON THE COORDINATION OF SPECIAL MEASURES CONCERNING THE MOVEMENT AND RESIDENCE OF FOREIGN NATIONALS WHICH ARE JUSTIFIED ON GROUNDS OF PUBLIC POLICY, PUBLIC SECURITY OR PUBLIC HEALTH TO INCLUDE NATIONALS OF A MEMBER STATE WHO EXERCISE THE RIGHT TO REMAIN IN THE TERRITORY OF ANOTHER MEMBER STATE AFTER HAVING PURSUED THEREIN AN ACTIVITY IN A SELF-EMPLOYED CAPACITY

THE COUNCIL OF THE EUROPEAN COMMUNITIES,   A13–01

Having regard to the Treaty establishing the European Economic Community, and in particular Article 56 (2) and Article 235 thereof;

Having regard to the proposal from the Commission;

Having regard to the Opinion of the European Parliament;[1]

Having regard to the Opinion of the Economic and Social Committee;[2]

Whereas Directive No 64/221/EEC[3] coordinated special measures concerning the movement and residence of foreign nationals which are justified on grounds of public policy, public security or public health and whereas Directive No 75/34/EEC laid down conditions for the exercise of the right of nationals of a Member State to remain in the territory of another Member State after having pursued therein an activity in a self-employed capacity;

Whereas Directive No 64/221/EEC should therefore apply to persons to whom Directive No 75/34/EEC applies,

HAS ADOPTED THIS DIRECTIVE:

Article 1

Directive No 64/221/EEC shall apply to nationals of Member States and members of their families who have the right to remain in the territory of a Member State pursuant to Directive No 75/34/EEC.

---

[1] OJ No C 14, 27.3.1973, p. 21.
[2] OJ No C 142, 31.12.1972, p. 10.
[3] OJ No 56, 4.4.1964, p. 850/64.

Article 2

Member States shall, within twelve months of notification of this Directive, bring into force the measures necessary to comply with its provisions and shall forthwith inform the Commission thereof.

Article 3

This Directive is addressed to the Member States.

COUNCIL DIRECTIVE 90/364/EEC OF 28 JUNE 1990 ON THE RIGHT OF RESIDENCE

THE COUNCIL OF THE EUROPEAN COMMUNITIES,   **A14–01**

Having regard to the Treaty establishing the European Economic Community, and in particular Article 235 thereof,

Having regard to the proposal from the Commission,[1]

Having regard to the opinion of the European Parliament,[2]

Having regard to the opinion of the Economic and Social Committee,[3]

Whereas Article 3(c) of the Treaty provides that the activities of the Community shall include, as provided in the Treaty, the abolition, as between Member States, of obstacles to freedom of movement for persons;

Whereas Article 8a of the Treaty provides that the internal market must be established by 31 December 1992; whereas the internal market comprises an area without internal frontiers in which the free movement of goods, persons, services and capital is ensured in accordance with the provisions of the Treaty;

Whereas national provisions on the right of nationals of the Member States to reside in a Member State other than their own must be harmonized to ensure such freedom of movement;

Whereas beneficiaries of the right of residence must not become an unreasonable burden on the public finances of the host Member State;

Whereas this right can only be genuinely exercised if it is also granted to members of the family;

Whereas the beneficiaries of this Directive should be covered by administrative arrangements similar to those laid down in particular in Directive 68/360/EEC[4] and Directive 64/221/EEC[5];

Whereas the Treaty does not provide, for the action concerned, powers other than those of Article 235,

HAS ADOPTED THIS DIRECTIVE:

---

[1] OJ No C 191, 28. 7. 1989, p. 5; and OJ No C 26, 3. 2. 1990, p. 22.
[2] Opinion delivered on 13 June 1990 (not yet published in the Official Journal).
[3] OJ No C 329, 30. 12. 1989, p. 25.
[4] OJ No L 257, 19. 10. 1968, p. 13.
[5] OJ No 56, 4. 4. 1964, p. 850/64.

Article 1

1. Member States shall grant the right of residence to nationals of Member States who do not enjoy this right under other provisions of Community law and to members of their families as defined in paragraph 2, provided that they themselves and the members of their families are covered by sickness insurance in respect of all risks in the host Member State and have sufficient resources to avoid becoming a burden on the social assistance system of the host Member State during their period of residence.

The resources referred to in the first subparagraph shall be deemed sufficient where they are higher than the level of resources below which the host Member State may grant social assistance to its nationals, taking into account the personal circumstances of the applicant and, where appropriate, the personal circumstances of persons admitted pursuant to paragraph 2.

Where the second subparagraph cannot be applied in a Member State, the resources of the applicant shall be deemed sufficient if they are higher than the level of the minimum social security pension paid by the host Member State.

2. The following shall, irrespective of their nationality, have the right to install themselves in another Member State with the holder of the right of residence:

(a) his or her spouse and their descendants who are dependants;

(b) dependent relatives in the ascending line of the holder of the right of residence and his or her spouse.

Article 2

1. Exercise of the right of residence shall be evidenced by means of the issue of a document known as a 'Residence permit for a national of a Member State of the EEC', the validity of which may be limited to five years on a renewable basis. However, the Member States may, when they deem it to be necessary, require revalidation of the permit at the end of the first two years of residence. Where a member of the family does not hold the nationality of a Member State, he or she shall be issued with a residence document of the same validity as that issued to the national on whom he or she depends.

For the purpose of issuing the residence permit or document, the Member State may require only that the applicant present a valid identity card or passport and provide proof that he or she meets the conditions laid down in Article 1.

2. Articles 2, 3, 6 (1) (a) and (2) and Article 9 of Directive 68/360/EEC shall apply mutatis mutandis to the beneficiaries of this Directive.

The spouse and the dependent children of a national of a Member State entitled to the right of residence within the territory of a Member State shall be entitled to take up any employed or self-employed activity anywhere within the territory of that Member State, even if they are not nationals of a Member State.

Member States shall not derogate from the provisions of this Directive save on grounds of public policy, public security or public health. In that event, Directive 64/221/EEC shall apply.

3. This Directive shall not affect existing law on the acquisition of second homes.

Article 3

The right of residence shall remain for as long as beneficiaries of that right fulfil the conditions laid down in Article 1.

Article 4

The Commission shall, not more than three years after the date of implementation of this Directive, and at three-yearly intervals thereafter, draw up a report on the application of this Directive and submit it to the European Parliament and the Council.

Article 5

Member States shall bring into force the laws, regulations and administrative provisions necessary to comply with this Directive not later than 30 June 1992. They shall forthwith inform the Commission thereof.

Article 6

This Directive is addressed to the Member States.

COUNCIL DIRECTIVE 90/365/EEC OF 28 JUNE 1990 ON THE RIGHT OF RESIDENCE FOR EMPLOYEES AND SELF-EMPLOYED PERSONS WHO HAVE CEASED THEIR OCCUPATIONAL ACTIVITY

THE COUNCIL OF THE EUROPEAN COMMUNITIES,

Having regard to the Treaty establishing the European Economic Community, and in particular Article 235 thereof,

Having regard to the proposal from the Commission,[1]

Having regard to the opinion of the European Parliament,[2]

Having regard to the opinion of the Economic and Social Committee,[3]

Whereas Article 3 (c) of the Treaty provides that the activities of the Community shall include, as provided in the Treaty, the abolition, as between Member States, of obstacles to freedom of movement for persons;

Whereas Article 8a of the Treaty provides that the internal market must be established by 31 December 1992; whereas the internal market comprises an area without internal frontiers in which the free movement of goods, persons, services and capital is ensured, in accordance with the provisions of the Treaty;

Whereas Articles 48 and 52 of the Treaty provide for freedom of movement for workers and self-employed persons, which entails the right of residence in the Member States in which they pursue their occupational activity; whereas it is desirable that this right of residence also be granted to persons who have ceased their occupational activity even if they have not exercised their right to freedom of movement during their working life;

Whereas beneficiaries of the right of residence must not become an unreasonable burden on the public finances of the host Member State;

Whereas under Article 10 of Regulation (EEC) No 1408/71,[4] as amended by Regulation (EEC) No 1390/81,[5] recipients of invalidity or old age cash benefits or pensions for accidents at work or occupational diseases are entitled to continue to receive these benefits and pensions even if they reside in the territory of a Member State other than that in which the institution responsible for payment is situated;

---

[1] OJ No C 191, 28. 7. 1989, p. 3; and OJ No C 26, 3. 2. 1990, p. 19.
[2] Opinion delivered on 13 June 1990 (not yet published in the Official Journal).
[3] OJ No C 329, 30. 12. 1989, p. 25.
[4] OJ No L 149, 5. 7. 1971, p. 2.
[5] OJ No L 143, 29. 5. 1981, p. 1.

Whereas this right can only be genuinely exercised if it is also granted to members of the family;

Whereas the beneficiaries of this Directive should be covered by administrative arrangements similar to those laid down in particular by Directive 68/630/EEC[6] and Directive 64/221/EEC[7];

Whereas the Treaty does not provide, for the action concerned, powers other than those of Article 235,

HAS ADOPTED THIS DIRECTIVE:

Article 1

1. Member States shall grant the right of residence to nationals of Member States who have pursued an activity as an employee or self-employed person and to members of their families as defined in paragraph 2, provided that they are recipients of an invalidity or early retirement pension, or old age benefits, or of a pension in respect of an industrial accident or disease of an amount sufficient to avoid becoming a burden on the social security system of the host Member State during their period of residence and provided they are covered by sickness insurance in respect of all risks in the host Member State.

The resources of the applicant shall be deemed sufficient where they are higher than the level of resources below which the host Member State may grant social assistance to its nationals, taking into account the personal circumstances of persons admitted pursuant to paragraph 2.

Where the second subparagraph cannot be applied in a Member State, the resources of the applicant shall be deemed sufficient if they are higher than the level of the minimum social security pension paid by the host Member State.

2. The following shall, irrespective of their nationality, have the right to install themselves in another Member State with the holder of the right of residence:

(a) his or her spouse and their descendants who are dependants;

(b) dependent relatives in the ascending line of the holder of the right of residence and his or her spouse.

Article 2

1. Exercise of the right of residence shall be evidenced by means of the issue of a document known as a 'Residence permit for a national of a Member State of the EEC', whose validity may be limited to five years on a renewable basis. However, the Member States may, when they deem it to be necessary, require revalidation of the permit at the end of the first two years of residence. Where a member of the family does not hold the nationality of a Member State, he or she shall be issued with a

---

[6] OJ No L 257, 19. 10. 1968, p. 13.
[7] OJ No 56, 4. 4. 1964, p. 850/64.

residence document of the same validity as that issued to the national on whom he or she depends.

For the purposes of issuing the residence permit or document, the Member State may require only that the applicant present a valid identity card or passport and provide proof that he or she meets the conditions laid down in Article 1.

2. Articles 2, 3, 6 (1) (a) and (2) and Article 9 of Directive 68/360/EEC shall apply mutatis mutandis to the beneficiaries of this Directive.

The spouse and the dependent children of a national of a Member State entitled to the right of residence within the territory of a Member State shall be entitled to take up any employed or self-employed activity anywhere within the territory of that Member State, even if they are not nationals of a Member State.

Member States shall not derogate from the provisions of this Directive save on grounds of public policy, public security or public health. In that event, Directive 64/221/EEC shall apply.

3. This Directive shall not affect existing law on the acquisition of second homes.

Article 3

The right of residence shall remain for as long as beneficiaries of that right fulfil the conditions laid down in Article 1.

Article 4

The Commission shall, not more than three years after the date of implementation of this Directive, and at three-yearly intervals thereafter, draw up a report on the application of this Directive and submit it to the European Parliament and the Council.

Article 5

Member States shall bring into force the laws, regulations and administrative provisions necessary to comply with this Directive not later than 30 June 1992. They shall forthwith inform the Commission thereof.

Article 6

This Directive is addressed to the Member States.

Done at Luxembourg, 28 June 1990.

COUNCIL DIRECTIVE 93/96/EEC OF 29 OCTOBER 1993 ON THE RIGHT OF RESIDENCE FOR STUDENTS

THE COUNCIL OF THE EUROPEAN COMMUNITIES,   A16–0

Having regard to the Treaty establishing the European Economic Community, and in particular the second paragraph of Article 7 thereof,

Having regard to the proposal from the Commission,[1]

In cooperation with the European Parliament,[2]

Having regard to the opinion of the Economic and Social Committee,[3]

Whereas Article 3 (c) of the Treaty provides that the activities of the Community shall include, as provided in the Treaty, the abolition, as between Member States, of obstacles to freedom of movement for persons;

Whereas Article 8a of the Treaty provides that the internal market must be established by 31 December 1992; whereas the internal market comprises an area without internal frontiers in which the free movement of goods, persons, services and capital is ensured in accordance with the provisions of the Treaty;

Whereas, as the Court of Justice has held, Articles 128 and 7 of the Treaty prohibit any discrimination between nationals of the Member States as regards access to vocational training in the Community; whereas access by a national of one Member State to vocational training in another Member State implies, for that national, a right of residence in that other Member State;

Whereas, accordingly, in order to guarantee access to vocational training, the conditions likely to facilitate the effective exercise of that right of residence should be laid down;

Whereas the right of residence for students forms part of a set of related measures designed to promote vocational training;

Whereas beneficiaries of the right of residence must not become an unreasonable burden on the public finances of the host Member State;

Whereas, in the present state of Community law, as established by the case law of the Court of Justice, assistance granted to students, does not fall within the scope of the Treaty within the meaning of Article 7 thereof;

---

[1] OJ No C 166, 17. 6. 1993. p. 16.
[2] OJ No C 255, 20. 9. 1993, p. 70 and OJ No C 315, 22. 11. 1993.
[3] OJ No C 304, 10. 11. 1993, p. 1.

Whereas the right of residence can only be genuinely exercised if it is also granted to the spouse and their dependent children;

Whereas the beneficiaries of this Directive should be covered by administrative arrangements similar to those laid down in particular in Council Directive 68/360/EEC of 15 October 1968 on the abolition of restrictions on movement and residence within the Community for workers of Member States and their families[4] and Council Directive 64/221/EEC of 25 February 1964 on the coordination of special measures concerning the movement and residence of foreign nationals which are justified on grounds of public policy, public security or public health[5];

Whereas this Directive does not apply to students who enjoy the right of residence by virtue of the fact that they are or have been effectively engaged in economic activities or are members of the family of a migrant worker;

Whereas, by its judgment of 7 July 1992 in Case C-295/90, the Court of Justice annulled Council Directive 90/366/EEC of 28 June 1990 on the right of residence for students,[6] while maintaining the effects of the annulled Directive until the entry into force of a directive adopted on the appropriate legal basis;

Whereas the effects of Directive 90/366/EEC should be maintained during the period up to 31 December 1993, the date by which Member States are to have adopted the laws, regulations and administrative provisions necessary to comply with this Directive,

HAS ADOPTED THIS DIRECTIVE:

Article 1

In order to lay down conditions to facilitate the exercise of the right of residence and with a view to guaranteeing access to vocational training in a non-discriminatory manner for a national of a Member State who has been accepted to attend a vocational training course in another Member State, the Member States shall recognize the right of residence for any student who is a national of a Member State and who does not enjoy that right under other provisions of Community law, and for the student's spouse and their dependent children, where the student assures the relevant national authority, by means of a declaration or by such alternative means as the student may choose that are at least equivalent, that he has sufficient resources to avoid becoming a burden on the social assistance system of the host Member State during their period of residence, provided that the student is enrolled in a recognized educational establishment for the principal purpose of following a vocational training course there and that he is covered by sickness insurance in respect of all risks in the host Member State.

---

[4] OJ No L 257, 19. 10. 1968, p. 13. Directive as last amended by the Act of Accession of 1985.
[5] OJ No 56, 4. 4. 1964, p. 850/64.
[6] OJ No L 180, 13. 7. 1990, p. 30.

Article 2

1. The right of residence shall be restricted to the duration of the course of studies in question.

The right of residence shall be evidenced by means of the issue of a document known as a 'residence permit for a national of a Member State of the Community', the validity of which may be limited to the duration of the course of studies or to one year where the course lasts longer; in the latter event it shall be renewable annually. Where a member of the family does not hold the nationality of a Member State, he or she shall be issued with a residence document of the same validity as that issued to the national on whom he or she depends.

For the purpose of issuing the residence permit or document, the Member State may require only that the applicant present a valid identity card or passport and provide proof that he or she meets the conditions laid down in Article 1.

2. Articles 2, 3 and 9 of Directive 68/360/EEC shall apply mutatis mutandis to the beneficiaries of this Directive.

The spouse and the dependent children of a national of a Member State entitled to the right of residence within the territory of a Member State shall be entitled to take up any employed or self-employed activity anywhere within the territory of that Member State, even if they are not nationals of a Member State.

Member States shall not derogate from the provisions of this Directive save on grounds of public policy, public security or public health; in that event, Articles 2 to 9 of Directive 64/221/EEC shall apply.

Article 3

This Directive shall not establish any entitlement to the payment of maintenance grants by the host Member State on the part of students benefiting from the right of residence.

Article 4

The right of residence shall remain for as long as beneficiaries of that right fulfil the conditions laid down in Article 1.

Article 5

The Commission shall, not more than three years after the date of implementation of this Directive, and at three-yearly intervals thereafter, draw up a report on the application of this Directive and submit it to the European Parliament and the Council. The Commission shall pay particular attention to any difficulties to which the implementation of Article 1 might give rise in the Member States; it shall, if appropriate, submit proposals to the Council with the aim of remedying such difficulties.

Article 6

Member States shall bring into force the laws, regulations and administrative provisions necessary to comply with this Directive not later than 31 December 1993. They shall forthwith inform the Commission thereof.

For the period preceding that date, the effects of Directive 90/366/EEC shall be maintained. When Member States adopt those measures, they shall contain a reference to this Directive or shall be accompanied by such a reference on the occasion of their official publication. The methods of making such references shall be laid down by the Member States.

Article 7

This Directive is addressed to the Member States.

DIRECTIVE 2004/38/EC OF THE EUROPEAN PARLIAMENT AND OF THE COUNCIL OF 29 APRIL 2004 ON THE RIGHT OF CITIZENS OF THE UNION AND THEIR FAMILY MEMBERS TO MOVE AND RESIDE FREELY WITHIN THE TERRITORY OF THE MEMBER STATES AMENDING REGULATION (EEC) NO 1612/68 AND REPEALING DIRECTIVES 64/221/EEC, 68/360/EEC, 72/194/EEC, 73/148/EEC, 75/34/EEC, 75/35/EEC, 90/364/EEC, 90/365/EEC AND 93/96/EEC (TEXT WITH EEA RELEVANCE)

THE EUROPEAN PARLIAMENT AND THE COUNCIL OF THE EUROPEAN UNION,

Having regard to the Treaty establishing the European Community, and in particular Articles 12, 18, 40, 44 and 52 thereof,   **A17–01**

Having regard to the proposal from the Commission[1],

Having regard to the Opinion of the European Economic and Social Committee[2],

Having regard to the Opinion of the Committee of the Regions[3],

Acting in accordance with the procedure laid down in Article 251 of the Treaty[4],

Whereas:

(1) Citizenship of the Union confers on every citizen of the Union a primary and individual right to move and reside freely within the territory of the Member States, subject to the limitations and conditions laid down in the Treaty and to the measures adopted to give it effect.

(2) The free movement of persons constitutes one of the fundamental freedoms of the internal market, which comprises an area without internal frontiers, in which freedom is ensured in accordance with the provisions of the Treaty.

(3) Union citizenship should be the fundamental status of nationals of the Member States when they exercise their right of free movement and residence. It is therefore necessary to codify and review the existing Community instruments dealing separately with workers, self-employed persons, as well as students and other inactive persons in order to simplify and strengthen the right of free movement and residence of all Union citizens.

---

[1] OJ C 270 E, 25.9.2001, p. 150.
[2] OJ C 149, 21.6.2002, p. 46.
[3] OJ C 192, 12.8.2002, p. 17.
[4] Opinion of the European Parliament of 11 February 2003 (OJ C 43 E, 19.2.2004, p. 42), Council Common Position of 5 December 2003 (OJ C 54 E, 2.3.2004, p. 12) and Position of the European Parliament of 10 March 2004 (not yet published in the Official Journal).

(4)   With a view to remedying this sector-by-sector, piecemeal approach to the right of free movement and residence and facilitating the exercise of this right, there needs to be a single legislative act to amend Council Regulation (EEC) No 1612/68 of 15 October 1968 on freedom of movement for workers within the Community,[5] and to repeal the following acts: Council Directive 68/360/EEC of 15 October 1968 on the abolition of restrictions on movement and residence within the Community for workers of Member States and their families,[6] Council Directive 73/148/EEC of 21 May 1973 on the abolition of restrictions on movement and residence within the Community for nationals of Member States with regard to establishment and the provision of services,[7] Council Directive 90/364/EEC of 28 June 1990 on the right of residence,[8] Council Directive 90/365/EEC of 28 June 1990 on the right of residence for employees and self-employed persons who have ceased their occupational activity[9] and Council Directive 93/96/EEC of 29 October 1993 on the right of residence for students.[10]

(5)   The right of all Union citizens to move and reside freely within the territory of the Member States should, if it is to be exercised under objective conditions of freedom and dignity, be also granted to their family members, irrespective of nationality. For the purposes of this Directive, the definition of "family member" should also include the registered partner if the legislation of the host Member State treats registered partnership as equivalent to marriage.

(6)   In order to maintain the unity of the family in a broader sense and without prejudice to the prohibition of discrimination on grounds of nationality, the situation of those persons who are not included in the definition of family members under this Directive, and who therefore do not enjoy an automatic right of entry and residence in the host Member State, should be examined by the host Member State on the basis of its own national legislation, in order to decide whether entry and residence could be granted to such persons, taking into consideration their relationship with the Union citizen or any other circumstances, such as their financial or physical dependence on the Union citizen.

(7)   The formalities connected with the free movement of Union citizens within the territory of Member States should be clearly defined, without prejudice to the provisions applicable to national border controls.

(8)   With a view to facilitating the free movement of family members who are not nationals of a Member State, those who have already obtained a residence card should be exempted from the requirement to obtain an entry visa within the meaning of Council Regulation (E.C.) No 539/2001 of 15 March 2001 listing the third countries whose nationals must be in possession of visas when crossing the external borders and those whose nationals are exempt from that requirement[11] or, where appropriate, of the applicable national legislation.

(9)   Union citizens should have the right of residence in the host Member State for a period not exceeding three months without being subject to any conditions or any formalities other than the requirement to hold a valid identity card or pass-

---

[5] OJ L 257, 19.10.1968, p. 2. Regulation as last amended by Regulation (EEC) No 2434/92. (OJ L 245, 26.8.1992, p. 1).
[6] OJ L 257, 19.10.1968, p. 13. Directive as last amended by the 2003 Act of Accession.
[7] OJ L 172, 28.6.1973, p. 14.
[8] OJ L 180, 13.7.1990, p. 26.
[9] OJ L 180, 13.7.1990, p. 28.
[10] OJ L 317, 18.12.1993, p. 59.
[11] OJ L 81, 21.3.2001, p. 1. Regulation (E.C.) No 453/2003 (OJ L 69, 13.3.2003, p. 10).

port, without prejudice to a more favourable treatment applicable to job-seekers as recognised by the case-law of the Court of Justice.

(10) Persons exercising their right of residence should not, however, become an unreasonable burden on the social assistance system of the host Member State during an initial period of residence. Therefore, the right of residence for Union citizens and their family members for periods in excess of three months should be subject to conditions.

(11) The fundamental and personal right of residence in another Member State is conferred directly on Union citizens by the Treaty and is not dependent upon their having fulfilled administrative procedures.

(12) For periods of residence of longer than three months, Member States should have the possibility to require Union citizens to register with the competent authorities in the place of residence, attested by a registration certificate issued to that effect.

(13) The residence card requirement should be restricted to family members of Union citizens who are not nationals of a Member State for periods of residence of longer than three months.

(14) The supporting documents required by the competent authorities for the issuing of a registration certificate or of a residence card should be comprehensively specified in order to avoid divergent administrative practices or interpretations constituting an undue obstacle to the exercise of the right of residence by Union citizens and their family members.

(15) Family members should be legally safeguarded in the event of the death of the Union citizen, divorce, annulment of marriage or termination of a registered partnership. With due regard for family life and human dignity, and in certain conditions to guard against abuse, measures should therefore be taken to ensure that in such circumstances family members already residing within the territory of the host Member State retain their right of residence exclusively on a personal basis.

(16) As long as the beneficiaries of the right of residence do not become an unreasonable burden on the social assistance system of the host Member State they should not be expelled. Therefore, an expulsion measure should not be the automatic consequence of recourse to the social assistance system. The host Member State should examine whether it is a case of temporary difficulties and take into account the duration of residence, the personal circumstances and the amount of aid granted in order to consider whether the beneficiary has become an unreasonable burden on its social assistance system and to proceed to his expulsion. In no case should an expulsion measure be adopted against workers, self-employed persons or job-seekers as defined by the Court of Justice save on grounds of public policy or public security.

(17) Enjoyment of permanent residence by Union citizens who have chosen to settle long term in the host Member State would strengthen the feeling of Union citizenship and is a key element in promoting social cohesion, which is one of the fundamental objectives of the Union. A right of permanent residence should therefore be laid down for all Union citizens and their family members who have resided in the host Member State in compliance with the conditions laid down in this Directive during a continuous period of five years without becoming subject to an expulsion measure.

(18) In order to be a genuine vehicle for integration into the society of the host Member State in which the Union citizen resides, the right of permanent residence, once obtained, should not be subject to any conditions.

(19) Certain advantages specific to Union citizens who are workers or self-employed persons and to their family members, which may allow these persons to acquire a right of permanent residence before they have resided five years in the host Member State, should be maintained, as these constitute acquired rights, conferred by Commission Regulation (EEC) No 1251/70 of 29 June 1970 on the right of workers to remain in the territory of a Member State after having been employed in that State[12] and Council Directive 75/34/EEC of 17 December 1974 concerning the right of nationals of a Member State to remain in the territory of another Member State after having pursued therein an activity in a self-employed capacity.[13]

(20) In accordance with the prohibition of discrimination on grounds of nationality, all Union citizens and their family members residing in a Member State on the basis of this Directive should enjoy, in that Member State, equal treatment with nationals in areas covered by the Treaty, subject to such specific provisions as are expressly provided for in the Treaty and secondary law.

(21) However, it should be left to the host Member State to decide whether it will grant social assistance during the first three months of residence, or for a longer period in the case of job-seekers, to Union citizens other than those who are workers or self-employed persons or who retain that status or their family members, or maintenance assistance for studies, including vocational training, prior to acquisition of the right of permanent residence, to these same persons.

(22) The Treaty allows restrictions to be placed on the right of free movement and residence on grounds of public policy, public security or public health. In order to ensure a tighter definition of the circumstances and procedural safeguards subject to which Union citizens and their family members may be denied leave to enter or may be expelled, this Directive should replace Council Directive 64/221/EEC of 25 February 1964 on the coordination of special measures concerning the movement and residence of foreign nationals, which are justified on grounds of public policy, public security or public health.[14]

(23) Expulsion of Union citizens and their family members on grounds of public policy or public security is a measure that can seriously harm persons who, having availed themselves of the rights and freedoms conferred on them by the Treaty, have become genuinely integrated into the host Member State. The scope for such measures should therefore be limited in accordance with the principle of proportionality to take account of the degree of integration of the persons concerned, the length of their residence in the host Member State, their age, state of health, family and economic situation and the links with their country of origin.

(24) Accordingly, the greater the degree of integration of Union citizens and their family members in the host Member State, the greater the degree of protection against expulsion should be. Only in exceptional circumstances, where there are imperative grounds of public security, should an expulsion measure be taken against Union citizens who have resided for many years in the territory of the host Member State, in particular when they were born and have resided there throughout their life. In addition, such exceptional circumstances should also apply to an expulsion measure taken against minors, in order to protect their links with their family, in accordance with the United Nations Convention on the Rights of the Child, of 20 November 1989.

---

[12] OJ L 142, 30.6.1970, p. 24.
[13] OJ L 14, 20.1.1975, p. 10.
[14] OJ 56, 4.4.1964, p. 850. Directive as last amended by Dir. 75/35/EEC (OJ 13, 20.1.1975, p. 14.

(25) Procedural safeguards should also be specified in detail in order to ensure a high level of protection of the rights of Union citizens and their family members in the event of their being denied leave to enter or reside in another Member State, as well as to uphold the principle that any action taken by the authorities must be properly justified.

(26) In all events, judicial redress procedures should be available to Union citizens and their family members who have been refused leave to enter or reside in another Member State.

(27) In line with the case-law of the Court of Justice prohibiting Member States from issuing orders excluding for life persons covered by this Directive from their territory, the right of Union citizens and their family members who have been excluded from the territory of a Member State to submit a fresh application after a reasonable period, and in any event after a three year period from enforcement of the final exclusion order, should be confirmed.

(28) To guard against abuse of rights or fraud, notably marriages of convenience or any other form of relationships contracted for the sole purpose of enjoying the right of free movement and residence, Member States should have the possibility to adopt the necessary measures.

(29) This Directive should not affect more favourable national provisions.

(30) With a view to examining how further to facilitate the exercise of the right of free movement and residence, a report should be prepared by the Commission in order to evaluate the opportunity to present any necessary proposals to this effect, notably on the extension of the period of residence with no conditions.

(31) This Directive respects the fundamental rights and freedoms and observes the principles recognised in particular by the Charter of Fundamental Rights of the European Union. In accordance with the prohibition of discrimination contained in the Charter, Member States should implement this Directive without discrimination between the beneficiaries of this Directive on grounds such as sex, race, colour, ethnic or social origin, genetic characteristics, language, religion or beliefs, political or other opinion, membership of an ethnic minority, property, birth, disability, age or sexual orientation,

HAVE ADOPTED THIS DIRECTIVE:

CHAPTER I

GENERAL PROVISIONS

Article 1—Subject

This Directive lays down:

(a) the conditions governing the exercise of the right of free movement and residence within the territory of the Member States by Union citizens and their family members;

(b) the right of permanent residence in the territory of the Member States for Union citizens and their family members;

(c) the limits placed on the rights set out in (a) and (b) on grounds of public policy, public security or public health.

Article 2—Definitions

For the purposes of this Directive:

1) "Union citizen" means any person having the nationality of a Member State;

2) "Family member" means:

    (a) the spouse;

    (b) the partner with whom the Union citizen has contracted a registered partnership, on the basis of the legislation of a Member State, if the legislation of the host Member State treats registered partnerships as equivalent to marriage and in accordance with the conditions laid down in the relevant legislation of the host Member State;

    (c) the direct descendants who are under the age of 21 or are dependants and those of the spouse or partner as defined in point (b);

    (d) the dependent direct relatives in the ascending line and those of the spouse or partner as defined in point (b);

3) "Host Member State" means the Member State to which a Union citizen moves in order to exercise his/her right of free movement and residence.

Article 3—Beneficiaries

1. This Directive shall apply to all Union citizens who move to or reside in a Member State other than that of which they are a national, and to their family members as defined in point 2 of Article 2 who accompany or join them.

2. Without prejudice to any right to free movement and residence the persons concerned may have in their own right, the host Member State shall, in accordance with its national legislation, facilitate entry and residence for the following persons:

(a) any other family members, irrespective of their nationality, not falling under the definition in point 2 of Article 2 who, in the country from which they have come, are dependants or members of the household of the Union citizen having the primary right of residence, or where serious health grounds strictly require the personal care of the family member by the Union citizen;

(b) the partner with whom the Union citizen has a durable relationship, duly attested.

The host Member State shall undertake an extensive examination of the personal circumstances and shall justify any denial of entry or residence to these people.

CHAPTER II

RIGHT OF EXIT AND ENTRY

Article 4—Right of Exit

1. Without prejudice to the provisions on travel documents applicable to national border controls, all Union citizens with a valid identity card or passport and their family members who are not nationals of a Member State and who hold a valid passport shall have the right to leave the territory of a Member State to travel to another Member State.

2. No exit visa or equivalent formality may be imposed on the persons to whom paragraph 1 applies.

3. Member States shall, acting in accordance with their laws, issue to their own nationals, and renew, an identity card or passport stating their nationality.

4. The passport shall be valid at least for all Member States and for countries through which the holder must pass when travelling between Member States. Where the law of a Member State does not provide for identity cards to be issued, the period of validity of any passport on being issued or renewed shall be not less than five years.

Article 5—Right of Entry

1. Without prejudice to the provisions on travel documents applicable to national border controls, Member States shall grant Union citizens leave to enter their territory with a valid identity card or passport and shall grant family members who are not nationals of a Member State leave to enter their territory with a valid passport. No entry visa or equivalent formality may be imposed on Union citizens.

2. Family members who are not nationals of a Member State shall only be required to have an entry visa in accordance with Regulation (E.C.) No 539/2001 or, where appropriate, with national law. For the purposes of this Directive, possession of the valid residence card referred to in Article 10 shall exempt such family members from the visa requirement.

Member States shall grant such persons every facility to obtain the necessary visas. Such visas shall be issued free of charge as soon as possible and on the basis of an accelerated procedure.

3. The host Member State shall not place an entry or exit stamp in the passport of family members who are not nationals of a Member State provided that they present the residence card provided for in Article 10.

4. Where a Union citizen, or a family member who is not a national of a Member State, does not have the necessary travel documents or, if required, the necessary visas, the Member State concerned shall, before turning them back, give such persons every reasonable opportunity to obtain the necessary documents or have them brought to them within a reasonable period of time or to corroborate or prove by other means that they are covered by the right of free movement and residence.

5. The Member State may require the person concerned to report his/her presence within its territory within a reasonable and non-discriminatory period of time. Failure to comply with this requirement may make the person concerned liable to proportionate and non-discriminatory sanctions.

CHAPTER III

RIGHT OF RESIDENCE

Article 6—Right of Residence for up to Three Months

1. Union citizens shall have the right of residence on the territory of another Member State for a period of up to three months without any conditions or any formalities other than the requirement to hold a valid identity card or passport.

2. The provisions of paragraph 1 shall also apply to family members in possession of a valid passport who are not nationals of a Member State, accompanying or joining the Union citizen.

Article 7—Right of Residence for More than Three Months

1. All Union citizens shall have the right of residence on the territory of another Member State for a period of longer than three months if they:

(a) are workers or self-employed persons in the host Member State; or

(b) have sufficient resources for themselves and their family members not to become a burden on the social assistance system of the host Member State during their period of residence and have comprehensive sickness insurance cover in the host Member State; or

(c) – are enrolled at a private or public establishment, accredited or financed by the host Member State on the basis of its legislation or administrative practice, for the principal purpose of following a course of study, including vocational training; and

– have comprehensive sickness insurance cover in the host Member State and assure the relevant national authority, by means of a declaration or by such equivalent means as they may choose, that they have sufficient resources for themselves and their family members not to become a burden on the social assistance system of the host Member State during their period of residence; or

(d) are family members accompanying or joining a Union citizen who satisfies the conditions referred to in points (a), (b) or (c).

2. The right of residence provided for in paragraph 1 shall extend to family members who are not nationals of a Member State, accompanying or joining the Union citizen in the host Member State, provided that such Union citizen satisfies the conditions referred to in paragraph 1(a), (b) or (c).

3. For the purposes of paragraph 1(a), a Union citizen who is no longer a worker or self-employed person shall retain the status of worker or self-employed person in the following circumstances:

(a) he/she is temporarily unable to work as the result of an illness or accident;

(b) he/she is in duly recorded involuntary unemployment after having been employed for more than one year and has registered as a job-seeker with the relevant employment office;

(c) he/she is in duly recorded involuntary unemployment after completing a fixed-term employment contract of less than a year or after having become involuntarily unemployed during the first twelve months and has registered as a job-seeker with the relevant employment office. In this case, the status of worker shall be retained for no less than six months;

(d) he/she embarks on vocational training. Unless he/she is involuntarily unemployed, the retention of the status of worker shall require the training to be related to the previous employment.

4. By way of derogation from paragraphs 1(d) and 2 above, only the spouse, the registered partner provided for in Article 2(2)(b) and dependent children shall have the right of residence as family members of a Union citizen meeting the conditions under 1(c) above. Article 3(2) shall apply to his/her dependent direct relatives in the ascending lines and those of his/her spouse or registered partner.

Article 8—Administrative Formalities for Union Citizens

1. Without prejudice to Article 5(5), for periods of residence longer than three months, the host Member State may require Union citizens to register with the relevant authorities.

2. The deadline for registration may not be less than three months from the date of arrival. A registration certificate shall be issued immediately, stating the name and address of the person registering and the date of the registration. Failure to comply with the registration requirement may render the person concerned liable to proportionate and non-discriminatory sanctions.

3. For the registration certificate to be issued, Member States may only require that

– Union citizens to whom point (a) of Article 7(1) applies present a valid identity card or passport, a confirmation of engagement from the employer or a certificate of employment, or proof that they are self-employed persons;

– Union citizens to whom point (b) of Article 7(1) applies present a valid identity card or passport and provide proof that they satisfy the conditions laid down therein;

– Union citizens to whom point (c) of Article 7(1) applies present a valid identity card or passport, provide proof of enrolment at an accredited establishment and of comprehensive sickness insurance cover and the declaration or equivalent means referred to in point (c) of Article 7(1). Member States may not require this declaration to refer to any specific amount of resources.

4. Member States may not lay down a fixed amount which they regard as "sufficient resources", but they must take into account the personal situation of the person concerned. In all cases this amount shall not be higher than the threshold below which nationals of the host Member State become eligible for social assistance, or, where this criterion is not applicable, higher than the minimum social security pension paid by the host Member State.

5. For the registration certificate to be issued to family members of Union citizens, who are themselves Union citizens, Member States may require the following documents to be presented:

(a)   a valid identity card or passport;

(b)   a document attesting to the existence of a family relationship or of a registered partnership;

(c)   where appropriate, the registration certificate of the Union citizen whom they are accompanying or joining;

(d)   in cases falling under points (c) and (d) of Article 2(2), documentary evidence that the conditions laid down therein are met;

(e)   in cases falling under Article 3(2)(a), a document issued by the relevant authority in the country of origin or country from which they are arriving certifying that they are dependants or members of the household of the Union citizen, or proof of the existence of serious health grounds which strictly require the personal care of the family member by the Union citizen;

(f)   in cases falling under Article 3(2)(b), proof of the existence of a durable relationship with the Union citizen.

Article 9—Administrative Formalities for Family Members who are not Nationals of a Member State

1. Member States shall issue a residence card to family members of a Union citizen who are not nationals of a Member State, where the planned period of residence is for more than three months.

2. The deadline for submitting the residence card application may not be less than three months from the date of arrival.

3. Failure to comply with the requirement to apply for a residence card may make the person concerned liable to proportionate and non-discriminatory sanctions.

Article 10—Issue of Residence Cards

1. The right of residence of family members of a Union citizen who are not nationals of a Member State shall be evidenced by the issuing of a document called "Residence card of a family member of a Union citizen" no later than six months from the date on which they submit the application. A certificate of application for the residence card shall be issued immediately.

2. For the residence card to be issued, Member States shall require presentation of the following documents:

(a)   a valid passport;

(b)   a document attesting to the existence of a family relationship or of a registered partnership;

(c)   the registration certificate or, in the absence of a registration system, any other proof of residence in the host Member State of the Union citizen whom they are accompanying or joining;

(d)   in cases falling under points (c) and (d) of Article 2(2), documentary evidence that the conditions laid down therein are met;

(e)   in cases falling under Article 3(2)(a), a document issued by the relevant authority in the country of origin or country from which they are arriving certifying that they are dependants or members of the household of the Union citizen, or proof of the existence of serious health grounds which strictly require the personal care of the family member by the Union citizen;

(f)   in cases falling under Article 3(2)(b), proof of the existence of a durable relationship with the Union citizen.

Article 11—Validity of the Residence Card

1. The residence card provided for by Article 10(1) shall be valid for five years from the date of issue or for the envisaged period of residence of the Union citizen, if this period is less than five years.

2. The validity of the residence card shall not be affected by temporary absences not exceeding six months a year, or by absences of a longer duration for compulsory military service or by one absence of a maximum of twelve consecutive months for important reasons such as pregnancy and childbirth, serious illness, study or vocational training, or a posting in another Member State or a third country.

Article 12—Retention of the Right of Residence by Family Members in the Event of Death or Departure of the Union Citizen

1. Without prejudice to the second subparagraph, the Union citizen's death or departure from the host Member State shall not affect the right of residence of his/her family members who are nationals of a Member State.
Before acquiring the right of permanent residence, the persons concerned must meet the conditions laid down in points (a), (b), (c) or (d) of Article 7(1).

2. Without prejudice to the second subparagraph, the Union citizen's death shall not entail loss of the right of residence of his/her family members who are not nationals of a Member State and who have been residing in the host Member State as family members for at least one year before the Union citizen's death.

Before acquiring the right of permanent residence, the right of residence of the persons concerned shall remain subject to the requirement that they are able to show that they are workers or self-employed persons or that they have sufficient resources for themselves and their family members not to become a burden on the social assistance system of the host Member State during their period of residence and have comprehensive sickness insurance cover in the host Member State, or that they are members of the family, already constituted in the host Member State, of a person satisfying these requirements. "Sufficient resources" shall be as defined in Article 8(4). Such family members shall retain their right of residence exclusively on a personal basis.

3. The Union citizen's departure from the host Member State or his/her death shall not entail loss of the right of residence of his/her children or of the parent who has actual custody of the children, irrespective of nationality, if the children reside in the host Member State and are enrolled at an educational establishment, for the purpose of studying there, until the completion of their studies.

Article 13—Retention of the Right of Residence by Family Members in the Event of Divorce, Annulment of Marriage or Termination of Registered Partnership

1. Without prejudice to the second subparagraph, divorce, annulment of the Union citizen's marriage or termination of his/her registered partnership, as referred to in point 2(b) of Article 2 shall not affect the right of residence of his/her family members who are nationals of a Member State.

Before acquiring the right of permanent residence, the persons concerned must meet the conditions laid down in points (a), (b), (c) or (d) of Article 7(1).

2. Without prejudice to the second subparagraph, divorce, annulment of marriage or termination of the registered partnership referred to in point 2(b) of Article 2 shall not entail loss of the right of residence of a Union citizen's family members who are not nationals of a Member State where:

(a) prior to initiation of the divorce or annulment proceedings or termination of the registered partnership referred to in point 2(b) of Article 2, the marriage or registered partnership has lasted at least three years, including one year in the host Member State; or

(b) by agreement between the spouses or the partners referred to in point 2(b) of Article 2 or by court order, the spouse or partner who is not a national of a Member State has custody of the Union citizen's children; or

(c) this is warranted by particularly difficult circumstances, such as having been a victim of domestic violence while the marriage or registered partnership was subsisting; or

(d) by agreement between the spouses or partners referred to in point 2(b) of Article 2 or by court order, the spouse or partner who is not a national of a Member State has the right of access to a minor child, provided that the court has ruled that such access must be in the host Member State, and for as long as is required.

Before acquiring the right of permanent residence, the right of residence of the persons concerned shall remain subject to the requirement that they are able to show that they are workers or self-employed persons or that they have sufficient resources for themselves and their family members not to become a burden on the social assistance system of the host Member State during their period of residence and have comprehensive sickness insurance cover in the host Member State, or that they are members of the family, already constituted in the host Member State, of a person satisfying these requirements. "Sufficient resources" shall be as defined in Article 8(4).

Such family members shall retain their right of residence exclusively on personal basis.

Article 14—Retention of the Right of Residence

1. Union citizens and their family members shall have the right of residence provided for in Article 6, as long as they do not become an unreasonable burden on the social assistance system of the host Member State.

2. Union citizens and their family members shall have the right of residence provided for in Articles 7, 12 and 13 as long as they meet the conditions set out therein.

In specific cases where there is a reasonable doubt as to whether a Union citizen or his/her family members satisfies the conditions set out in Articles 7, 12 and 13, Member States may verify if these conditions are fulfilled. This verification shall not be carried out systematically.

3. An expulsion measure shall not be the automatic consequence of a Union citizen's or his or her family member's recourse to the social assistance system of the host Member State.

4. By way of derogation from paragraphs 1 and 2 and without prejudice to the provisions of Chapter VI, an expulsion measure may in no case be adopted against Union citizens or their family members if:

(a) the Union citizens are workers or self-employed persons, or

(b) the Union citizens entered the territory of the host Member State in order to seek employment. In this case, the Union citizens and their family members may not be expelled for as long as the Union citizens can provide evidence that they are continuing to seek employment and that they have a genuine chance of being engaged.

Article 15—Procedural Safeguards

1. The procedures provided for by Articles 30 and 31 shall apply by analogy to all decisions restricting free movement of Union citizens and their family members on grounds other than public policy, public security or public health.

2. Expiry of the identity card or passport on the basis of which the person concerned entered the host Member State and was issued with a registration certificate or residence card shall not constitute a ground for expulsion from the host Member State.

3. The host Member State may not impose a ban on entry in the context of an expulsion decision to which paragraph 1 applies.

CHAPTER IV

RIGHT OF PERMANENT RESIDENCE

SECTION I

ELIGIBILITY

Article 16—General Rule for Union Citizens and their Family Members

1. Union citizens who have resided legally for a continuous period of five years in the host Member State shall have the right of permanent residence there. This right shall not be subject to the conditions provided for in Chapter III.

2. Paragraph 1 shall apply also to family members who are not nationals of a Member State and have legally resided with the Union citizen in the host Member State for a continuous period of five years.

3. Continuity of residence shall not be affected by temporary absences not exceeding a total of six months a year, or by absences of a longer duration for compulsory military service, or by one absence of a maximum of twelve consecutive months for important reasons such as pregnancy and childbirth, serious illness, study or vocational training, or a posting in another Member State or a third country.

4. Once acquired, the right of permanent residence shall be lost only through absence from the host Member State for a period exceeding two consecutive years.

Article 17—Exemptions for Persons no Longer Working in the Host Member State and Their Family Members

1. By way of derogation from Article 16, the right of permanent residence in the host Member State shall be enjoyed before completion of a continuous period of five years of residence by:

(a) workers or self-employed persons who, at the time they stop working, have reached the age laid down by the law of that Member State for entitlement to an old age pension or workers who cease paid employment to take early retirement, provided that they have been working in that Member State for at least the preceding twelve months and have resided there continuously for more than three years.
If the law of the host Member State does not grant the right to an old age pension to certain categories of self-employed persons, the age condition shall be deemed to have been met once the person concerned has reached the age of 60;

(b) workers or self-employed persons who have resided continuously in the host Member State for more than two years and stop working there as a result of permanent incapacity to work.

If such incapacity is the result of an accident at work or an occupational disease entitling the person concerned to a benefit payable in full or in part by an institution in the host Member State, no condition shall be imposed as to length of residence;

(c)   workers or self-employed persons who, after three years of continuous employ-ment and residence in the host Member State, work in an employed or self-employed capacity in another Member State, while retaining their place of residence in the host Member State, to which they return, as a rule, each day or at least once a week.

For the purposes of entitlement to the rights referred to in points (a) and (b), periods of employment spent in the Member State in which the person con-cerned is working shall be regarded as having been spent in the host Member State.

Periods of involuntary unemployment duly recorded by the relevant employment office, periods not worked for reasons not of the person's own making and absences from work or cessation of work due to illness or accident shall be regarded as periods of employment.

2. The conditions as to length of residence and employment laid down in point (a) of paragraph 1 and the condition as to length of residence laid down in point (b) of paragraph 1 shall not apply if the worker's or the self-employed person's spouse or partner as referred to in point 2(b) of Article 2 is a national of the host Member State or has lost the nationality of that Member State by marriage to that worker or self-employed person.

3. Irrespective of nationality, the family members of a worker or a self-employed person who are residing with him in the territory of the host Member State shall have the right of permanent residence in that Member State, if the worker or self-employed person has acquired himself the right of permanent residence in that Member State on the basis of paragraph 1.

4. If, however, the worker or self-employed person dies while still working but before acquiring permanent residence status in the host Member State on the basis of para-graph 1, his family members who are residing with him in the host Member State shall acquire the right of permanent residence there, on condition that:

(a)   the worker or self-employed person had, at the time of death, resided continu-ously on the territory of that Member State for two years; or

(b)   the death resulted from an accident at work or an occupational disease; or

(c)   the surviving spouse lost the nationality of that Member State following mar-riage to the worker or self-employed person.

Article 18—Acquisition of the Right of Permanent Residence by Certain Family Members who are not Nationals of a Member State

Without prejudice to Article 17, the family members of a Union citizen to whom Articles 12(2) and 13(2) apply, who satisfy the conditions laid down therein, shall acquire the right of permanent residence after residing legally for a period of five consecutive years in the host Member State.

SECTION II

ADMINISTRATIVE FORMALITIES

Article 19—Document Certifying Permanent Residence for Union Citizens

1. Upon application Member States shall issue Union citizens entitled to permanent residence, after having verified duration of residence, with a document certifying permanent residence.

2. The document certifying permanent residence shall be issued as soon as possible.

Article 20—Permanent Residence Card for Family Members who are not Nationals of a Member State

1. Member States shall issue family members who are not nationals of a Member State entitled to permanent residence with a permanent residence card within six months of the submission of the application. The permanent residence card shall be renewable automatically every ten years.

2. The application for a permanent residence card shall be submitted before the residence card expires. Failure to comply with the requirement to apply for a permanent residence card may render the person concerned liable to proportionate and non-discriminatory sanctions.

3. Interruption in residence not exceeding two consecutive years shall not affect the validity of the permanent residence card.

Article 21—Continuity of Residence

For the purposes of this Directive, continuity of residence may be attested by any means of proof in use in the host Member State. Continuity of residence is broken by any expulsion decision duly enforced against the person concerned.

CHAPTER V

PROVISIONS COMMON TO THE RIGHT OF RESIDENCE AND THE RIGHT OF PERMANENT RESIDENCE

Article 22—Territorial Scope

The right of residence and the right of permanent residence shall cover the whole territory of the host Member State. Member States may impose territorial restrictions on the right of residence and the right of permanent residence only where the same restrictions apply to their own nationals.

Article 23—Related Rights

Irrespective of nationality, the family members of a Union citizen who have the right of residence or the right of permanent residence in a Member State shall be entitled to take up employment or self-employment there.

Article 24—Equal Treatment

1. Subject to such specific provisions as are expressly provided for in the Treaty and secondary law, all Union citizens residing on the basis of this Directive in the territory of the host Member State shall enjoy equal treatment with the nationals of that Member State within the scope of the Treaty. The benefit of this right shall be extended to family members who are not nationals of a Member State and who have the right of residence or permanent residence.

2. By way of derogation from paragraph 1, the host Member State shall not be obliged to confer entitlement to social assistance during the first three months of residence or, where appropriate, the longer period provided for in Article 14(4)(b), nor shall it be obliged, prior to acquisition of the right of permanent residence, to grant maintenance aid for studies, including vocational training, consisting in student grants or student loans to persons other than workers, self-employed persons, persons who retain such status and members of their families.

Article 25—General Provisions Concerning Residence Documents

1. Possession of a registration certificate as referred to in Article 8, of a document certifying permanent residence, of a certificate attesting submission of an application for a family member residence card, of a residence card or of a permanent residence card, may under no circumstances be made a precondition for the exercise of a right or the completion of an administrative formality, as entitlement to rights may be attested by any other means of proof.

2. All documents mentioned in paragraph 1 shall be issued free of charge or for a charge not exceeding that imposed on nationals for the issuing of similar documents.

Article 26—Checks

Member States may carry out checks on compliance with any requirement deriving from their national legislation for non-nationals always to carry their registration certificate or residence card, provided that the same requirement applies to their own nationals as regards their identity card. In the event of failure to comply with this requirement, Member States may impose the same sanctions as those imposed on their own nationals for failure to carry their identity card.

CHAPTER VI

RESTRICTIONS ON THE RIGHT OF ENTRY AND THE RIGHT OF RESIDENCE ON GROUNDS OF PUBLIC POLICY, PUBLIC SECURITY OR PUBLIC HEALTH

Article 27—General Principles

1. Subject to the provisions of this Chapter, Member States may restrict the freedom of movement and residence of Union citizens and their family members, irrespective of nationality, on grounds of public policy, public security or public health. These grounds shall not be invoked to serve economic ends.

2. Measures taken on grounds of public policy or public security shall comply with the principle of proportionality and shall be based exclusively on the personal conduct of the individual concerned. Previous criminal convictions shall not in themselves constitute grounds for taking such measures.

The personal conduct of the individual concerned must represent a genuine, present and sufficiently serious threat affecting one of the fundamental interests of society. Justifications that are isolated from the particulars of the case or that rely on considerations of general prevention shall not be accepted.

3. In order to ascertain whether the person concerned represents a danger for public policy or public security, when issuing the registration certificate or, in the absence of a registration system, not later than three months from the date of arrival of the person concerned on its territory or from the date of reporting his/her presence within the territory, as provided for in Article 5(5), or when issuing the residence card, the host Member State may, should it consider this essential, request the Member State of origin and, if need be, other Member States to provide information concerning any previous police record the person concerned may have. Such enquiries shall not be made as a matter of routine. The Member State consulted shall give its reply within two months.

4. The Member State which issued the passport or identity card shall allow the holder of the document who has been expelled on grounds of public policy, public security, or public health from another Member State to re-enter its territory without any formality even if the document is no longer valid or the nationality of the holder is in dispute.

Article 28—Protection Against Expulsion

1. Before taking an expulsion decision on grounds of public policy or public security, the host Member State shall take account of considerations such as how long the individual concerned has resided on its territory, his/her age, state of health, family and economic situation, social and cultural integration into the host Member State and the extent of his/her links with the country of origin.

2. The host Member State may not take an expulsion decision against Union citizens or their family members, irrespective of nationality, who have the right of permanent residence on its territory, except on serious grounds of public policy or public security.

3. An expulsion decision may not be taken against Union citizens, except if the decision is based on imperative grounds of public security, as defined by Member States, if they:

(a) have resided in the host Member State for the previous ten years; or

(b) are a minor, except if the expulsion is necessary for the best interests of the child, as provided for in the United Nations Convention on the Rights of the Child of 20 November 1989.

Article 29—Public Health

1. The only diseases justifying measures restricting freedom of movement shall be the diseases with epidemic potential as defined by the relevant instruments of the World Health Organisation and other infectious diseases or contagious parasitic diseases if they are the subject of protection provisions applying to nationals of the host Member State.

2. Diseases occurring after a three-month period from the date of arrival shall not constitute grounds for expulsion from the territory.

3. Where there are serious indications that it is necessary, Member States may, within three months of the date of arrival, require persons entitled to the right of residence to undergo, free of charge, a medical examination to certify that they are not suffering from any of the conditions referred to in paragraph 1. Such medical examinations may not be required as a matter of routine.

Article 30—Notification of Decisions

1. The persons concerned shall be notified in writing of any decision taken under Article 27(1), in such a way that they are able to comprehend its content and the implications for them.

2. The persons concerned shall be informed, precisely and in full, of the public policy, public security or public health grounds on which the decision taken in their case is based, unless this is contrary to the interests of State security.

3. The notification shall specify the court or administrative authority with which the person concerned may lodge an appeal, the time limit for the appeal and, where applicable, the time allowed for the person to leave the territory of the Member State. Save in duly substantiated cases of urgency, the time allowed to leave the territory shall be not less than one month from the date of notification.

Article 31—Procedural Safeguards

1. The persons concerned shall have access to judicial and, where appropriate, administrative redress procedures in the host Member State to appeal against or seek review of any decision taken against them on the grounds of public policy, public security or public health.

2. Where the application for appeal against or judicial review of the expulsion decision is accompanied by an application for an interim order to suspend enforcement of that decision, actual removal from the territory may not take place until such time as the decision on the interim order has been taken, except:

– where the expulsion decision is based on a previous judicial decision; or

– where the persons concerned have had previous access to judicial review; or

– where the expulsion decision is based on imperative grounds of public security under Article 28(3).

3. The redress procedures shall allow for an examination of the legality of the decision, as well as of the facts and circumstances on which the proposed measure is based. They shall ensure that the decision is not disproportionate, particularly in view of the requirements laid down in Article 28.

4. Member States may exclude the individual concerned from their territory pending the redress procedure, but they may not prevent the individual from submitting his/her defence in person, except when his/her appearance may cause serious troubles to public policy or public security or when the appeal or judicial review concerns a denial of entry to the territory.

Article 32—Duration of Exclusion Orders

1. Persons excluded on grounds of public policy or public security may submit an application for lifting of the exclusion order after a reasonable period, depending on the circumstances, and in any event after three years from enforcement of the final exclusion order which has been validly adopted in accordance with Community law, by putting forward arguments to establish that there has been a material change in the circumstances which justified the decision ordering their exclusion.

The Member State concerned shall reach a decision on this application within six months of its submission.

2. The persons referred to in paragraph 1 shall have no right of entry to the territory of the Member State concerned while their application is being considered.

Article 33—Expulsion as a Penalty or Legal Consequence

1. Expulsion orders may not be issued by the host Member State as a penalty or legal consequence of a custodial penalty, unless they conform to the requirements of Articles 27, 28 and 29.

2. If an expulsion order, as provided for in paragraph 1, is enforced more than two years after it was issued, the Member State shall check that the individual concerned is currently and genuinely a threat to public policy or public security and shall assess whether there has been any material change in the circumstances since the expulsion order was issued.

CHAPTER VII

FINAL PROVISIONS

Article 34—Publicity

Member States shall disseminate information concerning the rights and obligations of Union citizens and their family members on the subjects covered by this Directive, particularly by means of awareness-raising campaigns conducted through national and local media and other means of communication.

Article 35—Abuse of Rights

Member States may adopt the necessary measures to refuse, terminate or withdraw any right conferred by this Directive in the case of abuse of rights or fraud, such as marriages of convenience. Any such measure shall be proportionate and subject to the procedural safeguards provided for in Articles 30 and 31.

Article 36—Sanctions

Member States shall lay down provisions on the sanctions applicable to breaches of national rules adopted for the implementation of this Directive and shall take the measures required for their application. The sanctions laid down shall be effective and proportionate. Member States shall notify the Commission of these provisions not later than . . .[15] and as promptly as possible in the case of any subsequent changes.

Article 37—More Favourable National Provisions

The provisions of this Directive shall not affect any laws, regulations or administrative provisions laid down by a Member State which would be more favourable to the persons covered by this Directive.

Article 38—Repeals

1. Articles 10 and 11 of Regulation (EEC) No 1612/68 shall be repealed with effect from . . . [16].

2. Directives 64/221/EEC, 68/360/EEC, 72/194/EEC, 73/148/EEC, 75/34/EEC, 75/35/EEC, 90/364/EEC, 90/365/EEC and 93/96/EEC shall be repealed with effect from . . . . [17].

---

[15] Two years from the date of entry into force of this Directive.
[16] Two years from the date of entry into force of this Directive.
[17] Two years from the date of entry into force of this Directive.

3. References made to the repealed provisions and Directives shall be construed as being made to this Directive.

Article 39—Report

No later than. . . [18] the Commission shall submit a report on the application of this Directive to the European Parliament and the Council, together with any necessary proposals, notably on the opportunity to extend the period of time during which Union citizens and their family members may reside in the territory of the host Member State without any conditions. The Member States shall provide the Commission with the information needed to produce the report.

Article 40—Transposition

1. Member States shall bring into force the laws, regulations and administrative provisions necessary to comply with this Directive by . . . . [19]

When Member States adopt those measures, they shall contain a reference to this Directive or shall be accompanied by such a reference on the occasion of their official publication. The methods of making such reference shall be laid down by the Member States.

2. Member States shall communicate to the Commission the text of the provisions of national law which they adopt in the field covered by this Directive together with a table showing how the provisions of this Directive correspond to the national provisions adopted.

Article 41—Entry into Force

This Directive shall enter into force on the day of its publication in the Official Journal of the European Union.

Article 42—Addressees

This Directive is addressed to the Member States.

---

[18] Four years from the date of entry into force of this Directive.
[19] Two years from the date of entry into force of this Directive.

AGREEMENTS WITH THIRD COUNTRIES

AGREEMENT ON THE EEA (EXCERPTS): ARTICLES 28–35

[1992] O.J. L1/3

CHAPTER 1

WORKERS AND SELF-EMPLOYED PERSONS

Article 28

A18–01

1. Freedom of movement for workers shall be secured among E.C. Member States and EFTA States.

2. Such freedom of movement shall entail the abolition of any discrimination based on nationality between workers of E.C. Member States and EFTA States as regards employment, remuneration and other conditions of work and employment.

3. It shall entail the right, subject to limitations justified on grounds of public policy, public security or public health:

(a) to accept offers of employment actually made;

(b) to move freely within the territory of E.C. Member States and EFTA States for this purpose;

(c) to stay in the territory of an E.C. Member State or an EFTA State for the purpose of employment in accordance with the provisions governing the employment of nationals of that State laid down by law, regulation or administrative action;

(d) to remain in the territory of an E.C. Member State or an EFTA State after having been employed there.

4. The provisions of this Article shall not apply to employment in the public service.

5. Annex V contains specific provisions on the free movement of workers.

Article 29

In order to provide freedom of movement for workers and self-employed persons, the

Contracting Parties shall, in the field of social security, secure, as provided for in Annex VI, for workers and self-employed persons and their dependants, in particular:

(a) aggregation, for the purpose of acquiring and retaining the right to benefit and of calculating the amount of benefit, of all periods taken into account under the laws of the several countries;

(b) payment of benefits to persons resident in the territories of Contracting Parties.

Article 30

In order to make it easier for persons to take up and pursue activities as workers and self-employed persons, the Contracting Parties shall take the necessary measures, as contained in Annex VII, concerning the mutual recognition of diplomas, certificates and other evidence of formal qualifications, and the coordination of the provisions laid down by law, regulation or administrative action in the Contracting Parties concerning the taking up and pursuit of activities by workers and self-employed persons.

CHAPTER 2

RIGHT OF ESTABLISHMENT

Article 31

1. Within the framework of the provisions of this Agreement, there shall be no restrictions on the freedom of establishment of nationals of an E.C. Member State or an EFTA State in the territory of any other of these States. This shall also apply to the setting up of agencies, branches or subsidiaries by nationals of any E.C. Member State or EFTA State established in the territory of any of these States.

Freedom of establishment shall include the right to take up and pursue activities as self-employed persons and to set up and manage undertakings, in particular companies or firms within the meaning of Article 34, second paragraph, under the conditions laid down for its own nationals by the law of the country where such establishment is effected, subject to the provisions of Chapter 4.

2. Annexes VIII to XI contain specific provisions on the right of establishment.

Article 32

The provisions of this Chapter shall not apply, so far as any given Contracting Party is concerned, to activities which in that Contracting Party are connected, even occasionally, with the exercise of official authority.

Article 33

The provisions of this Chapter and measures taken in pursuance thereof shall not prejudice the applicability of provisions laid down by law, regulation or administrative action providing for special treatment for foreign nationals on grounds of public policy, public security or public health.

Article 34

Companies or firms formed in accordance with the law of an E.C. Member State or an EFTA State and having their registered office, central administration or principal place of business within the territory of the Contracting Parties shall, for the purposes of this Chapter, be treated in the same way as natural persons who are nationals of E.C. Member States or EFTA States.

"Companies or firms" means companies or firms constituted under civil or commercial law, including cooperative societies, and other legal persons governed by public or private law, save for those which are non-profit-making.

Article 35

The provisions of Article 30 shall apply to the matters covered by this Chapter.

ANNEX V

FREE MOVEMENT OF WORKERS

LIST PROVIDED FOR IN ARTICLE 28

Introduction

When the acts referred to in this Annex contain notions or refer to procedures which are specific to the

Community legal order, such as:

- preambles;
- the addressees of the Community acts;
- references to territories or languages of the E.C.;
- references to rights and obligations of E.C. Member States, their public entities, undertakings or individuals in relation to each other; and
- references to information and notification procedures;

Protocol 1 on horizontal adaptations shall apply, unless otherwise provided for in this Annex.

Sectoral Adaptations

For the purposes of this Annex and notwithstanding the provisions of Protocol 1, the term "Member State(s)" contained in the acts referred to shall be understood to include, in addition to its meaning in the relevant E.C. acts, Austria, Finland, Iceland, Liechtenstein, Norway, Sweden.[1]

The provisions in the SECTORAL ADAPTATIONS in Annex VIII concerning Liechtenstein shall apply, as appropriate, to this Annex.[2]

Transition Period[3]

The transitional arrangements set out in the Annexes to the Act of Accession of 16 April 2003 for the Czech Republic (Annex V, Chapter 1), Estonia (Annex VI, Chapter 1), Latvia (Annex VIII, Chapter 1), Lithuania (Annex IX, Chapter 2), Hungary (Annex X, Chapter 1), Malta (Annex XI, Chapter 2), Poland (Annex XII, Chapter 2), Slovenia (Annex XIII, Chapter 2) and the Slovak Republic (Annex XIV, Chapter 1) shall apply.

With regard to the safeguard mechanisms contained in the transitional arrangements referred to in the previous paragraph, with the exception of the arrangements for Malta, PROTOCOL 44 ON SAFEGUARD MECHANISMS CONTAINED IN THE ACT OF ACCESSION OF 16 APRIL 2003 shall apply.

Acts Referred to

1.   **364 L 0221:** Council Directive 64/221/EEC of 25 February 1964 on the co-ordination of special measures concerning the movement and residence of foreign nationals which are justified on grounds of public policy, public security or public health (OJ No 56, 4.4.1964, p.850/64).

     The provisions of the Directive shall, for the purposes of the present Agreement, be read with the following adaptation:

     Article 4(3) shall not apply.

2.   **368 R 1612:** Council Regulation (EEC) No 1612/68 of 15 October 1968 on freedom of movement for workers within the Community (OJ No L 257, 19.10.1968, p.2), as amended by:

     –   **376 R 0312:** Council Regulation (EEC) No 312/76 of 9 February 1976 (OJ No L 39, 14.2.1976, p.2),

---

[1] Words "and Switzerland" deleted by the Adjusting Protocol.
[2] Text added by Decision No 191/1999 (OJ No L 74, 15.3.2001, p. 29 and EEA Supplement No 14, 15.3.2001, p. 130 (Norwegian) and p. 217 (Icelandic)), e.i.f. 1.6.2000.
[3] Heading and text added by the EEA Enlargement Agreement (OJ L 130, 29.4.2004, p. 3 and EEA Supplement No 23, 29.4.2004, p. 1), e.i.f. 1.5.2004.

–[4] **392 R 2434:** Council Regulation (EEC) No 2434/92 of 27 July 1992 (OJ No L 245, 26.8.1992, p.1).

The provisions of the Regulation shall, for the purposes of the present Agreement, be read with the following adaptations:

[ ][5]

(b) Article 40 shall not apply;

(c) Article 41 shall not apply;

(d) Article 42(1) shall not apply;

(e) In Article 42(2), the reference to Article 51 of the EEC Treaty shall be replaced by reference to Article 29 of this Agreement;

(f) Article 48 shall not apply.

3. **368 L 0360:** Council Directive 68/360/EEC of 15 October 1968 on the abolition of restrictions on movement and residence within the Community for workers of Member States and their families (OJ No L 257, 19.10.1968, p.13), as amended by:

–[6] **1 03 T:** Act concerning the conditions of accession of the Czech Republic, the Republic of Estonia, the Republic of Cyprus, the Republic of Latvia, the Republic of Lithuania, the Republic of Hungary, the Republic of Malta, the Republic of Poland, the Republic of Slovenia and the Slovak Republic and the adjustments of the Treaties on which the European Union is founded adopted on 16 April 2003.

The provisions of the Directive shall, for the purposes of the present Agreement, be read with the following adaptations:

(a) in Article 4(2), the words "Residence Permit for a national of a Member State of the EEC" shall be replaced by "Residence Permit";

(b) in Article 4(3), the words "Residence Permit for a national of a Member State of the EEC" shall be replaced by "Residence Permit";

(c) Article 11 shall not apply;

(d) Article 13 shall not apply;

(e) in the Annex:

    (i) the first paragraph of the statement shall be replaced by the following:

    "This permit is issued pursuant to Regulation (EEC) No 1612/68 of 15 October 1968 and to the measures taken in implementation of Directive 68/360/EEC as integrated into the EEA Agreement.";

    [7](ii) the footnote shall be replaced by the following:

    "Belgian, Czech, Danish, German, Estonian, Greek, Icelandic, Spanish, French, Irish, Italian, Cypriot, Latvian, Liechtenstein, Lithuanian, Luxembourg, Hungarian, Maltese, Netherlands, Norwegian, Austrian, Polish, Portugese, Slovenian, Slovakian, Finnish, Swedish and British according to the country issuing the permit.";

4. **370 R 1251:** Commission Regulation (EEC) No 1251/70 of 29 June 1970 on the

---

[4] Indent added by Decision No 7/94.

[5] Adaptation deleted by Decision No 7/94.

[6] Indent and words ", as amended by:" added by the EEA Enlargement Agreement (OJ L 130, 29.4.2004, p.3 and EEA Supplement No 23, 29.4.2004, p.1) e.i.f. 1.5.2004.

[7] Adaptation (e)(ii) replaced by the EEA Enlargement Agreement (OJ L 130, 29.4.2004, p.3 and EEA Supplement No. 23, 29.4.2004, p.1), e.i.f. 1.5.2004.

right of workers to remain in the territory of a Member State after having been employed in that State (OJ No L 142, 30.6.1970, p.24).

The provisions of the Regulation shall, for the purposes of the present Agreement, be read with the following adaptation:

Article 9 shall not apply.

5.   **372 L 0194:** Council Directive 72/194/EEC of 18 May 1972 extending to workers exercising the right to remain in the territory of a Member State after having been employed in that State the scope of Directive 64/221/EEC (OJ No L 121, 26.5.1972, p.32).

6.   **377 L 0486:** Council Directive 77/486/EEC of 25 July 1977 on the education of the children of migrant workers (OJ No L 199, 6.8.1977, p.32).

7.[8] **32003 D 0008:** Commission Decision 2003/8/EC of 23 December 2002 implementing Council Regulation (EEC) No 1612/68 as regards the clearance of vacancies and applications for employment (OJ L 5, 10.1.2003, p.16).

---

[8] Point (Commission Decision 93/569/EC) inserted by Decision No 7/94, and replaced by Decision No 7/2004 (OJ No L 116, 22.4.2004, p.52 and EEA Supplement No 20, 22.4.2004, p.10), e.i.f. 7.2.2004.

AGREEMENT BETWEEN THE EUROPEAN COMMUNITY AND ITS MEMBER STATES, OF THE ONE PART, AND THE SWISS CONFEDERATION, OF THE OTHER, ON THE FREE MOVEMENT OF PERSONS

[2002] O.J. L114/6

THE SWISS CONFEDERATION, of the one part,

and

THE EUROPEAN COMMUNITY, THE KINGDOM OF BELGIUM, THE KINGDOM OF DENMARK, THE FEDERAL REPUBLIC OF GERMANY, THE HELLENIC REPUBLIC, THE KINGDOM OF SPAIN, THE FRENCH REPUBLIC, IRELAND, THE ITALIAN REPUBLIC, THE GRAND DUCHY OF LUXEMBOURG, THE KINGDOM OF THE NETHERLANDS, THE REPUBLIC OF AUSTRIA, THE PORTUGUESE REPUBLIC, THE REPUBLIC OF FINLAND, THE KINGDOM OF SWEDEN, THE UNITED KINGDOM OF GREAT BRITAIN AND NORTHERN IRELAND, of the other part, HEREINAFTER referred to as 'the Contracting Parties',

Convinced that the free movement of persons between the territories of the Contracting Parties is a key factor in the harmonious development of their relations,

A19–01

Resolved to bring about the free movement of persons between them on the basis of the rules applying in the European Community,

Have decided to conclude this Agreement:

I. BASIC PROVISIONS

Article 1

Objective

The objective of this Agreement, for the benefit of nationals of the Member States of the European Community and Switzerland, is:

(a) to accord a right of entry, residence, access to work as employed persons, establishment on a self-employed basis and the right to stay in the territory of the Contracting Parties;

(b) to facilitate the provision of services in the territory of the Contracting Parties, and in particular to liberalise the provision of services of brief duration;

(c) to accord a right of entry into, and residence in, the territory of the Contracting Parties to persons without an economic activity in the host country;

(d) to accord the same living, employment and working conditions as those accorded to nationals.

Article 2

Non-discrimination

Nationals of one Contracting Party who are lawfully resident in the territory of another Contracting Party shall not, in application of and in accordance with the provisions of Annexes I, II and III to this Agreement, be the subject of any discrimination on grounds of nationality.

Article 3

Right of entry

The right of entry of nationals of one Contracting Party into the territory of another Contracting Party shall be guaranteed in accordance with the provisions laid down in Annex I.

Article 4

Right of residence and access to an economic activity

The right of residence and access to an economic activity shall be guaranteed unless otherwise provided in Article 10 and inaccordance with the provisions of Annex I.

Article 5

Persons providing services

1. Without prejudice to other specific agreements between the Contracting Parties specifically concerning the provision of services (including the Government Procurement Agreement in so far as it covers the provision of services), persons providing services, including companies in accordance with the provisions of Annex I, shall have the right to provide a service in the territory of the other Contracting Party for a period not exceeding 90 days' of actual work in a calendar year.

2. Providers of services shall have the right of entry into, and residence in, the territory of the other Contracting Party:

(a) where they have the right to provide a service under paragraph 1 or by virtue of the provisions of an agreement mentioned in paragraph 1;

(b) or, if the conditions specified in (a) are not fulfilled, where they have received authorisation to provide a service from the competent authorities of the Contracting Party concerned.

3. Nationals of a Member State of the European Community or Switzerland entering the territory of a Contracting Party solely to receive services shall have the right of entry and residence.

4. The rights referred to in this Article shall be guaranteed in accordance with the provisions laid down in Annexes I, II and III. The quantitative limits of Article 10 may not be relied upon as against persons referred to in this Article.

Article 6

Right of residence for persons not pursuing an economic activity

The right of residence in the territory of a Contracting Party shall be guaranteed to persons not pursuing an economic activity in accordance with the provisions of Annex I relating to non-active people.

Article 7

Other rights

The Contracting Parties shall make provision, in accordance with Annex I, for the following rights in relation to the free movement of persons:

(a) the right to equal treatment with nationals in respect of access to, and the pursuit of, an economic activity, and living, employment and working conditions;

(b) the right to occupational and geographical mobility which enables nationals of the Contracting Parties to move freely within the territory of the host state and to pursue the occupation of their choice;

(c) the right to stay in the territory of a Contracting Party after the end of an economic activity;

(d) the right of residence for members of the family, irrespective of their nationality;

(e) the right of family members to pursue an economic activity, irrespective of their nationality;

(f) the right to acquire immovable property in so far as this is linked to the exercise of rights conferred by this Agreement;

(g) during the transitional period, the right, after the end of an economic activity or period of residence in the territory of a Contracting Party, to return there for the purposes of pursuing an economic activity and the right to have a temporary residence permit converted into a permanent one.

Article 8

Coordination of social security systems

The Contracting Parties shall make provision, in accordance with Annex II, for the coordination of social security systems with the aim in particular of:

(a)   securing equality of treatment;

(b)   determining the legislation applicable;

(c)   aggregation, for the purpose of acquiring and retaining the right to benefits, and of calculating such benefits, all periods taken into consideration by the national legislation of the countries concerned;

(d)   paying benefits to persons residing in the territory of the Contracting Parties;

(e)   fostering mutual administrative assistance and cooperation between authorities and institutions.

Article 9

Diplomas, certificates and other qualifications

In order to make it easier for nationals of the Member States of the European Community and Switzerland to gain access to and pursue activities as employed and self-employed persons and to provide services, the Contracting Parties shall take the necessary measures, in accordance with Annex III, concerning the mutual recognition of diplomas, certificates and other qualifications, and coordination of the laws, regulations and administrative provisions of the Contracting Parties on access to and pursuit of activities as employed and self-employed persons and the provision of services.

II. GENERAL AND FINAL PROVISIONS

Article 10

Transitional provisions and development of the Agreement

1. For five years after the entry into force of the Agreement, Switzerland may maintain quantitative limits in respect of access to an economic activity for the following two categories of residence: residence for a period of more than four months and less than one year and residence for a period equal to, or exceeding, one year. There shall be no restriction on residence for less than four months.

From the beginning of the sixth year, all quantitative limits applicable to nationals of the Member States of the European Community shall be abolished.

2. For a maximum period of two years, the Contracting Parties may maintain the controls on the priority of workers integrated into the regular labour market and wage and working conditions applicable to nationals of the other Contracting Party, including the persons providing services referred to in Article 5. Before the end of the first year, the Joint Committee shall consider whether these restrictions need to be maintained. It may curtail the maximum period of two years. The controls on the priority of workers integrated into the regular labour market shall not apply to providers of services liberalised by a specific agreement between the Contracting Parties concerning the provision of services (including the Agreement on certain aspects of government procurement in so far as it covers the provision of services).

3. On entry into force of this Agreement and until the end of the fifth year, each year Switzerland shall reserve, within its overall quotas, for employed and self-employed

persons of the European Community at least 15 000 new residence permits valid for a period equal to, or exceeding, one year and 115 500 valid for more than four months and less than one year.

4. Notwithstanding the provisions of paragraph 3, the Contracting Parties have agreed on the following arrangements: if, after five years and up to 12 years after the entry into force of the Agreement, the number of new residence permits of either of the categories referred to in paragraph 1 issued to employed and self-employed persons of the European Community in a given year exceeds the average for the three preceding years by more than 10 %, Switzerland may, for the following year, unilaterally limit the number of new residence permits of that category for employed and self-employed persons of the European Community to the average of the three preceding years plus 5 %. The following year, the number may be limited to the same level.

Notwithstanding the provisions of the previous subparagraph, the number of new residence permits issued to employed and self-employed persons of the European Community may not be limited to fewer than 15 000 per year valid for a period equal to, or exceeding, one year and 115 500 per year valid for more than four months and less than one year.

5. The transitional provisions of paragraphs 1 to 4, and in particular those of paragraph 2 concerning the priority of workers integrated into the regular labour market and controls on wage and working conditions, shall not apply to employed and self-employed persons who, at the time of this Agreement's entry into force, are authorised to pursue an economic activity in the territory of the Contracting Parties. Such persons shall in particular enjoy occupational and geographical mobility. The holders of residence permits valid for less than one year shall be entitled to have their permits renewed; the exhaustion of quantitative limits may not be invoked against them. The holders of residence permits valid for a period equal to, or exceeding, one year shall automatically be entitled to have their permits extended. Such employed and self-employed persons shall therefore enjoy the rights to free movement accorded to established persons in the basic provisions of this Agreement, and in particular Article 7 thereof, from its entry into force.

6. Switzerland shall regularly and promptly forward to the Joint Committee any useful statistics and information, including measures implementing paragraph 2. A Contracting Party may request a review of the situation within the Joint Committee.

7. No quantitative limits may be applied to frontier workers.

8. The transitional provisions on social security and the retrocession of unemployment insurance contributions are laid down in the Protocol to Annex II.

Article 11

Processing of appeals

1. The persons covered by this Agreement shall have a right of appeal to the competent authorities in respect of the application of the provisions of this Agreement.

2. Appeals must be processed within a reasonable period of time.

3. Persons covered by this Agreement shall have the opportunity to appeal to the competent national judicial body in respect of decisions on appeals, or the absence of a decision within a reasonable period of time.

Article 12

More favourable provisions

This Agreement shall not preclude any more favourable national provisions which may exist for both nationals of the Contracting Parties and their family members.

Article 13

Standstill

The Contracting Parties undertake not to adopt any further restrictive measures vis-à-vis each other's nationals in fields covered by this Agreement.

Article 14

Joint Committee

1. A Joint Committee composed of representatives of the Contracting Parties is hereby established. It shall be responsible for the management and proper application of the Agreement. To that end it shall issue recommendations. It shall take decisions in the circumstances provided for in the Agreement. The Joint Committee shall reach its decisions by mutual agreement.

2. In the event of serious economic or social difficulties, the Joint Committee shall meet, at the request of either Contracting Party, to examine appropriate measures to remedy the situation. The Joint Committee may decide what measures to take within 60 days of the date of the request. This period may be extended by the Joint Committee. The scope and duration of such measures shall not exceed that which is strictly necessary to remedy the situation. Preference shall be given to measures that least disrupt the working of this Agreement.

3. For the purposes of proper implementation of the Agreement, the Contracting Parties shall regularly exchange information and, at the request of either of them, shall consult each other within the Joint Committee.

4. The Joint Committee shall meet as and when necessary and at least once a year. Either Party may request the convening of a meeting. The Joint Committee shall meet within 15 days of a request under paragraph 2.

5. The Joint Committee shall establish its rules of procedure which shall contain, inter alia, provisions on the convening of meetings, the appointment of the chairman and the chairman's term of office.

6. The Joint Committee may decide to set up any working party or group of experts to assist it in the performance of its duties.

Article 15

Annexes and Protocols

The Annexes and Protocols to this Agreement shall form an integral part thereof. The Final Act shall contain the declarations.

Article 16

Reference to Community law

1. In order to attain the objectives pursued by this Agreement, the Contracting Parties shall take all measures necessary to ensure that rights and obligations equivalent to those contained in the legal acts of the European Community to which reference is made are applied in relations between them.

2. Insofar as the application of this Agreement involves concepts of Community law, account shall be taken of the relevant case-law of the Court of Justice of the European Communities prior to the date of its signature. Case-law after that date shall be brought to Switzerland's attention. To ensure that the Agreement works properly, the Joint Committee shall, at the request of either Contracting Party, determine the implications of such case-law.

Article 17

Development of law

1. As soon as one Contracting Party initiates the process of adopting a draft amendment to its domestic legislation, or as soon as there is a change in the case-law of authorities against whose decisions there is no judicial remedy under domestic law in a field governed by this Agreement, it shall inform the other Contracting Party through the Joint Committee.

2. The Joint Committee shall hold an exchange of views on the implications of such an amendment for the proper functioning of the Agreement.

Article 18

Revision

If a Contracting Party wishes to have this Agreement revised, it shall submit a proposal to that effect to the Joint Committee. Amendments to this Agreement shall enter into force after the respective internal procedures have been completed, with the exception of amendments to Annexes II and III, which shall be adopted by decision of the Joint Committee and may enter into force immediately after that decision.

Article 19

Settlement of disputes

1. The Contracting Parties may bring a matter under dispute which concerns the interpretation or application of this Agreement to the Joint Committee.

2. The Joint Committee may settle the dispute. Any information which might be of use in making possible an in-depth examination of the situation with a view to finding an acceptable solution shall be supplied to the Joint Committee. To this end, the Joint Committee shall consider every possible means to maintain the good functioning of this Agreement.

Article 20

Relationship to bilateral social security agreements

Unless otherwise provided for under Annex II, bilateral social security agreements between Switzerland and the Member States of the European Community shall be suspended on the entry into force of this Agreement, in so far as the latter covers the same subject-matter.

Article 21

Relationship to bilateral agreements on double taxation

1. The provisions of bilateral agreements between Switzerland and the Member States of the European Community on double taxation shall be unaffected by the provisions of this Agreement. In particular, the provisions of this Agreement shall not affect the double taxation agreements' definition of 'frontier workers'.

2. No provision of this Agreement may be interpreted in such a way as to prevent the Contracting Parties from distinguishing, when applying the relevant provisions of their fiscal legislation, between taxpayers whose situations are not comparable, especially as regards their place of residence.

3. No provision of this Agreement shall prevent the Contracting Parties from adopting or applying measures to ensure the imposition, payment and effective recovery of taxes or to forestall tax evasion under their national tax legislation or agreements aimed at preventing double taxation between Switzerland, of the one part, and one or more Member States of the European Community, of the other part, or any other tax arrangements.

Article 22

Relationship to bilateral agreements on matters other than social security and double taxation

1. Notwithstanding the provisions of Articles 20 and 21, this Agreement shall not affect agreements linking Switzerland, of the one part, and one or more Member States of the European Community, of the other part, such as those concerning

private individuals, economic operators, cross-border cooperation or local frontier traffic, in so far as they are compatible with this Agreement.

2. In the event of incompatibilities between such agreements and this Agreement, the latter shall prevail.

Article 23

Acquired rights

In the event of termination or non-renewal, rights acquired by private individuals shall not be affected. The Contracting Parties shall settle by mutual agreement what action is to be taken in respect of rights in the process of being acquired.

Article 24

Territorial scope

This Agreement shall apply, on the one hand, to the territory of Switzerland and, on the other hand, to the territories in which the Treaty establishing the European Community is applicable and under the conditions laid down by that Treaty.

Article 25

Entry into force and duration

1. This Agreement shall be ratified or approved by the Contracting Parties in accordance with their own procedures. It shall enter into force on the first day of the second month following the last notification of deposit of the instruments of ratification or approval of all seven of the following agreements:

Agreement on the free movement of persons

Agreement on air transport

Agreement on the carriage of passengers and goods by road and rail

Agreement on trade in agricultural products

Agreement on the mutual recognition of conformity assessment

Agreement on certain aspects of government procurement

Agreement on scientific and technological cooperation.

2. This Agreement shall be concluded for an initial period of seven years. It shall be renewed indefinitely unless the European Community or Switzerland notifies the other Contracting Party to the contrary before the initial period expires. In the event of such notification, paragraph 4 shall apply.

3. The European Community or Switzerland may terminate this Agreement by notifying its decision to the other Party. In the event of such notification, the provisions of paragraph 4 shall apply.

[551]

FREE MOVEMENT OF PERSONS

I. GENERAL PROVISIONS

Article 1

Entry and exit

1. The Contracting Parties shall allow nationals of the other Contracting Parties and members of their family within the meaning of Article 3 of this Annex and posted persons within the meaning of Article 17 of this Annex to enter their territory simply upon production of a valid identity card or passport.

No entry visa or equivalent requirement may be demanded save in respect of members of the family and posted workers within the meaning of Article 17 of this Annex who do not have the nationality of a Contracting Party. The Contracting Party concerned shall grant these persons every facility for obtaining any necessary visas.

2. The Contracting Parties shall grant nationals of the Contracting Parties, and members of their family within the meaning of Article 3 of this Annex and posted workers within the meaning of Article 17 of this Annex, the right to leave their territory simply upon production of a valid identity card or passport. The Contracting Parties may not demand any exit visa or equivalent requirement from nationals of the other Contracting Parties.

The Contracting Parties, acting in accordance with their laws, shall issue to such nationals, or renew, an identity card or passport, which shall state in particular the holder's nationality.

The passport must be valid at least for all the Contracting Parties and for the countries through which the holder must pass when travelling between them. Where the passport is the only document on which the holder may lawfully leave the country, its period of validity may not be less than five years.

Article 2

Residence and economic activity

1. Without prejudice to the provisions for the transitional period, which are laid down in Article 10 of this Agreement and Chapter VII of this Annex, nationals of a Contracting Party shall have the right to reside and pursue an economic activity in the territory of the other Contracting Party under the procedures laid down in Chapters II to IV. That right shall be substantiated through the issue of a residence permit or, for persons from frontier zones, by means of a special permit.

Nationals of a Contracting Party shall also have the right to visit another Contracting Party or to remain there after a period of employment of less than one year in order to seek employment and to reside there for a reasonable amount of time, which may be up to six months, to allow them to find out about the employment opportunities corresponding to their professional qualifications and, if necessary, take the appropriate steps to take up employment. Those seeking employment shall have the right, in the territory of the Contracting Party concerned, to receive the same assistance as employment agencies in that state grant to its own nationals. They may be excluded from social security schemes for the duration of such residence.

2. Nationals of the Contracting Parties not pursuing any economic activity in the host State who do not have a right of residence pursuant to other provisions of this Agreement shall, provided they fulfil the preconditions laid down in Chapter V, have a right of residence. That right shall be substantiated through the issue of a residence permit.

3. The residence or special permit granted to nationals of the Contracting Parties shall be issued and renewed free of charge or on payment of a sum not exceeding the charges or taxes which nationals are required to pay for the issue of identity cards. The Contracting Parties shall take the necessary measures to simplify the formalities and procedures for obtaining those documents as far as possible.

4. The Contracting Parties may require nationals of the other Contracting Parties to report their presence in the territory.

Article 3

Members of the family

1. A person who has the right of residence and is a national of a Contracting Party is entitled to be joined by the members of his family. An employed person must possess housing for his family which is regarded as of normal standard for national employed persons in the region where he is employed, but this provision may not lead to discrimination between national employed persons and employed persons from the other Contracting Party.

2. The following shall be regarded as members of the family, whatever their nationality:

(a) his spouse and their relatives in the descending line who are under the age of 21 or are dependent;

(b) his relatives in the ascending line and those of his spouse who are dependent on him;

(c) in the case of a student, his spouse and their dependent children.

The Contracting Parties shall facilitate the admission of any member of the family not covered by the provisions of this paragraph under (a), (b) and (c), if that person is a dependant or lives in the household of the national of a Contracting Party in the country of provenance.

3. When issuing a residence permit to members of the family of a national of a Contracting Party, the Contracting Parties may require only the documents listed below:

(a) the document by virtue of which they entered the territory;

(b) a document issued by the competent authority of the state of origin or provenance proving their relationship;

(c) for dependants, a document issued by the competent authority of the state of origin or provenance certifying that they are dependants of the person referred to in paragraph 1 or that they live in his household in that state.

4. The period of validity of a residence permit issued to a member of the family shall be the same as that of the permit issued to the person on whom he is dependent.

5. The spouse and the dependent children or children aged under 21 of a person having a right of residence shall have the right to take up an economic activity whatever their nationality.

6. The children of a national of a Contracting Party, whether or not he is pursuing or has pursued an economic activity in the territory of the other Contracting Party, shall be admitted to general education, apprenticeships and vocational training courses on the same basis as nationals of the host state, if those children are living in its territory.

The Contracting Parties shall promote initiatives to enable such children to follow the abovementioned courses under the best conditions.

Article 4

Right to stay

1. Nationals of a Contracting Party and members of their family shall have the right to stay in the territory of another Contracting Party after their economic activity has finished.

2. In accordance with Article 16 of the Agreement, reference is made to Regulation (EEC) No 1251/70 (OJ L 142, 1970, p. 24) ([1]) and Directive 75/34/EEC (OJ L 14, 1975, p. 10) ([1]).

Article 5

Public order

1. The rights granted under the provisions of this Agreement may be restricted only by means of measures which are justified on grounds of public order, public security or public health.

2. In accordance with Article 16 of the Agreement, reference is made to Directives 64/221/EEC (OJ L 56, 4.4.1964, p. 850/64) ([1]), 72/194/EEC (OJ L 121, 26.5.1972, p. 32) ([1]) and 75/35/EEC (OJ L 14, 20.1.1975, p. 14) ([1]).

([1]) As in force at the date of signing the Agreement.

II. EMPLOYED PERSONS

Article 6

Rules regarding residence

1. An employed person who is a national of a Contracting Party (hereinafter referred to as 'employed person') and is employed for a period of one year or more by an employer in the host state shall receive a residence permit which is valid for at least five years from its date of issue. It shall be extended automatically for a period of at least five years. When renewed for the first time, its period of validity may be limited, but not to less than one year, where its holder has been involuntarily unemployed for more than 12 consecutive months.

2. An employed person who is employed for a period of more than three months but less than one year by an employer in the host state shall receive a residence permit for the same duration as his contract.

An employed person who is employed for a period of up to three months does not require a residence permit.

3. When issuing residence permits, the Contracting Parties may not require an employed person to produce more than the following documents:

(a) the document by virtue of which he entered their territory;

(b) a contractual statement from the employer or a written confirmation of engagement.

4. A residence permit shall be valid throughout the territory of the issuing state.

5. Breaks in residence of less than six consecutive months and absences for the purposes of fulfilling military service obligations shall not affect the validity of the residence permit.

6. A valid residence permit may not be withdrawn from an employed person merely on the grounds that he is no longer working, either because he has become temporarily unable to work owing to an accident or illness, or because he is involuntarily unemployed as certified by the competent employment office.

7. Completion of the formalities for obtaining a residence permit shall not prevent an applicant immediately taking up employment under the contract he has concluded.

Article 7

Employed frontier workers

1. An employed frontier worker is a national of a Contracting Party who has his residence in the territory of a Contracting Party and who pursues an activity as an employed person in the territory of the other Contracting Party, returning to his place of residence as a rule every day, or at least once a week.

2. Frontier workers shall not require a residence permit.

The competent authorities of the state of employment may nevertheless issue the frontier worker with a special permit for a period of at least five years or for the duration of his employment where this is longer than three months and less than one year. It shall be extended for at least five years provided that the frontier worker furnishes proof that he is actually pursuing an economic activity.

3. Special permits shall be valid throughout the territory of the issuing state.

Article 8

Occupational and geographical mobility

1. Employed persons shall have the right to occupational and geographical mobility throughout the territory of the host state.

2. Occupational mobility shall include changes of employer, employment or occupation and changing from employed to self-employed status. Geographical mobility shall include changes in the place of work and residence.

Article 9

Equal treatment

1. An employed person who is a national of a Contracting Party may not, by reason of his nationality, be treated differently in the territory of the other Contracting Party from national employed persons as regards conditions of employment and working conditions, especially as regards pay, dismissal, or reinstatement or re-employment if he becomes unemployed.

2. An employed person and the members of his family referred to in Article 3 of this Annex shall enjoy the same tax concessions and welfare benefits as national employed persons and members of their family.

3. He shall also be entitled on the same basis and on the same terms as national employed persons to education in vocational training establishments and in vocational retraining and occupational rehabilitation centres.

4. Any clause in a collective or individual agreement or in any other collective arrangements concerning access to employment, employment, pay and other terms of employment and dismissal, shall be automatically void insofar as it provides for or authorises discriminatory conditions with respect to foreign employed persons who are nationals of the Contracting Parties.

5. An employed person who is a national of a Contracting Party and is employed in the territory of the other Contracting Party shall enjoy equal treatment in terms of membership of trade union organisations and exercise of union rights, including the right to vote and right of access to executive or managerial positions within a trade union organisation; he may be precluded from involvement in the management of public law bodies and from holding an office governed by public law. He shall, moreover, have the right to be eligible for election to bodies representing employees in an undertaking.

These provisions shall be without prejudice to laws or regulations in the host state which confer more extensive rights on employed persons from the other Contracting Party.

6. Without prejudice to the provisions of Article 26 of this Annex, an employed person who is a national of a Contracting Party and employed in the territory of the other Contracting Party shall enjoy all the rights and all the advantages accorded to national employed persons in terms of housing, including ownership of the housing he needs.

Such a worker shall have the same right as nationals to register on the housing lists in the region in which he is employed, where such lists exist; he shall enjoy the resultant benefits and priorities.

If his family has remained in his state of provenance, it shall be considered for this purpose as residing in the said region, where national workers benefit from a similar presumption.

Article 10

Public service employment

A national of a Contracting Party pursuing an activity as an employed person may be refused the right to take up employment in the public service which involves the exercise of the state or other public bodies.

Article 11

Cooperation in relation to employment services.

The Contracting Parties shall cooperate, within the EURES (European Employment Services) network, in particular in setting up contacts, matching job vacancies and applications and exchanging information on the state of the labour market and living and working conditions.

III. SELF-EMPLOYED PERSONS

Article 12

Rules regarding residence

1. A national of a Contracting Party wishing to become established in the territory of another Contracting Party in order to pursue a self-employed activity (hereinafter referred to as a 'self-employed person') shall receive a residence permit valid for a period of at least five years from its date of issue, provided that he produces evidence to the competent national authorities that he is established or wishes to become so.

2. The residence permit shall be extended automatically for a period of at least five years, provided that the self-employed person produces evidence to the competent national authorities that he is pursuing a self-employed economic activity.

3. When issuing residence permits, the Contracting Parties may not require self-employed persons to produce more than the following:

(a)   the document by virtue of which he entered their territory;

(b)   the evidence referred to in paragraphs 1 and 2.

4. A residence permit shall be valid throughout the territory of the issuing state.

5. Breaks in residence of less than six consecutive months and absences for the purposes of fulfilling military service obligations shall not affect the validity of the residence permit.

6. Valid residence permits may not be withdrawn from persons referred to in paragraph 1 merely because they are no longer working owing to temporary incapacity as a result of illness or accident.

Article 13

Self-employed frontier workers

1. A self-employed frontier worker is a national of a Contracting Party who is resident in the territory of a Contracting Party and who pursues a self-employed activity in the territory of the other Contracting Party, returning to his place of residence as a rule every day or at least once a week.

2. Self-employed frontier workers shall not require a residence permit.

The relevant authorities of the state concerned may nevertheless issue a self-employed frontier worker with a special permit valid for at least five years provided that he produces evidence to the competent national authorities that he is pursuing or wishes to pursue a self-employed activity. The permit shall be extended for at least five years, provided that the frontier worker produces evidence that he is pursuing a self-employed activity.

3. Special permits shall be valid throughout the territory of the issuing state.

Article 14

Occupational and geographical mobility

1. Self-employed persons shall have the right to occupational and geographical mobility throughout the territory of the host state.

2. Occupational mobility shall include change of occupation and changing from self-employed to employed status. Geographical mobility shall include changes in the place of work and residence.

Article 15

Equal treatment

1. As regards access to a self-employed activity and the pursuit thereof, a self-employed worker shall be afforded no less favourable treatment in the host country than that accorded to its own nationals.

2. The provisions of Article 9 of this Annex shall apply mutatis mutandis to the self-employed persons referred to in this Chapter.

Article 16

Exercise of public authority

A self-employed person may be denied the right to pursue an activity involving, even on an occasional basis, the exercise of public authority.

IV. PROVISION OF SERVICES

Article 17

Persons providing services

With regard to the provision of services, the following shall be prohibited under Article 5 of this Agreement:

(a) any restriction on the cross-frontier provision of services in the territory of a Contracting Party not exceeding 90 days of actual work per calendar year;

(b) any restriction on the right of entry and residence in the cases covered by Article 5(2) of this Agreement concerning:

(i) persons providing services who are nationals of the Member States of the European Community or Switzerland and are established in the territory of a Contracting Party other than that of the person receiving services;

(ii) employees, irrespective of their nationality, of persons providing services, who are integrated into one Contracting Party's regular labour market and posted for the provision of a service in the territory of another Contracting Party without prejudice to Article 1.

Article 18

The provisions of Article 17 of this Annex shall apply to companies formed in accordance with the law of a Member State of the European Community or Switzerland and having their registered office, central administration or principal place of business in the territory of a Contracting Party.

Article 19

A person providing services who has the right or has been authorised to provide a service may, for the purposes of its provision, temporarily pursue his activity in the state in which the service is provided on the same terms as those imposed by that state on its own nationals, in accordance with the provisions of this Annex and Annexes II and III.

Article 20

1. Persons referred to in Article 17(b) of this Annex who have the right to provide a service shall not require a residence permit for periods of residence of 90 days or less. Such residence shall be covered by the documents referred to in Article 1, by virtue of which they entered the territory.

2. Persons referred to in Article 17(b) of this Annex who have the right or have been authorised to provide a service for a period exceeding 90 days shall receive, to substantiate that right, a residence permit for a period equal to that of the provision of services.

3. The right of residence shall apply throughout the territory of Switzerland or the Member State of the European Community concerned.

4. For the purposes of issuing residence permits, the Contracting Parties may not require of the persons referred to in Article 17(b) of this Annex more than:

(a)   the document by virtue of which they entered the territory;

(b)   evidence that they are providing or wish to provide a service.

Article 21

1. The total duration of provision of services under Article 17(a) of this Annex, whether continuous or consisting of successive periods of provision, may not exceed 90 days of actual work per calendar year.

2. The provisions of paragraph 1 shall be without prejudice to the discharge by the person providing a service of his legal obligations under the guarantee given to the person receiving the service or to cases of force majeure.

Article 22

1. The provisions of Articles 17 and 19 of this Annex shall not apply to activities involving, even on an occasional basis, the exercise of public authority in the Contracting Party concerned.

2. The provisions of Articles 17 and 19 of this Annex and measures adopted by virtue thereof shall not preclude the applicability of laws, regulations and administrative provisions providing for the application of working and employment conditions to

employed persons posted for the purposes of providing a service. In accordance with Article 16 of this Agreement, reference is made to Directive 96/71/EC of 16 December 1996 concerning the posting of workers in the framework of the provision of services (OJ L 18, 21.1.1997, p. 1) ([1]).

3. The provisions of Articles 17(a) and 19 of this Annex shall be without prejudice to the applicability of the laws, regulations and administrative provisions prevailing in all Contracting Parties at the time of this Agreement's entry into force in respect of:

(i) the activities of temporary and interim employment agencies;

(ii) financial services where provision is subject to prior authorisation in the territory of a Contracting Party and the provider to prudential supervision by that Contracting Party's authorities.

4. The provisions of Articles 17(a) and 19 of this Annex shall be without prejudice to the applicability of the Contracting Parties' respective laws, regulations and administrative provisions concerning the provision of services of 90 days of actual work or less required by imperative requirements in the public interest.

Article 23

Persons receiving services

1. A person receiving services within the meaning of Article 5(3) of this Agreement shall not require a residence permit for a period of residence of three months or less. For a period exceeding three months, a person receiving services shall be issued with a residence permit equal in duration to the service. He may be excluded from social security schemes during his period of residence.

2. A residence permit shall be valid throughout the territory of the issuing state.

V. PERSONS NOT PURSUING AN ECONOMIC ACTIVITY

Article 24

Rules regarding residence

1. A person who is a national of a Contracting Party not pursuing an economic activity in the state of residence and having no right of residence pursuant to other provisions of this Agreement shall receive a residence permit valid for at least five years provided he proves to the competent national authorities that he possesses for himself and the members of his family:

(a) sufficient financial means not to have to apply for social assistance benefits during their stay;

(b) all-risks sickness insurance cover ([2]).

([1]) As in force at the date of signing the Agreement.
([2]) In Switzerland, sickness insurance for persons who do not elect to make it their domicile must include accident and maternity cover.

The Contracting Parties may, if they consider it necessary, require the residence permit to be revalidated at the end of the first two years of residence.

2. Financial means shall be considered sufficient if they exceed the amount below which nationals, having regard to their personal situation and, where appropriate, that of their family, can claim social security benefits. Where that condition cannot be applied, the applicant's financial means shall be regarded as sufficient if they are greater than the level of the minimum social security pension paid by the host state.

3. Persons who have been employed for less than one year in the territory of a Contracting Party may reside there provided they comply with the conditions set out in paragraph 1 of this Article. The unemployment benefits to which they are entitled under national law which is, where appropriate, complemented by the provisions of Annex II, shall be considered to be financial means within the meaning of paragraphs 1(a) and 2 of this Article.

4. A student who does not have a right of residence in the territory of the other Contracting Party on the basis of any other provision of this Agreement shall be issued with a residence permit for a period limited to that of the training or to one year, if the training lasts for more than one year, provided he satisfies the national authority concerned, by means of a statement or, if he chooses, by any other at least equivalent means, that he has sufficient financial means to ensure that neither he, his spouse nor his dependent children will make any claim for social security of the host state during their stay, and provided he is registered in an approved establishment for the purpose of following, as his principal activity, a vocational training course and has all-risks sickness insurance cover. This Agreement does not regulate access to vocational training or maintenance assistance given to the students covered by this Article.

5. A residence permit shall automatically be extended for at least five years provided that the eligibility conditions are still met. Residence permits for students shall be extended annually for a duration equal to the remaining training period.

6. Breaks in residence of less than six consecutive months and absences for the purposes of fulfilling military service obligations shall not affect the validity of the residence permit.

7. A residence permit shall be valid throughout the territory of the issuing state.

8. The right of residence shall obtain for as long as beneficiaries of that right fulfil the conditions laid down in paragraph 1.

VI. Purchase of Immovable Property

Article 25

1. A national of a Contracting Party who has a right of residence and his principal residence in the host state shall enjoy the same rights as a national as regards the purchase of immovable property. He may set up his principal residence in the host state at any time in accordance with the relevant national rules irrespective of the duration of his employment. Leaving the host state shall not entail any obligation to dispose of such property.

2. The national of a Contracting Party who has a right of residence but does not have his principal residence in the host state shall enjoy the same rights as a national as regards the purchase of immovable property needed for his economic activity. Leaving the host state shall not entail any obligation to dispose of such property. He may also be authorised to purchase a second residence or holiday accommodation. This Agreement shall not affect the rules applying to pure capital investment or business of unbuilt land and apartments.

3. A frontier worker shall enjoy the same rights as a national as regards the purchase of immovable property for his economic activity and as a secondary residence. Leaving the host state shall not entail any obligation to dispose of such property. He may also be authorised to purchase holiday accommodation. This Agreement shall not affect the rules applying in the host state to pure capital investment or business of unbuilt land and apartments.

VII. TRANSITIONAL PROVISIONS AND DEVELOPMENT OF THE AGREEMENT

Article 26

General provisions

1. When the quantitative restrictions laid down in Article 10 of this Agreement are applied, the provisions contained in this Chapter shall supplement or replace the other provisions of this Annex, as the case may be.

2. When the quantitative restrictions laid down in Article 10 of this Agreement are applied, the pursuit of an economic activity shall be subject to the issue of a residence and/or a work permit.

Article 27

Rules relating to the residence of employed persons

1. The residence permit of an employed person who has an employment contract for a period of less than one year shall be extended for up to a total of 12 months provided that the employed person furnishes proof to the competent national authorities that he is able to pursue an economic activity. A new residence permit shall be issued provided that the employed person furnishes proof that he is able to pursue an economic activity and that the quantitative limits laid down in Article 10 of this Agreement have not been reached. There shall be no obligation to leave the country between two employment contracts in accordance with Article 24 of this Annex.

2. During the period referred to in Article 10(2) of this Agreement, a Contracting Party may require that a written contract or draft contract be produced before issuing a first residence permit.

3.   (a) Persons who have previously held temporary jobs in the territory of the host state for at least 30 months shall automatically have the right to take

up employment for an unlimited duration (¹). They may not be denied this right on the grounds that the number of residence permits guaranteed has been exhausted.

(b) Persons who have previously held seasonal employment in the territory of the host state for a total of not less than 50 months during the last 15 years and do not meet the conditions of entitlement to a residence permit in accordance with the provisions of subparagraph (a) above shall automatically have the right to take up employment for an unlimited duration.

Article 28

Employed frontier workers

1. An employed frontier worker is a national of a Contracting Party who has his normal place of residence in the frontier zones of Switzerland or neighbouring states and who pursues an activity as an employed person in the frontier zones of another Contracting Party returning as a rule to his principal residence every day, or at least once a week. For the purposes of this Agreement, frontier zones shall mean the zones defined in the agreements concluded between Switzerland and its neighbours concerning movement in frontier zones.

2. The special permit shall be valid throughout the frontier zone of the issuing state.

Article 29

Employed persons' right to return

1. An employed person who, on the date this Agreement entered into force, was holding a residence permit valid for at least one year and who has then left the host country shall be entitled to preferential access to the quota for a new residence permit within six years of his departure provided he proves that he is able to pursue an economic activity.

2. A frontier worker shall have the right to a new special permit within six years of the end of his previous employment over an uninterrupted period of three years, subject to verification of his pay and working conditions if he is employed for the two years following the Agreement's entry into force, provided he proves to the competent national authorities that he is able to pursue an economic activity.

3. Young persons who have left the territory of a Contracting Party after residing there for at least five years before the age of 21 shall have the right for a period of four years to return to that country and pursue an economic activity.

(¹) They shall not be subject to the priority accorded to workers integrated into the regular labour market or monitoring of compliance with wage and employment conditions in a particular sector or place.

Article 30

Employed persons' occupational and geographical mobility

1. An employed person holding a residence permit valid for less than one year shall, for the twelve months following the commencement of his employment, have the right to subject to compliance with Article 10 of this Agreement.

2. Special permits issued to employed frontier workers shall confer the right to occupational and geographical mobility within all the frontier zones of Switzerland or its neighbouring states.

Article 31

Rules relating to the residence of self-employed persons

A national of a Contracting Party wishing to become established in the territory of another Contracting Party in order to pursue a self-employed activity (hereinafter referred to as a 'self-employed worker') shall receive a residence permit valid for a period of six months. He shall receive a residence permit valid for at least five years provided that he proves to the competent national authorities before the end of the six-month period that he is pursuing a self-employed activity. If necessary, the six-month period may be extended by a maximum of two months if there is a genuine likelihood that he will produce such proof.

Article 32

Self-employed frontier workers

1. A self-employed frontier worker is a national of a Contracting Party who is ordinarily resident in the frontier zones of Switzerland or neighbouring states and who pursues a self-employed activity in the frontier zones of the other Contracting Party returning as a rule to his principal residence in principle every day or at least once a week. For the purposes of this Agreement, frontier zones shall mean the zones defined in the agreements concluded between Switzerland and its neighbouring states concerning movement in frontier zones.

2. A national of a Contracting Party who wishes in his capacity as a frontier worker to pursue a self-employed activity in the frontier zones of Switzerland or its neighbouring states shall receive a preliminary six-month special permit in advance. He shall receive a special permit for a period of at least five years provided that he proves to the competent national authorities, before the end of that six-month period, that he is pursuing a self-employed activity. If necessary, the six-month period may be extended by a maximum of two months if there is a genuine likelihood that he will produce such proof.

3. Special permits shall be valid throughout the frontier zone of the issuing state.

Article 33

Self-employed persons' right to return

1. A self-employed person who has held a residence permit valid for a period of at least five years and who has left the host state shall have the right to a new permit within six years of his departure provided he has already worked in the host country for an uninterrupted period of three years and proves to the competent national authorities that he is able to pursue an economic activity.

2. A self-employed frontier worker shall have the right to a new special permit within a period of six years of the termination of previous activity lasting for an uninterrupted period of four years provided he proves to the competent national authorities that he is able to pursue an economic activity.

3. Young persons who have left the territory of a Contracting Party after residing there for at least five years before the age of 21 shall have the right for a period of four years to return to that country and pursue an economic activity.

Article 34

Self-employed persons' occupational and geographical mobility

Special permits issued to self-employed frontier workers shall confer the right to occupational and geographical mobility within the frontier zones of Switzerland or its neighbouring states. Preliminary six-month residence permits issued in advance (in the case of frontier workers, special permits) shall confer the right only to geographical mobility.

E.C.-TURKEY ASSOCIATION AGREEMENT, 1963 (EXCERPTS), PREAMBLE: ARTICLES 7, 12–14

PREAMBLE

HIS MAJESTY THE KING OF THE BELGIANS,

THE PRESIDENT OF THE FEDERAL REPUBLIC OF GERMANY,

THE PRESIDENT OF THE FRENCH REPUBLIC,

THE PRESIDENT OF THE ITALIAN REPUBLIC,

HER ROYAL HIGHNESS THE GRAND DUCHESS OF LUXEMBOURG,

HER MAJESTY THE QUEEN OF THE NETHERLANDS,

and

THE COUNCIL OF THE EUROPEAN ECONOMIC COMMUNITY,

of the one part, and

THE PRESIDENT OF THE REPUBLIC OF TURKEY,

of the other part,

DETERMINED to establish ever closer bonds between the Turkish people and the peoples brought together in the European Economic Community;

RESOLVED to ensure a continuous improvement in living conditions in Turkey and in the European Economic Community through accelerated economic progress and the harmonious expansion of trade, and to reduce the disparity between the Turkish economy and economies of the Member States of the Community;

MINDFUL both of the special problems presented by the development of the Turkish economy and of the need to grant economic aid to Turkey during a given period;

RECOGNIZING that the support given by the European Economic Community to the efforts of the Turkish people to improve their standard of living will facilitate the accession of Turkey to the Community at a later date;

RESOLVED to preserve and strengthen peace and liberty by joint pursuit of the ideals underlying the Treaty establishing the European Economic Community;

HAVE DECIDED to conclude an Agreement establishing an Association between the European Economic Community and Turkey in accordance with Article 238 of the Treaty establishing the European Economic Community, and to this end have designated as their Plenipotentiaries:

HIS MAJESTY THE KING OF THE BELGIANS:
        Mr Paul-Henri SPAAK,
        Deputy Prime Minister and Minister for Foreign Affairs;

THE PRESIDENT OF THE FEDERAL REPUBLIC OF GERMANY,
        Dr. Gerhard SCHRODER,
        Minister for Foreign Affairs;

THE PRESIDENT OF THE FRENCH REPUBLIC,
        Mr Maurice COUVE DE MURVILLE,
        Minister for Foreign Affairs;

THE PRESIDENT OF THE ITALIAN REPUBLIC,
   Mr Emilio COLOMBO,
   Minister for the Treasury;

HER ROYAL HIGHNESS THE GRAND DUCHESS OF LUXEMBOURG,
   Mr Eugène SCHAUS,
   Vice-President of the Government and Minister for Foreign Affairs;

HER MAJESTY THE QUEEN OF THE NETHERLANDS,
   Mr Joseph M. A. H. LUNS,
   Minister for Foreign Affairs;

THE COUNCIL OF THE EUROPEAN ECONOMIC COMMUNITY,
   Mr Joseph M. A. H. LUNS,
   President in Office of the Council of the European Economic Community and
   Minister for Foreign Affairs in the Netherlands;

THE PRESIDENT OF THE REPUBLIC OF TURKEY,
   Mr Feridun Cemal ERKN,
   Mininster for Foreign Affairs;

WHO, having exchanged their Full Powers, found in good due form,

HAVE AGREED AS FOLLOWS:

Article 7

The Contracting Parties shall take all appropriate measures, whether general or particular, to ensure the fulfilment of the obligations arising from this Agreement.

They shall refrain from any measures liable to jeopardize the attainment of the objectives of this Agreement.

Article 12

The Contracting Parties agree to be guided by Articles 48, 49 and 50 of the Treaty establishing the Community for the purpose of progressively securing freedom of movement for workers between them.

Article 13

The Contracting Parties agree to be guided by Articles 52 to 56 and Article 58 of the Treaty establishing the Community for the purpose of abolishing restrictions on freedom of establishment between them.

Article 14

The Contracting Parties agree to be guided by Articles 55, 56 and 58 to 65 of the Treaty establishing the Community for the purpose of abolishing restrictions on freedom to provide services between them.

ADDITIONAL PROTOCOL TO E.C.-TURKEY ASSOCIATION AGREEMENT (EXCERPTS): ARTICLES 36–41, 58–59

Article 36

Freedom of movement for workers between Member States of the Community and Turkey shall be secured by progressive stages in accordance with the principles set out in Article 12 of the Agreement of Association between the end of the twelfth and the twenty-second year after the entry into force of that Agreement.

A21–01

The Council of Association shall decide on the rules necessary to that end.

Article 37

As regards conditions of work and remuneration, the rules which each Member State applies to workers of Turkish nationality employed in the Community shall not discriminate on grounds of nationality between such workers and workers who are nationals of other Member States of the Community.

Article 38

While freedom of movement for workers between Member States of the Community and Turkey is being brought about by progressive stages, the Council of Association may review all questions arising in connection with the geografical and occupational mobility of workers of Turkish nationality, in particular the extension of work and residence permits, in order to facilitate the employment of those workers in each Member State.

To that end, the Council of Association may make recommendations to Member States.

Article 39

1. Before the end of the first year after the entry into force of this Protocol the Council of Association shall adopt social security measures for workers of Turkish nationality moving within the Community and for their families residing in the Community.

2. These provisions must enable workers of Turkish nationality, in accordance with arrangements to be laid down, to aggregate periods of insurance or employment completed in individual Member States in respect of old-age pensions, death benefits and invalidity pensions, and also as regards the provision of health services for workers and their families residing in the Community. These measures shall create no obligation on Member States to take into account periods completed in Turkey.

3. The abovementioned measures must ensure that family allowances are paid if a worker's family resides in the Community.

4. It must be possible to transfer to Turkey old-age pensions, death benefits and invalidity pensions obtained under the measures adopted pursuant to paragraph 2.

5. The measures provided for in this Article shall not affect the rights and obligations arising from bilateral agreements between Turkey and Member States of the Community, in so far as these agreements provide more favourable arrangements for Turkish nationals.

Article 40

The Council of Association may make recommendations to Member States and Turkey for encouraging the exchange of young workers; the Council of Association shall be guided in the matter by the measures adopted by Member States in implementation of Article 50 of the Treaty establishing the Community.

Article 41

1. The Contracting Parties shall refrain from introducing between themselves any new restrictions on the freedom of establishment and the freedom to provide services.

2. The Council of Association shall, in accordance with the principles set out in Articles 13 and 14 of the Agreement of Association, determine the timetable and rules for the progressive abolition by the Contracting Parties, between themselves, of restrictions on freedom of establishment and on freedom to provide services.

The Council of Association shall, when determining such timetable and rules for the various classes of activity, take into account corresponding measures already adopted by the Community in these fields and also the special economic and social circumstances of Turkey. Priority shall be given to activities making a particular contribution to the development of production and trade.

Article 58

In the fields covered by this Protocol:

– the arrangements applied by Turkey in respect of the Community shall not give rise to any discrimination between Member States, their nationals or their companies or firms;

– the arrangements applied by the Community in respect of Turkey shall not give rise to any discrimination between Turkish nationals or Turkish companies or firms.

Article 59

In the fields covered by this Protocol Turkey shall not receive more favourable treatment than that which Member States grant to one another pursuant to the Treaty establishing the Community.

DECISION NO 1/80 OF THE ASSOCIATION COUNCIL OF 19 SEPTEMBER 1980 ON THE DEVELOPMENT OF THE ASSOCIATION
(EXCERPTS)

THE ASSOCIATION COUNCIL,

Having regard to the Agreement establishing an Association between the European Economic Community and Turkey, **A22–01**

WHEREAS the revitalization and development of the Association must, as agreed on 5 February 1980, cover the entire range of current Association problems; whereas the search for solutions to these problems must take account of the specific nature of the Association links between the Community and Turkey;

WHEREAS in the agricultural sector, the elimination of customs duties applicable to Turkish products imported into the Community will make for the achievement of the desired result and for the alleviation of Turkey's concern as to the effects of the enlargement of the Community; whereas, moreover, Article 33 of the Additional Protocol should be implemented as a prior condition for the introduction of free movement of agricultural products; whereas the arrangements provided for must be implemented with due regard for the principles and mechanisms of the common agricultural policy;

WHEREAS, in the social field, and within the framework of the international commitments of each of the Parties, the above considerations make it necessary to improve the treatment accorded workers and members of their families in relation to the arrangements introduced by Decision No 2/76 of the Association Council; whereas, furthermore, the provisions relating to social security should be implemented as should those relating to the exchange of young workers;

WHEREAS development of the Association justifies the establishment of such economic, technical and financial co-operation as will help to attain the objectives of the Association Agreement, in particular by means of a Community contribution to the economic development of Turkey in various sectors,

HAS DECIDED AS FOLLOWS:

CHAPTER II

SOCIAL PROVISIONS

SECTION 1

QUESTIONS RELATING TO EMPLOYMENT AND THE FREE MOVEMENT OF WORKERS

Article 6

1. Subject to Article 7 on free access to employment for members of his family, a Turkish worker duly registered as belonging to the labour force of a Member State:

– shall be entitled in that Member State, after one year's legal employment, to the renewal of his permit to work for the same employer, if a job is available;

– shall be entitled in that Member State, after three years of legal employment and subject to the priority to be given to workers of Member States of the Community, to respond to another offer of employment, with an employer of his choice, made under normal conditions and registered with the employment services of that State, for the same occupation;

– shall enjoy free access in that Member State to any paid employment of his choice, after four years of legal employment;

2. Annual holidays and absences for reasons of maternity or an accident at work or short periods of sickness shall be treated as periods of legal employment. Periods of involuntary unemployment duly certified by the relevant authorities and long absences on account of sickness shall not be treated as periods of legal employment, but shall not affect rights acquired as the result of the preceding period of employment.

3. The procedures for applying paragraphs 1 and 2 shall be those established under national rules.

Article 7

The members of the family of a Turkish worker duly registered as belonging to the labour force of a Member State, who have been authorized to join him:

– shall be entitled-subject to the priority to be given to workers of Member States of the Community—to respond to any offer of employment after they have been legally resident for at least three years in that Member State;

– shall enjoy free access to any paid employment of their choice provided they have been legally resident there for at least five years.

Children of Turkish workers who have completed a course of vocational training in the host country may respond to any offer of employment there, irrespective of the length of time they have been resident in that Member State, provided one of their parents has been legally employed in the Member State concerned for at least three years.

Article 8

1. Should it not be possible in the Community to meet an offer of employment by calling on the labour available on the employment market of the Member States and should the Member States, within the framework of their provisions laid down by law, regulation or administrative action, decide to authorize a call on workers who are not nationals of a Member State of the Community in order to meet the offer of employment, they shall endeavour in so doing to accord priority to Turkish workers.

2. The employment services of the Member State shall endeavour to fill vacant positions which they have registered and which the duly registered Community labour force has not been able to fill with Turkish workers who are registered as unemployed and legally resident in the territory of that Member State.

Article 9

Turkish children residing legally in a Member State of the Community with their parents who are or have been legally employed in that Member State, shall be admitted to courses of general education, apprenticeship and vocational training under the same educational entry qualifications as the children of nationals of that Member State. They may in that Member State be eligible to benefit from the advantages provided for under the national legislation in this area.

Article 10

1. The Member States of the Community shall as regards remuneration and other conditions of work grant Turkish workers duly registered as belonging to their labour forces treatment involving no discrimination on the basis of nationality between them and Community workers.

2. Subject to the application of Articles 6 and 7, the Turkish workers referred to in paragraph 1 and members of their families shall be entitled, on the same footing as Community workers, to assistance from the employment services in their search for employment.

Article 11

Nationals of the Member States duly registered as belonging to the labour force in Turkey, and members of their families who have been authorized to join them, shall enjoy in that country the rights and advantages referred to in Articles 6, 7, 9 and 10 if they meet the conditions laid down in those Articles.

Article 12

Where a Member State of the Community of Turkey experiences or is threatened with disturbances on its employment market which might seriously jeopardize the standard of living or level of employment in a particular region, branch of activity or occupation, the State concerned may refrain from automatically applying Articles 6 and 7. The State concerned shall inform the Association Council of any such temporary restriction.

Article 13

The Member States of the Community and Turkey may not introduce new restrictions on the conditions of access to employment applicable to workers and members of their families legally resident and employed in their respective territories.

Article 14

1. The provisions of this section shall be applied subject to limitations justified on grounds of public policy, public security or public health.

2. They shall not prejudice the rights and obligations arising from national legislation or bilateral agreements between Turkey and the Member States of the Community where such legislation or agreements provide for more favourable treatment for their nationals.

Article 15

1. So as to be in a position to ensure the harmonious application of the provisions of this section and determine that they are applied in such a way as to exclude the danger of disturbance of the employment markets, the Association Committee shall periodically exchange information in order to improve mutual knowledge of the economic and social situation, including the state of and outlook for the labour market in the Community and in Turkey.

It shall each year present a report on its activities to the Association Council.

2. The Association Committee shall be authorized to enlist the assistance of an ad hoc Working Party in order to implement paragraph 1.

Article 16

1. The provisions of this section shall apply from 1 December 1980.

2. From 1 June 1983, the Association Council shall, particularly in the light of the reports on activities referred to in Article 15 examine the results of application of the provisions of this section with a view to preparing solutions which might apply as from 1 December 1983.

SECTION 2

SOCIAL AND CULTURAL ADVANCEMENT AND THE EXCHANGE OF YOUNG WORKERS

Article 17

The Member States and turkey shall co-operate, in accordance with their domestic situations and their legal systems, in appropriate schemes to promote the social and cultural advancement of Turkish workers and the members of their family, in particular literacy campaigns and courses in the language of the host country, activities to maintain links with Turkish culture and access to vocational training.

Article 18

The Association Committee shall prepare a recommendation to be forwarded by the Association Council to the Member States of the Community and Turkey with a view to the implementation of any action that may enable young workers who have received their basic training in their own country to complement their vocational training by participating in in-service training, under the conditions set out in Article 40 of the Additional Protocol.

It shall monitor the actual implementation of this provision.

CHAPTER III

ECONOMIC AND TECHNICAL CO-OPERATION

Article 19

Co-operation shall be established between the Contracting Parties in order to contribute to the development of Turkey by complementing the country's own efforts to strengthen the economic ties between Turkey and the Community on as broad a basis as possible and to the mutual benefit of the Parties.

AGREEMENT BETWEEN E.C. AND BULGARIA (EXCERPTS): PREAMBLE, ARTICLES 1, 38–56, 59

AGREEMENT establishing an association between the European Communities and   **A23–01**
their Member States, of the one part, and the Republic of Bulgaria, of the other
part THE KINGDOM OF BELGIUM, THE KINGDOM OF DENMARK,
THE FEDERAL REPUBLIC OF GERMANY, THE HELLENIC REPUBLIC,
THE KINGDOM OF SPAIN, THE FRENCH REPUBLIC, IRELAND,
THE ITALIAN REPUBLIC, THE GRAND DUCHY OF LUXEMBOURG,
THE KINGDOM OF THE NETHERLANDS, THE PORTUGUESE
REPUBLIC, THE UNITED KINGDOM OF GREAT BRITAIN AND
NORTHERN IRELAND, Contracting Parties to the Treaty establishing the
EUROPEAN ECONOMIC COMMUNITY, the Treaty establishing the
EUROPEAN COAL AND STEEL COMMUNITY, and the Treaty establishing the
EUROPEAN ATOMIC ENERGY COMMUNITY, hereinafter referred to as
'Member States', and The EUROPEAN ECONOMIC COMMUNITY, the
EUROPEAN ATOMIC ENERGY COMMUNITY AND THE EUROPEAN COAL
AND STEEL COMMUNITY, hereinafter referred to as 'the Community', of the
one part, and THE REPUBLIC OF BULGARIA, hereinafter referred to as
'Bulgaria', of the other part,

CONSIDERING the importance of the traditional links existing between the
Community, its Member States and Bulgaria and the common values that they share,

RECOGNIZING that the Community and Bulgaria wish to strengthen these links
and to establish close and long lasting relations, based on mutual interest and reciprocity, which would allow Bulgaria to take part in the process of European integration, thus strengthening and widening the relations established in the past notably by
the Agreement on Trade and Commercial and Economic Cooperation, signed on 8
May 1990,

CONSIDERING the opportunities for a relationship of a new quality offered by the
emergence of a new democracy in Bulgaria,

CONSIDERING the commitment of the Community and its Member States and of
Bulgaria to strengthening the political and economic freedoms which constitute the
very basis of the association,

RECOGNIZING the fundamental character of the democratic changes in Bulgaria,
taking place in a peaceful manner and aimed at building a new political and economic
system, based on the rule of law and human rights, political pluralism, and a pluralist multi-party system involving free and democratic elections and the creation of the
legislative and economic conditions, necessary for the development of a market economy, as well as the need to continue and complete that process with the assistance of
the Community,

CONSIDERING the firm commitment of the Community and its Member States
and of Bulgaria to the rule of law and human rights, including those of persons
belonging to minorities, and to the full implementation of all other principles and

provisons contained in the Final Act of the Conference on Security and Cooperation in Europe (CSCE), the concluding documents of Vienna and Madrid, the Charter of Paris for a new Europe, as well as to the principles and provisions of the European Energy Charter,

WILLING to promote improved contacts among their citizens as well as the free flow of information and ideas, as agreed by the Parties in the framework of the CSCE,

CONSCIOUS of the importance of this Agreement to establishing and enhancing in Europe a system of stability based on cooperation, with the Community as one of the cornerstones,

BELIEVING that a link should be made between full implementation of association, on the one hand, and continuation of the actual accomplishment of Bulgaria's political, economic and legal reforms on the other hand, as well as the introduction of the factors necessary for cooperation and the actual rapprochement between the Parties' systems, notably in the light of the conclusions of the CSCE Bonn Conference,

DESIROUS of establishing regular political dialogue on bilateral and international issues of mutual interest to enhance and complete the association,

TAKING ACCOUNT of the Community's willingness to provide decisive support for the completion of the transition towards a market economy in Bulgaria and to help Bulgaria cope with the economic and social consequences of structural readjustment,

TAKING ACCOUNT furthermore of the Community's willingness to set up instruments of cooperation and economic, technical and financial assistance on a global and multiannual basis,

CONSIDERING the commitment of the Community and Bulgaria to free trade, and in particular in respect of the General Agreement on Tariffs and Trade principles,

BEARING in mind the economic and social disparities between the Community and Bulgaria and thus recognizing that the objectives of this association should be reached through appropriate provisions of this Agreement,

CONVINCED that this Agreement will create a new climate for their economic relations and in particular for the development of trade and investment, instruments which are indispensable for economic restructuring and technological modernization of the Bulgarian economy,

DESIROUS of establishing cultural cooperation and developing exchanges of information,

RECOGNIZING the fact that Bulgaria's ultimate objective is to become a member of the Community, and that this association, in the view of the Parties, will help Bulgaria to achieve this objective,

HAVE DECIDED to conclude this Agreement and to this end have designated as their plenipotentiaries,

THE KINGDOM OF BELGIUM: Robert URBAIN, Minister for Foreign Trade and European Affairs; THE KINGDOM OF DENMARK: Jørgen ØSTRØM MØLLER, State Secretary for Foreign Affairs; THE FEDERAL REPUBLIC OF GERMANY: Klaus KINKEL, Federal Minister for Foreign Affairs; THE HELLENIC REPUBLIC: Michel PAPACONSTANTINOU, Minister for Foreign Affairs;

THE KINGDOM OF SPAIN: Javier SOLANA, Minister for Foreign Affairs; THE FRENCH REPUBLIC: Elisabeth GUIGOU, Minister responsible for European Affairs; IRELAND: Dick SPRING, Minister for Foreign Affairs; THE ITALIAN REPUBLIC: Valdo SPINI, State Secretary for Foreign Affairs; THE GRAND DUCHY OF LUXEMBOURG: Jacques POOS, Minister for Foreign Affairs; THE KINGDOM OF THE NETHERLANDS: P. KOOIJMANS, Minister for Foreign Affairs; THE PORTUGUESE REPUBLIC: J. M. DURAO BARROSO, Minister for Foreign Affairs; THE UNITED KINGDOM OF GREAT BRITAIN AND NORTHERN IRELAND: Douglas HURD, Secretary of State for Foreign and Commonwealth Affairs; THE EUROPEAN ECONOMIC COMMUNITY, THE EUROPEAN ATOMIC ENERGY COMMUNITY AND THE EUROPEAN COAL AND STEEL COMMUNITY: Niels HELVEG PETERSEN, Minister for Foreign Affairs of the Kingdom of Denmark, President-in-Office of the Council of the European Communities; Sir Leon BRITTAN, Member of the Commission of the European Communities; Hans VAN DEN BROEK, Member of the Commission of the European Communities; THE REPUBLIC OF BULGARIA: Luben BEROV, Prime Minister and Minister for Foreign Affairs; WHO, having exchanged their full powers, formed in good and due form, HAVE AGREED AS FOLLOWS:

Article 1

1. An association is hereby established between the Community and its Member States on the one part, and Bulgaria on the other part.

2. The objectives of this association are:

–   to provide an appropriate framework for the political dialogue between the Parties allowing the development of close political relations,

–   to establish gradually a free trade area between the Community and Bulgaria covering substantially all trade between them,

–   to promote the expansion of trade and the harmonious economic relations between the Parties and so to foster the dynamic economic development and prosperity in Bulgaria,

–   to provide a basis for economic, financial, cultural and social cooperation, as well as for the Community's assistance to Bulgaria,

–   to support Bulgaria's efforts to develop its economy and to complete the transition into a market economy,

–   to provide an appropriate framework for the gradual integration of Bulgaria into the Community. To this end new rules, policies and practices will be established in compliance with market mechanisms, and Bulgaria shall work towards fulfilling the necessary requirements in this respect,

–   to set up institutions suitable to make the association effective.

TITLE IV

MOVEMENT OF WORKERS, ESTABLISHMENT, SUPPLY OF SERVICES

CHAPTER I

MOVEMENT OF WORKERS

Article 38

1. Subject to the conditions and modalities applicable in each Member State:

– the treatment accorded to workers of Bulgarian nationality, legally employed in the territory of a Member State shall be free from any discrimination based on nationality, as regards working conditions, remuneration or dismissal, as compared to its own nationals,

– the legally resident spouse and children of a worker legally employed in the territory of a Member State, with the exception of seasonal workers and of workers coming under bilateral Agreements in the sense of Article 42, unless otherwise provided by such Agreements, shall have access to the labour market of that Member State, during the period of that worker's authorized stay of employment.

2. Bulgaria shall, subject to the conditions and modalities applicable in that country, accord the treatment referred to in paragraph 1 to workers who are nationals of a Member State and are legally employed in its territory as well as to their spouse and children who are legally resident in the said territory.

Article 39

1. With a view to coordinating social security systems for workers of Bulgarian nationality, legally employed in the territory of a Member State and for the members of their family, legally resident there, and subject to the conditions and modalities applicable in each Member State,

– all periods of insurance, employment or residence completed by such workers in the various Member States shall be added together for the purpose of pensions and annuities in respect of old age, invalidity and death and for the purpose of medical care for such workers and such family members,

– any pensions or annuities in respect of old age, death, industrial accident or occupational disease, or of invalidity resulting therefrom, with the exception of non-contributory benefits, shall be freely transferable at the rate applied by virtue of the law of the debtor Member State or States,

– the workers in question shall receive family allowances for the members of their family as defined above.

2. Bulgaria shall accord to workers who are nationals of a Member State and legally employed in its territory, and to members of their families legally resident there, treatment similar to that specified in the second and third indents of paragraph 1.

Article 40

1. The Association Council shall by decision adopt the appropriate provisions to implement the objective set out in Article 39.

2. The Association Council shall by decision adopt detailed rules for administrative cooperation providing the necessary management and control guarantees for the application of the provisions referred to in paragraph 1.

Article 41

The provisions adopted by the Association Council in accordance with Article 40 shall not affect any rights or obligations arising from bilateral Agreements linking Bulgaria and the Member States where those Agreements provide for more favourable treatment of nationals of Bulgaria or of the Member States.

Article 42

1. Taking into account the labour market situation in the Member State, subject to its legislation and to the respect of rules in force in that Member State in the area of mobility of workers,

–   the existing facilities for access to employment for Bulgarian workers accorded by Member States under bilateral Agreements ought to be preserved and if possible improved,

–   the other Member States shall consider favourably the possibility of concluding similar Agreements.

2. The Association Council shall examine granting other improvements including facilities of access for professional training, in conformity with rules and procedures in force in the Member States, and taking account of the labour market situation in the Member States and in the Community.

Article 43

During the second stage referred to in Article 7, or earlier if so decided, the Association Council shall examine further ways of improving the movement of workers, taking into account inter alia the social and economic situation in Bulgaria and the employment situation in the Community. The Association Council shall make recommendations to such end.

Article 44

In the interest of facilitating the restructuring of labour resources resulting from the economic restructuring in Bulgaria, the Community shall provide technical assistance for the establishment of a suitable social security system in Bulgaria as set out in Article 89.

CHAPTER II

ESTABLISHMENT

Article 45

1. Each Member State shall grant, from entry into force of the Agreement, for the establishment of Bulgarian companies and nationals and for the operation of Bulgarian companies and nationals established in its territory, a treatment no less favourable than that accorded to its own companies and nationals, save for matters referred to in Annex XVa.

2. Bulgaria shall

(i)   grant, from entry into force of the Agreement, for the establishment of Community companies and nationals a treatment no less favourable than that accorded to its own companies and nationals, save for the sectors and matters referred to in Annexes XVb and XVc, where such treatment shall be granted at the latest by the end of the transitional period referred to in Article 7;

(ii) grant, from entry into force of the Agreement, in the operation of Community companies and nationals established in Bulgaria a treatment no less favourable than that accorded to its own companies and nationals.

3. The provisions contained in paragraph 2 of this Article shall not apply to the matters listed in Annex XVd.

4. Bulgaria shall, during the transitional period referred to in paragraph 2 (i), not adopt any new regulations or measures which introduce discrimination as regards the establishment of Community companies and nationals in its territory in comparison to its own companies and nationals.

5. For the purposes of this Agreement

(a)   'establishment' shall mean

(i)   as regards nationals, the right to take up and pursue economic activities as self-employed persons and to set up and manage undertakings, in particular companies, which they effectively control. Self-employment and business undertakings by nationals shall not extend to seeking or taking employment in the labour market or confer a right of access to the labour market of the other Party. The provisions of this chapter do not apply to those who are not exclusively self-employed;

    (ii)   as regards companies, the right to take up and pursue economic activities by means of the setting up and management of subsidiaries, branches and agencies;

(b)   'subsidiary' of a company shall mean a company which is effectively controlled by the first company;

(c)   'economic activities' shall in particular include activities of an industrial character, activities of a commercial character, activities of craftsmen and activities of the professions.

6. The Association Council shall, during the transitional period referred to in paragraph 2 (i), examine regularly the possibility of accelerating the granting of national treatment in the sectors referred to in Annexes XVb and XVc and the inclusion of areas or matters listed in Annex XVd within the scope of application of the provisions of paragraph 2 (i) of this Article. Amendments may be made to these Annexes by decision of the Association Council.

Following the expiration of the transitional period referred to in paragraph 2 (i), the Association Council may exceptionally, upon request by Bulgaria, and if the necessity arises, decide to prolong the duration of exclusion of certain areas or matters listed in Annexes XVb and XVc for a limited period of time.

Article 46

1. Subject to the provisions of Article 45 with the exception of financial services described in Annex XVb, each Party may regulate the establishment and operation of companies and nationals on its territory, in so far as these regulations do not discriminate against companies and nationals of the other Party in comparison to its own companies and nationals.

2. In respect of financial services, described in Annex XVb, this Agreement does not prejudice the right of the Parties to adopt measures necessry for the conduct of the Party's monetary policy, or for prudential grounds in order to ensure the protection of investors, depositors, policy holders, or persons to whom a fiduciary duty is owed, or to ensure the integrity and stability of the financial system. These measures shall not discriminate on grounds of nationality against companies and nationals of the other Party in comparison to its own companies and nationals.

Article 47

In order to make it easier for Community nationals and Bulgarian nationals to take up and pursue regulated professional activities in Bulgaria and the Community respectively, the Association Council shall examine which steps are necessary to be taken to provide for the mutual recognition of qualifications. It may take all necessary measures to that end.

Article 48

The provisions of Article 46 do not preclude the application by a Party of particular rules concerning the establishment and operation in its territory of branches and agencies of companies of another Party not incorporated in the territory of the first Party, which are justified by legal or technical differences between such branches and agencies as compared to branches and agencies of companies incorporated in its territory, or, as regards financial services, for prudential reasons. The difference in treatment shall not go beyond what is strictly necessary as a result of such legal or technical differences, or, as regards financial services, described in Annex XVb, for prudential reasons.

Article 49

1. A 'Community company' and a 'Bulgarian company' respectively shall, for the purpose of this Agreement, mean a company or a firm set up in accordance with the laws of a Member State or of Bulgaria respectively and having its registered office, central administration, or principle place of business in the territory of the Community or Bulgaria respectively. However, should the company or firm, set up in accordance with the laws of a Member State or of Bulgaria respectively, have only its registered office in the territory of the Community or Bulgaria respectively, its operations must possess a real and continuous link with the economy of one of the Member States or Bulgaria respectively.

2. With regard to international maritime transport, a national or a shipping company of the Member States or of Bulgaria, respectively established outside the Community or Bulgaria respectively and controlled by nationals of a Member State, or Bulgarian nationals respectively, shall also be beneficiaries of the provisions of this chapter and Chapter III of this title, if their vessels are registered in that Member State or in Bulgaria respectively in accordance with their respective legislations.

3. A 'Community national' and a 'Bulgarian national' respectively shall, for the purpose of this Agreement, mean a natural person who is a national of one of the Member States or of Bulgaria respectively.

4. The provisions of this Agreement shall not prejudice the application by each Party of any measure necessary to prevent the circumvention of its measures concerning third country access to its market, through the provisions of this Agreement.

Article 50

For the purpose of this Agreement 'financial services' shall mean those activities described in Annex XVb. The Association Council may extend or modify the scope of Annex XVb.

Article 51

During the first five years following the date of entry into force of this Agreement, or for the sectors referred to in Annex XVb and XVc during the transitional period referred to in Article 7, Bulgaria may introduce measures which derogate from the provisions of this chapter as regards the establishment of Community companies and nationals if certain industries:

- are undergoing restructuring, or

- are facing serious difficulties, particularly where these entail serious social problems in Bulgaria, or

- face the elimination or a drastic reduction of the total market share held by Bulgarian companies or nationals in a given sector or industry in Bulgaria, or

- are newly emerging industries in Bulgaria.

Such measures:

(i) shall cease to apply at the latest two years after the expiraton of the fifth year following the date of entry into force of this Agreement; and

(ii) shall be reasonable and necessary in order to remedy the situation; and

(iii) shall only relate to establishments in Bulgaria to be created after the entry into force of such measures and shall not introduce discrimination concerning the operations of Community companies or nationals already established in Bulgaria at the time of introduction of a given measure compared to Bulgarian companies or nationals.

The Association Council may exceptionally, upon request by Bulgaria, and if the necessity arises, decide to prolong the period referred to in indent (i) for a given sector for a limited period of time not exceeding the duration of the transitional period referred to in Article 7.

While devising and applying such measures, Bulgaria shall grant whenever possible to Community companies and nationals a preferential treatment, and in no case a treatment less favourable than that accorded to companies or nationals from any third country.

Prior to the introduction of these measures, Bulgaria shall consult the Association Council and shall not put them into effect before a one month period following the notification to the Association Council of the concrete measures to be introduced by Bulgaria, except where the threat of irreparable damage requires the taking of urgent measures in which case Bulgaria shall consult the Association Council immediately after their introduction.

Upon the expiration of the fifth year following the entry into force of the Agreement, or for the sectors referred to in Annexes XVb and XVc upon expiration of the transitional period referred to in Article 7, Bulgaria may introduce such measures only with the authorization of the Association Council and under conditions determined by the latter.

Article 52

1. The provisions of this chapter shall not apply to air transport services, inland-waterways transport services and maritime cabotage transport services.

2. The Association Council may make recommendations for improving establishment and operations in the areas covered by paragraph 1.

Article 53

1. Notwithstanding the provisions of Chapter I of this title, the beneficiaries of the rights of establishment granted by Bulgaria and the Community respectively shall be entitled to employ, or have employed by one of their subsidiaries, in accordance with the legislation in force in the host country of establishment, in the territory of Bulgaria and the Community respectively, employees who are nationals of Community Member States and Bulgaria respectively, provided that such employees are key personnel as defined in paragraph 2, and that they are employed exclusively by such beneficiaries or their subsidiaries. The residence and work permits of such employees shall only cover the period of such employment.

2. Key personnel of the beneficiaries of the rights of establishment, herein referred to as 'organization', are:

(a) senior employees of an organization who primarily direct the management of the organization, receiving general supervision or direction principally from the board of directors or shareholders of the business, including:

  – directing the organization or a department or sub-division of the organization,
  – supervising and controlling the work of other supervisory, professional or managerial employees,
  – having the authority personally to engage and dismiss or recommend engaging, dismissing or other personnel actions.

(b) persons employed by an organization who possess high or uncommon:

  – qualifications referring to a type of work or trade requiring specific technical knowledge,
  – knowledge essential to the organization's service, research equipment, techniques or management.

These may include, but are not limited to, members of accredited professions.

Each such employee must have been employed by the organization concerned for at least one year preceding the detachment by the organization.

Article 54

1. The provisions of this chapter shall be applied subject to limitations justified on grounds of public policy, public security or public health.

2. They shall not apply to activities which in the territory of each party are connected, even occasionally, with the exercise of official authority.

Article 55

Companies which are controlled and exclusively owned jointly by Bulgarian companies or nationals and Community companies or nationals shall also be beneficiaries of the provisions of this chapter and Chapter III of this title.

CHAPTER III

SUPPLY OF SERVICES BETWEEN THE COMMUNITY AND BULGARIA

Article 56

1. The Parties undertake in accordance with the provisions of this chapter to take the necessary steps to allow progressively the supply of services by Community or Bulgarian companies or nationals who are established in a Party other than that of the person for whom the services are intended taking into account the development of the services sectors in the Parties.

2. In step with the liberalization process mentioned in paragraph 1, and subject to the provisions of Article 59 (1), the Parties shall permit the temporary movement of natural persons providing the service or who are employed by the service provider as key personnel as defined in Article 53 (2), including natural persons who are representatives of a Community or Bulgarian company or national and are seeking temporary entry for the purpose of negotiating for the sale of services or entering into Agreements to sell services for that service provider, where those representatives will not be engaged in making direct sales to the general public or in supplying services themselves.

3. The Association Council shall take the measures necessary to implement progressively the provisions of paragraph 1 of this Article.

CHAPTER IV

GENERAL PROVISIONS

Article 59

1. For the purpose of Title IV, nothing in the Agreement shall prevent the Parties from applying their laws and regulations regarding entry and stay, work, labour conditions and establishment of natural persons and supply of services, provided that, in so doing, they do not apply them in a manner as to nullify or impair the benefits accruing to any Party under the terms of a specific provision of the Agreement. The above provision does not prejudice the application of Article 54.

2. The provisions of Chapters II, III and IV of Title IV shall be adjusted by decision of the Association Council in the light of the result of the negotiations on services taking place in the Uruguay Round and in particular to ensure that under any provision of this Agreement a Party grants to the other Party a treatment no less favourable than that under any provision of this Agreement a Party grants to the other Party a treatment no less favourable than that accorded under the provisions of a future General Agreement on Trade and Services (GATS).

Pending Bulgaria's accession to a future GATS Agreement, and without prejudice to any decisions the Association Council may take,

(i)   the Community shall grant to Bulgarian companies and nationals a treatment no less favourable than that accorded under the provisions of a future GATS Agreement to companies and nationals of other members of that Agreement;

(ii)   Bulgaria shall grant Community companies and nationals a treatment no less favourable than that accorded by Bulgaria to companies and nationals from any third country.

3. The exclusion of Community companies and nationals established in Bulgaria in accordance with the provisions of Chapter II of Title IV from public aid granted by Bulgaria in the areas of public education services, health-related and social services and cultural services shall, for the duration of the transitional period referred to in Article 7, be deemed compatible with the provisions of Title IV and with the competition rules referred to in Title V.

UK LEGISLATION

IMMIGRATION ACT 1988
(EXCERPTS)

NOTES

An Act to make further provision for the regulation of immigration into the United Kingdom; and for connected purposes. **A24–01**

[MAY 10, 1988]

BE IT ENACTED by the Queen's most Excellent Majesty, by and with the advice and consent of the Lords Spiritual and Temporal, and Commons, in this present Parliament assembled, and by the authority of the same, as follows:

s 7 Persons Exercising Community Rights and Nationals of Member States

(1) A person shall not under the principal Act require leave to enter or remain in the United Kingdom in any case in which he is entitled to do so by virtue of an enforceable Community right or of any provision made under Section 2(2) of the European Communities Act 1972.

(2) The Secretary of State may by order made by statutory instrument give leave to enter the United Kingdom for a limited period to any class of persons who are nationals of member States but who are not entitled to enter the United Kingdom as mentioned in subsection (1) above; and any such order may give leave subject to such conditions as may be imposed by the order.

(3) References in the principal Act to limited leave shall include references to leave given by an order under subsection (2) above and a person having leave by virtue of such an order shall be treated as having been given that leave by a notice given to him by an immigration officer within the period specified in paragraph 6(1) of Schedule 2 to that Act.[1,2,3,4]

END NOTES

[1] In relation to the Isle of Man:

7.— Persons exercising Community rights and nationals of member States.

(1) A person shall not under the principal Act require leave to enter or remain in the Isle of Man where he is entitled to enter or remain in the United Kingdom by virtue of an enforceable Community right or of any provision made under Section 2(2) of the European Communities Act 1972.

(2) The Lieutenant-Governor may by order give leave to enter the Isle of Man for a limited period to any class of persons who are nationals of member States but who are not entitled to enter the United Kingdom as mentioned in subsection (1) above; and any such order may give leave subject to such conditions as may be imposed by the order.

(3) References in the principal Act to limited leave shall include references to leave given by an order under subsection (2) above and a person having leave by virtue of such an order shall be

treated as having been given that leave by a notice given to him by an immigration officer within the period specified in paragraph 6(1) of Schedule 2 to that Act.

[2] In relation to Jersey:

7.— Persons exercising Community rights and nationals of member States.

(1) A person shall not under the principal Act require leave to enter or remain in the Bailiwick of Jersey in circumstances in which he would be entitled to enter or remain in the United Kingdom by virtue of an enforceable Community right or of any provision made under Section 2(2) of the European Communities Act 1972.

(2) The Lieutenant-Governor may by directions give leave to enter the Bailiwick of Jersey for a limited period to any class of persons who are nationals of member States but who would not be entitled to enter the United Kingdom as mentioned in subsection (1) above; and any such order may give leave subject to such conditions as may be imposed by the order.

(3) References in the principal Act to limited leave shall include references to leave given by directions under subsection (2) above and a person having leave by virtue of such directions shall be treated as having been given that leave by a notice given to him by an immigration officer within the period specified in paragraph 6(1) of Schedule 2 to that Act.

[3] In relation to Guernsey:

7.— Persons exercising Community rights and nationals of member States.

(1) A person shall not under the principal Act require leave to enter or remain in the Bailiwick of Guernsey in circumstances in which he would be entitled to enter or remain in the United Kingdom by virtue of an enforceable Community right or of any provision made under Section 2(2) of the European Communities Act 1972.

(2) The Board with the concurrence of the Lieutenant-Governor may by order give leave to enter the Bailiwick of Guernsey for a limited period to any class of persons who are nationals of member States but who would not be entitled to enter the United Kingdom as mentioned in subsection (1) above; and any such order may give leave subject to such conditions as may be imposed by the order.

(3) References in the principal Act to limited leave shall include references to leave given by an order under subsection (2) above and a person having leave by virtue of such an order shall be treated as having been given that leave by a notice given to him by an immigration officer within the period specified in paragraph 6(1) of Schedule 2 to that Act.

[4] Modified by SI 1993/1796 (Immigration (Guernsey) Order), Sch 1 (III) Para 2.

IMMIGRATION RULES HC 395 PARAS 255–257 (EXCERPTS)

EEA NATIONALS AND THEIR FAMILIES

SETTLEMENT

255. Any person (other than a student) who under, either the Immigration (European **A25–01** Economic Area) Order 1994, or the 2000 EEA Regulations has been issued with a residence permit or residence document valid for 5 years, and who has remained in the United Kingdom in accordance with the provisions of that Order or those Regulations (as the case may be) for 4 years and continues to do so may, on application, have his residence permit or residence document (as the case may be) endorsed to show permission to remain in the United Kingdom indefinitely.

255A. This paragraph applies where a Swiss national has been issued with a residence permit under the 2000 EEA Regulations and, prior to 1st June 2002, remained in the United Kingdom in accordance with the provisions of these Rules and in a capacity which would have entitled that Swiss national to apply for indefinite leave to remain after a continuous period of 4 years in that capacity in the United Kingdom. Where this paragraph applies, the period during which the Swiss national remained in the United Kingdom prior to 1st June 2002 shall be treated as a period during which he remained in the United Kingdom in accordance with the 2000 EEA Regulations for the purpose of calculating the 4 year period referred to in paragraph 255.

255B. This paragraph applies where an Accession State national has been issued with a residence permit under the 2000 EEA Regulations and, prior to 1st May 2004, remained in the United Kingdom in accordance with the provisions of these Rules and in a capacity which would have entitled that Accession State national to apply for indefinite leave to remain after a continuous period of 4 years in that capacity in the United Kingdom.

Where this paragraph applies, the period during which the Accession State national remained in the United Kingdom prior to 1st May 2004 shall be treated as a period during which he remained in the United Kingdom in accordance with the 2000 EEA Regulations for the purpose of calculating the 4 year period referred to in paragraph 255.?.

256. DELETED

257. In addition, the following persons will be permitted to remain in the United Kingdom indefinitely in accordance with Commission Regulation 1251/70:

(i) an EEA national who has been continuously resident in the United Kingdom for at least 3 years, has been in employment in the United Kingdom or any other

Member State of the EEA for the preceding 12 months, and has reached the age of entitlement to a state retirement pension;

(ii)   an EEA national who has ceased to be employed owing to a permanent incapacity for work arising out of an accident at work or an occupational disease entitling him to a state disability pension;

(iii)   an EEA national who has been continuously resident in the United Kingdom for at least 2 years, and who has ceased to be employed owing to a permanent incapacity for work;

(iv)   a member of the family of an EEA national to whom (i), (ii) or (iii) above applies;

(v)   a member of the family of an EEA national who dies during his working life after having resided continuously in the United Kingdom for at least 2 years, or whose death results from an accident at work or an occupational disease.

For the purposes of this paragraph:

"EEA National"

(a) "EEA national means a national of a Member State, other than the United Kingdom, or Norway, Iceland or Liechtenstein, but for the purposes of (iv) and (v) includes a national of the United Kingdom where the conditions set out in Regulation 11 of the 2000 EEA Regulations are satisfied. A Swiss national shall also be treated as an EEA national for the purposes of these Rules."; and

A *"member of the family"* is a family member as defined in Regulation 6 of the 2000 EEA Regulations, or a person whom it has been decided to treat as a family member in accordance with the principles set out in Regulation 10 of those Regulations. So far as this paragraph relates to a Swiss national no account will be taken of any period of residence before 1st June 2002, a cessation of employment before that date, or a death before that date.

(b) "So far as this paragraph relates to an Accession State national no account will be taken of any period of residence before 1st May 2004, a cessation of employment before that date, or a death before that date.".

257A. This paragraph applies where a Swiss national was admitted to the United Kingdom before 1st June 2002 for an initial period not exceeding 12 months pursuant to paragraph 282 and on or after that date became a qualified person or the family member of a qualified person under the 2000 EEA Regulations. Where this paragraph applies the Swiss national may, on application, have his residence permit endorsed to show permission to remain in the United Kingdom indefinitely if he meets the requirements set out in paragraph 287.

"**257B.** This paragraph applies where an Accession State national was admitted to the United Kingdom before 1st May 2004 for an initial period not exceeding 12 months pursuant to paragraph 282 and on or after that date became a qualified person or the family member of a qualified person under the 2000 EEA Regulations. Where this paragraph applies the Accession State national may, on application, have his residence permit endorsedto show permission to remain in the United Kingdom indefinitely if he meets the requirements set out in paragraph 287.".

IMMIGRATION (EUROPEAN ECONOMIC AREA) REGULATIONS 2000

Made: August 30, 2000
Laid before Parliament: September 1, 2000
Coming into force: October 2, 2000

The Secretary of State, being a Minister designated[1] for the purposes of Section 2(2) **A26–01** of the European Communities Act 1972 in relation to measures relating to rights of entry into, and residence in, the United Kingdom, in exercise of the powers conferred on him by the said Section 2(2), and of the powers conferred on him by Section 80 of the Immigration and Asylum Act 1999, hereby makes the following Regulations:

Regulation 1 Citation, Commencement and Revocation

(1) These Regulations may be cited as the Immigration (European Economic Area) Regulations 2000 and shall come into force on 2nd October 2000.

(2) Subject to paragraph (3), the Immigration (European Economic Area) Order 1994[2] is hereby revoked.

(3) Article 19 of the Order continues to have effect until the commencement of the repeal by the 1999 Act of the Immigration (Carriers' Liability) Act 1987.[3]

Regulation 2 General

(1) In these Regulations—

"the 1971 Act" means the Immigration Act 1971;

"the 1999 Act" means the Immigration and Asylum Act 1999;

"the Accession Regulations 2004" means the Accession (Immigration and Worker Registration) Regulations 2004;

"the 2002 Act" means the Nationality, Immigration and Asylum Act 2002;

"decision-maker" means the Secretary of State, an immigration officer or an entry clearance officer (as the case may be);

---

[1] S.I. 2000/1813.
[2] Amended by S.I. 1997/2981.
[3] Amended by S.I. 1991/1497, article 2, and by section 12 of the Asylum and Immigration Appeals Act 1993. See the 1999 Act, Schedule 16 (repeals).

"EEA decision" means a decision under these Regulations, or under Regulation 1251/70,[4] which concerns a person's—

(a) removal from the United Kingdom;

(b) entitlement to be admitted to the United Kingdom; or

(c) entitlement to be issued with or to have renewed, or not to have revoked, a residence permit or residence document;

"EEA family permit" means a document issued to a person, in accordance with Regulation 10 or 13, in connection with his admission to the United Kingdom;

"EEA national" means a national of an EEA State;

"EEA State" means a Member State, other than the United Kingdom, or Norway, Iceland or Liechtenstein;[5]

"economic activity" means activity as a worker or self-employed person, or as a provider or recipient of services;

"entry clearance officer" means a person responsible for the grant or refusal of entry clearances;

"military service" means service in the armed forces of an EEA State;

"Regulation 1251/70" means Commission Regulation (EEC) No. 1251/70 on the right of workers to remain in the territory of a Member State after having been employed in that State;[6]

"residence document" means a document issued to a person who is not an EEA national, in accordance with Regulation 10 or 15, as proof of the holder's right of residence in the United Kingdom;

"residence permit" means a permit issued to an EEA national, in accordance with Regulation 10 or 15, as proof of the holder's right of residence in the United Kingdom;

"spouse" does not include a party to a marriage of convenience;

"United Kingdom national" means a person who falls to be treated as a national of the United Kingdom for the purposes of the Community Treaties;

---

[4] Commission Regulation (EEC) No. 1251/70 on the right of workers to remain in the territory of a Member State after having been employed in that State (OJ No. L 142, 30.6.70, p.24); "Regulation 1251/70" is defined in regulation 2(1) of the Immigration (European Economic Area) Regulations 2000.
[5] Definition substituted by SI 2004/1219 (Accession (Immigration and Worker Registration) Regulations), Pt 2 Regulation 3.
[6] OJ No. L 142, 30.6.70, p.24 (OJ/SE 1st Series 1970 vol. II, p.402).

"visa national" means a person who requires a visa for the United Kingdom because he is a national or citizen of one of the countries or territorial entities for the time being specified in the immigration rules.[7]

(2) In these Regulations unless the context otherwise requires a reference to a regulation is a reference to a regulation of these Regulations; and within a regulation a reference to a paragraph is to a paragraph of that regulation.

Regulation 3 "Worker", "Self-employed Person", "Provider" and "Recipient" of Services, "Self-sufficient Person", "Retired Person" and "Student"

(1) In these Regulations—

(a) "worker" means a worker within the meaning of Article 39 of the E.C. Treaty;

(b) "self-employed person" means a person who establishes himself in order to pursue activity as a self-employed person in accordance with Article 43 of the E.C. Treaty, or who seeks to do so;

(c) "provider of services" means a person who provides, or seeks to provide, services within the meaning of Article 50 of the E.C. Treaty;

(d) "recipient of services" means a person who receives, or seeks to receive, services within the meaning of Article 50 of the E.C. Treaty;

(e) "self-sufficient person" means a person who—

    (i) has sufficient resources to avoid his becoming a burden on the social assistance system of the United Kingdom; and

    (ii) is covered by sickness insurance in respect of all risks in the United Kingdom;

(f) "retired person" means a person who—

    (i) has pursued an activity as an employed or self-employed person;

    (ii) is in receipt of—

        (aa) an invalidity or early retirement pension;

        (bb) old age benefits;

        (cc) survivor's benefits; or

        (dd) a pension in respect of an industrial accident or disease;

        sufficient to avoid his becoming a burden on the social security system of the United Kingdom; and

    (iii) is covered by sickness insurance in respect of all risks in the United Kingdom;

(g) "student" means a person who—

    (i) is enrolled at a recognised educational establishment in the United Kingdom for the principal purpose of following a vocational training course;

---

[7] See Appendix 1 to the Statement of Changes in Immigration Rules (HC 395) laid before Parliament on 23 May 1994; the Appendix was substituted from 4 April 1996 (HC 329) and renamed Appendix 1 with effect from 11 May 1998 (Cmnd 3953), and paragraph 2(b) was substituted from 1 November 1996 (HC 31).

(ii) assures the Secretary of State by means of a declaration, or by such alternative means as he may choose that are at least equivalent, that he has sufficient resources to avoid him becoming a burden on the social assistance system of the United Kingdom; and

(iii) is covered by sickness insurance in respect of all risks in the United Kingdom.

(2) For the purposes of paragraph (1)(e), where family members of the person concerned reside in the United Kingdom and their right to so reside is dependent upon their being family members of that person-

(a) the requirement for that person to have sufficient resources to avoid becoming a burden on the social assistance system of the United Kingdom shall only be satisfied if his resources and those of the family members are sufficient to avoid him and the family members becoming such a burden;

(b) the requirement for that person to be covered by sickness insurance in respect of all risks in the United Kingdom shall only be satisfied if he and the family members are so covered.

(3) For the purposes of paragraph (1)(f) where family members of the person concerned reside in the United Kingdom and their right to so reside is dependent upon their being family members of that person-

(a) the requirement for that person to be in receipt of a pension or benefits sufficient to avoid his becoming a burden on the social security system of the United Kingdom shall only be satisfied if that pension or those benefits are sufficient to avoid him and the family members becoming such a burden;

(b) the requirement for that person to be covered by sickness insurance in respect of all risks in the United Kingdom shall only be satisfied if he and the family members are so covered.

(4) For the purposes of paragraph (1)(g), where family members of the person concerned reside in the United Kingdom and their right to so reside is dependent upon their being family members of that person, the requirement for that person to assure the Secretary of State that he has sufficient resources to avoid him becoming a burden on the social assistance system of the United Kingdom shall only be satisfied if he assures the Secretary of State that his resources and those of the family members are sufficient to avoid him and the family members becoming such a burden.

(5) For the purposes of paragraph (1)(e) and (f) and paragraphs (2) and (3) the resources of the person concerned and, where applicable, any family members are to be regarded as sufficient if they exceed the level below which social assistance might be granted under the United Kingdom benefit system to a United Kingdom national in the same circumstances.[8]

---

[8] Regulation 3(2)-(5) substituted for Regulation 3(2) by SI 2004/1236 (Immigration (European Economic Area) and Accession (Amendment) Regulations), Regulation 2 (3).

Regulation 4 *"Self-employed Person who has Ceased Activity"*

(1) In these Regulations, "self-employed person who has ceased activity" means—

(a) a person who—

    (i) on the day on which he terminates his activity as a self-employed person has reached the age at which he is entitled to a state pension;

    (ii) has pursued such activity in the United Kingdom for at least the twelve months prior to its termination; and

    (iii) has resided continuously in the United Kingdom for more than three years;

(b) a person who—

    (i) has resident continuously in the United Kingdom for more than two years; and

    (ii) has terminated his activity there as a self-employed person as a result of a permanent incapacity to work;

(c) a person who—

    (i) has resided and pursued activity as a self-employed person in the United Kingdom;

    (ii) has terminated that activity as a result of a permanent incapacity to work; and

    (iii) such incapacity is the result of an accident at work or an occupational illness which entitles him to a pension payable in whole or in part by the state;

(d) a person who—

    (i) has been continuously resident and continuously active as a self-employed person in the United Kingdom for three years; and

    (ii) is active as a self-employed person in the territory of an EEA State but resides in the United Kingdom and returns to his residence at least once a week.

(2) But, if the person is the spouse of a United Kingdom national—

(a) the conditions as to length of residence and activity in paragraph (1)(a) do not apply; and

(b) the condition as to length of residence in paragraph (1)(b) does not apply.

(3) For the purposes of [paragraph (1)(a), (b) and (c)][9] periods of activity completed in an EEA State by a person to whom paragraph (1)(d)(ii) applies are to be considered as having been completed in the United Kingdom.

(4) For the purposes of paragraph (1)—

(a) periods of absence from the United Kingdom which do not exceed three months in any year or periods of absence from the United Kingdom on military service are not to be taken into account; and

---

[9] Words substituted by SI 2001/865 (Immigration (European Economic Area) (Amendment) Regulations), Regulation 3 (2).

(b) periods of inactivity caused by circumstances outside the control of the self-employed person and periods of inactivity caused by illness or accident are to be treated as periods of activity as a self-employed person.

Regulation 5 "Qualified Person"

(1) In these Regulations, "qualified person" means a person who is an EEA national and in the United Kingdom as—

(a) a worker;

(b) a self-employed person;

(c) a provider of services;

(d) a recipient of services;

(e) a self-sufficient person;

(f) a retired person;

(g) a student; or

(h) a self-employed person who has ceased activity;

or who is a person to whom paragraph (4) applies.

(2) A worker does not cease to be a qualified person solely because—

(a) he is temporarily incapable of work as a result of illness or accident; or

(b) he is involuntarily unemployed, if that fact is duly recorded by the relevant employment office.

(3) A self-employed person does not cease to be a qualified person solely because he is temporarily incapable of work as a result of illness or accident.

(4) This paragraph applies to—

(a) the family member of a qualified person referred to in paragraph (1)(h), if—

    (i) the qualified person has died; and
    (ii) the family member was residing with him in the United Kingdom immediately before his death;

(b) the family member of a qualified person referred to in paragraph 1(b) where—

    (i) the qualified person has died;
    (ii) the family member resided with him immediately before his death; and
    (iii) either—

        (aa) the qualified person had resided continuously in the United Kingdom for at least the two years immediately before his death; or
        (bb) the death was the result of an accident at work or an occupational disease; or
        (cc) his surviving spouse is a United Kingdom national.

(5) For the purposes of paragraph (4)(b), periods of absence from the United Kingdom which do not exceed three months in any year or periods of absence from the United Kingdom on military service are not to be taken into account.

Regulation 6 "Family Member"

(1) In these Regulations, paragraphs (2) to (4) apply in order to determine the persons who are family members of another person.

(2) If the other person is a student, the persons are—

(a)   his spouse; and

(b)   his dependent children.

(2A) If the other person has divorced his spouse, the person is his divorced spouse provided she is the primary carer of their dependent child who is under 19 and attending an educational course in the United Kingdom.

(2B) If the other person has ceased to be a qualified person on ceasing to reside in the United Kingdom, the persons are—

(a)   his spouse or his divorced spouse, provided she is the primary carer of their dependent child who is under 19 and attending an educational course in the United Kingdom; and

(b)   descendants of his or of his spouse who are under 21 or are their dependants, provided that they were attending an educational course in the United Kingdom when the qualified person was residing in the United Kingdom and are continuing to attend such a course.[10]

(2C) For the purposes of paragraphs (2A) and (2B), "educational course" means a course within the scope of Article 12 of Regulation (EEC) No. 1612/68 of the Council of the European Communities on freedom of movement for workers within the Community.[11]

(2D) For the purposes of these Regulations, a person to whom paragraph (2B) applies shall be treated as the family member of a qualified person, notwithstanding that the other person has ceased to be a qualified person.

(4) In any other case, the persons are—

(a)   his spouse;

(b)   descendants of his or of his spouse who are under 21 or are their dependants;

(c)   dependent relatives in his ascending line or that of his spouse.

---

[10] Substituted by SI 2003/3188 (Immigration (European Economic Area) (Amendment No. 2) Regulations), Regulation 2 (2).
[11] OJ No. L 257, 19.10.68, p.2 (OJ/SE 1st series 1968, vol. II, p.475).

Regulation 7 Carriers' Liability

For the purposes of satisfying a requirement to produce a visa under Section 40(1)(b) of the 1999 Act (charges to carriers in respect of passengers without proper documents), a "valid visa of the required kind" includes a family permit or residence document required for admission as a visa national under Regulation 12.

Regulation 8 Persons not Subject to Restriction on the Period for Which They may Remain

(1) For the purposes of the 1971 Act[12] and the British Nationality Act 1981,[13] the following are to be regarded as persons who are in the United Kingdom without being subject under the immigration laws to any restriction on the period for which they may remain—

(a)   a self-employed person who has ceased activity;

(b)   the family member of such a person who was residing with that person in the United Kingdom immediately before that person ceased his activity in the United Kingdom;

(c)   a family member to whom Regulation 5(4) applies;

(d)   a person who has right Regulation 1251/70;

(e)   a person who has been granted permission to remain in the United Kingdom indefinitely.

(2) However, a qualified person or family member who is not mentioned in paragraph (1) is not, by virtue of his status as a qualified person or the family member of a qualified person, to be so regarded for those purposes.

Regulation 9 General

Subject to Regulations 10 and 11 (and to [Regulations 24(1), 25(1), 26(1), 28 and 33][14]) these Regulations apply solely to EEA nationals and their family members.

Regulation 10 Dependants and Members of the Household of EEA Nationals

(1) If a person satisfies any of the conditions in paragraph (4), and if in all the circumstances it appears to the decision-maker appropriate to do so, the decision-maker may issue to that person an EEA family permit, a residence permit or a residence document (as the case may be).

---

[12] See in particular section 33(2A) of the 1971 Act (definition of "settled in the United Kingdom"), inserted by section 39(6) of, and paragraph 7 of Schedule 4 to, the British Nationality Act 1981 (c.61).

[13] See in particular section 50(2) (definition of "settled in the United Kingdom").

[14] Words substituted by SI 2003/549 (Immigration (European Economic Area) (Amendment) Regulations), Regulation 2 (4)

(2) Where a permit or document has been issued under paragraph (1), these Regulations apply to the holder of the permit or document as if he were the family member of an EEA national and the permit or document had been issued to him under Regulation 13 or 15.

(3) Without prejudice to Regulation 22, a decision-maker may revoke (or refuse to renew) a permit or document issued under paragraph (1) if he decides that the holder no longer satisfies any of the conditions in paragraph (4).

(4) The conditions are that the person[is a relative of an EEA national or his spouse and][15]

(a)   is dependent on the EEA national or his spouse;

(b)   is living as part of the EEA national's household outside the United Kingdom; or

(c)   was living as part of the EEA national's household before the EEA national came to the United Kingdom.

(5) However, for those purposes "EEA national" does not include—

(a)   an EEA national who is in the United Kingdom as a self-sufficient person, a retired person or a student;

(b)   an EEA national who, when he is in the United Kingdom, will be a person referred to in sub-paragraph (a).

Regulation 11 Family Members of United Kingdom Nationals

(1) If the conditions in paragraph (2) are satisfied, these Regulations apply to a person who is the family member of a United Kingdom national returning to the United Kingdom as if that person were the family member of an EEA national.

(2) The conditions are that—

(a)   after leaving the United Kingdom, the United Kingdom national resided in an EEA State and—

(i)   was employed there (other than on a transient or casual basis); or
(ii)   established himself there as a self-employed person;

(b)   the United Kingdom national did not leave the United Kingdom in order to enable his family member to acquire rights under these Regulations and thereby to evade the application of United Kingdom immigration law;

(c)   on his return to the United Kingdom, the United Kingdom national would, if he were an EEA national, be a qualified person; and

---

[15] Words inserted by SI 2001/865 (Immigration (European Economic Area) (Amendment) Regulations), Regulation 5.

(d) if the family member of the United Kingdom national is his spouse, the marriage took place, and the parties lived together in an EEA State, before the United Kingdom national returned to the United Kingdom.

Regulation 12 Right of Admission to the United Kingdom

(1) Subject to Regulation 21(1), an EEA national must be admitted to the United Kingdom if he produces, on arrival, a valid national identity card or passport issued by an EEA State.

(2) Subject to Regulation 21(1) and (2), a family member of an EEA national who is not himself an EEA national must be admitted to the United Kingdom if he produces, on arrival—

(a) a valid national identity card issued by an EEA State, or a valid passport; and

(b) either—

    (i)   where the family member is a visa national or a person who seeks to be admitted to instal himself with a qualified person, a valid EEA family permit or residence document; or

    (ii) in all other cases (but only where required by an immigration officer) a document proving that he is a family member of a qualified person.[16,17]

Regulation 13 Issue of EEA Family Permit

(1) An entry clearance officer must issue an EEA family permit, free of charge, to a person who applies for one if he is a family member of—

(a) a qualified person; or

(b) a person who is not a qualified person, where that person—

---

[16] In relation to the Channel Tunnel:

12.— Right of admission to the United Kingdom

(1) Subject to regulation 21(1), an EEA national must be admitted to the United Kingdom if he produces, on arrival, a valid national identity card or passport issued by an EEA State.

(2) Subject to regulation 21(1) and (2), a family member of an EEA national who is not himself an EEA national must be admitted to the United Kingdom if he produces, on arrival—

(a) a valid national identity card issued by an EEA State, or a valid passport; and

(b) either—

    (i) where the family member is a visa national or a person who seeks to be admitted to instal himself with a qualified person, a valid EEA family permit or residence document; or

    (ii) in all other cases (but only where required by an immigration officer) a document proving that he is a family member of a qualified person.

(3) Any passport, identity card, family permit, residence document or document proving family membership which is required to be produced under this regulation as a condition for admission to the United Kingdom ("the required documents") may, for the same purpose, be required to be produced in a control zone or a supplementary control zone.

[17] Added by SI 1993/1813 (Channel Tunnel (International Arrangements) Order), Sch 4 Para 5 (a).

    (i)   will be travelling to the United Kingdom with the person who has made the application within a year of the date of the application; and

    (ii)   will be a qualified person on arrival in the United Kingdom.

(2) But paragraph (1) does not apply if—

(a)   the applicant; or

(b)   the person whose family member he is

falls to be excluded from the United Kingdom on grounds of public policy, public security or public health.

Regulation 14 Right of Residence

(1) A qualified person is entitled to reside in the United Kingdom, without the requirement for leave to remain under the 1971 Act, for as long as he remains a qualified person.

(2) A family member of a qualified person is entitled to reside in the United Kingdom, without the requirement for such leave, for as long as he remains the family member of a qualified person.

(3) A qualified person and the family member of such a person may reside and pursue economic activity in the United Kingdom notwithstanding that his application for a residence permit or residence document (as the case may be) has not been determined by the Secretary of State.

(4) However, this regulation is subject to Regulation 21(3)(b).

Regulation 15 Issue of Residence Permits and Residence Documents

(1) Subject to Regulations 16 and 22(1), the Secretary of State must issue a residence permit to a qualified person on application and production of—

(a) a valid identity card or passport issued by an EEA State; and

(b) the proof that he is a qualified person.

(2) Subject to Regulation 22(1), the Secretary of State must issue a residence permit to a family member of a qualified person (or, where the family member is not an EEA national, a residence document) on application and production of—

(a) a valid identity card issued by an EEA State or a valid passport;

(b) in the case of a family member who required an EEA family permit for admission to the United Kingdom, such a permit; and

(c) in the case of a person not falling within sub-paragraph (b), proof that he is a family member of a qualified person.

(3) In the case of a worker, confirmation of the worker's engagement from his employer or a certificate of employment is sufficient proof for the purposes of paragraph (1)(b).

Regulation 16 *Where no Requirement to Issue Residence Permit*

(1) The Secretary of State is not required to grant a residence permit to—

(a) a worker whose employment in the United Kingdom is limited to three months and who holds a document from his employer certifying that his employment is so limited;

(b) a worker who is employed in the United Kingdom but who resides in the territory of an EEA State and who returns to his residence at least once a week;

(c) a seasonal worker whose contract of employment has been approved by the Department for Education and Employment; or

(d) a provider or recipient of services if the services are to be provided for no more than three months.

(2) The requirement in paragraph (1)(a) to hold a document does not apply to workers coming within the provisions of Council Directive 64/224/EEC of 25 February 1964 concerning the attainment of freedom of establishment and freedom to provide services in respect of activities of intermediaries in commerce, industry and small craft industries.[18]

Regulation 17 *Form of Residence Permit and Residence Document*

(1) The residence permit issued to a worker or a worker's family member who is an EEA national must be in the following form:

"Residence Permit for a National of an EEA State

This permit is issued pursuant to Regulation (EEC) No 1612/68 of the Council of the European Communities of 15 October 1968[19] and to the measures taken in implementation of the Council Directive of 15 October 1968.[20]

In accordance with the provisions of the above-mentioned Regulation, the holder of this permit has the right to take up and pursue an activity as an employed person in the territory of the United Kingdom under the same conditions as United Kingdom national workers.".

(2) A residence document issued to a family member who is not an EEA national may take the form of a stamp in that person's passport.

Regulation 18 *Duration of Residence Permit*

(1) Subject to the following paragraphs and to Regulations 20 and 22(2), a residence permit must be valid for at least five years from the date of issue.

---

[18] OJ No. 56, 4.4.64, p. 869 (OJ/SE 1st series 1963–64, p. 126).
[19] OJ No. L 257, 19.10.68, p.2 (OJ/SE 1st series 1968, vol. II, p. 475).
[20] Council Directive 68/360/EEC; OJ L 257, 19.10.68, p. 13 (OJ/SE 1st series 1968, vol. II, p. 485).

(2) In the case of a worker who is to be employed in the United Kingdom for less than twelve but more than three months, the validity of the residence permit may be limited to the duration of the employment.

(3) In the case of a seasonal worker who is to be employed for more than three months, the validity of the residence permit may be limited to the duration of the employment if the duration is indicated in the document confirming the worker's engagement or in a certificate of employment.

(4) In the case of a provider or recipient of services, the validity of the residence permit may be limited to the period during which the services are to be provided.

(5) In the case of a student, the residence permit is to be valid for a period which does not exceed the duration of the course of study; but where the course lasts for more than one year the validity of the residence permit may be limited to one year.

(6) In the case of a retired person or a self-sufficient person, the Secretary of State may, if he deems it necessary, require the revalidation of the residence permit at the end of the first two years of residence.

(7) The validity of a residence permit is not to be affected by absence from the United Kingdom for periods of no more than six consecutive months or absence from the United Kingdom on military service.

Regulation 19 Renewal of Residence Permit

(1) Subject to paragraphs (2) and (3) and to Regulations 20 and 22(2), a residence permit must be renewed on application.

(2) On the occasion of the first renewal of a worker's residence permit the validity may be limited to one year if the worker has been involuntarily unemployed in the United Kingdom for more than one year.

(3) In the case of a student whose first residence permit is limited to one year by virtue of Regulation 18(5), renewal may be for periods limited to one year.

Regulation 20 Duration and Renewal of Residence Permit or Residence Document Granted to a Family Member

(1) Subject to paragraph (2), the family member of an EEA national is entitled to a residence permit or residence document of the same duration as the residence permit granted to the qualified person of whose family he is a member; and the family member's residence permit or residence document is subject to the same terms as to renewal.

(2) In the case of a family member of an EEA national to whom Regulation 6(2A) or 6(2B)(a) applies, the validity of the residence permit or residence document may be limited to the period during which the family member is the primary carer of the dependent child who is under 19 and attending an educational course in the United Kingdom.[21]

---

[21] Existing regulation 20 renumbered as regulation 20(1), words are inserted and regulation 20(2) is added by SI 2003/549 (Immigration (European Economic Area) (Amendment) Regulations), Regulation 2 (5).

Regulation 21 Exclusion and Removal from the United Kingdom

(1) A person is not entitled to be admitted to the United Kingdom by virtue of Regulation 12 if his exclusion is justified on grounds of public policy, public security or public health.

(2) A person is not entitled to be admitted to the United Kingdom by virtue of Regulation 12(2) if, at the time of his arrival, he is not the family member of a qualified person.

(3) A person may be removed from the United Kingdom—

(a)   if he is not, or has ceased to be—

    (i)   a qualified person; or
    (ii)   the family member of a qualified person;

(b)   if he is a qualified person or the family member of such a person, but the Secretary of State has decided that his removal is justified on the grounds of public policy, public security or public health.[22,23]

Regulation 22 Refusal to Issue or Renew Residence Permit or Residence Document, and Revocation of Residence Permit, Residence Document or EEA Family Permit

(1) The Secretary of State may refuse to issue a residence permit or residence document (as the case may be) if the refusal is justified on grounds of public policy, public security or public health.

(2) The Secretary of State may revoke, or refuse to renew, a residence permit or residence document if—

(a)   the revocation or refusal is justified on grounds of public policy, public security or public health; or

(b)   the person to whom the residence permit or residence document was issued—

    (i)   is not, or has ceased to be, a qualified person;
    (ii)   is not, or has ceased to be, the family member of a qualified person.

---

[22] In relation to the Channel Tunnel:
21.— Exclusion and removal from the United Kingdom
(1) A person is not entitled to be admitted to the United Kingdom by virtue of regulation 12 if his exclusion is justified on grounds of public policy, public security or public health.
(2) A person is not entitled to be admitted to the United Kingdom by virtue of regulation 12(2) if, at the time of his arrival or the time of his production of the required documents in a control zone or a supplementary control zone, he is not the family member of a qualified person.
(3) A person may be removed from the United Kingdom—
(a)   if he is not, or has ceased to be—
    (i)   a qualified person; or
    (ii)   the family member of a qualified person;
(b)   if he is a qualified person or the family member of such a person, but the Secretary of State has decided that his removal is justified on the grounds of public policy, public security or public health.
[23] Words inserted by SI 1993/1813 (Channel Tunnel (International Arrangements) Order), Sch 4 Para 5 (b).

(3) An immigration officer may, at the time of the arrival in the United Kingdom of a person who is not an EEA national, revoke that person's residence document if he is not at that time the family member of a qualified person.

(4) An immigration officer may, at the time of a person's arrival in the United Kingdom, revoke that person's EEA family permit if—

(a) the revocation is justified on grounds of public policy, public security or public health; or

(b) the person is not at that time the family member of a qualified person.[24,25]

Regulation 23 Public Policy, Public Security and Public Health

Decisions taken on grounds of public policy, public security or public health ("the relevant grounds") must be taken in accordance with the following principles—

(a) the relevant grounds must not be invoked to secure economic ends;

(b) a decision taken on one or more of the relevant grounds must be based exclusively on the personal conduct of the individual in respect of whom the decision is taken;

(c) a person's previous criminal convictions do not, in themselves, justify a decision on grounds of public policy or public security;

(d) a decision to refuse admission to the United Kingdom, or to refuse to grant the first residence permit or residence document, to a person on the grounds that he has a disease or disability may be justified only if the disease or disability is of a type specified in Schedule 1 to these Regulations;

---

[24] In relation to the Channel Tunnel:
22.— Refusal to issue or renew residence permit or residence document, and revocation of residence permit, residence document or EEA family permit
(1) The Secretary of State may refuse to issue a residence permit or residence document (as the case may be) if the refusal is justified on grounds of public policy, public security or public health.
(2) The Secretary of State may revoke, or refuse to renew, a residence permit or residence document if—
(a) the revocation or refusal is justified on grounds of public policy, public security or public health; or
(b) the person to whom the residence permit or residence document was issued—
  (i) is not, or has ceased to be, a qualified person;
  (ii) is not, or has ceased to be, the family member of a qualified person.
(3) An immigration officer may, at the time of the arrival in the United Kingdom of a person who is not an EEA national or the time of his production of the required documents in a control zone or a supplementary control zone, revoke that person's residence document if he is not at that time the family member of a qualified person.
(4) An immigration officer may, at the time of a person's arrival in the United Kingdom or the time of his production of the required documents in a control zone or a supplementary control zone, revoke that person's EEA family permit if—
(a) the revocation is justified on grounds of public policy, public security or public health; or
(b) the person is not at that time the family member of a qualified person.
[25] Words inserted by SI 1993/1813 (Channel Tunnel (International Arrangements) Order), Sch 4 Para 5 (b).

(e) a disease or disability contracted after a person has been granted a first residence permit or first residence document does not justify a decision to refuse to renew the permit or document or a decision to remove him;

(f) a person is to be informed of the grounds of public policy, public security or public health upon which the decision taken in his case is based unless it would be contrary to the interests of national security to do so.

Regulation 24 Persons Claiming Right of Admission

(1) This regulation applies to a person who claims a right of admission to the United Kingdom under Regulation 12 as—

(a) the family member of an EEA national, where he is not himself an EEA national; or

(b) an EEA national, where there is reason to believe that he may fall to be excluded from the United Kingdom on grounds of public policy, public security or public health.

(2) A person to whom this regulation applies is to be treated as if he were a person seeking leave to enter the United Kingdom under the 1971 Act and paragraphs 2 to 4, 7, 16 to 18 and 21 to 24 of Schedule 2 to the 1971 Act (administrative provisions as to control on entry etc)[26] apply accordingly, except that—

(a) the reference in paragraph 2(1) to the purpose for which the immigration officer may examine any persons who have arrived in the United Kingdom is to be read as a reference to the purpose of determining whether he is a person who is to be granted admission under these Regulations; and

(b) the references in paragraph 4(2A) and in paragraph 7 to a person who is, or may be, given leave to enter are to be read as references to a person who is, or may be, granted admission under these Regulations.

(3) For so long as a person to whom this regulation applies is detained, or temporarily admitted or released while liable to detention, under the powers conferred by Schedule 2 to the 1971 Act, he is deemed not to have been admitted to the United Kingdom.

Regulation 25 Persons Refused Admission

(1) This regulation applies to a person who is in the United Kingdom and has been refused admission to the United Kingdom—
(a) because he does not meet the requirements of Regulation 12 (including where he does not meet those requirements because his residence document or EEA family permit has been revoked by an immigration officer in accordance with Regulation 22); or

---

[26] Schedule 2 has been amended, inter alia, by the Criminal Justice Act 1972 (c. 71); the Justices of the Peace Act 1979 (c. 55); the British Nationality Act 1981 (c. 61); the Police and Criminal Evidence Act 1984 (c. 60); the Immigration Act 1988 (c. 14); the Asylum and Immigration Act 1996 (c. 49); and the 1999 Act.

(b) in accordance with Regulation 21(1) or (2).

(2) A person to whom this regulation applies is to be treated as if he were a person refused leave to enter under the 1971 Act, and the provisions set out in paragraph (3) apply accordingly.

(3) Those provisions are—

(a) paragraphs 8, 10, 11, 16 to 18 and 21 to 24 of Schedule 2 to the 1971 Act;

(b) paragraph 19 of Schedule 2 to the 1971 Act, except that the reference in that paragraph to a certificate of entitlement, entry clearance or work permit is to be read as a reference to an EEA family permit or residence document[.][27]

[. . .][28]

Regulation 26 Persons Subject to Removal

(1) This regulation applies to a person whom it has been decided to remove from the United Kingdom in accordance with Regulation 21(3).

(2) Where the decision is under sub-paragraph (a) of Regulation 21(3), the person is to be treated as if he were a person to whom Section 10(1)(a) of the 1999 Act applied, and Section 10 of that Act (removal of certain persons unlawfully in the United Kingdom) is to apply accordingly.

(3) Where the decision is under sub-paragraph (b) of Regulation 21(3), the person is to be treated as if he were a person to whom Section 3(5)(a) of the 1971 Act (liability to deportation) applied, and section 5 of that Act (procedure for deportation) and Schedule 3 to that Act (supplementary provisions as to deportation) are to apply accordingly.

Regulation 26A Requirement to State Grounds Under Section 120 of the 2002 Act

26A. Requirement to state grounds under Section 120 of the 2002 Act

Section 120 of the 2002 Act shall apply to a person if an EEA decision has been taken or may be taken in respect of him and, accordingly, the Secretary of State or an immigration officer may require a statement from that person under subsection (2) of that section.[29]

---

[27] Repealed by SI 2003/549 (Immigration (European Economic Area) (Amendment) Regulations), Regulation 2 (6).
[28] Repealed by SI 2003/549 (Immigration (European Economic Area) (Amendment) Regulations), Regulation 2 (6).
[29] Added by SI 2003/549 (Immigration (European Economic Area) (Amendment) Regulations), Regulation 2 (7).

Regulation 27 Interpretation of Part VII

27.— Interpretation of Part VII

(1) In this Part—

"adjudicator" has the same meaning as in the 2002 Act;

"Commission" has the same meaning as in the Special Immigration Appeals Commission Act 1997;[30]

"the Human Rights Convention" has the same meaning as "the Convention" in the Human Rights Act 1998; and

"the Refugee Convention" means the Convention relating to the Status of Refugees done at Geneva on 28th July 1951 and its Protocol.

(2) For the purposes of this Part, and subject to paragraphs (3) and (4), an appeal is to be treated as pending during the period beginning when notice of appeal is given and ending when the appeal is finally determined, withdrawn or abandoned.

(3) An appeal is not to be treated as finally determined while a further appeal may be brought; and, if such a further appeal is brought, the original appeal is not to be treated as finally determined until the further appeal is determined, withdrawn or abandoned.

(4) A pending appeal is not to be treated as abandoned solely because the appellant leaves the United Kingdom.[31]

Regulation 28 Scope of Part VII

28. Scope of Part VII

This Part applies to persons who have, or who claim to have, rights under these Regulations or under Regulation 1251/70.[32]

Regulation 29 Appeal Rights

29.— Appeal rights

(1) Subject to paragraphs (2) to (4), a person may appeal under these Regulations against an EEA decision.

---

[30] 1997 c.68; amended by paragraphs 20 to 26 of Schedule 7 to the Nationality, Immigration and Asylum Act 2002.

[31] Existing Part VII, consisting of regulations 27–36, is substituted for a new Part VII consisting of regulations 27–32 subject to transitional provisions specified in SI 2003/549 regulation 3(1)–(2) by SI 2003/549 (Immigration (European Economic Area) (Amendment) Regulations), Regulation 2 (8).

[32] Existing Part VII, consisting of regulations 27–36, is substituted for a new Part VII consisting of regulations 27–32 subject to transitional provisions specified in SI 2003/549 regulation 3(1)–(2) by SI 2003/549 (Immigration (European Economic Area) (Amendment) Regulations), Regulation 2 (8).

(2) If a person claims to be an EEA national, he may not appeal under these Regulations unless he produces—

(a)   a valid national identity card; or

(b)   a valid passport, issued by an EEA State.

(3) If a person claims to be the family member of another person, he may not appeal under these Regulations unless he produces—

(a)   an EEA family permit; or

(b)   other proof that he is related as claimed to that other person.

(4) For the purposes of paragraphs (2) and (3), a document—

(a)   is to be regarded as being what it purports to be provided that this is reasonably apparent; and

(b)   is to be regarded as relating to the person producing it unless it is reasonably apparent that it relates to another person.

(5) A person may not rely on a ground in an appeal under these Regulations if the Secretary of State or an immigration officer certifies that the ground was considered in a previous appeal brought by that person under these Regulations or under Section 82(1) of the 2002 Act.

(6) Except where an appeal lies to the Commission, an appeal under these Regulations lies to an adjudicator.

(7) The sections of the 2002 Act set out in Schedule 2 shall have effect for the purposes of appeals under these Regulations to an adjudicator in accordance with that Schedule.[33]

Regulation 30 Out-of-Country Appeals

30.— Out-of-country appeals

(1) Regulation 29 does not entitle a person to appeal while he is in the United Kingdom against an EEA decision—

(a)   to refuse to admit him to the United Kingdom;

(b)   to refuse to revoke a deportation order made against him;

(c)   to refuse to issue him with an EEA family permit.

(2) Paragraph (1) also applies to a decision to remove someone from the United Kingdom which is consequent upon a refusal to admit him.

(3) But paragraphs (1)(a) and (2) do not apply—

---

[33] Existing Part VII, consisting of regulations 27–36, is substituted for a new Part VII consisting of regulations 27–32 subject to transitional provisions specified in SI 2003/549 regulation 3(1)–(2) by SI 2003/549 (Immigration (European Economic Area) (Amendment) Regulations), Regulation 2 (8).

(a) where the right of appeal is to the Commission;

(b) where a ground of the appeal is that, in taking the decision, the decision-maker acted in breach of the appellant's rights under the Human Rights Convention or the Refugee Convention; or

(c) where the person held an EEA family permit, or a residence permit or residence document, on his arrival in the United Kingdom.[34]

Regulation 31 Appeals to the Commission

31.— Appeals to the Commission

(1) An appeal against an EEA decision lies to the Commission where paragraphs (2) and (4) applies.

(2) This paragraph applies if the Secretary of State certifies that the EEA decision was taken—

(a) by the Secretary of State wholly or partly on a ground listed in paragraph (3), or

(b) in accordance with a direction of the Secretary of State which identifies the person to whom the decision relates and which is given wholly or partly on a ground listed in paragraph (3).

(3) The grounds mentioned in paragraph (2) are that the person's exclusion or removal from the United Kingdom is—

(a) in the interests of national security, or

(b) in the interests of the relationship between the United Kingdom and another country.

(4) This paragraph applies if the Secretary of State certifies that the EEA decision was taken wholly or partly in reliance on information which in his opinion should not be made public—

(a) in the interests of national security,

(b) in the interests of the relationship between the United Kingdom and another country, or

(c) otherwise in the public interest.

(5) In paragraphs (2) and (4) a reference to the Secretary of State is to the Secretary of State acting in person.

(6) Where a certificate is issued under paragraph (2) or (3) in respect of a pending appeal to an adjudicator the appeal shall lapse.

---

[34] Existing Part VII, consisting of regulations 27–36, is substituted for a new Part VII consisting of regulations 27–32 subject to transitional provisions specified in SI 2003/549 regulation 3(1)–(2) by SI 2003/549 (Immigration (European Economic Area) (Amendment) Regulations), Regulation 2 (8).

(7) An appeal against an EEA decision lies to the Commission where an appeal lapses by virtue of paragraph (6).

(8) The Special Immigration Appeals Commission Act 1997 shall apply to an appeal to the Commission under these Regulations as it applies to an appeal under Section 2 of that Act to which subsection (2) of that section applies (appeals against an immigration decision) but paragraph (i) of that subsection shall not apply in relation to such an appeal.[35]

Regulation 32 Effect of Appeals to an Adjudicator

32.— Effect of appeals to an adjudicator

(1) If a person in the United Kingdom appeals under these Regulations against an EEA decision to refuse to admit him to the United Kingdom, any directions previously given by virtue of the refusal for his removal from the United Kingdom cease to have effect, except in so far as they have already been carried out, and no directions may be so given while the appeal is pending.

(2) If a person appeals under these Regulations against an EEA decision to remove him from the United Kingdom, any directions given under Section 10 of the 1999 Act or Schedule 3 to the 1971 Act[36] for his removal from the United Kingdom are to have no effect, except in so far as they have already been carried out, while the appeal is pending.

(3) But the provisions of Part I of Schedule 2, or as the case may be, Schedule 3 to the 1971 Act with respect to detention and persons liable to detention apply to a person appealing under these Regulations against a refusal to admit him or a decision to remove him as if there were in force directions for his removal from the United Kingdom, except that he may not be detained on board a ship or aircraft so as to compel him to leave the United Kingdom while the appeal is pending.

(4) In calculating the period of two months limited by paragraph 8(2) of Schedule 2 to the 1971 Act for—

(a)   the giving of directions under that paragraph for the removal of a person from the United Kingdom, and

(b)   the giving of a notice of intention to give such directions,

any period during which there is pending an appeal by him under these Regulations is to be disregarded.

(5) If a person appeals under these Regulations against an EEA decision to remove him from the United Kingdom, a deportation order is not to be made against him under Section 5 of the 1971 Act[37] while the appeal is pending.

---

[35] Existing Part VII, consisting of regulations 27–36, is substituted for a new Part VII consisting of regulations 27–32 subject to transitional provisions specified in SI 2003/549 regulation 3(1)–(2) by SI 2003/549 (Immigration (European Economic Area) (Amendment) Regulations), Regulation 2 (8).
[36] Schedule 3 has been amended by the Criminal Justice Act 1982 (c.48); the Immigration Act 1988 (c.14); the Asylum and Immigration Act 1996 (c.49); and the 1999 Act.
[37] Section 5 has been amended by the British Nationality Act 1981 (c.61); the Immigration Act 1988 (c.14); and the Asylum and Immigration Act 1996 (c.49).

(6) Paragraph 29 of Schedule 2 to the 1971 Act (grant of bail pending appeal) applies to a person who has an appeal pending under these Regulations as it applies to a person who has an appeal pending under Section 82(1) of the 2002 Act.

(7) This regulation does not apply to an appeal which lies to the Commission.[38]

Regulation 33

[. . .][39]

Regulation 34

[. . .][40]

Regulation 35

[. . .][41]

Regulation 36

[. . .][42]

Regulation 33 Appeals Under the 2002 Act

(1A) A person who has been issued with a residence permit, a residence document or a registration certificate or whose passport has been stamped with a family member residence stamp shall have no right of appeal under Section 82(1) of the 2002 Act. Any existing appeal shall be treated as abandoned.

---

[38] Existing Part VII, consisting of regulations 27–36, is substituted for a new Part VII consisting of regulations 27–32 subject to transitional provisions specified in SI 2003/549 regulation 3(1)–(2) by SI 2003/549 (Immigration (European Economic Area) (Amendment) Regulations), Regulation 2 (8).

[39] Existing Part VII, consisting of regulations 27–36, is substituted for a new Part VII consisting of regulations 27–32 subject to transitional provisions specified in SI 2003/549 regulation 3(1)–(2) by SI 2003/549 (Immigration (European Economic Area) (Amendment) Regulations), Regulation 2 (8).

[40] Existing Part VII, consisting of regulations 27–36, is substituted for a new Part VII consisting of regulations 27–32 subject to transitional provisions specified in SI 2003/549 regulation 3(1)–(2) by SI 2003/549 (Immigration (European Economic Area) (Amendment) Regulations), Regulation 2 (8).

[41] Existing Part VII, consisting of regulations 27–36, is substituted for a new Part VII consisting of regulations 27–32 subject to transitional provisions specified in SI 2003/549 regulation 3(1)–(2) by SI 2003/549 (Immigration (European Economic Area) (Amendment) Regulations), Regulation 2 (8).

[42] Existing Part VII, consisting of regulations 27–36, is substituted for a new Part VII consisting of regulations 27–32 subject to transitional provisions specified in SI 2003/549 regulation 3(1)–(2) by SI 2003/549 (Immigration (European Economic Area) (Amendment) Regulations), Regulation 2 (8).

(1B) Subject to paragraph (1C), a person may appeal to an adjudicator under Section 83(2) of the 2002 Act against the rejection of his asylum claim where–

(a) that claim has been rejected, but

(b) he has a right to reside in the United Kingdom under these Regulations.

(1C) Paragraph (1B) shall not apply if the person is an EEA national and the Secretary of State certifies that the asylum claim is clearly unfounded.

(1D) The Secretary of State shall certify the claim under paragraph (1C) unless satisfied that it is not clearly unfounded.

(2) In addition to the national of a State which is a contracting party to the Agreement referred to in Section 84(2) of the 2002 Act, the national of a State which is a contracting party to any other agreement forming part of the Community Treaties which confers rights of entry to or residence in the United Kingdom shall also be treated as an EEA national for the purposes of Section 84(1)(d) of that Act.

(3) An appeal under these Regulations against an EEA decision made on or after 1st April 2003 shall be treated as an appeal under Section 82(1) of the 2002 Act against an immigration decision for the purposes of sections 96(1)(a), (2)(a) and (2)(c) of the 2002 Act and such an EEA decision shall be treated as an immigration decision for the purposes of Section 96(2)(b) of that Act.

(4) A ground considered in an appeal under these Regulations against an EEA decision made on or after 1st April 2003 shall be treated as a ground considered in an appeal under Section 82(1) of the 2002 Act for the purposes of Section 96(3) of that Act.

(5) In paragraph (1A),

(a) "registration certificate" has the same meaning as in Regulation 1(2)(h) of the Accession Regulations 2004;

(b) "family member residence stamp" means a stamp in the passport of a family member who is not an EEA national confirming that the family member of an accession state worker requiring registration has a right of residence under these Regulations as the family member of that worker; and in this paragraph reference to family member is to a family member who is not an EEA national and "accession state worker requiring registration" has the same meaning as in Regulation 2 of the Accession Regulations 2004.[43]

Para 1

The following diseases may justify a decision taken on grounds of public health—

(a) diseases subject to quarantine listed in International Health Regulation No. 2 of the World Health Organisation of 25th May 1951;

---

[43] Added by SI 2004/1236 (Immigration (European Economic Area) and Accession (Amendment) Regulations), Regulation 2 (4) (b).

(b) tuberculosis of the respiratory system in an active state or showing a tendency to develop;

(c) syphilis;

(d) other infectious diseases or contagious parasitic diseases, if they are the subject of provisions for the protection of public health in the United Kingdom.

Para 2

The following diseases or disabilities may justify a decision taken on grounds of public policy or public security—

(a) drug addiction;

(b) profound mental disturbance; manifest conditions of psychotic disturbance with agitation, delirium, hallucinations or confusion.

Para 1

[. . .]⁴⁴

Para 2

[. . .]⁴⁵

Para 3

[. . .]⁴⁶

---

⁴⁴ Existing Sch.2 consisting of paras.1–3 substituted for a new Sch.2 consisting of one unnumbered paragraph subject to transitional provisions specified in SI 2003/549 regulation 3(1)–(2) by SI 2003/549 (Immigration (European Economic Area) (Amendment) Regulations), Regulation 2 (10).

⁴⁵ Existing Sch.2 consisting of paras.1–3 substituted for a new Sch.2 consisting of one unnumbered paragraph subject to transitional provisions specified in SI 2003/549 regulation 3(1)–(2) by SI 2003/549 (Immigration (European Economic Area) (Amendment) Regulations), Regulation 2 (10).

⁴⁶ Existing Sch.2 consisting of paras.1–3 substituted for a new Sch.2 consisting of one unnumbered paragraph subject to transitional provisions specified in SI 2003/549 regulation 3(1)–(2) by SI 2003/549 (Immigration (European Economic Area) (Amendment) Regulations), Regulation 2 (10).

Para 1

The following provisions of, or made under, the 2002 Act have effect in relation to an appeal under these Regulations to an adjudicator as if it were an appeal against an immigration decision under Section 82(1) of that Act:

section 84(1) (except paragraphs (a) and (f)) and (2);

sections 85 to 87;

sections 101 to 103;

section 105 and any regulations made under that section; and

section 106 and any rules made under that section.[47]

---

[47] Substituted by SI 2003/3188 (Immigration (European Economic Area) (Amendment No. 2) Regulations), Regulation 2 (4).

EUROPEAN UNION (ACCESSIONS) ACT 2003

An Act to make provision consequential on the treaty concerning the accession of the Czech Republic, the Republic of Estonia, the Republic of Cyprus, the Republic of Latvia, the Republic of Lithuania, the Republic of Hungary, the Republic of Malta, the Republic of Poland, the Republic of Slovenia and the Slovak Republic to the European Union, signed at Athens on 16th April 2003; and to make provision in relation to the entitlement of nationals of certain acceding States to enter or reside in the United Kingdom as workers.

[NOVEMBER 13, 2003]

BE IT ENACTED by the Queen's most Excellent Majesty, by and with the advice and consent of the Lords Spiritual and Temporal, and Commons, in this present Parliament assembled, and by the authority of the same, as follows:-

Section 1 Accession Treaty

(1) In Section 1(2) of the European Communities Act 1972 (c. 68), in the definition of "the Treaties" and "the Community Treaties", after paragraph (p), insert

"and

(q) the treaty concerning the accession of the Czech Republic, the Republic of Estonia, the Republic of Cyprus, the Republic of Latvia, the Republic of Lithuania, the Republic of Hungary, the Republic of Malta, the Republic of Poland, the Republic of Slovenia and the Slovak Republic to the European Union, signed at Athens on 16th April 2003;".

(2) For the purpose of Section 12 of the European Parliamentary Elections Act 2002 (c. 24) (ratification of treaties), the treaty concerning the accession of the Czech Republic, the Republic of Estonia, the Republic of Cyprus, the Republic of Latvia, the Republic of Lithuania, the Republic of Hungary, the Republic of Malta, the Republic of Poland, the Republic of Slovenia and the Slovak Republic to the European Union, signed at Athens on 16th April 2003, is approved.

Section 2 Freedom of Movement for Workers

(1) The Secretary of State may by regulations provide that a specified enactment relating to–

  (a) the entitlement of a national of an EEA State to enter or reside in the United Kingdom as a worker, or

  (b) any matter ancillary to that entitlement,

applies in relation to a national of a relevant acceding State as it applies in relation to a national of an EEA State.

(2) Regulations under this section in respect of a specified enactment may apply that enactment subject to specified exceptions or modifications.

(3) Regulations under this section—

    (a)   may include incidental, supplementary, consequential or transitional provision;

    (b)   may make different provision for different cases.

(4) Regulations under this section do not have effect so as to apply an enactment in relation to a national of a relevant acceding State which has not ratified the treaty mentioned in Section 1(2).

(5) The power to make regulations under this section is exercisable by statutory instrument.

(6) Regulations may not be made under this section unless a draft has been laid before and approved by a resolution of each House of Parliament.

(7) But, in the case of regulations other than the first set of regulations under this section, subsection (6) does not apply if it appears to the Secretary of State that by reason of urgency they should be made without being approved in draft.

(8) Where by virtue of subsection (7) regulations are made without being approved in draft, the regulations—

    (a)   must be laid before Parliament, and

    (b)   cease to have effect at the end of the period mentioned in subsection (9) unless they are approved during that period by resolution of each House of Parliament.

(9) The period referred to in subsection (8)(b) is the period of 40 days—

    (a)   beginning with the day on which the regulations are made, and

    (b)   ignoring any period during which Parliament is dissolved or prorogued or during which both Houses are adjourned for more than four days.

(10) The fact that regulations cease to have effect by virtue of subsection (8)—

    (a)   does not affect the lawfulness of anything done before the regulations cease to have effect, and

    (b)   does not prevent the making of new regulations.

(11) In this section—

"EEA State" means a State (other than the United Kingdom) which is a contracting party to the Agreement on the European Economic Area signed at Oporto on 2nd May 1992, as adjusted by the Protocol signed at Brussels on 17th March 1993;

"enactment" includes an enactment comprised in subordinate legislation (within the meaning of the Interpretation Act 1978 (c. 30));

"relevant acceding State" means any of the following—

(a) the Czech Republic,

(b) the Republic of Estonia,

(c) the Republic of Latvia,

(d) the Republic of Lithuania,

(e) the Republic of Hungary,

(f) the Republic of Poland,

(g) the Republic of Slovenia,

(h) the Slovak Republic;

"specified" means specified in regulations under this section; and

"worker" means the same as it does for the purposes of Article 39 of the Treaty establishing the European Community.

Section 3 Short Title

This Act may be cited as the European Union (Accessions) Act 2003.

THE ACCESSION (IMMIGRATION AND WORKER REGISTRATION) REGULATIONS 2004

SI 2004 No. 1219

Made   *28th April 2004*

Coming into force   *1st May 2004*

The Secretary of State, being a Minister designated[1] for the purposes of Section 2(2) **A28–01**
of the European Communities Act 1972 in relation to measures relating to the right
of entry into, and residence in, the United Kingdom and access to the labour market of
the United Kingdom, in exercise of the powers conferred on him by Section 2(2), and
in exercise of the powers conferred upon him by Section 2 of the European Union
(Accessions) Act 2003, hereby makes the following Regulations, a draft of which has
been approved by resolution of each House of Parliament:

PART 1

GENERAL

Citation, Commencement and Interpretation

1.—(1) These Regulations may be cited as the Accession (Immigration and Worker
Registration) Regulations 2004 and shall come into force on 1st May 2004.

(2) In these Regulations –

(a) "the 1971 Act" means the Immigration Act 1971;

(b) "the 2000 Regulations" means the Immigration (European Economic Area)
Regulations 2000;

(c) "accession period" means the period beginning on 1st May 2004 and ending on
30th April 2009;

(d) "accession State worker requiring registration" shall be interpreted in accordance with regulation 2;

(e) "authorised employer" shall be interpreted in accordance with regulation 7;

(f) "EEA State" means a Member State, other than the United Kingdom, or
Norway, Iceland or Liechtenstein, and "EEA national" means a national of an
EEA State;

---

[1] S.I. 200/1813 and S.I. 2004/706.

(g) "employer" means, in relation to a worker, the person who directly pays the wage or salary of that worker;

(h) "registration certificate" means a certificate issued under regulation 8 authorising an accession State worker requiring registration to work for an employer;

(i) "relevant accession State" means the Czech Republic, the Republic of Estonia, the Republic of Latvia, the Republic of Lithuania, the Republic of Hungary, the Republic of Poland, the Republic of Slovenia and the Slovak Republic;

(j) "self-sufficient person" has the same meaning as in regulation 3 of the 2000 Regulations;

(k) "worker" means a worker within the meaning of Article 39 of the Treaty establishing the European Community, and "work" and "working" shall be construed accordingly.

"Accession State Worker Requiring Registration"

2.—(1) Subject to the following paragraphs of this regulation, "accession State worker requiring registration" means a national of a relevant accession State working in the United Kingdom during the accession period.

(2) A national of a relevant accession State is not an accession State worker requiring registration if on 30th April 2004 he had leave to enter or remain in the United Kingdom under the 1971 Act and that leave was not subject to any condition restricting his employment.

(3) A national of a relevant accession State is not an accession State worker requiring registration if he was legally working in the United Kingdom on 30th April 2004 and had been legally working in the United Kingdom without interruption throughout the period of 12 months ending on that date.

(4) A national of a relevant accession State who legally works in the United Kingdom without interruption for a period of 12 months falling partly or wholly after 30th April 2004 shall cease to be an accession State worker requiring registration at the end of that period of 12 months.

(5) A national of a relevant accession State is not an accession State worker requiring registration during any period in which he is also a national of–

(a)   the United Kingdom;

(b)   another EEA State, other than a relevant accession State; or

(c)   Switzerland.

(6) A national of a relevant accession State is not an accession State worker requiring registration during any period in which he is –

(a)   a posted worker; or

(b)   a family member of a Swiss or EEA national who is in the United Kingdom as–

   (i)   a worker, other than as an accession State worker requiring registration;
   (ii)   a self-sufficient person;

    (iii) a retired person; or

    (iv) a student.

(7) For the purpose of this regulation–

(a) a person working in the United Kingdom during a period falling before 1st May 2004 was legally working in the United Kingdom during that period if–

    (i) he had leave to enter or remain in the United Kingdom under the 1971 Act for that period, that leave allowed him to work in the United Kingdom, and he was working in accordance with any condition on that leave restricting his employment; or

    (ii) he was entitled to reside in the United Kingdom for that period under the 2000 Regulations without the requirement for such leave;

(b) a person working in the United Kingdom on or after 1st May 2004 is legally working during any period in which he is working in the United Kingdom for an authorised employer;

(c) a person shall also be treated as legally working in the United Kingdom on or after 1st May 2004 during any period in which he falls within paragraph (5) or (6).

(8) For the purpose of paragraphs (3) and (4), a person shall be treated as having worked in the United Kingdom without interruption for a period of 12 months if he was legally working in the United Kingdom at the beginning and end of that period and any intervening periods in which he was not legally working in the United Kingdom do not, in total, exceed 30 days.

(9) In this regulation–

(a) "retired person" and "student" have the same meaning as in Regulation 3 of the 2000 Regulations;

(b) "posted worker" means a person whose employer is not established in the United Kingdom and who works for that employer in the United Kingdom for the purpose of providing services on his employer's behalf;

(c) "family member" means–

    (i) in relation to a worker, his spouse and his children who are under 21 or dependent on him[2];

    (ii) in relation to any other person, his spouse and his children who are dependent on him.

---

[2] Substituted by SI 2004/1236 (Immigration (European Economic Area) and Accession (Amendment) Regulations), Regulation 3 (2) (b).

PART 2

IMMIGRATION

Amendment of the 2000 Regulations

3.—In Regulation 2(1) of the 2000 Regulations, for the definition of "EEA State" substitute–

" "EEA State" means a Member State, other than the United Kingdom, or Norway, Iceland or Liechtenstein.".

Right of Residence of Work Seekers and Workers from Relevant Acceding States During the Accession Period

4.—(1) This regulation derogates during the accession period from Article 39 of the Treaty establishing the European Community, Articles 1 to 6 of Regulation (EEC) No. 1612/68 on freedom of movement for workers within the Community and Council Directive (EEC) No. 68/360 on the abolition of restrictions on movement and residence within the Community for workers of Member States and their families.

(2) A national of a relevant accession State shall not be entitled to reside in the United Kingdom for the purpose of seeking work by virtue of his status as a work seeker if he would be an accession State worker requiring registration if he began working in the United Kingdom.

(3) Paragraph (2) is without prejudice to the right of a national of a relevant accession State to reside in the United Kingdom under the 2000 Regulations as a self-sufficient person whilst seeking work in the United Kingdom.

(4) An accession State worker requiring registration shall only be entitled to reside in the United Kingdom in accordance with the 2000 Regulations as modified by Regulation 5.

Application of 2000 Regulations in Relation to an Accession State Worker Requiring Registration

5.—(1) The 2000 Regulations shall apply in relation to an accession State worker requiring registration subject to the modifications set out in this regulation.

(2) An accession State worker requiring registration shall be treated as a worker for the purpose of the definition of "qualified person" in Regulation 5(1) of the 2000 Regulations only during a period in which he is working in the United Kingdom for an authorised employer.

(3) Subject to paragraph (4), Regulation 5(2) of the 2000 Regulations shall not apply to an accession State worker requiring registration who ceases to work.

(4) Where an accession State worker requiring registration–

(a) begins working for an authorised employer on or after 1st May 2004; and

(b) ceases working for that employer in the circumstances mentioned in Regulation 5(2) of the 2000 Regulations during the one month period beginning on the date on which the work begins,

that regulation shall apply to that worker during the remainder of that one month period.

(5) An accession State worker requiring registration shall not be treated as an EEA national for the purpose of the power in Regulation 10 of the 2000 Regulations (dependants and members of the household of EEA nationals)[3] to issue a residence permit or a residence document to a relative of an EEA national or his spouse.

(6) An accession State worker requiring registration shall not be treated as a qualified person for the purpose of Regulation 15 of the 2000 Regulations (issue of residence permits and residence documents).

Transitional Provisions Applying to the Application of the 2000 Regulations to Nationals of the Accession States and Their Family Members

6.—(1) Where before 1st May 2004 a qualified person or the family member of a qualified person has been given leave to enter or remain in the United Kingdom under the 1971 Act subject to conditions, those conditions shall cease to have effect on and after that date.

(2) Where before 1st May 2004 directions have been given for the removal of a qualified person or the family member of a qualified person under paragraphs 8 to 10A of Schedule 2 to the 1971 Act[4] or Section 10 of the 1999 Act, those directions shall cease to have effect on and after that date.

(3) Where before 1st May 2004 the Secretary of State has made a decision to make a deportation order against a qualified person or the family member of a qualified person under Section 5(1) of the 1971 Act –

(a) that decision shall, on and after 1st May 2004, be treated as if it were a decision under Regulation 21(3)(b) of the 2000 Regulations; and

(b) any appeal against that decision, or against the refusal by the Secretary of State to revoke the deportation order, made under Section 63 of the 1999 Act or Section 82(2)(j) or (k) of the 2002 Act before 1st May 2004 shall, on and after that date, be treated as if it had been made under Regulation 29 of the 2000 Regulations.

(4) In this regulation–

(a) "the 1999 Act" means the Immigration and Asylum Act 1999

---

[3] Regulation 10(4) has been amended by regulation 5 of S.I. 2001/865.
[4] Paragraphs 8 to 10 have been amended by the Schedule to the Immigration Act 1988 (c. 14), Schedule 2 to the Asylum and Immigration Act 1996 (c. 49), and Schedule 7 to the Nationality, Immigration and Asylum Act 2002(c. 41) and paragraph 10A was inserted by section 73 of the 2002 Act.

(b) "the 2002 Act" means the Nationality, Immigration and Asylum Act 2002;

(c) Regulation 6 of the 2000 Regulations shall apply for the purpose of determining whether a person is the family member of another person;

(d) any reference to a qualified person or to the family member of a qualified person is a reference to a person who becomes for the purpose of the 2000 Regulations a qualified person or the family member of a qualified person, as the case may be, on 1st May 2004 by virtue of Regulation 3.

PART 3

ACCESSION STATE WORKER REGISTRATION

Requirement for an Accession State Worker Requiring Registration to be Authorised to Work

7.—(1) By way of derogation from Article 39 of the Treaty establishing the European Community and Articles 1 to 6 of Regulation (EEC) No. 1612/68 on freedom of movement for workers within the Community, an accession State worker requiring registration shall only be authorised to work in the United Kingdom for an authorised employer.

(2) An employer is an authorised employer in relation to a worker if–

(a) the worker was legally working for that employer on 30th April 2004 and has not ceased working for that employer after that date;

(b) the worker–

    (i) during the one month period beginning on the date on which he begins working for the employer, applies for a registration certificate authorising him to work for that employer in accordance with Regulation 8; and

    (ii) has not received a valid registration certificate or notice of refusal under Regulation 8 in relation to that application or ceased working for that employer since the application was made;

(c) the worker has received a valid registration certificate authorising him to work for that employer and that certificate has not expired under paragraph (5); or

(d) the employer is an authorised employer in relation to that worker under paragraph (3) or (4).

(3) Where a worker begins working for an employer on or after 1st May 2004 that employer is an authorised employer in relation to that worker during the one month period beginning on the date on which the work begins.

(4) Where a worker was, before 1st May 2004, issued with leave to enter the United Kingdom under the 1971 Act as a seasonal worker at an agricultural camp and the worker begins working for an employer on or after 1st May 2004 as a seasonal worker at such a camp, that employer is an authorised employer in relation to that worker during the period beginning on the date on which the work begins and ending on the date on which the worker ceases working for that employer, or on 31st December 2004, which ever is the earlier.

(5) A registration certificate –

(a) is invalid if the worker is no longer working for the employer specified in the certificate on the date on which it is issued;

(b) expires on the date on which the worker ceases working for that employer.

(6) Regulation 2(7)(a) shall apply for the purpose of determining whether a person is legally working on 30th April 2004 for the purpose of this regulation.

Registration Card and Registration Certificate

8.—(1) An application for a registration certificate authorising an accession State worker requiring registration to work for an employer may only be made by an applicant who is working for that employer at the date of the application.

(2) The application shall be in writing and shall be made to the Secretary of State.

(3) The application shall state –

(a) the name, address, and date of birth of the applicant;

(b) the name and address of the head or main office of the employer;

(c) the date on which the applicant began working for that employer;

(d) where the applicant has been issued with a registration card, the reference number of that card.

(4) Unless the applicant has been issued with a registration card under paragraph (5), the application shall be accompanied by –

(a) a registration fee of £50;

(b) two passport size photographs of the applicant;

(c) the applicant's national identity card or passport issued by the applicant's State;

(d) a letter from the employer concerned confirming that the applicant began working for the employer on the date specified in the application.

(5) In the case of an application by an applicant who has not been issued with a registration card under this paragraph, the Secretary of State shall, where he is satisfied that the application is made in accordance with this regulation and that the applicant—

(a) is an accession State worker requiring registration; and

(b) began working for the employer on the date specified in the application,

send the applicant a registration card and a registration certificate authorising the worker to work for the employer specified in the application, and shall return the applicant's national identity card or passport.

(6) In the case of any other application, the Secretary of State shall, if he is satisfied as mentioned in paragraph (5), send the applicant a registration certificate authorising the worker to work for the employer specified in the application.

(7) A registration card issued under paragraph (5) shall contain –

(a)   the name, nationality and date of birth of the applicant;

(b)   a photograph of the applicant;

(c)   a reference number.

(8) A registration certificate issued under paragraph (5) or (6) shall contain–

(a)   the name of the applicant;

(b)   the reference number of the applicant's registration card;

(c)   the name and address of the head or main office of the employer, as specified in the application;

(d)   the date on which the applicant began working for the employer, as specified in the application; and

(e)   the date on which the certificate is issued.

(9) Where the Secretary of State receives an application made in accordance with this regulation and he is not satisfied as mentioned in paragraph (5), he shall–

(a)   send the applicant a notice of refusal; and

(b)   return any documents and fee that accompanied the application to the applicant.

(10) Where the Secretary of State sends a registration certificate or notice of refusal to an applicant under this regulation he shall, at the same time, send a copy of the certificate or notice to the employer concerned at the address specified in the application for that employer.

(11) Certificates and notices, and copies of these documents, sent under this regulation shall be sent by post.

Restriction on Employers of Relevant Accession State Workers Requiring Registration

9.—(1) Subject to paragraph (2), if an employer employs an accession State worker requiring registration during a period in which the employer is not an authorised employer in relation to that worker, the employer shall be guilty of an offence.

(2) Subject to paragraph (4), in proceedings under this regulation it shall be a defence to prove that –

(a)   there was produced to the employer during the one month period beginning on the date on which the worker began working for the employer a document that appeared to him to establish that the worker was not an accession State worker requiring registration; and

(b)   the employer took and retained a copy of that document.

(3) Subject to paragraph (4), in proceedings under this regulation it shall be a defence to prove that –

(a)   there was produced to the employer during the one month period beginning on the date on which the worker began working for the employer a document that appeared to him to establish that the worker had applied for a registration certificate in accordance with Regulation 8 authorising the worker to work for that employer;

(b)   the employer took and retained a copy of that document; and

(c)   the employer has not received a copy of a registration certificate or notice of refusal in relation to that application.

(4) The defence afforded by paragraph (2) or (3) shall not be available in any case where the employer knew that his employment of the worker would constitute an offence under this regulation.

(5) A person guilty of an offence under this regulation shall be liable on summary conviction to a fine not exceeding level 5 on the standard scale.

(6) Where an offence under this regulation committed by a body corporate is proved to have been committed with the consent or connivance of, or to be attributable to any neglect on the part of –

(a)   any director, manager, secretary or other similar officer of the body corporate; or

(b)   any person purporting to act in such a capacity,

he as well as the body corporate shall be guilty of the offence and shall be liable to be proceeded against and punished accordingly.

(7) Where the affairs of a body corporate are managed by its members, paragraph (6) shall apply in relation to the acts and defaults of a member in connection with his functions of management as if he were a director of the body corporate.

(8) Where an offence under this regulation is committed by a partnership (other than a limited partnership) each partner shall be guilty of the offence and shall be liable to be proceeded against and punished accordingly.

(9) Paragraph (6) shall have effect in relation to a limited partnership as if –

(a)   a reference to a body corporate were a reference to a limited partnership; and

(b)   a reference to an officer of the body corporate were a reference to a partner.

(10) Section 28(1) of the 1971 Act (extended time limit for prosecution) shall apply in relation to an offence under this regulation.

(11) An offence under this regulation shall be treated as –

(a)   a relevant offence for the purpose of sections 28B and 28D of that Act[5] (search, entry and arrest); and

(b)   an offence under Part III of that Act (criminal proceedings) for the purposes of sections 28E, 28G and 28H[6] (search after arrest).

---

[5] Sections 28B was inserted by section 129 of the Immigration and Asylum Act 1999(c. 33) and 28D was inserted by section 131 of that Act; both sections have been amended by sections 144 and 150 of the Nationality, Immigration and Asylum Act 2002(c. 41).
[6] Sections 28E, 28G and 28H were inserted by sections 132, 134 and 135 of the Immigration and Asylum Act 1999 respectively.

THE IMMIGRATION (EUROPEAN ECONOMIC AREA) AND ACCESSION (AMENDMENT) REGULATIONS 2004

SI 2004 No. 1236

Made   *28th April 2004*

Laid before Parliament   *30th April 2004*

Coming into force   *1st May 2004*

The Secretary of State, being a Minister designated[1] for the purposes of Section 2(2) of the European Communities Act 1972 in relation to measures relating to rights of entry into, and residence in, the United Kingdom, in exercise of the powers conferred on him by the said Section 2(2), and of the powers conferred on him by Section 109 of the Nationality, Immigration and Asylum Act 2002, hereby makes the following Regulations: **A29–01**

Citation and Commencement

1.—These Regulations may be cited as the Immigration (European Economic Area) and Accession (Amendment) Regulations 2004 and shall come into force on 1st May 2004.

Amendment of Immigration (European Economic Area) Regulations 2000

2.—(1) The Immigration (European Economic Area) Regulations 2000[2] are amended as follows.

(2) In Regulation 2(1) (general interpretation), after the definition of "the 1999 Act" there is inserted "the Accession Regulations 2004" means the Accession (Immigration and Worker Registration) Regulations 2004".

(3) In Regulation 3 (interpretation of "worker", "self-employed person" etc), for paragraph (2) substitute –
    " (2) For the purposes of paragraph (1)(e), where family members of the person concerned reside in the United Kingdom and their right to so reside is dependent upon their being family members of that person –

      (a) the requirement for that person to have sufficient resources to avoid becoming a burden on the social assistance system of the United Kingdom shall

---

[1] S.I. 2000/1813.
[2] The relevant amending instrument is S.I. 2003/3188.

only be satisfied if his resources and those of the family members are sufficient to avoid him and the family members becoming such a burden;

(b) the requirement for that person to be covered by sickness insurance in respect of all risks in the United Kingdom shall only be satisfied if he and the family members are so covered.

(3) For the purposes of paragraph (1)(f) where family members of the person concerned reside in the United Kingdom and their right to so reside is dependent upon their being family members of that person –

(a) the requirement for that person to be in receipt of a pension or benefits sufficient to avoid his becoming a burden on the social security system of the United Kingdom shall only be satisfied if that pension or those benefits are sufficient to avoid him and the family members becoming such a burden;

(b) the requirement for that person to be covered by sickness insurance in respect of all risks in the United Kingdom shall only be satisfied if he and the family members are so covered.

(4) For the purposes of paragraph (1)(g), where family members of the person concerned reside in the United Kingdom and their right to so reside is dependent upon their being family members of that person, the requirement for that person to assure the Secretary of State that he has sufficient resources to avoid him becoming a burden on the social assistance system of the United Kingdom shall only be satisfied if he assures the Secretary of State that his resources and those of the family members are sufficient to avoid him and the family members becoming such a burden.

(5) For the purposes of paragraph (1)(e) and (f) and paragraphs (2) and (3) the resources of the person concerned and, where applicable, any family members are to be regarded as sufficient if they exceed the level below which social assistance might be granted under the United Kingdom benefit system to a United Kingdom national in the same circumstances.".

(4) In Regulation 33 (appeals under the 2002 Act) –

(a) for paragraph (1A) there is substituted –

" (1A) A person who has been issued with a residence permit, a residence document or a registration certificate or whose passport has been stamped with a family member residence stamp shall have no right of appeal under Section 82(1) of the 2002 Act. Any existing appeal shall be treated as abandoned.".

(b) at the end of that regulation there is inserted –

" (5) In paragraph (1A),

(a) "registration certificate" has the same meaning as in Regulation 1(2)(h) of the Accession Regulations 2004;

(b) "family member residence stamp" means a stamp in the passport of a family member who is not an EEA national confirming that the family member of an accession state worker requiring registration has a right of residence under these Regulations as the family member of that worker; and in this paragraph reference to family member is to a family member who is not an EEA national and "accession state worker requiring registration" has the same meaning as in Regulation 2 of the Accession Regulations 2004.".

Amendment of the Accession (Immigration and Worker Registration)
Regulations 2004

3.—(1) The Accession (Immigration and Worker Registration) Regulations 2004 are amended as follows.
(2) In Regulation 2 ("Accession State worker requiring registration") –

(a) for paragraph (6)(b) there is substituted –

" (b) a family member of a Swiss or EEA national who is in the United Kingdom as –

(i) a worker, other than as an accession State worker requiring registration;
(ii) a self-sufficient person;
(iii) a retired person;
(iv) a self-employed person; or
(v) a student.";

(b) For paragraph (9)(c)(i) there is substituted –

" (i) in relation to a worker or a self-employed person, his spouse and his children who are under 21 or dependent on him;".

TABLES

THE CITIZENS' DIRECTIVE

Directive 2004/38/EC of the European Parliament and of the Council of April 29, 2004 on the rights of citizens of the Union and their family members to move and reside freely within the territory of the Member States must be implemented by Member States by April 30, 2006. Article 38 of the Citizens' Directive provides that Directives 64/221/EEC, 68/360/EEC, 73/148/EEC, 75/34/EEC, 75/35/EEC, 90/364/EEC, 90/365/EEC and 93/96/EEC as well as Articles 10 and 11 of Regulation 1612/68 will be repealed on April 30, 2006. The Citizens' Directive is intended to consolidate secondary legislation on the free movement of persons and to some extent the ECJ's guidance on that legislation into one document. Its inception will not represent the end of the evolution of the law relating to the free movement of persons in the European Union and undoubtedly the provisions of the Directive will cause as much comment and interpretation by the ECJ as the secondary legislation that it replaces.

The table below identifies corresponding provisions in the Citizens' Directive to those in the Regulation and Directives that it replaces. Where the provisions in the Citizens' Directive differ from the equivalent provisions in the preceding secondary legislation, additions or changes to the text are identified in the observations column. Only substantive provisions of the Citizens' Directive are included in the table. The table is not intended as a commentary on the text of the Citizens' Directive but simply as a short guide. Many of the provisions of the Citizens' Directive replicate closely the provisions of the secondary legislation that it replaces or reflect case law of the ECJ which has been the subject of discussion in Part II of this book.

Provision in Citizens' Directive	Equivalent Provision in repealed legislation	Observations: Additions and changes made by provisions in Citizens' Directive
Article 2(1)	*New provision*	Replicates the provision in Article 17 E.C. Treaty
Article 2(2)	Article 10 Regulation 1612/68 Article 1 Directive 73/148 Article 1(2) Directive 90/364 Article 1(2) Directive 90/365 Article 1 Directive 93/96	A uniform definition of "family members" applies to all free movers, to include spouses, unmarried partners (see below), descendants who are dependant (or under 21) and ascendants. The word "direct" is inserted before both descendant and ascendant. For the unmarried partner to have the right to join an E.U. national they must have contracted registered partnerships which are treated in the host Member State as equivalent to marriage.

Provision in Citizens' Directive	Equivalent Provision in repealed legislation	Observations: Additions and changes made by provisions in Citizens' Directive
Article 3(2)	Article 10(2) Regulation 1612/68	The duty to facilitate the entry or residence of "other family members" previously applicable to workers only is applicable to other free movers. The definition of "other family member" is extended to those whose serious health needs require the care of the principal. The duty to facilitate entry or residence is also extended to unmarried partners in a "duly attested" durable relationship. The duty to facilitate entry includes a requirement to justify any denial of entry.
Article 4	Article 2 Directive 68/360 Article 2 Directive 73/148	
Article 5	Articles 3 and 9 Directive 68/360 Articles 3 and 7 Directive 73/148	Entry visas for family members are to be issued as soon as possible and on the basis of an accelerated procedure. Member States must not place entry or exit stamps in the passports of family members if they present a residence card. Specific provision is made for Union citizens and their family members who travel without the necessary documentation reflecting the ECJ's judgment in *MRAX*. Any requirement that persons report their presence in a Member State shall be applied in a non-discriminatory fashion with proportionate sanctions for failure to comply.
Article 6	Article 8 Directive 68/360 Article 4 Directive 73/148	Any Union citizen, regardless of the reason for being in the host Member State, has the right of residence in that Member State without formality for up to 3 months.

Provision in Citizens' Directive	Equivalent Provision in repealed legislation	Observations: Additions and changes made by provisions in Citizens' Directive
Article 7	Regulation 1612/68 Directive 73/148 Directive 90/364 Directive 90/365 Directive 93/96	Article 7 generally reflects the substantive provisions as regards rights of residence contained in previous secondary legislation. The broad categories of economically active and inactive free mover are maintained. Rights of residence provided for are reflective of general established principles, although not identical to previous provisions. For example the scope of "family members" is extended by the Directive.
Article 8	Article 4 Directive 68/360 Article 6 Directive 73/148 Article 2 Directive 90/364 Article 2 Directive 90/365 Article 2 Directive 93/96	Nationals of Member States are to be issued with "registration certificates" by the host Member State which may require the obtaining of such certificate for periods of residence of longer than 3 months. Family members are also to be issued with registration certificates if they are E.U. nationals themselves. Failure to obtain a registration certificate can only result in a proportionate and non-discriminatory sanction. Registration certificates have no fixed duration.
Article 9	Article 4 Directive 68/360 Article 6 Directive 73/148 Article 2 Directive 90/364 Article 2 Directive 90/365 Article 2 Directive 93/96	Non-E.U. national family members who plan to be resident in the host Member State for longer than 3 months are to be issued with "residence cards". Only proportionate and non-discriminatory sanctions may be applied to those who fail to comply with requirements to apply for residence cards.
Article 10	Article 5 Directive 64/221	Those who apply for residence cards are to be issued with a certificate confirming that an application has been made immediately.

Provision in Citizens' Directive	Equivalent Provision in repealed legislation	Observations: Additions and changes made by provisions in Citizens' Directive
Article 11	Articles 6 and 7 Directive 68/360 Article 4 Directive 73/148	Residence cards will be valid for 5 years or for the envisaged period of the principal. One absence of a maximum of 12 months is permitted for "important" reasons such as pregnancy, child birth, posting in a third country or training.
Article 12	Article 3 Regulation 1251/70 Article 3 Directive 75/34	A family member retains the right to reside after the death of the principal providing that the family member had resided for one year as a family member in the host Member State. These provisions are extended to apply to the family members of all categories of free mover. Reflective of the ECJ's judgment in *Baumbast* parents of children retain the right to reside in the host Member State following the death or departure from that Member State of the principal if the children are enrolled at an educational establishment.
Article 13	*New provision*	In the event of divorce, annulment of marriage or termination of a registered partnership the right of residence of E.U. national family members is not affected. If the family member is a non-E.U. national the right of residence is retained in certain circumstances.
Article 14	Article 3 Directive 90/364 Article 3 Directive 90/365 Article 4 Directive 93/96	The right of residence for the first 3 months is secured provided that the E.U. national and his family do not become unreasonable burdens on the host Member State. Thereafter verification is permitted where there is reasonable doubt that conditions of residence are being met. Reflective of the ECJ's judgment in *Gryzelcyk* recourse to public funds cannot automatically result in expulsion for the economically inactive.

Provision in Citizens' Directive	Equivalent Provision in repealed legislation	Observations: Additions and changes made by provisions in Citizens' Directive
		Workers, work-seekers and self-employed persons may not be expelled except on public policy, public security or public health grounds.
Article 15	Articles 8 and 9 Directive 64/221	Expiry of identity documents does not constitute a ground for expulsion.
Article 16	*New provision*	The right of permanent residence is granted to all E.U. nationals and their family members who have lawfully resided in a host Member State for 5 years.
Article 17	Article 2 Regulation 1251/70 Article 2 Directive 75/34	
Article 18	Article 3 Regulation 1251/70 Article 3 Directive 73/34	The right to reside permanently following the death of the E.U. national free mover (or departure or divorce under conditions laid down in Article 13(2)) is only acquired by the family member after 5 years legal residence.
Article 19	*New provision*	E.U. nationals acquiring the right of permanent residence are to be issued with a document certifying this right
Article 20	Article 5 Regulation 1251/70 Article 6 Directive 75/34	Non-E.U. national family members acquiring the right of permanent residence are to be issued with a permanent residence card. This is renewable automatically every 10 years. Failure to apply for such card may only result in proportionate and non-discriminatory sanctions. Interruptions in residence of up to 2 years do not affect the right of permanent residence.
Article 21	*New provision*	Continuity in residence is broken by an enforced expulsion.
Article 22	Article 6 Directive 68/360 Article 5 Directive 73/148	

Provision in Citizens' Directive	Equivalent Provision in repealed legislation	Observations: Additions and changes made by provisions in Citizens' Directive
Article 23	Article 11 Regulation 1612/68 Article 2 Directive 90/364 Article 2 Directive 90/365 Article 2 Directive 93/96	Family members of all free movers are entitled to take up employed or self-employed activities.
Article 24	Article 7(2) Regulation 1612/68	The right of equal treatment is guaranteed to all free movers and their family members. Access to social assistance may be restricted in the first 3 months or whilst the E.U. national is a work seeker. Access to maintenance aid for students may also be denied.
Article 25	Articles 5 and 9 Directive 68/360 Article 7 Directive 73/148	The declaratory effect of certificates of permanent residence and residence cards is formalised
Article 26	*New provision*	Reflective of the ECJ's judgment in *Commission v Belgium* (1989) Member States may retain internal controls and checks on residence documents of non-nationals providing that such controls exist for own nationals.
Article 27	Articles 2 and 3 Directive 64/221	Consistent with the ECJ's judgment in *Calfa*, Member States cannot make expulsion or exclusion decisions on general preventative grounds. Host Member States may consult other Member States in relation to previous criminal records provided this is not done routinely.
Article 28	*New provision*	Expulsion decisions are to be proportionate and take into account human rights. E.U. nationals who have resided in a host Member State for 10 years are protected against expulsion except on imperative national security grounds. Minors are protected against expulsion except where the best interests of the child dictate otherwise.

Provision in Citizens' Directive	Equivalent Provision in repealed legislation	Observations: Additions and changes made by provisions in Citizens' Directive
Article 29	Annex to Directive 64/221	Diseases with epidemic potential may justify restriction on free movement rights (replacing the list of diseases in the Annex to Directive 64/221).
Article 30	Article 6 Directive 64/221	Information about an expulsion or exclusion decision must be comprehensible, full and in writing. Time allowed for leaving the territory is extended to one month (save in urgent cases).
Article 31	Articles 8 and 8 Directive 64/221	Redress procedures must be able to examine the substance and proportionality of any exclusion or expulsion decision. Whilst such procedures are not expressly suspensive, Member States may not prevent the person from submitting his defence in person (subject to certain exceptions).
Article 32	*New provision*	A person may apply to have an exclusion or expulsion decision lifted after 3 years.
Article 33	*New provision*	If two years elapse between the making and enforcement of an expulsion decision, it must be reviewed.
Article 34	*New provision*	Member States are to disseminate information about the rights contained in the Directive.
Article 35	*New provision*	Member States are permitted to adopt measures to combat fraud and marriages of convenience subject to procedural safeguards.
Article 37	*New provision*	Member States may have more favourable provisions in place, although no standstill clause is included.

INDEX

[649]